EASTERN EUROPE

Transformation and Revolution, 1945–1991

Sources in Modern History Series

EASTERN EUROPE

Transformation and Revolution, 1945–1991

Documents and Analyses

Lyman H. Legters

D. C. Heath and Company
Lexington, Massachusetts   Toronto

Address editorial correspondence to

D. C. Heath and Company
125 Spring Street
Lexington, MA 02173

Cover: Saxgre/Impact Visuals

Published simultaneously in Canada.

Printed in the United States of America.

International Standard Book Number: 0-669-24994-7

Library of Congress Catalog Number: 91-73739

10 9 8 7 6 5 4 3 2 1

♦

For Werner Philipp

Preface

✦ *This collection of materials on Eastern Europe is designed to make the current upheavals in the region until very recently called the Soviet bloc more readily understandable to students and interested general readers alike.*

It is virtually self-evident that a definite connection exists between the processes of change still under way in Eastern Europe and the record of past discord, most particularly the dramatic events of 1956, 1968, and 1980–1981 in Hungary, Czechoslovakia, and Poland, respectively. Accordingly these and other related signs of discontent with Soviet tutelage since World War II receive special prominence in this collection. But it does not follow, of course, that headline-catching events adequately portray profound social change. The analytical portions of the selections offered here, from eastern and western commentators, should suffice to draw the reader's attention to underlying structural processes that typically elude the daily news. Furthermore, it is extremely important to recognize that current developments are not merely extensions, still less culminations, of earlier upheavals. The transformation that began in 1989–1990 contains some strikingly new features, most notably those now at work in the Soviet Union itself, and it deserves to be considered sui generis, as a distinctive development with consequences and outcomes still hardly foreseeable.

Part I examines the relationship between the Soviet Union and the client states of Eastern Europe as that relationship evolved over some four decades. Cursory though the examination must be, the selections underscore the different stages of Soviet domination, down to the point when that domination ceased to be the paramount fact of life in the region.

Part II presents two early cases of disruption, the expulsion of Yugoslavia from the bloc in 1948 and the uprising in 1953 that threatened Ulbricht's East German regime. For both countries, the most salient subsequent developments are also covered briefly, since the two reenter the picture only in Part IV, as participants in the collapse of communism in Eastern Europe.

Part III features the three dramatic revolts against Soviet tutelage and against the domestic agents of that domination. Of all three it can be said (and often has been) that Soviet intervention and pressure by no means closed those particular chapters. The restoration of acceptable conduct, chronicled here as aftermaths of the respective revolts, has turned out to represent not a final outcome but rather an interlude. The memories of 1956, 1968, and 1980–1981 have proved, from our present perspective, to be very much alive.

Part IV depicts the developments of 1989–1990 (extended into 1991 where possible). The chapters devoted to Poland, Czechoslovakia, and Hungary follow from the accounts in Part III; those on East Germany and Yugoslavia take up where Part II left off. Romania, Bulgaria, and Albania thus appear in this section for the first time, each with some attempt at recapitulation of earlier developments. The organization of material reflects the logic of four decades of history in the area rather than a mechanical country-by-country treatment.

Part V offers a variety of viewpoints and interpretations, but no cross section of all available opinion. Quite a lot of commentary, especially but not exclusively from western sources, is essentially frivolous, either couched in the terms of an outmoded ideological clash or designed to justify mistaken earlier interpretations. The viewpoints offered here are ones that I regard as serious and thoughtful, however much their advocates may differ among themselves.

Regarding the selections in general, I have favored East European over western commentary where the choice was otherwise a toss-up, and have included documents only when they were brief enough or lively enough to maintain readability. For the sake of a readable and uncluttered text, footnotes have been omitted wherever possible; the reader looking for sources can always refer to the original.

With minor exceptions, the selections were made by the end of 1990. In a few cases, it has been possible to append more recent material to make Part IV as topical as possible. But the reader should always bear in mind that the developments depicted there are far from complete and the outcomes far from certain.

I would like to acknowledge the critical assistance of several reviewers whose comments on the manuscript aided significantly in creating this anthology: D. R. Dorondo, Western Carolina University; Richard Lewis, St. Cloud State University; and Paul Michelson, Huntington College. I would also like to thank the staff at D. C. Heath with whom I worked: Tina Beazer and Karen Wise, production editors; Martha Friedmann, photo researcher; James Miller, senior editor for history; Margaret Roll, permissions editor; and Jan Shapiro, designer.

L.H.L.

Contents

◆
Part IV
The Bloc
Transformed   297

Chronology of Major Events, 1945–1991

✦
1945

February: Allies agree at Yalta on a continuing Soviet presence in Eastern Europe.

April: Soviet Union and Yugoslavia sign treaty of friendship.

July: Potsdam Conference considers arrangements in defeated Germany.

November: Marshal Josip Broz Tito's National Front wins Yugoslav elections; republic declared. Hungarian elections won by Smallholders' party; sharp defeat for the Communist party.

✦
1946

January: Albania proclaimed a republic under Enver Hoxha.

February: Hungary declared a republic.

March: Winston Churchill's "iron curtain" speech at Fulton, Missouri.

May: Czechoslovak Communist Party gains 38% of vote in elections. Paris Peace Conference fixes territorial arrangements in Romania.

August: Soviet trade agreements with East European states.

October: Georgii Dimitrov forms Communist-dominated cabinet in Bulgaria.

November: Communist-dominated National Democratic Front wins Romanian elections.

✦
1947

January: Communist party wins Polish elections.

March: Announcement of Marshall Plan.

August: Communists gain control of Hungarian government and National Assembly.

September: Establishment of Cominform under Soviet domination.

December: Soviet forces leave Bulgaria after peace treaty is signed.

✦
1948

February: Klement Gottwald forms Communist-dominated cabinet in Czechoslovakia.

March: Death of Jan Masaryk, noncommunist foreign minister of Czechoslovakia. Eruption of Soviet-Yugoslav dispute.

May: Eduard Beneš resigns as Czechoslovak president after electoral victory of Communist-dominated National Front.

June: Soviets blockade Berlin; Allies respond with airlift.

September: Władysław Gomułka charged with nationalist deviation and removed as general secretary of Polish Communist Party.

December: Socialists and Communists merge to form Polish United Workers' Party. Dimitrov proclaims theory of People's Democracy.

✦
1949

January: Formation of Council for Mutual Economic Assistance (CMEA).

April: Foundation of NATO.

May: End of Berlin Blockade.

June: Purges begin in Hungary with arrest of Foreign Minister Lászlo Rajk.

October: Establishment of German Democratic Republic led by Walter Ulbricht.

November: Soviet Marshal Konstantin Rokossovski designated Polish defense minister.

✦
1950

March:	Mass expulsion of Germans from Polish western territories.
June:	Workers' Councils established in Yugoslav industry.
July:	At its third congress in Berlin, the Socialist Unity Party adopts a new constitution and a first Five-Year Plan.
August:	Mass expulsion of Turkish Muslims from Bulgaria.

✦
1951

January:	Mátyás Rákosi stresses importance of collectivization in Hungary.
May:	Yugoslav farmers allowed to sell on free market but warned against leaving collectives.
September:	Gottwald assumes general secretary's role in the Czechoslovak party.

✦
1952

March:	Soviet proposal for peace treaty endorsed by GDR parliament.
July:	Ulbricht announces plan emphasizing heavy industry.
August:	Hungarian National Assembly designates Rákosi prime minister.
November:	Trial and execution of Rudolf Slánský and other high Czechoslovak officials.

✦
1953

March:	Stalin dies, as does Gottwald in Czechoslovakia.
June:	Workers' uprising in East Berlin, protesting higher work norms, spreads throughout GDR but is put down by Soviet intervention.
July:	Imre Nagy becomes Hungarian prime minister, Rákosi retaining party post.
November:	Yugoslav ambassadors return to Hungary and Bulgaria.

◆
1954

March:	Todor Zhivkov becomes party secretary in Bulgaria.
April:	Gustav Husák sentenced on charge of Slovak separatism.
November:	East European states, meeting in Moscow, denounce Paris agreement on Germany.

◆
1955

March:	In Hungary, Rákosi begins to reassert power, resulting in denunciation of Nagy.
May:	In response to West German entry into NATO, Warsaw Pact organization is formed. Soviet Treaty with Austria. Khrushchev initiates rapprochement by visiting Yugoslavia.
September:	Soviet-GDR treaty acknowledges East German sovereignty.

◆
1956

February:	20th Party Congress in the Soviet Union; Khrushchev destalinization speech.
April:	Dissolution of the Cominform.
July:	Rákosi replaced by Ernő Gerő as general secretary in Hungary.
October:	Gomułka reinstated as general secretary in Poland, Rokossovski is dismissed, and Soviet intervention narrowly avoided. Nagy becomes prime minister; Soviets invade but then accept Nagy regime and replace Gerő with Kádár; Nagy announces democratic reforms and withdrawal from Warsaw Pact.
November:	Soviets invade again, replace Nagy with János Kádár; massive retaliation ensues against reform elements.

◆
1957

January:	Kádár announces hard line as strikes and stoppages continue.

May:	Soviet-Hungarian agreement on stationing Soviet troops in Hungary.
October:	Milovan Djilas sentenced to seven years because of his criticism of the party in Yugoslavia.

✦
1958

June:	Nagy executed, signaling end of post-Stalin liberalization.
July:	Soviet troops leave Romania.
November:	Khrushchev precipitates Berlin crisis, proposing GDR control of access routes to West Berlin.

✦
1959

January:	Zhivkov announces plan for full collectivization in Bulgaria.
April:	GDR proclaims that collectivization is completed.
July:	Soviet-Albanian trade agreement.

✦
1960

January:	Gomułka and Cardinal Stefan Wyszyński reach church-state accommodation.
February:	Warsaw Pact threatens separate peace treaties with GDR.

✦
1961

February:	Albania sides with China in Sino-Soviet dispute.
August:	Erection of Berlin Wall.
December:	A socialist division of labor is devised for the bloc, minus Albania.

✦
1962

March:	Romania registers dissent from Council of Mutual Economic Assistance (CMEA) division of labor.

November: Zhivkov prevails in Bulgarian party struggle.

◆
1963

March: Hungary amnesties most political prisoners.

April: New Yugoslav constitution.

September: Antonín Novotný asserts primacy in Czechoslovakia.

◆
1964

April: Romania offers to attempt resolution of Sino-Soviet dispute.

June: Romania proclaims release of political prisoners.

October: Brezhnev replaces Khrushchev as Soviet leader.

◆
1965

July: Romanian Party Congress adopts new constitution and party statute emphasizing the country's independent position within the bloc.

December: The Soviet Union and GDR report a new economic agreement.

◆
1966

March: Leaders of East European states record support for the Soviet Union against China, except for Romania's renewed offer to mediate.

July: Tito's expected successor, Alexander Ranković, is purged with others of his faction.

October: Yugoslav League of Communists reorganized.

◆
1967

January: Romania is first bloc state to establish relations with West Germany.

April: Yugoslavia develops plan for reducing the leading role of the party.

June: The Czechoslovak Writers' Union Congress voices criticism of party and government.

December: Leadership crisis threatens Novotný's position in Czechoslovakia.

◆
1968

January: Alexander Dubček replaces Novotný as Prague Spring begins.

March: Novotný also ousted from presidency, replaced by Ludvík Svoboda.

April: Action Program of basic reform is announced in Prague.

July: Warsaw Pact warns Czechoslovakia against excessive reform; Soviet and Czechoslovak leaders reach temporary agreement.

August: Invasion of Czechoslovakia by Soviet troops and other Warsaw Pact neighbors; Soviets fail to find alternative and reinstate Dubček.

September: Soviets proclaim doctrine of limited sovereignty, confirmed later in year by Brezhnev at Polish party congress.

◆
1969

January: Czechoslovak students protest occupation in Prague Manifesto after Jan Palach's self-immolation in Wenceslas Square.

March: Gustav Husák replaces Dubček.

June: Romania disagrees with Brezhnev Doctrine at Moscow meeting of world communist parties.

◆
1970

March: East and West Germany begin talks that lead to diplomatic recognition and agreement on access to Berlin.

June: Dubček expelled from Czechoslovak Communist Party.

December: Strikes and riots in coastal cities of Poland in response to price increases; Gomułka replaced by Edward Gierek.

✦
1971

May:	Ulbricht replaced by Erich Honecker in the GDR.
July:	CMEA announces plan for increased regional economic integration.
December:	Riots in Zagreb involving Croatian nationalists.

✦
1972

July:	Trials of Dubček supporters charged with subversion.
November:	GDR amnesties some 30,000 political prisoners.
December:	Croatian nationalists purged from Yugoslav party and state posts.

✦
1973

February:	The fourth postwar constitution enlarges powers of Yugoslav workers' councils. Britain and France recognize GDR.
June:	Romania's Nicolae Ceauşescu becomes first bloc head of state to visit West Germany.
July:	Helsinki Conference on Security and Cooperation in Europe.
December:	Moscow Conference of Nine Ruling Communist Parties.

✦
1974

March:	Purges reported from Albania following Hoxha's rejection of detente.
July:	Romania receives World Bank loan.
September:	United States and GDR open relations.

✦
1975

June:	Announcement of new Soviet gas pipeline to Eastern Europe.

August: Final Act of Helsinki accords is signed.

✦
1976

June: Riots in Poland over food prices. Tito ends 19-year boycott by attending East Berlin conference of Communist parties.

July: Polish food prices adjusted in response to riots.

October: Increase in price of Soviet crude oil causes difficulty for some East European states.

✦
1977

January: Charter 77 is signed by 240 intellectuals in Czechoslovakia.

February: Expensive grain imports add to Poland's mounting foreign debt.

August: Romanian miners strike over living standards.

✦
1978

May: Yugoslav Party Congress adopts plan for collective leadership.

July: China terminates economic assistance to Albania.

October: Cardinal Karol Wojtyla of Poland elected pope as John Paul II.

✦
1979

June: Pope John Paul's visit to Poland.

October: Imprisonment of Charter 77 dissenters in Czechoslovakia.

✦
1980

July: Widespread strikes and riots in Poland after meat price increase.

August: Workers take over Lenin Shipyard in Gdańsk; Gierek resigns.

September: Formation of Solidarity as independent trade union.

November: Warsaw Pact troops mass on Polish border.

December:	To avert invasion, Solidarity calls off strike; at the Lenin Shipyard, a memorial is unveiled honoring workers killed in 1970 protests.

◆
1981

February:	General Wojciech Jaruzelski becomes prime minister of Poland.
March:	Negotiations between government and Solidarity delay strike action, though union demands are not met. State of emergency in Kosovo, Yugoslavia.
May:	Warsaw court gives legal status to farmers' branch of Solidarity. Cardinal Wyszyński dies.
Summer:	Strikes continue throughout Poland, as do negotiations between union and government and between Polish government and Warsaw Pact leadership.
November:	Solidarity and government reopen negotiations.
December:	Solidarity presents new demands; Jaruzelski declares martial law, suspending civil rights and union operations.

◆
1982

March:	Warsaw Pact maneuvers in Poland.
May:	Mass demonstration in Warsaw against martial law.
November:	Brezhnev dies, succeeded by Yuri Andropov.
December:	Polish announcement that martial law will be suspended formally by year's end.

◆
1983

January:	Officially sponsored trade unions formed to replace Solidarity.
June:	Pope John Paul II visits Poland, meets with Jaruzelski and Lech Wałęsa.
July:	Martial law terminated with limited amnesty.
October:	Nobel Peace Prize to Wałęsa.

✦ 1984

February:	Andropov dies, replaced by Konstantin Chernenko.
July:	Poland announces broad amnesty.
September:	Soviet pressure results in postponement of Honecker's, and cancellation of Zhivkov's, visit to West Germany.

✦ 1985

March:	Chernenko dies, succeeded by Mikhail Gorbachev.
April:	General secretary of the Albanian party, Hoxha, dies, succeeded by Ramiz Alia.

✦ 1986

February:	Gorbachev addresses Communist Party Congress with proposals for radical reform in politics and economy.
Summer:	After May arrest of Zbigniew Bujak, underground Solidarity leader, a more general crackdown is launched; but then Bogdan Lis and Adam Michnik are released, with amnesty for remaining political prisoners in September.
September:	Helsinki Watch reports that ethnic Turks are being killed in Bulgaria.
November:	Gorbachev presses for reforms at CMEA meeting.

✦ 1987

March:	Demonstration in Budapest in behalf of liberalization. Husák backs Gorbachev's reforms in address to Czechoslovak Central Committee.
April:	Honecker denies applicability of Soviet reforms to the GDR. Gorbachev and Jaruzelski sign accord on Soviet-Polish cooperation.
May:	Zhivkov endorses reform program for Bulgaria.

July: GDR announces political amnesty.

December: Miloš Jakeš replaces Husák as general secretary in Czechoslovakia.

◆

1988

April: Polish government puts down steel strike vigorously.

May: Kádár removed in Hungary and replaced by collective presidium.

August: Polish interior minister suggests roundtable talks with opposition demanding reinstatement of Solidarity.

Autumn: Worsening relations between Hungary and Romania over latter's treatment of Hungarian minority.

November: Gorbachev announces cuts in Soviet armed forces and removal of some troops from Hungary, Czechoslovakia, and GDR.

◆

1989

January: Human rights protests in Czechoslovakia; Václav Havel and many others arrested.

February: Roundtable talks begin in Poland between government and opposition.

March: Mass demonstration in Budapest for free elections and Soviet withdrawal.

April: Solidarity and government reach agreement that some parliamentary seats will be contested at the polls.

May: Thousands of ethnic Turks forced to leave Bulgaria. Hungary begins to dismantle iron curtain along Austrian border. Havel released on parole.

June: Solidarity and independent candidates win all contested seats against party candidates in Polish election. Remains of former prime minister Nagy reinterred with state honors, one week after the death of Kádár.

July: Jaruzelski resigns as party secretary to become president of Poland.

August: Solidarity assumes task of forming a government, designating Tadeusz Mazowiecki as prime minister. Many arrests in Czechoslovakia after mass demonstrations celebrating the anniversary of the
1968 invasion.

September: Thousands of East Germans flee through West German embassies
in Prague and Warsaw or over the Hungarian border into Austria.
Hungarian government and opposition agree on multiparty system in 1990.

October: Honecker deposed in East Germany. The Hungarian party
renames itself the Hungarian Socialist Party and renounces Lenin-
sim. Riot police break up mass demonstration in Czechoslovakia.

November: GDR opens its borders; government and Politburo resign.
Zhivkov retires in Bulgaria, replaced by Petar Mladenov with
promises of reform. Romania and Czechoslovakia resist the
reforming tendency, but continuing protests bring down government and party in the latter country.

December: East German party leadership resigns and party renounces its leading role. Husák resigns the presidency in Czechoslovakia and is
replaced by the end of the month by Havel, with Dubček serving
as president of the Federal Assembly. Mass demonstrations in Sofia
elicit the promise of free elections and the end of party monopoly
of power. The clash of demonstrators and government in Romania leads to violence in Timişoara and Bucharest that turns into a
brief but bloody civil war, ending with the execution of
Ceauşescu and his wife.

◆

1990

January: Bulgarian Central Committee and Politburo replaced as orthodox
communists are defeated at party congress. Socialist Unity Party
becomes Party of Democratic Socialism in GDR as mass exodus
to West Germany continues. Wałęsa joins Czechoslovak and
Hungarian leaders in calling for withdrawal of Soviet troops.

February: Deepening crisis in GDR prompts increasing talk of reunification.
Romanian demonstrators charge that the National Salvation Front
has not sufficiently repudiated Ceauşescu regime.

March: Nearly half of East German voters prefer Alliance for Germany, the counterpart of the Christian Democrats in West Germany and a proponent of early reunification. Hungarian voters favor Hungarian Democratic Front and its appeal to nationalism over other parties; Socialists (former communist) poll only 10 percent. Serious clashes between Romanians and the Hungarian minority in Transylvania.

April: Hungarian Democratic Front begins attempt to form government. East Germany's first noncommunist government formed under Lothar de Maizière. Soviet government acknowledges responsibility for 1940 massacre of Polish officers in Katyn forest. Slovene multiparty election challenges communist rule. GDR party coalition, socialists and free democrats joining the Alliance for Germany.

May: Ion Iliescu and National Salvation Front win Romanian election, preserving Communist control. Jozef Antall, Hungarian prime minister, presents government program, emphasizing privatization and foreign investment.

June: Civic Forum and its Slovak counterpart, Public Against Violence, win decisive victory in Czechoslovak elections; Marián Čalfa continues as prime minister. Socialists (former Communists) prevail in Bulgarian elections. Announcement of Serbian plan to unite the League of Communists with the Socialist Alliance with Milošević as president.

July: Solidarity divides, the Civic Movement–Democratic Action forming as counter to Wałęsa's Center Alliance. East Germany joins the Federal Republic in economic and currency union. Slovenia and Kosovo both proclaim sovereignty; Serbia retaliates by dissolving Kosovo's provincial assembly.

September: Czechoslovak Federal Assembly approves program of economic reform, promoting privatization and mixed economy.

October: Croatia and Slovenia propose that Yugoslavia become a confederation of independent states. Treaty of union between the GDR and West Germany. Bulgarian prime minister announces plan for transition to market economy.

November: Wałęsa defeats Mazowiecki for the presidency of Poland. Prime Minister Andrey Lukanov resigns in Bulgaria.

◆
1991

January: Czechoslovak parliament inaugurates screening of members for past involvement with secret police.

February: In Poland, Solidarity's third national congress again debates issue of trade unionism vs. political action.

March: The military arm of the Warsaw Pact is dissolved. Albania's first multiparty election results in communist victory, though the opposition Democratic Party dominates cities. Serbia refuses to recognize authority of the Yugoslav federal presidency; removal of members from Kosovo, Voivodina, and Montenegro deprives that body of required quorum.

May: Soviet troops complete withdrawal from Czechoslovakia. Former communists Imre Pozsgay and Zoltán Biró form a new Hungarian party, the National Democratic Alliance. In the five new Länder formed from the former German Democratic Republic, unemployment has reached 30% and industrial production has fallen by 50%. Ethnic Serbs living in Croatia vote overwhelmingly for union with Serbia.

June: The Pope arrives to begin his fourth visit to Poland. German parliament votes to move capital from Bonn to Berlin. Hungary celebrates departure of Soviet troops. Croatia and Slovenia declare independence from Yugoslavia. In Albania, Prime Minister Fatos Nano forced to resign, ending 47 years of communist rule, in favor of a government of national salvation.

July: Nobel Prize winner Elie Wiesel, in Bucharest for commemoration of wartime massacre of Romania Jews, notes rash of antisemitic statements in Romanian press and warns of danger to the nation. A summit meeting in Ohrid breaks down, failing to halt ethnic turmoil in Yugoslavia.

August: The truce between Serbia and Croatia appears to be holding, but Macedonia announces a September referendum on independence.

Eastern Europe

Former East European members of the Warsaw Pact

Boundaries and place names are given as of October 1, 1991. Estonia, Latvia, and Lithuania have achieved independence, relations among the other Soviet republics and the future of the union are in flux. In Yugoslavia, the republics of Slovenia, Croatia, and Macedonia are seeking independence.

NORWAY

SWEDEN

FINLAND

Helsinki

St. Petersburg

Russia (RSFSR)

Oslo

Stockholm

Baltic Sea

ESTONIA

Moscow

LATVIA

North Sea

DENMARK

LITHUANIA

Copenhagen

Gdańsk

RSFSR

Belorussia

Berlin

POLAND

NETH.

GERMANY

Warsaw

Kiev

BELG.

Bonn

Leipzig

Kraków

Ukraine

LUX.

Prague

CZECH.

FRANCE

LIECH.

Vienna

Bratislava

Moldavia

SWITZ.

AUSTRIA

Budapest

HUNGARY

ROMANIA

Ljubljana

Timişoara

Zagreb

Belgrade

Bucharest

Black Sea

YUGOSLAVIA

Sofia

BULGARIA

ITALY

Plovdiv

Tiriana

TURKEY

ALBANIA

GREECE

Mediterranean Sea

0   250   500
Miles

Yugoslavia

0   50   100
Miles

ROMANIA

HUNGARY

AUSTRIA

BULGARIA

GREECE

ALBANIA

ITALY

ADRIATIC SEA

Danube R.

Subotica

Voivodina

Nova Sad

Tisa R.

Drava R.

SLOVENIA

LJUBLJANA

ISTRIA

TRIESTE

Piran

Opatija

Pula

VENICE

Po R.

ZAGREB

Karlovac

Krajna

Rijeka

C R O A T I A

Sava R.

Una R.

Banja Luka

Bihać

Slavonski Brod

Sremska
Mitrovica

Ruma

BELGRADE

Pančevo

Radmilovac

Smederevo

Bor

ŠUMADIJA

Maladenovac

Topola

Morava

Kraljevo

Niš

Leskovac

Radmilovac

SERBIA

Drina R.

Bosna R.

B O S N I A

Zenica

Jajce

Drvar

Travnik

Livno

Knin

Zadar

Šibenik

Trogir

Split

Neretva R.

Mostar

HERCEGOVINA

Polče

Ploče

D A L M A T I A

Dubrovnik

Ercegnovi

Budva

Kotor

Cetinje

TITOGRAD

M O N T E N E G R O

Peć

Dečani

Kosmet

SKOPJE

Tetovo

MACEDONIA

Ohrid

Bitolj

Djevdjelija

Crna R.

L. Scutari

SARAJEVO

Introduction

◆ *Revolution is an ambiguous word. For some, any major change beyond the limits of prescribed routine may be, and often is, called a revolution. Others prefer to restrict the word's meaning to the comprehensive social transformation that formed the core of Marx's concept of revolution. In the looser usage, we can recognize a revolution almost immediately, even though we may not be able to anticipate its outcome. In the more restrictive sense, we cannot identify a revolution with any certainty until it has run its course.*

In 1917 in Russia, some held that a revolution occurred early in that year when tsarism was overthrown and replaced by a provisional government. It was enough, according to the looser view, that a style of governance and its autocratic protagonist had given way to a more responsive style and a different set of leaders. But it could also count as a revolution in the more precise sense if one held that the substitution of constitutional government for autocracy was equivalent to social transformation.

Later that year the reins of power were seized by the Bolsheviks, with their proclaimed revolutionary intentions. For those of critical or skeptical bent, this was merely a seizure of power, at least until Bolshevik intentions had been translated into an effective, implemented program. And for some close observers, it eventually became clear that an authentic revolution had indeed occurred in the early years of Bolshevik rule—but that it had happened in the countryside when, without benefit of Bolshevik supervision, peasants seized the land. In important ways, this transformation in fact ran counter to the central principles of socialist revolutionary doctrine. There were thus three events in 1917 that could be immediately identified, in the uncritical view, as revolutions. All three could also be identified as revolutions in the restrictive meaning of the term, but only after enough time had elapsed to permit a confident grasp of the implications and consequences of the initial event.

As we observe contemporary developments in Eastern Europe, we confront a similar problem of interpretation. We may sense intuitively, even in the restrictive view, that we are witnessing revolutionary events, but it is far too early to glimpse the outcomes—to know, in other words, what kinds of revolutions these are. The processes of and impulses to change are of course by no means new—if we include the whole history of striving for autonomy in the area. If, on the other hand, we limit our outlook to 1989–1990, the processes we are witnessing are very new indeed. There are powerful reasons for emphasizing this newness: it is already clear that the events of 1989–1990 are different in kind from the eruptions of 1956 or 1968 or 1980, that current upheavals are not just reenactments of earlier strivings for autonomy.

And that gives us some warrant for what could seem a premature judgment on the question of revolution, despite the fact that we find ourselves in an early stage of transformation. Even as we admit that outcomes are uncertain, we can quite confidently say that processes of change now under way will run some course or other. They will not simply be terminated, with the status quo ante *restored.*

If we may speak unabashedly of current events in Eastern Europe as revolutionary, as a new revolution, the question remains: What was the old revolution? And this brings us back to the Soviet Union. Ever since Lenin established his dominant role, through the Third International, over a global movement for socialist revolution, down to the enunciation of the so-called Brezhnev Doctrine in 1968 (in the aftermath of the invasion of Czechoslovakia), official Soviet doctrine has favored a peculiar understanding of revolution. It has insisted, as a negative constraint on independent revolutionary efforts, that the requirements and interests of the "homeland of revolution" be paramount considerations in any revolutionary strategy anywhere. And on the positive side, it has advocated a notion of "revolution by association," suggesting that an alliance with the Soviet Union, if coupled with adoption of Soviet tutelage in socioeconomic matters, could confer revolutionary status on another society, irrespective of the means by which the alliance occurred.

A variant of this notion operated within the Soviet Union to abrogate the principle of self-determination and the right of secession, claiming for "socialism" and "the revolution" many territories that had no opportunity to give or withhold their assent. It is no accident (as Marxist-Leninists have been wont to say) that the consequences of Soviet policy toward domestic nationalities have come to a head, threatening the dissolution of the USSR itself, even as the Soviet bloc in Eastern Europe disintegrates.

Beginning in 1945, the countries of Eastern Europe had their "first" revolutions in the same manner: revolutionary status was conferred by association, not by choice or independent action, and the association was imposed by the Soviet army within a framework that East Europeans still refer to as the Yalta system. As the war ground to a close, Stalin made good on his sphere of influence in Eastern Europe by imposing puppet regimes on the countries that lay on the path to Berlin, dominated by old communists trained in Moscow and held in readiness through World War II. One exception to the pattern of takeover was Yugoslavia, which asserted its autonomy against Soviet wishes as early as 1948; another was East Germany, which remained a zone of Soviet occupation until 1948–1949, but whose rulers conformed to the general East European pattern; and Albania never came fully under Soviet control.

Thus, the revolutions of the postwar period in Eastern Europe (again excepting Yugoslavia and Albania) were initially as specious as the revolutionary status conferred on the Baltic states by amalgamation a few years before—or, one might add, the notion of Bolshevik revolution in the Russian countryside in 1917. In all these cases, however, the artificial quality of the initial, Soviet-imposed "revolution" did nothing to prevent real social transformation thereafter. The ensuing measures to eradicate private ownership, collectivize agriculture, and confer privileges on formerly exploited classes did produce genuine social transformation, whether or not they conformed to a particular conception of socialism. In the East European countries, as in the Soviet Union, changes of such fundamental character may in turn be altered or even superseded, but they cannot be undone.

The eruptions of 1956, 1968, and 1980 revealed of course that the Soviet model was immune even to modest alteration, at least so long as the Soviet authorities remained unyielding. Fortunately for Eastern Europe, however, a crucial difference appeared after 1985 between the erstwhile Soviet satellites on the one hand and the restive Soviet republics on the other. In all cases, the flaw in the presumptive initial revolution was that it had not been chosen by its citizenry and, especially in Eastern Europe, that it had been imposed by an alien power. But when that power relaxed its hold, when tutelary restriction turned into encouragement of significant political and social change, the way opened for East Europeans to reclaim control over their own affairs. In some cases the first moves came, as they had in 1956 and 1968, from within the ruling party; in others, as in 1980–1981, from a reviving civil society. But ultimately, the dam burst everywhere, and in greatest force in places (notably East Germany and Romania) where civil society had previously enjoyed the smallest opportunity to fulfill the functions it sought to recapture from a state monopoly of all public affairs—otherwise known as the Soviet model.

It is of course possible to argue that the program, initiated throughout the Soviet bloc as soon as communist control was firmly established, amounted eventually to a revolution. The so-called building of socialism undoubtedly transformed the societies in question, whether they were predominantly agrarian like Bulgaria or industrially advanced like Czechoslovakia.

But there is a powerful reason, stemming from within the tradition of social thought that the Soviet Union claimed to represent and was purportedly extending to fortunate recipients, for denying these transformations the status of revolution. The Marxist revolutionary tradition has always held, except of course where it has been perverted, that the people (that is, the working class) must make their own revolution. Such a revolution may not be conferred from above or from outside. If that is true, then the transformations imposed on the countries of Eastern Europe were fatally flawed unless the affected peoples themselves freely embraced and willingly implemented them.

Viewed in this way, the steady East European resistance to the Soviet model and program, and the periodic revolts in which that resistance culminated here and *there, do not necessarily repudiate the particular measures promoting social change; they certainly do repudiate the manner of their imposition. Put another way, even people who favor some kind of socialism will not endorse a socialism that is inflicted involuntarily. This is not to suggest that the peoples of Eastern Europe did favor socialism; the majority of them probably did not. But we can never know whether or not they might have been persuaded, by force of argument rather than force of arms, for the simple reason that they had no opportunity to register their preference. That fact deprived the client regimes and their policies of legitimacy and, after decades of inflicted "socialism" and the debased rhetoric accompanying it, resulted in the power-ful backlash we are witnessing today—not just against particular policies or their agents but against any reminder whatsoever of forty-some years of alien repressive force exerted in behalf of the Soviet version of socialism.*

That is why it seems useful to resort to the less elevated notion of "takeover" as a way of calling attention to the probability that East Europeans would have wel-comed no program, socialist or otherwise, that was inflicted on them. The Soviet leadership began to practice this maneuver soon after the initial seizure of power in 1917. They attempted takeovers first in what became the border republics of the Soviet Union (which helps to account for some similarities visible today between those republics and the former client states of Eastern Europe in relation to central authority in Moscow), and also in countries like Finland and Poland. Soviet leaders were without question far more cynical in employing this device after 1945, but the tech-nique was essentially the same. A cadre of disciplined communists, native to the target country or locale, was held in readiness to become the government, or at least crucial elements of the government, of a territory newly won for the revolution. Even in the early years, when revolutionary zeal was still operative, the essential thing was to assure responsiveness to the needs, wishes, and experience of the Bolsheviks. In the late years of Stalin's rule, when his armed forces were "liberating" the German-occupied countries of Eastern Europe, little of revolutionary fervor remained except its rhetoric. Control was left as virtually the sole preoccupation.

With the Soviet army on the scene everywhere (except Yugoslavia and Alba-nia), Stalin could proceed confidently with the business of most pressing concern: the extraction of reparations to assist in the rebuilding of the war-torn Soviet economy and the formation of joint companies to exploit local resources to Soviet advantage. Such pursuits took precedence over the establishment of socialist regimes, and Stalin could afford to be more patient about actual takeovers, which served their purpose better if cloaked in the trappings of consent and legality. The subject populations were seldom deceived by takeover tactics, but the gradual undermining of more or less popular native government suited the needs of diplomacy so long as the wartime alliance survived.

When that alliance broke down and was replaced by overt hostility in 1947–1948, Soviet designs could become more open. At this point the overt fashioning of "people's democracies" could and did proceed. That meant the elimination of national communisms, which, to Stalin, were associated with the less trustworthy leaders who had, for one reason or another, not had the benefit of schooling in wartime Moscow for their postwar tasks. Władysław Gomułka in Poland was the pre-eminent national communist, one who resisted collectivization of agriculture and proclaimed a distinctive Polish path of development.

The issue took acute form in Yugoslavia, however, not so much because Tito and his associates differed ideologically from Stalin but because, having gained their own triumph unaided in Yugoslavia, they objected to Stalin's "junior partner" treatment that reduced them to parity with the states that became people's democracies by Soviet military force. The break that ensued just as Stalin was consolidating the Soviet bloc in the rest of Eastern Europe, and Yugoslavia's subsequent success in developing a distinctive form of socialism, upset Stalin's calculations but also undoubtedly fortified him in his mistrust of native leaders. For the balance of his tenure, until his death in 1953, Stalin clamped a rigid system of control over the region, subjecting it through the military and his trusted native agents to much the same tyranny that marked his domestic regime.

Because he had established his ideological sympathizers in power in all the satellites (as the client states were called in the West), and because those henchmen owed their positions entirely to Soviet influence and not at all to popular support, the softening of Soviet policy toward the region, advertised as the "New Course," came as a shock to the East European Stalinists. This was the first instance of the Soviet Union's acting in behalf of liberalization against the wishes of its client regimes. (The second instance would come when Gorbachev launched his perestroika program in the late 1980s.) The relaxation was favorable to native advocates of reform such as Imre Nagy in Hungary, but uncomfortable for unreconstructed hardliners like Walter Ulbricht, who nearly lost his position in 1953 when a spontaneous strike in East Germany broke out after he had refused to grant workers any benefits of liberalization. This, incidentally, was a rare situation in which local protest was aimed exclusively at the domestic regime without admixture of anti-Soviet feeling, at least until Soviet troops intervened to end the strike.

The rapid East German reaction notwithstanding, the change from Stalin to new leadership in the Soviet Union was felt only quite gradually in Eastern Europe. But Khrushchev's exposure of Stalin's transgressions in 1956 encouraged the moderate elements of communism in the region to move further toward autonomy in the choice of policies leading to further socialization, especially in Poland and Hungary. The Polish crisis was resolved without major conflict when Khrushchev accepted the *return of Gomułka. Hungary, on the other hand, discovered the limits of Soviet tolerance. When it appeared that they had another defection to deal with, Soviet forces intervened and crushed the Hungarian uprising most brutally, installed a tractable new regime, and simply ignored the condemnation of world opinion.*

The intervention of 1956 essentially settled the question of Soviet liberality. Twelve years later the Czechoslovaks thought they had taken the necessary precautions to avoid a repetition of 1956, but they were confounded when intervention prevented acceptance of a sharp departure from the Soviet model and demonstrated concern about the leading role of the Czechoslovak ruling party. Even as late as 1980–1981 and the Solidarity period in Poland, a Soviet intervention loomed as a distinct possibility—a fear that the Soviet leadership did not hesitate to encourage for its own purposes.

In dwelling on particular events and episodes that can be described as outbreaks of resistance, oppositional actions aimed either at Soviet domination or at unpopular domestic regimes or at both together, we risk overlooking two developments of another type that surfaced in the early 1960s. The first was the decision by Albania to side with China against the Soviet Union in the Sino-Soviet dispute of that era. This move made Albania (willingly it would seem) a pariah in Eastern Europe. And, Albania being Albania, this hardly posed a life-or-death challenge to Soviet hegemony. At worst it impaired the image of correctness that the Soviet Union sought to cultivate in everything from tactics and policies to global strategy.

The other development, much closer to the geopolitical heart of the Soviet bloc, was Romania's growing tendency to strike out on paths of its own, first manifested in its resistance to the Soviet-sponsored economic division of labor for the region, a scheme that cast Romania in a role subservient to the more developed states of the alliance. That was followed by the adoption of an independent line in foreign relations, resulting eventually in Romanian initiatives toward Western Europe that seemed to operate at cross-purposes with the Soviet Union's own moves in that direction. By the end of the 1960s, Romania's Ceauşescu had become an outspoken critic of the Brezhnev Doctrine—the formal Soviet response (in fact simply an enunciation of prevailing policy) to the Czechoslovak upheaval of 1968. It was often startling to hear Ceauşescu stating with impunity a line that had cost other leaders so dearly in former times.

Both the Albanian and the Romanian gestures of independence, however much they challenged the notion of Soviet infallibility, underscore the rule that "resistance" or "opposition" is in fact defined by the target of that action. If the target chooses to regard an act or policy as permissible, it is hard to argue for its oppositional nature. This may seem a weak basis for the distinction, but it is simply what separates tolerated deviations from those evoking reprisal or penalty.

The balance of the postwar East European story is told, often with eloquence, in the texts that make up the body of this book. Not to be confused with narrative history, an anthology has the particular merit of allowing participants and observers of diverse viewpoints to convey the flavor of events in their own time. The last phase, the one that is still unfolding from day to day, is undoubtedly of greatest interest to present readers. It must be approached as an unfinished chapter, the full import of which can be revealed only in years to come. We must also accept as an abiding mystery the dynamics of social transformation. No scientific rule explains why major changes occur just when they do or just what elements of social mobilization suffice to accomplish at one time what has eluded the grasp at other times. The readings that make up this book are simply one way of telling the story or, better, of letting the story tell itself.

Part I

The Soviet Bloc

◆ *Given the duration and complexity of the Soviet bloc in postwar Eastern Europe, it is possible here to offer only a small sample of texts that illustrate either stages or turning points in its development or describe it in quite general terms. The matter of duration is important here: the Soviet Union's postwar alliance system lasted well over a generation. Only people born in the 1930s or earlier can remember the time before the advent of Soviet domination in Eastern Europe. We of course want to dwell on the end of that system now that the downfall of communism appears to be irreversible. And we properly harbor congratulatory sentiments toward the East European peoples. But we dare not lose sight of the extent to which habits are formed and institutional practices internalized in forty years. True, the spirit of resistance never died and was there to be mobilized. Yet it takes more than that to overcome four decades of history. A sympathetic view of Eastern Europe must therefore recognize the enormous difficulties left as a legacy of Soviet preponderance.*

The selections begin by defining the concept of takeover. *Thomas T. Hammond indicates the long history of that maneuver in Soviet practice and compares East European instances. Takeover produced a set of "people's democracies," a locution that conveyed certain meanings at the time. Eugene Varga, whose definition appears here, was a professionally trained Hungarian economist and a revolutionary socialist who worked for the international communist movement during the Stalinist era. The Khrushchev passage is from his dramatic 1956 "secret speech" exposing the underside of Stalinism at the Twentieth Soviet Party Congress, a turning point of great significance for Eastern Europe.*

The next two selections both characterize, though with different emphases, the implications of Soviet domination for any independent action attempted in the client states of that era. Another selection assesses the impact of glasnost *on those states. The concluding entry epitomizes the immense change in Soviet perspectives on the region by the latter half of the 1980s.*

Communist Takeover

✦

Thomas T. Hammond

Thomas T. Hammond, a historian at the University of Virginia, offers here a synthesis of the technique utilized by the Soviet Union to extend its power into adjacent areas. This essay concluded a book of case studies that Hammond published in 1975 at a time of the Cold War when additional instances of takeover seemed a distinct possibility to many observers.

✦

THE TYPOLOGY OF COMMUNIST TAKEOVERS

It is clear . . . that Communists have taken power under a great variety of circumstances, with tactics differing from country to country and from time to time. There are, however, some remarkable similarities. It might be useful at this point, therefore, to group the various takeovers according to type and see which ones fall into each category.

One major dividing line can be noted at the start—between exported revolutions and indigenous ones. There have been three types of *exported revolutions*—i.e., revolutions imposed from without by foreign armies:

Type 1—*Outright Annexation of Territory by a Communist State*. The instances of this type are numerous. For example, during the first years of the Bolshevik regime the Red Army was continuously engaged in conquering and re-annexing the borderlands of the former Tsarist empire—areas such as the Ukraine, the Caucasus, and Central Asia, where non-Russian peoples had established independent states. Many years later, as a result of the Nazi-Soviet pact of 1939, several more areas were annexed—western Ukraine, western Belorussia, the Baltic States, Bessarabia, northern Bukovina, and parts of Finland. During and after World War II other territories were annexed— Tannu Tuva, Carpatho-Ukraine, the Königsberg area of East Prussia, the Kurile Islands, and Southern Sakhalin. In this same category might also be included the absorption of Tibet by Communist China and the annexation by Poland of German lands east of the Oder-Neisse line.

Thomas T. Hammond, "The Typology of Communist Takeovers," from *The Anatomy of Communist Takeovers,* Yale University Press, 1975, pp. 638–643.

Type 2—*Installation of a Communist Regime Outside of Russia by the Soviet Army.* The first cases of this type were in Outer Mongolia and Tannu Tuva in 1921, while the others came in the aftermath of World War II—in Poland, East Germany, Hungary, Bulgaria, Rumania, and North Korea. This was the most common way in which countries became Communist during the period from 1944 to 1947.

Type 3—*Counter-Revolutions in Heretical Communist Countries by the Soviet Army.* There have been three of these so far—in East Germany in 1953, Hungary in 1956, and Czechoslovakia in 1968.

The remaining types of Communist takeovers have been entirely or mainly *indigenous;* that is, they have been carried out primarily by native forces, although they may have received some help from abroad.

Type 4—*A Revolution in the Urban Centers, Based Largely on the Proletariat, Followed by Conquest of the Countryside.* This type of Communist takeover has occurred in only one country—Russia.

Type 5—*A Revolution in the Countryside, Based Mainly on the Peasants, Followed by Conquest of the Urban Centers.* This pattern of tactics was outlined by Mao in 1938 when he said: "Basically the task of the Communist Party here is not to . . . seize the big cities first and then occupy the countryside, but to take the other way round." Such revolutions have occurred not only in China but also in Yugoslavia, Albania, and North Vietnam.

Type 6—*A Completely Legal Takeover Through Free Elections.* So far Communists have been freely voted into power in only three small areas—San Marino, Kerala, and West Bengal—and in all three they were subsequently voted out. None of them are truly independent states.

Type 7—*A Semi-Legal Takeover Through Considerable Popular Support, Combined with Armed Threats.* In Czechoslovakia the Communists hoped to take power through free elections, but never quite made it. Instead they threatened the country with civil war by mobilizing the police forces, the "Workers Militia," and the trade unions, while at the same time intimating that Soviet troops would intervene if necessary. Fearing bloodshed, President Beneš gave legal sanction to a Communist-controlled government. Czechoslovakia thus followed in many respects the pattern set by Hitler's takeover.

Type 8—*A Non-Communist Leader Seizes Power and Then Decides to Adopt Communism.* Cuba so far offers the only example of this type of takeover, which has been described by Prof. Robert C. Tucker as "communism by conversion." Similarities have been displayed elsewhere, however: Sukarno in Indonesia and Arbenz in Guatemala seemed to be moving in this direction until they fell from power, and it once seemed possible that Allende would become the Castro of Chile.

◆

WHY COMMUNIST TAKEOVERS
HAVE SUCCEEDED OR FAILED

1. Military Force. The most striking conclusion that emerges from this survey of Communist takeovers is that military force has been the key to success in almost every case, and usually this has meant the Red Army. Out of a total of twenty-two Communist takeovers beginning in 1917, the Red Army played some role in fifteen and played the leading role in twelve. Where the Red Army was not decisive, native armed forces generally were used, as in Yugoslavia, Albania, China, Vietnam, and Cuba. Indeed, there were only three instances in which armed force was not the crucial element—in the tiny states of San Marino, Kerala, and West Bengal. Moreover, in each of these three states the Communists were subsequently removed from office. Thus it can be said that armed force was the determinant of victory in *all* cases in which Communists have not only seized power but have managed to retain it.

If Lenin and Stalin emphasized the importance of military power, Mao stressed it even more. Indeed, since Mao was forced to fight a civil war for more than twenty years in order to gain power, his attachment to military power became an obsession. In 1938 he made his famous statement:

> Political power grows out of the barrel of a gun. . . . Anything can grow out of the barrel of the gun. . . . Whoever wants to seize and hold on to political power must have a strong army. Some people have ridiculed us as advocates of the "theory of the omnipotence of war"; yes, we are, we are advocates of the theory of the omnipotence of revolutionary war. This is not a bad thing; it is good and it is Marxist. With the help of guns, the Russian Communists brought about socialism. . . . The working class and the toiling masses cannot defeat the armed bourgeois and landlord except by the power of the gun; in this sense we can even say that the whole world can be remolded only with the gun.

Pointing out the importance of organized armed force may seem to some a case of belaboring the obvious. However, many people still have highly romantic notions about revolutions—they have visions of the poor, downtrodden masses, unable any longer to bear the poverty and tyranny under which they suffer, rising up spontaneously to overthrow their reactionary oppressors. Such has not been the case in a single Communist revolution. A similar mistake made by some writers has been to ignore or underestimate the importance of the Red Army. For example, Gar Alperovitz writes: ". . . revolutions are caused by the inability of governments to deal with their problems (rarely, in any serious sense, as Che Guevara's failure [in Bolivia] illustrates, by 'outside agitators' and 'foreign powers'). . . ." Such a statement is obviously nonsense if applied to Communist revolutions, as the figures given above about the Red Army illustrate.

Military force imported from outside has also played a key role in Communist defeats. In the first few years after the Bolshevik revolution, armed intervention from other countries helped to prevent Communist revolutions from succeeding in Finland, Estonia, Latvia, Lithuania, Poland, and Hungary. In the aftermath of World War II, military intervention (or the threat of intervention) was important in defeating attempted Communist takeovers in Greece, northern Iran, Malaya, South Korea, South Vietnam, Laos, Cambodia, and Guatemala.

2. Geographical Contiguity. Since Communist victory or defeat has been determined in most cases by armed intervention from outside, the physical location of a country and the political complexion of its neighbors have naturally been important. Countries that have become Communist since 1917 have bordered on an established Communist state in every case except one—Cuba. Geography has been of equal importance in Communist defeats. To cite just two of the most striking examples: the Hungarian Soviet Republic of 1919 was overthrown largely because it was surrounded by hostile neighbors, while the attempt to make Guatemala Communist was foiled in part because of the proximity of anti-Communist neighbors, including the United States.

3. War. Almost all Communist takeovers have occurred either during international wars or in the aftermath of such wars—wars which undermined the old political, economic, and social order and which, in many cases, provided an opportunity for a foreign Communist army (usually the Red Army) to intervene. Examples are numerous. The Bolsheviks' opportunity to seize power in Russia came because of World War I. Eastern Europe became Communist mainly because of World War II. "The decisive factor in undermining the Nationalist government in China and enabling the Chinese Communist Party to build up sufficient strength to overthrow it was the Sino-Japanese war."

4. Free Elections. Communists have been freely elected to power in only three small states—San Marino, Kerala, and West Bengal—and in all three cases the Communists subsequently fell from power. That these Communists gave up power peacefully can be explained by the fact that each of these states is located inside a larger political entity, ruled by democratic governments, which can intervene if necessary. (Indeed, the President of India did intervene and dismiss the Communist government of Kerala in 1959.) Aside from these three states where Communists have been voted into office, there are two countries of some importance—France and Czechoslovakia—where Communists have won pluralities (but not majorities) in free elections, and two others—Italy and Finland—where they have gotten about one-fourth of the votes.

5. Agrarian Countries. Marx was of course wrong in expecting that Communist revolutions would occur first in advanced, highly industrialized countries. So far they have taken place in only two such countries—Czechoslovakia and East Germany—while the rest have been predominantly agrarian.

6. Camouflage. No Communist Party has ever come to power on the basis of a platform which frankly admitted that it intended to introduce communism, including such measures as the collectivization of agriculture, the nationalization of small enterprises, and the establishment of a one-party dictatorship.

7. *Retaining Power.* It is a remarkable fact that only one Communist regime controlling a whole country has ever been overthrown—Hungary in 1919. The only other exceptions are *parts* of countries, such as San Marino, Kerala, and West Bengal, plus the puppet regimes of Azerbaijan and Kurdistan in northern Iran. Guatemala and Indonesia do not qualify because there the Communists were not yet in control. This remarkable stability of Communist governments points to the conclusion that communism is a science not only of how to seize power, but also of how to *retain* power. Once a Communist regime is fully ensconced, it is almost impossible to remove it, except perhaps by foreign intervention.

8. *Indigenous Revolutions.* Finally, it might be noted that the Soviet Union has had the greatest difficulty in controlling those Communist regimes which rose to power mainly through their own efforts, rather than through the Soviet army. The examples are obvious—Yugoslavia, Albania, China, Cuba, and North Vietnam. Moscow has undoubtedly drawn the appropriate lesson from this fact—namely, that Communist revolutions carried out by the Soviet army and subject to Soviet control are usually desirable from the point of view of Russia's national interests, while indigenous Communist revolutions generally are not. The implications of such a conclusion for present Soviet foreign policy are clear—another Communist takeover in Latin America, for example, would be acceptable in Moscow's eyes only if there were reason to believe that the new regime would benefit the USSR or weaken the capitalist powers. No more Yugoslavias and Chinas are wanted, and perhaps no more Cubas either.

Thus Peking's charge that Moscow has abandoned the cause of world revolution is largely true. Since 1917 the Soviet Union has followed a dual policy—promoting revolutions when favorable opportunities arise, while at the same time promoting peaceful relations with capitalist states when it is advantageous to do so. In recent years the former goal has been almost completely sacrificed to the latter. Whether in the Middle East, Africa, Asia, Latin America, or Europe, the Soviet Union today seems to feel that its interests are usually better served by dealing with existing non-Communist regimes than by trying to overthrow them.

The "People's Democracies"

✦

Eugene Varga

A veteran communist, economist, and theoretician associated with the Communist International before World War II, the Hungarian-born Varga used this 1947 article to define the notion of "people's democracy" in keeping with the official view of the place of new socialist societies within the Soviet sphere of influence in Eastern Europe.

One of the most important political results of the Second World War is the emergence of democratic states of a new type: Yugoslavia, Bulgaria, Poland, Czechoslovakia and, also, Albania. We understand by a "democracy of a new type" a state of affairs in a country where feudal remnants—large-scale landownership—have been eliminated, where the system of private ownership of the means of production still exists but large enterprises in the spheres of industry, transport and credit are in state hands, while the state itself and its apparatus of coercion serve not the interests of a monopolistic bourgeoisie but the interests of the working people in town and countryside.

The social structure of these states differs from all those hitherto known to us; it is something totally new in the history of mankind. It is neither a bourgeois dictatorship nor a proletarian dictatorship. The old state apparatus has not been smashed, as in the Soviet Union, but re-organized by means of a continuous inclusion in it of the supporters of the new regime. They are not capitalist states in the ordinary sense of the word. Neither, however, are they Socialist states. The basis for their transition to Socialism is given by the nationalization of the most important means of production and by the essential character of the state. They may, with the maintenance of the present state apparatus, gradually pass over to Socialism, developing to an ever-increasing extent the socialist sector which already exists side by side with the simple commodity sector (peasant and artisan) and the capitalist sector, which has lost its dominant position. . . .

The change in the character of the state—its transformation from a weapon of domination in the hands of the propertied classes into the state of the working

Eugene Varga, "The 'People's Democracies,' " from *A Documentary History of Communism,* Robert V. Daniels, ed., vol. 2, Vintage Press, 1962, pp. 151–155.

people—this is what determines the real significance of the transfer of a decisive part of the means of production into the hands of the state in the countries of a democracy of a new type.

The change in the character of the state explains also why the influence of nationalization on the distribution of the national revenue is totally different in the democratic states of a new type from that in the bourgeois-democratic countries such as Great Britain.

Nationalization in the new democratic states signifies a special sort of economic revolution. The property of traitors to the country, of fascist capitalists, was confiscated without compensation. Other big capitalists received compensation, but their income after compensation was only a small part of the surplus value which they previously appropriated. . . .

The second important feature of the economies of the countries of democracy of a new type is the complete and final elimination of large-scale landlordism, of this feudal survival inside the capitalist system of economy. The social and political power of the big landowners, dating back a thousand years, has been destroyed. The big landed properties were confiscated by the state and distributed among peasants having little land and landless agricultural laborers. The number of peasant households (i.e., private owners of land) increased very considerably in these countries.

The division of the lands among many hundreds of thousands of peasants who had little or no land has converted the overwhelming majority of these peasants into loyal supporters of the new regime. The mistake made by the Hungarian Communists in 1919, when they wanted to leap over an essential historical stage by converting the confiscated large landed properties into state farms, instead of dividing them up among the peasants and so satisfying the land hunger, has nowhere been repeated.

The cultivation of land by the peasants using their own resources and giving them the opportunity of selling their produce on the market (in some countries only after fulfilling tax payments and deliveries to the state) make possible the preservation or re-emergence of commodity capitalist relations in the economy of the country. As Lenin pointed out, "Small-scale production engenders capitalism and the bourgeoisie continuously, daily, hourly, spontaneously and on a mass scale."

Thus, the social order in the states of democracy of a new type is not a socialist order, but a peculiar, new, transitional form. The contradiction between the productive forces and relations of production becomes mitigated in proportion as the relative weight of the socialist sector increases. . . .

As regards the class struggle, however, there exists a difference in principle between the states of democracy of a new type and the old bourgeois countries. In the old bourgeois countries the state is a weapon of domination in the hands of the propertied classes. The entire state apparatus—officials, judges, police and as a last resort, the standing army—is on the side of the propertied classes.

The opposite is to be seen in the countries of new democracy. Here the state protects the interests of the working people against those who live by appropriating surplus value. When conflicts arise the armed forces of the State are to be found, not on the side of the capitalists, but on the side of the workers. . . .

The Stalin Cult. From the advent of the people's democracies until 1956, Joseph Stalin enjoyed officially sponsored adulation everywhere in Eastern Europe except Yugoslavia. This 1954 May Day parade in Bucharest, Romania, was a typical scene. (Eastfoto)

In this connection an important theoretical question arises: the idea was widely held in the Communist parties that the political domination of the working people, as is the case in the Soviet Union, could only be realized in the form of soviet power. This is not correct, nor is it an expression of Lenin's opinion. . . .

The rise of the states of new democracy shows clearly that it is possible to have political rule by the working people even while the outward forms of parliamentary democracy are still maintained. . . .

It is equally understandable that these countries maintain close, friendly relations with the Soviet Union. This is so not only because it was precisely the victorious troops of the Soviet Union that liberated their countries (Yugoslavia being, in part, an exception) from German occupation, and not only because they are all Slav states, but primarily because the present social order brings them close to the Soviet Union, because of all the great powers the Soviet Union alone is interested in the maintenance and further progressive development of the social order and political regime existing in these countries and can afford them diplomatic support against the reactionary offensive from outside.

The Soviet Union is at the same time interested in the maintenance by these countries of the existing regime and their further development in a progressive direction. The present regime in these countries provides the guarantee that they will not, in the future, again voluntarily serve as a *place d'armes* for any power which tries to attack the Soviet Union. . . .

"De-Stalinization"

✦

Nikita Khrushchev

In February 1956, Nikita Khrushchev, First Secretary of the Soviet Communist Party, rocked the Soviet Union and the rest of the communist world with his "secret speech" at the Twentieth Party Congress. In his speech he denounced Stalin's crimes against the people and the loyal party comrades. News of this dramatic development circulated rapidly, destroying confidence in the places where reverence for Stalin had been obligatory and contributing to the crises of 1956 in Poland and Hungary.

At the present we are concerned with a question which has immense importance for the party now and for the future—[we are concerned] with how the cult of the person of Stalin has been gradually growing, the cult which became at a certain specific stage the source of a whole series of exceedingly serious and grave perversions of party principles, of party democracy, of revolutionary legality. . . .

When we analyze the practice of Stalin in regard to the direction of the party and of the country, when we pause to consider everything which Stalin perpetrated, we must be convinced that Lenin's fears were justified. The negative characteristics of Stalin, which, in Lenin's time, were only incipient, transformed themselves during the last years into a grave abuse of power by Stalin, which caused untold harm to our Party.

We have to consider seriously and analyze correctly this matter in order that we may preclude any possibility of a repetition in any form whatever of what took place during the life of Stalin, who absolutely did not tolerate collegiality in leadership and

Nikita Khrushchev, "De-Stalinization," from *A Documentary History of Communism*, Robert V. Daniels, ed., vol. 2, Vintage Press, 1962, pp. 224–231.

in work, and who practiced brutal violence, not only toward everything which opposed him, but also toward that which seemed to his capricious and despotic character, contrary to his concepts.

Stalin acted not through persuasion, explanation, and patient co-operation with people, but by imposing his concepts and demanding absolute submission to his opinion. Whoever opposed this concept or tried to prove his viewpoint, and the correctness of his position, was doomed to removal from the leading collective and to subsequent moral and physical annihilation. This was especially true during the period following the XVIIth Party Congress [1934], when many prominent party leaders and rank-and-file party workers, honest and dedicated to the cause of Communism, fell victim to Stalin's despotism.

We must affirm that the party had fought a serious fight against the Trotskyites, rightists and bourgeois nationalists, and that it disarmed ideologically all the enemies of Leninism. This ideological fight was carried on successfully, as a result of which the Party became strengthened and tempered. Here Stalin played a positive role. . . .

Worth noting is the fact that even during the progress of the furious ideological fight against the Trotskyites, the Zinovievites, the Bukharinites and others, extreme repressive measures were not used against them. The fight was on ideological grounds. But some years later when socialism in our country was fundamentally constructed, when the exploiting classes were generally liquidated, when the Soviet social structure had radically changed, when the social basis for political movements and groups hostile to the party had violently contracted, when the ideological opponents of the party were long since defeated politically—then the repression directed against them began.

It was precisely during this period (1935–1937–1938) that the practice of mass repression through the government apparatus was born, first against the enemies of Leninism—Trotskyites, Zinovievites, Bukharinites, long since politically defeated by the party, and subsequently also against many honest Communists, against those party cadres who had borne the heavy load of the Civil War and the first and most difficult years of industrialization and collectivization, who actively fought against the Trotskyites and the rightists for the Leninist Party line.

Stalin originated the concept "enemy of the people." This term automatically rendered it unnecessary that the ideological errors of a man or men engaged in a controversy be proven; this term made possible the usage of the most cruel repression, violating all norms of revolutionary legality, against anyone who in any way disagreed with Stalin, against those who were only suspected of hostile intent, against those who had bad reputations. This concept, "enemy of the people," actually eliminated the possibility of any kind of ideological fight or the making of one's views known on this or that issue, even those of a practical character. In the main, and in actuality, the only proof of guilt used, against all norms of current legal science, was the "confession" of the accused himself; and, as subsequent probing proved, "confessions" were acquired through physical pressures against the accused.

This led to glaring violations of revolutionary legality, and to the fact that many entirely innocent persons, who in the past had defended the party line, became victims.

We must assert that in regard to those persons who in their time had opposed the party line, there were often no sufficiently serious reasons for their physical annihilation. The formula, "enemy of the people," was specifically introduced for the purpose of physically annihilating such individuals. . . .

. . . Many party, soviet and economic activists who were branded in 1937–1938 as "enemies" were actually never enemies, spies, wreckers, etc., but were always honest Communists; they were only so stigmatized, and often, no longer able to bear barbaric tortures, they charged themselves (at the order of the investigative judges—falsifiers) with all kinds of grave and unlikely crimes. The commission [for investigation of the purge] has presented to the Central Committee Presidium lengthy and documented materials pertaining to mass repressions against the delegates to the XVIIth Party Congress and against members of the Central Committee elected at that Congress. These materials have been studied by the Presidium of the Central Committee.

It was determined that of the 139 members and candidates of the Party's Central Committee who were elected at the XVIIth Congress, 98 persons, i.e., 70 percent, were arrested and shot (mostly in 1937–1938). (*Indignation in the hall*) . . . The same fate met not only the Central Committee members but also the majority of the delegates to the XVIIth Party Congress. Of 1,966 delegates with either voting or advisory rights, 1,108 persons were arrested on charges of antirevolutionary crimes, i.e., decidedly more than a majority. This very fact shows how absurd, wild and contrary to common sense were the charges of counterrevolutionary crimes made out, as we now see, against a majority of participants at the XVIIth Party Congress. (*Indignation in the hall*) . . .

We have examined the cases and have rehabilitated Kossior, Rudzutak, Postyshev, Kosarev and others. For what causes were they arrested and sentenced? The review of evidence shows that there was no reason for this. They, like many others, were arrested without the Prosecutor's knowledge. In such a situation there is no need for any sanction, for what sort of a sanction could there be when Stalin decided everything? He was the chief prosecutor in these cases. Stalin not only agreed to, but on his own initiative issued, arrest orders. We must say this so that the delegates to the Congress can clearly undertake and themselves assess this and draw the proper conclusions.

Facts prove that many abuses were made on Stalin's orders without reckoning with any norms of party and Soviet legality. Stalin was a very distrustful man, sickly suspicious; we knew this from our work with him. He could look at a man and say: "Why are your eyes so shifty today?" or "Why are you turning so much today and avoiding to look me directly in the eyes?" The sickly suspicion created in him a general distrust even toward eminent party workers whom he had known for years. Everywhere and in everything he saw "enemies," "two-facers" and "spies."

Possessing unlimited power he indulged in great willfulness and choked a person morally and physically. A situation was created where one could not express one's own will.

When Stalin said that one or another should be arrested, it was necessary to accept on faith that he was an "enemy of the people." Meanwhile, Beria's gang, which ran the organs of state security, outdid itself in proving the guilt of the arrested and the truth of materials which it falsified. And what proofs were offered? The confessions of the arrested, and the investigative judges accepted these "confessions." And how is it possible that a person confesses to crimes which he has not committed? Only in one way—because of application of physical methods of pressuring him, tortures, bringing him to a state of unconsciousness, deprivation of his judgment, taking away of his human dignity. In this manner were "confessions" acquired. . . .

The willfulness of Stalin showed itself not only in decisions concerning the internal life of the country but also in the international relations of the Soviet Union.

The July Plenum of the Central Committee studied in detail the reasons for the development of conflict with Yugoslavia. It was a shameful role which Stalin played here. The "Yugoslav Affair" contained no problems which could not have been solved through party discussions among comrades. There was no significant basis for the development of this "affair"; it was completely possible to have prevented the rupture of relations with that country. This does not mean, however, that the Yugoslav leaders did not make mistakes or did not have shortcomings. But these mistakes and shortcomings were magnified in a monstrous manner by Stalin, which resulted in a break of relations with a friendly country.

I recall the first days when the conflict between the Soviet Union and Yugoslavia began artificially to be blown up. Once, when I came from Kiev to Moscow, I was invited to visit Stalin who, pointing to the copy of a letter lately sent to Tito, asked me, "Have you read this?" Not waiting for my reply he answered, "I will shake my little finger—and there will be no more Tito. He will fall." . . .

But this did not happen to Tito. No matter how much or how little Stalin shook, not only his little finger but everything else that he could shake, Tito did not fall. Why? The reason was that, in this case of disagreement with the Yugoslav comrades, Tito had behind him a state and a people who had gone through a severe school of fighting for liberty and independence, a people which gave support to its leaders.

You see to what Stalin's mania for greatness led. He had completely lost consciousness of reality; he demonstrated his suspicion and haughtiness not only in relation to individuals in the USSR, but in relation to whole parties and nations. . . .

Some comrades may ask us: Where were the members of the Political Bureau of the Central Committee? Why did they not assert themselves against the cult of the individual in time? And why is this being done only now?

First of all we have to consider the fact that the members of the Political Bureau viewed these matters in a different way at different times. Initially, many of them backed Stalin actively because Stalin was one of the strongest Marxists and his logic, his strength and his will greatly influenced the cadres and party work. . . .

Later, however, Stalin, abusing his power more and more, began to fight eminent party and government leaders and to use terroristic methods against honest Soviet people. As we have already shown, Stalin thus handled such eminent party and government leaders as Kossior, Rudzutak, Eikhe, Postyshev and many others.

Attempts to oppose groundless suspicions and charges resulted in the opponent falling victim of the repression. This characterized the fall of Comrade Postyshev.

In one of his speeches Stalin expressed his dissatisfaction with Postyshev and asked him, "What are you actually?"

Postyshev answered clearly, "I am a Bolshevik, Comrade Stalin, a Bolshevik."

This assertion was at first considered to show a lack of respect for Stalin; later it was considered a harmful act and consequently resulted in Postyshev's annihilation and branding without any reason as a "people's enemy."

In the situation which then prevailed I have talked often with Nikolai Alexandrovich Bulganin; once when we two were traveling in a car, he said, "It has happened sometimes that a man goes to Stalin on his invitation as a friend. And when he sits with Stalin, he does not know where he will be sent next, home or to jail."

It is clear that such conditions put every member of the Political Bureau in a very difficult situation. And when we also consider the fact that in the last years the Central Committee plenary sessions were not convened and that the sessions of the Political Bureau occurred only occasionally, from time to time, then we will understand how difficult it was for any member of the Political Bureau to take a stand against one or another injust or improper procedure, against serious errors and shortcomings in the practices of leadership. . . .

Comrades: We must abolish the cult of the individual decisively, once and for all; we must draw the proper conclusions concerning both ideological-theoretical and practical work.

It is necessary for this purpose: . . . to return to and actually practice in all our ideological work the most important theses of Marxist-Leninist science about the people as the creator of history and as the creator of all material and spiritual good of humanity, about the decisive role of the Marxist Party in the revolutionary fight for the transformation of society, about the victory of Communism.

In this connection we will be forced to do much work in order to examine critically from the Marxist-Leninist viewpoint and to correct the widely spread erroneous views connected with the cult of the individual in the sphere of history, philosophy, economy and of other sciences, as well as in literature and the fine arts. . . .

[It is necessary] to restore completely the Leninist principles of Soviet socialist democracy, expressed in the Constitution of the Soviet Union, to fight willfulness of individuals abusing their power. The evil caused by acts violating revolutionary socialist legality, which have accumulated during a long time as a result of the negative influence of the cult of the individual, has to be completely corrected. Comrades! The XXth Congress of the Communist Party of the Soviet Union has manifested with a new strength the unshakable unity of our party, its cohesiveness around the Central Committee, its resolute will to accomplish the great task of building Communism. (*Tumultuous applause*) And the fact that we present in all their ramifications the basic problems of overcoming the cult of the individual which is alien to Marxism-Leninism, as well as the problem of liquidating its burdensome consequences, is an evidence of the great moral and political strength of our party. (*Prolonged applause*)

We are absolutely certain that our party, armed with the historical resolutions of the XXth Congress, will lead the Soviet people along the Leninist path to new successes, to new victories. (*Tumultuous, prolonged applause*)

Long live the victorious banner of our party—Leninism! (*Tumultuous, prolonged applause ending in ovation. All rise.*)

Pax Sovietica Without Peace

✦

Robert L. Hutchings

This essay forms the conclusion of a study of Soviet–East European relations. First published in 1983, it was reissued in 1987
by Robert L. Hutchings, a specialist on Eastern Europe who has
combined government service with academic pursuits. His work
underscores the failure of the Soviet Union to fashion a stable
alliance with its client states in Eastern Europe.

To the extent that a single line of development characterizes Soviet–East
European relations in the period 1968–1980, it is this: in the aftermath of the invasion
of Czechoslovakia, the Soviet leaders moved to restore unity and cohesion in Eastern
Europe through the reassertion of Soviet authority in the region, the reinstitution of
domestic orthodoxy, and the elaboration of a comprehensive integrationist program
in every sphere of Soviet–East European relations. Soviet in inspiration but collective
in practice, these combined measures yielded a degree of stability in Eastern Europe
during the early 1970s. In the latter half of the decade, however, efforts toward Soviet–
East European consolidation were eroded by new political conflicts—between East
and West, between the Soviet Union and its East European allies, and within the East
European societies—and the grandiose integrationist designs of a few years earlier
proved largely irrelevant to the pressing political and economic challenges confronting
Eastern Europe.

Beyond this general line of development were a number of interrelated trends
and factors affecting Soviet–East European relations in the era of détente. In the early
1970s, Soviet and East European diplomacy aimed at regulating the process of détente
so as to maximize its political and economic benefits while minimizing the potentially
destabilizing tendencies inherent in expanded contacts with the West; toward the end
of the decade it was geared to keeping détente alive in the face of growing misgivings
in the West. Even while engaging in an energetic post-Helsinki "peace offensive"
designed to reinvigorate détente, however, the Soviet and East European regimes
were grappling with the consequences of its ambiguous legacy. Despite their anxious
countermeasures, the rapid expansion of contacts with the West had exposed the East

Robert L. Hutchings, "Pax Sovietica Without Peace," from *Soviet-East European Relations*, University of
Wisconsin Press, 1987, pp. 229–235. Reprinted by permission of University of Wisconsin Press.

European societies as never before to the cultural and economic lure of the West. The emergence of self-styled human rights and "Helsinki watch" groups were but the most visible manifestations of this influence; more important still were the diffuse consequences of Western cultural penetration and the belated "demonstration effect" of sustained economic prosperity in Western Europe.

Even the eagerly sought expansion of trade with the West had failed to live up to its early promise. Seen as the motor of economic regeneration and prosperity in Eastern Europe, trade with the West began to founder at mid-decade under the impact of soaring energy costs and their attendant disruptions on the global economy. By decade's end, economic growth rates were sharply down throughout Eastern Europe, balance of payments reversals were acute, and debts to Western lenders huge and still growing. Everywhere in Eastern Europe, the buoyant optimism surrounding the import-led growth strategies of a few years earlier had given way to profound concern over the mounting economic crisis confronting the entire region. For all this, Western trade, credits, and technology remained central to any hopes of economic recovery, and trade with the West had been introduced as a key, seemingly permanent feature of East European economic life.

One further consequence of the détente process was that it afforded scope for East European diplomatic activity on a scale unthinkable in the 1950s or early 1960s. It was the East Europeans who took the lead in promoting European détente—before their initiatives were subsumed within a Soviet-directed Warsaw Pact Westpolitik; and it was they who sought most urgently to revive it a decade later, when they saw their carefully cultivated contacts with the West threatened by superpower conflicts not of their making. In the interim, the Soviet leaders sought to channel and control this activity, and contain the continued independent-mindedness of the Romanians, through the Warsaw Pact's Political Consultative Committee and Committee of Foreign Ministers, annual summit meetings in the Crimea, and other forums for foreign policy coordination. Far from amounting to a genuine conciliar system, these combined measures were part of a Soviet effort to ensure "directed consensus" in Eastern Europe by according the junior allies new consultation privileges and giving a degree of political and institutional expression to their growing role in East-West affairs.

A similar pattern was revealed in intrabloc affairs during the period, as some of the dysfunctional control devices of the past were replaced by a more collectivist and participatory, though still Soviet-dominated, pattern of relations. In this regard, the Soviet leaders confronted the tasks of alliance management rather more creatively than in the past, supervising various integrationist schemes and erecting new multilateral forums for consultation and joint action. Soviet influence in alliance affairs remained paramount, of course, and there could be no demur in matters where vital Soviet interests were at stake; but considerable, sometimes decisive, East European influence was evident in a host of lesser issues, ranging from defense expenditures and joint economic ventures to the broader questions of Warsaw Pact decisionmaking and the shaping of an economic integration program.

If interstate relations in Eastern Europe during the era of détente were marked by a certain flexibility and innovation, at least initially, the same cannot be said of domestic policies in the region. At the beginning of the 1970s Soviet and East European domestic strategies were shaped, above all, by the legacy of the Prague Spring of 1968 and the outbreak of workers' riots along Poland's Baltic coast in protest against food price increases in late 1970. If the Prague Spring had persuaded the Soviet leaders and their more orthodox East European comrades that economic reform was fraught with unacceptable political risks, the convulsions in Poland just two years later revealed the dangers inherent in prolonged suppression of material living standards. Accordingly, Party programs for the 1970s stressed domestic orthodoxy and eschewed reformism in social and economic policy, but they also aimed at satisfying the material demands of the populations by shifting economic priorities toward the production of consumer goods.

This domestic orientation, in turn, fueled another, less conspicuous development affecting Soviet–East European relations in the era of détente: the decline of ideology as an energizing element in East European political life. The ideology of Soviet-style socialism, as the Italian Communists were to conclude in 1982, was a "spent force," and the strenuous but largely ritualistic paeans to ideology could not disguise its steady erosion, even (or especially) within the ruling apparats. The crushing of the Prague Spring had dealt the final blow to any residual revolutionary élan in Eastern Europe; after 1968, Party programs were based on an increasingly cynical combination of rigid orthodoxy and overt consumerist appeals. For the East German, Polish, Czechoslovak, and Hungarian regimes especially, "goulash Communism" supplanted the vision of socialist development as the linchpin of a new "social contract," which sought to win popular acquiescence in return for steady improvements in material living standards. In Hungary the process was broadened to embrace a cautious reformist course and conciliatory social policy; elsewhere a reorientation of economic policy was seen as a palliative—a substitute for, rather than concomitant of, social or economic reform.

To achieve the economic goals on which their rule came increasingly to be judged, the East European regimes (with the notable exception of the Czechoslovak) relied heavily on Western trade, credits, and technology, which were expected to propel the East European economies along the path of rapid growth and material abundance. Consequently, when East–West trade began to founder in the late 1970s, so too did East European economic strategies for the 1970s, and Eastern Europe was facing a political as well as an economic crisis. Unable to fulfill the early promises of a bright socialist future or even the far more limited aims embodied in the new social contract, the East European regimes were confronted with a new crisis of legitimacy, entrapped by their pledges of a few years earlier and the fundamental insecurity of their rule.

Within the East European societies, meanwhile, a parallel and largely subterranean transformation was taking place. For large segments of those societies, the liquidation of the Czechoslovak reform movement had ended all hopes for the self-regeneration of Soviet-style socialism. The resulting disillusionment was felt most keenly in Czechoslovakia, of course, where the euphoria of the Prague Spring gave way to pessimism and apolitical resignation, but it was present to one degree or another throughout Eastern Europe. Ideological disaffection was variously manifested in apathy, enervation, alienation, corruption (both official and unofficial), and overt dissent, the last being largely confined to human rights or "Helsinki watch" groups who pressed demands on the authorities, generally on specific and limited humanitarian issues. In Poland, however, the seeds were planted of a genuine Democratic Opposition, which grew and flourished in the fertile soil of Gierek's misrule.

As early as 1970, the conviction was growing among Polish dissident circles that the only hope for fundamental political change lay outside the ruling establishment, through social self-organization. The suppression of the Radom and Ursus strikes in 1976 sealed their conviction: they (or their political forebears) had trusted Gomulka in 1956 and had been betrayed; they had trusted Gierek in 1970 and were betrayed; they would not trust or be betrayed again. Emboldened by the conspicuous weakness of the Gierek leadership after 1976, dissidents, Catholic intellectuals, and disaffected Party members coalesced within a nascent Democratic Opposition, which began to acquire organization and purpose and gather mass support among industrial workers and even the rural peasantry. Perhaps most important, the election of Cardinal Karol Wojtyla as Pope John Paul II in 1978, and the massive outpouring of public affection accorded him on his visit to his native land a year later, served to galvanize a disillusioned Poland around an alternative, but as yet not fully defined, vision of its national future.

It was against this background that the price increases of July 1980—themselves a reflection of the failure of the Gierek leadership's economic strategy and a violation of its fragile "social contract" with a disillusioned population—touched off a wave of strikes and protest demonstrations. Within weeks, the protest had grown to a full-scale, organized assault on established methods of Party rule and a challenge to the entire interstate system in Eastern Europe, and neither martial law in Poland nor countermeasures elsewhere could erase its legacy.

Since the Second World War, the Soviet Union has seen Eastern Europe as a buffer, military and ideological, against the West, as a base for the projection of Soviet power and influence over all of Europe, and as a laboratory for the vindication of Soviet ideological and internationalist aspirations. The relative weight assigned to these factors undoubtedly has changed over time—military security considerations have perhaps receded, while ideological concerns are greater than ever—but the importance of the East European interstate system remains undiminished in Soviet perceptions. And the Soviet Union has sought to make this arrangement durable, stable, viable, organic; to establish a permanent Pax Sovietica over the entire region. This latter aim has proved elusive.

In Stalin's time, unity and stability in Eastern Europe was achieved through a rigidly controlled empire imposed by Moscow and brutally administered by East European leaderships thoroughly subordinate to the Soviet Union. It was a unified, seemingly monolithic system but a brittle one, whose surface stability concealed an underlying unviability. After Stalin's death in 1953 and the Hungarian and Polish upheavals in 1956, the Khrushchev leadership in the USSR sought to reshape the legacy of the Stalinist interstate system by eliminating the more glaring manifestations of Soviet hegemony in Eastern Europe and by trying to weld a new, more resilient alliance system, whose chief pillars were to be Comecon and the Warsaw Pact. More than that, Khrushchev encouraged his East European counterparts to overcome their Stalinist excesses and attempt to bridge the gap between rulers and ruled in Eastern Europe under a more attractive and conciliatory pattern of domestic authority. In so doing, however, Khrushchev failed to grasp the fundamental bankruptcy of Soviet-style socialism. His inconsistency and experimentation served to introduce a period of drift and disarray in Eastern Europe, whose most obvious manifestations were Romania's semi-autonomous foreign policy and Czechoslovakia's experiment in "socialism with a human face."

It was not until the Prague Spring and its forcible liquidation, nearly four years after Khrushchev's ouster, that the new Soviet leadership under Brezhnev undertook to restore unity and cohesion in Eastern Europe through a comprehensive drive toward "socialist integration." This effort demanded a rather more creative application of Soviet power and authority than in the past: aware that unity could no longer be imposed by fiat from the Kremlin, the Soviet leaders sought instead to promote cohesion by constructing new multilateral forums and integrative links susceptible to Soviet control or manipulation. Described by one Soviet commentator as the "creation of thousands of unbreakable bonds" within the region, this Soviet-led integrationist drive aimed toward the creation of a system of consultation so pervasive and an interdependence so thorough that independent action by the East Europeans would be severely circumscribed.

The nature and scope of Soviet integrationist policies after 1968 have been described at some length in the chapters above. If these aspects of Soviet integrationist efforts are more or less readily discernible, their results and significance are far less so. Indeed, no question of interest to observers of Soviet–East European relations is more slippery than that of "integration" in the region. In some respects, the interstate system in Eastern Europe is almost totally integrated, yet on closer inspection the notion of an integrated interstate system seems inappropriate. Nor does the concept of integration as a process hold much promise, for the pattern of interaction in Soviet–East European relations seems to move in an altogether different direction.

Militarily, the countries of the Warsaw Pact share common (i.e., Soviet) doctrine, organizational structure, regulations, and even uniforms; they employ standardized equipment and weaponry (down to ammunition of the smallest caliber); and they engage in joint training exercises purportedly designed to foster "combat solidarity." Yet military integration is largely confined to the upper echelons of the Warsaw Pact: even in large multinational exercises there is little contact among national forces except at the staff level, and East European units customarily maneuver side-by-side or in proximity with their allied counterparts rather than as an integrated operational force. The Warsaw Pact possesses neither a standing army nor a central body with decisionmaking authority, and recommendations issued by any pact organ must be submitted to the national governments concerned for approval. It does not even have an operational command in the usual sense of the term, for the functions of the Joint Command have been limited to matters of administration, training, and organization.

As to economic relations, CMEA [Council for Mutual Economic Assistance] has been divided for years between "plan" and "market" conceptions of socialist economic integration—between a conception which would create central planning bodies and invest them with supranational authority and one which would free "market" forces in intra-CMEA trade by facilitating direct contacts between firms and reducing trade barriers. Out of this conflict emerged the hybrid "Comprehensive Program" of 1971 and a pattern of interaction which links the CMEA economies in various ways but which lacks a clear vision of the economic (as opposed to organizational or procedural) prerequisites for integration. Thus for all the efforts toward multilateral cooperation in CMEA, Soviet–East European trade relations can best be characterized as "multiple bilateralism," a pattern in which an elaborate multilateral superstructure has been erected over an essentially unaltered system of bilateral economic relations in the region. As in the Warsaw Pact, CMEA possesses no central body with decisionmaking power; indeed, so restrictive were the procedural rules governing CMEA bodies that they had to be hastily amended just to permit the opening of collective dialogue with the EEC [Europe Economic Community]. Domestic economic decisions are partially based on regionwide considerations, it is true, but such limited interdependence and foreign trade coordination can hardly be said to constitute integration in any accepted sense of the term.

The integrationist drive of the early 1970s was designed to remedy some of these deficiencies by strengthening the consultative mechanisms of the Warsaw Pact, promoting multilateral economic cooperation, especially in the energy sector, and forging new ties in the realms of ideology and culture. In every sphere of Soviet–East European relations—political, economic, military, ideological, and cultural—and at every level of activity, new multilateral forums were created and new links established. To call this process integration, however, may do some violence to the concept, for the process lacks the sense of free and independent states voluntarily relinquishing portions of their sovereignty to achieve some common purpose or shared goal. The sovereignty of the East European states was relinquished more than three decades ago, and integration in Eastern Europe has amounted chiefly to a kind of Soviet-directed "apparat integration" linking the several Party and state bureaucracies and facilitating consultation among them.

The cumulative effect of these measures was to improve the nominal access of the East European junior allies to the levers of decisionmaking, while at the same time strengthening Soviet control and supervision through a tighter alliance infrastructure. These improved mechanisms for consultation, in turn, facilitated the forging of a coordinated Westpolitik in the era of détente, afforded a measure of political and military consolidation in the Warsaw Pact, and permitted the elaboration of new programs for economic collaboration. But neither these measures nor their associated integrationist schemes offered any solution to the pressing challenges facing Eastern Europe in the late 1970s: severe economic deterioration, ideological erosion and political malaise, and the widening gulf between the East European regimes and their disaffected populaces.

Thus the vision of a durable and viable Pax Sovietica remained in 1980 as elusive as ever. For all its external assertiveness, the Soviet-led alliance system in Eastern

Europe was still beset by the internal contradictions and fundamental instability of an empire held together by force. It had failed to submerge national aspirations beneath the façade of internationalism, and it had not won popular allegiance by ideological persuasion or political achievement. It had failed to bridge the gap between rulers and ruled or arrest the growing enervation and immobility of its ruling parties. It had not even assured law and order in its half of the continent, for the chief threats to European peace since World War II had arisen in Eastern Europe itself—Hungary in 1956, Czechoslovakia in 1968, and Poland after August 1980—in nationalist outbursts aimed directly or indirectly at Soviet hegemony in the region. After thirty-five years, Pax Sovietica remained neither stable, secure, nor peaceful.

The Outlook for Reform in Eastern Europe

✦

János Bak and Lyman H. Legters

In this 1983 essay, two historians, from the University of British Columbia and the University of Washington respectively, provide a framework for viewing Soviet hegemony in Eastern Europe, emphasizing the limitations that Soviet rigidity placed on reforming impulses in the client states of the region.

Serious discussions of the status of socialism in Eastern Europe, i.e., in the "peoples' democracies" whose governments and ruling parties proclaim them to be at some stage along the road to perfected socialism or communism, tend to begin with the verification or refutation of that claim and thereby risk exhausting themselves in that exercise without getting beyond it. By opting for a different way of posing the question of future development in this area, addressing the prospects and possibilities for reform, we hope to have found a more manageable, though no less controversial, point of departure. Our vantage point is that of sympathetic observer with preferences for most of the programs and principles that traditionally fall under the heading of socialism, but also with an awareness of the limitations on independent or unsanctioned action in present-day Eastern Europe, and of the enormous mortgage carried

János Bak and Lyman H. Legters, "The Outlook for Reform in Eastern Europe," from *Praxis International*, April 1983, pp. 62–72. Reprinted by permission of Basil Blackwell Ltd.

by the very term, socialism, among populations exposed for more than a generation to the official rhetoric of "the building of socialism."

The limitations are, not exclusively but to a very large extent, a function of the client status occupied by the states of the region under review in relation to the superpower of the area, the USSR. If reminders are needed, we have only to look at the successive upheavals of the post-war period, all of which failed (or recorded marginal gains) within the shifting boundaries of what the Soviet Union was prepared to tolerate. Stating the same proposition in more immediate terms, the known or conjectured limits of Soviet tolerance are always the first consideration in assessing the chances of any reform, the success of which never depends solely on the forces and resources arrayed for or against it in a single more or less autonomous society.

The Soviet presence in the area and the political and strategic interests perceived by the Soviet government thus necessarily circumscribe the outlook for social change and require, quite aside from the theoretical difficulties of doing otherwise, that the discussion be restricted to gradual and partial kinds of transformation. Tempting and intellectually gratifying as it might be to consider the full range of possibilities within the concept of social change—from full-dress revolution, through what we might call temporal irridentism (undoing the recent past in favor of some more distant but arguably better one), to outright counterrevolution—such a discussion might easily be as hollow and abstract as many of the official claims for "developed socialism." Granting that reform is necessarily conservative from one perspective and incorrigibly optimistic from another, system-rejection is merely romantic, as much so in its revolutionary as in its restorationist form, for it does not at present fall within the range of entertainable propositions in Eastern Europe. Moreover, one cannot, in good conscience, recommend suicidal decisions to peoples who, in their majority, do not apparently regard the present system as altogether unbearable; nor can one disregard the lessons well learned in Eastern Europe, by the older generation from experience and by the younger in schools, that make options of an openly restorative character unacceptable.

The notion of reform of course presupposes a present system that is in some sense usable and salvageable; otherwise the very suggestion of reform is either hypocritical or quixotic. The official claim of the regimes in question is that the postwar transformations, centering on the abolition of private property, amounted to a social revolution that has laid the foundations for the building of socialism. Except for the radical agrarian reforms in many of these countries, redistributing the sometimes substantial remnants of feudal-latifundial estates among the peasants, nothing of the sort really happened. Even the near-revolutionary rural transformation was in a way cancelled out a few years later by the more or less complete, more or less coercive, collectivization of agriculture. Thus, the revolutionary claim, even in comparison with the avowed model—the Great October Revolution, which did in fact grow from the Bolshevik seizure of power into a country-wide peasant revolt and civil war—is untenable. The ensuing three decades have, to be sure, brought about a substantial measure of transformation in the working classes and several changes in the ruling élites, but what has happened, taken overall, has been more nearly a variant of military occupation than of revolution, accompanied by a program of social reform imposed from above, a phenomenon well known in these countries at least since the times of Joseph II and Catherine the Great. The general pattern of development in the region has, then, little to do with social revolution and much more with what Ernst Bloch referred to as the "epoch" of worldwide urbanization and industrialization, flight from the countryside, decline in population growth in advanced countries, and so on. Marx's admonition that the abolition of private property is a prerequisite of socialist revolution but hardly its total program has thus retained its validity for these countries too.

But it may be less important to demolish official claims than to propose a counterclaim, namely, that a regime asserting its legitimacy as a spokesman for popular or working class interests is to be held accountable precisely in those terms. If that is so, the exceptional circumstances that serve these regimes as excuses need not be accepted; instead, the "postrevolutionary" record has to be judged within a normative tradition that is quite explicit on a number of fundamental principles habitually ignored in Eastern Europe.

Within this perspective in which the East European governments enjoy no exemptions from a critique based on their own ostensible informing principles, it becomes possible to consider the prospect for reform either as a putative route back to those informing principles or simply as a way of improving the life circumstances of millions of people. It can remain an open question, temporarily at least, whether the reforms would constitute a preparation for authentic social transformation or a move in the direction of fulfilling the revolutionary aims that are heard at present only as official incantations. With these questions set aside, we can also acknowledge that all of the at least minimally effective forces discernible in the societies under review stand for some version of reform. In stating this, we are aware of the clash of incompatible reform programs and of the uncertain outcome of such clashes. Still, the universal endorsement of social change, at least in the controlled variant that we generally mean by reform, does establish a basis for legitimate discussions of outlook and strategies.

Among the several advocates of reform in Eastern Europe, first place belongs— on grounds of efficacy and control over the mechanisms of change—to the regimes themselves. It has become a commonplace, especially in commentary from the left, to regard these governments as essentially conservative, content to preserve an unsatisfactory status quo. It is doubtless true that *some* elements of the ruling apparatus in each of these societies think only of protecting their own privileged status; it is also true, probably, that *all* elements of the ruling groups give first priority, among the policy options facing them, to courses of action that will keep them in power, whether on purely cynical grounds or because they really cannot believe that another kind of leadership would perform the task as well. And it is certainly a permissible conjecture that these nomenclatura-cliques, having so long maintained an essentially defensive posture vis-à-vis both a hostile capitalist encirclement (partly a fact of life, partly a convenient myth) and the incalculable moves of the neighboring Soviet leadership, have become habitually cautious and rigid.

Yet we cannot forget or overlook the fact that all of the ruling parties and governmental machines in the region are fully committed to a continuing process of social change. The remnants of informing principle still claimed from the original revolutionary project, the official announcements and justifications of social policy, and the rhetoric of self-characterization on the traditional revolutionary continuum—all proclaim this commitment to change. Whether the target of such changes would be nearer to the revolutionary (socialist) model proclaimed or only make the system work better in the sense of fulfilling the genuine needs of the population, is a question connected to the definition of socialism which we proposed to bracket for this inquiry. It seems entirely plausible to consider the regimes themselves not only as initiators of reform but also, on grounds that must be obvious, as the likeliest architects of the future social orders in the area, even if that required of them at least tacit admission of having overstated the completion of a revolutionary transformation to date.

The second set of advocates of reform in the countries of Eastern Europe comprises the critics and dissenters who, standing outside the ruling groups, manage in some fashion to articulate their criticisms and thereby create a kind of public discourse, however subterranean and surreptitious it may at times have to be. (This formulation rules out the incalculable volume of generalized discontent within the populations in question, not because it is unimportant but because it is only a potentiality awaiting actualization by some action—calculated or fortuitous—taken in public.) Dissent, as we all know, runs the gamut from particularistic claims and demands for repair of specific deficiencies to insistence upon a complete dismantling of the "revolutionary" order. Under discussion here is, of course, only that element of dissent that stops short of system-rejection and seeks, usually by some from of suasion, either modifications of the system or a more consistent observance of the system's own professed norms. These advocates of reform, too, are for from being unanimous in their objectives or priorities. Further, and unhappily for any discussion of perspectives, their success in focusing attention on political actualities of their respective societies coincides depressingly with the incidence of exile and imprisonment as a standard official response.

Scarcely more promising, strategically speaking, is the advocacy of reform that comes from abroad, primarily from the West. It is usually a bit difficult to discern just what sorts of reform would satisfy this clamor. Not openly restorationist in recent years, it has mainly contented itself with appeals for the recognition of human and civil rights, appeals which—on the strength of East European dissenters' testimony rather more than on the basis of consistent advocacy elsewhere in the world—one should regard with seriousness. Beyond that, however, it seems pointless to search for a Western agenda of reform in Eastern Europe, not because the appropriate sentiments are lacking, but because the enunciated principles fail to carry conviction. They are not very well observed by those doing the enunciating, and they seldom connect, except on the matter of human rights, with actualities in the societies being admonished for their shortcomings. On the other hand, there is—or lately has been—a Western source of reform advocacy that has made its critique more pertinent. This refers of course to the stated uneasiness of Western communists and socialists with developments in Eastern Europe, a form of critique that is not so easy to dismiss as fundamentally hostile or to ignore as irrelevant. The Eurocommunist commentary, which reached its dramatic high point in 1968 with respect to Czechoslovakia, has continued, in statements by Enrico Berlinguer, Santiago Carrillo, and others, to provide external sustenance to indigenous critics and reforming sentiments. Fragile as Eurocommunism may turn out to be, its fraternal status allows for important features of dialogue with East European intellectuals that is not automatically equated with subversion.

One might add a fourth source of reform advocacy, a compound of East European and external thrusts that does not fit neatly into a parallel relationship with the three enumerated so far. It consists of the challenges to the international tutelary system presided over by the Soviet Union, a client-state arrangement that is rebuked as much by Yugoslavia and Romania as by West Germany and the United States. Knowingly, astutely, and perhaps disastrously, Lenin transferred the problem of revolution from the domestic to the international plane and in so doing, aside from prefiguring the Brezhnev Doctrine, opened up for challenge and criticism not only the domestic postrevolutionary order but also the international system erected to both buttress and enlarge that order. One consequence, which muddies the waters conceptually even as it enhances the strategic possibilities, is that a regime that is more Catholic than the Pope domestically can be a veritable renegade internationally. Conversely, a client state that seeks to reform itself too dramatically on the domestic level is in no way protected by professed loyalty to the international bloc system.

Out of this muddle perhaps only the foolhardy will seek to derive any sweeping conclusions. Yet, since it is clear that all parties to the situation intend some kind of social change, and since these changes, domestic and international, are bound to have significant consequences, we must attempt to understand the possibilities at hand. Furthermore, the future of socialism is hardly to be conceived, the Brezhnev Doctrine notwithstanding, as a monopoly of those societies that have formally abolished private property. The Soviet Union and its emulators deserve our concern, but they must also allow outside observers their critical perspectives. And the forces of constructive change, in East and West alike, will only fortify each other's and the common effort through continuing dialogue. The lessons we seek to derive from East European experience do not, in any case, depend on external intervention, nor do they entail irresponsible exhortations encouraging other people to put their lives on the line for purposes that are not necessarily their own.

The history of Eastern Europe in the period of Soviet domination suggest a starting point for the consideration of reform perspectives. Among the officially sponsored reforms and periods of reform, the most substantial have occurred behind a screen of unquestioning fidelity to Soviet precept. Hungary under Kádár after the widespread repression following the 1956 uprising, Czechoslovakia before 1968, and East Germany in the middle span of Ulbricht's regime and now under Honecker have been the scenes of rather far-reaching economic reform and, at least at times, some significant relaxation in the cultural realm. Partly, of course, these successes have been a function simply of the relaxation of tutelary rigidity in the post-Stalin era. But beyond that factor, it is significant that those reform programs were all so neatly contained and controlled by the regimes in question that the Soviet Union had no reason to fear that autonomous tendencies would get out of hand. When, in the case of Czechoslovakia, they finally did, control was quickly reasserted by the tutelary power. We can now observe in Poland, even as the most daring initiative of the postwar period moves toward an as yet uncertain outcome, how carefully all actors in that situation conditioned their actions to maintain a balance between meaningful change and the risk of intervention.

When we look to the character of the reforms so far tolerated in Eastern Europe, the verdict can only be a mixed one. Given that the maintenance of central direction and party control seem to be essential prerequisites for tolerable reform, even the measures that involve some degree of devolution, contributing to a more efficient and productive variant of "socialism," do not entail steps toward democratization, citizen participation, or worker control—those steps, in short, that most of us would want to regard as characteristics of genuine socialism. Although the regimes do stand for certain kinds of change, especially in the realm of economic improvement, and although some of these would be welcomed as gains in just about any thinkable scheme for constructive social development, the outlook for basic reform remains generally bleak. In the case where a popular reform movement sought to go beyond the measures officially tolerated—whether by the Soviet leadership or by their obedient clients in the region—military intervention quickly demonstrated the boundary of tolerability. Yet even as that lesson of realism is stated, we are prompted to recall that high risks have been taken in contemporary Poland on the strength of a massively popular conviction that officially sanctioned change will not suffice, either substantively as a response to authentic needs and interests of the populace or procedurally as an effective articulation of those needs and interests in public discourse. It thus becomes equally compelling, without forgetting the pessimistic lessons of recent history, to examine more carefully the actualities of changes already wrought in the societies of the region and to weigh the possibility that still more far-reaching reform can be added to that record.

The most modest beginnings of reform, registered more by default than by design, are to be found in the attempts by popular constituencies to recapture ranges of social activity from the state and for the private sectors of societies that supposedly have no private sectors. As an outgrowth of an intellectual tradition seeking historically to make the private sector—civil society—answerable to the common weal, this is a supremely ironical development and one that has some discomfiting features for Marxists. The statist version of socialist tradition, triumphant in Eastern Europe, produced unbearable consequences, thereby occasioning spontaneous demands for different answers even if they were associated with altogether different traditions of social thought. But it testifies to the pervasiveness of statist solutions in the region, and to a continuity of statism across the watershed of "revolution" and irrespective of shifting labels, that such a "reprivatization," far from signifying anything like a return to capitalism, represents simply a reappropriation of elements of social life in a form that is responsive to the needs and interests of the population.

The appearance in all the countries of the region (including the Soviet Union) of extra-legal markets outside the purview of central planning mechanisms is perhaps the most striking example, not only because these economic entities perform essential services for the populace on a private basis but also because they have become essential to the functioning of the official economies. These more or less tolerated private economies, usually designated as "second" or "third" ones, begin with the utilization of kitchen garden plots on collective or state farm land for small-scale production of cash crops, to which correspond, in towns and villages, the small repair and retail shops, that respond to people's needs more effectively than do any of the features of the centrally planned economies. This "reprivatized" sector then shades over into more ambitious enterprises, undertaken both in towns and the countryside by workers and farmers using their skills to supplement official earnings (or even to replace them in some cases), that in the more extreme cases may depend on the appropriation (read: theft) of state-owned materials and constantly risk running afoul of the law. This whole continuum, where government attitudes ranging from approval through toleration to inability to control and service to the actual needs of the population stand in inverse relation to each other, scarcely suggests a bright future for socialism in East Europe. It would be difficult to find a definition or theory of socialism that could accommodate these elements of the region's economies and social configurations.

A less basic example, but one that is closer to the needs and interests of intellectual critics, is afforded by the organization and circulation of literary, historical, and sociological studies outside the state publishing system. Known in its Soviet variant as *samizdat* (self-publication), it is, of course, a vehicle for expressing protest and dissent but, more than that, it signals the recapture from the state of a vital social function, one that contributes in a negative way by limiting the efficacy of censorship, but also in a positive way by helping to form an unofficial public opinion. As Michnik has put it, "Instead of trying to control the power of the state, these movements simply removed certain social activities from under the control of the state; they do something that can not be done in the official frames. . . . Together with publications abroad, such a movement can establish a whole system which may grow into a second public opinion." The importance of such a realm of public discourse under private auspices, filling a need deliberately neglected by public authorities, is of course nowhere better illustrated than in Poland, where samizdat-style and Church-sponsored networks of private communication were so vital to the rapid growth of Solidarity.

A third example, reported from Hungary, involves the private organization of quite elaborate social welfare activities, from benefit concerts to the distribution of outright financial assistance, that supplement and correct the official system. Once again, we see private initiative meeting an officially ignored need in an extra-legal way, challenging the system ever more overtly until it becomes downright oppositional in its implications.

Besides standing as reproaches to central planning, the state monopoly of publishing, and official welfare systems, such beachheads of private activity—stopgaps though they may be—also represent the reappearance of civil society (where, with minor exceptions, it had never existed in classical form) as counterweight to an oppressive monopoly of social life by the state. Unexpected as this development may seem in light of the usual Marxian anticipations, it can be regarded as, among other things, the refashioning of participatory preconditions for more radical social change. That they recur at the "wrong place" in an anticipated sequence of developments should not diminish their significance, for they may function as belated substitutes for historical experience that was simply not a part of the earlier stages of social development. And this is as good a place as any to observe that, although there undoubtedly have been places where even parts of the working population have wanted to return to a system in which a national bourgeoisie flourished while distributing morsels of their imperialist largesse to the working class, in Eastern Europe societies that barely experienced capitalism in the full sense, the official charges of "restoration of capitalism" hurled at proponents of civil spheres of action serve only as means of denunciation. The only "return" here would be to half-feudal, half-dependent capitalism laced with memories of authoritarian dictatorship, which is certainly not a promising expectation to anyone but the reactionary fringe.

Considerations such as these lead us to the thorniest problem of all, that of democracy, or, as Svetozar Stojanović and others have insisted, of democratization—recognising that democracy is a condition reached only at the end of a lengthy historical process. These private initiatives just mentioned can be viewed as instances of grass-roots participatory democracy made necessary by the negligence of the socialist regimes. Or they can be regarded as belated outcroppings of a democratic impulse that fell victim, stating the matter in rather sweeping retrospective terms, to the historical error of placing the building of socialism ahead of the cause of democratization on the revolutionary agenda. Either way the problem is to generalize these grass-roots models into acceptable forms for nationwide adoption, or to discover in the classical texts of Marxism a pertinent democratic imperative, or to invoke an external model that will not register as subversive. Yugoslavia aside (where the break with the Soviet Union virtually dictated the adoption of some novel alternative to the tutelary prescription), East Europeans have been overtaxed in general just to maintain the unofficial expressions of a democratic impulse, let alone to apply them to society at large. The classical texts are at hand and have been creatively reinterpreted by coteries of dissident intellectuals in various countries, but with very little chance to prevail against official Marxism-Leninism. And the external models either play into the hands of the authorities who rejoice when they can find scapegoats or they evoke serious misgivings in the native critics themselves.

Few living East Europeans have a memory of actual democratic functioning, even of the proximate kind known as bourgeois democracy. What most can remember is either an unbroken lineage of autocracies sailing under different ideological banners or, for the younger people, just the various stages of socialism advertised as democracy. The serious intellectuals of these societies are caught, in their efforts at democratic spokesmanship, in the bind of acknowledging, necessarily, that Western societies afford certain civic freedoms missing in their own polities while attenuating democratic principle by restricting it to certain procedural safeguards or to carefully delimited sectors of public life. This is the bourgeois democracy they have been taught to disparage and a limited conception that they cannot conscientiously advocate even as they envy the relative freedom it allows.

It is, in short, the age-old problem of Central Europeans too sophisticated to accept a narrow Western concept of democracy and too oppressed not to yearn for that degree of freedom. The Hungarian poet, Endre Ady, prefigured the dilemma almost a century ago when he opposed the backward, antidemocratic climate of Central Europe while also rejecting the corrupt and money-grubbing politics of Western Europe. Ady's heirs, in Hungary and elsewhere, have not transcended the dilemma: a Western model seems totally inadequate because of the inequality and imperialism associated with it, yet there is no other that offers a specific remedy for the unfreedom of their own social environment. The dilemma of East European intellectuals is self-evident when an oppositional poet, István Eörsi, is rebuked by his associates for citing Chomsky on the derelictions of the West's "friendly fascism" on grounds that he may give unwitting ("objective") sustenance to the official anti-American posture. We should not, then, be unduly surprised if it turns out that they prefer either to build open-endedly on their own grass-roots initiatives, however feeble, or to adopt an alternative, such as the Yugoslav, that addresses their own problems and their own stage of social development more immediately. They would probably all agree, however, that a solution to the question of democratization is prior, theoretically and practically, to the question of socialism if they wish to discuss the latter at all. What remains in doubt, as regards a strategy of reform, is whether democratization can be attained, introduced belatedly and allowed to redefine what is to count as socialism in societies that have, for several decades, professed to be socialist in the only extant realization of that term.

It is at this point that we encounter workers, the working class of original Marxism, and their advocacy of interests that are explicitly those of the working class in opposition to the government or party that claims to speak for those interests. In short, we arrive at Poland and confront the singular features of that current crisis.

Historically, the labor movements of Eastern Europe have been tardy and weak, excepting possibly those of Czechoslovakia and East Germany, and notwithstanding the lively history of Polish socialism, in keeping with the region's prevailing tempo of social development. We should not forget that the abolition of serfdom preceded the peoples' democracies by less than a century. The strained Leninist analysis that rendered Russia ripe for revolution, resting its case on a small minority of working class people and the assumption by a vanguard party of the task of enunciating working class interests, would still have been strained for most of Eastern Europe even as late as the end of World War II. Therefore, the absorption of trade union functions into the machinery of state was not the wrenching experience that it would have been had the trade union tradition been deeper and more resistant to the Soviet model.

When labor unrest surfaced, as it did in East Germany in 1953, it was far more a spontaneous protest than a rekindling of independent trade union spirit. Further, the active involvement of workers in the Hungarian upheaval of 1956 and in the Czechoslovak reform movement of 1968, while certainly to be counted as a sign of an increasingly pervasive, and even organized, working class disenchantment with the orthodox regimes, was largely a response to initiatives and leadership provided by intellectuals. There was, in short, little reason to think of working class resistance to governmental dictate as anything more substantial or far-reaching than the aforementioned attempts to reclaim a piece of civil society from the state monopoly.

But recent developments in Poland have introduced a qualitatively new dimension into the region's oppositional patterns, not just because of the magnitude of the movement known as Solidarity or the comprehensiveness of its demands, but because, for the first time on any major scale, the direction of a challenge to the workers' state was assumed initially by, and then firmly maintained in the hands of, workers. Symbolically at least, the mass movement, in which intellectuals affiliated with workers rather than the other way round, completed the task of discrediting, and not just in Poland, the official claims regarding democracy and socialism. It is too soon to know whether or not this particular development will reach beyond the symbolic realm to become a genuine political victory. But even if such a victory proves elusive, becomes ambiguous, or is indefinitely postponed, the effects of a full-blown workers' movement have by now been implanted in Eastern European consciousness. All of the many inhabitants of the societies organized according to Soviet precept—workers, intellectuals, ordinary citizens—have acquired a renewed sense of what it is possible to achieve in the way of a more humane and democratic socialism if they have the patience to nudge, push, and generally outmaneuver the discredited regimes at every opportunity, even challenging them directly, perhaps in the Polish manner, but, in any event, pressing the case for reforms that serve people's needs rather than official designs.

Such an outlook for reform on the domestic front is of course slow and tedious, not exciting or heroic. It involves, at a minimum and irrespective of directions chosen, a marked increase in productivity and work discipline. While governments and managers argue that the prerequisite for this is more central planning and rigid control, the underpaid and disenfranchised workers reply—either in the silent ways, described by Haraszti in *A Worker in a Workers' State,* or in open protests the peak of which was Gdansk—that the road to higher production figures leads through democratization and workers' participation. Their chances of minor victories are not completely hopeless, but it is most unlikely that a genuine and radical democratization would ever receive from a regime the priority that it merits. When, on the other hand, a popular local initiative takes place, no matter how modest its scale, there is at least a potential or embryonic experience of democratic participation to record in a region that has known all too little of such participation.

On the international plane it is possible to identify a pair of interrelated tendencies that, while they offer little of the substance to reform themselves, could prove exceedingly important as external supports for domestic initiatives. Having opted for a system of client states rather than for outright annexation, the Soviet Union assumed a permanent burden (along with the many benefits) of maintaining a viable international alliance or coalition. Strict control worked nicely for a time, but as the client states became individually viable (as they had to do if the system were not to be an albatross), their heterogeneity, cultural to be sure but above all economic, made the alliance increasingly problematical. With or without Stalin, its viability depended more and more on voluntary allegiance, less and less on the threat of intervention.

Most of us who were wrong in 1968 calculated, presumably, that the Soviet Union had adjusted more fully than it had in fact to the necessity for change within its client-state system. Our current uneasiness about Poland testifies that we are still unsure how much adjustment has in fact occurred. But Soviet reluctance to intervene (and assume all of the resulting burdens) is already clear, no matter what may unfold in future, and this suggests that, just as the Prague Spring has become a part, however ill-starred, of postwar East European experience, so will the Polish reform movement register even more strongly and regardless of immediate outcomes. And it thus becomes increasingly manifest that the Soviet client-state system, if it is to have any utility for its dominant member, will have to continue, grudgingly no doubt, to allow for increasing autonomy on the part of its diverse subordinate members.

That tendency is joined by another, almost the reverse side of the same medal. All of the client-state regimes seek constantly for ways to enlarge the range and autonomy of their international relationships. The second tendency is obscured at times, as when the GDR and Poland agitate for repression in Czechoslovakia or when the GDR and Czechoslovakia urge that Poland not get out of hand. The clients' striving for autonomy is not, and may never be, synchronized. But it is not the possibility of a united bloc turning on its tutelary power that is most interesting in this connection. It is rather the possibility, already implicit in cultural and economic relations with the West, that regimes and subject populations may one day acknowledge a common interest. The focal point could be so simple a matter as improving product quality in order to attain a competitive status in the international market. A common stake in increased worker productivity is easy to discern, *in potentia,* in contemporary Poland. Whatever the common cause, it would render the regime dependent on popular mobilization and collaboration. In such a situation, the *quid pro quo* could easily widen out to include the whole of a grass-roots agenda of desired social change. The patience of the advocates of domestic reform could then be rewarded in surprising measure.

How Eastern Europe Looks at Glasnost

✦

Peter Michielsen

This survey of the East European states by a Dutch journalist details different responses in the region to Soviet initiatives of reform and examines the varied reasons for fearful and supportive reactions by the several governments.

The Soviet Union is trying to reform. Under the term *perestroika* (restructuring), attempts are being made by Soviet leader Mikhail Gorbachev to get some movement in the rusty machine—politically, economically, and culturally. The process has until now been largely confined to the verbal field. Few practical breakthroughs have been reached, and no guarantees for success exist. Thousands of party and state functionaries have been purged but millions have not.

Glasnost (openness) is one of the most striking features of the new course. An average but attentive Soviet citizen is surprised day after day by impossibilities that have become possible: Newspapers write about problems in general; blundering bureaucrats, *apparatchiks* and managers; failures to carry out rational policies; even the Stalinist past. Disasters are reported; previously taboo subjects like the number of psychiatric patients, crime, prostitution, minority problems, corruption, and mismanagement are discussed; controversial books appear; films are shown after years on dusty shelves. Openness alone, of course, achieves no practical solutions—though it can introduce and facilitate them. But the process is breathtaking in itself.

The Eastern European states are following this process with special attention. After all, changes in Moscow never leave the small partners untouched. From Warsaw to Sofia, from East Berlin to Bucharest, whenever the wind from Moscow changes, the small socialist countries have to follow suit. This dogma may have lost some of its meaning because economic pressure from Moscow has been growing: The economically stagnating USSR needs the assistance of its allies—their technological help, manpower, consumer goods, and financial investments. And with the balance of power between Gorbachev and the conservatives a precarious one, he needs even political support from the allies.

Has Gorbachev's *perestroika* affected the small states of Eastern Europe? How have Gorbachev's Eastern European colleagues reacted to his calls for reform? Most of those colleagues came to power in Leonid Brezhnev's or even Nikita Khrushchev's time. In the past most of them have followed a general Soviet model that sharply differed from the one Gorbachev strives for now, and they are faced with a difficult dilemma: Should they follow the young Soviet leader, with all the risks involved, not only in their own countries but also for their own future if Gorbachev stumbles and falls? Or should they wait and see how *perestroika* develops? And does Gorbachev indeed expect his Eastern European colleagues to follow him?

As a general principle, and limited to their internal policies, the leaders of Eastern Europe are more interested in a weak and stagnating Soviet Union than in one that radiates strength and self-confidence, one that not only demands but also enforces obedience. In recent years, Soviet stagnation has tended to enlarge the maneuvering space of the small allies. They have been skillful in handling this space.

Earlier than the USSR itself, the small states recognized the connection between sticking stubbornly to ideological dogma and a threatening economic isolation in the computer age. Worried about the general chill between East and West, they have drawn their conclusions by adopting a kind of *Westpolitik* of their own. Hungary and East Germany have tightened their links to Western Europe. Twice, Moscow pressured East German leader Erich Honecker to cancel visits to West Germany; Bulgarian leader Todor Zhivkov was pressed into canceling such a trip once. While Moscow involved itself in angry confrontations with the West, the Eastern Europeans welcomed one Western leader after another. In the East German and Czechoslovak press, unusually critical remarks appeared about the deployment of new Soviet missiles there; Poland witnessed the birth and death of Solidarity and welcomed twice a pope of its own; and in some countries economic reforms had very much a matter-of-fact character.

Consultation with Moscow was out, and when there had to be any, the arguments of the small countries pulled more weight. Moscow was neglected, sometimes ignored. Moscow, after all, could not function as an example. Moscow was too busy with the succession of one old man by another. It had nothing to offer.

That erosion of Moscow's authority led to consternation among the conservatives in Moscow, first in the party's foreign and ideological departments, but also in the Foreign Ministry, then under Andrei Gromyko. But they had neither sticks nor carrots to bring the small states back into line. The pressure on Honecker and Zhivkov had an emergency character. Shady excuses had to be found to justify the cancellation of those visits to Bonn. And such concessions from East Berlin and Sofia had a price. In the end, Soviet interventions enlarged the political space for the Eastern Europeans rather than limiting it.

Now that Gorbachev has gained ground in Moscow, the Soviets are slowly activating their Eastern Europe policy. Gorbachev wants to force the unwilling partners back into line. The moment of choice has come close to the leaders in the capitals of Eastern Europe.

◆

ROMANIA

The Romanians have cared least about Gorbachev's *perestroika*—knowing full well they can get away with that attitude better than most. It would be exaggerated to state that the independent line the Romanians have been following since the 1960s has loosened the country from the Eastern bloc. It has not. But it has resulted in an erosion of political solidarity vis-à-vis the stubbornly independent Romanians. On the one hand, Romanians have lost credibility and moral credit within the bloc because of the extremely severe policies of party leader Nicolae Ceauşescu and the economic malaise in Romania. On the other hand, no one any longer expects the Romanians to fall into line. This psychological condition allows Ceauşescu to ignore Gorbachev's calls for obedience and economic reform.

It is worthwhile for Gorbachev to force his line upon the other partners. He cannot and will not expect obedience in Bucharest.

However, Romanian independence enjoys less and less attention and sympathy abroad. It is old hat in East and West: A habituation process has eroded the effectiveness of Romanian efforts. Most Western governments doubt the realism of the many disarmament proposals that come from Bucharest. The further they go, the less credible they become and the less seriously they are considered. Ceauşescu's stature abroad, in East and West, is also undermined by the serious economic crisis of Romania—for which he alone is responsible—and even more by the way he deals with that crisis: by forcing the population to pay the price. Romania has become the poorhouse of Europe. It can be extremely cold there in winter. There is very little to buy, very little to eat even, and generally very little to look forward to or to enjoy.

This, however, does not mean that Ceauşescu has changed the principles of his independent line. The crisis has not brought about any change in the Romanian reluctance to give way to Soviet demands, and Romania generally cares very little about what its formal partners say or think.

And what Gorbachev is trying to realize in the Soviet Union is, in every way, anathema to the Romanian leader. Romania is a very centralized country—politically, economically, culturally, and socially. Private economic activity, independence of companies, responsibility for managers, economic and political democratization, self-government, and fundamental critical attitudes in press and cultural circles are all taboo.

In two recent speeches, Ceauşescu has called these and other changes in the Soviet Union "contrary to scientific socialism" and thus negative. "The new activity of small private entrepreneurs" in the Soviet Union will lead to "the existence of groups which exploit inequality among people." Capitalist ownership of means of production may be large or small; it still is capitalism. Without naming the Soviet Union, Ceauşescu said that "our practice has shown that socialist ownership is the only way to reach equality and social justice and to guarantee the powerful development of productive forces, the safeguarding of welfare and the independence of every nation."

Ceauşescu may have his own unorthodox ways to guarantee "socialist owner-ship" (some years ago he invented a system that obliged Romanian workers to buy stocks in the factories, which according to Marxist theory they already owned), but the message is clear: There will be no privatization in Romania.

Gorbachev's model, in Ceauşescu's eyes, is unacceptable because it erodes the leading role of the party. That, after all, is the consequence of self-government for workers and independence of companies and of openness in the cultural, scientific, and media spheres. Such concepts, Ceauşescu said, mean "a step back." Glasnost is very much out in Romania. There is no criticism and no openness in the press, litera-ture, or any other field. On the contrary, problems are not discussed or even hinted at; usually they are just ignored or even bluntly denied. The only person for whom this does not apply is Ceauşescu himself: He, and only he, may criticize.

✦

CZECHOSLOVAKIA

Skepticism and distrust about Gorbachev's policies also dominate in Prague. Some Czechoslovak leaders, with a courage unseen since the Prague Spring was crushed by Soviet tanks in 1968, have already openly distanced themselves from it. Chief ideologist (and chief conservative) Vasil Bilak has even said he "hopes" that Gorbachev "leaves the basic rules of communism intact." In other words, he fears Gorbachev may do the opposite.

Prague has reason to worry. If anywhere in the bloc, Romania excepting, there is fear of reform, it is in Prague. The leaders who called in the tanks in 1968 or came to power in their wake are still today's leaders. Death has somewhat reduced their ranks, but very few newcomers have been added to the team since the followers of the 1968 reform course were purged in a cruel normalization process. This team is afraid of any kind of structure touching reform because it reminds them (and their people) of the 1968 drama. Even the word *reform* is taboo and is replaced by euphemisms like *changes* or *measures*. In the economy, they have gotten away with that for quite some time, mainly because the regime of Gustav Husák had a large advantage when it came into power—a highly developed industrial base—and because it has never succumbed to the temptation of easy Western credits (which were also less easily offered anyway because of the political desert in which Prague found itself at that time). Furthermore, the regime could afford—or thought it could afford—to banish its reform-minded intellectuals, the backbone of the Prague Spring, to manual labor. Even now, nearly two decades later, they wash windows, dig graves, clean dead bodies in hospitals, work as stokers, sell ice cream, or at best, live abroad.

But 1987 is not 1970. The trauma of the 1970s has not grown less intensive, but the economic situation has changed radically. The developed industry of those days is now outmoded. Technologically, Czechoslovakia has been surpassed even within the Eastern bloc. Centralized organization is just as amorphous as the regime itself. But there is widespread fear of reforms. Only during the last two years has the conscious-ness gained ground that the country has no choice: It will have to reform if it wants to survive. Up until now, however, this consciousness has been limited to small circles of economic specialists, and every time they plead their cause they get their knuckles rapped by the political leadership.

The only attempt Czechoslovakia has undertaken in this field is an experiment in some companies allowing managers to make their own decisions. This modest experiment will be incorporated in the next five-year plan if it succeeds. Until 1990, Prague wants to continue the course it has taken since 1970.

Glasnost is no issue. Even when discussions are reported, there are severe rebukes in papers like the party paper *Rudé Pravo,* which can bluntly claim that there are no shortages in Czechoslovakia, only "surpluses that are not distributed evenly." Criticism is dangerous not only because it threatens the position of the present leaders but also because its contents remind them of what Alexander Dubček tried to realize. In a recent speech Bilak said the Soviet example must not be copied "mechanically" and "opportunistically." He compared Czechoslovak adherents to Soviet-type reforms with the purged leaders of the Prague Spring. These people, Bilak said, try to "conceal their antisocialist behavior." The fact that youngsters demonstrated recently in Plzeň for "a Czechoslovak Gorbachev" can only have strengthened the belief among the present leaders that following the Soviet line may be the beginning of the end.

✦

EAST GERMANY

East Germany is quite worried about Gorbachev. Not only has it strengthened its ties to Western Europe in recent years but it also feels it has nothing to learn from Moscow. East German leaders can rightly claim to have realized reforms that have been crowned with relative success. Their economy is the best organized, most efficient, and most streamlined in the bloc, and East Berlin knows that it is far ahead of the USSR in this field. If anyone has lessons to teach, it is East Germany, they feel.

That may be true in the economic field, but not in the political field. An "open" socialism, democratization, glasnost, and cultural liberalization are quite different from streamlining the economy, and East German leader Erich Honecker has repeatedly stated that such political reforms are not welcome.

The East German party congress last year was attended by Gorbachev, who shortly before had confronted the delegates at his own congress with a barrage of criticism. In East Berlin, the dynamic Soviet leader repeated that criticism. He was promptly brushed off by Honecker: The East German party boss had nothing but unqualified praise for his own country, his own party, and his own performance. Criticism and self-criticism, so popular now in the Soviet Union, were very much absent in East Berlin. It was an incident that had not been witnessed since "people's power" was established in the East: A Soviet leader, the highest boss from the leading center, the chairman of the board, was publicly humiliated by the local branch's chief.

Since then the East Germans have pursued their opposition. Gorbachev's speeches are censored in their press. Soviet media are quoted positively when they criticize Soviet developments, and East German developments are praised to high heaven. The party paper *Neues Deutschland* virtually ignored the February Plenum in Moscow, while eight full pages were devoted to a speech in which Honecker made quite plain that Gorbachev's *perestroika* was not something East Berlin was prepared to copy. Every country, Honecker said, must determine its own course, "which of course leads to differences in approach." The East German economy and social policy are sensibly related, he was saying. The results are excellent and the party is supported by ever more millions of workers, so there is no need for reforms.

Most of Honecker's statements may be true to a certain extent, but they cannot but frustrate the man in Moscow. So striking is this break with traditional Eastern practice that in Bonn and elsewhere speculations have arisen whether Honecker may be maneuvering himself into a position in which his predecessor Walter Ulbricht found himself in the early 1970s: on the way out.

◆

BULGARIA

Bulgaria was the first among the allies in Eastern Europe to be corrected in a rather ungentle way by the new Kremlin leader. The Bulgarians are usually proud of their special family relationship with the Russians. Bulgarians and Russians have been blood brothers for centuries. In Bulgaria, 60,000 copies of the Moscow edition of *Pravda* are sold each day, as well as 250,000 copies of other Soviet periodicals each week.

That special tie was cultivated during Brezhnev's tenure. Brezhnev and Zhivkov got on so well together that Zhivkov sometimes spoke of two lungs within one body, and from time to time speculation arose whether Bulgaria wanted to become the 16th Soviet republic. Under Gorbachev, however, this harmony quickly evaporated. Gorbachev's rise to power after Konstantin Chernenko's death was greeted in Sofia by a deep silence, which was ended by the new Soviet ambassador, Grekov. In a very unusual and public way—an interview—Grekov vented Moscow's displeasure about the state of affairs in Bulgaria, especially in the economy. No painful subject was avoided. The Bulgarian economy was badly organized, the quality was too low, means of production were not used, and there was no innovation or streamlining. When shortly afterwards Gorbachev came to Sofia, he repeated that criticism. His relation with Zhivkov, the bloc's veteran, was clearly quite uncomfortable.

Since that visit, the Gorbachev line has received more favorable attention in the Bulgarian press, and the Bulgarians have diligently started on a road of economic renewal. Before, during and after the Bulgarian party congress of March 1986, personnel changes were made in the administrative and economic fields, from top to bottom, as well as many organizational changes in the economic system. But much of this Bulgarian solidarity with *perestroika* and glasnost is verbal and somewhat half-hearted. The more they change, the more things remain the same. There is no dynamism, reorganizations tend to have an alibi character or remain unfinished. There is little glasnost, little discussion, little criticism. It is a renewal without conviction, and distrust dominates. Sofia is quite shaken.

◆

HUNGARY

The Hungarians have fewer problems with Gorbachev. On the whole, his line does not contradict the one they started much earlier. What is new in Moscow is not new in Budapest. From Gorbachev, there is little to learn, either economically or politically. And so the Hungarians wish him well, expecting an encouraging and helping hand in their own attempts to further modernize.

The only Hungarian worry is that Gorbachev might pressure them to integrate their economy more with his. For years, Budapest has cultivated its links with the West; it is very much dependent on world trade and could suffer if this direction were suddenly changed.

The Hungarians have been decentralizing and streamlining their economy for years: giving factory managers independence; promoting private economic activity; respecting the relation between costs and prices and the market mechanism in general; and using criteria like profit, liquidity, and efficiency. The magic center, which used to dictate policy and hand out orders, gradually has been curtailed to a coordinating, supporting role. The "new manager," whose education will still cause Gorbachev many headaches in the USSR, has a firm place in Hungarian economy. The Hungarian consumer is more satisfied than his counterparts elsewhere in the bloc, and no average participant in the production process in Eastern Europe is as active (though especially when working privately) as the one in Hungary.

It would be an exaggeration to call this policy a success story. The Hungarian reforms are pursued with a catalogue of compromises. Not only are the Hungarians dependent on developments in world trade, there is also still much resistance among lower-level bureaucrats as well as nasty side effects in the form of social problems that the Hungarians have not even begun to solve. Private economic activity is beautiful for those who can pursue it; it is less beautiful for those who can't—like retirees, people in the countryside, women, and those with a low education. There is poverty in Hungary, and the country threatens to be split between haves and have-nots. That will be Hungary's main problem in the 1990s, and no one in Budapest really knows how to solve it.

For the time being—surely until party leader János Kádár passes from the scene—this course will be followed. The political will that is lacking elsewhere in the bloc exists in Hungary.

In glasnost as well, the Hungarians do not fear lessons from Moscow. They have opened up and decentralized in this area, too. There are few political taboos. In elections, even dissidents have tried to become candidates. Discussions are quite open, and in March 1987 there was even a demonstration of 2,000 people demanding more liberty and the departure of Soviet troops. Of course, liberty has its boundaries—the regime and the writers are just now locked in a quite bitter ideological struggle—but policies are, in general, quite open. It is no wonder that on March 15, while in another part of the Hungarian capital demonstrators were demanding the departure of Soviet troops, Imre Pozsgay, the reform-minded leader of the Patriotic People's Front, went out of his way to praise Gorbachev. In the nineteenth century, Hungarians looked to Paris for progressive reforms, he said. Now they look to Moscow.

✦

POLAND

Apart from Hungary, Poland is the only country in Eastern Europe where Gorbachev has received open and unqualified support. Party boss Wojciech Jaruzelski might well be the most clever politician in Eastern Europe. No one is faced with more difficulties than he is: an angry and unwilling people, a tainted past, and a desperate economic situation. And yet he has succeeded in silencing the opposition and increasing stabilization, without the open terror Kádár used until 1960 or the hidden terror Husák used in the 1970s. Gorbachev recognized Jaruzelski's political gifts quite early, and the Polish leader has become a kind of best pupil in the class.

On the other hand, law and order do not mean that things go well in Poland. In fact, things are going quite wrong in Poland. The country desperately needs to reform. That reform, which exists on paper but on paper only, is wanted very much by Jaruzelski. But reforms cannot be realized without sacrifices, and those sacrifices must be made in the first place by the many millions of ordinary Poles, who have to bear the social costs of the reforms in the form of higher prices and harder work.

Jaruzelski is, however, a prisoner in his own country—a prisoner not only of the party conservatives on the middle level whom he had to promote in 1982 to realize his goal of repressing Solidarity, but even more a prisoner of his own past. The suppression of Solidarity made him immensely unpopular. It also saddled him with a trauma, a great fear of popular resistance. He does not know his boundaries and he is quite unwilling to test where they are. He simply is not in the position to ask anything, let alone sacrifice, from the Poles. Thus, Poland stagnates.

One way of convincing the millions of angry or indifferent Poles that the state of the country is very bad is glasnost. Glasnost in Poland goes further than anywhere else in the bloc, including the Soviet Union. Papers can write virtually everything, and they use that freedom freely. With one exception—the legitimacy of the system—there are no taboos. Polish papers serialize *Doctor Zhivago,* ridicule the government, call for "a revolution" to bring Poland back on its feet, and write that things were better organized in pre-war Poland. The function of all this liberty is to convince the party and the people that reforms must be made. Participation is the big issue in Poland.

And it will remain an issue, because there is no way to convince the Poles. Participation is a two-way process; it suggests that influence has been acknowledged. And Jaruzelski is not prepared to grant that influence. A sociologist said: "The regime has no concept to win over the Poles because it is afraid of them, afraid to get Solidarity back under another name. They want participation, but on their terms, and controlled. But there is no such thing as controlled participation. Participation is spontaneous and uncontrolled, otherwise it is not participation."

No East European leader has praised Gorbachev more than Jaruzelski. In a recent speech, he called the Soviet reforms "breathtaking." They deserve, he added, the "ardent" support and "the honest sympathy" of all Poles. The Polish leader made clear: The wind from the east is favorable, and this "is a constellation Poland has not witnessed in a thousand years."

It is quite clear, prominent Solidarity adviser Professor Bronisław Geremek said in an interview, that Jaruzelski wants and needs reforms like Gorbachev's but cannot realize them. "Gorbachev has given him the green light. He can do in Poland as he pleases. But he does not use that green light because he is, like everybody, unsure of what will happen with Gorbachev. Much is going on in Moscow, but there are no breakthroughs. He wants to wait until he is sure Gorbachev is firmly in the saddle and the reform course is on its way. Only then he will feel safe to act, by enforcing reforms in Poland. Until then he can do nothing."

That seems to be the prevailing opinion in Warsaw, among observers and even in government and party circles.

Gorbachev's *perestroika* is judged quite differently in each of the small Eastern European states. Each regime has different reasons to fear or to support it. Even where judgments coincide, the reasons can differ, which is quite an illuminating illustration of Eastern bloc differentiation. In some countries political and economic decentralization is taboo as contrary to socialism; in other countries it is a part of the system. Ideas vary about glasnost; other (alibi-) parties; criticism from below; and autonomy for artists, the press, scientists, and common citizens. A peculiar phenomenon has thus been introduced: Ideological conservatives who have always condemned the "own way principle" of the Romanians have now suddenly discovered that principle for themselves.

What Moscow thinks about all this has been most clearly articulated by the Soviet ambassador in Bonn, Yuli Kvitsinsky. He recently said that "revolutionary reforms [in the Soviet Union] make socialism more attractive." Of course, he added, that is "a task for all of us, wherever we are, in the GDR, in the Soviet Union, or in Poland." Of course, Kvitsinsky went on, every party has its own tasks and circumstances. How the new principles must be put into practice is a matter for each individual party. But the ambassador left no real doubt that there is only one socialism and that the new principles must be applied everywhere.

A Soviet View of Eastern Europe

✦

Staff of the Institute of Economics of the World Socialist System (Moscow)

This document, prepared by the staff of the Institute of Economics of the World Socialist System in Moscow and printed in *Problems of Communism,* reveals the striking change in Soviet thinking about Eastern Europe that emerged in the era of Gorbachev's restructuring campaign. It reflects the sharp and in some ways ironic shift from the inhibition to the promotion of political and economic change in the area.

The countries of Eastern Europe constitute an international and political community of states marked by contradictions. Not only are they heterogeneous ethnically and linguistically, and in their levels of cultural, economic, and political development, but they lie within a region that has historically been in the magnetic fields of different major powers. This circumstance has imparted particular features to the policies of the East European countries. Over the centuries, they maneuvered between different power centers and blocs and exerted tremendous influence on the destiny of Europe.

After World War II, the East European countries were united by the path of socialist development. But even socialism was incapable of eliminating the region's historical and new interstate contradictions, especially those regarding territorial and national questions. Thus, the administrative-state model of socialism, established in the majority of East European countries during the 1950's under the influence of the Soviet Union, has not withstood the test of time, thereby showing its socio-political and economic inefficiency. Moreover, the Soviet model erected serious barriers to direct communication among the nations of these states, impeding the intertwining of their political, economic, scientific, and cultural interests. The process of reform and renewal of socialism in East European countries was further hindered for a long time by the stagnation of the Soviet system and the related conceptual inertia and dogma-

"A Soviet View of Eastern Europe," from *Problems of Communism,* May–August 1988, U.S. Information Agency, pp. 60–67.

tism of Soviet policy in the 1960's and 1970's. As a result, internal socio-political and economic contradictions accumulated in many countries of Eastern Europe and were not resolved in time. This only aggravated previous interstate controversies and domestic problems.

Today, the socialist countries of Eastern Europe are at a turning point in their development—a turning point characterized by societal understanding of the compelling necessity to change radically the political and economic structures, and to undertake profound reforms in all spheres of public life.

The scope of work to be done is enormous indeed. It ranges from the recovery of an economy distorted by the administrative-command methods of the past, to the democratization of a society emerging with difficulty from the suppression of the Stalinist period, to the improvement of cooperation among socialist countries—a cooperation based on true partnership and mutual respect. Not only present-day problems, but those inherited from the past, must be solved.

The profound socio-political and economic reforms that have been started in a number of East European countries are intended to create radically new conditions for economic, social, and scientific-technological progress, and for the free development of the individual. The aim is to create in these countries a qualitatively new model of socialism that would be truly humane in nature. This would lead to drastic changes in the role of these countries in the all-European process and in the system of East-West relations that, in turn, would substantially enhance their importance and influence on international politics.

◆

THE USSR AND THE EAST
EUROPEAN SOCIALIST COUNTRIES

The establishment and development of relations between the Soviet Union and its neighbors in Eastern Europe have been complicated and contradictory. The conditions for good-neighborly relations were, frankly speaking, very unfavorable. As is well known, after World War I, the sponsors of the Versailles Treaty system tried to erect a "cordon sanitaire" around the young Soviet Russian state, and the system's bulwark in Eastern Europe was the Little Entente. The anti-Soviet orientation of the ruling circles of the countries of Eastern Europe in the interwar period caused considerable damage to the security of the Soviet Union. Serious collisions and conflicts also took place among the East European countries over national, territorial, and other issues.

A new situation arose in Europe after World War II as a result of the defeat of the Axis powers and the downfall of the pro-fascist regimes in Eastern Europe, creating favorable conditions for a radical reorganization of relations between the Soviet Union and the East European states on the basis of neighborly and mutually beneficial cooperation. The course of events in Europe had been such that conservative bourgeois circles and the capitalist order were seriously discredited. At the same time, there was the unprecedented rise of a mass movement for social renewal, which had its origins in the context of wartime resistance. These two developments placed revolutionary transformations of the socio-economic system of the East European countries on the agenda. Clearly, the sympathy and support of the Soviet Union were with the mass movement; this led at first to the formation of the people's democracy regime, and then to the victory of the socialist system in the countries of Eastern Europe.

Once socialism moved beyond the borders of one country, the issue of the theoretical and practical foundations on which international relations among socialist countries were to rest became a pressing one. The Soviet Union and the other socialist countries faced a number of new and complicated problems which the international workers' movement and Marxist-Leninist theory had not previously encountered. The primary issue was how to align the specific national features and the ensuing political and economic interests of independent sovereign states with the international interests of the community of socialist states as a whole—in other words, how to synchronize the specific interests of individual socialist countries that differed from one another in territorial size; in endowment with natural resources; in national habits, traditions, and historical experience; in the level of development of productive forces, as well as in production relations, social structures, forms of political organization, extent of democratic experience, etc.

In dealing with these problems, the Soviet Union and the other socialist countries embarked on an uncharted path in a difficult "cold war" climate marked by military, economic, and propaganda pressures from the West. It is quite understandable that everything did not turn out well immediately. There were illusions that had to be overcome, and mistakes, sometimes grave ones, were made which had serious consequences. For example, great damage was caused by the naive concepts prevailing in the 1950's and 1960's about the noncontradictory and conflictless character both of the socio-political and economic development of socialist states and of relations among them. The theory of "non-conflict" made it impossible to understand the nature and sources of contradictions and crises in the socialist community, and to elaborate mechanisms and procedures for their timely detection, prevention, and elimination. This, in turn, led to incorrect decisions that brought on deformations in the mutual relations of socialist states.

Still greater difficulties and problems arose in applying the principles of equal partnership among socialist states. For objective reasons, the Soviet Union, as the first socialist state in the world, was in a special position relative to other socialist countries. When the Third International was in existence, solidarity with the Soviet Union and acceptance of its leading role in the world communist movement was regarded by communist parties as natural. But even at that time, this view hindered the realization of the principle of independence on the part of working-class parties and prevented the understanding of their role as a national force in their own countries. Moreover, it was inadmissible to extend the postulate of the primary role of the Communist Party of the Soviet Union (CPSU) to relations among socialist states. The urge of the Stalin leadership to do so resulted in a conflict between the Soviet Union and Yugoslavia (as well as other socialist states) and affected the entire system of links among socialist countries and communist parties. Closely related to this erroneous policy was the practice of thoughtlessly copying and mechanically transferring the Soviet experience to the different social and historic situations of the East European countries.

The period of the 1940's and 1950's, when relations between the Soviet Union and the socialist countries of Eastern Europe were being established, was unfortunately marked by many of the above-mentioned mistakes and distortions of the principles of socialism, a process aggravated by the voluntaristic practices and violations of law by Stalin. After his death, a process of eliminating deformations and purging the mutual relations of the socialist countries of unhealthy phenomena commenced. The need to observe strictly the principles of full equality, good will, respect for national sovereignty, and consideration for specific national features was acknowledged. The recognition that different roads of socialist development were rightful was also of great significance.

However, the process of "rejecting evil" initiated after the 20th CPSU Congress was of a contradictory nature. It was influenced by a desire to overcome past inertia, by rigid stereotypes, by a dogmatic incomprehension of change and the new requirements for social development. Moreover, this process was interrupted after 1964, when the leadership of Leonid Brezhnev and Mikhail Suslov came to power and the era of stagnant neo-Stalinism began. Even reversion to the past, to Stalinist practices, became noticeable. Major deformations of socialism in East European countries, major mistakes in their internal policies, together with the hegemonic aspirations of the Soviet leadership of that period, were among the main reasons for the deep political crises in Hungary in 1956, in Czechoslovakia in 1968, and in Poland in 1956, 1970, and 1980. These crises acquired an international dimension and seriously tested military and political stability in Europe. The negative consequences of Stalinist distortions in the domestic policies of the socialist countries and in the system of relations among them are being felt even today.

The *perestroyka* initiated in the Soviet Union when the Gorbachev leadership came to power marked not only a drastic turn in Soviet internal policy away from the Stalinist model of state-bureaucratic socialism in the direction of a qualitatively new model of democratic socialism; it also introduced profound changes in the system of political and economic relations among the socialist countries belonging to the Warsaw Treaty Organization and the Council for Economic Mutual Assistance (CEMA). New thinking, free of outlived stereotypes and dogma, underlies the policy of the Soviet Union with respect to the countries of Eastern Europe. The policy is directed toward a harmonious development of true good-neighborliness with these countries; toward a relationship free from dictate, pressure, and interference in each other's internal affairs; and toward strict observance of the principles of equal partnership, independence, and attentive respect for the national interests and the national forms of socialist development of each country. The countries of Eastern Europe now have broad opportunities to realize unhindered their national interests both within the framework of the socialist community and in relations with the West.

✦

POLITICAL *PERESTROYKA* OF THE SOCIALIST SYSTEM AND ITS EFFECT ON EAST-WEST RELATIONS

In many countries of Eastern Europe, *perestroyka* of the system of political power has begun. The model for the existing system was created in the Soviet Union during the 1930's and 1940's. This model was profoundly influenced by Stalin's perverted concepts of the character of political mechanisms in socialism, as well as by the insufficient political maturity on the part of Soviet society and a lack of democratic traditions and political culture. The administrative-command system of power started in the USSR was replicated in other socialist countries. It was characterized by hypercentralism, an absolute monopoly on decision-making, monolithic thinking, a disdain for the masses (who were seen as "small crews" and as objects of management), and isolation from the outside world. Political institutions aimed at securing political stability primarily through suppression and the leveling of diversity. This system, which demanded servile obedience, undermined the foundations of societal dynamism and viability.

The pyramidal, monocentric model of power could not help but affect the behavior of socialist states in the sphere of international relations. A similar hierarchic structure, based on subordination of everybody to a "single center," long prevailed in relations among the socialist countries. Development in these countries was undertaken according to the same model; that is, national specificity was ignored. In relations with the West, the administrative-command system of power was oriented first of all toward its own preservation, and toward counteraction and self-isolation. The existence of interests of civilization common to the two systems and requiring their cooperation and interaction was rejected. Dialogue as a form and means of international coexistence was neglected. The principle of *kto kogo* ("who bests whom") was mechanically applied to the external sphere.

The image of the capitalist "enemy" impressed itself on the public psyche. To some extent, this image was used as a means to effect the internal consolidation and mobilization of the masses in individual socialist countries. However, its utilization as the motive force for vital actions undermined the creative stimuli, and the economic and democratic regulators, of socialism. The defensive reaction of the political system long delayed the formation of a civil society in socialist countries, the growth of the political maturity of the masses, and their creative progress. It should be noted, however, that this behavior was due largely to external reasons, to the constant pressure exerted by the West, a genuine external menace to socialism. The perpetuation of the administrative system of socialism was thus, in part, a consequence of the policies of some Western circles and their blatant anticommunism.

The essence of the new model of power can be defined as the delegation of considerable responsibility to the local level, to labor and territorial collectives; the expansion of pluralism in public life; and the democratization of all institutions, including the vanguard party. The aim is to create more effective guarantees against the power monopoly of the layer of managers and professional politicians—against the bureaucratic apparatus.

The process of *perestroyka* is already shaping a new multifaceted political reality, one full of contradictions and conflicts, of collisions of interests of individuals and social groups. The renewal is just beginning, and there is a long road ahead before a new political system will be formed. The resistance of old, but still unbroken mechanisms is quite strong, and the force of inertia is quite great both "at the top" and "at the bottom." But the process of *perestroyka* has been started, and there are signs that it is becoming irreversible, and that a return to Stalinist methods is becoming impossible.

The formation of a qualitatively new political system of socialism is occurring to some extent under the influence of international realities, of the general progress of civilization and technology. In the socialist countries, there is enhanced understanding that it is necessary to promote East-West cooperation to ensure the survival of humanity, and that such cooperation requires mutual confidence between the two systems. This, in turn, calls for a new quality in foreign policy, for a reconsideration of its priorities. This reappraisal is directly linked to the *perestroyka* of the entire system of power. The shift to the new model is intended to bring about not only greater efficiency and effectiveness in political decision-making; it is intended also to create conditions for the democratization of the foreign policy process, its control by society, so as to prevent a repetition of the past, namely, the taking of voluntaristic and, in many cases, quite risky steps in international relations. Legislative and institutional guarantees of public control over foreign policy must be elaborated.

The results of political reform ought to include a more comprehensive evaluation by the socialist countries of the diversity of interests existing in the international arena, of different "balances of forces," and a renunciation of attempts at their equalization so as to preclude the development of hegemonistic intentions on the part of anyone. This stimulates greater flexibility, openness, and tolerance, which also result directly from the new atmosphere in individual countries. A country that rids itself of the command methods of management is unlikely to impose its position on others. This, however, does not mean renouncing one's own ideal values.

In the socialist countries, the formation of a new political thinking is now under way—in particular, the view of the West as a hostile force is being revised. This is reflected in a gradual retreat from the stress on autarky, on the defensive function in exercising power inside the country. Opportunities for exchange of ideas and experience are opening up, and justification of unpredictable actions in both domestic and foreign affairs is being eliminated. If society becomes more transparent, more democratic, if power is controllable, then a basis will be formed for greater mutual understanding in the international sphere as well.

It should be noted, however, that the processes of renovation occurring in the Soviet Union and other socialist countries need suitable international conditions. Pressure, blackmail, derailment of agreements by the Western side can work in favor of the adversaries of *perestroyka,* may lead to restoration of the former order. This would also mean the aggravation of international tensions. For this reason, the successful renovation of socialism is one of the guarantees for the establishment of new international relations, and above all, of a qualitatively new East–West relationship.

✦

PERESTROYKA OF THE ECONOMIC COOPERATION MECHANISM AND EAST-WEST ECONOMIC RELATIONS

All the shortcomings and difficulties in the development of cooperation among the East European countries within the CEMA framework, as well as in economic relations with the West, stem from the old mechanism of managing the national economy. With slight variations, the mechanism was copied from the Soviet model created in the 1930's and 1940's. Its specific features were rigid centralism; administrative methods of management; arbitrary methods of price formation; the ignoring of the role of the market, of the intimate link between production and consumption, and of economic methods of management; and a primitive and simplified understanding of the character and functions of ownership under socialism.

These features determined the nature of integrational cooperation among CEMA countries. Cooperation was based on macroeconomic decisions made by higher power echelons and, accordingly, on the basis of administrative methods of regulating the integrational processes and economic interaction. This doomed to inertia, passivity, and lack of entrepreneurship the micro-economic units of the economies of socialist countries, that is, the overwhelming majority of working people directly engaged in industry, agriculture, science, and services. This led to an abnormal situation, whereby there existed no direct contacts and business relations between cooperating collectives of enterprises and organizations of the CEMA countries. As a result, there was no real interest in the progress of economic cooperation and in deriving benefits from it. Integration in CEMA took an administrative-bureaucratic route. Instead of working for a true economic partnership leading to the extensive interweaving of genuine economic interests and the creation of cooperative links among basic units of the national economy and the entire social organism of socialist countries, spurious and pretentious measures and projects were substituted by the higher power echelons. The process of integration was reduced to one of bureaucratic organization of economic interaction among the state systems of self-contained individual countries which were separated from one another by virtually insurmountable administrative, financial, economic, legal, and other barriers. With time, these barriers grew even higher. The swollen bureaucratic apparatus could not keep up with, let alone regulate, the growing and increasingly complicated economic ties between individual enterprises, associations, and organizations of the CEMA countries. This led to reduced effectiveness in economic, scientific, and technological cooperation, to growing dissatisfaction with existing economic relations, and to the collapse of CEMA's prestige. In terms of the scale and depth of integration processes and the intensity of the interweaving of economic, scientific, and technological interests and relations, the CEMA countries turned out to be far behind the countries of the European Economic Community.

The main imperative at the present stage of mutual economic cooperation among CEMA countries is to shift from interstate barter to direct commercial links between enterprises as economic entities. In fact, the process of transforming the directive-distributive model of labor division within the CEMA framework into a qualitatively new model of a market type, including the indispensable "rehabilitation" of price and currency tools, has begun. In this process, the Council for Economic Mutual Assistance should turn into a body maximizing favorable conditions for the realization of direct cooperative relations among enterprises, associations, and organizations in the national economies of the socialist countries. It is necessary to create in all CEMA countries favorable legal, administrative, financial, and other conditions and prerequisites for economic, scientific, and technological contacts at the microeconomic level to match the national economic mechanisms. CEMA should also be sure to remove existing or emerging obstacles and barriers to setting up and realizing direct cooperative links. Special emphasis should be placed on the unimpeded movement across borders of all factors of production, including manpower, commodities, capital, and information.

According to the new model of cooperation, the principals in economic interactions would be the producers and consumers of the supplied products; they would enter into contracts not because of a command from "the top," but because of the mutual expectations of economic benefits. The partners would naturally become the real "subjects" of price formation, setting prices according to contractual principles. The contract price itself, being part of an actual deal, would acquire a structure-forming function that is now lacking, i.e., it would contribute in practice to the formation of a progressive structure of mutual exchanges. Since the contract price would be governed by demand-and-supply relations, this would ensure that only those products that meet real public needs and are manufactured at the lowest possible cost would be involved in mutual trade. The process of forming foreign trade prices would no longer be performed according to a predetermined rigid scheme but would allow for considerable freedom of maneuver.

To ensure the viability of the new price-formation mechanism, the CEMA countries have to introduce radical changes in the monetary sphere of cooperation. First of all, it is essential to introduce mutual convertibility (though limited in the initial stages) of the currencies of the countries concerned, at exchange rates reflecting their real purchasing power. In practice, this will mean the use of national currencies in mutual accounting and in setting mutual trade prices. Under such conditions, a truly unified market of the CEMA countries will begin to take shape with mechanisms for ensuring multilateral (not just bilateral, as things now stand) balancing of commodity deliveries. The need for genuine convertibility of the currencies of the CEMA countries, including convertibility into hard currencies, will grow as their internal domestic mechanisms are rearranged to foster the proliferation of market relations.

The step-by-step implementation of the concept of a CEMA common market should not be seen as economic isolation of its members from the rest of the world. On the contrary, the course of forming such a market and, in the long run, a monetary and customs union of the CEMA countries is related to a considerable extent to the need to involve their economies more effectively in world economic relations. A successful implementation of the commodity-money model of economic interaction among the socialist countries will surely give a powerful impetus to the growth of East–West economic relations.

This model will make it possible to overcome the isolation of the economies of the CEMA countries not only from one another but from the West as well. It will make possible more joint East–West economic ventures. The creation of a market setting in which the actual subjects of external economic activity become the enterprises themselves creates favorable conditions for them to carry out various mutually beneficial transactions with foreign medium- and small-size firms, thus providing truly unlimited opportunities for East–West economic cooperation.

Reform of the economic cooperation mechanism by the CEMA countries will hinge directly on the success of the *perestroyka* of the political and economic system in the USSR and other CEMA members.

◆

THE UNITED STATES AND EASTERN EUROPE

The policy of the United States toward the socialist countries of Eastern Europe, both conceptually and in practice, is characterized by a certain contradictoriness. To a considerable extent, this stems from the inconsistent general methodological approach the United States takes to these countries. On the one hand, for nearly three decades, American scholars and politicians have been declaring that diversity and differences are inherent in the countries of Eastern Europe and, hence, that the US approach to each of them should be differentiated. On the other hand, there is an impression that in practice matters are quite different, that Washington takes the same approach to all the East European countries. Since Eastern Europe is, in fact, internationally one political region despite the considerable specificity of each East European country, it objectively forms one sphere for implementing a particular line in the foreign political strategy and tactics of the United States. In this context, it may be noted that there does exist a regional—East European—area in US foreign policy whose specific features are determined by common goals and interests in the approach to all the countries of the region, by an overall policy conception, and by the general doctrinal setup. This does not exclude differentiation in US foreign policy, which naturally occurs in relations with the East European countries. Indeed, to a great extent, it explains the differences that exist in the US approach to the Soviet Union and to other countries of the socialist community.

As is known, the core of the most extensively elaborated, tested, and still operational US foreign policy doctrine of "building bridges" to Eastern Europe is a differentiated, long-term policy whose goal is to develop varied relations of differing intensity with individual states in this region so as to gradually and carefully weaken the ties of the socialist community. This would, first of all, enfeeble the position of the Soviet Union by creating a situation in the East European community that would fully preoccupy the Soviet Union with maintaining its coherence and prevent the Soviet Union from competing with the United States in other parts of the world.

It is frequently alleged in American scholarly literature and the press that the

United States has but limited possibilities for exerting influence in Eastern Europe. Hence, the conclusion is reached that it would be advisable to encourage European countries allied to the United States through the North Atlantic Treaty Organization to utilize their long-established and broad contacts with the East European states to exercise influence. Such reliance on Western Europe is hardly warranted. Although the interests of the allies on both sides of the Atlantic do coincide to some extent in this region, there are also significant differences between them. These differences are revealed in the general assessments of both sides concerning the importance of relations with socialist countries (out of security considerations and in terms of economic cooperation), and of such problems of particular importance to Europe as the German issue, the "legacy of Yalta," the varied and contradictory ideas about the restoration on the political map of the European continent of some sort of neutral interstate formation called "Central Europe," the further development of the all-European process and of disarmament, and so forth.

There is a desire on the part of the United States to use the fact that Eastern Europe is, on the one hand, an integral part of the socialist community, and on the other, a part of a European system of ties. The desire is to obtain political advantages in relations with the Soviet Union, which reflects the obsolete stereotype of a bipolar evaluation of global politics. This oversimplified understanding of East-West relations does not correspond to today's complicated international realities.

This US approach is also improper in the sense that it assigns to the states of Eastern Europe the function of serving as a means to exert influence on the main rival of the United States—the Soviet Union. It unilaterally seeks to define the national and state interests of the East European countries, and thereby artificially narrows their positions and restricts their sovereign role in global relations, especially in the socialist community and the all-European process. This approach to Eastern Europe is especially dangerous today, since the present stage of the development of these countries is characterized by considerable difficulties in connection with reforms, aggravation of conflict regarding reform, and, in a number of countries, even crisis tendencies.

In today's era of growing interdependence, no region, and especially not Eastern Europe, should be the arena of interstate rivalry of the two systems, of the two great powers—the USA and the USSR. After all, in Eastern Europe—as in all of Europe—their basic interests coincide, regardless of the acuteness of the contradictions existing between America and the Soviet Union. This confluence of interests derives above all from the need to prevent conflictual processes in international affairs, to maintain stability, and to strengthen international security.

◆

CRISES IN SOCIALIST COUNTRIES
AND EAST-WEST RELATIONS

The experience of recent decades clearly shows that crises in the countries of Eastern Europe have never been confined within the borders of the country in which they originated. Rather, they have quickly drawn into their orbit a whole number of actors on the international scene—first of all, the USSR and the other East European allies who wanted to prevent the military-political, ideological, and economic destabilization of the socialist community. Crises in Eastern Europe also affected the Western powers, especially the United States, which has traditionally viewed the dramatic collisions inside the "Soviet bloc" in terms of the potential damage they might do to the bloc's consolidation and of the opportunities they offered for weakening Soviet positions in this region and/or Soviet control over its East European allies, thus negatively affecting the interests of socialism in Eastern Europe. The clash between the main objectives of the two sides has its origins in the acute military-political, ideological, and economic rivalry of the two social systems that has existed throughout the entire postwar period. This clash was intensified by the nuclear confrontation between the USA and USSR, and by the division of Europe into opposing military and political groupings. Inevitably, this meant that a crisis situation in any East European country was globalized and aggravated, and that it seriously destabilized East-West relations irrespective of whether the international political barometer registered calm or storm when the crisis erupted.

Two vitally important circumstances require that East and West, and the USSR and the USA above all, must thoroughly rethink both the history of past East European crises and their response to present and future crises. First, unfortunately there is no reason to believe that crises in East European countries are a thing of the past. The present period in socialist countries—where the new coexists with the old and the cumbersome but ingrained forms and methods of political and economic activity are still being overcome—is pregnant with crises. Even the reforms as such, which aim at the eventual recovery of society and the improvement of socialism, might become in the course of their implementation new sources of public discontent and conflict.

Second, not the USSR, not the USA, nor any other country can afford to make the success of normalization of East-West relations, dictated as it is by the nuclear imperative, dependent on crisis phenomena in any country—including a socialist one. The stakes are too high. This necessitates an open-minded revision by each side of many aspects of traditional policy behavior during crisis situations in Eastern Europe.

What particular traits of the "crisis" policy of the USA and USSR (as the most representative and influential powers in the two systems) appear from past experience to be most dangerous and destructive for a normal development of relations between the two systems? First, and this applies to both sides, is a tendency toward the excessive globalization and ideologization of any given crisis situation. Both the United States and the Soviet Union have tended in recent years to regard every crisis in the context of their global policies, from the perspective of an inter-bloc confrontation, from the perspective of American-Soviet rivalry. (For justice's sake, it should be noted that in early stages of the existence of the world socialist system, the United States did not exclude the possibility of restoring capitalism in the countries where crises took place.) In their analyses of crisis situations in East European countries, American official circles placed the main responsibility for their origin on the USSR and explained them mainly as a rejection by these countries of the Soviet model of socialism "imposed" on them; they made much less effort to understand the domestic reasons for the crises.

Soviet policy also frequently demonized the "subversive activity" of the opposite side to the detriment of a sober-minded analysis of the reasons for certain conflicts and crises in the allied countries. A dogmatic understanding of the essence of socialism and the fear in the USSR of novel solutions in the course of building socialism prevented the socialist countries from eliminating in time the causes of ripening crises. Once a crisis developed, the role played by the Western powers, above all the USA, in the situation was exaggerated. The more so when Western countries provided pretexts for doing so.

A specific feature of American policy toward East European crises was not to try to normalize the situation but to maintain a so-called "controlled tension" in close vicinity to the Soviet Union's borders for an extended period. As the situation became aggravated during crisis, a more realistic US policy came to the fore; in the initial stages of crises, however, propagandistic activities of a provocative character were generally carried out (which, by the way, were often resumed when the crises de-escalated). Under present circumstances, such a policy could have a destabilizing effect on the development of Eastern Europe and on the European continent as a whole. It could also result in undesirable complications—for the United States as well—in East-West relations, including in the field of arms control and arms reduction. Such diplomacy also does not correspond to the moral principles and political ethical norms espoused by the United States.

The risk this policy posed for stability in Europe during recent years was well understood by the European allies of the United States. This was clearly evidenced by their markedly different approach to the Polish crisis of the early 1980's. Today, it is quite clear that Central and Eastern Europe, and Europe as a whole, is not the place for experimenting with maintaining a state of tension, especially when this involves countries belonging to different systems and military-political groupings.

Interest in preserving peace, a prerequisite for which is the positive development of relations between the two systems, necessitates that new political thinking guide the policies of the great powers with respect to crisis situations in the whole world, including those in the socialist countries of Eastern Europe. First, it is inadmissible that either side interfere in the internal problems of a country finding itself in a difficult position. Second, it is necessary to avoid globalizing crises, or attempting to use them to damage the interests of the opposite side and promote one's own interests.

Should crisis situations develop, they should under no circumstances be allowed to deter progress in East-West relations. On the contrary, improvement of these relations should be the factor that facilitates the quick localization of the crisis. Moreover, cooperation between the USSR and the USA is possible in rendering assistance to East European countries that find themselves in difficult straits. Should this happen, everyone wins: a focal point of potential destabilization in Europe is eliminated, the country more easily comes out of the crisis, and the USSR and the USA expand the sphere of their cooperation—so much needed for the improvement of international relations and the strengthening of peace.

Part II

Strains in the Bloc

✦ *Those who direct the affairs of major powers on the global stage are rather like new parents: they have had little or no training for the tasks thrust upon them and must learn their roles on the job.*

In the first postwar decade, with Stalin dominating the scene on the Soviet side of international politics, both of the states that would become known as superpowers were learning to conduct themselves as dominant global forces. Furthermore, from 1947 onward, their on-the-job training occurred in an atmosphere of unrelieved Cold War hostility, a set of circumstances that must be borne in mind if one is to understand superpower behavior at the time and for many years after.

By any manner of reckoning, Stalin's handling of relations with Yugoslavia was profoundly mistaken, resulting in a permanent fissure in an otherwise unbroken pattern of regional domination. The needless affront to Tito and Yugoslavia put in place an East European socialist system that consciously differentiated itself from the Soviet model prevailing elsewhere and deliberately pursued independent policies on the international plane.

The other exception to the regional system under Soviet direction was the Soviet Zone of Occupation in Germany that became the German Democratic Republic. Here it was the neophyte's uncertainty rather than his mistakes that produced an exception. Stalin took his time to decide what the Soviet interest in Germany really was: whether ambition might extend to all of Germany or whether East Germany was to become just another satellite in the regional system. Developments in the west made this choice for him: Stalin proceeded with the formation of the GDR in response to the western sponsorship of the Federal Republic formed from the three western zones of occupation.

At this point, hard as it was for western observers to accept, East Germany became a full-fledged member of the Soviet bloc, eventually, indeed, a member of great importance to the regional economy. Only the continuation of a special relationship with West Germany made the GDR a partial exception in the East European scheme. The postwar slogan of German reunification lost its currency, and for many years the ties to the Federal Republic seemed rather unimportant. Only when the regional system collapsed in 1989–1990 did this exception reappear as a factor of significance.

YUGOSLAVIA 1948

◆ *Tito's Yugoslavia, unwilling to assume the subservient role to which Stalin wanted to assign it along with the other East European states, broke with Stalin just as the Soviet bloc was first consolidated. Stalin expected expulsion from the Cominform to bring about Tito's downfall, but Tito prevailed, and eventually the Soviet Union had to take the initiative in trying to heal the old wound. In the meantime, however, Yugoslavia invented a new style of socialism and forged a new foreign policy. Hostility could be muted, but genuine rapprochement was out of the question.*

The dispute points up the singular position of Yugoslavia as the only state in the region that secured its own victory over the German occupiers and the only one functioning under a government that, unpopular as it might be in some circles, was undeniably Yugoslav and beholden to no external power. It also reveals the motives uppermost in Stalin's mind: his concern for security and reliability among his allies, his unwillingness to entertain partnership on any basis resembling parity, and his disdain for any "revolutionary" enterprise (such as Tito's regional ambitions) not firmly under Soviet control. In that sense, the Yugoslav case is as instructive about the development of the Soviet bloc as is the history of countries termed satellites.

In searching out possibilities for democratization in Yugoslavia, Stojanović, a leading member of the Praxis group that has been so critical of official practices in its country, deftly summarizes the stages and crises through which Yugoslavia has passed. Furthermore, he illustrates how authentic Marxist principles have been applied critically to the institutions of official Marxism-Leninism—and not only in Yugoslavia.

The next selection excerpts the lengthy record of communications leading up to Yugoslavia's expulsion. Milovan Djilas then appears in two successive roles: as the spokesman for the official rejection of Stalinist tutelage and, some years later, as the severely penalized defector from Tito's inner circle turned critic of the ruling party. His second role as dissident united him (despite considerable disagreement) with the group of scholars at the University of Belgrade who were victimized in an academic freedom case because they would not confine themselves to purely academic issues. And finally, a fairly early examination of the growing nationality problem anticipates the convulsions that would overtake Yugoslavia at the end of the 1980s.

Opportunities for Socialist
Democratization in Yugoslavia

✦

Svetozar Stojanović

Professor of philosophy in Belgrade, and now also at the University of Kansas, Stojanović here sketches the possibilities for democratization in a Yugoslavia that was, at the beginning of the 1980s, still relatively stable and, seemingly, capable of progressive development. This critique may be taken as representative of those authored throughout Eastern Europe by Marxist thinkers of democratic persuasion who rejected the claims of reigning communist ideology.

The Communist Party of Yugoslavia [CPY] led an independent War of National Liberation in the years 1941–45 and succeeded in broadening and deepening that war into a revolution. Upon coming to power it proceeded to construct a new socio-economic system on the model of the USSR. So long as the Party's Stalinist dimension is not acknowledged, it is impossible to understand why it carried over this statist paradigm of social organization into the Yugoslav context.

Stalinism had an extraordinarily strong impact on *all* communist parties. The Third International, at the time a Stalinist transmission belt, confirmed or even installed national party leaderships throughout the world, and Yugoslavia was no exception in this regard.

For these reasons it is especially urgent to subject a whole range of issues in the Party's history to systematic, scientific examination. Among these are the "Bolshevization" (the then current expression for Stalinization) of the CPY, sectarianism within the Party, Party attacks on anti-Stalinist left intellectuals before the war, the crushing of resistance to the Stalinization of the Party, the relationships among the CPY's leaders during the purges in the USSR, and revolutionary terror during the wartime and post-war periods.

Svetozar Stojanović, "Opportunities for Socialist Democratization in Yugoslavia," from *In Search of Democracy in Socialism*, Prometheus Books, 1981, pp. 77–88. Copyright © 1981 by Svetozar Stojanović. Reprinted by permission of Prometheus Books.

Josip Broz Tito. During World War II, Tito led a guerrilla resistance against the German and Italian occupiers of Yugoslavia, indigenous Croatian fascists, and traditionalist-minded Serbian forces. Having won power largely on their own, Tito and many other Yugoslav communists refused to accept the role of Soviet clients after the war. In this 1949 photograph—taken about a year after he had begun defying the Kremlin—Tito addresses a political meeting. (Topham/ The Image Works)

The CPY's accomplishment of 1948 was all the greater in that its protagonists had to liberate themselves from both external Stalinism and from their own as well. If the existence of the CPY's Stalinist dimension is denied, there is also no way of explaining the difficult struggle that had to be waged against the Cominformists at even the highest levels of the Party, state, and military.

At times the latent contradiction between the independence of the Yugoslav Revolution and Stalinism's influence on it was bound to develop into overt conflict. After all, to this day there has not been a single independent socialist revolution which has not sooner or later offered resistance to the hegemonistic aspirations of the "international revolutionary center." The potential counterexample of Cuba should not confuse the issue, for Cuba's development would probably have been much more independent were it not for the dangers presented by its proximity to the USA.

From the very beginning, Stalin tried to smash the independence of the Yugoslav Revolution in order to subordinate it to the great-power interests of the

USSR. During the war he reprimanded the CPY leadership for leftist sectarianism. It is interesting that Moscow perfidiously induced that same leadership to criticize the communist parties of France and Italy at the first meeting of the Cominform in 1947, thus putting the CPY into the position of unwittingly contributing to its own isolation in the years that were to follow. And in 1948 Stalin accused the Yugoslav leadership of deviations in both directions, albeit more of a leftist than of a rightist character.

The Yugoslav leadership reacted ambivalently to Stalin's charges in 1948. And this was understandable in light of the psychological tendency described by William James: people are unable to accept anything new as true so long as they incorporate it into the stock of existing truths with a *minimum of dissonance* and a *maximum of continuity*. And the CPY leadership indignantly rejected all the charges and proclaimed that it would demonstrate through its actions that it had been slandered.

From this there flowed a series of ultraleftist measures that the CPY would later regret—the nationalization of the last remnants of small-scale trade, services, and weekend cottages; the intensification of policies toward the peasantry through increasingly crude forms of forced procurement of agricultural produce and pressure to enter into peasant work communes; the purge of "bourgeois elements" from the Popular Front. Through this self-criticism in practice the CPY's leaders attempted to prove their loyalty to Stalin and simultaneously to deprive Stalin of all his "arguments" in the belief that with time, they would win.

Thus there was a Stalinist quality to the CPY's resistance to Stalin. How else, indeed, to explain the brutality of the conflict with their comrades-in-arms who had come out for Stalin?

How much can truly be understood and justified on the basis of the size of the stakes and the gravity of the situation in 1948? I believe that future generations will also appreciate that the repression and isolation of the Stalinists was unavoidable. For how much terror would there have been had Stalin succeeded in bringing a Quisling clique to Yugoslavia? Thus there can be no question of any rehabilitation of the real Cominformists. Nevertheless there is no defense for the inhuman conditions and torture in the prisons. And what shall we say of repressive measures employed against the families of Cominformists? And finally there were more than a few who were arrested in haste, completely innocent of any wrongdoing.

The CPY's leaders did not know at the outset how far-reaching their decision to resist Stalin would be. They entered the fray in order to protect their independence and dignity, not out of commitment to any conception of an alternative internal socialist order. The real theoretical groundwork and justification were constructed retrospectively and gradually. The workers' councils, as the touchstone and framework of the new socialism, were created only two years later.

Had the Yugoslav Communists capitulated to Stalin like so many others before and after them, the Yugoslav Revolution of 1941–45 would have been recorded in history as an occurrence of more or less local significance. Events having happened as they did, however, it acquired a world-historical dimension as well. This was the first socialist revolution to break out of the "socialist" (statist) encirclement. Within this encirclement all subsequent attempts at radical change in Eastern Europe were destined to collapse. The Yugoslavs' triumph in their clash with Stalin falls among the most important events of international communism from the October Revolution to the present day.

All this remains indisputable even after one has taken into account the fact that the bearers of the 1948 break later abandoned their own commitment to Stalinism. It is of course true that history is shaped by both objective facts as well as human commitments. Yet some of the leaders of the 1948 break have been inconsistent in retrospect, explaining the conflict with Stalin as the result of their *commitment,* while rationalizing the Stalinist features of their previous policies as deriving from the action of *objective* circumstances.

But in what sense was the period of the terrible political, economic, and military blockade of Yugoslavia on the part of the Eastern bloc more favorable for, say, the creation of workers' councils than the period immediately after the war? It is quite clear that the crucial role in this respect was played by the statist conception of socialism with which the CPY came to power, not by any objective necessity independent of that conception. It can be seen that the notions of "objective necessity" and "objective fact" are well suited to the ideological distortion of history when separated from the commitments of its principal actors.

Yugoslavia affirmed that a small country cannot create anything historically significant in this world of massive concentrations of material and military power unless it is prepared for resistance and sacrifice in order to protect its independence. That small countries are not beyond hope provided that they possess these qualities was convincingly shown by the example of the Vietnamese Revolution. And this was, among other things, the catalyst for the antiwar movement and the New Left in the West, just as Yugoslavia's example stimulated differentiation within the Eastern camp and in general among the communist parties of the world.

The concepts of authoritarian and pauperistic communism had the upper hand in the Yugoslav Revolution. It formulated its authoritarianism under the influence of Stalinism. But its pauperism harkened back to the War Communism of Lenin's Bolsheviks, for the heroic morality of the Partisans was ascetic, collectivist, and egalitarian.

The copying of the statist model after the war led to the appearance of serious symptoms of degeneration on the part of the new regime. The broad masses of the people lived ascetically, collectivistically, and in an egalitarian manner. But in the inner circles of the party-state apparatus, privilege, the high life, differentiated housing and settlement patterns, and similar phenomena began to spread. In today's terms these privileges were not conspicuous. But they were most painful to see for the people, who lived in dire need.

The conflict with Stalin moved the CPY leadership to subject the authoritarian-statist conception of socialism to re-examination. Since the blockade of Yugoslavia imposed further renunciations, the pauperistic aspect of communist politics and ideology became a subject of critical inquiry only somewhat later.

After the 1948 break an anti-Stalinist social bloc in Yugoslavia was gradually created. Through the end of the 1950s it appeared to be homogeneous. But then it began to become sharply differentiated, confronted with new trials and temptations and changed circumstances. Thenceforth several conflicting tendencies in Yugoslavia went under the common appellation of *self-managing socialism*. For our purposes, the most important were these three: *liberalized statism, bourgeois socialism,* and *democratic socialism*.

The party-state leadership was the first to expound and elaborate the basic ideas of the program of de-statization. These ideas were workers' and social self-management, the withering away of the state and the transcendence of politics as alienated social power, and the transformation of the Communist Party of Yugoslavia into the League of Communists in Yugoslavia [LCY]. What was accomplished?

The most important legacy of de-statization was the development of self-management *at the workplace*. It was first instituted in the economy and then broadened to other areas as well. In practice, however, self-management has been limited to problems of production and distribution. Genuinely political questions are tacitly reserved for the organizations of the LCY, particularly its leadership.

In the vertical organization of society there were also created a series of forms and institutions which were termed "self-managing"—assemblies of delegates from the commune, republic, and federal levels; communities of interest; and diverse associations and chambers. Since there are no *real* elections for these bodies, all this is merely *formal* self-management. Were such elections to take place, the resulting system, encompassing some two million delegates of various sorts, would be democratic almost second to none.

Self-management is the democratic component of the existing system. But it is also exploited as the ideology of the status quo. Along with genuine self-management *in work collectives* there has been cultivated an ideological picture of Yugoslavia as a "*society* of workers' and social self-management." Such *summary* pronouncements about self-management are ideological. Real self-management is measured by concrete freedoms and rights, as well as by the opportunities that exist for the citizen to use them.

From the ideological pretense of a "self-managing society" the conclusion necessarily follows, by simple deduction, that every major institution and organization in that society is self-managing in character. On this logic any pressure from below to change these institutions and organizations, or even merely to subject them to fundamental criticism, can *by definition* be characterized as an attack on self-management. All this is intended to prevent the authoritarian-statist conception of the *political* system of socialism from being brought seriously into question.

The slogan "Factories to the workers!" heralded, in its own time, the beginnings of de-statization in Yugoslavia. Today what should be demanded is nothing less than radical socialist democratization, which means workers' and social self-management from top to bottom. This is the major watershed between democratic socialism and liberalized statism.

There is no more urgent need than for Marxists to set to work in constructing the political theory of socialism. The founders of bourgeois democracy knew in advance that power corrupts. Consequently, they proceeded realistically from personal and group interests, attempting to bring them face to face and into equilibrium as much as possible, and to divide power. Astonishingly, many Marxists have become helpless moralists, seeking the sole guarantee against the abuse of the new power that has fallen into their hands in the personal qualities of those who exercise that power. While the former have woven variations on the Marxist theme of the withering away of the state, the latter have seized a monopoly of power in the name of Marxism. Before the state withers away, it must be lived in just the same. But the distinction between the good and the bad state has also been forgotten. Nothing of any consequence has been done to design and create defenses and counterbalances to this political monopoly. And it is not true that nothing can be done in this respect so long as only one party continues to rule.

The record to date offers no basis for the official assessment that in Yugoslavia the historical process has begun of the withering away of the state and of the transcendence of politics as alienated social power dominated by a particular professional group. After the victorious revolution the state appropriated the key resources of production and management of all areas of social life. At that time an *enormous* party-state apparatus was created. From 1950 to the present this apparatus has been considerably *decentralized* and its *competences reduced*. It is true that the role of the political-state apparatus in Yugoslavia is smaller than in any other country governed by a communist party. But by the same token it is substantially larger than in many other countries, the capitalist countries in particular.

Much effort and even more words have been invested in the process of de-statization in Yugoslavia. To grasp our situation by the root, however, means to grasp the role of the ruling party. The Yugoslavs live in a political society. In it the Party is the basic factor of rule, continuity, and change. No further democratization is possible in such a society so long as democracy in the Party is still in its infancy. Any critique of statism which sidesteps the Party concerns itself with its secondary aspect—state administration. Any attempt to approach the problem of de-statization independently of the Party testifies to the failure of the investigator to liberate himself from the Party's charismatic grasp.

In order to place themselves at a distance from other systems ruled by communist parties, our official spokesmen assert that Yugoslavia is not a one-party system (although neither, obviously, is it a multi-party system). In fact, Yugoslavia is distinguished from these countries not by virtue of its party structure, but by virtue of more liberal policies and more liberal relations within the Party, the development of self-management at the workplace, a market economy. . . .

A critical analysis of the Party must be preceded by an acknowledgment that the idea of the Party's transformation into a League of Communists accomplished nothing of substance. The numerous proclamations of radical Party reform have ended in more than modest results: reorganizations.

Not only does the Party relate to the workers as a "class in itself" incomparably more than as a "class for itself;" within the Party, too, there is in practice a division between a kind of Party for itself (the leadership) and a Party in itself (the membership). The dominant influence on its policies and on all political life in Yugoslavia is exercised by people who were educated in the spirit of the communism of the late Third International. Not even in the LCY, which according to newspaper accounts is superior to all other ruling communist parties, has intraparty democracy attained the level known in the Bolshevik Party prior to its Tenth Congress in 1921.

Those who belong to the Party are people of very heterogeneous social origins, interests, and thoughts. Other factors, too, operate against monolithism: the degree of economic development, the general level of education, the country's openness to ideological and political influences from the rest of the world, as well as differentiation within the international communist movement. Sooner or later the monolithic conception of the Party will have to be abandoned and reconciled with the diversity of its composition and of the composition of the environment in which it acts, as well as with the developmental needs of Yugoslavia. Hitherto, it has always been efforts to reconcile reality with the monolithic and centralistic principle that have predominated. Thanks to the domination of this principle, all currents and orientations in the Party have publicly adopted the same platform, but only *in the abstract.*

In the LCY there is still no attempt made to verify whether a majority of the members do, in fact, stand behind a given policy decision. In the Party true elections do not exist and virtually without exception there is one candidate for each major position. The leadership renews itself in accordance with its own taste. All really serious conflicts in the political summit are resolved within that narrow circle and never has an extraordinary Party Congress been called to deal with such questions. The public learns of these conflicts only when news of the corresponding expulsions or resignations is officially released.

What would happen if, at a future Party Congress, there were elected several leading organs which were truly independent of each other and responsible only to the Congress—say, executive, auditing, and informational? Let us leave little to the imagination: in addition to these organs, in which professional politicians must necessarily participate, the Congress might also elect a body composed of "ordinary" members who would take part in the total range of work of these organs (apart from voting) and who would set forth an independent evaluation of the state of affairs within the Party prior to the next Congress.

In the Party the right of the minority openly to advocate changes in adopted policies is not recognized. It is maintained that this would lead to Party paralysis. But this claim is unjustified, for a democratically adopted policy would be in force by mandate so long as the minority has not become a majority.

The members of Party organizations are internally divided and this makes it possible for the leading circles to exercise a monopoly of power. They are an ineluctable mediating force, since "ordinary" communists do not have the right to communicate *directly* in efforts to influence Party policies. Since the leading circles can expel members and even dissolve entire Party organizations, this means that the leadership determines their behavior in an essential way, rather than the other way around. The theoretical possibility exists that in this manner the leading circles can vitally alter the Party's composition. In the history of communism this has certainly happened on occasion.

While "ordinary" Party members are politically atomized, this is also true of workers and of citizens in general. The professional political apparatus still has the final word in the Party and in society at large. Proclamations about the deprofessionalization of politics are insufficient when the monopoly of professional politicians and qualitative differences among them are there to be seen.

If in its internal life a communist party is still largely a party typical of the Third International, then its relations with other organizations and institutions can certainly be no different. This evaluation is not affected by the fact that the Party's leading circles are no longer identical with those of the state administration or of mass political organizations in a personal sense. There is a real division of labor and jurisdiction between the Party and other organizations. But it is no less accurate to say that the other components of the system are still the Party's transmission belts. The Party is guaranteed influence in them in advance by virtue of the assignment of its discipline cadres to *all important* posts. In these posts it is almost unheard of to find someone who is not a Party member.

The Party is not obliged to struggle for influence through argument alone. This situation is in conflict with the idea that the Party ought to act as an internal, rather than an external, vanguard. To be sure, there have been sincere attempts to exert the Party's influence primarily through force of argument, but the Party, afraid of the consequences of operating in this manner, has returned to the old method of direction whenever serious disagreements have surfaced.

We have argued that Yugoslavia is just beginning to face the prospect of a coming of age in a transition from *authoritarian* to democratic communism. On the other side of the coin, *pauperistic* communism has been abandoned in record time.

Of asceticism not so much as a trace has remained; everyone is involved in trying to achieve a high material standard of living. During and immediately after the war, collectivism held in check the aspiration for the satisfaction of individual and group interests, but "interest" was thereafter rapidly conceived as a stimulus to social progress and as an individual and group right. Serious differences in wages and incomes have long been permitted without reservation in order to stimulate productivity, creativity, and educational achievement.

But in place of the former asceticism, substantial inroads have been made by a vulgar consumerist hedonism. And at times it seems as if individual and group egoism is the sole realistic alternative to the collectivism which has since been transcended. Egalitarianism in material distribution has been rejected, but nowadays any and all principles of social equality are in constant jeopardy. Alongside of the critique of the "egalitarian syndrome," a truly antiegalitarian syndrome has developed and flourished.

Uravnilovka [leveling], of course, is unjustified both on its own merits and because it inhibits economic and social progress. But does this really also justify excessive differences between individual categories and strata of the population? What would remain of socialism were we to attempt increasingly to divide ourselves into a consumer society on the one hand, and a society of want on the other?

To say that equality is the foundation of communism assumes, according to

Marx, that it is politically justified. Social equality belongs to the network of ideals of Marxist socialism; inequality does not. We are not speaking here of primitive egalitarianism, but of distribution according to work combined with guarantee of a minimum standard of living and greater equalization of opportunity for education, health care, and the cultural uplifting of each individual, regardless of his or her labor contribution.

How else are we to carry out further modernization, instead of hindering it, if we do not increase the prospects of social equality and justice as well as the participation of the broad masses in public life? How much social differentiation constitutes a truly *unavoidable* price for the deliverance from want? We will not, one hopes, be told that there is some iron law of social differentiation analogous to Michels' "iron law of oligarchy." Discussions of the stratification of Yugoslav society concern themselves as a rule with the economic side of the problem, forgetting that the existing distribution of political power is also a potent source of social differentiation.

De-statization in the economy would certainly not have been possible without the reaffirmation of the market. Even Lenin sensed that socialism would not be in any position simply to eliminate the commodity character of production. This is why he sought salvation from the economic dead-end of War Communism in the NEP [New Economic Policy]. To be sure, Lenin had wanted the market confined to the sphere of small property-holders and viewed NEP as a temporary retreat from socialism. But even this was too great a sacrilege for the dogmatists among the Bolsheviks, who quickly replaced NEP with an economy that was totally centralized, distributive, and statist.

The CPY laid this dogma, too, to rest in the museum of antiquities, showing that economics in socialism must possess market characteristics. But those who construed de-statization in a bourgeois manner were not satisfied with this and began to make a fetish of *market spontaneity* as an end in itself. In Yugoslavia in the second half of the 1960s, this went so far as to generate a resurgence of the *laissez-faire* conception of the market.

The market began to be seen as a collection of mutually opposed self-managing enterprises and banks that were totally protected from broader social influence and that had legitimate interests in increasing their income on the market *at any price*. The next move was the demand to introduce market measures into all other areas, including the school system, culture, housing policy, and health care. And all of this was purportedly for the sake of the further socialization of property and the development of self-management. In reality this path was leading to *group* property and *group-particularistic* self-management. The technocratic strata firmly embraced economic liberalism because they sensed that the prospects for oligarchic groups would be very bright in self-management so conceived.

The most extreme advocates of the market sought freedom for "self-managing capital" and proposed the introduction of "self-managing stockholding." By transforming the producers into stockholders of some sort, they were to be given a greater stake in the fate of their enterprises. But what kind of a society would it be that, after a short-lived idyll of egalitarian and "self-managing" stockholding, become divided into those with shares and those without?

A true picture of the potential scope of unbridled economic liberalism was available only beyond Yugoslavia's borders. Several Yugoslav firms were registered abroad in the names of their managers, who proceeded to behave quite like proprietors; the purchasing, export, and exploitation of labor power was expanded; and there was increased pressure to eliminate all substantive controls on export and import as well as on foreign investment.

Capitalism, in historical perspective, has developed from classical, anti–statist liberalism to neoliberalism, which not only permits but demands state intervention in the economy, the bridling of market spontaneity, and attempts to resolve the mass of accumulated social problems through the "welfare state."

In Yugoslavia in the 1960s there were increasingly strong tendencies toward movement in the opposite direction: from statism to an economic liberalism with strong affinities with liberalism of the *laissez-faire* variety.

As the antithesis of the feudal state, classical liberalism played a revolutionary role throughout the world. In time, however, it became such a fetter to progress that its advocates have long since been targeted as conservatives. Contrary to classical liberalism, neoliberalism exhibits a certain similarity to statism, as well as to socialism.

In Yugoslavia economic liberalization, as the opposite of statist economics, also had a positive function. But economic liberalism quickly revealed its own dark side: the establishment of a peculiar variety of *capitalist* relationships between work collectives.

Economic liberalism necessarily created market anarchy, a new form of contradiction between the social character of production and group-private ownership, as well as unacceptable social differences. The statists, naturally, sought relief from such crises in state intervention. In turn, once the economy was smothered with accelerated state-imposed measures, the economic liberals appeared anew on the scene.

The social pendulum will swing like this between the state and market spontaneity so long as there is not constructed an all-embracing system of workers' and social self-management that would unite market competition with democratic social planning and direction. Insofar as such an economy and such a society are without historical precedent, it is understandable that it is not easy to find the right solution on the basis of our existing knowledge.

Nevertheless, liberalized statism and bourgeois socialism are not equally well rooted in the Yugoslav soil. Whenever the opportunity of directly measuring both has presented itself, the latter has proved to be the weaker. On these occasions the statists have easily taken advantage of the dissatisfaction of the broad masses with the consequences of market spontaneity and have vitally restricted the political freedom won during the process of de-statization heretofore.

It can be said without exaggeration that for Yugoslavia the past three and a half decades have represented not only an historical period, but an historical epoch. Without the Communist Party of Yugoslavia the rebirth of Yugoslavia from the ruins left by foreign occupation as well as civil and religious war would not have been possible. The revolution strongly accelerated the course of historical development in this corner of the world.

In the Yugoslav federation there is considerable autonomy and equality of the component units, nations, and national minorities. From a backward agrarian country, Yugoslavia has been transformed in these thirty-five years into an industrial-agrarian country nearly at the middle stage of development. Because the CPY rejected the dogma of the forced collectivization of the countryside, Yugoslavia's agriculture has been considerably modernized. In the production of consumer goods, in terms of assortment as well as quantity, Yugoslavia hardly lags at all behind the nearly developed Western countries. Schooling, health care, and social services are accessible to the broad masses. Employee self-management is developing in work collectives. Individual areas of art, science, and philosophy have blossomed. Finally, Yugoslavia is the only open state in the world that is ruled by a communist party. And this is one of the reasons for the growth of the ambitious expectations of the population at large.

We Yugoslavs, therefore, live in a society which, according to material indicators, has very nearly approached the middle tier of developed countries. But there is also considerable political poverty in Yugoslav society. Under pressure from the progressive element of the leadership and membership, the Party's conservative wing periodically agrees to make democratic promises and declarations. But ideology always establishes attractive goals whose real and concrete meaning is revealed only in practice. "It turns out that words are not the eye of a needle, but doors that are wide open to all. One passes through them easily, as from darkness to the morning light." Whether a regime is for real democratization or not is to be measured by whether it is prepared to accept the unavoidable consequences of democratization: criticism of its own work, the possibility of being replaced, the appearance of "undesirable" people in the public political arena. . . :

There will be no escape from the cycle of alternating political "relaxation" and "tightening" so long as the Party fails to transform itself from the guardian of the existing order into the initiator of the *socialist movement*. For Marx, communism was preeminently a movement. And many communists still treat "the party" as synonymous with "the movement." Yet in all socialist revolutions to the present day the militant movement was broader than the communist party alone. Only after the seizure of power has the party eliminated the movement's other participants from the political stage. How is the revolutionary and post-revolutionary dictatorship to be democratized unless communists return to the idea of a "movement"? In the socialist movement the Party would have no advance guarantees; it would have to struggle for influence through example, persuasion, and argument.

Fundamental political reform will be as elusive as a mirage so long as democratic-socialist pressure is not articulated from below. It is clear that only a political movement can draw people out of their state of practical inertia. There are plenty of people in the Party who secretly hope for the development of some sort of socialist movement, but when its first traces begin to appear many are seized with fear of innovation and risk.

This is why the student movement of 1968 was so thoroughly crushed. This was the first time that the party-state hierarchy had experienced a mass challenge from the democratic left and it was decided to smash it while it was still in the "group fusion" stage. It was asserted by some at the time that the closing off of the leftist outlet from political crises usually leads to shifts to the right. And how else to explain the extent of the breakthrough of the nationalist right two years later?

The real question is not, "Why should the working class *as a class* be enabled to enter onto the political stage?" but rather, "In whose real interest is it?" In Yugoslavia the Party, by forcing the pace of industrialization, has merely created the conditions for the rapid development of the working class. But what was created in this process was a working class—fragmented—that corresponded to the Party's political monopoly. How can the working populace truly become a class for itself unless it does not organize and engage itself, particularly in politics? The point is precisely that it is not enough to have a workers' ideology; what is needed is a workers' politics. But the best guarantee of a workers' politics is mass participation by the workers in political decision-making at all levels.

The inadequate developmental level and lack of education of the working people can no longer be used to justify the state of affairs in Yugoslavia. We have long had mighty industrial centers, yet the working people's participation in their political life has been minimal. And as far as education is concerned, Yugoslav workers on the average have now attained a higher educational level than the bourgeoisie when it became the ruling class, not only within Yugoslavia's boundaries but in the West as well.

It is to be hoped that the democratic current within the Party will finally become strong enough vis-à-vis the guardians of past and present that it will come to rely on pressure from below and commit itself to the creation of a socialist movement. This will not happen easily or quickly. And how could it, when the goal is a radical transformation? The preservation of a minimum of stability is only one of the things about which a small country situated between the two global blocs need be concerned. All the intelligent and progressive forces of the people must gather together to conceptualize and put into effect a realistic program of socialist democratization. Yugoslavia, of all the countries ruled by communist parties, has the greatest prospects in this regard.

The Soviet-Yugoslav Break

✦

The expulsion of Yugoslavia from the Cominform, precipitated by Stalin in June 1948, was preceded by an increasingly acrimonious exchange of letters in which Tito was asked in effect to accept Soviet tutelage on the same footing as the states of Eastern Europe that had not, as Yugoslavia had, achieved their own independence from Nazi occupation rule. The exchange culminated, after Yugoslavia rejected the Soviet position, in a resolution of the Cominform inviting Yugoslav communists to overthrow Tito. That resolution and the official Yugoslav response are encapsulated in the excerpts that follow.

✦

A) THE COMINFORM RESOLUTION

. . . The leaders of the Communist Party of Yugoslavia have taken a stand unworthy of Communists, and have begun to identify the foreign policy of the Soviet Union with the foreign policy of the imperialist powers, behaving toward the Soviet Union in the same manner as they behave to the bourgeois states. Precisely because of this anti-Soviet stand, slanderous propaganda about the "degeneration" of the CPSU [Communist Party of the Soviet Union], about the "degeneration" of the USSR, and so on, borrowed from the arsenal of counter-revolutionary Trotskyism, is current within the Central Committee of the Communist Party of Yugoslavia.

The Information Bureau denounces this anti-Soviet attitude of the leaders of the Communist Party of Yugoslavia, as being incompatible with Marxism-Leninism and only appropriate to nationalists.

In home policy, the leaders of the Communist Party of Yugoslavia are departing from the positions of the working class and are breaking with the Marxist theory of classes and class struggle. They deny that there is a growth of capitalist elements in their country, and consequently, a sharpening of the class struggle in the countryside. This denial is the direct result of the opportunist tenet that the class struggle does not become sharper during the period of transition from capitalism to socialism, as

"The Soviet-Yugoslav Break," from Robert V. Daniels, ed., *A Documentary History of Communism*, vol. 2, Vintage Press, 1962, pp. 169–174.

Marxism-Leninism teaches, but dies down, as was affirmed by opportunists of the Bukharin type, who propagated the theory of the peaceful growing over of capitalism into socialism.

The Yugoslav leaders are pursuing an incorrect policy in the countryside by ignoring the class differentiation in the countryside and by regarding the individual peasantry as a single entity, contrary to the Marxist-Leninist doctrine of classes and class struggle, contrary to the well-known Lenin thesis that small individual farming gives birth to capitalism and the bourgeoisie continually, daily, hourly, spontaneously and on a mass scale. Moreover, the political situation in the Yugoslav countryside gives no grounds for smugness and complacency. In the conditions obtaining in Yugoslavia, where individual peasant farming predominates, where the land is not nationalized, where there is private property in land, and where land can be bought and sold, where much of the land is concentrated in the hands of kulaks, and where hired labour is employed—in such conditions there can be no question of educating the Party in the spirit of glossing over the class struggle and of reconciling class contradictions without by so doing disarming the Party itself in face of the difficulties connected with the construction of socialism. . . .

. . . The Information Bureau unanimously concludes that by their anti-Party and anti-Soviet views, incompatible with Marxism-Leninism, by their whole attitude and their refusal to attend the meeting of the Information Bureau, the leaders of the Communist Party of Yugoslavia have placed themselves in opposition to the Communist Parties affiliated to the Information Bureau, have taken the path of seceding from the united Socialist front against imperialism, have taken the path of betraying the cause of international solidarity of the working people, and have taken up a position of nationalism.

The Information Bureau condemns this anti-Party policy and attitude of the Central Committee of the Communist Party of Yugoslavia.

The Information Bureau considers that, in view of all this, the Central Committee of the Communist Party of Yugoslavia has placed itself and the Yugoslav Party outside the family of the fraternal Communist Parties, outside the united Communist front and consequently outside the ranks of the Information Bureau.

The Information Bureau considers that the basis of these mistakes made by the leadership of the Communist Party of Yugoslavia lies in the undoubted fact that nationalist elements, which previously existed in a disguised form, managed in the course of the past five or six months to reach a dominant position in the leadership of the Communist Party of Yugoslavia, and that consequently the leadership of the Yugoslav Communist Party has broken with the international traditions of the Communist Party of Yugoslavia and has taken the road of nationalism.

Considerably overestimating the internal, national forces of Yugoslavia and their influence, the Yugoslav leaders think that they can maintain Yugoslavia's independence and build socialism without the support of the Communist Parties of other countries, without the support of the people's democracies, without the support of the Soviet Union. They think that the new Yugoslavia can do without the help of these revolutionary forces.

Showing their poor understanding of the international situation and their intimidation by the blackmailing threats of the imperialists, the Yugoslav leaders think that by making concessions they can curry favor with the Imperialist states. They think they will be able to bargain with them for Yugoslavia's independence and, gradually, get the people of Yugoslavia orientated on these states, that is, on capitalism. In this they proceed tacitly from the well-known bourgeois–nationalist thesis that "capitalist states are a lesser danger to the independence of Yugoslavia than the Soviet Union."

The Yugoslav leaders evidently do not understand or, probably, pretend they do not understand, that such a nationalist line can only lead to Yugoslavia's degeneration into an ordinary bourgeois republic, to the loss of its independence and to its transformation into a colony of the imperialist countries.

The Information Bureau does not doubt that inside the Communist Party of Yugoslavia [CPY] there are sufficient healthy elements, loyal to Marxism-Leninism, to the international traditions of the Yugoslav Communist Party and to the united socialist front.

Their task is to compel their present leaders to recognize their mistakes openly and honestly and to rectify them; to break with nationalism, return to internationalism; and in every way to consolidate the united socialist front against imperialism.

Should the present leaders of the Yugoslav Communist Party prove incapable of doing this, their job is to replace them and to advance a new internationalist leadership of the Party.

The Information Bureau does not doubt that the Communist Party of Yugoslavia will be able to fulfill this honourable task.

✦

B) THE YUGOSLAV REPLY

In connection with the publication of the Resolution of the Information Bureau, the Central Committee [CC] of the Communist Party of Yugoslavia makes the following statement:

1. The criticism contained in the Resolution is based on inaccurate and unfounded assertions and represents an attempt to destroy the prestige of the CPY both abroad and in the country, to arouse confusion amongst the masses in the country and in the international workers' movement, to weaken the unity within the CPY and its leading role. . . .

2. The Resolution maintains, without citing any proof, that the leadership of the CPY carried out a hostile policy towards the USSR. The statement that Soviet military specialists in Yugoslavia have been treated with scant respect, and that Soviet civilian citizens have been under the surveillance of state security agents does not in the least correspond to the truth. . . .

On the contrary, it is correct, as stated in the letter to the CC of the CPSU of 13 April, and based on numerous reports of members of the CPY to their Party organizations as well as on statements of other citizens of our country, that from the liberation up to date the Soviet intelligence service sought to enroll them. The CC of the

CPY considered and considers that such an attitude towards a country where the communists are the ruling party and which is advancing toward socialism is impermissible. . . .

4. The CC of the CPY cannot but reject with deep indignation the assertions that the leading ranks in the CPY are deviating to the course of a kulak party, to the path of the liquidation of the Communist Party of Yugoslavia, that there is no democracy in the Party, that methods of military leadership are fostered within the Party, that the most basic rights of Party members are trampled upon by the Party and that the mildest criticism of irregularities in the Party is answered by sharp reprisals, etc. Could the members of the Party who dauntlessly faced death in thousands of battles, tolerate in the Party a state of affairs unworthy of both men and communists? The assertion that criticism is not allowed in the Party and similar statements are a terrible insult to every member of our Party, a degradation of the heroic and glorious past of the Party and its present heroic struggle for the reconstruction and development of the country. . . .

8. . . . The Information Bureau has committed a breach of the principles on which it was based and which provide for the voluntary adoption of conclusions by every Party. The Information Bureau, however, not only forces the leaders of the CPY to admit errors which they did not commit but also calls members of the CPY to rebellion within the Party, to shatter the unity of the Party. The CC of the CPY can never agree to a discussion about its policy on the basis of inventions and uncomradely behavior without mutual confidence. Such a basis is not one of principle and in this and only in this sense the CC of the CPY considered that it was not on an equal footing in the discussion and that it could not accept discussion on that basis. Further, in connection with the above, the CC of the CPY resolutely rejects the accusation that the CPY has passed on to positions of nationalism. By its entire internal and foreign policy, and especially by its struggle during the national liberation war and the proper solution of the national question in Yugoslavia, the CPY has given proof of the exact opposite.

By the above-mentioned unjust charges, the greatest historical injustice has been done to our Party, our working class and working masses, the peoples in Yugoslavia in general and their unselfish and heroic struggle. . . .

The CC of the CPY calls upon the Party membership to close their ranks in the struggle for the realization of the Party line and for even greater strengthening of Party unity, while it calls upon the working class and other working masses, gathered in the People's Front, to continue to work even more persistently on the building of our socialist homeland. This is the only way, the only method to prove in full and by deeds the unjustness of the above-mentioned charges.

The Titoist Critique of Stalinism

◆

Milovan Djilas

In 1950, Djilas was vice premier in Tito's government and often-
times the regime's spokesman on matters of communist theory.
This statement of the Yugoslav position two years after the
break comes from a speech that Djilas delivered to a rally of
Belgrade students and reflects the recasting of the official
Yugoslav viewpoint necessitated by the break.

. . . Taking as a point of departure the economic laws of development toward
communism, Marx and Lenin foresaw two dangers threatening the triumphant working class in socialism: from the overthrown bourgeoisie on the one hand and its own
bureaucracy on the other. It was not accidental that Marx asked that civil service
employees be elected and that only for a certain period of time after which they were
to go into production. Engels and Lenin emphasized often that with the change in
economic relations, that is, with the liquidation of private capitalist ownership over
the means of production, changes in political relationships do not come about immediately, easily and automatically. The development of dictatorship of the proletariat,
socialist democracy, can therefore go in two directions: in the direction of its own
disappearance to the extent that socialism itself strengthens, or in the direction of
strengthening and transformation of bureaucracy into a privileged caste which lives at
the expense of society as a whole. . . .

The development of production forces in the Soviet Union has reached a point
where social relations no longer correspond to it. Neither does the method of management of the process of production itself or the method of distribution of the goods
produced. The classic antagonism between productive forces and relationships in production has arisen. But this antagonism in the Soviet Union is not the same as that in
earlier class social formations, for the relationships of property are different than they
were then. Although we have there the existence of capitalist, and even pre-capitalist
remnants, they do not play an essential role in social development, for property relationships have been destroyed and it is on these that remnants could base their further
development. This is therefore a new historical phenomenon in which new, socialist

Milovan Djilas, "The Titoist Critique of Stalinism," from Robert V. Daniels, ed., *A Documentary History of
Communism,* vol. 2, Vintage Press, 1962, pp. 189–193.

relationships of ownership and new development of production forces no longer suit the method of management of that property itself and the production forces themselves.

Let us see the forms in which this process appears: introduction of unequal relations and exploitation of other socialist countries; un-Marxist treatment of the role of the leader which often takes the shape of even vulgar, historical falsifications and idolatries similar to those in absolute monarchies; differences in pay which are greater than in bourgeois bureaucracies themselves, ranging from 400 to 15,000 rubles; ideological promotion of Great-Russian nationalism and underestimation and subordination of the role, culture and history of other peoples; a policy of division of spheres of influence with the capitalist states; monopolization of the interpretation of Marxist ideology and the tactics of the international working class movement; introduction of lying and slandering methods into the working-class movement; neglect of study of Marx, Engels and Lenin, and especially their premises about the laws of the transition period and communist society; underestimation of the role of consciousness—especially the consciousness of the masses—in the struggle for a new society; tendencies toward actual liquidation of socialist democracy and transforming it into a mere form; rendering impossible a struggle of opinions and putting brakes on the initiative of the masses, that is, the basic productive forces, and by that very fact productive forces in general; revision of the philosophical foundations of Marxism, etc., etc. Seeing all this, drawing conclusions from the conflict between the Central Committee of the Communist Party of the Soviet Union and the Soviet Government and the Central Committee of the Yugoslav Communist Party and the Yugoslav Government and seeking theoretical explanations both of the phenomenon and practice, many comrades pose the question: whence such phenomena, in every way characteristic of class formations; what do they mean and why must they exist in socialism? Further, where, actually, are the roots of these phenomena? Is what is taking place in the Soviet Union some new kind of class society, is it state capitalism, or "deviations" within socialism itself?

. . . The basis which is the point of departure (socialist revolution and dictatorship of the proletariat, nationalization of capitalist property and struggle for socialist construction) is the same here and in the USSR. Both here and there, these bases are progressive as beginnings. But the tendencies of development, which came about as the result of different general historic conditions and dissimilar conditions in both countries, are unlike. There we see the creation of a privileged bureaucratic stratum, bureaucratic centralism, temporary transformation of the state into "a force above society." (Some of the reasons for this are the fact that the USSR was for a long time the only socialist country, that it was backward, surrounded by capitalism, that the masses had a relatively weak conscious role in the struggle for socialist building and that there were relatively weak foreign and internal revolutionary forces.) Here, in our country, there is also a tendency toward domination by bureaucracy for, as we see in Marx, it is a law that this becomes a danger, a necessarily conditioned phenomenon, a necessary remnant of the old class society in the struggle for the creation of a new classless society. But here, these tendencies will not and cannot win, because historical conditions are different, because the relationship of forces, which changes in struggle every day, is different, because the tendencies of development are different—toward accelerating the decrease of the role of bureaucracy, toward giving greater initiative to the masses and actual power (to put it that way) to the direct producers in the process of production. . . .

. . . Bureaucratic elements in the USSR who have frozen their privileged position, are attempting to find the solution to the internal crisis in the outside world, that is, to hush it temporarily by foreign successes, by exploitation and subordination of other socialist countries. And since methods of exploitation and subordination of peoples in the contemporary world, which is divided and in which the world market is still dominated by capitalism, can only be capitalistic, they inevitably appear as a struggle for spheres of influence and as a brake to the further development of socialism, as a struggle for the victory of socialism, only there, to that extent and in that form that suits the narrow, hegemonistic interests of that privileged stratum. That is why what is directly advantageous to that stratum becomes, for it, theoretically true and justified. Thence the ever broader and more ruthless orientation toward Great-Russian nationalism, the backwardness of the masses and their obscure instincts, inherited from the past, which were always stimulated and appealed to by the bourgeoisie. But this has a new, different character here—the character of bureaucratic, imperialist expansion and domination by the bureaucracy of one nation over other nations. Reliance on historic nationalistic backwardness, in the given conditions, is possible only for the biggest nation where these remnants are the strongest precisely because it has long been the ruling nation. Thence subjective idealism—despite its materialistic and dialectic phraseology—in the philosophy and science of the USSR, which is unfolding on the basis of untrue and undialectic proclamations to the effect that there are no more internal contradictions there. It is on this erroneous basis that their scientific methodology and practice is founded and it must substitute apologetics for scientific work, and routine for revolutionary practice. . . .

Tried by the Party

✦

Milovan Djilas

In the early 1950s, Djilas became increasingly critical of the
Yugoslav party and government in which he had played such a
prominent role. He published a series of articles setting forth his
criticisms and in January 1954 he was subjected to a trial before the Central Committee of the League of Communists. The
excerpts that follow include the accusations by Tito and Kardelj,
Dedijer's defense of Djilas, and Djilas's own statements, first
seeking reconciliation but then resolutely accepting the "impossibility" of bowing to party dictate. As a result, he was stripped
of governmental and party posts and ultimately imprisoned.

[. . .] And just as victory by slander arouses the triumphant ardor of
the victor, it leaves the slandered person in a hopeless position. He finds himself arguing pointlessly, trying to prove his point with primarily moral
evidence—moral evidence that is monotonous and colorless, as all evidence
is, and that becomes pale under the flood of slanders. [. . .] For slanders are
infinite in number but there is only one truth. It is possible to slander indefinitely because one can always invent more lies, but the truth cannot be
invented.

The "beauty" of slander lies in the imagination of the person who con-
ceives it and in the obvious discomfort of the person defending himself. And
its "advantage" lies in its unlimited possibilities. Slander progresses gradually,
with calculation, and employs the vast power of tragedy. But the truth is
sudden and involuntary, it is unpracticed and it is judged upon itself alone.

Slander comes forth in the name of the most beautiful ideals, with
seeming passion and ardor, while in fact it is cold and deliberate. Truth is
otherwise. The beauty and the advantage of slander lie in its forms and its
possibilities. Truth is naked and powerless.

It will be said, Truth always wins in the end. Yes, but only in the
end. . . .

Diary of Thoughts, 1953–1954 (unpublished)

Milovan Djilas, "Tried by the Party," from *Parts of a Lifetime,* Harcourt Brace Jovanovich, 1975, pp.
223–237.

◆

THE ACCUSATION
"Djilas Has Gone Too Far" (Tito)

The articles of Comrade Milovan Djilas were his own doing, were his own ideas. It has been asked why we didn't do something about this matter earlier. Since he was a member of the Executive Committee of the Central Committee of the League of Communists of Yugoslavia, couldn't we have resolved the problem with less commotion and less damage?

When the question is put this way, I must admit that to a certain extent we are guilty. Comrade Djilas had written articles before and last fall when he asked me, "Old Man, what do you think about what I'm writing?" I replied, "You know that you say certain things I can't agree with, but I don't think this is a reason for you not to write. On the contrary. Mostly you have valuable things to say; keep on writing." I said that because in his articles Djilas had presented matters about which we had already written.

Only in December, when I read all his later articles, did I realize that Djilas had gone too far. When I saw that Comrade Djilas directly attacked the League of Communists (I will not mention other positions he took which are invalid from a theoretical viewpoint—Comrade Kardelj will speak about them later), I realized that he was proposing the liquidation of the League of Communists and the abolition of discipline—proposals which could inflict enormous damage not only upon the unity of our party but also upon the unity of the country. [. . .]

Comrade Djilas was aware of my opinion before he published his last article in *Nova Misao*. He hurried to get it published. [. . .]

Are the articles in *Borba,* written at the rate of three articles per week, some new original theory? Are these new ideas about our development, new ideas about our reality? They are not, comrades! And when today some of our comrades ask us, "Why did you attack him, why do you hold a Special Plenum, when he only writes about things that you yourselves have talked about?" I answer, "Correct. They contain some ideas and formulations of my own, of Kardelj's, and also of some other comrades, ideas and formulations which we have discussed publicly. I was the first one to talk about the withering away of the party and of the Socialist Alliance. But I did not say that this will take place within six months or a year or two, but that it is a long-range process." [. . .]

Why did Comrade Djilas part ways with the comrades with whom he had worked closely for seventeen years? Within our circle Comrade Djilas has always had an opportunity to say whatever he wanted—even more than he has written. We all knew him and discussed matters with him. We also joked, and a man can say many things when joking. But the questions raised in his articles were not discussed within our circle in the form in which they appeared in the press, nor did he consider it necessary even to mention them at meetings of the Executive Committee or of the Secretariat or to tell us what he was planning to write about. [. . .]

Up to now we have worked collectively and in the future we must do the same.

Exchanges of opinion, heated discussions take place—and then what is deemed by the majority to be the most correct is accepted. That principle should continue to be followed within our circle. [. . .]

It is very curious—and revealing—that in his articles Comrade Djilas failed to mention the working class even once, as if it does not exist. [. . .]

If I see revisionism in Djilas's articles, it is not too hard to see why, comrades. [. . .] He is advocating democracy at any price, which is exactly the position of Bernstein, and of a whole set of revisionist circles in the West. Comrade Djilas does not see that. He fails to see that this is revisionism of the worst kind, reformist opportunism, and not the revolutionary dynamism that he tries to make it out to be. [. . .]

"Djilas's Theses—Shallow and Unscientific" (Kardelj)

Comrade Tito has already explained the position taken by the Executive Committee in regard to the articles of Comrade Djilas, that is, concerning their ideological and political character. The theoretical arguments in Djilas's articles are extraneous and unimportant. They are unimportant principally because Djilas starts with a political thesis and only later does he tack onto it hastily a schematic theoretical explanation—essentially superficial, unscientific and garbled—in order to make his theses appear more significant. Because they are unimportant, the Central Committee would not have interfered in the purely theoretical contemplations of Comrade Djilas unless his articles also had political significance.

However, since some are of the opinion that, although Comrade Djilas's theory is quite harmful in our concrete political situation because it is premature, it is nonetheless a "new" contribution to socialist theory, a "new" socialist idea, it is necessary to look at the theoretical side of these articles. It is clear that we have no time for a detailed analysis of these articles at this plenum. Therefore, on the basis of Djilas's articles, following the order in which he wrote them, I shall attempt to answer the following three questions:

1. Is the theory presented in the articles of Comrade Djilas really "new"?

2. Does his theory represent a contribution to socialist thought or does it drag socialist thought backward?

3. What is the significance of his theory in our situation, for our struggle for socialism and socialist democracy? [. . .]

I shall cite the content of one of my longer conversations with Comrade Djilas, that on December 22 of last year. A few days before that date I had mentioned to him my disagreement—as well as the disagreement of many other Communists—with the thesis set forth in his articles. On December 22 we met so that I could tell him the essence of my disagreement. In a friendly, comradely form, I presented my critical observations.

Comrade Djilas was very upset by my comments and, showing that he was hurt, he set forth the following theses:

1. that Comrade Tito defends bureaucratism and that sooner or later he will clash with him;

2. that Comrade Ranković and I are in agreement with him, Djilas, but that we are opportunists, and thus are evading a quarrel with Comrade Tito;

3. that within our movement—whether we like it or not—there exists some socialist "left";

4. that we must not exclude the possibility of developing two socialist parties simultaneously in our country.

Understandably those statements shocked me and I refuted all four of his theses. During our conversation—at least this is my impression—Comrade Djilas retracted all four theses, explaining that they were only ideas off the top of his head and that he himself knew that they were absurd. But I have no clear perception of how our conversation ended on the subject of his articles in *Borba*. I did not mention Djilas's new theses to Comrade Tito. I believed they were just one of those foolish and fanciful journeys which were one of Djilas's familiar traits. I expected that in his future articles he would show more respect for the opinions of his comrades from the Central Committee. [. . .]

However, today, since Djilas's theory reached full expression through his articles, it is possible to say that the theses expressed during our conversation have a close connection with the theses in his articles. If there were not such a connection, I would not discuss them. And conversely: the theses that he presented in our conversation affirm what I just said—that Djilas's conception of democracy is not ours, it is not socialist but a mixture of anarchism and bourgeois-liberalistic forms. [. . .]

In opposition to the struggle for socialist democracy there exists still another process. Hiding behind the word democracy are petty bourgeois and anarchistic tendencies, all kinds of little socialist yearnings and various negative influences from abroad. Their goal is not democracy, although they hide behind its name. The pressure is very strong and it is no less dangerous for socialist democracy than are bureaucratic tendencies. Comrade Djilas, instead of opposing them, collapsed under their pressure. Here, in my opinion, is the source of the political conceptions of Comrade Djilas. [. . .]

Comrade Djilas reopens the dispute that Bernstein started fifty years ago and that was continued by many other writers and politicians, whether right social-democrats or left bourgeoisie. Bernstein formulated his conceptions in the well-known sentence: "What is commonly called the ultimate goal of socialism is nothing for me; the movement is everything." [. . .] From this position Bernstein concluded that the primary goal of the workers' movement is the struggle for democracy, the struggle to transform Germany into a democratic nation. [. . .] Although I am convinced that Comrade Djilas has never read Bernstein, did we not find the same ideas in the articles of Comrade Djilas?

Milovan Djilas: I did not read Bernstein, but I agree with him that the goal is nothing and the movement everything.

Edvard Kardelj: Plekhanov, Rosa Luxemburg, Bebel, Parvus and other social democrats, even Kautsky attacked Bernstein (later Kautsky joined him). Lenin also stood against the revisionist thesis. As is known, Bernstein was expelled from the Social-Democratic party at the Hannover Congress in 1899 because of such views. I don't want to make some historical analogies. [. . .] But it is fair to compare several of Bernstein's sentences with those of Djilas, and to note the amazing similarity between the two. Djilas's theory is an old theory which has been restated in every conceivable manner in the last fifty years. [. . .]

If we want to draw any conclusion from all this, we shall have to state that the theory of Comrade Djilas not only failed to contribute to the development of scientific socialist thought, but that it represents a step backward, and that in its political essence it can only harm the ideological unity of the League of Communists in the struggle for socialism and socialist democracy.

What was the impact of Djilas's articles in our country? The impact did not derive from the theoretical content but from the general tendency toward uncontrollable anarchistic disorder. Such disorder is always acceptable to one stratum of people who want us to leap over the present phase—the effort to create the material conditions for socialism and socialist democracy—and to find ourselves overnight in the "land of plenty."

We have always had such tendencies. I must say that up to now we underestimated them and for this reason the present case has occurred. We must struggle against those tendencies by the further building of democratic organs of social self-management and other democratic forms and by the better work of the League of Communists and of the Socialist Alliance of Working People. *We must be aware that we have to battle on two fronts—against bureaucratic tendencies and against the tendencies of uncontrollable anarchistic forces.* Both can threaten the further development of socialism and socialist democracy. [. . .]

I do not believe that every Yugoslav citizen must be a Marxist or that every citizen must believe in the Marxist dialectic. But the League of Communists and its Central Committee definitely hold the Marxist position and consider Marxism to be a necessary scientific weapon of the working class and of socialism. Comrade Djilas can renounce the dialectic, but he has no right as a member of the Central Committee to force his opinions upon members of the League of Communists, and even less right to do so under the imprimatur of Marxism.

In "Reply" he writes:

> And precisely because it is "socialist," our bureaucracy cannot avoid being a little Stalinist, and to some extent, a Yugoslav Stalinism. It therefore stinks of the same ideology and it proclaims the same "civilized" and "peace-loving" methods loudly and clearly. These methods, however, are still not directed at those who are "on top" but at those who are "below."

The tone of his answer to his comrades is characteristic of Djilas's democratism. People who want to fight for democracy should first learn to speak democratically. This tone is typical of the language of the *pogrom* used against all who disagree. And the conclusion of Djilas's "Reply" expresses intolerance toward any other opinion and a shocking immodesty which has lost all sense of time and place. We read there,

I am not writing in order to make a name for myself, nor out of juvenile pigheadedness, and still less out of a desire to bask in democratic glory. I must write because, like many others, I am the "victim" of objective social processes which compel me to do so. And therein lie my sources of passion and belief. Because of that, and precisely because I respect and want open, comradely socialist criticism of these ideas, I can have only contempt for any other kind of criticism.

This tone needs no comment. Comrade Djilas was unaccustomed to criticism. He was criticized for the first time—and from below. It is precisely that which he could not stand. With his reply he wanted to cut off all further criticism. And finally, doesn't the reaction itself show quite clearly that Djilas's conception is not a contribution to our struggle for socialist democracy but is instead a blow against it? I think that these facts put into proper perspective Djilas's statements about freedom and his so-called descending the "bureaucratic ladder" to be among the people. They also show that the fear of some people that, after this plenum, socialist democracy will not be able to develop is unfounded. On the contrary, this plenum will put tendencies which are contrary to that goal in their places and in that way will decisively contribute to our further struggle for socialism and socialist democracy.

◆

THE REPLY
"To Remain a Free Man and a Communist" (Djilas)

When I look over my past, I cannot say that I have been one of the most disciplined Communists, but neither was I one who violated discipline or failed to carry out tasks entrusted to him. Discipline was for me a conscious act and never conflicted with my feelings or wishes or with my social action. I was the kind of Communist who conscientiously performs his duty without thinking too much about discipline. I did not make any "retreats" or act "hastily."

However, during the last several months I gradually began to be aware of my ideological disagreement with the accepted theoretical views of our movement on a series of fundamental questions. This is the real—and basic—cause for my personal alienation from my closest comrades in the Executive Committee of the Central Committee.

I reached these conclusions after long and deep reflection. I was aware that my views have their weaknesses and for that very reason I presented them as thoughts for discussion. Not even today do I maintain that all those ideas were absolutely correct, although I believe that in the main they are. It is probable that most of them, or at least a good portion of them, should be changed or rephrased during the course of further discussion and the struggle of ideas.

Although in the top leadership there was no formal requirement to present speeches and articles to be read by others, I did violate a long-established rule, which amounts to a violation of discipline, although not a formal one. [. . .] That violation is

Milovan Djilas. A fiery Montenegrin radical, Djilas had been a communist since his youth in prewar Yugoslavia, fought loyally in the wartime partisan movement, and served as a prominent minister in Tito's communist government. This photograph depicts him in his days as one of Tito's closest postwar comrades. But in the early 1950s Djilas began to criticize the emergence of a privileged communist elite, and eventually he became the first prominent East European dissident against Marxist-Leninist orthodoxy. (Topham/The Image Works)

obvious because I was conscious that certain of my views, especially on theoretical matters, differ from those of other members of the leadership.

I thought, especially recently, that the differences among us could be eliminated during a discussion (better yet, a public discussion). I was convinced that as a movement and as a society we had already entered the phase where such discussions could be conducted without any danger for the unity of the movement—for unity is certain in all political, organizational and foreign-policy matters. I was not sure then, nor am I even now, that any of my political conclusions are either good or feasible. Insofar as I had time, I criticized all areas of our system, but I am not now nor will I be in the foreseeable future opposed to the system as a whole. [. . .]

During the entire period, including today, I have never been aware of any differences between myself and the leadership on questions of foreign policy or of the brotherhood and unity of our peoples. This is demonstrated by my recent election speeches.

However, looking over the past, especially in recent times, on philosophical and esthetic questions my views did differ in essence from the views of most of our theoretical workers. But I cannot understand nor can I accept the criticism that I abandoned materialism and dialectics (Marxism), or that I have become a skeptic or an agnostic. On the contrary, I believed that in our new progressive social and cultural development we try to expand upon and even to change significantly the previous ideological views, including those of Lenin. Marx's views were for me always and remain today the foundation of all my interpretations. [. . .]

My greatest mistake was failing to consult with my comrades. [. . .] Doubtless that was not only the proximate cause but also the essential cause of the present difficulties which could seriously harm the movement.

Stories are circulating that I am against Comrade Tito. I cannot accept that. Not one of my criticisms is directed against a particular person, and least of all against Comrade Tito. Comrade Tito was and, regardless of the present dispute, remains for me an incomparable figure in Yugoslav national and social development, the strongest and most active force for unity in our movement and in our country.

I shall always work with discipline to fulfill the decisions of the League of Communists and government organs just as I have in the past. Regardless of what I think, I am ready to renounce the publication of those of my positions that the leadership considers potentially politically damaging. You may think what you will about me or my work, but I cannot and could not imagine that socialism could be realized in our country outside the framework of the League of Communists, the Socialist Alliance and the governmental and economic organs.

I must say that my writing in "Anatomy of a Moral" in *Nova Misao* is too general and overdone—like all satirical pamphlet literature. Even more important, it deals with periods and with phenomena that are in many ways a matter of the past. Under certain circumstances that article could cause political harm. But I do not agree that my article is directed against any specific person or that it describes any concrete situation. Such a view of literature is naïve. If anyone feels insulted, I am ready to apologize in any manner that he wishes.

To me the unity of the movement is above all else, and I consider this to be the duty of every Communist and every citizen. In my opinion that unity does not contradict free thought but is realized with its aid.

Since my early youth I have always been a free man and a Communist and I hope to remain so till the end of my life. I cannot see that these two things contradict one another or that they could be separated from one another. And not only for me, but it seems to me that they are inseparable elements of the movement also: to say what one thinks and to do what is agreed or ordered. I shall do what is required without complaining and I shall speak without preconceived thoughts. I learned the one in the revolutionary movement and the other I was taught by a humanistic culture throughout my entire life.

I considered it my human and my political duty to send this statement first to Comrade Tito and to ask him his opinion. He has given his answer. Without asking his permission, I will read it:

> I think that you failed to understand the consequences of what you call "retreat" and "hastiness." I consider this basic to the entire affair, because just those consequences prove most clearly that such public discussions as you began in your articles are dangerous not only for the unity of the League of Communists but also for the development of socialism.

I will not try to interpret the words of Comrade Tito, because they are clearly stated. I pledge myself to carry them out in my political work. That is my statement. [. . .]

Now I should like to answer your statement very briefly, Comrade Tito.

I cannot accept some of the criticisms of my positions. I have stated that I did violate discipline. And it is correct that ninety per cent of those ideas, as Comrade Tito observes, are not mine but are taken from him or Kardelj or elsewhere.

It is clear that I cannot straighten out everything. I will dwell here only on the question of revisionism. In order to clarify some matters and to leave no doubt about what is involved here, I want to state some things clearly. I am a revisionist in relation to Leninism. I am of the opinion, and have no reason to hide it, that such an "ideology" no longer fits our country. Comrades, I am not a supporter of some bourgeois or Western social-democratic idea. I am not by my education or by my way of life, nor have I read about social democracy. If some of my ideas resemble those of some social democrats or those of Bernstein, which will be discussed later, that is not the result of copying those authors but the result of some objective conditions expressed in my mind, perhaps some possibly bourgeois tendency.

In order to understand each other clearly: I do not see any differences between myself and the leadership in regard to the policy, or the sharpness of that policy, of our party, our government and our economic organs toward the bourgeois elements in our country or in regard to the ideological struggle against those bourgeois elements. If our Central Committee or our Parliament [. . .] considers that our policy should be sharpened, and passes corresponding measures, I do not disagree. I never differed with our leadership on that question and have no differences even today.

Other differences are obvious and one should not hide them when they in fact exist. These differences concern the ideological questions about which we have already spoken.

I am convinced that many of my articles created a great stir within the League of Communists. I am not for liquidating the League. I am for organizational changes within the League of Communists. That is briefly what I wanted to say.

"The Party Needs His Strength and Talent" (Dedijer)

I have a feeling, comrades, that all of us will agree that we have never been through more difficult days in our lives than those today. [*A voice:* It depends. We had some pretty difficult days.] We found ourselves in a new situation. [. . .] I have become a persecuted animal. I was accused of being a traitor and also of disliking Comrade Tito. I felt this way until two days ago when Comrade Tito invited me to visit him. I found him also disturbed. Calmly, like a father, he let me tell him what was bothering me. [. . .]

Now, comrades, let me express my opinion concerning the articles of Comrade Djilas published in *Borba*. [. . .]

I thought it was good to have these articles published; the whole paper looked better with them, it had more substance. [. . .] I warned Djilas especially concerning the article "Is There a Goal?" mainly because it is very difficult to deal with such deep philosophical concepts in a newspaper article. Concerning his "Reply," I criticized his method. He was very upset by the comment of a comrade that he was trying to have Tito deposed. [. . .]

On December 25 I asked Kardelj . . . whether there was any fundamental disagreement between Djilas's articles and his own. He left me under the impression that there were no essential differences. [. . .] During these last few days, I have read all the articles written during the last two years by Comrades Tito, Kardelj and Djilas and I have concluded [. . .] that in essence there are no basic disagreements. [. . .] We elected Comrade Djilas as president of the Parliament on December 25. Up to that date he had already published 14 of his 18 or 19 articles. That means that he had already presented his thoughts. Yet with a unanimous vote we elected him president of the Parliament. [. . .]

I discussed the matter for an entire ten days with many comrades who are sitting among us, and the majority of them accepted more or less the articles of Comrade Djilas. Of course, the majority of comrades accepted those articles because they thought he was writing them in agreement with comrades from the Secretariat and that the Executive Committee stood behind him. But then the question arises, why do people accept articles without regard for their content, paying attention only to the authority behind them? Now we have a new situation. The Executive Committee examined the articles, reached its decision, and now these same people change their opinions. [. . .]

Finally, comrades, I am convinced that we must find a sensible solution. We have few people of Djilas's caliber. Such men are not born every day [*laughter*]. Yugoslavia and the party need his strength and his talent. If I am faced with a terrible choice, which finger of my hand I should cut off—Tito, Kardelj, Ranković or Djilas—which banner of the revolution I should pull out, I must answer: I cannot tear apart the body of my party. I would cut off my head to prevent my hand from doing it. We should rejoice that our revolution lives on, that it did not devour its children, that the children of this revolution are honest. [. . .]

"I Have Separated Myself from the Party" (Djilas)

I will dissociate myself from Dedijer's speech [. . .] because it is emotional. [. . .] I cannot hold it against you, comrades, if you consider that I have also separated myself sharply from the party. It is clear that I have dissociated myself from the party. I am aware of that today. But I did not do it because of any hostile intent, but for ideological reasons.

In that connection, Kardelj's speech is new both in tone and in the manner of exposition. We did not speak in this way [. . .] about Hebrang and Žujović. Regardless of how much I disagree with his opinion, Kardelj did discuss my theses. [. . .] I accept ninety per cent of Kardelj's theses and can state that Kardelj criticized my work solidly. There are some points I cannot agree with, but I cannot categorically state that Kardelj might find something useful in some of my ideas. All in all, this is a struggle of opinions, and history teaches us that no one thesis is always right.

One area where Kardelj and Tito interpreted me wrongly is their contention that I neglect the role of the working class and that I fail to mention it. [. . .] In the trade-union periodical in 1951 or 1952 I stated that the working class is the major force in the building of socialism. [*Voices:* That was earlier.] I stand by the same thesis today regardless of my unfinished articles. [. . .] Because whether I say socialism or socialist forces or the city, as you saw in my articles, that concept is for me almost identical with the working class. [. . .]

Some people speak about my skepticism and lack of faith. There is one thing that is absolutely true. [. . .] I do not really believe in the League as it is today. I do not want to say that all Communists are bureaucrats; but a large number in my opinion are not Communists. In my opinion peasant Communists are not Communists but are allies of Communists; peasant party members are our form of alliance with the village. Second, I think there is too much of the petty official element in the party in the city and that it plays too large a role within the party. I think that the role of the party apparatus is too vast to be democratized. [. . .] I think that things should be reorganized so that people at the lower level exercise initiative rather than receiving direct orders from committees. Thus, comrades, if our discussion were to lead to the reorganization of the League along these lines, all my differences with my comrades in the Executive Committee would vanish. [. . .]

Comrades, it has been stated that I sought to legalize factions. [. . .] That is not correct. [. . .] I did say that [. . .] neither socialism nor socialist theory makes the principle of one party an absolute. Kardelj said that this view was a retreat. [. . .]

When Comrade Kardelj says that I believe that the League of Communists is the chief obstacle to the development of democracy in our country, this is only partially correct; but I do maintain that the League of Communists, as it is today, is the chief obstacle to democratic socialist development in our country. [. . .]

Comrade Roćko told me that I have to repent. It is hard for me to understand this terminology in the League of Communists today. I have nothing to repent. If I made a mistake, I made a mistake and will be rewarded as I deserve. But I say openly what I think. To repent is a moral act appropriate to religion and not to our Communist organization.

"I Have Nothing More to Say" (Djilas)

Comrades, Communist self-criticism is very difficult. Mainly because there is a large complex of mistakes. [. . .] During these last two days in some way a devil broke in me. [. . .]

Today I am convinced that holding this Special Plenum was the best way to end the matter.

I have a strange feeling that this will be the most useful event for the Communist party of Yugoslavia since the Cominform conflict. [. . .] Last night [. . .] for the first time I slept normally. [. . .] From the criticism by Minić as well as Kardelj and Tito, I felt that the plenum is following an antibureaucratic course in struggling against my concepts. [. . .] I am in a situation here at the plenum where either I have definitely to part from Communist practice and Communist ideology and everything Communist or I have to try, at least as a private citizen, in some way to turn my face toward you, toward your work, toward Communists, toward the League, toward our entire politics. [. . .]

One of the comrades said that the article in *Nova Misao* is an integral part of the earlier articles, is even the conclusion. Quite correct. It is an integral part and carries things to the end, except for about ten more articles I intended to publish in *Borba*. That is the end and the entire whole. Comrades who say that is the case are correct.

After the Brioni Plenum I was not convinced that the plenum had chosen the correct path. I constantly had the feeling that the plenum was one-sided, that it neglected the struggle against bureaucratism. When I wrote my articles, I felt that someone should correct in some way the Brioni Plenum. [. . .]

Comrade Tito [. . .] said that there are men who are afraid of difficulties. I cannot accept this formulation as pertaining to me. [. . .] I was afraid of the victory of bureaucratism. I participated in the anti-Cominform campaign. Thereafter I started applying some of those criticisms to events in Yugoslavia. [. . .] In the Executive Committee I did not have any specific duty. Either I did not have one or I could not find out what it was or I preferred not to have one. This must have happened primarily because I always did intellectual work in the party. Those administrative-economic matters were hard for me to understand. But somehow I found myself in the situation that has already been discussed here.

Moša Pijade: As far as I recall, you were in charge of social questions in the Executive Council.

Djilas: That was done by Bobi. I traveled here and there. I had scarcely any contact with Bobi. I met him twice. But it does not matter. I had that job but I was attracted toward abstract intellectualism, and in the final analysis it doesn't make any difference. [. . .]

I only saw the external phenomena [. . .] but I did not see the entire process as a whole. [. . .] As I looked at those phenomena, I was afraid of bureaucratism . . . and I created an abstract theory which applied concretely means exactly what the comrades say it means: the mobilization of the petty bourgeoisie, of social democracy and the West, all of the things I really said. [. . .]

This plenum has convinced me that bureaucratism will not be victorious in Yugoslavia. My faith in the League of Communists is restored, the faith I openly denied yesterday. With this my faith in the Central Committee of the League of Communists and the Central Committee as the chief antibureaucratic force is restored. Obviously when confronted with these facts that I heard really do exist, my theory cannot operate in practice and nothing will remain of my theory. [. . .]

I have nothing more to say, comrades, unless someone else has something to ask me.

An Appeal from the Belgrade Philosophers

◆

The first major school of critical, humanistic Marxist thought in Eastern Europe was centered in Belgrade and Zagreb in the 1950s and 1960s and sharply opposed to official Marxism-Leninism. As this group of scholars advanced from purely philosophical concerns to involvement with public affairs, it made itself and its journal *Praxis* increasingly unpopular with the authorities. In 1975, the Belgrade branch of the school was removed from university positions by special action of the Serbian government, and eight affected professors issued this appeal, supported in large part by their university colleagues and by scholars around the world. Ultimately they were reinstated.

◆

TO THE ASSEMBLY OF THE SOCIALIST REPUBLIC OF SERBIA, BELGRADE

The seven-year campaign against us, in which—in a way unprecedented in the postwar history of this country—all repressive propaganda means were used and many political authorities were mobilised, both the present ones and some past ones, has by the force of mechanical necessity reached its climax: by an *arbitrary* decision which is contrary to the basic legal acts and the principles of self-government on which the very foundations of the existing order should rest—we have been ousted from our teaching positions at the Faculty of Philosophy of the University of Belgrade.

This was done because all the pressures and threats used against us during those seven years, intended to split us and to compel us to capitulate, eventually failed. Banning books and journals, eliminating us from mass media, from official cultural and scholarly institutions and indeed from all public life, suspending finances for the projects of research in which we participated, spreading insulting rumours, confiscating passports, harassing and arresting the students who dared to support us, attempts at corruption, threats of closing the Faculty of Philosophy, of splitting it into two parts, of abolishing self-management and introducing compulsory management—none of

"An Appeal from the Belgrade Philosophers," from Mihailo Marković and Robert S. Cohen, eds., *Yugoslavia: The Rise and Fall of Socialist Humanism,* Spokesman Books, 1975, pp. 86–93.

these measures turned out to be sufficient to ensure either our voluntary withdrawal or our democratic dismissal by the self-governing bodies of the Faculty.

The Faculty of Philosophy in Belgrade, although exposed to long, constant pressure, refused to act against its beliefs and to bow under sheer arbitrary force. With an impressive dignity and courage the Faculty has upheld its firm conviction that it must take its decisions in an independent, democratic way with full moral integrity. It evaluated all proposals and demands only with respect to offered reasons and evidence, only on the grounds of the basic principles of socialist forms of self-government and university self-management and not in deference to the political authorities behind them. In the history of Yugoslav socialism the Faculty of Philosophy is the first, and until this moment, the only institution that has been able to resist bureaucratic pressure and to defend successfully the basic freedom of the university and fundamental human rights: the right to the freedom of research and scholarly publication, the right to assume a critical attitude towards existing social reality and towards every ideology, the right to be equal with any political spokesman, the right to autonomous decision-making. As a consequence of the need to adjust the law to an arbitrary bureaucratic will, the University law was drastically changed twice within one year, and exclusively for the Republic of Serbia. First, in 1973, a demand was incorporated into law that the university professors must satisfy moral and political criteria in addition to schol-arly ones. At the same time, university *self*-management was transformed into co-management by including outside members to the extent of half the composition of the Faculty Council. The second change of the University law, in November 1974, made complete violation of self-management possible by giving a right to the Repub-lican Assembly to dismiss all those professors who allegedly "damaged social interests."

Until this very day the Yugoslav mass media, which has disseminated an incredi-ble amount of misinformation and untruth about us, has never confirmed the result of a legally prescribed, self-governing procedure examining our "moral and political suitability": namely that committees composed of thirty-five outstanding scholars from various Yugoslav universities wrote very favourable reports about our activity and that these reports were accepted by an overwhelming majority in all the self-governing bodies of the Faculty in July 1974. Although, according to the Constitution and the existing laws that decision had to be considered final, it did not satisfy the political authorities. They continued to demand our elimination from the Faculty.

In the interest of the normalization of work at the Faculty of Philosophy we have expressed readiness to abstain temporarily from teaching and to take leave for scientific research. We only requested minimal guarantees that persecution of the stu-dents and further pressures on the Faculty would be stopped. But the authorities were not satisfied with anything but unconditional capitulation. The political campaign was continued with redoubled abusiveness, the University law was again adjusted and sup-plemented. This act of bureaucratic violence constitutes a heavy blow to Yugoslav culture, to self-management, to the reputation of socialism in the contemporary world.

Our crime consists in taking democratic socialism seriously, in expressing pub-licly the truth about the present crisis of Yugoslav society, about its causes and the possibilities of its future development.

We are accused of "corrupting the youth" and of being engaged in political activity. The first of these two accusations is as old as the history of philosophy: its victims have been precisely those who have contributed most to the development of the human mind and the discovery of truth: of knowledge about men and about the world. The second accusation is grotesque: it has been put forward in a country in which the active political commitment of every citizen, his active participation in all political decision-making, is the basic assumption of its economic and political system. Unless perhaps our professional political leaders consider that everyone should be politically engaged except Marxist philosophers and sociologists? Naturally, any relevant critical social theory has certain political implications. To accuse scholars of political engagement in the sense of struggling for power on that ground solely, without any other clear supporting evidence, only reveals a bureaucratic obsession with power and a poorly hidden intention to create an atmosphere in which any repressive measures may be justified.

We have been accused of creating a "monopoly in scientific and cultural activity." In a manner worthy of the heroes of Orwell's novels, those who have a complete monopoly of the mass media, of publishing houses, of funds for cultural and scientific activity and indeed of all socialised property, accuse of monopoly those who have no power, no property, whose basic human rights have been violated, who are not even allowed, contrary to the law, to reply publicly to all the public attacks and the most outrageous insults which have been heaped upon them.

We have also been accused of cultivating "connections with foreigners"—in a country that one decade ago adopted a policy of "opening toward the world" as one of its basic goals. It is true, we have many connections abroad, but these are with scholars and progressive people all over the world and not with politicians, businessmen, financial magnates, generals, kings or emperors. Those numerous persons in various other countries who have been supporting us, expressing their concern and dismay because of this deplorable development of repression, are not enemies of socialism—as the official propaganda tries to present them—but some of the most active and most brilliant defenders of socialism and democracy, some of the greatest friends of Yugoslavia and its socialist future. Utterly vague, unsubstantiated allegations about growing enemy forces, about ever present, "hostile activities" invariably serve a single purpose: to scare, to suppress any dissident thought, to silence all those who refuse to conform.

One of the most absurd accusations is that we deny the revolutionary character of the working class. The truth is however, that we deny the revolutionary character of all those social forces, above all of political bureaucracy, which prevent the working class from becoming a real historical subject. And this is the real reason for the present conflict, and for similar conflicts between bureaucratic leaderships and the theoreticians of the International labour movement. We claimed the freedom not to merely serve bureaucracy, but to speak up as Marxists, as the theoreticians of a democratic socialism. We defended that freedom consistently, not merely for ourselves and for some particular practical purpose but for everyone and as a principle. On the other hand, there are and there always have been powerful forces in the labour movement which have tended to win complete freedom for themselves but to prevent it among their followers. In his letter to Trier of 18 December 1889, Engels very clearly formulated the nature of the problem:

> "The labour movement rests on the sharpest critique of the existing society. Critique is its life principle. How then can the labour movement avoid criticism and stop debate? Do we demand freedom of speech only in order to destroy it in our own ranks?"

Two years later, after the news had reached him that the German Social Democratic Party intended to introduce censorship of its own newspaper *Vene Teit,* Engels wrote to Kenchi (on 25th February 1891): "This is really a brilliant idea, to impose a new anti-socialist law on German socialist science, just after it has been liberated from Bismarck's law against socialists. And this new law has to be introduced and implemented by the Social Democratic Party's leadership itself."

In the letter to Bebel of 12 May 1891, and to Kenchi of 11 February 1891, Engels described in the following way the attitude of the theoretician who found himself under attack from the leadership of his own movement.

"No party in any country can condemn me to silence if I decide to speak up. It is high time that people once and for all stop wearing silken gloves in all their relationships with Party functionaries, who are in fact their servants and that they stop behaving humbly instead of critically toward those infallible bureaucrats."

Already Marx and Engels, whose Party friends Bebel and Kenchi attempted to prevent the publication of the *Critique of the Gotha programme,* found themselves in a situation which was to become typical for theoreticians of socialism whenever they took the ideals of the revolutionary movement seriously, whenever they took the liberty of searching for truth and of expressing critical statements about the errors and inconsistencies of the functionaries of the movement, whenever they refused to keep silent and to stand humbly and obediently in front of those powerful and infallible bureaucrats.

Together with Marx and Engels we have held the view that criticism is the life principle of the labour movement "not only in capitalism but also in socialism."

How can there be a genuine workers' movement and a really socialist society which forbids discussion and criticism, or which treats free speech as a hostile act to be punishable according to the norms of the Criminal code?

All our critical remarks: against the professionalisation of politics, against bureaucratic privileges as a form of exploration [*sic; exploitation* is meant] of the working class, against the reduction of self-government to a distintegrated cluster of councils which play an inferior role in the distribution of social power and represent only an appendix of the Party and the State, against the utterly uncritical transfers of the "laissez-faire" model of a market economy with its well known consequences (such as the rise of social inequality, the growth of the new middle class, the generation of irrational competition among socialist enterprises, the destruction of the solidarity of the working class, the creation of artificial needs and the dominance of a new petty bourgeois consumerist mentality), against incomprehensible neglect of workers' education, against authoritarian relationships within the League of Communists, against the introduction of censorship and bureaucratic pressures for self-censorship, against increasing repression in the field of culture—all those critical remarks are clearly in the spirit of the basic principles of a classless socialist society, and furthermore, remain in the spirit of the 1958 Programme of the Yugoslav League of Communists. That Programme requests members of the League of Communists to fight bureaucratism. It is nearer to truth that in this respect we have done less than was possible, than that we have done more than is needed. On the other hand, there is hardly any doubt that the Party leadership has given up most of its own programme. It experienced our criticism as the voice of its own uneasy conscience and that is perhaps its main motive in trying to silence us. Its accusation that a couple of philosophers are eager to seize power is not only an utterly unconvincing rationalisation but also the expression of its own obsession with power.

Rejecting all such wild accusations, which not only endanger a few of us personally but imperil the freedom and the socialist culture of the whole country, we wish to emphasise as strongly as possible that every theoretical idea which moves solely within the framework of the existing structure, which conforms and adjusts to it instead of transcending it—deprives socialism of its *future*. Such a thought can hardly be anything but a superficial and mystifying apologetic for what is given. Such a thought is not guided by the interests of the working-class movement and of humanity at large, but by the shortsighted particular interests of the ruling apparatus of power. It is characteristic that, parallel with the development of the campaign against us, there is an obvious growth of influence of the ideologies of Stalinist dogmatism which have patiently waited for their hour of revenge, ready to justify every upsurge of voluntarism, every twist and turn of daily politics, and on the other hand, ready to attack savagely any attitude, any idea if it is merely *different* from that of the infallible leadership.

In the long run this bureaucratic, apparently legitimate violence turns against those who use it. Nothing weakens a ruling elite more than an order to bring about acts which can no longer be convincingly ideologically justified, which lack any proper legal basis, and which no longer rest on any other authority than the authority of power. On the other hand, no party in any country can condemn to silence a person who has decided to speak up. Ideas cannot be defeated by preventing them being expounded from a professor's chair. We are convinced that such a bold, dignified and truthful scholarly community as the Faculty of Philosophy in Belgrade will not be demoralised and prevented from continuing to defend the great principles of freedom and the integrity of scholarly research simply because it has temporarily lost eight of its members.

Belgrade, *Zagorka Golubović, Trivo Indjić, Mihailo Marković, Dragoljub Mićunović, Nebojša Popov, Svetozar Stojanović, Ljubomir Tadić, Miladin Životić.*

28th January, 1975.

Yugoslavia's National Question

◆

Viktor Meier

Originating as a federation of distinct South Slavic peoples, Yugoslavia has never been without ethnic tension and has often experienced bloody violence issuing from nationality conflict. Although Tito's regime kept such conflict more or less under control, the old strains reappeared and worsened throughout the 1980s. This essay by a knowledgeable German journalist characterizes the situation early in that decade and prefigures the more serious issues besetting Yugoslavia today.

At the end of March 1981, disturbances broke out in the Yugoslav autonomous province of Kosovo, inhabited primarily by Albanians but part of the Republic of Serbia. Since that time, the Kosovo region has effectively been subject to combined military and police rule under the control of the federal authorities. The cause of the disturbances in Kosovo is alleged to have been "Albanian nationalism." Thus, the nationality question in the multi-national state of Yugoslavia erupted once again in a sensitive area, approximately 10 years after the national crisis in the Republic of Croatia. The events in Kosovo in turn stimulated nationalist reactions in Serbia. One gets a strong impression that the situation is turning into a traditional Balkan nationality struggle and that it will be waged in the traditional way. Communists in Yugoslavia have been claiming in their propaganda for years, even decades, that they had solved the nationality problem in Yugoslavia thanks largely to socialism and socialist self-management. Yet, today they are confronted by national problems that are hardly less serious than those of the interwar Yugoslav state.

◆

IDEOLOGICAL BACKGROUND

One may well ask whether a movement like communism can by its very nature arrive at real solutions to the nationality question in a multi-national state. The Yugoslav Communists could find little encouragement in the ideas of their ideological

Viktor Meier, "Yugoslavia's National Question," from *Problems of Communism,* March–April 1983, pp. 47–60.

mentors. Multi-national states were an abomination for Lenin. Agreeing with Karl Kautsky, he postulated in 1914 that "both the example of all progressive mankind and the example of the Balkans" demonstrated that the national state is the rule and norm under capitalism. "The state of diverse composition is something backward or an anomaly." For the proletariat, Lenin continued, national demands are generally subordinate to the interests of the class struggle; for the proletariat it is important "to ensure the development of its class."

Communist Yugoslav writers admit now that it was not easy for their party to arrive at adequate solutions for the nationality question, probably due in part to such concepts as Lenin's. Gavro Altman writes that in the Yugoslav as in the other Communist parties the idea had prevailed that "the national question was in substance a peasant question." From this it was tempting to conclude "that this problem was peculiar to capitalist countries and that under socialism it would tend to disappear by itself." Sima Marković, the first leader of the Communists in Yugoslavia, believed that he was doing justice to Lenin's precepts by opposing a federal solution for Yugoslavia and by displaying complete indifference about whether the three peoples making up the state at that time—the Serbs, Croats, and Slovenes—were three nations or three branches of a single nation. Thus, contrary to Tito's remarks at the 8th Congress of the League of the Communists of Yugoslavia in 1964, it is not accurate to say that the party had a correct "Leninist" position toward the nationality question since 1924— when it stipulated the principle of "equal rights up to secession" for every nation.

Such declarations mean little. At the time they were proclaimed, the Comintern found it useful to favor the dissolution of all existing states in the Balkans and their replacement by one or more federations. This position could even be traced to the ideas of the old Serbian socialist, Svetozar Marković. Nevertheless, some Yugoslav observers have claimed that these prewar federative concepts led to the adoption of a federal structure for the postwar Yugoslav state.

On the other hand, there have always been—and continue to be—Yugoslav Communists who cling as a matter of principle to Lenin's original thesis that multi-national states are awkward and backward. Their beliefs led them either to try to form separate Communist parties and toy with the idea of dismembering the country, or to advocate an integral Yugoslav nation, such as King Alexander had proclaimed in 1929, and thereby leap over the national contradictions in Yugoslavia. In 1937, independent Communist parties arose in Croatia and Slovenia; for Macedonia, the same was at least contemplated. At the same time, in view of the dangers on the European horizon in the 1930's, other Yugoslav Communists became prey to patriotic impulses in the sense of advocating the integrity of the Yugoslav state. Yet, after the occupation of Yugoslavia by the Germans in April 1941, the Comintern, as well as wide circles of the Yugoslav party itself, leaned toward accepting the dissolution of the state, not only in Macedonia but also in Croatia. In Zagreb in July 1941, an agent of the Comintern named Kopinić was promoting the creation of an independent Communist party for the "Independent State of Croatia."

For a long time there was only vague knowledge of this interlude. Vladimir Dedijer was the first to publish details in his "new contributions" to the biography of

Tito that was published in 1981. As a result of these efforts, which could have been interpreted as treason, the agent Kopinić in no way lost Tito's friendship. He extricated himself from the situation by claiming communications problems, and merely had to be content with subordinate posts after the war. Separatism evidently was not a transient phenomenon in Croatia. Even in 1944, Milovan Djilas noted "little prominence for Yugoslavia and an overemphasis on Croatian peculiarities" in the headquarters of the Communists of Croatia. Dedijer claims that his portrayal of the activities of the Croatian party during the war made Vladimir Bakarić and other high Croatian party functionaries hostile toward the publication of his book.

◆

EVOLUTION OF YUGOSLAV FEDERALISM

Prewar Yugoslavia did not have autonomous territorial sub-units. There were merely administrative districts in various forms, although the nations—at least the three leading nations—were recognized as constituting the state. This was expressed in the very name of the country adopted in 1918, "Kingdom of the Serbs, Croats and Slovenes." Politically, the nations were represented by parties in prewar Yugoslavia. The more important ones succeeded in becoming "national" parties with leading roles among the nations concerned: the Radicals and their auxiliary and successor organizations among the Serbs; the Croatian Peasant Party among the Croats; and the clerical People's Party among the Slovenes. Even the Bosnian Moslems had a kind of national representation at certain times. These parties received recognition even in public law. For example, the so-called *sporazum* (agreement) of August 1939 that was to resolve the Croatian question was concluded between Yugoslav Prime Minister Dragiša Cvetković and the leader of the Croatian Peasant Party, Vladko Maček.

The new Communist Yugoslavia that was conceived at the second session of AVNOJ—the Anti-Fascist Council for the National Liberation of Yugoslavia—in November 1943 at Jajce was based on the principle of federalism. The territory of the country was to be divided into six republics, according to both historic and ethnic considerations. Within the Republic of Serbia two autonomous regions, Kosovo-Metohija (later called just Kosovo, or in Albanian, Kosova) and Vojvodina, came into being. The relations of the Yugoslav nations and nationalities were put under the slogan "unity-brotherhood"—a description which lends itself well to papering over problems.

The federal constitution of postwar Yugoslavia, following the Soviet pattern, was probably supposed to have a primarily declarative character in the eyes of the Yugoslav Communists. In Article 1 of the constitution of 1946, the member republics even received the formal right to secede from the federation. One of the ideological pillars of the "Croatian Spring" of 1968–71, Zagreb University professor Sima Djodan—later sentenced to a long prison term at Tito's insistence—said with regard to this conception: "For us the federation was first created as a state and assumed exclusive competence over all spheres it deemed important for state sovereignty and for socioeconomic life. The republics, as a kind of ethnic form, were left with the less important and the local communities with the least important functions."

Djodan is not entirely correct in this definition of Yugoslav federalism. In one sense, and perhaps the most important one, the republics quickly grew into considerable and to a certain extent autonomous power centers, namely in regard to the Communist party and its apparatus. As we shall see, the relative independence of the republic party apparatuses was to prove of great importance for the subsequent development of Yugoslavia. (In the Soviet Union, where similar tendencies were bloodily liquidated by Stalin, matters were different.)

The republics in Yugoslavia, however, are not coterminous with the nations. Of all the republics, only Slovenia is ethnically homogeneous. Croatia has a large Serbian minority. Many Croats live in Bosnia-Hercegovina and Vojvodina. Macedonia too has large ethnic minorities within its boundaries, as does Serbia, above all in the two autonomous regions. Similarly, Serbs live in Bosnia-Hercegovina and in Croatia. Montenegro is not clearly defined from an ethnic standpoint, and Bosnia-Hercegovina is a historically determined unit inhabited by Moslems, Serbs, and Croats. Of the two autonomous regions created in Serbia, Kosovo has an Albanian majority while Vojvodina has a large Hungarian minority, although in Vojvodina the Serbs predominate numerically and politically.

The lack of congruence between the republics and the nations has occasionally led to situations whereby ethnic animosities found outlets within the boundaries of a specific republic and did not affect the state as a whole. Furthermore, despite the federal state, the nations remained an additional category, separate from the republic structure. As nationalist impulses were expressed once again in Yugoslavia, the old irritation of the Communists with this phenomenon that they could not master also returned.

Moreover, from the very inception of Communist rule in Yugoslavia, the category of nation contained politically conditioned ambiguities. There were what might be called "good" and "bad" nations and even "good" and "bad" nationalisms. The newly created Macedonian nation with its ethnic consciousness has been favored: this new nation has been allowed to pursue irredentism abroad, in Bulgaria as well as in Greece. In the same way, the ethnic feelings of the Slovenes have enjoyed understanding and support. The Slovenes are permitted to bring up continuously the issue of their fellow nationals in Carinthia (Austria) and in the area around Trieste (Italy). Serbian and Croatian national aspirations, on the other hand, have long been regarded negatively; the former are equated with "hegemonism" and the latter with "separatism."

Nevertheless, eventually it seemed advisable to accord greater recognition to the nations under constitutional law. In the new "basic principles" preceding the revised constitution of 1963, "the nations of Yugoslavia," without being expressly enumerated, were called the constituent parts of the country; they—and not the republics—were granted the fictitious right to secede. This construction has been retained in all subsequent revisions of the constitution including that of 1974, now in effect. However, the "nations and nationalities" (formerly "national minorities") are neither enumerated nor recognized as legal subjects. Articles 245–247 simply set forth the principle of equal rights for the nations and nationalities, including the right to use their various languages. The difference between nations and nationalities is also not specifically defined. In practice, it seems that the nations of Yugoslavia are those that have their ethnic center within the boundaries of Yugoslavia, while the nationalities have their center outside the borders. Thus, in the census results of 1981, the 577,000 Montenegrins are listed as a "nation," while the over 1.7 million Albanians are considered a "nationality" ("national minority" according to previous usage).

✦
NATIONAL TENSIONS, 1957–1980

In the second half of the 1950's, nationally related tensions made themselves felt in Yugoslavia, particularly among the individual republics. At first, the tensions were economically conditioned. The separate power centers of the Communist leadership in the individual republics had an impact for the first time. Their economic interests had come to coincide with those of the population, including the non-Communists, within the individual republics. For example, general dissatisfaction prevailed in Slovenia because large funds were channeled from this developed republic via the federal budget to the less developed parts of Yugoslavia. The Slovenes felt threatened by stagnation and feared that their republic might fall behind the neighboring Western countries with which it was compared. At the 7th Congress of the League of Communists of Yugoslavia in 1958, therefore, Slovene politicians called for a compromise that would guarantee further advances for the developed parts of Yugoslavia. The economic discussions arising from this issue led many Yugoslavs, including many Communists, to the conclusion that a new nationalism based exclusively on unresolved economic problems could arise. From this it followed that acceptable economic solutions would dampen ethnic stirrings. Such views were still being voiced when the so-called "Croatian Spring" of 1968–71 was already under way in Zagreb.

This diagnosis proved to be another Communist mistake. While it cannot be denied that economic problems and a sense of economic backwardness played a large role during the onset of the malaise in Croatia, and came up again and again in discussions at that time, it was also apparent that in the final analysis these economic discussions were actually only a starting point for the articulation of a much more general and deeply felt emotional current. In other words, at issue was classical nationalism with all its ramifications. Furthermore, the polemics which broke out among the historians of the individual republics and regions coincided with, rather than followed, the discussions about the distribution of the national income.

The uncertainty of the Communists in the face of the revival of national movements and conflicts caused the party to look for theoretical concepts that might resolve these contradictions in the multi-national state of Yugoslavia. Somehow, it was felt, a "Yugoslav consciousness" must be created that could appeal to both patriotic and ethnic feelings. In 1957, Edvard Kardelj attempted to direct this search into politically acceptable channels. In the foreword to the second edition of his work on the Slovenian national question, written before World War II, he spoke in favor of a socialistically determined "Yugoslavness" (*Jugoslovenstvo*) that should form a "consciousness" above national feelings among the different peoples of Yugoslavia.

According to Kardelj, national conflicts could arise only if a "nationalistic" position was adopted, if "Yugoslavness" was understood as national integralism (as King Alexander had understood it in 1929), or if a "bureaucratic" standpoint was taken.

This was a very complicated definition. It is no wonder that some party members simply took Kardelj's "Yugoslavness" to mean overcoming particular nationalism by cultivating a new Yugoslav national feeling, that is, precisely by promoting Yugoslav national integralism. This interpretation corresponded also with Lenin's view on how to overcome the "backward" multi-national state. The Zagreb sociologist Dušan Bilandžić recalled in a 1982 interview with the Zagreb *Vjesnik* that at the 7th Congress of the League of Communists in 1958, some delegates had spoken out "for the formation of a Yugoslav nation and the abolition of the republics." Tito, too, was apparently influenced by such views. In 1963, out of the blue, he advocated Yugoslav integralism, at least in the cultural sense: "If we want to create a socialist culture," he said in an address to the Yugoslav journalists' association, "we must also have a common program. It must be Yugoslav. Not every republic or every nationality can create its own socialist culture, for this would again mean separation." Such theses were soon dropped since they encountered resistance. In 1967, Tito stated before the Communists of Belgrade that the term "Yugoslav" meant "membership in our socialist community but not a nationality."

Nevertheless, it is probable that the attempts to stimulate a renewed Yugoslav integralism played a large role in the rise of the national movement in Croatia during 1968–71. In part, this movement consisted of a very emotional reaction against "unitarism" and "centralism" in any form. It stressed the independence and equal rights of the nations within the federal structure to the point of reviving the "right to secede," which the constitution had granted first to the republics and later to the nations. There were proposals to transform the federation into a confederation. In this connection, the principle of statehood for the individual republics was also advocated. This demand was important because it basically involved, at least for Croatia, the revival of the idea of national sovereignty within Yugoslavia and its linkage to the republic. The Croatian crisis was a crucial turning point in the evolution of the nationality question in Yugoslavia. It spelled the end of propagandistic slogans and Leninist flourishes, as well as of notions that socialism made nationalism inconceivable.

Although Tito ordered a thorough crackdown on nationalist manifestations in 1971, national aspirations were accorded more consideration in the ensuing years. The principle of statehood for the individual republics became accepted and adopted first in the constitutional amendments of 1971 and then in the constitution of 1974. Even the autonomous provinces within Serbia were recognized as constituent elements of Yugoslavia and were granted autonomous rights, recognized in the constitution. The difference in comparison to the republics lay in the fact that the statehood of the regions was not recognized. Article 4 characterizes the regions simply as "autonomous, socialist, self-managed, democratic, socio-political communities"—in which, to be sure, "the nations and nationalities realize their sovereign rights." This is the point on which the authorities of Kosovo and Vojvodina base their claims in the struggle against centralizing tendencies in the Republic of Serbia.

It is often asked why federalism in Yugoslavia came to be especially emphasized and anchored in the constitution in a veritably "bourgeois" manner after the crisis in Croatia. The explanation can only lie in Tito's belief at the time that he had discovered a new political concept for Yugoslavia. He apparently thought it possible to accommodate the new realities on the *state* level through a federalism solidly anchored in the constitution and the legal system, while a more disciplined and centralized *party* would buttress both the state and the regime. In two speeches in Split and Zadar as early as the summer of 1970, Tito characterized as an error the attempt (at the 6th Congress of the Yugoslav League of Communists in 1952) to obliterate the centralist organizational principle of a Leninist Communist party. The 10th party congress in 1974 emphasized, as had not been done for a long time, the centralist and Leninist nature of the party; it took an explicit stance against the party's "federalization."

This concept of Tito's—which, like Kardelj's, sought to mix "socialist internationalism" with an unclearly defined "Yugoslavness"—failed, since it aggravated national and federal problems in the post-Tito period. Because the Communist party apparatuses in the individual republics constitute relatively independent power centers, a centralist conception of the party could not prevail over them. While Tito did succeed, in conjunction with the purge in Croatia, in ousting from their posts in the Serbian, Slovenian, and Macedonian republics proponents of policies that he disliked, he was forced to rely even in the Croatian case on alliances with the various republic leaderships. Aside from the fact that these purges caused the Yugoslav party to lose many outstanding personalities, whose absence is still felt today, Tito's actions precipitated a general decline in the authority and prestige of the party as an institution.

◆

POST-TITO DEVELOPMENTS

These developments—the further strengthening of the republics and the decline of the party's importance in the spectrum of Yugoslav institutions—continued at an accelerated pace after Tito's death. They reached their high point thus far at the 12th Congress of the League of Communists of Yugoslavia in 1982. Both developments were closely linked to growing economic difficulties, which could not be overcome by party resolutions alone. It also became clear that all the problems, including the Kosovo problem, did not lead to strong solidarity within the Yugoslav party but rather to an intensification of conflicts. In September 1982, the new party chairman, Mitja Ribičić, spoke openly about the lamentable state of cohesion within the party and threatened his listeners with "democratic centralism."

As far as the Republic of Croatia is concerned, Tito's crackdown in the early 1970's left it in an unsatisfactory state, indicative of Communist inability to cope with the phenomenon of nation. The new leadership was of second-rate quality. While they did defend the economic interests of the republic, the new leaders in Zagreb could not bring about an identification between republic and nation. This left the mounting Croatian national consciousness without an outlet. The situation was not improved by the fact that the roughly 15 percent Serbian minority within the republic has been accorded preferential treatment. These Serbs live in the economically more backward areas and favored strong Yugoslav centralism as far back as the pre-war period. They were afraid—as it turns out justifiably—of Croatian nationalism. In 1941, these Serbs were driven into the arms of the Communist partisans by the operations of the Croatian Ustaše, and it is probably no exaggeration to say that after 1945 and again after 1971, the Serbs behaved like conquerors. The share of Serbs in the membership of the Croatian Communist party was around 28 percent in 1958 and was still 24 percent in 1978. This is far more than their proportion of the population. One also gets the impression that the Serbs are overrepresented in the political police of Croatia.

The Catholic church was able to fill the national vacuum in Croatia. It succeeded in making itself the guardian of the historical traditions of the Croats. The massive gathering of about 200,000 participants in Nin (Dalmatia) on September 1 and 2, 1979, to celebrate the Croats' 1,100 year-old affiliation with Roman Christianity constituted the high point of this effort. The success of this celebration and of other activities by the Church made the regime nervous and led to an anticlerical campaign in 1980 and 1981, including police harassment of the clergy extending even into Bosnia-Hercegovina. Jakov Blažević, then president of the Presidium of the Croatian Republic and the chief procurator in the 1946 trial of the Archbishop of Zagreb, Aloys Stepinać, reopened old wounds by publishing his memoirs in January 1981. At the same time, nationalistically inclined Croatian intellectuals such as Franjo Tudjman, Vlado Gotovac, Zlatko Tomičić, Dobroslav Paraga, and Marko Veselica were put on trial. To this day, many expressions of national feeling that have long been a matter of course in the other republics of Yugoslavia are apparently taboo in Croatia.

The percentage of party members among the individual nations or nationalities seems to have become more and more the measure of the tolerance and understanding that the Communist regime is ready to display in specific instances, including on the issue of nationality. The percentages of party membership were long secret, but in June 1982, official statistics were published. With a "Communist density" of only 4.62 percent, the Albanians are the black sheep among the Yugoslav nations, even if one takes into account that the proportion of minors among this nation is especially high. The Croatians, with 7 percent, are not much better off. As for the Slovenes, only 6.4 percent belong to the party. However, in addition to the strength of Catholicism there, low party membership is probably due to a higher living standard and relatively tranquil conditions, which make political involvement seem rather superfluous. Among the Montenegrins, on the other hand, almost 20 percent are Communists, and among the Serbs over 12 percent. Of the Macedonians, 10.5 percent are Communists. Of those who designate themselves ethnically as "Yugoslavs," more than 11 percent belong to the party.

This last-named ethnic designation gave rise to many comments and discussions in the spring of 1982, and brought the dilemma of the Yugoslav Communists vis-à-vis the nationality question back to its starting point. When the results of the 1981 census were published, it turned out that a surprisingly large number of Yugoslav citizens—around 1.22 million or 5.42 percent of the total population—designated themselves as

"Yugoslavs" by national affiliation. This was 4.3 times as many as in 1971. It is interesting to note how this phenomenon manifested itself in different parts of the country. In Bosnia-Hercegovina, the number of "national Yugoslavs" rose in comparison to the 1971 census from around 44,000 to 326,000; one can assume that the figure was for the most part made up of Moslems who do not care for the formal identification of religion and nationality. In the autonomous region of Vojvodina, the "Yugoslavs" increased from 47,000 to 167,000; on the other hand, the number of Hungarians declined by 40,000, and that of Croats fell also. In the Republic of Croatia, the percentage of Serbs sank from 14.2 to 11.5 percent, while there were suddenly 8.2 percent "Yugoslavs," a figure more than four times as great as in 1971. In Kosovo, the share of "national Yugoslavs," 0.2 percent, was the lowest percentage in all of Yugoslavia.

Did the tremendous increase in the number of national Yugoslavs come about because the party carried out direct or indirect propaganda to the effect that "Yugoslav" as a national category was "more progressive" in the socialist sense than Croat, Slovene, or Serb? Obviously, this must have played a role. Dušan Bilandžić met with excited denials when he tried to explore this question. The fear of conflict that many citizens might have harbored so soon after Tito's death, the wish to resolve personal dilemmas such as mixed marriages, or a preference for unity and centralism undoubtedly influenced the choice of some respondents. In addition, some groups who are minorities in their area might have sought to protect themselves by "national Yugoslavness." In any event, in Bilandžić's opinion, the huge increase in "national Yugoslavs" shows that "something is wrong in our society." Bilandžić also suggested that the striving for a Yugoslav nation was an "illusion."

The ugly way in which some party activists, notably Serbs from Croatia, conducted polemics against Bilandžić supports the assumption that, now as before, there are many Yugoslav Communists—and perhaps non-Communist Yugoslav patriots as well—who seek to overcome Yugoslavia's national diversity and occasional discord through a supranational "Yugoslavism." The unease over this declarative Yugoslavism so evident in the Bilandžić interview, however, indicates that the traditional nations of Yugoslavia still constitute the basic components of that country, and cannot be pushed into the background or bypassed. Bilandžić is probably correct in saying that "national Yugoslavism" is primarily a product of specific regional or personal idiosyncrasies and thus a limited phenomenon. Indeed, developments since Tito's death seem to have strengthened rather than weakened the assertiveness of individual nations, nationalities, and republics.

◆

THE ALBANIAN QUESTION

Nowhere has this assertiveness been expressed more conspicuously than in Kosovo. The events in Kosovo clearly show the limits of national integralism in contemporary Yugoslavia. At the same time, they could also signify an unequivocal and perhaps irrevocable dashing of hopes that national contradictions in the Balkans might be overcome by means of "supranational" socialist doctrine. The very name "Yugoslavia" signifies the land of the Southern Slavs. The Albanians—of whom more than 2.5 million live in the Albanian Socialist People's Republic and another 1.73 million, according to the 1981 census, live in Yugoslavia—are not Slavs. According to modern scholarship, they are the descendants of the ancient Illyrians. This hypothesis is accepted today by all Albanian scholars and by a large number of non-Albanian Balkan specialists. The Albanians were the last Balkan nation to acquire a modern national consciousness in the 19th century and form a national state. In Tirana, the visitor is always told that the religious diversity of the Albanians (Moslem, Orthodox, and Catholic) hindered the process of becoming a nation. This is given, among other reasons, as the explanation for the massive antireligious campaign of 1967–68 and the designation of Albania as the world's "first atheistic state." It is probably also true that the late coalescence of the Albanians into a modern nation led them at first to prefer the continued existence of the 19th-century Ottoman Empire, which at least tried to protect the Albanian settlement areas against the territorial claims of the new Balkan Christian states of Serbia, Greece, and Montenegro. The "League of Prizren," the first united political association of the Albanians which sought to make the Berlin Congress of 1878 understand their interests, certainly contained this tendency along with an emancipatory one.

The first Balkan War then brought precisely what the Albanians had feared: the victorious young Balkan states appropriated large parts of the Albanian settlement area, with Serbia and Montenegro dividing between them Kosovo and today's western Macedonia. The Albanians of Kosovo fought against this annexation but were unable to prevent it. Of the 1.73 million Albanians in Yugoslavia today, 1.23 million live in Kosovo where, according to the 1981 census, they make up 77.7 percent of the population. In Macedonia, there are 374,000 Albanians making up 19 percent of the population; not quite 38,000 live in Montenegro.

Kosovo is dear not only to the Albanians; it was also the heart of the medieval Serbian kingdom. Many important Serbian cultural monuments are located here, and the landmark battle of 1389 against the Turks was fought on Kosovo Field. This Serbian defeat forms the subject of the national epic literature. In Prizren, the great memorials of both Albanians and Serbs are found only a short distance apart: in the city is the villa in which the "League of Prizren" met in 1878; two miles up the valley is the monastery on the site where Tsar Dušan, the greatest ruler of medieval Serbia, was buried. It is also beyond doubt that in this early period Kosovo was settled primarily by Serbs. In the western part of Kosovo, that is, along the border with contemporary Albania, Metohija and its cities Peć and Prizren may have always been partly settled by Albanians; but in eastern Kosovo, where Priština is located, the Albanians came to settle only toward the end of the 18th century and later.

These historical points are important because the Kosovo conflict has increasingly become a purely national dispute between Serbs and Albanians, as well as between the authorities of the Republic of Serbia and those of the autonomous region of Kosovo. The rest of Yugoslavia seems to play the role of an irritated and concerned spectator. The authorities of the Republic of Serbia and the Serbian press concentrate their attention to an ever greater extent on the problem of the emigration of the Serbs out of Kosovo. At the request of Serbia, the Federal Parliament has also taken up this problem but obviously has difficulty finding solutions.

Even a casual visitor to Kosovo can easily see that relations between the two groups of inhabitants are quite tense. Outmigration of Serbs has been a persistent phenomenon there since 1966, when the authorities and police in Kosovo were "Albanianized" after the fall of the internal affairs minister, Aleksandar Ranković. As a result of the Serbian outmigration and the higher birthrate of the Albanians, the population ratio has changed since World War II. In 1953, the Albanians made up not quite 65 percent of the population of Kosovo, while Serbs and Montenegrins together accounted for over 26 percent. Today, the corresponding figures are 77.7 and not quite 15 percent. Thus, Albanian nationalists are tangibly realizing the goal of an "ethnically pure Kosovo," despite federal intervention and massive police pressure. There is little doubt that the outmigration of many Serbs, especially from the villages, is hastened by the behavior of segments of the Albanian population. Although only incomplete statistics on the exact number of Serbs and Montenegrins that have left are available, the Belgrade newspaper *Politika* estimates the migration losses of these two groups in Kosovo between 1971 and 1981 to be about 102,000 persons. The absolute number of Serbs in Kosovo declined during this period from 228,000 to just under 310,000, while the number of Albanians grew from 916,000 to 1.23 million.

The present situation is just a phase in a long process. The governments of Serbia and interwar Yugoslavia—both dominated by Serbs—viewed the annexation of Kosovo after the first Balkan War and World War I as a return of places sacred to the Serbian national past; they attempted to bring Serbs into Kosovo again and to push back the Albanians through colonization. Most Albanians in Kosovo therefore welcomed the breakup of Yugoslavia by fascist Italy and the uniting of Kosovo and western Macedonia to Albania proper, even if they presumably would have preferred to see this "liberation" take place in different circumstances.

In this connection, a former high official of the Yugoslav Communist party, Vukmanović-Tempo, vividly described the precarious conditions in which the Communists had to try to build their resistance movement during World War II. There was always the risk that the few Albanians who found their way to the Communists would begin to discuss unification plans with the Communists of Albania. Quite possibly, it was the substantial dependence of Enver Hoxha's Albanian partisan movement on Tito's Yugoslav partisans that prevented greater complications in this sphere. The scant joy of the Albanians over the reestablishment of Yugoslavia was again expressed in armed resistance after 1944, prompting Tito's government to introduce a brutal police regime in Kosovo that oppressed the Albanian population, despite the formal autonomy of the region. This regime was supported by many of the Serbs and Montenegrins living in Kosovo, some of whom avenged grievances accumulated during the Albanian domination in World War II.

When repression eased after 1966, the feeling of liberation on the part of the Albanians was expressed in the demonstrations of 1968. Subsequently, the Albanians succeeded in creating a national intellectual center for Kosovo in the University of

Priština. In addition, a generation of young, nationally conscious teachers for all school levels reached maturity. These people were the instigators of the nationalist revolts of 1981, and they firmly maintain their national positions. The police and military repression, as well as the arrests and convictions of so many young Albanians—often out of all proportion to their transgressions—contribute to hostility toward the Serbian and Montenegrin population. The situation appears insoluble today since all suggested measures can ultimately be undermined by the Albanian population of Kosovo, which reacts to repression with solidarity and a conspiracy of silence.

What do the young Albanian rebels of Kosovo want? One can get some idea of their goals only through personal impressions; the conspiracy of silence also applies to their objectives. They feel themselves to be Albanians, for whom the unification process of the Albanian nation is the determining national experience. A corollary of this is a feeling of indifference to the problems of Yugoslavia. Just as 19th-century Serbs thought about national unity first culturally and then politically, today the Albanians of Kosovo, above all the younger generation, are doing the same. This, however, does not necessarily imply an unconditional desire for union with present-day Albania.

Immediately after the events, Stane Dolanc, a member of the Presidium of the League of Communists of Yugoslavia and minister of internal affairs, dismissed the notion that the unrest was instigated by Tirana. Subsequently, Albania generally, and Enver Hoxha personally, were accused of "agitating" the young Albanians in Kosovo with irredentist sentiments. Yet, from visits and conversations in Tirana, one gains the impression that this has not been the case. On the contrary, there is unease in Tirana about the developments in Kosovo. The Albanians in Kosovo are perceived to be national "purists" whose intensifying nationalism is unsettling to authorities in Tirana because it is not subject to their control. There is also fear that the Kosovars—who have a freer life, practice their religion, and can travel abroad—might cause unrest in Albania by stimulating desires for similar conditions there. Furthermore, Tirana appreciates the importance of Yugoslavia as one of the few countries with which Albania has contacts, as its most important trading partner, and as a rampart against the Soviets. In principle, so a visitor is always told, Albania wants good relations with Yugoslavia, but naturally cannot remain silent when the "brothers on the other side of the border" are oppressed by Serbian or Macedonian nationalism.

It would seem that the time for true Albanian irredentism in Kosovo, in the sense of a movement for unification with Albania, has not yet come. Rather, one has the impression that the young Kosovars feel that their mission includes lighting the torch of national unity on a "realistic" basis in Albania proper. Enver Hoxha is respected as a national leader, a sort of "anti-Tito," but hardly as anything more. As long as the current regime and the current system exist in Albania, the Kosovo problem will remain a domestic problem for Yugoslavia. The young Kosovars in no way dispute the fact that they have more freedom and a higher standard of living in Yugoslavia than do their brothers in Albania. They think, however, that they owe it to their Albanian national consciousness to place these advantages in the service of eventual Albanian unification.

The Communist authorities in Kosovo who are Albanian are in danger of falling between two stools. Under the former party secretary Mahmud Bakali, a kind of state-socialist regime was in effect in Kosovo, with capital investments coming from the central government. Today, the much weaker political leadership of Kosovo is under pressure from the authorities of Serbia, who would like to reduce the constitutional prerogatives of the province and who threaten "personnel changes." The Serbian leadership, especially Dragoslav Marković, can and does capitalize on Serbian frustrations unleashed by the Kosovo question. Statements expressive of low esteem for the national achievements of the Albanians are pouring out of Serbia; even the Illyrian ancestry of the Albanians is presented as a political problem (and thus denied) in the Serbian Central Committee. This overt anti-Albanian bias also found its way into the platform on Kosovo adopted at the 12th Congress of the League of Communists.

Thus, the nationality question has become again a rivalry between nationalisms in socialist Yugoslavia, as it had been in prewar Yugoslavia. This development is regarded with concern by many people in Yugoslavia, in and out of the party. In the wake of the 12th party congress in the summer of 1982, there were some criticisms of the political leadership in Serbia on this point. The question remains whether Serbia, which is strong in both population and power, can be circumvented or induced to change its policies. According to some views the Yugoslav federation, including the party, is not sufficiently strong to bring this about. With regard to Kosovo, the policy of the federation at the present time amounts simply to keeping the situation under some degree of physical control through a massive show of force. A political solution, however, would have to include recognition that the Albanians are the majority in Kosovo, and perhaps even a change of the present constitutional arrangements. Because of the specter of separatism, there is reluctance to give Kosovo republic status. Yet, postponement of a political solution might necessitate greater concessions in the future. Meanwhile, the Kosovo problem reveals the limited room for maneuver at the disposal of the post-Tito leadership of Yugoslavia.

EAST GERMANY 1953

◆ *The relaxation Stalin's successors announced after the dictator's death in 1953 had differential echoes in Eastern Europe. The Ulbricht regime in the German Democratic Republic was one that resisted the so-called New Course. Instead of adopting measures calculated to ease the situation of workers and consumers, the ruling party in East Germany imposed new and higher work norms unaccompanied by corresponding wage increases.*

The resulting indignation produced a spontaneous outburst, a strike by industrial workers in Berlin that quickly turned into a set of demands for political as well as economic change. The strike spread overnight to other cities and, while it never took on the proportions of a popular nationwide protest, seemed for a time to endanger Ulbricht's position. The strike itself was rapidly overcome by Soviet troops and tanks, the native police having shown some unreliability. Ulbricht was saved but at the price of instituting a measure of economic reform. Baring and Lowenthal provide an account of the uprising and a retrospective interpretation of events that retained symbolic importance, not least because it was so clearly a case of workers reacting against a purported government of the working class.

Although East Germany produced fairly isolated instances of dissent, by the party intellectual Wolfgang Harich, for example, and by the scientist Robert Havemann, the popular satirist Wolf Biermann, and the Marxist critic Rudolf Bahro, the Socialist Unity Party led by Ulbricht and his successor Erich Honecker was successful on the whole in preventing the emergence of major sectors of dissidence. The late GDR expert Peter Ludz offers some explanations for the long-standing quiescence of the East German populace.

The spell was broken by a change unique in postwar Eastern Europe, an authentic peace movement arising in the churches and representing a broad challenge to the regime by reason of its ability to galvanize a popular following. As described by Wensierski, this phenomenon prefigured the massive unrest that surfaced at the end of the 1980s.

The East German Uprising of 1953

✦

Arnulf Baring

This summary of the events of 1953 is taken from the standard scholarly account of the uprising, first published in Germany more than a decade afterward and thus free of the exaggerations that marred some of the first published accounts.

✦

EXTENT OF THE RISING

Eastern and western sources are more or less in agreement as to the extent of the strike action of June 17. In July 1953 Grotewohl stated officially that strikes had occurred in 272 towns and that 300,000 workers had been involved, while western estimates list 274 towns and 372,000 strikers. The total work force in the GDR (excluding apprentices) at that time was 5.5 million. It is immediately apparent, therefore, that only a relatively small proportion of the work force took part in the events of June 17: according to Grotewohl's version 5.5 per cent, according to the western version 6.8 per cent.

There are no official estimates, either from the East or from the West, as to how many members of the general public joined in the workers' demonstrations. The estimates made by eyewitnesses, which cannot of course be verified, are highly contradictory. For example, the number of people taking part in the demonstration at the Hallmarkt in Halle (Saale) was variously assessed at 60,000, 70,000, 80,000 and even 90,000.

But do such estimates really matter? There is a danger in paying too much attention to the large scale demonstrations which took place in certain towns, for they tend to create the impression that June 17 was a popular rising. In fact, the eyewitness reports prove conclusively that this was not the case. It was the industrial workers— actively supported by the youth of the GDR—who were responsible for the events of June 17. They started the rising and they were the dominant factor in every major demonstration. By contrast, the farmers were involved only in isolated incidents, and the middle classes and the intelligentsia played little or no part in the day's events. There were a few towns (Görlitz, for example) where intellectuals joined in the demonstrations, but these were the exception rather than the rule. On the face of it, this seems surprising, for the middle classes, the intelligentsia and the farmers were even more harshly treated than the workers. Why, then, were the workers the ones to strike?

Some twelve months before the June rising, Professor Hans Köhler published a paper in which he argued that, far from being undermined by their bitter experiences, the solidarity of the workers in the eastern zone had actually been reinforced. This was why they had resisted the collective agreements so resolutely and why all attempts at intimidation on the part of the regime were bound to miscarry for, since the workers had nothing to lose, oppressive measures would only strengthen them in their opposition. Köhler detected a similar attitude among the farmers of the GDR, most of whom were in any case natural conservatives and consequently anti-SED [Sozialistische Einheitspartei Deutschlands, the Socialist Unity Party], and all of whom had good reason to hate the communist state, which was seeking to confiscate their property and deprive them of their independence. But, as Köhler pointed out, the conditions of rural life were such that it was much easier for the authorities to keep a close watch on the activities of individuals in the country with the result that, at least apparently, the farmers had been obliged to conform to a far greater degree than had the industrial workers. As for the middle classes and the old intelligentsia, whose numbers had been greatly diminished by the flight of so many of their members to the West and whose social position had been undermined as a result of the economic and political programs instituted by the regime, Köhler regarded them as a completely demoralized force. Having allowed themselves to be intimidated by government pressures and threats, these two groups were prepared to make a deal with the regime in the hope of preserving what was left of their former status. Köhler wrote at the time: "The workers are prepared to act, the middle classes are not; they are hoping for help from outside." In my view Köhler's assessment of the workers' attitude in 1952–1953 was entirely correct. Long before June 17, 1953, he pointed to the underlying reason why even those farmers who heard the strike call in time found it difficult to show their solidarity with the industrial workers. This, coupled with the fact that small rural communities simply do not lend themselves to strikes and demonstrations (which need the kind of mass audience provided by the big city if they are to be really effective), explains the farmers' failure to participate. As for Köhler's assessment of the middle classes, this was completely endorsed by the events of June 17. It has been suggested that the reticence shown by the middle classes on June 17 was because the higher quotas, which had been the original bone of contention, were primarily a matter of concern to the workers and that consequently the rising had "nothing to do with the middle classes." But this argument is specious. It has also been said that the middle classes were unaware that a strike had been called until the Soviet troops appeared on the streets. This simply is not true. It is quite obvious from the eyewitness accounts that news of what was happening spread with almost unbelievable speed.

Bricks Against Tanks. This famous photograph of two East Berliners hurling broken bricks at Soviet tanks on June 17, 1953, was widely published in the West. (AP/Wide World Photos)

The indecisiveness of the middle classes on June 17 seems to have been characteristic of their general attitude. Köhler tells us that, even prior to 1953, the members of this social group seldom became involved in political disputes. Was this because they had formed a more accurate assessment of future developments in the GDR or was it because they were afraid to take risks? Foresight and fear are often interdependent, and it could well be that the middle classes of East Germany were motivated by both. Nevertheless, the fact remains that they were far too enervated to enter into any commitment on their own account. They had seen that the wind of change was blowing in the GDR and had decided to knuckle under in the interests of survival. Instead of placing their trust in their own endeavors, they waited in the hope that things would improve, either as a result of a change in the leadership or as a result of western intervention.

◆

CENTERS OF REVOLT

Apart from Berlin and its environs, the principal centers of revolt were to be found in the industrial areas of Central Germany (Bitterfeld, Halle, Leipzig, and Merseburg), in the Magdeburg district and, to a lesser extent, in the districts of Jena/ Gera, Brandenburg, and Görlitz. 61,000 workers struck in and around East Berlin, 121,000 in the industrial areas of Central Germany, 38,000 in Magdeburg, 24,000 in Jena, 13,000 in Brandenburg and 10,000 in Görlitz. The strikes in all these districts and towns started in large industrial installations, which was the principal reason for their initial success. When the personnel of these big industrial concerns, such as the Leuna plant (28,000 men), the Buna plant (18,000 men), the Wolfen Paint Factory (12,000 men), and the Hennigsdorf plant (12,000 men), marched on to the streets in an orderly fashion, the local party and government functionaries were at a total loss. In other places, where there were no large factories or where these disregarded the strike call (in Dresden, for example), the demonstrations were either suppressed before they could get under way or were dispersed by SED functionaries skilled in the art of argument, who entered into discussions with the demonstrators and then talked them to a standstill.

There was almost no liaison between the various strike centers, although an ineffectual attempt was made to coordinate the strike action in the towns of Halle, Merseburg and Bitterfeld: the workers in Halle tried to get pamphlets printed, they discussed the feasibility of proclaiming a general strike for the whole of the GDR and they made telephone contact with the strike leaders in neighboring towns. But time ran out on them long before their initiatives could influence the course of events.

◆

INDUSTRIES INVOLVED IN THE STRIKE

Of the many branches of East German industry involved in the strike by far the most prominent were the construction industry, the mining industry, the machine construction industry, and the chemical and iron-ore-producing industries. I have already mentioned the construction workers in the section dealing with the events of June 16 but there are two further points which need to be made in this connection.

The vast majority of the East German construction workers who struck on June 17 belonged to the industrial construction unions, which were engaged on special construction projects forming part of the general program of socialist development. Many of the construction sites concerned were situated in isolated areas, where nobody had ever built before and where the regime had decided to erect industrial installations and socialist new towns in the early 1950's. The workers who came to build these ideal socialist homes of the future were themselves accommodated in extremely primitive huts. Moreover, in these desolate and remote districts there were no diversions (such as cinemas or dance halls), very few women and, on the not infrequent occasions when there was a breakdown in organization, not even adequate food. It is hardly surprising that in such conditions and in such a milieu—a perfect breeding ground for discontent and resentment—the higher quotas stipulated by the government should have led to strike action.

Those construction workers employed in the provincial towns struck for an entirely different reason: when they heard that their colleagues in East Berlin had been demonstrating, the construction workers in numerous towns throughout the GDR came out in sympathy. Thus, the feeling of solidarity that had been such an important factor on June 16 at a site level re-emerged on June 17 at an inter-site level, which meant that the workers of a whole industry were united by this common bond. But this feeling of unity went still further, for the personnel of various other industries also demonstrated their solidarity with the construction workers of East Berlin.

This was an important development and one that casts a significant light on the situation in the GDR for its shows that, although the unions had lost their original function and no longer served as a vehicle for united action, a large number of workers had evidently retained their sense of solidarity.

If we consider the strike situation in the mining industry we find that in both the iron ore and the potassium mines there were extensive stoppages whereas in the coal and uranium mines there was practically no strike action at all. This is accounted for, in part at least, by certain essential differences between these branches of the mining industry. In the copper mining industry, with its centuries-old tradition, the workers revealed a high degree of solidarity that enabled them to join forces and offer concerted resistance to the regime. (Not surprisingly the town of Mansfeld, where copper mining has been going on for the past six hundred years, was one of the major centers of the strike.) By contrast, the uranium mines, which were started after the Second World War at the instigation of the Soviet Control Commission and which drew their labor from all parts of the GDR, had inspired no real sense of community, which precluded all possibility of solidarity among the workers. Moreover, the uranium miners received far higher wages and far better food than most other categories of workers, which meant that they had little personal incentive for taking strike action. In the coal mines of Saxony, which were expanded and modernized after the war, the situation was much the same.

On the face of it, therefore, it would appear that the failure of the uranium and coal miners to take strike action on June 17 was due to a combination of material welfare and a lack of solidarity. This seems all the more likely if we consider the iron industry, for example: a new and extremely large foundry (Eisenhüttenkombinat Ost) built after the war where the workers enjoyed conditions comparable to those obtaining in the uranium and coal mines, also continued work on June 17.

It is also true that the workers in the uranium district were notorious for their riotous behavior. Until quite late in the 1950's they regularly attacked police stations and beat up SED functionaries. However, these actions were hardly ever prompted by political considerations, and it was only on relatively rare occasions that the uranium miners protested against their economic situation. The truth of the matter is that, in this particular district of the GDR, conditions were rather like those found in the western United States at the time of the gold-rush: money was quickly earned and just as quickly lost, morals were lax, and heavy drinking often led to brawls and even bloodshed. Prior to June 17 there had been more stoppages in the uranium mines than in any other industry in the GDR, and in the circumstances, one would have expected these workers to have been the first to strike.

One factor in their apparent inertia was that, in those days, it was almost impossible to receive western radio transmissions in the Erzgebirge, which is where the uranium mines were situated. As a result it was several days before many of the miners heard about the July [sic] 16 demonstrations in East Berlin, and by then it was too late.

But the principal reason why the uranium and, for that matter, the coal miners of Saxony played such a minor part in the strike was that in Saxony, as in the harbors on the Baltic coast, the Soviets intervened very quickly to nip any incipient disturbances in the bud. It seems that, even during their June maneuvers, the Soviets maintained garrisons in areas of major importance such as the uranium district of southern Saxony and the shipyards on the Baltic. Consequently, they were able to act at a moment's notice in these areas, whereas in other parts of the GDR there was a time lag of several hours because the troops had to be transported from their field maneuvers to the various trouble spots.

Along with the iron ore and potassium miners and the construction workers, the workers in heavy industry also played an important part in the strike. So too did those in various essential industries. In nine out of ten of the major iron and steel works in the GDR, for example, there were stoppages or riots. At first sight it seems surprising to find that it was these highly paid workers who took strike action and not those employed in the less remunerative sectors of the economy, such as the state controlled trading concerns or the hotel, food and textile industries. But there were good reasons for this.

In the first place, the workers in the essential industries had been subjected to particularly heavy pressure during the government's propaganda campaign for a voluntary increase in work quotas. The state economists had argued forcibly that, since wages were high in these industries, productivity should be correspondingly high. Between January 1952 and June 1953 *Der Neue Weg,* a journal concerned with the practical application of party policy, published twenty-three articles on productivity in the iron and steel producing plants in the GDR, twenty-six articles on productivity in the coal, electricity and gas industries and in various works producing raw materials for the chemical industry, thirty-six articles on productivity in works engaged in heavy machine construction but only one article on productivity in a branch of the publicly owned HO.

However, the pressure brought to bear on these workers to increase their productivity (despite the progressive decline in their living standards) was only one of the reasons why they opted for strike action. They also struck because they knew they were indispensable.

Like the construction workers on the Stalin-Allee, they were fully aware that the regime needed them in order to fulfill its economic plans. If necessary, administrative and commercial workers could be replaced. So could the workers in the consumer industries. And if the quantity and quality of the consumer goods produced in the GDR failed to meet the people's needs or if the efficiency of the state trading organizations constantly declined, then these were not matters of great concern to the SED regime. But the program for heavy industry was of the utmost importance, and it could not be achieved without skilled workers. This was why higher wages had been paid in the essential industries, and it was why special shops had been installed on factory and work sites in February 1953 when there was a shortage of food. It was also why the SED had been forced to accept the fact that far fewer industrial workers had become party members than it would have liked. Undoubtedly, these workers would have known that the regime depended absolutely on their loyal cooperation and simply could not afford to have them shot down in the streets, since this would have resulted in the total collapse of the economic structure of the GDR.

Over and above this, of course, the workers must also have known that, for purely ideological reasons, the regime would want to avoid using force at all costs. For the SED campaign for the build-up of heavy industry had been conceived as a program of socialist industrialization. In other words, it was to have established socialist working conditions in the GDR. Opposition on the part of independent craftsmen or small commercial firms would merely have served to confirm the government's thesis that the transition to socialism would necessarily involve a bitter class struggle. But resistance by the workers—especially those employed in essential industries—would undermine its whole conception of the state, in which the working and agricultural classes were to have become the ruling class and to have played the central role. After all, the GDR was supposed to be a workers' state and the government of the GDR merely an instrument for the representation of the workers' interests.

There was only one big works engaged in heavy industry that did not join the strike. This was the Eisenhüttenkombinat Ost, the new foundry then in course of construction at Stalinstadt (now Eisenhüttenstadt) near Frankfort on the Oder, where it was ideally situated to receive supplies of coal from the East and iron ore from Sweden.

In 1953, Stalinstadt was the largest industrial installation in the GDR. But, quite apart from its importance to the economy, this enormous project—which was described at the time as "the first socialist town in Germany"—also fulfilled a political function, for it constituted the first systematic attempt to restructure a cross-section of German society. Stalinstadt was supposed to become what Stammer has called a "socialist fortress," in other words a model of the new socialist way of life that would break down the old capitalist structure and then reshape it along entirely different lines.

In 1953 the wages in Stalinstadt were higher than those in any other town in the GDR. Because of this and because of the novelty value of living in a "socialist town" there was a large influx of workers. Most of these were young men, many of whom came from the former German territories east of the Oder. In 1954, the proportion of refugee workers living in Stalinstadt was estimated at nearly 50 per cent of the total work force. Previously, when they had been living in other towns in the GDR, these refugees had found it difficult to compete with the indigenous workers and had tended to get the worst-paid jobs. This explains why they showed a greater willingness to offer themselves as guinea pigs for this socialist experiment than their native counterparts, most of whom preferred to remain in their familiar and trusted environment, even when a financial sacrifice was involved.

We see, therefore, that the workers in Stalinstadt had little financial incentive to join the strike. But they were not only far better paid than the other workers in the GDR; they also lacked the sort of cohesion found among the personnel of established concerns, which is one of the prerequisites of concerted action. This was due partly to the fact that the entire work force consisted of newcomers, the vast majority of whom had been strangers to one another before their arrival, and partly to the sharp watch kept by the party on the political attitudes of these workers. Neither of these factors made for close human relationships and it is hardly surprising that the industrial workers of Stalinstadt showed no sense of solidarity with their colleagues in other parts of the GDR. The only demonstrations in this town on June 17 were those staged by the itinerant construction workers.

Consequently, when the troubles were over, the regime was able to comfort itself with the thought that the new experimental town at least had remained true to its socialist principles. In actual fact, of course, the reason why the industrial workers of Stalinstadt failed to strike was that they lacked the necessary sense of solidarity. Unlike the workers in so many of the older industrial centers (who were also receiving comparatively high wages but who nonetheless took strike action on June 17) they were rendered incapable of concerted action by their feelings of isolation. It remains to be seen whether the workers of the large new industrial centers that have now been developed in the GDR acquire a sense of solidarity in the years to come. If they do, and if they should decide to oppose the government *en bloc,* the SED could find itself in a highly precarious situation.

✦

THE SIGNIFICANCE OF TRADITION

The solidarity of the workers, whose effectiveness had already been demonstrated in the dispute over the collective agreements, was the principal reason for the initial success of the events of June 16 and 17.

It is difficult to assess the extent to which this new postwar solidarity was influenced by trade union or political tradition. Certainly, the biggest demonstrations were mounted in places like Magdeburg, Leipzig and Halle, which had always been centers of the working class movement. And even if the members of the younger generation—who were responsible for setting up most of the strike committees and were in fact the mainstay of the whole strike—had no firsthand knowledge of the old working class movement, they may quite conceivably have been told about the aims and beliefs of the movement by their parents and older colleagues. Nonetheless, I have been unable to discover in the reports to which I had access any reference to the "traditional accounts of the old social and political working class movement" which, according to Willy Brandt, exerted a considerable influence on the events of June 17. Perhaps they did. But there is no way of proving it.

What is quite certain, however, is that the demonstrations in the traditionally communist districts of the GDR were no less vehement than those in the old Social Democrat districts. It seems as if all ancient conflicts were resolved by the common bond of opposition to the new regime. This was already apparent at the elections for the Berlin municipal parliament in 1946 when the communists, who had obtained more votes than the Social Democrats in Berlin during the closing phase of the Weimar Republic, suffered a heavy defeat at the hands of the German Social Democratic Party (SPD): 48.7 per cent of the valid votes cast went to the SPD and only 19.8 per cent to the SED.

At the first postwar election in the Russian zone the SPD and the German Communist Party (KPD) shared the same platform, which meant that the electors in the zone—unlike those in Berlin—were not able to vote SPD without voting KPD. Nonetheless, the bourgeois parties did remarkably well, for in none of the provincial assemblies did the SED obtain an absolute majority. In Sachsen-Anhalt, a province consisting of a sparsely populated, mainly agricultural area in the north and a densely populated, industrial area in the south (centered on the towns of Magdeburg, Halle, Merseburg and Bitterfeld), the SED received 45.8 per cent of the valid votes in the provincial election, the Christian Democratic Union (CDU) 21.9 per cent and the Farmer's Association for Mutual Aid (VdgB) 2.4 per cent. With its bourgeois majority the provincial assembly of Sachsen-Anhalt had a Liberal Democratic Prime Minister in 1946. In view of the success of the bourgeois parties and the high percentage of spoiled votes cast at that time it seems reasonable to assume that a considerable number of the workers will have voted for the CDU or Liberal Democratic Party (LDP) or else have spoiled their ballot papers.

In any event, it was in the district of Halle and Merseburg, where the communists had been the strongest single party during the Weimar period, that the largest demonstrations were staged. Other strike centers, such as Magdeburg and Leipzig, had of course been Social Democrat strongholds prior to 1933. In the early 1950's when they heard Ernst Reuter speaking on the radio, many Magdeburgers will have recalled their former Oberbürgermeister. Only a month before the rising—on May 19, 1953—the Central Committee published a detailed resolution, in which it censured the local SED leaders in the Magdeburg district for failing to pursue the socialist restructuring of the city with sufficient force. And, after June 17, Otto Grotewohl was obliged to explain that "in certain towns, such as Magdeburg, Leipzig and others" there were "illegal organizations of former SPD members, who still cling to Social Democrat conceptions that are inimical to the workers." This theme was one that was subsequently taken up by the Central Committee of the party.

We know from various sources—many of them unimportant in themselves—that in both the former communist district of Halle (where the Leuna Works are situated) and in the former Social Democrat district of Magdeburg even the SED party members were no more than lukewarm in their advocacy of the SED brand of socialism. Thus, in its issue of December 1952, *Der Neue Weg* severely criticized the party members employed at the Leuna Works and those living in the towns of Halle and Magdeburg for buying so few communist journals. It appears that only 19.5 per cent of all party members in Halle, 18.7 per cent in Magdeburg and 11.8 per cent at the Leuna Works were regular subscribers to *Der Neue Weg*. These were the lowest figures in the whole of the GDR, which meant that Halle, Magdeburg and Leuna were failing in their duty to support this important organ for the dissemination of information about the practical aspects of party work.

The Uprising in Retrospect

◆

Richard Lowenthal

The late Richard Lowenthal, longtime faculty member at the Free University in Berlin, was one of Europe's most incisive commentators on developments in the Soviet Union and Eastern Europe. This 1965 essay appeared as the introduction to the Baring volume and affords an additional perspective on the meaning of the uprising.

The first comprehensive accounts of the East German rising of June 17 were written under the direct impact of events. Inevitably, every line of these works reflected the feelings of contemporary West Germans, who had witnessed the revolutionary incidents in the German Democratic Republic (GDR) as deeply sympathetic but powerless bystanders. No matter how conscientiously these early writers strove after objectivity, they could not avoid expressing their sense of human and political solidarity with the oppressed workers of the GDR, their indignation over the coercive methods that had provoked the demonstrations, their satisfaction at finding people capable of attempting the impossible by taking such sudden and completely spontaneous action, and their bitter disappointment over their own impotence—or failure?—and over the fruitless outcome of the rising.

Twelve years later, most of us still entertained such feelings. But, because we expressed them so often, they became unbearably hackneyed: protestations of indignation which do not lead to action must inevitably degenerate into meaningless rhetoric. At this time such rhetoric, far from illuminating the events of June 17, tends to obscure their true significance, especially for the younger generation that has grown

Richard Lowenthal, "The Uprising in Retrospect," from Arnulf M. Baring, *Uprising in East Germany, June 17, 1953*, pp. xix–xxvii. Translated from the German by Gerald Onn, with an introduction by David Schoenbaum and a foreword by Richard Lowenthal. Copyright © 1972 by Cornell University. Used by permission of the publisher, Cornell University Press.

up in the post-Stalin era. In his objective study, however, Baring deals with the historical aspects of June 17. He explains what actually happened, he analyzes the factors underlying the rising, and he discusses its consequences. And, having done so, he allows the reader to make his own value judgments.

It is now left to me to sketch in the international background of the specific events dealt with by Baring. This involves two principal factors: the economic and political crisis that began to emerge in the Soviet bloc in the months immediately following Stalin's death and the discussions entered into at that time with a view to reopening negotiations between the four great powers in order to resolve the German question.

When Stalin died on March 5, 1953, the economic resources of the Soviet Union and its European satellites were dangerously overstretched. Instead of trying to bring about a relaxation of tension following the breakdown of his postwar offensive in Europe in 1948–1949, Stalin had reacted to the failure of the Berlin Blockade, the secession of Yugoslavia, the ending of the Greek civil war, and the founding of NATO by persecuting the Titoist sympathizers in eastern Europe and by promoting the Korean War in 1950. His unwillingness to bring this war to an end was one of the principal reasons why the western powers, especially America, embarked on a massive rearmament program and made the decision to rearm the Federal Republic. In the closing years of his life Stalin vacillated between half-hearted attempts to establish a détente and frenzied efforts to rearm. And the peoples of the Soviet bloc had to pay for this policy. Quotas for armaments and heavy industries were increased again and again even though, once industrial reserves and reserves of raw materials had been used up, these projects could only be pursued by reducing to an absolute minimum the production program of the consumer goods and agricultural industries, which presupposed a similar reduction in the standard of living of the population. In the winter of 1952–1953 the growing food crisis led, in one satellite state after another, to a reduction of productivity even in heavy industries, where the workers were receiving preferential treatment. At this point Stalin's rearmament policy reached its absolute limit. The "combing out" of small industrial concerns, freelance craftsmen, and commercial firms in the Soviet zone of Germany within the framework of Ulbricht's program for the "establishment of socialism," which had such a tangible effect on East German living standards, was just a special instance of the general crisis in the Soviet bloc.

Because of this crisis Stalin's heirs received calls for help and warnings of impending disaster from the satellite states within months of taking office. They were quick to react to the worsening situation. In April 1953, Moscow began to evolve a new line which provided for concessions to the farmers, workers, and consumers and for foreign policy initiatives aimed at bringing about a relaxation of tension in international relations with a view to slowing down the arms race. Internal concessions went hand in hand with attempts to achieve an external détente. Thus, the speedy conclusion of the long-drawn-out armistice negotiations in Korea and Malenkov's assurances that, given the necessary good will, all international problems could be peacefully resolved were in complete accord with the new developments taking place throughout the Soviet bloc. These included the change of course forced on the Socialist Unity

Party (Sozialistische Einheitspartei Deutschlands, SED) leadership on June 9; the relaxation of government pressure on the Czech workers following the disturbances in Pilsen, which were sparked off at the beginning of June by the confiscatory "currency reform" introduced by the Czech communist party; the establishment in Hungary on July 4 of Imre Nagy's first government, which proposed to increase the production of consumer goods and to allow the Hungarian farmers to opt out of the agricultural collectives; and, finally, "Malenkov's gifts" to the Soviet farmers (remission of tax arrears and the reduction of taxes on privately owned land), which were coupled with the announcement by the Soviet Premier to the Supreme Soviet, on August 8, of a decision to step up the production of consumer goods in the USSR. The decision made by the new leaders in Moscow to combat the crisis by reducing the economic pressure on the workers was also reflected in the changes effected in other Soviet bloc countries, where overambitious projects for heavy industry were canceled and concessions were granted to the working population.

But these proposed changes in Soviet economic and foreign policy had to be carried out in conditions of considerable uncertainty by men who were embroiled in an internal struggle for the succession. Under a leadership that was still far from firmly established and whose authority had been greatly diminished, to retreat too far from Stalin's policies could easily be interpreted as a sign of weakness. How far could the new men go with their liberalization plans without losing control of the situation? The attempt to bring about a détente abroad raised a similar question: to what extent were the western powers prepared to collaborate and what would they demand in return? Both in Moscow and, to a lesser degree, in the satellite states, power struggles within the communist leadership arose out of the question of how much liberalization should be allowed at home and how much détente abroad. It was the confluence of these and other related factors—as Baring points out in his study—that provoked the rising of June 17 in the GDR: the pent-up bitterness that was the legacy of the preceding period of extreme economic pressure, the abruptness of the change following Semyonov's directive of June 9, the arguments between Ulbricht and his critics in the Politburo of the SED over the extent of the change and the uncertainty that this created among the rank and file of the SED all combined to produce a revolutionary situation. Elsewhere in the Soviet bloc similar circumstances also led to a resurgence of individualistic activity, although not on the same scale as in the GDR: following the sudden change of government and the introduction of the new line in Hungary countless farmers decided to leave the agricultural collectives, with the result that the country's agricultural land, equipment, and stock were divided up in the middle of the harvest and in a completely haphazard fashion. Meanwhile, when the news of the East German rising reached the Soviet Union—where the authority of the state in general and the power of the secret police in particular had been greatly undermined following Beria's overthrow—it triggered a wave of strikes in the penal colonies, most of which were subsequently closed down as a direct consequence. Eventually the mass exodus from the collective farms in Hungary played an important part in the power struggle between the reform-minded head of the Hungarian government, Imre Nagy, and the Stalinist party leader, Rakosi, just as the rising of June 17 became one of the crucial factors in Ulbricht's victory over his rivals and in all probability contributed to Beria's downfall in Moscow.

The particularly close connection between the internal struggles fought out in the summer of 1953 by the leaders of the SED, on the one hand, and the leaders of the Soviet communist party, on the other, was due to the key position occupied by East Germany in the Soviet Union's policy of détente. Ever since the autumn of 1950 Stalin had been trying, without success, to prevent the rearming of the Federal Republic within the framework of NATO by making more or less vague offers of negotiations. When he died, the Bonn and Paris treaties had been signed but had not yet come into effect. Consequently, Stalin's heirs had to decide whether to enter into new negotiations with the other great powers on the German question and, if necessary, offer reunification in freedom in return for guarantees of German neutrality under the terms of a definitive peace treaty. By then they knew—from Churchill's speech of May 11, 1953—that the English Prime Minister wanted a four-power conference in the near future to negotiate just such a treaty. In this connection Churchill had spoken of a German Locarno.

There are many indications that, at the beginning of June 1953, not only Beria, but a majority of the Soviet party presidium led by Malenkov, was in favor of this proposal. The fact that Khrushchev subsequently accused his two vanquished rivals of wanting to sell out to the West in this way means little in itself. But everything that is known about Semyonov's behavior in Berlin in the days just before the rising fits in with this hypothesis. It seems certain, for example, that he encouraged Herrnstadt and Zaisser in their opposition to Ulbricht. Moreover, the rumors circulating at that time—even among the top functionaries of the SED—to the effect that the party might well have to go into opposition and might even be declared illegal seem to have originated in suggestions made by the Soviet High Commissar after his return from Moscow. The failure to discipline Semyonov after Beria's downfall suggests that his actions had been approved, not only by Beria, but also by the competent official departments. Moreover, this would explain why Herrnstadt and Zaisser, who were subsequently deprived of their party membership for forming factions within the party, were not also arraigned on a criminal charge of seditious complicity with Beria.

It seems that only after the events of June 17 did the majority of the Soviet party presidium, and especially Malenkov, come out against the proposed policy for the settlement of the German question, which was then condemned as "capitulationary" and, for a while, ascribed to Beria alone. Although Beria's arrest was not announced to the public until July 9, we know from subsequent official statements that the decision to move against him was made on June 26. The other members of the presidium doubtless had many reasons for wanting to overthrow the powerful chief of the secret police. But the time chosen for this action would suggest that he had been isolated at a critical moment by the failure of the German policy that he had been actively promoting. What is quite certain is that Ulbricht's opponents in the Politburo of the SED continued their struggle even after June 17 and were not subdued until after Beria's downfall. In short, the Soviet leadership began to have second thoughts about the proposal for a "Solution of the German Question through Negotiations" after the East German rising and finally rejected it following Beria's elimination.

Does it follow from this that the popular rising of June 17 was the principal reason for the Soviets' change of course? If so, it would mean that the striking and demonstrating workers in the Soviet zone had tragically achieved the precise opposite of what they had come to regard in the course of the rising as their ultimate aim. Certainly, the Soviet leaders were influenced by the events of June 17. But these were no more than the proximate cause of their change of policy. The underlying and far more important cause was the passivity of western and West German foreign policy in the critical months following Stalin's death. Moscow had taken note of Churchill's initiative; the western and West German government departments had not. The State Department and the Office of the Federal Chancellor, the Quai D'Orsay, and even Churchill's own Foreign Office showed no inclination to jeopardize the incorporation of the Federal Republic into the western alliance, which had already been decided but still awaited ratification, by entering into discussions of the German question at a four-power conference. Meanwhile, Churchill himself was taken ill shortly after making his speech of May 11, and was unable to pursue this proposal any further. Under the circumstances the prospects of a compromise settlement of the German question, which his initiative had seemed to hold out, must have appeared less promising from week to week. And the dangers of adopting a vacillatory policy over Germany, which were clearly demonstrated on June 17, would have impressed themselves on the Soviet leaders all the more forcefully the more these prospects faded.

Considered in these terms, June 17 was not only a day of crisis for the Soviet Union but also a missed opportunity for the western powers. Such opportunities never recur in the same form, but they do contain lessons for those prepared to learn from them. At the present writing Russia again has a collective government, in which the distribution of power still seems uncertain and temporary. One of the problems on which its members will have to adopt a common attitude is the same as that which faced Stalin's heirs: the extent of a possible détente between East and West and the significance of the German question within that process. Today, of course, there are no signs of a popular rising in the German Democratic Republic or of a new opportunity to resolve the whole of the German question by diplomatic measures. But even the more modest opportunities open to us can only be put to profitable use if, instead of waiting for the Soviet leadership to clarify its position, the western powers try to influence that process by putting forward constructive proposals. In Germany today people have far greater knowledge of the factors involved than they had in 1953; by studying this history of June 17 they can increase their knowledge still further.

Why Is There No Political Change in the GDR?

✦

Peter Ludz

Based on his 1968 lectures at Harvard, the late Peter Ludz attempts here to answer the question posed in his title, a perennial puzzle to students of East Germany in that era.

In 1963–1964, various observers of the GDR expected that the economic reforms would sooner or later bring about basic political changes as well. They were fascinated by the prospect that dynamic economic changes might automatically set loose new forces in other areas of the society, especially in politics. Others believed that the economic reforms were themselves to be equated with political liberalization.

These vain hopes and false predictions were understandable, for the "professional pessimists" in the Federal Republic of Germany had for all too long predicted that everything would continue to go badly in the GDR. From a psychological point of view, the time for a basic reassessment seemed to have come. However, as so often happens, the reassessment went too far. Since the GDR had for so long enjoyed such low repute in the FRG and elsewhere in the West, observers have in recent years tended to exaggerate the potential for economic and educational modernization in East Germany.

In starting to discuss the question of why there is and has been no political change in the GDR, we should first of all make clear what we mean by the term "change." Change is a sociological concept as well as one in general use in the social sciences. In research about Eastern Europe, this term serves to characterize sociopolitical processes leading to a situation in which different social and political factions can articulate interests and organize themselves. Political change involving a *de facto* authoritarian one-party state would in this framework of analysis denote a change toward a more pluralistic political system. If we take the concept of "political change" to its logical conclusion, it means a very basic alteration of the structures and attitudes of government, both within the present political elite and in the populace.

Realistically speaking, there would seem to be little prospect for such a funda-

Peter Ludz, "Why Is There No Political Change in the GDR?" from *The German Democratic Republic from the Sixties to the Seventies,* Harvard University Press, 1970, pp. 52–57. Reprinted by permission of the Harvard University Center for International Affairs and the University Press of America.

mental political change in the ruling structures of the GDR as presently constituted. The SED [Sozialistische Einherlspartei Deutschlands, or Socialist Unity Party] leadership exercises such tight control over GDR society that such a thoroughgoing political transformation of the system seems out of the question, for the present at least.

On the other hand, we must not be overly pessimistic in this regard. If we project the present processes of increased upward social mobility (the "career society" motivations inculcated in society), plus the trends of present economic expansion, we can see certain long-range prospects for gradual, evolutionary changes *in* (not *of*) the system. If this is a valid assumption, we should consider the "vulnerability zones" of the party's power, that is, how closely it *must* or *can* control the processes it set in motion during most of the 1960s. Put another way, how far should the dictates of efficiency intrude upon purely political-power considerations of preserving the present system of government?

More specific questions also arise in this context. For example, within the Politburo proper, what policies advocated by representatives of the party's technical experts should be accepted, albeit grudgingly, by its dogmatist members, and to what extent? Also, to what degree should the "experts" in the Politburo accommodate to the policies formulated by those representing the dogmatic strains? As far as we can determine, the "specialist" wing in the Politburo has not been able to attain unquestioned preeminence, largely because of Ulbricht's tactical ability. On the other hand, this wing is influential to the degree that a consensus now prevails in the SED's ruling body that any further change in the system must not be at the high political cost of widespread terror.

Major problems in both foreign and domestic policy face the leadership. In foreign policy they are: political and economic pressures from the Soviet Union, the continuing effects of communist polycentrism, and the influence, basically psychological, of the FRG. The problems rooted in the GDR domestic situation are even more complicated. The two sets of factors influence each other.

✦

SOURCES OF POLITICAL INSTABILITY

As we have already asserted, the *political* system of the GDR has remained unstable. We can adduce a variety of reasons to substantiate this line of argument.

First and foremost, substantial segments of the population continue to withhold unqualified, active support from the party and its policies. In fact many are still either openly hostile to the SED or totally uninvolved in political matters.

Secondly, there has not been any widespread development of a "national consciousness," of any widely accepted system of social behavioral norms, or of the "socialist" style of life propounded by the party. Therefore, the average citizen remains insecure in his conceptions of "correct" everyday political behavior—though one must concede that the overall atmosphere in this respect is now far from being as oppressive as it was in 1961 and 1962.

Finally, the GDR remains locked into step with the Soviet Union as far as foreign policy is concerned. Only in recent years, moreover, has it achieved a certain autonomy in matters of domestic policy.

We shall now go into these arguments in more detail. Put briefly, it is our thesis that the present situation in the GDR is one of political instability combined with some degree of socio-economic stability. One of the most important factors in the tendency toward socio-economic stability has been the development of the concept of a "career society." For the people to regard careers in society as offering promise for the future, there must first of all be a basic confidence in the country and society in which these careers are to be pursued. This confidence is necessarily related to the "dependability" or "predictability" of the standards and criteria for occupational and social advancement established by the state or the party. Ample reason for such confidence evidently exists today for hundreds of thousands of ambitious working people in the GDR.

However, when one turns to the political scene, one finds confidence in the political rulers and in the basic precepts of the system in general sorely lacking. This is true even for many of those who represent political power. It is not without good reason that the "independence" or "autonomy" of the GDR are monotonously paraded at every opportunity. One gets the impression that this continuous self-assertion is rooted in deep feelings of insecurity and anxiety. Ulbricht's patent political dependence on the USSR has helped both to create and to reinforce this impression; the close identification of SED Politburo policies with the course of the Soviet Union has, in the twenty years since the founding of the GDR, only gradually given way to a somewhat more independent policy, and really only in domestic matters. There are good reasons for this. As has already been pointed out, Ulbricht and the other political leaders know that their close identification with the Soviet Union represents their only chance to assume a relatively important position in the Eastern Bloc, and to a certain degree in European politics as well. They know that this international position can only be consolidated if the GDR proves itself an especially reliable partner of the Soviet Union. A concurrent disadvantage of this policy is, however, a heavy political and economic dependence on the Soviets. Psychologically, this dependency has had a double effect: on the one hand, the SED leadership follows the directives of Moscow or at least waits until the positions adopted by the Kremlin are clear, when it usually adopts them itself with no prompting. On the other hand, the people do not consider the GDR a sovereign state because they feel the result of this dependency deeply. In the light of these psychological and political considerations, the GDR can hardly be considered a sovereign state. In the GDR we find no "national" consciousness in the traditional sense of the term.

◆

THE STRUGGLE AGAINST REVISIONISM

A further factor influencing both domestic and foreign policy is the SED leadership's phobia against any type of revisionism. The men in power define the term "revisionism" as standing for any type of thinking having to do with political and social change which does not originate within the SED leadership itself. Ulbricht, in particular, fears the discussion of ideological principles—insofar as he cannot initiate and control such debate himself. This is, on the one hand, a reflection of the authoritarian ruling style of the SED's First Secretary. On the other hand, however, the phenomenon has roots in the history of the KPD [Kommunistische Partei Deutschlands, the Communist Party of Germany] and the SED.

In his career Ulbricht has always made prominent individuals in the party scapegoats for political deviations. As early as in the forties and fifties, discussion of political principles had resulted in conflict among SED factions. In the period from 1954 to 1958, Zaisser and Herrnstadt, Schirdewan, Wollweber and Oelssner, and even the political utopian, Harich, were eliminated in such struggles. Some discussion of principle is permitted, but the ultimate verdict is rendered solely by Ulbricht. This was true, for example, in the case of a series of practical suggestions for the reorganization of the economic system which had been formulated as early as 1956–1957 by such "revisionist" economists as Professor Fritz Behrens, one of the outstanding men in this field in the GDR. At that time, Behrens had called for the greater autonomy of enterprises and the delegation of day-to-day economic decision-making to subordinate bodies—thus proving himself to be a precurser of the Liberman reforms in the USSR in the mid 1960s. His suggestions were rejected by the party leadership as "revisionist" and were dismissed without any serious discussion. A few years later, at a time which was politically far more auspicious, Ulbricht adopted Behrens' suggestions and in part implemented them. Therefore, the complex history of East German revisionism must be considered whenever one speaks of politically or ideologically deviant thought in that country, as must all the nuances and connotations which the word "revisionism" has in communist usage.

The rejection of revisionist thinking extends to all segments of the leading groups of the SED, though for different motives. Ulbricht and the conservative party leaders have committed themselves ideologically so strongly that they can not accept or even discuss a clearly deviant political or ideological line. Thus, they sift out and attack all conceptions which deviate from the existing official line. Even younger, ideologically more flexible party leaders, the specialists, managers, and technocrats, have a deep aversion to ideological revisionism, at least in its traditional forms. These men have always seen themselves mainly as pragmatic reformers of the system. They are filled with a deep mistrust of the literary representatives of utopian revisionism, who often had few misgivings about supporting Stalinism. Actually, Stalinism and the literary variants of utopian revisionism were worlds apart. However, in their abstract-dogmatic and totalitarian features, and in their styles of viewing the world and its problems, they were similar. The long-time giants among revisionists—Georg Lukács, Ernst Bloch, Robert Havemann, even their most famous representative in the younger generation, Wolfgang Harich—for a time had, each in his own way, supported Stalinism ideologically—and morally as well, in the eyes of the critical generation of technocrats. The abstract utopias of humanistic socialism had apparently been compatible with a political maneuverability. The critical younger party leaders would probably be more attracted by such authors as Christa Wolf, whose marxistic "morality" would seem more honest intellectually.

However, the younger specialists in the party, like Günter Mittag, reject utopian revisionism in its classical definition for other reasons as well. They do not feel that abstract philosophical theorems about the nature of man and society can be translated into forward-looking policies in this day and age. The political theories of representatives of this utopian thinking—such as Wolfgang Harich's "Platform"—are lacking in concreteness and in political judgment about the potentials and limitations of political action. Thus, to men like Mittag, demands made in 1956 for the abolition of the National People's Army and for the "liberalization of the SED" betray a lack of sensitivity to the political realities of the GDR. The younger specialists realize that in general there is in East Germany a weariness with ideological slogans. For the "new men" in the party the real questions involve concrete, incremental improvements, such as decentralization of the decision-making process and a more direct participation in the economic process on the part of all those involved. On the whole, however, it is not likely that the younger groups will fight "revisionism" in the way the dogmatists have done and—given an appropriate situation—would presumably do again.

These considerations lead us to ask whether, at present or in the foreseeable future, there is any chance for revisionist thinking in the GDR at all. In the context of our analysis we would briefly answer this question as follows: the major goals of the party's leadership in foreign policy—attainment of wide international recognition plus a continuing close relationship with the Soviet Union—are by now so firmly established that they can hardly be questioned, even in the context of discussions which would officially be labelled "revisionist." The same holds true for some basic issues of domestic policy.

However, revisionist approaches still exist, in ideology, literature, the philosophy of arts, and so on. If they gained a certain prominence, they would probably be fought by the party leaders in the traditional way. On the other hand, a new kind of revisionism is emerging, to which the party leadership reacts in a different way, thus widening the range of intra-party discussion.

The Unofficial Peace Movement in the GDR

✦

Peter Wensierski

This study, presented in 1983 at a symposium on the GDR by a researcher from Berlin, offers a succinct account of an East German phenomenon almost unique in Eastern Europe, a grass-roots movement for peace that by implication challenges the official claim by governments of the region that their stand for peace renders popular movements redundant.

If an atomic bomb were to detonate directly over the Brandenburg Gate, then within a fraction of a second all auto bodies in Charlottenburg [West Berlin] and Pankow [East Berlin] would evaporate. In more distant city districts such as Marzahn [East Berlin] and Märkisches Viertel [West Berlin] the cars would melt. Even the concrete pilings of the bridge over the Spree near the Friedrichstrasse train station would vanish. In Wannsee or Königswusterhausen on the outskirts of Berlin—many kilometers from groundzero—the clothing of pedestrians would catch fire."

This vision of a possible atomic inferno was painted by a twenty-two-year-old woman at a peace meeting in East Berlin in July 1983. Such concrete descriptions made it clear to all those present that in Berlin, which lies directly on the seismic fault between East and West, the consequences of a nuclear war would be particularly absurd. A young woman from Potsdam added, "Since the politicians of the past thirty years have not succeeded in bringing us closer to peace, we will have to introduce new concepts of peace ourselves."

Such an opinion is no longer rare in the GDR. An awakening which seemed impossible only a few years ago is occurring among the younger generation. The GDR is presently in the midst of one of the most interesting political and cultural transitions it has ever experienced. Thanks to a sufficient degree of government stability and continuity, on the one hand, and changes in consciousness and perceived needs in some parts of the population, on the other, a process has come into being in the 1980s, the political significance of which has not yet been fully recognized in the West.

The state's unusual toleration of non-official peace activities within the church in recent years must be seen in this light. (In spite of the sporadic repression of individuals there has been no direct confrontation with the church as an institution.) That is, the system is moving in the direction of a more relaxed and more flexible domestic policy. Today one encounters the most varied attitudes in the GDR: both amazing political tolerance and traditional conservative *Sicherheitspolitik*. Using the example of the unofficial peace movement, I will discuss these developing tendencies and thus attempt to shed light on the situation of the GDR in the 1980s.

Terms such as "peace movement" and "peace" have been monopolized by the GDR state since its founding in 1949; the mandate to "serve the cause of peace" is anchored in the constitution. For decades, virtually on a daily basis, the mass media have appealed to the individual to make his personal contribution. One means of supporting peace is the "all-around strengthening of socialism," which implies primarily that the population work ever more productively in order to develop an economically strong state. An SED [Sozialistische Einheitspartei Deutschlands, or Socialist Unity Party] slogan reads: "The stronger socialism becomes, the more secure peace will be." Another method is much more direct: long-term military service in the National People's Army (NVA). Here the motto is "Peace must be armed."

Today several tens of thousands of primarily young people in the GDR have their own personal conception of meaningful peace initiatives. They are not seeking confrontation with the state, and do not dispute that the government's desire for peace is genuine, but they differ from the state in regard to the mode of securing peace and the concept of peace itself. Instead of relying on military strength and deterrence, they envision the joint securing of peace by means of gradual disarming and confidence-building measures. They believe that external peace depends on the internal peace of a society. Thus the concept of peace is broadened to include societal and environmental well-being.

This unofficial peace movement cannot be defined as classically dissident and isn't hiding behind some popular issue while in reality desiring something entirely different (i.e., a complete change of the system or "Sturz der Herrschenden"); it is not pro-West in its orientation. These peace activists are unorganized—precisely because everything else in the GDR is. Still, they are very much a movement; their concerns bind them together in a non-institutionalized manner, and they believe that collectively they can bring about political change. The existential threat of nuclear war has awakened in them a feeling of co-responsibility for the securing of peace.

It was not possible for the young people to form their own peace organization, to open their own offices, hold their own demonstrations, etc. They could and did however join forces with the one relatively autonomous mass organization in the GDR, the evangelical churches, to which half of the GDR population—approximately eight million people—still belongs. The new peace initiative merged with that of the church. This is a source of conflicts within church peace groups: conflicts between Christian-motivated and politically motivated peace engagement.

The GDR church has been nurturing its own peace conceptions for decades.

The church's definition of peace is rooted in the Gospel; its essentials include non-violence, love of one's enemies, and trust. In spite of the common utopian vision of an unarmed and non-violent future, fundamental tensions between the Christian and socialist understanding of peace still remain. The characteristic stringency of the socialist definition of peace excludes the possibility of any other position. Still, the churches in the GDR, as the only organizations which have retained their autonomy in the face of the SED's virtual monopoly in representing the populace, have a unique role in GDR society, a role which churches in the West, where there are many autonomous social institutions, do not play.

Two examples of church peace work during the past two decades seem particularly pertinent: the church's strong support of the right of conscientious objection during the 1960s and its present support of a non-military alternative form of service ("Sozialer Friedensdienst"); and its struggle against the introduction of military instruction ("Wehrkundeunterricht") as a required course for ninth and tenth graders in the schools in the late 1970s.

The months prior to the introduction of "Wehrkundeunterricht" in September 1978 were filled with waves of petitions ("Eingaben") from individuals and groups addressed to the state authorities. Appeals were also made to the churches in the hope that they might aid in the struggle to convince the authorities to cancel their plans to instate this new school course. The ensuing church protest failed. This relatively stormy and public dispute between church and state did result however in increased sensitivity on the part of the church and population in regard to subsequent state measures which have led to an ever greater militarization of GDR society.

Since the introduction of military instruction for ninth and tenth graders in 1978, military "fitness-making procedures" have been extended to include eleventh graders and apprentices. All students (including not only theologians, but also women) at state universities are now required to attend paramilitary sports camps during school vacations. The campaign to encourage voluntary longer enlistment in the army has been strengthened; obligating oneself to serve three years, instead of eighteen months, in the military is, for example, sometimes made a condition for boys' being allowed to go on to the *Erweiterte Oberschule*.

The fight against this militarization of society has played a major role in the peace work of the church as well as of the youth groups on the fringe of church activities. An example is the initiative requesting the creation of a "Sozialer Friedensdienst," an alternative form of service completely outside the military. In May 1981 three co-workers of the Evangelical Lutheran Church of Saxony composed a petition, which was circulated throughout the country and had collected 5,000 signatures by the fall. Church leaders presented the case to the government, which responded with a resounding "no" on the issue.

A second example is the open letter to Erich Honecker written by the East Berlin pastor Rainer Eppelmann and made public in September 1981. In this appeal Eppelmann demanded an end to certain militaristic aspects of GDR society including: the distribution of war toys, the glorification of soldiers in school classes, school visits to army barracks, the presence of military hardware at carnivals, and military parades on national holidays. He also demanded the elimination of all measures against persons who express pacifist views.

Such demands are typical. They show that the GDR non-state peace movement is rooted in the specific conditions of GDR society and was not imported from the West. This peace initiative existed long before the missile dispute and the Western mass demonstrations.

The church protest against the introduction of military instruction in the schools in 1978 was not a hand-picked act of peace; it was rather a simple reflex action to measures taken by the state. This dispute evoked, however, the desire for a long-term and well-planned peace effort. Peace committees were set up in churches; one of the slogans they devised: "Education for Peace." In the following I will sketch the development of the church-supported peace movement in the 1980s, giving some of the milestones, and then go on to discuss the peace activities and concepts of the young people.

A thesis paper, written in 1979 by the Friedensreferat der Theologischen Studienabteilung beim DDR-Kirchenbund and addressed to peace groups, criticizes the tactics of the state peace movement:

> Public appeals, mass demonstrations, and propagandistic statements in the press and radio concerning disarmament and the restriction of these statements to specific stereotypical thought patterns and political options have led to massive over-saturation. The result is that the true core of these statements is frequently no longer heard. Media campaigns are in danger of producing resentment and rejection, thereby achieving the opposite of what they initially intended.

The paper, pointing out the lack of concern with disarmament issues on the part of a broad spectrum of the church population, demanded that the church gain a new critical awareness of disarmament. This awareness should: 1) probe the causes of arms escalation; 2) criticize all concepts of security which are based solely on the might of weaponry; 3) support peace education; 4) demonstrate a concrete direction for the future through personal peace efforts.

An example of this resolution was given that same year at the synod of the Evangelical Church of the Church Province Saxony in Halle, where the discrepancy between the peace ovations of the SED and its call for increasing military readiness was noted. A statement from its summary paper reads: "We approve of and support the efforts of our government to attain disarmament and peace. But we cannot reconcile this with certain developments in our society, such as the introduction of military education, the forced expansion of civil defense programs, and the fostering of hate effigies ["Feindbilder"]."

The first peace week ("Friedensdekade"), initiated by the evangelical churches of the GDR, took place from November 9–19, 1980. Its motto, which was to reflect a basic idea of the GDR non-state peace movement, was "Make peace without arms" ("Friedenschaffen ohne Waffen"). Material prepared for this event urged people to articulate their "new perceptions" in conversations with both the church and the government. The suggestion was made that letters with the following message be sent to the Volkskammer: We thank you for all past efforts regarding disarmament and ask for their continuation in the form of "significant steps taken right here in this country."

The "Friedensdekade" has come to be a central annual activity of the churches. It has been held four times (1980–1983) so far, without state intervention. According to statements made by representatives of the GDR Kirchenbund in conversation with the author, approximately 90% of all parishes have participated. That is to say, even in the villages and small towns, practically speaking wherever there's a church, there have been activities—attended, in my estimation, by several tens of thousands of people. The numbers have increased continuously. The participants are predominately members of the intelligentsia and people engaged in social professions; but many young workers also take part. Writing letters to state offices is only one of the many activities. The ten-day program includes such varied activities. The ten-day program includes such varied activities as poetry readings, fasting, peace services, discussions, exhibits, and theater performances.

The leitmotif "Frieden schaffen ohne Waffen" expresses the conviction that peace cannot be guaranteed by military strength and deterrence. This position of the church was expressed most clearly in declarations emanating from the Evangelical Church of the Church Province of Saxony, which convened in Halle in the fall of 1981. A special declaration formulated there protested against the concept of securing peace by means of military measures. The synod went so far as to propose that the Warsaw Pact governments take unilateral steps to encourage the process of disarmament, for example, the withdrawal of SS-20 missiles and the reduction of the Warsaw Pact's superiority in tanks. Some church representatives at the Halle synod let it be known that they would have liked to be even more precise, but that it had proven impossible to attain the necessary consensus among the various provincial churches in the GDR and the sister churches in the Federal Republic to formulate a clear rejection of the system of deterrence.

In January 1982 the East Berlin pastor Rainer Eppelmann issued an appeal which attracted attention around the world, the "Berliner Appell—Frieden schaffen ohne Waffen." The petition, which invited signatures from the GDR population, demanded the withdrawal of all occupation forces from German soil and the creation of zones without atomic weapons in Europe. The East Berlin church hierarchy could not support the appeal and expressed its reservations concerning both the style and content of Eppelmann's petition. The state lost no time in reacting to the "Berlin Appeal"; within hours of its publication in the Western press and a subsequent meeting of the Politbüro, security police arrested Eppelmann and numerous other signatories. All were however released after having been interrogated for two days, and the legal proceedings were halted.

Eppelmann's role in the church is disputed, not least of all because he has been an intermediary between the church and dissidents such as Robert Havemann, who was a co-signer of the "Berliner Appell." He has also been criticized within the church for not having properly informed the young pacifists who responded to the petition of the risks involved and the limitations of their engagement, and for not having encouraged them to use reason. The actions of the young people are indeed often evoked more by emotion than reason, a fact which is understandable given the grounds of their discontent.

The reasons for the protest of GDR youth against the militarization of their society are illustrated by handmade posters circulating among young GDR citizens. One displays the legs of marching soldiers and quotes from the book released by the military publishing house of the GDR: "A war for the defense of the socialist fatherland is beautiful. This is of course not due to the destruction of material goods and the loss of human lives, but rather to the high and lofty goal, the noble struggle, and the heroic deeds accomplished in the name of the people and the workers in the entire world. Such a war allows no vulgar sentiment to arise within the combatant, but rather evokes strong and pure passions producing beautiful and humane qualities within that person." Another poster done by an East Berlin youth cites Soviet Marshal Yeremenko: "A feeling of beauty arises within me when I observe an organized attack by troops. It is not coincidental that one speaks of the art of commanding troops. An orchestra conductor, the artistic director of a theater, and a military commander do not only supervise; they also receive aesthetic satisfaction thereby."

As long as official pronouncements of this kind exist, pacifists will react negatively to them. The GDR peace activists want an open discussion of these and other problems. The possibility of publicly expressing such opinions represents something new in the GDR. Today—at least at church-sponsored meetings—an unusual openness prevails. An early example of this was the 1981 "Dresdener Friedensforum."

On February 13, 1981, the thirty-sixth anniversary of the destruction of Dresden, 5,000 people gathered in Dresden's Kreuzkirche for a public discussion with church representatives on the subject of peace. Young people had come from all parts of the country. They had streamed out of arriving trains, clearly identifiable by the emblems they wore on their parkas and jackets. Some wore headbands with the inscription: "Make peace without arms." Here for the first time it was readily apparent that a new movement had been conceived. This meeting, which had come about thanks to the grass-roots pressure of the most sundry peace groups, received official church approval and was therefore spared from confrontation with government security forces; an independent youth meeting would have undoubtedly been brought to a halt.

This unusually candid discussion marked a milestone in the political landscape of the GDR. State fears of violent demonstrations had proven to be unfounded. After the meeting many of the participants walked to the ruins of the Frauenkirche, where they lighted candles and held vigil until midnight. In this way they commemorated the horrors of war and demonstrated their desire for peace, thereby showing the government that the means of their struggle for peace were to be peaceful also.

The growing disagreement over the question of peace was clearly visible in the wake of the second "Friedensdekade," which was held in November 1981. Young people had discovered the Old Testament saying "swords to plowshares" and supplemented it with a drawing of the statue representing this idea which was given to the United Nations by the Soviet Union. They sewed the emblem on their parkas and jeans, used it as a bookmarker, and pasted it on their mopeds.

The ever increasing distribution of this emblem, which coincided with a counter-campaign of the SED ("Peace must be defended, peace must be armed"), irritated the authorities and resulted in police overreaction and coercion. In Rostock, Halle, Dresden, and East Berlin, teachers forced students to remove the emblem from their clothing. Young people were picked up by the police and hauled off to the police station. A group of Christians who had arrived in Halle for a church event were prevented from leaving the train station until they removed their emblems. Car windows were pasted over when the emblem was attached on the inside; emblems on the outside were meticulously scratched off. The same was true for apartment doors. One East Berlin youth was required to pay a penalty of 150 marks. The charge read:

> You broke the law on March 3, 1982 by wearing in public a symbolic likeness inscribed with a pacifistic slogan. This gravely disregarded the public's desire for protection and disturbed socialist communality ["Zusammenleben"]. . . . With this act you have infringed upon the sensitivities of a socialist state and caused undue annoyance.

East Berlin's bishop, Gottfried Forck, who still today displays the celebrated emblem on one of his briefcases, complained in a message addressed to the congregations and dated April 14, 1982 that no clear information concerning the legal basis for the police action was proffered by the state. In a conversation with State Secretary Klaus Gysi on April 7, 1982, Bishop Werner Krusche and other officials of the Kirchenbund pointed out that the churches were at a loss to justify the government's position to their young people and that the methods employed by the government agencies gave reason to fear damage to the personal development of the young people involved. At the same time, the church leadership stressed that it was not interested in a further sharpening of the conflict.

This position is characteristic of the evangelical churches in the GDR today. The church serves as mediator between the government and critically-minded youth groups. It attempts to foster understanding in state circles for the good intentions of the young people, and, at the grass-roots level, it strives to bring about a realistic estimation of what can be achieved under the present conditions. Despite their broad commitment to peace, the churches do not want to place themselves at the head of an independent peace movement. Bishop Hempel of Saxony, for example, spoke of the "limitations" of the church at the first peace forum in Dresden; it had become clear already then that the church's integrative capability is conditional. The church carries out its own peace work, which at times overlaps with non-church initiatives, and is careful not to go beyond certain limits.

As mediator the church is mistrusted by both sides. From the one side come accusations of opportunism; from the other, accusations of being an opposition movement. Church leaders must live with this tension, for their political latitude is indeed limited. The church's eight million members form a political mélange, and the church leadership must take these differences into account.

The peace discussions and initiatives have continued since the development of the new missiles in the Federal Republic in the fall of 1983 and the subsequent additional deployment of Soviet missiles in the GDR. The church is concerned above all with the "renunciation of the spirit and logic of deterrence" ("Absage an Geist und Logik der Abschreckung"). In the course of the year 1983 the non-state peace movement in the GDR branched out. Church groups attempted—with varying degrees of success—to take part in official peace demonstrations with their own, sometimes pacifistic, slogans. Women's groups ("Frauen für den Frieden") were formed in several cities. Other groups participated in worldwide fasts.

In 1983 seven *Kirchentage,* attended by more than 200,000 people, were held in the GDR. At these meetings peace issues and other problems of GDR society were discussed with an openness reminiscent of Western freedom of speech. The year of the Luther celebration left deep marks in the GDR. The state will most likely continue to tolerate the church's peace activities—even though there will be occasional conflicts. The non-church groups will have a more difficult time of it. Some disappointed peace workers have chosen to leave the GDR; others turned to more radical acts and were arrested. But on February 13, 1984 several thousand young people gathered once again in Dresden for a peace service. Their quiet demonstration with candles and peace songs near the ruins of the Frauenkirche was not disturbed by the state security forces.

A closer look at the unofficial GDR peace movement shows that those involved are not only concerned with peace. The issue of an alternative lifestyle was raised already at the original peace forum in Dresden. It was pointed out that there is a logical connection between the peace movement and the movement to save the environment. After all, what would be gained if external peace were secured and the countryside nevertheless destroyed. Ecological awareness and interest in alternative lifestyles go hand-in-hand with the struggle for peace, the same being true vice versa.

Many who were present at the Dresden peace sessions in February 1982 also participated in church-sponsored ecological campaigns during the following months. Such small-scale campaigns have become tradition in cities such as Leipzig, Dresden, Schwerin, Rostock, Neustrelitz, and East Berlin. They usually entail young people meeting for a weekend to discuss ecological issues such as alternative agriculture and nuclear power, and to plant trees, occasionally with the support of the state-owned landscaping firm, VEB Stadtgrün. The GDR media rarely deal with environmental questions; the ecological campaigns attempt to compensate for this information deficit.

The third annual campaign "Mobile without Cars" took place June 4–5, 1983, and involved dozens of GDR cities. Independent bicycle demonstrations have occurred in East Berlin and Leipzig, among other places. Even though—as is the case in the West also—these forms of criticism of present-day civilization are limited to small groups of people, their effect upon GDR society should not be underestimated.

In 1980 an ecology group in Wittenberg formulated the view that human labor should no longer be primarily directed toward the additional accumulation and accelerated consumption of material goods but rather increasingly toward intellectual or cultural activities, social concern, and a responsible lifestyle instead. The group maintained that societal wealth includes not only material wealth but intellectual-cultural wealth as well, i.e., is the sum of all things that lead to the enrichment of human existence. The paper goes on to state that this interpretation of societal wealth requires a modification of both societal and individual goals; and that these changes would require sacrifice.

Sacrifice and renunciation are common topics at youth meetings. The young people express their willingness to forgo the achievements of their parents' generation in favor of human relationships and character traits such as openness, tolerance, and honesty. People are viewed as the greatest wealth.

A kind of youth counterculture exists in the GDR, too. Numerous thousands of young people in East Berlin, Dresden, Leipzig, and other large cities subsist in a sort of internal emigration. Their outlook on life conforms in many ways to that of the West Berlin youth scene. Characteristic of both is the gap between generations. For many of these young people in the GDR the traditional Western and Prussian-German values no longer have appeal. Material prosperity and the collecting of consumer items—be it living-room furniture or a weekend cottage with garden patch—have lost priority. A glance at recent GDR literature, the latest GDR films, or youth culture in the large metropolitan centers—this includes "punks" as well as other disenchanted young people—readily shows that this phenomenon is already a major social movement. Yet a state dialogue with this segment of GDR youth has not yet taken place.

In my opinion, the unofficial peace movement and the ecological movement, as well as the dissatisfaction of young people with the accomplishments and lifestyle of their parents, are here to stay. They have become a political factor with which the SED will have to learn to deal. In earlier years repressive measures could be counted on to silence individual dissidents; this is however no longer the case. Young people are insisting on the right to express independent opinions, opinions that originate at the bottom, i.e., at the grass-roots level, and not with the state.

Government peace policies could, I believe, profit from supplementation by independent disarmament and peace initiatives. In my view, the politics of détente in the 1980s will have to develop from the bottom to the top. The peace movement in the West and the independent peace movement in the GDR have much in common: both renounce the system of deterrence, the official position of both the FRG and GDR governments; in both countries, a reduction of values involving national, collective, and personal identity is noticeable among young people. Identification with their respective political and economic systems has subsided—without having been replaced by a shift to the other system as an alternative. The movements in East and West can no longer be—nor do they desire to be—classified using the traditional schematics of East versus West, capitalism versus socialism. The trauma of a basic dichotomy between the systems appears increasingly anachronistic. The hate effigies of the past are being reduced as people on both sides of the Wall discover a common point of reference, their interest in lasting peace.

Today there are many various groups in East and West desirous of the opportunity to engage in dialogue with one another. A new peace effort on this level—in contrast to the stalled official negotiations—is conceivable. This is a truly new dimension of détente.

The GDR peace movement can make a contribution here. As one churchman in Potsdam stated:

> If the participants in the new GDR peace movement could make the transition from letting off steam to a serious discussion of the actual issues, from the plowshare utopia to constructive imagination regarding possible new steps, then one could achieve genuine political relevance instead of expending oneself in fruitless skirmishes with the government.

Part III

The Bloc in Upheaval

✦ *The extremely dramatic character of the crises of 1956, 1968, and 1980–1981 made those upheavals emblematic of Eastern European resistance to Soviet domination. Until the end of the 1980s, this was so much the case that the crises may have taken on a mildly deceptive quality by obscuring other currents, positive and negative alike, that failed to find expression (at least until 1989– 1990).*

Because the transformations begun in that later stage have been so fundamental and far-reaching, an infinitely more complex array of forces and tendencies has emerged. At least in part, the result is a still greater deception. The upheavals in Hungary, Czechoslovakia, and earlier in Poland, though preserved in their symbolic significance, have been overshadowed and sometimes all but forgotten. To be sure, they were failures in the short run, in contrast to what seems like the success now. The task of working out that apparent success is clearly a very absorbing one.

However, just as acute observers of Eastern Europe have always understood that the episodes of 1956, 1968, and 1980–1981 were not finished chapters, so must we expect that the values embodied in the earlier revolts will surface again. They are too important to remain in eclipse. East Europeans will find them so; accordingly, we too must try to understand them.

HUNGARY 1956

◆ *The impact of Stalin's death and the ensuing relaxation of the stricter, more arbitrary forms of repression was felt everywhere in the bloc but nowhere more dramatically than in Hungary. Whereas some governments of the region resisted the relaxation, Imre Nagy spoke for those who welcomed the so-called New Course. His posture was too liberal for the old guard of the party, however, and he and his reforms fell victim to the Stalinist wing of the party. Tension between the factions continued until 1956, when popular sentiment was galvanized by intellectual and student protest. Nagy was reinstated and far-reaching demands for fundamental change, not least autonomy in relation to the Soviet Union, were unleashed.*

The accounts by Kecskeméti and Rhodes summarize the course of the ensuing upheaval, capped late in October by the Soviet declaration and a conclusive military intervention that established the hitherto uncertain limits of Soviet tolerance. De-Stalinization, it now became clear, did not leave room for diminution of the "leading role of the party," still less for withdrawal from the Warsaw Pact system.

Less threatening sorts of reform would eventually be sanctioned by the Kádár regime installed after the 1956 uprising, and Kádár came to be associated, in the West especially, with such flexibility. But the bloody reprisals visited upon the Hungarian rebels (those who did not escape abroad) were not forgotten. The famous Hungarian writer, George Konrád, was moved, in the Solidarity period when Poland was threatened by Soviet intervention, to caution the Poles about the danger of betrayal by recalling the bloodbath that claimed Imre Nagy and many others.

Something of the bleakness of Hungarian life under Kádár is captured by Imre Kovács, former secretary general of the National Peasant Party and member of Parliament. The interview with János Kis, founder of the Hungarian samizdat *journal* Beszélö, *conveys the reawakening of dissident sentiment and opposition tendencies that assumed overwhelming proportions in and after 1989.*

The "New Course" in Eastern Europe

✦

Imre Nagy

Becoming Hungarian premier in the Soviet-sponsored relaxation that followed Stalin's death, Imre Nagy welcomed the change and, in his speech to the National Assembly in July 1953, announced a set of far-reaching reforms.

Our advancement along the road of People's Democracy, of socialist industrialization, towards Socialism must be such as would bring with it the steady improvement of the living standard and the social and cultural conditions of the working people, first of all, of the working class, the main army of socialist construction. This should clearly outline one of the important tasks of the economic policy of the government, a substantial all-round reduction, in accordance with the capacity of the country, of the pace of development of our national economy and of the investments. Bearing this in mind, the government will revise the plan of national economy in the spheres of both production and investments and will make proposals for an appropriate reduction in it.

The trend of development in the national economy must be also modified. There is no reason whatever for any excessive industrialization or any efforts to achieve industrial autarchy, especially if the necessary sources of basic materials are wanting. . . .

The course of economic policy must be altered also with regard to the two main branches of national economy—industry and agriculture. With an excessive industrialization, particularly the too rapid development of heavy industry and the large scale investments involved, the material resources of the country were insufficient to provide for the development of agriculture. As a result of this, with the too rapid development of industry and, first of all almost solely, of heavy industry, agricultural production was brought to a standstill and could not secure the satisfaction of either the raw material requirements of a rapidly growing industry, or of the food requirements of the steadily increasing number of industrial workers and of the population as a whole. The Government considers it as one of its most important tasks to increase substantially the investments in agriculture, simultaneously with a cut in industrial

Imre Nagy, "The 'New Course' in Eastern Europe," from Robert V. Daniels, ed., *A Documentary History of Communism,* vol. 2, Vintage Press, 1962, pp. 212–214.

Imre Nagy Announces the New Course. In January 1954 the newly installed communist premier of Hungary, Imre Nagy, announced in Parliament a program of significant economic and political reforms aimed at easing the strain of building socialism. Seated beside him was the Communist party leader—and real ruler of Hungary—Mátyás Rákosi, a hard-line Stalinist. In less than three years, Nagy would be under arrest as an anticommunist rebel (and later hanged), and Rákosi an exile in the Soviet Union. (Eastfoto)

investments, in order to bring about the earliest and biggest possible boom in production. . . .

. . . The government believes that it is right and necessary to slow down the pace of the farmers' cooperative movement, and in order to secure a strict compliance with the voluntary principle, it will make it possible for cooperative farm members, who wish to return to individual farming because they believe that is their way to prosperity, to withdraw from the farmers' cooperative. Moreover, it will permit the winding up of cooperative farms, where the majority of the membership wishes it. . . .

During recent years the state extended its economic activity to certain fields where private initiative and enterprise might still have an important role and might better promote the satisfaction of the needs of the population. Retail trade and crafts are these fields. Although handicrafts cooperatives show considerable development, they cannot make up for the shortage experienced in handicrafts production.

This fact encourages the government to allow private enterprise and to issue trade licenses according to legal provisions to those who are entitled to such, and at the same time to grant them the conditions required for their trade, such as a supply of materials, credit, etc. . . .

Greater tolerance is to be shown in religious questions. The employment of administrative measures in this field—which, as a matter of fact, has occurred occasionally—is impermissible. In this question the government espouses the principle of tolerance, of action through enlightenment and education. The government condemns and will not permit administrative and other coercive measures. . . .

The consolidation of legality is one of the most urgent tasks of the government. By applying strict measures and, if this is of no avail, with strict punishment, getting rid of mistakes and slackness, it must be achieved in a short time that our judicial and police organs and local Councils be firm pillars and guarantees of the people's State, of legality and of law and order. . . .

. . . The government will move a bill which will provide for the release of all those people whose offense is not of such a grave nature that their discharge might jeopardize either the security of the state or public order. At the same time, the institution of internment will be abolished and the internment camps wound up. By this measure the government's intention is to make it possible for those granted amnesty and the internees to return to their homes, rejoin their family, to return to the community and through their work to become useful members in it. The government also wishes to settle the issue of resettled people, enabling them to choose their residence in compliance with legal provisions applying to all citizens.

The institution of police-courts, which means, in fact, that the investigating authorities themselves pass judgments, is incompatible with the fundamental principles of people's democratic administration of justice. The government will introduce legislation providing for the abolition of this relic of the past.

Anatomy of a Revolt

✦

Paul Kecskeméti

This extract from Kecskeméti's book, *The Unexpected Revolution,* discusses the social forces that prepared the way for and then participated in the 1956 uprising. The author was a senior researcher at the Rand Corporation.

✦

THE ELITE

For months before the [1956] revolt, the intra-Party opposition had been demanding the rehabilitation of [former Premier Imre] Nagy and the reorganization of the government under his leadership; otherwise, the opponents of the Old Guard warned, there would be an explosion. The opposition, however, had no thought of forcing the hand of those in power. To all Party men, however critical of the regime, a change in leadership not decided upon by the appropriate Party authorities was unthinkable. Events, however, outran the sluggish tempo of intra-Party developments. The explosion came, but the old leadership was still in place, and no preparations had been made for reshuffling the top positions in the Party.

Nagy himself was out of town when the students began preparing their mass demonstration. It was the wine harvest season, and he had gone to a small country place he owned in the wine district of western Hungary. There, on the evening of October 22, Nagy was guest of honor at a wine harvest festival, while the Budapest students were holding meetings and formulating revolutionary demands, including the one that called for a new government under his leadership. Nagy learned about this from the radio on the 23rd, and decided to return to Budapest. Nothing, however, was further from his thoughts than taking advantage of this irregular popular movement in his favor in order to crush his old Party antagonists and impose himself as leader. According to [Tibor] Méray, who himself was an active member of the intra-Party opposition and conversant with Nagy's political attitudes at that time, some of the students' demands, notably those directed against Soviet domination, were far too radical for Nagy to swallow. Moreover, Nagy would not have considered taking any political initiative outside Party channels.

Paul Kecskeméti, "Anatomy of a Revolt," from *East Europe,* November 1961, pp. 23–27.

The only Party people imaginative and undisciplined enough to take direct action to bring about a last-minute change of government were the journalists of the Party newspaper *Szabad Nép*. After an impromptu meeting at the newspaper's offices, they sent a delegation to the Central Committee, urging the leadership to bow to the will of the people. [Ernő] Gerő, who received the delegation, waved the suggestion aside.

During the afternoon of the 23rd, when the city was already in an uproar, Nagy stayed at home. With great difficulty, some of his supporters, including the novelist Tamas Aczel, persuaded him to go to the parliament building, in front of which a huge crowd was clamoring to hear him. Nagy, having no instructions from the Party authorities, at first refused to talk to the crowd. When, finally, he appeared on the balcony and spoke a few words, it was a near disaster. He began with the word "Comrades" and was roundly booed. In his short address, he stressed the need to proceed within the framework of "constitutional order and discipline." The crowd then began to disperse; many went to the radio building, where fighting broke out soon afterward.

During the night, the Central Committee finally decided to appoint Nagy Premier. Installed in power, however, Nagy did not, at first, act like a revolutionary leader. His primary endeavor upon taking office was to restore order and disarm the insurgents. His appeals to the fighters to lay down their arms were fruitless (understandably enough, since Soviet tanks were in action in the capital), and his initial popularity declined rapidly.

The Communist intellectuals, who had been the most radical and outspoken critics of the regime before the revolution, were thoroughly frightened by its outbreak and did everything in their power to steer events into a peaceful course. Gyula Háy, for example, spoke as follows in a broadcast to young Hungarians on October 25:

> There must be a change-over to peaceful methods without the slightest delay, the armed struggle must stop immediately. Even peaceful demonstrations are not suitable at this time, because they can be misconstrued. There must now begin an implacable, uncompromising, democratic clash of thoughts and ideas in which the spokesmen of the new, the young in age and spirit, will gain a brilliant, universally resounding victory.

According to Háy, Gerő's removal from power guaranteed that all legitimate revolutionary aspirations would be satisfied under the new government.

The Communist writers' efforts to call a halt to violent action indicated no change in their fundamental attitudes. They did not give up their convictions, either then or later. Their determination "never again to tell lies" held good, after the crushing of the revolution, under the Kádár regime. Háy, Déry, and other leading Communist critics of the pre-revolutionary regime who stayed in Hungary never recanted; they went to prison rather than submit. Their behavior showed a remarkable consistency before, during, and after the revolution: they wanted to reform the regime, to rid it of its aberrations, but they had no idea of discarding Marxist socialism as the basis of political order and starting out along entirely new lines.

Nagy, too, was consistent; he thought he could save the situation in 1956 by reviving the New Course of 1953. Only gradually did he perceive that the dynamism of the revolution had rendered that stage hopelessly obsolete. When he did recognize this fact, he prepared himself to make a revolutionary break with the past. The formation of a government of national union, announced on October 27, represented the beginning of such a break; it was followed by more radical steps in the same direction, culminating in the attempted withdrawal from the Soviet bloc. Nagy, however, did not choose this radical course spontaneously; he was forced into it by the uncontrollable, overwhelming upsurge of the masses' revolutionary *élan*.

✦

THE SOCIAL BACKGROUND OF THE COMBATANTS

The proportion of active fighters in the revolution varied from one social group to another. A survey conducted by the Audience Analysis Section of Radio Free Europe, Munich, gives the following breakdown of the proportion of active fighters within the various social categories: professionals, 14 per cent; white-collar, 2 per cent; industrial workers, 13 per cent; farmers and farmhands, 6 per cent; and others (including students), 20 per cent.

This breakdown shows the highest incidence of active fighting in the last group, the youngest in age, who were not yet classified in any occupational category other than that of students. The urban occupational groups, except clerical workers, follow next. The peasantry shows a much lower percentage, and the office workers the lowest of all. (Of the total white-collar group, 82 per cent are shown as having been "inactive"; that is, as not even having participated in non-fighting activities.)

The peasantry had its own pattern of revolutionary activity. This class seems to have been in sympathy with the most aggressive revolutionary groups, the active fighters; it did not want a "reformed" Communism but was seeking something radically different. The peasants showed their sympathy by supplying the fighters with food. Their own activity, however, was concentrated largely upon dismantling the kolkhozes, their constant objective throughout the Communist era. Their behavior, somewhat like that of "elite" rebels, showed continuity rather than an abrupt change from submission to rebellion.

Some continuity also could be observed in the behavior of the intelligentsia: the members of this category reveled in proclaiming publicly what they had long been saying *sotto voce* in private. They devoted much energy to creating a democratic political machinery. There was a proliferation of newspapers and political parties reflecting every shade of opinion. Interview material reveals that many of the fighters (students, in particular) felt this activity to be both excessive and premature; it deflected energies from the main task. The intelligentsia, however, were extremely active in every field of revolutionary endeavor, literary and organizational work as well as armed combat: the Radio Free Europe survey shows that the proportion of the "inactive" in this class was only 6 per cent, as compared to 61 to 82 per cent in the other classes.

The extremely low participation quota among office workers is striking: it suggests that this category remained demoralized even after the outbreak of revolution. The group as a whole was apparently unable to develop an organizational framework of its own, or to attach itself to the various councils in which the industrial workers, the intelligentsia, and the students ranged themselves.

Extreme combativeness manifested itself in the Hungarian Revolution primarily among three categories of people: street crowds who assembled in spontaneous fashion, the youngest age group, and industrial workers. Each group had its own characteristic style of revolutionary behavior.

◆

THE STREET CROWDS

In the crowds, tension built up gradually during the afternoon and evening of October 23. What attracted them to begin with was the sight of marching students; this was something entirely new and exhilarating. But at first the street crowds were mere onlookers, curious to see what would happen. As time went by, however, the people's mood gradually changed. When the crowds grew denser and showed no inclination to disperse, it dawned upon those in them that a historic moment was at hand. We find in the interviews such statements as: "We simply felt that it was impossible to leave without having done something decisive"; and "Something big was bound to happen." The crowds now sought outlets for this accumulated tension. The statue of Stalin offered itself as a target. Vast numbers converged upon the parliament building, clamoring for Imre Nagy, whom the street had designated premier, and upon the radio building, where they took up the students' demand that their manifesto be put on the air. When the police attacked, nobody thought of dispersing. The provocation drove the crowd to frenzy, and the possession of arms, obtained from sympathizers among the military, gave it a feeling of unlimited power. The crowd's ruling impulse was to destroy the symbols of Communist and Soviet domination and to get even with the terror and publicity apparatus of the regime. The offices of the Party newspaper (by then under the control of Communist dissidents) were wrecked; bonfires were built of Communist literature; the hated red star emblem was torn down everywhere. Above all, the crowd stormed the strongholds of the political police and overpowered the units manning them. There were many lynchings.

This phase of the revolution exhibited many of the well-known features of mob violence: rage, a passionate desire for revenge, cruelty. Yet one of the classic symptoms of mass action, the breakdown of cultural restraints and inhibitions, was lacking. Mass aggression was extremely selective, pinpointed upon the political police. There was no looting, no storming of shops, no general breakdown of discipline. The crowds did not even start an indiscriminate persecution of Communists. Even in small towns, where Party members were highly conspicuous, "decent" Communists were left unharmed. On the whole, destructive impulses were vented only upon the political police and the inanimate symbols of Communist rule.

✦

THE YOUNG PEOPLE

The revolution entered a new, fateful stage after the entry of Soviet occupation troops in the early morning of October 24. During this stage, the revolutionary struggle consisted mainly of street battles with Soviet tanks, and in these the youngest age group played the most conspicuous part. To a very considerable extent, the street battles were fought by the young: students, apprentices, and schoolchildren. A good many older people participated too, but it seems certain that the struggle would not have been sustained as long as it was if it had not been for the death-defying, desperate determination of the very young.

According to the above-mentioned survey of Radio Free Europe, 11 per cent of the population up to 20 years of age, and 19 per cent of those aged between 21 and 29, were active fighters in the revolution. Among those between 30 and 49 years old, however, only 5 per cent fought actively, and of those aged 50 years or more, 1 per cent. The fall-off after 29 years of age is significant. How can this be explained? Whereas it is not surprising that people aged 50 and over showed little inclination to participate in street battles, men in their 30's are not too old to fight. On the other hand, those aged 32 or more in 1956 were old enough to have seen military service in World War II. They had had experience with Soviet tanks and could estimate the odds against successful resistance. This, presumably, was the reason why they showed less inclination to fight than those who had not been in the war. A Hungarian war veteran whom I interviewed was very positive on this point. He said that ex-soldiers considered military resistance to the Russians hopeless; only boys too young to have seen service were ignorant enough to fight. This extreme formulation certainly overstates the case, but the general point seems valid.

The very young among the active fighters did not, in fact, base their action upon any sort of realistic weighing of odds. There was in their combativeness an element of psychic compulsion, as though they were caught in a somnambulistic trance. It did not matter whether they lived or died. Only one thing counted: getting weapons and using them as much and as long as possible.

How did such a pattern of behavior develop among children? Lack of suitable data makes it impossible to answer this question conclusively. On general grounds, however, it seems that decisive weight must be given to peer-group solidarity and imitation. When some children got weapons and went out to fight, this apparently started a teen-age epidemic: the others felt they could not remain behind. Not every child fought, of course; presumably, *all* parents did what they could to restrain their own children, and many succeeded. However, the Radio Free Europe figure of 11 per cent for active fighters in the age group up to 20 by no means gives the true measure of the scope of the teen-age epidemic in Budapest. For one thing, the sample is nationwide, but most of the active fighting took place in Budapest; for another, the age span includes the many children not yet in the teen-group who were immune to the epidemic or could be controlled by their parents.

Whereas children mostly fought in small gangs, the combat activity of more mature young men, particularly students, showed a more organized pattern. The students had organizations of their own to begin with. Within these, various teams were formed for specific purposes (the printing and distribution of leaflets; liaison with the workers, the army, and the government; active fighting; and logistic support). Interviews with students indicate that they considered themselves the nerve center of the revolution. They found that they could easily establish contact with any group—workers and peasants as well as government officials, professionals, and army officers. They used this easy access to all strata in order to coordinate revolutionary policies and activities.

✦

THE INDUSTRIAL WORKERS

It was the industrial workers whose revolutionary activity lasted longest and was the best organized. They were active in street battles in Budapest and elsewhere; but their weightiest contribution to the revolutionary struggle was the organization of workers' councils and, its principal outcome, the revolutionary general strike.

The first workers' council was set up at the Incandescent Lamp Factory in Budapest on October 24. From there, the movement spread rapidly; within three days, a network of councils covered the entire country. The council's activity was concentrated on national politics. For example, on October 26, one of the most articulate of the councils, that of the industrial region of Borsod County, north of Budapest, broadcast a manifesto of twenty-one points, which a delegation took to Budapest and submitted to Premier Nagy.

The Borsod program contained a number of demands reflecting the social welfare aims of organized labor (better wages, workers' control of plants, decentralization of industry, and so on), but the significant thing about it was that it put the greatest emphasis not on social but on national grievances. It urged revision of the trade treaties with the Soviet Union, the exploitation of the Hungarian uranium deposits for the country's benefit, and, above all, the withdrawal of Soviet occupation troops by January 1, 1957, at the latest. To give effect to these demands, the Borsod workers proclaimed a general strike, to last until the occupation was lifted. In the sequel, the activity of all workers' councils was concentrated upon this basic point. Work stopped in all plants. The workers knew that the strike would bring great hardships, but they did not care; if existing conditions could not be altered radically, they felt, life was not worth living anyway. When the revolution seemed to be victorious, the councils made preparations to end the strike. But after the second Soviet intervention, they decided to keep it up, and the condition for resuming work remained the same: the withdrawal of the Soviet troops. The workers simply disregarded the verdict of military action, refusing to believe that their collective effort could be frustrated by it.

To my knowledge, this was the first time in history that the syndicalist myth of the revolutionary general strike, as set forth by Georges Sorel, actually became the basis of sustained political action by the entire industrial population of a country. It is safe to say that the Hungarian workers who organized the councils and conceived the idea of a general strike against the Russian occupation had never heard of Sorel and his theory of the "myth," but they acted in accordance with it. There was only this difference: Sorel thought that the proletariat would rise to sweep away a rotten, degenerate bourgeois order, but to his unwitting Hungarian disciples the antithesis between "bourgeoisie" and "proletariat" was of no immediate interest. The significant antithesis was between "Soviet" and "Hungarian," and the social and political order to be swept away was not a bourgeois but a Communist one, set up by the disciples of Lenin whom Sorel had greatly admired. The idea of workers' councils seems to have been inspired by the example of Yugoslavia, where a new type of "industrial self-government," based upon the creation of plant councils, had been introduced in 1950. A council movement inspired by the same example arose in the autumn of 1956 in Poland, where the councils mobilized the industrial masses and created popular pressure strong enough to compel a relaxation of the dictatorship and some easing of Soviet control. In Poland, however, the councils never became supreme, because the Party apparatus was not smashed, but merely revamped under Władysław Gomułka's leadership. By contrast, the Hungarian councils were able to steer a radical revolutionary course. They insisted upon the total elimination of all Party influences from economic management as well as from national politics. The end of Soviet occupation was the underlying aim of all this, and the council movement became primarily a national liberation movement.

The workers' revolutionary behavior showed a sharp break in continuity. Outwardly quiet until the outbreak of street fighting in Budapest, the Hungarian industrial population instantly mobilized itself in a determined bid to wrest political power from the Party. This explosive transition from total discipline to total rebellion was characteristic of the "mass pattern" of the Hungarian Revolution, in contrast with the smooth, continuous nature of the "elite pattern." Not that the revolutionary behavior of the mass represented a completely new departure; the Hungarian Revolution consciously imitated historical models. The memories of 1848–49 (Kossuth's and Petöfi's revolution) were ever-present. In addition, the industrial workers in revolting against the Party were inspired by the Social Democratic traditions of the organized labor movement of Hungary. These traditions, suppressed under the Communist regime, suddenly came to the fore when the workers regained their freedom of action.

◆

THE MOTIVATION OF THE FIGHTING

Analysis of Hungarian revolutionary behavior, both in the elite and in the mass, suggests this over-all conclusion: combative impulses resulted, generally speaking, from a combination of two factors, namely, bitterness and frustration on the one hand, and a feeling of strength on the other. Hungarian revolutionary behavior was not a sudden desperate reaction to intolerable pressure and deprivation. It was, rather, a delayed reaction to all the negative experiences of the past, a reaction released when elements of weakness appeared in the image of the regime, and elements of strength bulked larger in one's own self-image.

Thus, it was the "thaw" originating in Soviet Russia, a loosening in the fabric of dictatorship, that sparked active opposition in the disaffected part of the elite. Similarly, the peasants responded to the regime's retreat in the summer of 1953 by active revolt. The mass revolt in Budapest broke out when the crowds saw that the students could demonstrate with impunity, and when numbers and excitement gave them a feeling of strength. Finally, it was the collapse of the Communist power structure that gave the signal for nationwide revolt.

A related point is that propensity for rebellious action was not directly proportional to the psychic distance separating the individual from the regime. Those who had the amplest grounds for complaint were not the most prone to rebel. People who had lost everything tended to be demoralized and passive, whereas revolutionary activity originated with groups who were partly privileged and partly frustrated. The writers, who were the first to rebel, had a highly privileged social and economic position, but suffered acutely from the loss of personal integrity and professional satisfaction; the students who followed suit were nurtured by the regime and could expect to rise into relatively high social brackets, but they resented regimentation and forced indoctrination. Both groups inevitably accepted certain features of the regime to which they owed their status. Even such ideological closeness to the regime, however, did not preclude radical political opposition to it. This was not surprising: although strong political antagonism to a system may have its origin in total rejection of the system's principles, it may also spring from dissatisfaction with the way in which the principles, accepted as such, are being carried out. In fact, disappointed expectations are particularly likely to result in violent hatred. One may learn to live with an enemy from whom one never expected anything but evil, but it is impossible not to feel aggressive impulses toward a treacherous friend.

The gulf between "promises" and "reality" is a recurrent motif in the interviews with Hungarians; numerous respondents described this contrast as the most difficult thing to endure. It was most glaring for the industrial workers, who had been promised not only a good life in general, but a dominant position in the state, and who in actual fact were subjected to a particularly relentless form of regimentation and harassment. As we have seen, the disciplinary control that the Communist economic authorities exercised over the workers was strong enough to inhibit open opposition. At the same time, the workers felt that they had claims upon the state which were theirs by right; that is, by virtue of basic principles proclaimed by the Communists themselves. They were prepared to present these claims as soon as disciplinary controls were shaken off. If their material position was weak and dependent, their moral position vis-à-vis the apparatus always remained strong; for, given the freedom to talk and act, they could attack the regime in the name of principles that the Communist rulers themselves had to recognize as unassailable. This was an important strategic factor in the revolution. It contributed to the breakup of the Communist elite, some sections of which were intensely aware of the weakness of their moral position. It also facilitated the coordination of revolutionary forces, since it gave the opposition a noncontroversial platform.

Hungary 1956

✦

Anthony Rhodes

This is an eyewitness account of the turbulence of fall 1956 in
Budapest, authored by a British journalist.

In the Stalin square the next morning,* the people of Budapest had not only
pulled down the dictator's statue, they were feverishly chopping it up into little bits, so
that not a trace should remain. Outside the Communist Party headquarters was a
mountain of cinders, consisting of burnt communist books and pamphlets. A ceaseless
hail of these came hurtling out of the windows, together with paintings and photographs of Stalin, Lenin and Rákosi, to keep the fires alight. Even gramophone records
of the leaders' speeches added to the blaze.

When these busy people realized who we were, they clustered around, beseech-
ing us to let our countrymen know the truth, suggesting that we should take photographs of a big oil painting of Stalin which had just been hideously defaced. They
slapped us on the back and shook our hands a dozen times, until we felt that we, not
they, had liberated their city. An old woman in tears kissed my hand as if I were a
Monsignore; and one of the Austrians suddenly found himself clasping two babies.

Meanwhile inside the building, a grim AVO [Allamvedelmi Osztaly, State Security Department] hunt was in progress. A number of AVO men had just been caught in
the sewers and hanged, I was told. Would I care to step inside and take some photographs of them, for the benefit of the West? But the sight of the hanged men the night
before had been enough, and I refused this invitation. The AVO men had evidently
imagined that their Russian masters would quickly dominate the situation, and they
had been waiting underground (literally) for this to happen. But when the lull came
and they appeared in public again, they found to their dismay not the Russians, but the
population of Budapest, in control. Their cruelties of the past were now expiated.
After execution, their bodies were left hanging for an hour or so, for all to see; then the
dust-carts came and took them away, and more were displayed. The Hungarians never
seemed to tire of looking at the corpses of their late masters. To see the hate combined

---

Anthony Rhodes, "Hungary 1956," from *Ten Years After: The Hungarian Revolution in the Perspective of
History,* Tamas Aczel, ed., 1967, pp. 83–85, 88–92.
*October 1956.

with glee on the faces of some of these people as they gazed on them was to realize what communism had done in ten years to the Hungarian mind.

It might be supposed from this audacious behaviour that the Russians had left, or had at least evacuated, the city. This was not so. They still surrounded it, and some were in the suburbs. The next day an English-speaking Hungarian who had offered to act as my interpreter said, "In the barracks I will take you to, you will see that the Russians are still here. Nagy is lying when he says they have gone. Several thousands. With their families."

For perhaps twenty minutes we walked towards the eastern part of the city, into an area which seemed like some shelled village from the Second World War. Russian tank artillery had been employed against large apartment houses; tram-wires were lying tangled on the ground; barriers of overturned trams and burnt-out armoured cars had been erected in the streets. At length we came to a long white wall about six feet high. "The barracks," he said. "The thing is to walk past as if you were indifferent. Don't stop at that gate, just glance in quickly."

We joined a small file of people hurrying past the barrack gates, which were guarded by a sentry and a group of Russian soldiers.

"As long as they stay in the barracks, our people don't mind," he said. "But yesterday when two armoured cars came out wagging their guns, everyone came into the street and threw stones at them."

As we passed the gates, we saw some armoured vehicles inside, with Russian soldiers working on them. At the end of the street we stopped and looked back as an armoured car of the *Honvédség,* waving the new Hungarian flag with the hole in it, lumbered slowly down to the barracks. People scattered quickly into doorways, and it seemed as if trouble was about to begin again. But the car stopped at the gate, and a soldier with a Hungarian armband got out, carrying two large metal cans which he handed over to the Russians. "Milk," explained my interpreter. "Milk for the Russian babies in the barracks. They have come to an agreement. Every day our people bring fifty litres for the Russian children."

This was typical of the curious relations existing between the populace and the Russian troops during this twilight period of the revolution. In some parts of the city they were still firing at one another; in others, giving one another milk, or throwing stones. Once we came upon a Russian armoured car at a street corner, with a crowd around it, half-hostile, half-curious. The Russian soldiers were grinning as if embarrassed, trying to talk, even to exchange cigarettes. It was not hard to believe the story that some of these men had defected to the Hungarians whom they had been ordered to fire upon—nor to realize this was a further sign that the revolt was working-class. Even the soldiers of the Russian proletariat knew it.

In short, relations between the populace and the Russian troops—who were often loath to open fire—were better than is generally supposed in the West. I was told later of a young Hungarian woman, visibly pregnant, at whom the Russian soldiers in the street cried "Baby! Baby!"—and insisted on her accepting their food and rations. And this at the height of the revolution.

The Hungarian Revolution, 1956. Among the many symbolic actions of the anticommunist insurgents was burning portraits of Communist party leader Rákosi, who himself fled to the Soviet Union. (Erich Lessing/Magnum)

All the same, it was clear the next morning that the Hungarians were intent on effacing every sign of communist influence from their city. It was this courageous, if perhaps imprudent, Hungarian violence which distinguished this revolt from that of their neighbours, the Poles who, a week before, had been prepared to advance to independence by easier stages. The people of Budapest seemed to have gone mad, intoxicated with their new liberty. Almost hourly for the next two days, the unfortunate Nagy, the new Prime Minister, found himself forced to make democratic concessions on Western lines. Here was a typical demand from the workers of the town of Komárom—which I was shown—crudely written and printed:

> We, the students, workers and peasants of Komárom have always shown our faith in Imre Nagy. This faith was weakened when he called in the Soviet forces to destroy us. We know now that it was not Nagy who did this; he was made to act and speak with a pistol at his throat. We therefore restore to him

our faith; but we do not hereby give him a blank cheque. Imre Nagy knows we are watching him. He must immediately expel the Russian paid criminals from the government, as well [as] make the Russian troops leave our country. He must immediately announce free elections, with secret ballots, under an international commission from the UNO. Within the limits in which he achieves this, we will support him. Otherwise, we reject him.

By 2 November it was clear that the most delicate phase of the revolution, diplomatically and politically, had been reached. Either the Russians would withdraw and democracy on Western lines would return—or the most rigid form of communism would be imposed to redress the situation. Imre Nagy was acting as a kind of middleman, between the insurgents and the Russians, moderating the demands of the former, persuading the latter that he was master of the situation. His wireless appeals, contrasted with those of Radio Györ which was still in the hands of the insurgents, revealed the dilemma:

> ". . . let us finish with this flow of blood!" he said that morning. "Let us finish with these murders! Let us finish with this destruction! The new government has been formed on the broadest basis, with the various parties represented. We have firmly decided to achieve profound economic, social and political reforms. We guarantee that the demands of the Hungarian people shall be satisfied. For this reason, the revolt no longer has meaning. We therefore warn all those in possession of arms that they must be laid down by 6 p.m., or they will be treated as bandits. . . ."

Meanwhile, at almost precisely the same moment, Radio Györ was saying:

> . . . we will not lay down arms, because we cannot believe in government promises. We will lay them down only when there is not a Russian soldier left in the country . . .

The decisive day, when these two demands seemed for a moment to be reconciled, was Thursday 1 November; and the time was 4 p.m. It was precisely at this moment, too, that Budapest seemed to have returned to something approaching normal conditions. People had come out again this sunny afternoon, to walk along the Danube; the Sunday afternoon crowd had brought their children; there was even a pram or two. The insurgents with their Tommy-guns and armbands were for the first time less in evidence. I passed the Parliament buildings and stood by the Danube watching the last Russian civilians leave in the big pleasure steamers, bound for Rumania. There were bulky men in square-cut overcoats and trilby hats, and fat peasant-type women in ill-fitting suits, with their suitcases, parcels and children.

I was standing near the Chain bridge watching these families leave, when an English journalist I had met the day before ran up to me and said, "If you want the story of your life, come to the Parliament buildings now! Nagy is about to make an important declaration about the Warsaw Pact."

I followed him to this building where, by showing his journalist's pass, he was able to take me upstairs, through salons and corridors full of the Biedermeyer furnishings, marble-mounted and ormolu mirrors from the last century, to the door of the cabinet room. Here, he said, the government had been in session for two hours, arguing about the weighty decision they were about to take.

On the first landing we were told to wait in a reception room, in which other journalists were walking up and down with notebooks. Suddenly the big doors opposite opened and we saw, for a moment, Kádár the new first secretary of the Communist Party, seated at a table, and at his shoulder the Prime Minister, Imre Nagy. Near the wall was the President, Tildy, whose voice seemed raised in argument. On the other side of the table, out of view, sat (we did not know it at the time), the Russian ambassador, Andropov.

A quarter of an hour later, an official from the Hungarian Foreign Office, whom my friend evidently knew, came out of the cabinet room quickly. Taking him by the arm he said in English, "Have you a motorcar? Well, leave Budapest immediately! Don't waste time here asking for more news. When it comes, you won't be able to leave."

He said that the government had decided to withdraw from the Warsaw Pact, and had appealed for help to the United Nations. Whatever Nagy might feel personally about the wisdom of this step, he felt it was the will of the Hungarian people. Some of the cabinet, and of course the Soviet ambassador, were trying to dissuade him; "And the pro-Russian forces in the cabinet will finally win," he said. "Nagy is now going to the radio building to make the announcement. But you see what will happen afterwards."

Five minutes later we saw the Russian ambassador leave hurriedly; and a half an hour later, Nagy went to make the courageous statement about withdrawing from the Warsaw Pact, which meant that Hungary was no longer a satellite—which was responsible virtually, too, for the second Russian intervention. But in the streets that evening the Hungarians were elated. "Nagy has cleaned his slate," they said. "We can support him, he's our man now."

They felt that Hungarian honour had been saved, that whatever happened now, their revolution had not been in vain. But along with this feeling of relief, went one of tension. The pacific crowds of the afternoon soon melted away, as quickly as they had formed; the barricades went up again; the determined looking youths and workers with Hungarian armbands and Tommy-guns appeared on the streets again. When dusk fell, these streets emptied, and although the night was fine, an eerie atmosphere of waiting, as before a thunderstorm, possessed the city.

I returned that evening to the British Legation, where I was told that our Minister, Mr Fry, had just been called to the Hungarian Foreign Office. In the little restaurant which had been improvised on the top floor of the Legation (where all the families of the British officials were now living), an atmosphere of forced good humour prevailed. We sat drinking and talking till 9 p.m., when the Minister returned and said he had an announcement to make. He had decided to send a convoy to

Vienna the next morning, with the less important members of the staff and all the wives (including his own). The convoy was to be led by Mr Russell, a third secretary. He said no more; but everyone knew what this meant.

When conversation again became general, he came up to me and asked if I would care to help Mr Russell, and accompany the convoy. As I had no work to do in Budapest, he saw no point in my remaining; the fewer Englishmen here at the moment, the better. He could not afford to send more than one of his diplomats, and would be glad of any help I could give. He asked the same of an Oxford undergraduate who had spent the last five days in Budapest, going about with the insurgents.

We agreed. But we went to bed that night wondering if the convoy would be able to leave. The tense hours before dawn when armies move, found us at the window looking out at the hill above Buda where the Russians were supposed to be encamped. But all was still. And at ten o'clock that morning, our convoy of eight vehicles—mostly British and French diplomats' private cars—crossed the big Chain bridge, moving west.

If this drive was less eventful than my journey into Budapest surrounded by the insurgents, it was in some ways more informative, because we now met the Russians who were preparing their assault on the city. No longer at the road-blocks were the armed, determined young men; they had now been formed into units well away from the roads, so as to avoid contact with the Russians. Their places had been taken by old men and women; sometimes, sixty-year-old men stood beside machine guns, and often the road-blocks were guarded by boys. We showed our papers at these blocks, and were allowed to pass.

A wintry gale from the south-east was now blowing, stripping off the leaves and sweeping them along in slanting squalls of snow and sleet. Not far from Győr, we ran into a heavy snow-storm and then, through the falling flakes, we saw ahead a large tank going in our direction. "A 50-ton Stalin," said one of the British officials in our party learnedly. "What splendid tanks the Russians have left the insurgents!"

It was difficult to pass this tank because it was moving west too: I blew the horn impatiently, to get it to withdraw to the side of the road. At length we managed to squeeze past, only to find ahead of it another Stalin tank of the same size. Again I blew the horn in irritation—and again at last we managed to pass. But there was yet another tank in front of this and then, as we rounded a corner, a whole line of them running out ahead, about fifteen, trundling along, wagging their guns and antennae.

"Really! These insurgent tanks ought to get off the roads to let us pass," said the British official again. But then as we passed one of them, a face appeared at the turret and looked down—a Mongolian face. ". . . they are Russians!" he finished lamely.

Our car was in fact sandwiched in a long column of Russian tanks. More Mongoloid faces peered down at us as we passed, blank, expressionless, slit-eyed, beneath bell-shaped helmets. The Russians were bringing up their eastern troops. With these not particularly reassuring road companions we remained for nearly three-quarters of an hour, trying to pass. It is understandable that to men in such machines the ordinary, standard motor-horn means little or nothing.

After Győr, we saw more Russians in a maize field at the side of the road—armoured cars with tents around them, soldiers eating their midday meal out of mess-tins in the snow. Young for the most part, the term "simple soldier" applied to these men admirably. Of the thirty or so I saw, twenty at least were Mongoloid, almost Chinese, in appearance; several had taken off their helmets and were scratching their shaven heads. These were the troops who were gathering around Budapest for the assault due to take place in two days' time. Although dirty and slovenly in appearance, there was a businesslike air about their equipment and vehicles. They could clearly move, fire and communicate with one another by wireless. And what more can you ask of the modern soldier?

We later learned that we were one of the last Western convoys these Russian troops allowed through. A few hours later, their tanks fanned out along the Austrian frontier, closing it completely, in preparation for the assault. To travellers from Budapest, Red Cross personnel, or journalists wishing to "file" their cables in Vienna, they repeated the two words, "*Niet Wien!*" stubbornly, and forced them to return to Győr, Magyaróvár, or Budapest itself. In this way we came to Nickelsdorf again, and left the people, who, by liberating themselves, were soon to liberate Eastern Europe from the excesses of communism.

The Soviet "30 October Declaration"

✦

This declaration by the Soviet government is the thinly disguised and thoroughly mendacious ideological justification for military intervention in Hungary. It reveals the stringent limits of Soviet tolerance for independent policy and action by its client states and the shallowness of the Soviet commitment to significant reform.

The unchangeable foundation of Soviet foreign relations has been and remains a policy of peaceful coexistence, of friendship, and of collaboration with all other states.

"The Soviet '30 October Declaration,' " from Noel Barber, *Seven Days of Freedom*, Stein & Day, 1975, pp. 239–242.

The most profound and the clearest expression of this policy is to be found in the relations between the socialist countries. Linked together by the common goal of building a socialist society and by the principles of proletariat internationalism, the countries of the great community of socialist nations can base their relations only on the principles of complete equality of rights, of respect for territorial integrity, of political independence and sovereignty, and of non-interference in the internal affairs of one state by the other. This does not preclude, but on the contrary assumes, a close fraternal collaboration and a mutual assistance between the countries of the socialist community in economic, political, and cultural matters.

It was on this foundation that, after World War II and the collapse of fascism, the democratic people's regime leaped ahead. It was on this foundation that the regime was strengthened and that it was enabled to demonstrate its vitality throughout numerous European and Asian countries.

In the course of establishing the new regime and in the course of establishing deep revolutionary changes in socialist relations, there have come to light several difficulties, several unsolved problems, and several downright mistakes, including mistakes in the relations among socialist states. These violations and these mistakes have demeaned the principle of equal rights in socialist interstate relationships.

The Twentieth Congress of the Communist Party of the Soviet Union strongly condemned these violations and errors and decided that the Soviet Union would base its relations with the other socialist countries on the strict Lenin principles of equal rights for the people. The Congress proclaimed the need for taking into account the history and the individual peculiarities of each country on its way towards building a new life.

The Soviet Government has systematically applied the historic decisions of the Twentieth Congress in creating the conditions for strengthening the amity and the cooperation between socialist countries. It has based its application of these decisions on the firm foundation of complete respect for the sovereignty of each socialist state.

As recent events have shown, it is apparently necessary to declare the position of the Soviet Union concerning its relations with the other socialist countries, and, above all, concerning its economic and military relations with such countries.

The Soviet Government is prepared to examine, along with the governments of the other socialist states, the measures that will make possible the further development and reinforcement of economic ties between the socialist countries, in order to remove any possibility of interference with the principles of national sovereignty, of reciprocal interest, and of equality of rights in economic agreements.

This principle must also be extended to cover the question of advisors. It is well known that during the period just past, when the new socialist regime was being formed, the Soviet Union, at the request of the governments of the people's democracies has sent into these countries many specialists, many engineers, and many agronomists and scientists and military advisors. Recently, the Soviet Government has frequently proposed to the socialist states the question of withdrawing those advisors.

Inasmuch as the people's democracies have trained their own personnel, who are now qualified to handle all economic and military matters, the Soviet Government believes that it is necessary to reconsider, together with the other socialist states, the question of whether it is still advantageous to maintain these advisors of the USSR in these countries.

As far as the military domain is concerned, an important basis for relations between the USSR and the people's democracies has been provided by the Warsaw Pact, under which the signatories have made political and military commitments with each other. They have committed themselves, in particular, to take "those concerted measures which are deemed necessary for the reinforcement of their capabilities for protecting the peaceful employment of their people, for guaranteeing the integrity of their frontiers and their territories, and for assuring their defence against any aggression."

It is well known that, under the Warsaw Pact and under agreements between the governments, Soviet troops are stationed in the republics of Hungary and Romania. In the republic of Poland, Soviet troops are stationed under the terms of the Potsdam Agreement with the other great powers, as well as under the terms of the Warsaw Pact. There are no Soviet troops in the other people's democracies.

In order to insure the mutual security of the socialist countries, the Soviet Government is prepared to review with the other socialist countries signing the Warsaw Pact the question of Soviet troops stationed on the territory of the above-mentioned countries.

In doing so, the Soviet Government proceeds from the principle that the stationing of troops of one member state of the Warsaw Pact on the territory of another state shall be by agreement of all the member states and only with the consent of the state on the territory of which, and on the demand of which, these troops are to be stationed.

The Soviet Government believes it is essential to make a declaration regarding the recent events in Hungary. Their development has shown that the workers of Hungary have, after achieving great progress on the basis of the people's democratic order, justifiably raised the questions of the need for eliminating the serious inadequacies of the economic system, of the need for further improving the material well-being of the people, and of the need for furthering the battle against bureaucratic excesses in the state apparatus. However, the forces of reaction and of counter-revolution have quickly joined in this just and progressive movement of the workers, with the aim of using the discontent of the workers to undermine the foundations of the people's democratic system in Hungary and to restore to power the landlords and the capitalists.

The Soviet Government and all the Soviet people deeply regret that these events in Hungary have led to bloodshed.

At the request of the People's Government of Hungary, the Soviet Government agreed to send Soviet military units into Budapest to help the Hungarian People's Army and the Hungarian Government to re-establish order in that city.

Being of the opinion that the continued presence of Soviet units in Hungary could be used as a pretext for further aggravating the situation, the Soviet Government has now given instructions to its military commanders to withdraw their troops from the city of Budapest as soon as the Hungarian Government feels that they can be dispensed with.

At the same time, the Soviet Government is prepared to engage in negotiations with the Hungarian People's Government and the other signatories of the Warsaw Pact regarding the question of the presence of Soviet troops elsewhere on the territory of Hungary.

The defence of socialist gains in the Hungarian People's Government is at the moment the primary and sacred task of the workers, the peasants, the intellectuals, and all the working people of Hungary.

The Soviet Government expresses its conviction that the people of the socialist countries will not allow reactionary forces, whether foreign or domestic, to undermine those foundations of the democratic People's Government which have been won and strengthened by the struggle and sacrifice and work of the people of this country. These people will, it believes, employ all their efforts to eliminate any obstacles in the way of strengthening the democratic foundations, the independence, and the sovereignty of their country. Such actions will, in turn, strengthen the socialist foundations of the economy and the culture of each country and will continue to increase the material well-being and the cultural level of all the workers. The Hungarian people will strengthen the brotherhood and the mutual cause of the socialist countries in order to consolidate the great and peaceful aims of socialism.

The Establishment in Hungary

◆

Imre Kovács

Writing almost a decade after the Hungarian revolt, Kovács describes the malaise gripping Kádár's Hungary as the objectives of 1956 were systematically obliterated.

Western papers portray János Kádár as a smiling, charming man, a face from the crowd, an impressive mediocrity. Yet he should not be underestimated, because he is also a shrewd politician, an excellent tactician and an able leader. It was no accident

Imre Kovács, "The Establishment in Hungary," from *East Europe,* May 1965, pp. 2–7.

that the Russians picked him in 1956 as the right man to re-establish communism in Hungary. For months the Budapest regime has been celebrating the twentieth anniversary of the country's liberation by the Russian armies. But the prolonged festivities have not been able to stifle the insistent question on the tongues of politically-minded people as to how much longer Kádár will last as Premier and head of the communist party. The real question, of course, is: Where is Hungary going?

The speculation began last October when Khrushchev was suddenly ousted from power in Moscow. His fall came as a shock to the nation and a serious blow to the prestige of Kádár, who after all had been put in power and kept there by the Soviet leader. As soon as the news reached Budapest, virtually everybody—friend and foe alike—abandoned Kádár on the assumption that he couldn't possibly survive the impact of the Moscow events. His enemies in the party and the government called each other joyfully on the telephone as if at last their day had come. It was thought that at best he might continue as party leader, releasing the Premiership to one of his most trusted comrades—Gyula Kállai, the chief ideologist, or Jenö Fock, the chief economic planner, or perhaps agricultural chief Lajos Fehér. Others took a gloomier view, predicting a radical overhaul of the whole leadership and a return to a hard line. These Cassandras thought that Kádár might lose both of his positions and be supplanted by someone like Antal Apró, an old stalinist who is now a Deputy Premier and Hungary's representative in Comecon, or even by András Hegedüs, who was Premier just before the revolution and now writes articles on the "science of leadership" for monthly journals.

But Kádár survived. Indeed, on October 18 when he returned to Budapest from Poland where he had been on a political visit, a crowd was on hand at the railroad station to welcome him—a spontaneous crowd, one which demonstrated what many Hungarians have come to feel about Kádár: that he is a better ruler than they had reason to expect. A hint of Kádár's own feelings was given in his speech to the parliament in February when he said that "those autumn days" had been "a good time to draw some conclusions also about the opinions of men in general . . . how firmly they stand on their feet. In such times it is apparent that our order not only has firm adherents and also waverers, but that there is an opposition, an enemy. On the right, they were talking about resignations, the downfall of the government; on the left, they were whispering of a return to a 'true, militant, hardfisted' leadership."

Kádár is certainly a devoted communist, even aspiring to be remembered as an ideologist. At least this is indicated by the title of his collected speeches and writings: *Forward on the Road of Marxism-Leninism.* He has stated repeatedly that his aim is a "positive relation" to the Soviet Union, and he is quick to attack any suggestion that his regime might in any way oppose Soviet interests. While he has pushed various internal reforms, these are not to be considered "liberalization," he insists, but "humanization"—that is, they are not a movement away from communism but simply an effort to make it more livable. The October 1964 issue of *Partelet* (Party Life) warned the membership that "the imperialists are hoping to defeat the socialist system by an internal process of 'transformation' and without war."

The imperialists are reckoning with remnants of nationalism, are feeding them and exploiting human weakness, because they hope to promote a turning away from socialist goals. . . . Such influences also appear in Hungary. They are expressed by illusions . . . by confused views . . . we frequently come across desires expressing hope in the harmonization and reconciliation of opposing ideologies.

In an effort to achieve some measure of reconciliation between the party and the nation, Kádár has been applying a policy of measured concessions. However, these are quite limited in extent and cannot be construed as meaning that the 1956 revolution is being carried out by those who suppressed it. Some Western circles have rashly concluded that many of the revolutionary demands—ranging from 15 percent up to 80 percent—have been implemented by Kádár, and French publicist Claude Bourdet has even described the situation as "victory in defeat." (*Les Temps Modernes,* March 1964.)

What is the truth? Between October 23 and November 9, 1956, the Hungarian radio stations under revolutionary control broadcast 225 major demands. Of these, 35 percent called for national independence; 31 percent for political reform; and 28 percent for economic reform. The revolutionary program might be condensed into three points: national independence, the withdrawal of Soviet troops, and free elections. Have these three major demands been met? The country is perhaps more autonomous, but it is certainly not independent. The government continues to be a monopoly of the communists; and there are still 80 thousand Soviet soldiers in Hungary. Thus no matter how the changes introduced by Kádár are appraised, the things he has left undone are precisely those which would bring Hungary its independence and freedom.

The party, with a membership of 550,000 (about five percent of the population, or a little over half its peak size in the Rákosi era), is the same power structure as in the other East European countries where communism was imposed by the Soviet army. But some of its functions and responsibilities have been transferred to various front organizations, including the trade unions and social, professional and cultural associations. Unlike Poland and East Germany, where several tame political parties are allowed to function alongside the communists, Hungary has only the People's Patriotic Front [PPF]—a firmly controlled, standard communist device intended to give a mass appeal to the party's election campaigns. Even so, at its last congress in March 1964 there was talk of the possibility of replacing the single ticket with separate election districts or constituencies in which two or more candidates would compete for office.

Hungarian politics today is haunted by the ghost of parliamentary democracy. Official spokesmen labor to convince the public that nothing essential is lacking and that—to quote Deputy Premier Gyula Kállai—"the Hungarian parliament is more democratic than that of any capitalist country." (*Népszabadsag* [People's Freedom], December 25, 1964.) But under these pronouncements runs a current of doubt. Kallai himself admitted at last year's congress of the PPF that not everyone was happy with single-list elections; on the other hand, in his December article he merely proposed to increase the number of candidates for the single ticket. "Since our society is led by the party of the revolutionary working class . . . we ourselves must simultaneously be the 'opposition' party." The idea is apparently to let more approved non-communist candidates onto the ticket, thus widening the regime's electoral base. It might conceivably open the way to broader policies reflecting the desires of the people, provided of course that the political status quo and the existing "social achievements" are not threatened.

Freer and more democratic electoral procedures are in fact being adopted in various political bodies, reluctantly but steadily, from the parliament and party down to local councils. The parliament is no longer just an assembly of yes-men; it has acquired a more business-like atmosphere in which the deputies talk frankly and critically (though not, of course, challenging the regime's basic policies). The question period has been brought back, when ministers must answer to the deputies, and the Budapest radio has a regular program ("Between Sessions") in which ministers and deputies are asked whether the promised actions were taken. The renovated parliamentary committees discuss special governmental issues such as the budget, education, foreign affairs, the planned economy, etc., in closed-door sessions, and groups of deputies hold regional meetings in their respective county seats.

While the backbone of the Kádár regime is still the party, the government's main support comes from an elite of bureaucrats and technocrats who know how to run the operations of a modern state. One of the most interesting phenomena of present-day Hungary is the quiet takeover of the state-run economy and important segments of the civil service by old-timers and various types of experts. "Proletarian origin" or "movement merits" no longer count, and party hacks who haven't enough education to meet the new standards are being pushed aside. In higher education, talent and ability now have priority; the graduate schools are open only to those who can pass the entrance examinations.

The appearance of the "organization man" in Hungary raises serious questions for the party. How much authority can be turned over to experts and technocrats without undermining the system, in terms both of power and ideology? "The currents of present-day bourgeois ideology which are the strongest in Hungary do not attack Marxism frontally," warned *Tarsadalmi Szemle* (Social Review) in November, "but try to reconcile Marxism and bourgeois ideology."

> One of these currents is the bourgeois approach to economic, sociological, political and other problems of socialist development, *e.g.,* the concept of a "united industrial society," which, with regard to technical and scientific development, ignores the differences between the social systems of capitalism and communism. Another characteristic of the bourgeois ideology is the existentialist concept of the individual. This expresses itself in the abstract and unhistorical treatment of ethical questions, in doctrinaire sermonizing, in confusion on the conflict between power and morals, and, finally, in the con-

frontation of an isolated personality with an alien society. And a claim of "neutrality" is frequently heard with regard to the ideological approach to science and neo-positivism.

The ideological confrontation has also led to friction between party members and non-party experts, the former complaining that they are being unjustly pushed aside and that the new intelligentsia are getting undeserved advantages and privileges. Party spokesmen reply that the policy is one of "national unity" aiming to win over the intelligentsia; if party loyalty is not enough for the task of building socialism in modern conditions, neither is technical expertise.

Nevertheless, Hungary has now been taken over by a new class, or more accurately a new bourgeoisie. The makeup of this socialist establishment, comprising about one percent of the population, is rather heterogeneous. It includes the upper strata of the party and civil service, the state-run economy, the planning office and the trade unions; senior officers of the armed forces and the security police; privileged scientists; highly qualified experts; and the usual upper crust of artists and writers. They have no common language, since communists and non-communists think and talk quite differently, but they do have a common past: almost all of them suffered under Rákosi in the days of Stalin, and some of them were his followers as well. And they share a common interest: to keep things running and to keep themselves in power.

The new Hungarian ruling class claims much the same perquisites—homes, villas, pleasures, cars, travel—as its prewar counterpart, and is equally selfish, detached, arrogant and corrupt. Below the top elite is another stratum of managers who run the state and local administration, the state enterprises, the collective farms, the banks, the educational and propaganda network, etc. They are tough, poorly educated and without manners; while they follow the orders of their superiors, they do not always have a sense of responsibility. Far, far below this feudal-communist hierarchy come the rest of the nation—the peasants and workers. Although the national income is better distributed than in prewar Hungary, this class lives just above the poverty line.

◆

THE YOUNG CYNICS

The feeling that something has gone wrong with Hungarian communism is widespread among party members, but is especially marked in the younger generation. "Politics is a dirty business," said one high school student in a recent radio discussion, and a commentator the next day agreed with him. "Our young friend took these words out of the mouths of adults. They often say that politics is a dangerous trade, a dirty thing. How often a reporter is told, 'Please, I am not interested in politics.' " (Radio Kossuth, January 26.)

This attitude among the young has made the battle of generations unusually intense, for added to the normal outrage of the young at the follies of their elders is a political disgust over the state of the nation which they are to inherit. Two years ago the young poet Ferenc Baranyi published some verses which shook the establishment.

> *For seventeen years, we busily filled*
> *Our heads with the wine of knowledge,*
> *And yet, from a high shelf, an*
> *Empty barrel-head arrogantly*
> *Echoes instructions for us . . . .*

The war continues. In the January issue of the avant-garde literary monthly *Uj Iras* (New Writing) another young poet, Ferenc Buda, speaks of the attitude of those between 25 and 30: "We were enthusiastic twice and disappointed twice, on both occasions so cruelly that we could hardly survive even with our elastic spirit. It is not easy for us to be enthusiastic; instead of ideas, we try to find strength within ourselves on which we can depend." (The "two occasions" are obviously the liberation of 1945 and the revolt of 1956. The latter is called "the counterrevolution" by the party, but it remains a vivid and inspiring memory to people in all walks of life.)

His comments are part of a series entitled "Confessions About Youth." Most of the articles are in effect an indictment of the older generation, including the political leaders. A young, idealistic man, argues Buda, cannot hope to make a career because he is always running up against "job security, professional or materialistic jealousy, a kind of bad mood which is impossible to define, and corruption." Buda feels that the younger generation is not understood; that it is underpaid and ignored. Especially hard is the lot of the young professional or intellectual forced to live in the countryside where his ideas and energy are launched in vain "against the massive walls of poverty, misery, conservatism, prejudice, resentment, heavy-handed bossism, and hidden hostility."

Peter Veres, an old establishment writer with a slight accent of nonconformity, observed in the December issue of *Kortars* (Contemporary) that a prevalent mood in Hungary is indifference, an "apolitical" attitude stemming from "weariness and disappointment." He analyzed its various causes, most of which seemed to lie in the conflict between the "Messianic" promises of Marxism and the uncomfortable facts of reality. This apolitical attitude, he declared, "is the biggest and most difficult problem facing Hungarian society."

Beneath the calm surface, dark currents are at work. In the late forties and early fifties the regimented writers and artists were made to express the "happiness" of the Hungarians; today, when life is relatively free and the writers and artists are able to create according to their talents and ideas, the new Hungarian literature and art reflect sadness and hopelessness, pessimism and despondency. Their pervasive themes are the unhappiness of man and the emptiness of life; they are obsessed with the horrors of the recent past and with the total absence of alternatives. There is no difference in this between the older and the younger generations.

◆
THE ADVANCE WESTWARD

While the atmosphere within the country is freer but not happier, Budapest's foreign policy remains essentially that of the Soviet Union. President Johnson's "bridge-building" approach to Eastern Europe is interpreted Moscow-style as a desire to make Hungary a "bridgehead" against the Soviet Union. Unlike the Rumanians and the Poles, the Hungarian communists have not exploited the new power relations in the communist world to achieve national ends of their own, and until now Kádár has been among Moscow's two or three most reliable supporters. This may perhaps be a symptom of the political vacuum in Hungary. Not one of the top leaders was educated in the West or even visited a free country before he acquired his official post. The technocrats are not interested in foreign affairs, and the better-educated non-communist supporters of the regime have no desire to venture into dangerous matters.

Nevertheless the Kádár regime is trying to improve its international image, and the red carpet is rolled out for every prominent visitor along with 21-gun salutes. In the last two years the state guests have included Khrushchev, Gomułka, Novotný of Czechoslovakia, Zhivkov of Bulgaria, Tito, Haile Selassie and the President of the Yemen Republic. Last year Budapest began to explore the opportunities for closer contacts with the West. It developed warm relations with Austria, reached an accord with the Vatican, signed a trade agreement with Britain and a cultural agreement with Belgium, and even flirted a little with de Gaulle's formula for a united Europe.

The *rapprochement* with Austria revived memories of the Habsburg era when Hungary played an important part in Europe. Receiving Hungary's Deputy Premier Jeno Fock in Vienna, Austrian Vice Chancellor Bruno Pitterman said: "For Austria, Hungary is like the neighbors' flower garden." Austrians and Hungarians talked hopefully of some new form of cooperation, and after they had settled their claims it was reported that the two countries were planning joint industrial operations and business deals with the underdeveloped world. Last May, at an international Congress of Historians in Budapest, the participants openly discussed the lessons to be drawn from the history of the Austro-Hungarian monarchy; some speakers even raised the question whether the Western powers had not been mistaken in pressing for its dissolution in 1918.

The biggest surprise was provided by Foreign Minister János Peter when he visited Paris in January. On his arrival at the Gare de l'Est this dull and opportunistic bureaucrat announced that he had come "to take a close look at France's idea of an independent, enlarged and 'European' Europe." After he had met with his French counterpart Couve de Murville, he told the press that "Hungary, despite the fact that she is a small country, can in her geographical position help to bring the opposing worlds closer to each other."

His visit to France was called "historic," and the slogan "Europe to the Urals" received great play in the Hungarian press. "Why not?" asked the Budapest radio. "Hungary is a European nation, and it is only natural that she express her interest in a

Europe the borders of which cannot be arbitrarily drawn; it stretches from the Atlantic to the Urals. The cultural heritage of Europe is still a force in our culture and traditions."

Premier Kádár was led to discuss the idea in his speech to parliament on February 11. "Class struggle has not invalidated geography," he said, but he went on—typically—to say that while Hungary is geographically part of Europe it belongs politically to the "socialist world system." On the question whether the two parts of Europe might be brought closer, he confined himself as usual to the line laid down by Moscow: recognition of the status quo in eastern Europe (including East Germany and a separate West Berlin); the requirement that a withdrawal of Soviet troops can take place only as part of a "give and take" arrangement between East and West; and the levelling of the tariff wall of the Common Market.

But his speech did contain one new and independent note that may be heard again in the future. This was the appeal for Hungarian neutrality implicit in his statement that the search for contact between two countries should never be directed against a third country.

Democratic Opposition in Hungary Today

✦

Josef Gorlice

Gorlice interviewed János Kis, editor of the prominent *samizdat* periodical *Beszélö,* in Budapest in 1986, at a time when opposition forces were mounting more noticeably in Hungary than anywhere else in the bloc. The substance of the interview gains significance in light of developments at the end of the decade.

J.G.: To some of us in the west the *Beszélö* "reform program" signaled a turn in the thinking of the opposition. Some thought it a response to the situation created by the Polish coup. What in fact were the events that led to the formulation of the "reform program"?

J.K.: The Polish crackdown, naturally presented a problem for everybody in

Josef Gorlice, "Democratic Opposition in Hungary Today" (interview with János Kis), from *Across Frontiers,* Fall 1986, pp. 21–22, 43–5. Reprinted by permission of the Across Frontiers Foundation.

the opposition and discussions about ways to continue took place. In a way this programmatic text is a tentative answer, or part of a tentative answer, to this problem.

I would say that this text is a tentative combination of Polish "new evolutionism" and Hungarian "reformism." From the Polish KOR opposition it takes over the idea of the necessity of putting pressure on the government in order to push democratic changes through while dropping the Polish idea that the opposition need not bother with the content of the reforms. For the Polish opposition the manner in which to proceed with reforms is the business of the government, while the business of society is to measure the consequences of government policy—to react to, and defend itself from the bad consequences of government policy—but not to put forward its own constructive programs of social and political change.

What we are now trying to do is to take up the first part of the KOR strategy and combine it with constructive proposals for conceivable and necessary political reforms. We are trying to demonstrate that the package of reforms that we have proposed, which are clearly political ones, are necessary in order for any real economic reforms to be put into effect.

J.G.: Several years ago a well known figure of the opposition stated that, "because economic issues remain a mere appendage to politics and ideology, no real reform, even purely economic is possible." The implication being that significant economic reforms would inevitably tend to unravel the entire political structure. It would seem that in the light of the *Beszélö* "program" the regime is no longer considered so politically rigid as to make real economic reforms impossible. Can the state in fact truly proceed with significant but controlled and limited economic reforms? Is economic reform now possible without radical political reorganization/democratization?

J.K.: I think that if by economic reform you mean a thoroughgoing institutional change creating a socialist market economy, then you have to presuppose that such an economic change is impossible without political changes. In my view the reason for this is that such a change in the institutional structure of the economy would imply a very thoroughgoing redistribution of power. I wouldn't say in favor of democracy, but anyway, a very important redistribution of power which goes against the interests and wishes of a very large and very powerful sector of the established power apparatus. As a consequence, if you want such an economic reform to go through you have to combine it with those political reforms that would enable some of the social forces behind reform to counter-balance the resistance of the power apparatuses. Practically speaking, this is our argument in *Beszélö*. Reform is impossible without breaking the resistance of the power apparatuses. As a consequence economic reform is only possible if accompanied by thoroughgoing political reforms which would stimulate the activity of some definite social forces and make it possible for them to act politically.

J.G.: In the west we have only a very crude conception of how politics actually works in Hungary. Could you explain which social forces could push through greater reforms and a greater opening up of the system? How might they deploy themselves politically to do so?

J.K.: I think it depends very much on the kind of reform that is conceived of.

The present reform, for example, is entirely separated from political changes even in the sense of some moderate trade union reforms. This reform is only supported by very limited groupings who are mostly linked to the state apparatus or to some parts (but only some parts) of the economic establishment and to those groups interested in small enterprises. Wider social stratas linked neither to the ruling apparatus nor to the very very tiny free enterprise sector have any interest at all in the reforms. These reforms are not seen by them as being something that could really change things or have the effect of overcoming the crisis and democratizing the economy and society.

So this is the present situation, but more radical reforms are conceivable if they are combined with political changes that could marshal wider social backing.

J.G.: How does the opposition help in marshalling those forces?

J.K.: Well I do not think that the role of the opposition in Hungary is to marshal social forces. My feeling is that the main thing to understand about the Hungarian opposition is that its conceivable role in the near future is not parallel to that of the Polish one in smaller dimensions. When the Polish opposition organized in the middle of the 1970's there was a clear polarization of power and society and clear decomposition of the power structure. In that situation the opposition could really marshal the majority of the politically attentive and active public behind it. In Hungary, the general mood, although rather pessimistic about the capacities of the government to overcome the crisis and to put serious and important reforms into effect, is that of a strong attachment to stability due to Hungary's special situation. This is mainly the result of a comparison with the situation in other East European countries.

The aim of most of the people who become active is not to create a rupture, but to gain a little bit more independence vis-à-vis the government. This means that social movements begin to form in Hungary not behind the opposition, but between the opposition and the government. So the aim of the opposition is rather more to try to elucidate the situation, to show alternatives, to stimulate discussion and political thinking. It is rather more like an effective independent press in the west than a social movement or an organization.

We see the possibility of the emergence of a social movement which would gradually make itself more and more independent of the government, not behind the opposition but between the opposition and the government. We are trying to stimulate and influence the change without trying to lead.

J.G.: One of the conclusions that has been drawn from the Polish state of war is that after all is said and done, in the societies of "Really Existing Socialism" the state cannot tolerate any real independent centers of social self-organization outside of its control, as they would tend to spread and leave very little for the state to do. In light of the *Beszélö* "program's" orientation, for Hungary at least, should this opinion be revised? Can a soviet-type society tolerate independent self-organization?

J.K.: I think that all such arguments are a little bit metaphysical because they take the ideology of the system, or its rough political structure, or the two combined, and then deduce this consequence from it without taking into account the fact that every ideology and every institutional structure is working in an economic, social and world political environment and has to struggle for survival under the selective pressures of these environments. So its real behavior is not the simple consequence of its very abstract internal structure, but of this interplay of environment and structure and environment and ideology. Although I think that it is true that the ideological structure is selecting against tolerating independent social movements, organizations, press and so on, the combination of the conjuncture between these internal structures and ideologies on the one side, and the environment in which it is put on the other, may be such that, not withstanding this structure, movements and forms of social expression may be half-tolerated, or $^3\{_4$ tolerated or even tolerated as such.

Let's take the example of the Polish church. As in all the other East European soviet-type regimes, in Poland too, the state tried to crush the church's independence. But it was unable to do so. Even though there were still attacks on the church into the early 1970's, it is now clear (and it is something that determines the behavior of the state and its attitude towards the church) that the state can harass the church but it cannot do away with it. As a consequence, the state has even developed attitudes that would have been inconceivable 20 years ago, namely, of building on the church's interests vis-à-vis the opposition. There is, for example, a tacit agreement between Glemp and the government. Glemp asks the parish priests not to get involved in politics, and in return the state gives such, such and such things to Glemp. That means that the state is partially building its stability on an uneasy cooperation with the church.

Now I don't want to evaluate the politics of either the government or the church in Poland. I simply want to show that the conjuncture may be such that the regime has to tolerate such phenomena in the long run. So the big question, which no one is able to answer, is whether the semi-toleration that now exists for small opposition groups in Hungary can be extended and stabilized, or whether it will prove to have been no more than a crisis phenomenon.

J.G.: It would seem that, without massive pressure arising independently from society, any kind of serious economic reforms would require a tactical alliance with pragmatists within the government (its liberal wing) in order to stimulate the participation of significant social forces to push the reforms through. Do the pragmatists actually have the will and the influence to do that? Or can you foresee the development of a movement of independent social forces forcing the government to put through reforms?

J.K.: As for the first part of your question I think the answer is no. Here I think I can build on the opinion of the reform economists who are not oppositionists at all and who did not share our conceptions as little as two years ago when we first proposed them. These economists are now utterly disillusioned with the government's reform politics and now, *grosso modo,* accept our analysis that this government, under this political configuration, is unable to put through thoroughgoing economic reforms. So the mood of pessimism about the capacities of the government to push through reforms is not something characteristic of the opposition alone.

As for the second part of the question. My feeling is that for the moment the main problem is that those social forces whose support would be necessary to push through the reforms are so disillusioned about it that no backing is there at all. The groups are mainly that part of the working class whose influence sometimes can be felt (the skilled workers in big factories), that part of the intelligentsia which has some opinion forming influence, and so on.

I am thoroughly convinced that although there are some common interests in pushing through economic reform in the sense that if the government wants stability, if it wants to overcome the crisis, it has to push economic reforms through. But nevertheless I think it will be unable to do so without real political reform and without building on some independent social forces for pushing that reform through.

So in order to get people interested in reforms I think the reform program should first of all be much more clear, much more definite. It should be much more clear to the public that the issue is something of real importance, and secondly, the program should be combined with conceivable solutions for the everyday problems that people face: inflation, unemployment . . . , social policy of distribution in general.

Furthermore, I think that one of the most important lessons of the Polish events is that workers begin to realize the importance of structural changes at the moment in which they perceive that they can get some power. So some pluralization of the trade union structure is absolutely necessary, even though a real pluralization of the trade union structure is clearly inconceivable now. But it is absolutely necessary that reforms be made that would make it clear to the workers that, at least on the factory level, the trade unions could become their own rather than just being an extension of the power apparatus. The workers will only be on the side of the reforms if they feel that they are able to contend with the unfavorable effects of economic changes.

J.G.: What are the limits to this kind of evolutionary reformism given the structure of Really Existing Socialism in Hungary?

J.K.: I wouldn't talk about absolute limits. I think it is more intelligent to talk about limits for the foreseeable future because nobody knows what type of evolution would be possible under a reformed economy and polity or what the external and economic constraints will be.

My feeling is that for the present, any realistic program that could be received as such by the public, should openly accept that in the sphere of public law, by which I mean the sphere comprising the state, the party and other organizations which have a public juridical definition, no pluralization is conceivable. What is conceivable on the other hand is a pluralization in the sphere of private law or what is commonly called civil society.

It is conceivable that some forms of independent press, which would be regulated in a special way, will be created on the margins of the official press. Although there will continue to be just one trade union, professional associations could be set up, although without those public law rights which trade unions as corporate institutions generally have. It is conceivable that the very idea of voluntary associations and organization in general will be allowed and so on. That kind of pluralization is conceivable in my view. I won't forecast that it will happen, but it is possible.

J.G.: The Hungarian regime has been able to give a freer rein to society (at least in the private sphere) than has any other E. European state. What accounts for this Hungarian singularity? Are similar evolutions foreseeable in the other countries of

E. Central Europe? Does the strategy of evolutionary reformism imply that the potential now exists for the Hungarian state to reestablish its connections with the organic evolution of Hungarian society and develop a "normal" and legitimatable basis for its reproduction?

J.K.: In a sense I think that there are similar and parallel trends in every East European country, perhaps with the exception of Rumania which restalinized and retotalitarianized itself in the early 1970's. The only exceptional thing about Hungary is that such trends are more organic and widespread here than in other countries and the change has been accompanied by some secondary ideological adjustments that made it possible for large segments of the population to accept the status quo as being something more than forced upon them.

But I don't think that the question is whether or not social changes are possible in other countries. I cannot answer that question except by saying that some such trends are there already. The question is whether things can continue like this in Hungary and my feeling is that they cannot. My feeling is that we are witnessing the slow decomposition of the consensus and that Hungary confronts a crisis situation. That is why we are arguing for the necessity of a package of political and economic reforms before that social crisis arrives.

So my feeling is that this Kádárist success has had some historical preconditions—a very rapid horizontal and vertical social mobility for one—that have been partially changed and partially eaten up and that they cannot reproduce themselves forever. In the early 1950's mobilized people could not reap the fruits of the reorganization because of the terror and the general misery, but they could do so in the 60's and early 70's.

So from peasants they became workers, from manual unskilled workers they became skilled, from skilled manual workers they became mental workers and so on. It was a very rapid development concomitant with the very rapid evolution and restructuring of the country itself. But this mobilization has now come to an end and as a consequence the stratas that were exceptionally satisfied are simply dying out and the new stratas are already in the situation into which they were born.

The generations that participated in the events following the crushing of the revolution and the concomitant terror were very deeply affected by it. The very deep comparison effects between then and now were decisive for these generations. It was really an unexpected gift for them that the same power that had crushed them later allowed them to reestablish a normal social life. As a result they didn't bother about putting pressure on the government. They simply didn't think in those terms.

But the last parts of these generations are passing away in this decade and new generations have since grown up for whom the Kádárian regime is already a precondition, not something they received as a present. This is a second very important change.

Then there are other kinds of changes. For example, in the 60's and early 70's there was a very good economic conjuncture which made the at least partial satisfaction of every social strata possible at the same time. So there was no serious conflict between social stratas about the division of the cake. This is not the situation now. It is the same here as in the United States and everywhere else in the world. Choices have to be made and as a consequence people are beginning to feel that they have to have some impact on the way choices are made if they do not want to be maltreated.

And then there is also the fact that in the 60's and early 70's the government was able to make many concessions to the population which were not costly in either economic or political terms but which were, nevertheless, important to the people. For example, there was some liberalization of the passport system without making it a right to have a passport; some liberalization of culture without tolerating independent centers of culture such as reviews, theaters and so forth; toleration of the second economy without really legalizing it, etc.

The opportunities to make concessions have now been reduced and the costs have begun to grow for every bit of conceivable change by the government, and the situation is approaching in which real structural reforms are necessary in order to have any real impact.

I can continue the list but what I want to say is that my feeling is that the conditions of a successful Kádárism, the formula of which is concessions without rights, is now going to be progressively reduced. As a consequence I think that the alternative becomes either decomposition of this consensus-like situation or thoroughgoing reforms.

J.G.: In a situation of decomposition of consensus what do you think are the government's opportunities to rule in a more "traditional" manner, manipulating one social group against another, etc. What are the government's crisis management abilities?

J.K.: You never can exclude such a possibility. This is one of the reasons for making propaganda for reforms now, before it becomes a reality. There is such a possibility in every society. Whether it succeeds or not is a question of the political conjuncture of forces and the relations between the contending parties. But yes, there is such a possibility.

J.G.: Several people we have talked to have expressed a certain amount of ambivalence about economic reform in so far as (at least in its present formulations) it would tend to exacerbate inequalities and open the way towards a super exploitation of segments of the population. It also seems that the government wishes to shake off many of the social responsibilities that it hitherto claimed as a major source of its legislation as the second economy increasingly fills the spaces that the command economy cannot respond to. The development of the second economy and withdrawal of direct state control from many sectors of economic life seems to be a sort of wild process, one that is growing and may not be able to be reined in by the state very easily, even if it tends to decompose state power. A rather great deal of social fragmentation seems to be developing as a result of this process. Is that an accurate perception, and if it is, what does that tend to mean vis-à-vis the possibilities of social cohesion and social movements in the future in Hungary?

J.K.: Let me make a preliminary remark which doesn't concern your question directly. The economic reforms that are demanded by reform economists are not concentrating on the legalization of the second economy. They are concentrating on a thoroughgoing reform of the first one. Although everybody agrees on the necessity of liberalizing the private economy, every reform economist (with whom I agree myself) knows quite well that without a thoroughgoing structural reform of the first one, of the state enterprises system, the result can only be a mutual parasitism of ineffective structures. The effects would not only be economic, there are social consequences as well, of which I will now speak about in reply to your question.

I think that given the present structure, the legalization of some form of private enterprise is a doubled-edged phenomenon. On the one hand, naturally, it is very important and very positive in the sense that it demolishes the fetish of the necessity, in a socialized economy, of having direct state control, over every organized economic and non-economic activity. In this sense its ideological effects would be very stimulating and positive. Secondly, it creates a means for many people to earn a living independently of the state hierarchy and this too is positive.

On the other side it is true that this is the sector that is the least interested in political reforms and it functions as a safety valve for enterprising people who, instead of struggling to reform the factory structure, go out and begin to work on their little private plots and so on.

Another negative effect is that in a very imperfect market, the consequences of such a liberalization are not always, at least in the short run, healthy. For example, there are a lot of illegal and immoral ways of handling partners and customers which are almost inevitable given such a situation. Secondly, there is an accumulation of riches resulting from the monopoly situation that would be impossible in a normal market where supply and demand are more balanced. Windfall profits are made that cannot be reinvested and as a consequence one has to consume it in a conspicuous way of living it up—and that is something that hurts people.

But I think you should see this complex of things in a really complex way. Not only its negative side effects but its positive too.

J.G.: There seems to be a debate now taking place within government circles about a proposed decentralization of social services spending. Could you explain what is at question here?

J.K.: What the government is now trying to do is not a decentralization of redistribution per se but a reduction in funding. Because of the huge budget deficit which is a consequence of the economic recession, less is to be siphoned off, less is to be redistributed. So the government is trying to decentralize the burdens of providing infrastructure, building schools, etc., but not the funding. What is now going on is that the government is decentralizing some responsibilities without decentralizing the whole structure of redistribution. The position of the reform sociologists and economists about this is that redistribution system itself has to be decentralized, that is partially decentralized, partially put on legal and publicly controllable footing, this is how I see it.

J.G.: So this "decentralization" is a method for the government to reduce its social welfare bill.

J.K.: Exactly. It is Hungarian style Thatcherism and Reaganism.

CZECHOSLOVAKIA 1968

✦ As in Hungary a dozen years earlier, the Czechoslovak reform movement arose within the ruling party. Although the country started the postwar period with the head start of industrial experience and the memory of a modern political order, the regime that presided over Czechoslovakia until 1968 was unimaginative, leaving a great deal of room for intellectuals, in and out of the party, to fashion schemes for improving the situation. Writers and philosophers were very active in the months leading up to the Prague Spring, discussing privately some of the liberalizing notions that would presently become an official program.

When the old party leadership was turned out and a new one emerged around Alexander Dubček, the reform program was accompanied by circumspect reassurances aimed at the Soviet Union and calculated to forestall the kind of alarm that precipitated the invasion of Hungary in 1956. Had these precautions proved adequate, the "socialism with a human face" that unfolded during the first half of 1968 would almost certainly have saved socialism from the massive ill repute that was so prominent a factor in the late 1980s. It would have proved enormously attractive elsewhere in the region (which was of course part of the problem it posed to the Soviet Union) and might have averted some of the explosiveness that built up as the Soviet model lost its last shreds of credibility. Nevertheless, although the reform movement fell victim to Soviet intervention, it had injected potent yeast into East European consciousness, an effect that was only temporarily obscured by the repression that followed when the invaders finally installed a tractable restorationist regime under Gustav Husák.

The first four entries below come from participants in the ferment of the Prague Spring; the fourth was composed by the novelist Ludvik Vaculík. Liehm, Šik, and Sviták all went into exile after the intervention. Following Suda's account of the invasion of August 1968, Selucký reflects on the episode retrospectively and two groups voice two of the many dissenting statements that kept 1968 alive in the grim interlude that lasted until 1989. Charter 77 is the most widely noticed such expression. It made its many signatories targets for repression in the short run but eventually also candidates for leading roles when the Husák regime collapsed.

Intellectual Origins of the Reform Movement

✦

Antonín Liehm

Liehm was a participant in the intellectual ferment that he describes in this essay and, since leaving Czechoslovakia after the invasion, has remained a trenchant commentator on developments in his homeland. He has divided his time between academic and journalistic activity.

To understand the role that Czechoslovak culture played in preparing the way for the momentous events of the Spring, we must begin by grappling with a paradox. In the early nineteen-fifties, the structure of Czechoslovak cultural life was precipitously re-organized to parallel the pattern of the Soviet model. As became only too painfully evident in retrospect, this process was carried out in total disregard of the basic differences between the two countries, differences in traditions, intellectual climate and conditions of life. Furthermore, it is now evident that the same structures which served to buttress the Stalinist pyramid in the USSR could not be exported wholesale to other countries without seriously upsetting the stability of the local systems of power.

The power pyramid typical of Stalinism happens to be founded on a very simple, unoriginal principle, derived from older social orders. At its pinnacle there rules a small group (ultimately a single individual), surrounded by a military, political and police apparatus. This apparatus is given the task of seeing to it that orders from the top are faithfully reproduced and transmitted down to the lowest levels of the pyramid. The actual transmission of the orders is carried out by a system of "societal" organizations which function as so-called "transmission-belts." Members of the power apparatus are given leading positions in these organizations, which thus become links between the ruling elite and the masses, between the apparatus and the population—or, in Stalinist jargon, "between the party and the unaffiliated." To enable the "transmission-belts" to perform their functions, the government subsidizes them generously.

In addition to ensuring that orders from the top are properly disseminated and unquestioningly obeyed, the pyramid and its power apparatus also serve the obverse

Antonín Liehm, "Intellectual Origins of the Reform Movement," from V. V. Kusin, ed., *The Czechoslovak Reform Movement,* Clio Press, 1973, pp. 67–78.

function, namely, to transmit a purified, filtered message of compliance and confirmation back to the top, an idealized echo of the initial order. The operation of the power pyramid is self-justifying. This is clearly bound to be the case under conditions where all citizens are virtually government employees directly dependent upon the pyramid, and where there is an absence of free dissemination of information and lack of democratic institutions.

The top issues orders which the apparatus reduces to their simplest essentials and conveys down. The functionaries at the bottom of the apparatus are supposed to inform their superiors that all orders were carried out to the letter—or, preferably, that they were carried out beyond all expectations. The well-being of the functionaries is not dependent upon the state of the country's economy nor upon the level of performance in any particular sector, rather, their career is measured by their ability to ensure a smooth, uninterrupted flow of orders up and down within the pyramid, and to see to it that messages from the bottom confirm the maximum expectations of the leaders. The most successful officials are those who can surmise the leaders' hopes with the greatest accuracy, and who can adjust their own reports accordingly. In order for this system to work, it is of course necessary that all participants play the game, and scrupulously follow the tacit rules of conspiracy, co-operation, mutual assistance and loyalty. In the end, it is impossible to tell to which segment of the apparatus a given functionary belongs. Not only are all departments extremely similar to one another, but any individual who manages to climb to the highest rungs of the ladder necessarily had to pass through all the units of the apparatus, to know their mechanisms and to establish ties of mutual alliance with their staffs. Since orders from above must in turn support themselves on reports manufactured below, a closed cycle is created wherein the same situation is reproduced over and over again. The mechanism feeds on itself, it is its own goal and purpose, and the smallest particle of external, living reality is a mortal danger to its existence.

Under these circumstances, two totally different orders of reality come into being. One is the thriving, faultlessly working pyramid, disgorging streams of orders and voraciously feeding on reams of reports. And side by side with this pyramid is "parallel reality"—the living, working, bustling country, with its real problems and its own economic and social structures, which have no legal existence yet are indisputably real all the same. The official pyramid cannot liquidate these structures, for it dare not touch the living roots of the country. The pyramid is thus forced to tolerate the existence of these extra-legal entities, and must content itself to keep them from assuming nation-wide influence. For example, it attempts to sever any horizontal connections between autonomous centres of authority as soon as they outgrow a merely local importance. During certain periods, the attempt to define permissible limits to the autonomy of the living, *de facto* structures of the country becomes the most demanding and delicate problem the power pyramid has to face. This was especially true during the era of neo-Stalinism; after all, it is in its pragmatic approach to this very question that neo-Stalinism differs most markedly from the rigid ideological puritanism of original Stalinism. Too liberal a concession to the pressure exerted by *de facto* structures would endanger the very core of the pyramid. On the other hand, too brutal an intervention against "parallel reality" would stifle a working, breathing organism, indispensable to the life of the country as we shall see later. This dilemma is at the root of the characteristic oscillation of the power pyramid between repression and liberalization. Now economic reforms are accepted, now they are rejected; now cultural policy is democratized, now it is made more autocratic. The same oscillation was evident with respect to such questions as personal freedom, the right to move freely within the country and to travel abroad, even to certain questions of foreign policy. For in this area, too, there inevitably arose two orders of reality, the reality represented by the official pyramid and the reality of autonomous, vital structures representing the true needs of the nation and of foreign countries.

Within the official pyramid, there is a system of transmission belts not only for every segment of the population, but for every type of pursuit and interest, no matter how trivial. Thus, for example, crossword enthusiasts and rabbit fanciers have their own government sponsored organizations, and these have fundamentally the same structure and purpose as any of the other transmission-belts. Naturally, such organizations cannot really function in any meaningful way except by playing a dual role. In addition to performing "official" duty as part of the transmission belt system, these organizations eventually assume a second, more vital existence and quietly begin the job of providing services not in response to orders from the central pyramid but in response to real social needs.

In Czechoslovakia, the most striking manifestation of the two parallel structures—*de jure* and *de facto*—was in the realm of culture. After 1948, the country's cultural enterprise was furnished with the same system of transmission-belts as all other areas of national life. For example, the former independent Association of Czechoslovak Writers was replaced by a Writers' Union with its own presidium, central committee, secretariat, and control commission. Similar organizations were created in other cultural spheres, such as the graphic arts, music and theatre. (Film was excepted, possibly because at that time the Soviet film-makers did not yet have a union themselves, or because film production was more or less concentrated in a few studios under tight government control.)

The state proved to be not only a vigilant guardian of culture, but a generous patron as well, and lavish government subsidies temporarily gave Czechoslovak artists and writers the hope that the long national tradition of respect for things of the mind was asserting itself, and that culture was once more to assume its rightful place in national life. But it didn't take them long to recognize that the state's enormous involvement in culture, its open-handed largesse in distributing careers, rewards, and glory had a very significant drawback. It became evident that all of cultural life was being relentlessly transformed into an integral part of the power pyramid, and that this process inevitably brought the arts and sciences into conflict with the political leadership. Culture characteristically is extremely sensitive to the discrepancy between official power and unofficial, parallel reality. The first stirrings of unrest were felt shortly after 1953. In the years 1955–1956, Czechoslovakia went through the same process of awakening that took place in Poland, Hungary and the Soviet Union, and this was followed by the first efforts at "normalization." But unlike Poland and Hungary, Czechoslovakia had not yet exhausted the legacy of its former economic pre-eminence, its economic crisis was far milder, and thus the voice of its intellectuals was not heard in the neighbouring two countries. Nevertheless, the cultural leaders in all the socialist lands were saying more or less the same things.

Shortly after the first "normalization," the Czechoslovak economy began to succumb to a severe crisis which undermined the very foundations of the power pyramid and strengthened the autonomy of parallel-reality structures. In the realm of culture, this also marked the beginning of that remarkable process affecting the core of the pyramid which many years later culminated in the so-called Czechoslovak Spring.

Unlike the Soviet intelligentsia after 1917, Czechoslovak artists and writers never knew the elation accompanying a revolutionary explosion, with its promise of cultural liberation. The Czechoslovak culture elite entered socialism through a pompous triumphal arch, leading to a fairy-land of palatial rest-centres for writers and musicians, honorary titles, prizes and awards, offices and stipends for services rendered. These services performed for the state were used as yardsticks of cultural quality, and honours, rewards and stipends were meted out accordingly. And vice versa, the hand of Maecenas was generous, very generous—but it wasn't open for nothing. In return for the distinguished place inside the power pyramid accorded to cultural workers the governmental Maecenas—and Stalinist government was a cultural Maecenas in the original, literal sense of the term—required unconditional service.

Historically, Czechoslovak culture was always closely connected with society and with politics, and for a while it seemed that inclusion of culture within the power pyramid might be a logical outgrowth of this tradition. But this illusion faded rapidly. This was so because of the inherent logic underlying intellectual and creative activity, the fundamental self-determination of all true art. In retrospect it is clear that only two possibilities existed under the given circumstances. The artist had the option of sacrificing his gifts on the altar of the pyramid, in the best of faith and in all sincerity, to incorporate his talent and his labour into the mechanism of the pyramid, to adjust his own creative imagination to the blueprints of the power structure. If this choice is made, an insurmountable internal conflict begins to develop between the artist and the man, between service to the pyramid and intrinsic creative ideas; the best, most vital forces within the individual perish. The artist dies, or the man, sometimes both. The second possibility is that the artist's talent, the inner demands of his work, his faith in the truth prove stronger than his desire to serve the pyramid. In that event, the parallel reality beyond the reach of the pyramid triumphs. The author and his work come into ever sharper conflict with the ruling power, a conflict for which the reasons are at first unclear to both sides. Opposition to the pyramid of course entails estrangement from Maecenas, with consequent narrowing of the material possibilities of existence as well as loss of privileges, titles and stipends. Given these two alternatives, the majority of writers and artists tend to follow the course which their predecessors have followed for centuries, the strategy used by Caravaggio in an Italy ruled by popes and aristocrats, the approach used by so many artists in so many epochs when culture lived by the grace of patronage and truth had to be presented in a religious or ideological guise.

The artists paid Maecenas his due by pretending to honour the external forms of their patrons' myths and ceremonies. Eventually, artists wearing a patron's livery joined forces in attempts to gain greater degrees of autonomy. Such autonomy goes under the names of "freedom of artistic expression" or simply "freedom of expression." The recent experience of Czechoslovak writers and artists thus provides still another instance of history repeating itself, and still another example showing members of the "new society" breaking down doors which had been open a long time ago.

How did the creative artists go about gaining more autonomy? There were several ways. The matter was simplest in the area of cinematography. The writer or musician is an individual creator who fashions his work in the hope that it finds a patron's favour, and who therefore passionately longs for a free market for cultural products. The situation of the film artist is quite different. The production of film is an industry, and as soon as this industry was converted into state enterprise, it automatically came under the control of the power pyramid. The film artist was converted into an industrial employee, a government employee, with a firm wage, regular bonuses, pensions, job security. The industry itself could be depended upon to see to it that its products reflected the norms and values established by the pyramid, and that they didn't come under the sway of parallel reality. The pressure on the cinematic artist was far greater than the pressure on the writer or musician. Inside the film industry, the machinery had to be kept rolling, the genesis of an autonomous work was virtually impossible, the schizophrenia was virtually continuous and permanent.

Nevertheless, Czechoslovak cinematography came to the conviction that in a relatively small, linguistically limited country, the production of high-quality films was impossible outside the framework of government patronage. For this reason, Czechoslovak film workers concentrated their efforts on the reorganization of the inner structure of the industry, on the creation of a number of smaller units so that through decentralization a certain measure of autonomy would be gained. These demands were made at a time when the power pyramid began to show signs of weakness, sapped by the economic crisis. By the early nineteen-sixties, the autonomy of the small films workshops was continually expanding, the products of their work were coming into ever sharper conflict with the pyramid, which was no longer strong enough to crush opposition in the bud as it had still been able to do in 1958. As the contest grew in intensity, there was mounting need for cooperation and coordination on the part of the film workers. Thus, under the pretext of filling a long-neglected gap in the country's cultural organization, the Union of Film and Television Artists came into being. The pyramid was still pretending to itself that this really represented a matter of correcting a gap in its own structure, but in fact this union marked the emergence of parallel reality in a sphere of power. For the first time under a Stalinist system a so-called social organization came into existence not merely as a transmission-belt of orders from above but as an entity defending the true interests of its members. And these interests were not merely narrowly professional (those were theoretically under the aegis of a withering "official" organ), but ideological and political as well. It is therefore not surprising that film artists gradually took over the vanguard of cultural political activity, culminating in the events of 1968. In achieving this dominant position, the film workers had the advantage of not having had to cope with a paralyzing inheritance of an old trade-union outlook, which plagued the majority of other cultural organizations and prevented them from transcending their role as transmission-belts for the power pyramid.

The union of Czechoslovak writers developed in a completely opposite way. It was created simultaneously with other components of the pyramid, as a classical transmission-belt. Its task was to administer the policies of the pyramid in every sphere of literary activity. For this purpose the union was given not only the internal structure of a political organization but material power as well. It had its own publishing enterprise, which for a long time constituted a virtual monopoly over the publishing of original Czech and Slovak literature and over literary journalism.

This publishing organization became the sole heir of the liberal press of the first republic. And though there was little resemblance to pre-war publishing in terms of content, the outer form and the emphasis upon the intelligentsia were sufficiently reminiscent of pre-Munich books and magazines for the new publishers to inherit a considerable segment of the old readership. As a result, the weekly literary paper *Literární noviny* as well as other publications of the Writers' Union achieved a remarkably large circulation, even in the early nineteen fifties. The Union was also responsible for the administration of the so-called Literary Fund, which was financed by assessments on royalties and by levies on classics which had passed into the public domain. The Literary Fund, in turn, paid for various facilities which were available to members of the Writers' Union, and distributed loans, prizes, and stipends. It is clear that even the Fund was originally designed as part and parcel of the power pyramid, and that its function had to some extent a corrupting influence.

During the years 1955–1956 this publishing colossus underwent the first real inner tremors, a movement which culminated during the second congress of Czechoslovak writers. Stalin's death, the disclosure of Beria's crimes, the 20th Soviet party congress—these were shattering developments, but in the period of relative economic stability their impact was largely limited to the intellectual front. The majority of the members of the Writers' Union were communists and until the 4th congress in 1967, the entire leadership and the entire central committee consisted of party members. The impending conflict therefore had the form of a typical intramural contest within the pyramid rather than a revolt against the pyramid. It was regarded by the writers as a struggle for a smoother, more effective, more "socialist" operation of their organization. However, the pyramid instinctively reacted against any such attempts at reform of its own structure. At first, this reaction was not conscious. The pyramid initially combatted reform as an automatic response in the name of ideological principles; after all, the Stalinist system of power had long been totally identified with socialism. Later, the struggle against reform became ever more deliberate, as the pyramid came to realize that the granting of inner autonomy was an exceedingly dangerous step, a grafting of an incompatible foreign body which could prove fatal. On the other hand, the pyramid was no longer strong enough at that stage to compel unconditional obedience without resort to brutal administrative measures, which by the nineteen sixties would have been entirely out of keeping with the temper of the · times.

During periods when the public is deprived of basic information, it is always the intelligentsia which is politicized first. This was confirmed in the course of the 20th party congress. In the countries under discussion the intelligentsia was predominantly communist, thus having the advantage of a ready-made political platform, albeit a platform of a somewhat limited nature. With regard to literature, the situation was especially favourable. In a political struggle—and practically all scientific and artistic struggles ultimately become political—scientists, artists and musicians could exert only the force of their own prestige, name or reputation; the limits of their opposition were fixed by their total dependence for their existence upon the pyramid, since in the last analysis the pyramid was their employer. The situation of the writers was quite different. They were practically the only members of society capable of independent production. The writers were entirely self-sufficient, since the publishing enterprise which they controlled virtually guaranteed an outlet for their work, while the Literary Fund provided a financial reserve ready to assist individuals who came into conflict with authority. Furthermore, by having the power of the press at their disposal, they had control over printed words of such quantity and quality (censorship notwithstanding) that they exerted considerable influence over the intelligentsia and over a steadily growing portion of the general public. And so, step by step, writers fighting for a restoration of their rights taken away under Stalinism gradually transformed their organization. Their union was initially a transmission-belt, a demanding authoritarian patron keeping close watch over the loyalty of a traditionally influential group of intellectuals, and buying allegiance through privileges and material benefits. Now the organization was changing into a political force, capable of conducting a struggle within the pyramid and of carrying the battle beyond the confines of the pyramid as well.

It took a relatively long time before the pyramid realized where the basic problem lay. The pyramid came to see that the process of self-awareness among writers had reached a level where the conflict could no longer be liquidated by formerly effective administrative measures. It had now become necessary to attack the material base of the revolt, the economic independence of the writers.

The pyramid promptly proceeded to carry out this friendly advice, and slapped a tax on the income of writers. (In this connection, it is interesting to note the remarkable conservativeness of the Czechoslovak tax structure of the time, in which there was only minimal gradation in the rates toward high incomes—hardly a "progressive" system in either sense of the term.) But the government's move came too late. The process of self-awareness among the writers had gone too far, it was no longer possible to destroy their solidarity, not even by means of stepped-up political pressure. The Writers' Union had thus definitely become the first autonomous entity of the Stalinist pyramid, a social organization that had entirely ceased to act as a mere transmission-belt. In a society undergoing a profound crisis the significance of this phenomenon was obvious. The writers extended an invitation to the pyramid: let us take the development of the Writers' Union as a model for study, let us explore this phenomenon together. After all, it may well provide us with an excellent model for reforming the system. . . .

The writers still hadn't understood that the pyramid's only dedication was to itself, it was only concerned with buttressing its own structures and mechanisms; the pyramid had no interest in reform, which would necessarily imply its own demise.

And so the conflict grew in intensity, and the emergence of parallel reality into the light of day became ever more evident. The pyramid had no alternative but to strike. The Writers' Union was deprived of the weekly *Literární Noviny*, it was threatened with the loss of all publishing rights as well as loss of control over the Literary Fund. Yet, once again, these moves—undertaken in the fall of 1967—came too late. In the Writers' Union the communists could no longer count on a majority which would automatically sanction actions against fellow members. In the end, such actions had to be taken by the very top of the pyramid, the central committee of the Czechoslovak communist party. Once again, too late. Parallel reality had infected even this ultimate sanctuary of power. The leadership struck, but its move against the writers proved to mark the last time the forces of the pyramid could be mustered for disciplined, cohesive action. A number of members of the central committee sympathized with the writers and shared their humiliation. These men were ready to rebel at the earliest opportunity.

The gradual transformation of the Czechoslovak Writers' Union into a political force has crucial significance for understanding the processes which shook the country's power structure in the nineteen-sixties, culminating in the Spring of 1968.

At the beginning, this metamorphosis was unintentional and without ultimate goal. The leadership as well as the majority of members were not concerned with reforming Stalinist society; they were simply demanding the right to run their own affairs within an organization structured along Stalinist lines. In fact, a number of attempts were made to separate the Union from larger social issues, but this proved to be impossible. The Union and its members were an integral part of the pyramid. But in the heat of the tension between the pyramid and parallel reality, the Union was like a piece of glowing metal, gradually forged into a blade by alternate blows from one side and the other. As this process was nearing its end, the pyramid showed unmistakable evidence of cracking.

As soon as the Union became aware of its own metamorphosis from a trade organization into a political entity, it sought to liquidate all traces of its former structure. In the Spring of 1968, it joined other cultural organizations in forming the so-called Co-ordinating Committee of the Arts. The writers thus ceded their political leadership to take part in a broader co-ordinated effort, representing the entire cultural and scientific intelligentsia of the nation. A congress was planned for the fall of 1968, which was supposed to finish the job of burying the last remnants of the pyramid. The chateau used by the writers was to be returned to the state as an obsolete symbol of Stalinist privileges. The Writers' Union was to be re-organized as a free association of various writers' groups, serving to safeguard creative freedom and to secure optimal conditions for the development of literature.

The transformations in the Writers' Union were only the most clear-cut and striking example of changes taking place in the entire Stalinist system of transmission-belts. Particularly since 1968, a movement was evident among all kinds of societies and organizations to break the narrow bonds imposed on them by old Stalinist roles and to become true representatives of the wishes and interests of their members. Organizations representing segments of society most sensitive to changing conditions—such as the students and intelligentsia—led the way, gradually followed by organizations representing a variety of other groups, such as workers, farmers, office employees.

The battle for freedom of the press thus provides an interesting comment on the relation between culture and politics. The Writers' Union as well as other organizations involved in publishing have fought for decades for freedom of the press, as well as for the right to form associations, to choose leaders in free elections, and to administer their own affairs. As was noted earlier, this was not a deliberate campaign, based on a clearly formulated programme. Rather, it was a struggle in response to an immediate situation; the writers were simply trying to safeguard a sphere of social activity for which they felt responsible. And as always happens in societies in which political activity is temporarily suspended and ceases to function as a link between the citizen and the state, between the individual and social interests—culture stepped into the breach and assumed a political role. Thus, writers and publishers ostensibly formulating purely cultural needs and demands were actually playing a vital political part and influenced the political struggle of large segments of the population.

The liquidation of censorship of the press, radio and television was practically equivalent to the liquidation of the Stalinist pyramid from an extremely significant area of public life. In the last, neo-Stalinist phase of its existence, the pyramid ruled solely through the power of the state apparatus. The political channels and transmission belts stopped functioning, and even the administrators which the pyramid had put at their head gradually began to rebel. Through the abolishment of censorship the last vestige of the old vertical power structure was eliminated, and freedom of information was established on a scope previously unknown in modern society. The old structure had crumbled, and a new one was just beginning to take form. For many months, the press, radio and television really belonged to the journalists and broadcasters. And this self-government proved remarkably successful. Except for a few marginal exceptions, there was no demagoguery, sensationalism or lust for revenge. The thousands of persons working in the various areas of communications showed not only a high degree of competence, but also a high degree of responsibility for the fate of the nation, country and society. They were conscious of the baleful consequences that an information black-out of three decades' duration had produced in the country. Since 1938, the Czechoslovak people had been without information, without meaningful public opinion, without any possibility of influencing policies from below, and now the country was groping in the dark, searching for orientation, avidly eager to learn its own situation. After several months of feverish work by people for whom the task of informing the public was not merely a job but a calling, the explosive tensions and resentments accumulated in the country over many years began to subside. The press and the broadcast media disarmed demagogues on both extremes of the spectrum, presented objective facts and encouraged people to draw their own conclusions, to find their own solutions. The information media unfrocked the quacks, who promised immediate miracle cures for political ills which had been neglected for decades. Above all, the press, radio and television helped to create a new type of citizen: a citizen assuming direct responsibility for all actions of society, capable of independent political action to a degree previously unknown. In short, a citizen exercising true self-government. It seems safe to say that in those months Czechoslovak magazines, radio and TV programmes achieved a level of professional excellence unmatched anywhere in the world. These developments merit the careful study of all persons interested in plumbing the miraculous phenomenon known as the Czechoslovak Spring, and in evaluating its full cultural contribution to the country and to the world.

With the help of the information media, another enormously significant development of the Czechoslovak Spring came into being, namely the re-establishment of horizontal structures. Horizontal links of any kind were unknown and intolerable to the Stalinist power pyramid. Direct contact from one compartment of the pyramid to another was considered suspicious and dangerous; it reeked of conspiracy. Such contacts were therefore explicitly forbidden, and the only communication permitted within the pyramid was the vertical movement of orders and reports. Two associations in related fields, such as the metal-workers' union and the miners' union, the writers' union and the playwrights union, a union of secondary school teachers and one of college teachers, could not establish direct communication except through the mediation of a higher unit of the pyramid to which both organizations were subordinate. In short, all normal professional and trade communications could only take place under the control of the pyramid. As a result, society was completely atomized. There was a dearth of verifiable information except of the most restricted, local kind; people were totally isolated from each other even when working in closely allied fields, and no individual or group had the slightest hope of affecting the course of events. Not only was information lacking, but there was no possibility of mutual consultation, confrontation or co-operative action.

The Spring of 1968 not only renewed horizontal ties, but it gave such links a new form. The most important of those ties were those established between organizations representing the intelligentsia and the workers. A common front was established between intellectuals and labour, resulting in an entirely new level of cross-influence and solidarity. (One of the basic policies of the "political activity" of the pyramid was the erection of barriers between the workers—"bearers of power"—and the intelligentsia. Intellectuals were intrinsically suspect, because their most characteristic mode of thinking and action willy-nilly tended toward disrupting ideological unity and thus endangering the pyramid.) But mutual contacts and connections were also established between a wide variety of other individuals and organizations representing a diversity of nationwide, regional and local interests. In this way, citizens of the Czechoslovak socialist state finally began to assume the rights which they theoretically always possessed. The masses constituting the "people's democracy" were at last on the move. And when the well-known Two-Thousand Word Manifesto was promulgated, proclaiming the need for giving the newly-won democracy concrete form through the creation of new institutions from the ground up, the pyramid realized that the end had come. And it acted accordingly—by requesting foreign military intervention.

The Economic Impact of Stalinism

✦

Ota Šik

While vice premier of the Czechoslovak Socialist Republic and member of the Central Committee of the Communist Party, Šik was principal designer of the Czechoslovak economic reform program installed from 1965 through 1968. Here he describes the situation in the heyday of Stalinism that made reform so essential. He left Czechoslovakia after the invasion and has been teaching economics at the University of Basel in Switzerland.

It is ironic that Soviet communism, which claims to be the sole exemplar and champion of a universal socialist evolution, has, in fact, become the most formidable obstacle to any advance toward a progressive and humane socialism. Those who might be potential adherents to socialism, particularly in developed capitalist states, must recoil with horror at the thought of socialism in its Soviet variant being established in their countries. They must surely be appalled by even the remote prospect of living under a Stalinist type of socialism characterized by an undemocratic political system; the subjugation of individuals to an all-powerful bureaucracy; the repression of criticism, discussion and new ideas; and a rigidly centralized system of state planning and administration of the economy, prone to weakness in the areas of technological development and foreign trade, and unable to satisfy consumer demands for goods and services. Refusing to grasp these realities, the present Soviet rulers persist in branding every critic of Soviet society as "antisocialist" and in perpetuating the Stalinist apotheosis of a Soviet-type "socialism" which brooks no rival.

Yet even more than the ideological enshrinement of Stalinist "socialism," it is the political practice of the Soviet rulers which repels potential socialist forces. The USSR has repeatedly seen fit to impose its model—invested with the authority of a moral absolute—by brute force on countries held in political subjugation, in total disregard of the individual peculiarities of those countries. In so doing, the Soviet rulers have discredited socialism among large numbers of people who have felt that, to be acceptable, socialism must be indivisibly connected with the historical development of a given country, its progressive democratic traditions, its economic level, and its wealth of indigenous customs, culture and ideas.

Ota Šik, "The Economic Impact of Stalinism," from *Problems of Communism,* May–June 1971, pp. 1–10.

The forceful intervention in 1968 against the emerging Czechoslovak model of a democratic and humane socialism was only the most recent and most flagrant example of such Soviet power plays. It marked the second time that the Soviet Union has interfered with the socialist development of Czechoslovakia by eliminating from power those progressive Czechoslovak Communists who had the courage to develop a socialist system in forms adapted to the specific conditions of Czechoslovakia and approved by her people—*i.e.*, a socialist system deviating from the Soviet model. As in the 1950's, the Communist leaders thus cast aside on Soviet orders are relentlessly accused of every imaginable antisocialist sin and denounced as enemies of socialism. Once again such leaders have been replaced by men who are totally subservient to Moscow and who are ready to reimpose a Stalinist centralized bureaucratic system on Czechoslovakia.

While the outrage of the recent Soviet action is much fresher in the reader's memory, it is to the imposition of a Stalinist system on Czechoslovakia in the early 1950's—an occurrence with equally devastating consequences for Czechoslovak internal developments—that I shall now turn. The tragedy of these earlier events was particularly stark in light of the fact that at the time Stalinism was forced upon it, Czechoslovak society was far more advanced than the Soviet "model" in terms of democratic traditions, level and composition of foreign trade, sophistication of industrial production, modern management experience, and standard of living.

Prior to World War II, Czechoslovakia was already a highly developed country, with industry accounting for more than half the national income. However, like most small industrial nations, prewar Czechoslovakia was dependent on imports for the major portion of its raw materials and therefore had to seek to export a large portion of its industrial output. This dependence on foreign markets caused serious structural problems for the Czechoslovak economy—*e.g.*, overemphasis on the production of certain heavy industrial lines—and thus a search had already begun for a concept of development that would ensure an expansion of Czechoslovak imports and exports and at the same time provide for growth in national income.

◆

POSITIVE POSTWAR TRENDS

The search for means to integrate the Czechoslovak economy more successfully into world trade grew more intense after World War II, although in a changed set of internal and external economic conditions. During and after the war, industry's share in Czechoslovakia's social product [roughly equivalent to gross national product— Ed.] continued to rise, reaching 61.7 percent by 1948. It was essential to devise a structure of industrial production that would enable Czechoslovakia to make optimal use of its national labor force, its intellectual capacities and experience, its technological and productive potential, and its domestic raw material resources, in order to expand its exports and thereby be able to import those raw materials not available domestically. One distinct possibility was to expand the production and export of machinery. Machinery production had increased during the war, but in occupied Czechoslovakia the output was concentrated in armaments and heavy machinery. In the immediate postwar period, Czechoslovakia moved toward the production of precision and light machinery, appliances and electronic products, as well as chemicals, ceramics, and construction materials. Exports of these new products to traditional Western markets were to be complemented on a mounting scale by exports to new East European markets. The latter policy was motivated by the hope of increasing overall exports and by the necessity of securing raw materials for domestic production of consumer goods and machines.

As important as economic factors in determining the development of any economy are the political institutions and objectives of the given society. In the early postwar period (1945–48) Czechoslovak developments in this area were promising. Hand-in-hand with profound modifications in property ownership and socio-economic relations—which, in retrospect, can be seen to have created the base for socialism in Czechoslovakia—there developed *a system of democratic administration of the economy.* Cooperative and large nationalized enterprises emerged rapidly alongside the private sector. Up to 1949, this mixed economy compelled the socialist enterprises to engage, on equal terms, in a healthy competition with private firms and to apply a democratic system of management, which was supplemented by democratic planning and guidance of the economy on the part of the state. These factors remained operative, although on a steadily diminishing scale, until 1952.

The large nationalized enterprises were administered by general directorates or enterprise directorates, headed by generally competent directors appointed by executive boards. The latter, in turn, were appointed, in part by the political parties comprising the National Front (the coalition of the Czechoslovak and Slovak Communist parties, the Czechoslovak Social Democrats, the National Socialists, the Czechoslovak People's Party, and the Slovak Democratic Party, which governed postwar Czechoslovakia until February 1948), and in part by the labor unions.

A national economic plan for the years 1946–48, which constituted the economic program of the government and which was considered a binding directive for government bodies dealing with the economy, gave macro-economic indicative guidance to the enterprises. The plan constituted a first attempt at combining a market system with economic planning on a macro (national) level. This plan was established democratically, through the cooperative and aggregative work of a number of committees comprising representatives of management, labor unions, and interested political and other public organizations. With the help of small professional staffs, these committees set targets and established a basic orientation of the economy which was responsive to the long-term interests of the workers, and which, at the same time, allowed for the independent operations of competing enterprises in a market environment.

The developments described above facilitated the postwar reconstruction of the economy, ensured a swift changeover to peacetime production, promoted a rapid advance of Czechoslovak products on foreign markets, created a favorable balance of payments, and led to a relatively quick rise in the standard of living. The government's policy sought to overcome as quickly as possible the effects of postwar inflation and was to a certain extent successful in reviving the regulating function of the market.

◆

ENTER STALINISM

However, before it was possible to restore the internal balance of the economy and to establish a true market based on demand, the development of this democratic economic system was brought to a halt by coercive means. Almost overnight, economic processes were subordinated to the political objectives of a new regime, in defiance of all economic logic. The instruments of power were utilized to impose on the CSSR [Czechoslovak Socialist Republic] an ineffective long-term structure of production which took no account of the economic requirements of the society at large and which hampered the advance of technology. Tremendous economic losses were suffered owing to the economically irrational actions of the political leadership.

What caused this dramatic shift? The political stage for the developments of the 1950's had been set in 1948 when a radical change brought to power a Communist regime—a regime oriented toward Moscow. But various other objective and subjective factors also combined to cause, inexorably, a distortion in the economies of Czechoslovakia and the other developing socialist countries.

Beginning in 1947, international relations came to be increasingly dominated by the Cold War, which brought both sides to the brink of a new, catastrophic struggle. In 1950 the Cold War actually flared into a hot war in Korea. The war crisis generated a need to strengthen the military forces of the socialist countries—a factor which in turn entailed in Eastern Europe an acceleration of industrialization, with particular emphasis on heavy industry.

The distortion of Czechoslovakia's economic development was due far less to the objective threat of war, however, than to the emergence of certain subjective political concepts which—in utter disregard of basic economic laws—became the decisive determinants of economic policy over a long period. Under Soviet influence, totally unrealistic goals were set—among them, "catching up with and overtaking" the developed capitalist states in per capita performance in all major production lines in a brief span of time, and constructing broad-based heavy industry in even the smallest of the socialist countries. At a meeting with Czechoslovakia's new Communist leadership early in 1950, Stalin personally demanded a shift in the orientation and structure of Czechoslovakia's production and export trade 180 degrees toward the East, a rapid increase in the output of its heavy industry, and massive deliveries of heavy industry products to other socialist countries (in particular, the USSR). In February 1950 the Central Committee of the Czechoslovak Communist Party compliantly voted to increase the planned growth rate for industrial production—particularly the output of heavy industry—by a substantial margin.

In implementing this decision, the regime rapidly accelerated investment in heavy industry. The share of investment in the three major branches of heavy industry alone accounted for almost one-half of aggregate industrial investment in Czechoslovakia for the years 1948–53, as indicated below:

INDUSTRIAL INVESTMENT, 1948–53

Branch	Share of Total (%)
Coal mining	9.1
Metallurgy	18.0
Machine building	19.5
All other branches	53.4
Total	100.0

The orientation of export trade was also radically changed. Whereas in 1948 Czechoslovakia's exports to capitalist and non-Communist developing countries had been much larger than those to Communist countries, the opposite was true in 1953:

EXPORT TRADE

Trading partners	1948	1953
Socialist states	39.7	78.5
Capitalist states	45.7	14.9
Developing economies	14.6	6.6
Total	100.0	100.0

The precipitate and insufficiently calculated alteration of the structure of industrial production, investment and foreign trade demanded by Stalin proved disastrous to the Czechoslovak economy. This departure from the original concept adopted by all political groups prior to the Communist takeover in 1948 set in motion long-run economic processes which disregarded the basic laws of economic development. Expansion of heavy industry was pushed at the expense of development of all other productive and nonproductive sectors of the economy—agriculture, light industry, consumer goods and food products industries, transportation, services, trade, and housing construction. The result was growing inefficiency of production, failure to modernize production technology, a decline in the quality of once-valued Czechoslovak exports, a loss of markets, and a drop in the effectiveness of foreign trade. The economy experienced a severe and continuing inflation and a serious lag in the tertiary sphere of economic services—an area of great importance to labor productivity. The public was subjected to a depressed rate of growth in the standard of living, mounting shortages of goods, and insufficient service facilities, which had a particularly adverse impact on the leisure time available to women.

Such a radical and rapid change in the structure and orientation of the Czechoslovak economy required extensive political and ideological preparation, as well as a thorough transformation of the system of economic planning and administration. The political phase of this preparation consisted of the prosecution of a broad array of Czechoslovak political and economic leaders in the show trials of the 1950's—part of a wave of such trials staged by the Stalinist power apparatus in all the People's Democracies for the express purpose of rendering the leaderships of those countries completely subservient to Moscow's bidding. Those who had pioneered in Czechoslovakia's postwar economic adjustment and had helped create a democratic economic system were tried as enemies of socialism and were executed, imprisoned, or removed from key positions in the government, economy, and important institutions—to be replaced by a set of party functionaries of mediocre caliber, who would not or could not devise independent political concepts for Czechoslovakia or find solutions for the country's mounting economic problems.

Only a handful of experts, whose names cannot be revealed even now, were able at the outset of the 1950's to guess at the disastrous consequences which were to ensue from these drastic political and economic changes. Most of them were silenced in one way or the other, and all independent economic and sociological research was suppressed. The bulk of economic data was declared secret; the press and other information media were subjected to strict censorship; and the flow of information from the West was shut off. A propaganda campaign of unprecedented dimensions sought to identify all concrete political, administrative and economic measures of the government with the interests of the people, and to brand all divergent views and opinions as hostile to socialism. The barrage of one-sided or restricted information, the continuous pressure of political and administrative repressions, and the absence of basic democratic freedoms combined to deprive the people for many years of the possibility of judging the merits or drawbacks of the political and economic system and the truth or falsity of official claims.

◆

THE COMMAND STRUCTURE

Simultaneously, the existing system of economic planning and administration was discarded as a "relic of capitalism," ill-adapted to the solution of accumulating economic problems. In its place, the regime adopted the centralized, bureaucratic Soviet system. During the years 1951–52 an apparatus was created for centralizing all economic decision-making, as a result of which the enterprises ceased for all practical purposes to function as independent, responsible economic units—in the process losing their market orientation. The general directorates were replaced by numerous economic ministries and even more numerous central administrative offices. Operating through this vast bureaucratic apparatus and relying on plans elaborated from the top on the basis of artificial formulas, the state began to fix the total volume of production and the volume of specific key products to be manufactured by each enterprise, to assign these targets by administrative directive to individual enterprises and trading organizations, as well as to determine the volume and orientation of all investments, to allocate manpower, and to attempt to force growth of productivity and control production costs. The state also determined the volume, structure and orientation of export trade, fixed the prices of all products, and conducted all financing operations.

Under the new administrative system prices became mere accounting units or indicators and ceased to perform the economic functions of expressing true production costs and reflecting the market situation. Retail prices included turnover taxes which ranged from zero to several hundred percent. The profitability of product lines and enterprises varied widely, since it depended not on the efficiency of operations or the satisfaction of consumer demands but on the particular prices set by the bureaucracy for given products. Even large profits brought no advantages to enterprises— indeed profits ceased to have any bearing on the survival or even the operation of enterprises. Similarly, losses entailed no disadvantages for enterprises, since it was impossible to determine whether such deficits were the result of inefficient operations or of the price system. The state administered the redistribution of funds from those enterprises which enjoyed profits to those enterprises showing deficits. Even when the incentive bonuses for managers were later tied to profits, they failed to stimulate a genuine interest in increasing labor productivity and overall effectiveness of production. The official practice of assigning production tasks by mandatory directives and of siphoning off excess funds from enterprises as soon as they began to accumulate had the effect of killing any interest enterprise managers might otherwise have had in improving efficiency.

Although prices no longer served as market signals, they did exercise a negative influence on day-to-day decisions at the enterprise level. The centrally-assigned gross output targets for production were imposed on enterprises in terms of aggregate prices. As these production quotas escalated mechanically and relentlessly with each passing year, enterprises responded by changing their product mix, giving preference to the manufacture of those products which permitted the producer to show greater aggregate output in terms of prices—either because the products required more costly material inputs (which were automatically reflected in higher output prices) or because the official price for the selected product was higher than for an alternative item requiring the same input of labor. The result was a continuing decline in the manufacture of products with low material costs and disadvantageous prices. Thus, despite the command character of the completely centralized economic plans, prices did continue to influence the development of the microstructure of production. Enterprises were, in effect, attracted to the most wasteful utilization of materials and production capital. This may be seen in the table below, which gives a comparison of the consumption of energy and of steel per unit of production in the CSSR and in various non-Communist countries in 1966.

RESOURCE CONSUMPTION AND GNP IN 1966

Country	Energy units per $1,000 of GNP	Kg. steel per $1,000 of GNP
CSSR	5,023	485
USA	2,498	174
FRG	2,130	255
France	1,471	169
UK	2,689	202
Holland	2,105	191
Sweden	1,853	237
Switzerland ..	1,111	135

In addition to encouraging wasteful utilization of materials and capital equipment, the distorted system of pricing and administrative control of production fostered the output of an assortment of goods which was totally unrelated to the structure of demand, *i.e.,* the needs of consumers and customers. Growing quantities of unneeded products were forced on consumers either by direct administrative pressure or by the economic pressure of shortages or nonavailability of other, more necessary goods. Despite these pressures, stocks of useless and unsalable goods continued to grow from one year to the next. Some of these goods were periodically sacrificed at a sharp loss on less sophisticated markets (*i.e.,* in developing countries), while others were liquidated without being put to any use. Yet the producers continued to turn out such products, confident that as long as they reached their planned gross-output targets, they would receive all needed funds from the state.

The overriding interest of enterprises in expanding the *volume* of production militated against any consistent concern with quality, innovation, or technological improvement. The inflexible, politically-imposed structure of production likewise put heavy brakes on technological advance and modernization of the production base. Furthermore, the growing shortage of convertible currencies and the orientation of trade toward the USSR impeded the importation of modern technology from the more advanced non-Communist countries. As a consequence, the machines and equipment installed in newly-erected plants reached, at best, the world average of technology and lagged far behind the level in the most advanced countries. Older plants failed to replace amortized equipment, resulting in obsolescence of the production base—a condition that was particularly marked in the consumer goods and food products industries. In 1966, some 45 percent of the productive equipment of heavy industry and 60 percent of the equipment of light industry had been amortized (*i.e.,* had outlived its actuarial life and yet had not been replaced).

The continued use of obsolete and fully amortized production equipment contributed to a growing disparity between labor productivity in the CSSR and in industrially advanced Western countries. In 1966, the labor productivity rate in Czechoslovakia was approximately half that in Belgium, West Germany and the United Kingdom, two-fifths that in Switzerland and Sweden, and about one-fourth that in the United States.

✦
ON A TREADMILL

Technological backwardness, the distorted production structure (with its emphasis on heavy industry, where the time required to recoup investments in terms of output was longer than in other sectors), the wasteful utilization of material inputs, and the decelerating growth of labor productivity—all combined to produce a decline in the rate of growth of national income in the early 1960's. The regime found itself compelled to engage in an ever-expanding program of capital investment merely to sustain a flagging rate of growth in output.

The burgeoning capital construction program had a serious impact in a number of areas. Since the decision had been to expand rather than modernize the capital plant, there was a growing manpower shortage. Instead of improving the capital stock at the disposal of the existing labor force, the regime attempted to recruit new labor from the ranks of housewives or from non-preferred branches of industry, with the latter inevitably experiencing further slowdowns as a result of the loss of manpower.

The huge investment demand placed intolerable stress on the construction industry, which was not an officially favored economic sector and was therefore subject to shortages of labor, modern equipment and materials. As the demand for construction facilities outstripped the capacity, projects became fragmented, construction delays were more frequent and prolonged, and the average period for completion of projects grew longer. By 1966, the estimated time required to build a new industrial unit in the CSSR was, on the average, five to six years. This was two to three times as long as in developed Western countries. As a result, materials and labor were frozen in incompleted capital construction at enormous cost to the economy.

The expanded investment program and the continued emphasis on heavy industry inevitably generated inflationary pressures. The state countered with increasingly heavy restraints on the growth of average wages, but the labor force—particularly in heavy industry where wages were paid on a premium scale—kept growing, thereby fueling a rapid rise in the total wage bill of the economy. The supply of consumer goods increasingly failed to meet this rising purchasing power both in terms of quantity (due to priorities placed on heavy industry) and in terms of mix and quality. Particularly in the area of services and durable consumer goods—automobiles, housing, and home furnishings—consumer demand went unsatisfied. Due to administrative controls over pricing, this inflation was generally a "hidden" inflation—that is, it did not express itself in soaring prices (although there was a gradual price rise in recent years). Instead, it manifested itself indirectly in a rapid increase of personal and enterprise savings, which represented frozen or deferred purchasing power.

Nor could the inflationary pressures be eased by importing consumer goods. Terms of trade were deteriorating with the decline in the quality and relative technological sophistication of Czechoslovak industrial and consumer-goods exports. Increasing volumes of exports were required to maintain necessary imports, mainly of raw materials and semifinished goods for Czechoslovak industry. In 1954 it took 14 *korunas* worth of Czechoslovak exports to earn a dollar of foreign exchange; by 1967 this figure had risen to 31 *korunas*. As the gap widened, the balance of payments with the capitalist countries became negative, and foreign exchange reserves were depleted. It therefore became increasingly difficult to import needed consumer goods from the West, and socialist countries were unable to fill the vacuum. In fact, Czechoslovakia was forced to be a net exporter of consumer goods. In 1967 such goods accounted for 16.8 percent of CSSR exports to socialist countries, compared to 5.9 percent of imports from these countries. In trade with capitalist countries in the same year the comparable figures were 24 and 5 percent.

The relentless pressures to export, particularly heavy industrial products, militated against any modification in the structure of industry. Furthermore, producers felt no pressure to update or improve their output for the reason that they were effectively insulated from the impact of foreign competition by the state's foreign trade organizations. The latter purchased goods for export at domestic prices and absorbed the difference between these prices and the lower prices which the goods brought on foreign markets. The trade organizations were also prohibited from passing these costs on to domestic consumers of imports by raising the prices on imports—instead, imports were charged to domestic enterprises at domestic prices. The mounting deficits of the trade organizations were covered by subsidies from the state budget, a process which glossed over the inefficiency of production and of foreign trade, but which could not eliminate the resulting losses of national income and reductions in domestic consumption.

◆

SIGNS OF CRISIS

The accumulated problems of a distorted industrial structure, an adverse trade situation, an aging or obsolete production base, relatively low labor productivity, and wasteful utilization of production resources had by the early 1960's assumed such huge proportions that any quick resolution of Czechoslovakia's economic problems was out of the question. This was clearly evidenced by a decline in the rate of growth of the Czechoslovak economy. In the period 1948–58 the social product of Czechoslovakia grew 8.6 percent per annum. In 1958–68 it grew only 5.6 percent per annum, and in 1961–64 the rate of growth was particularly slow—2.1 percent per annum.

By the latter period it was clear that an alteration of the structure of the economy—toward the end of developing effective competitive lines of production, increasing the share of consumer goods and food products in output, expanding the construction and building-materials industries and housing, and modernizing transportation—would require enormous investments and large increments of labor, both of which would have to be achieved without relative retrenchments in heavy industry. The process might be speeded by large infusions of foreign credit, by the purchase of licenses, or by cooperation with progressive foreign companies, but there was no assurance that such foreign credits and contacts would actually be used to develop maximally efficient branches of production or to bring about the expansion of effective exports necessary to ensure repayment of credits in convertible currencies.

In the final analysis, it could be seen that the structural deformations which plagued the Czechoslovak economy were inextricably linked with the centralized, bureaucratic system of economic control. While every negative economic phenomenon in the CSSR could be traced to some "objective" or "technical" economic problem, ultimately it was the command system of administration—with its tight control over planning and the allocation of supplies and its counterproductive and distorting initiatives—which had become the insurmountable obstacle to any structural reform.

The mounting crisis culminated in an absolute decline in Czechoslovak national income and in the real wages of the Czechoslovak worker in 1963. There was palpable dissatisfaction among the working people, and a number of progressive economists openly and courageously began to criticize the existing economic model. As a result, the regime appointed a special party-government commission under the leadership of the present author, which worked out a reform model for the organization, planning and stimulation of the economy. After protracted ideological and political debate, and under the pressures generated by the adverse economic situation, even those conservative forces who were committed to the old system—both intellectually and through motives of self-interest—gave their grudging acceptance to the concept of a new system of economic administration. The reform was finally adopted by a majority of the CPCS [Communist Party of Czechoslovakia] Central Committee in 1965.

◆

REFORM OF THE ECONOMY

As envisaged, the reform was to eliminate the centralized-bureaucratic system of planning and administering the economy by commands from the center. The old structure was to be replaced by a system consisting of a modern macro-economic plan conceived as a set of general indicators, supplemented by indirect economic measures through which the government would seek to achieve its economic goals. The government was to limit its direct investments to measures aimed at improving the society's infrastructure. The reform anticipated the revitalization of the economic functions of the market, of prices, and of money. Socialist enterprises were to be transformed back into independent, profit-oriented market entities, while the state was to limit itself to blocking monopolistic tendencies among the enterprises and seeing to it that pressures of domestic and foreign competition acted to force enterprises to operate efficiently. The administrative foreign trade monopoly was to be abolished and foreign trade activities decentralized within general state policies on trade and foreign exchange. A capital market was to be re-created on the basis of a relatively independent banking system, and it was expected that the Czechoslovak *koruna* would eventually become a convertible currency.

A system of self-administration was to be introduced in all sectors of the economy. Enterprise councils were to be elected by the workers at each enterprise for the purpose of socialist administration of the enterprises, and the work force in each enterprise was to assume the risks inherent in the entrepreneurial activities of the given economic unit—*i.e.,* the possibility of bankruptcy and cessation of operations if the unit incurred repeated losses. Application of the new system was seen to entail major staffing changes and a new method and set of criteria for selection and training of top managerial personnel and economic policymakers.

The need for new attitudes and new leaders clearly presented a challenge to those entrenched in power—the Novotný regime. A fundamental change in the political ground rules was called for if there was to be any meaningful alteration of the economic structure and of the whole administrative system. Yet, although a growing number of responsible political and economic figures, supported by large segments of the population, came to realize the necessity for radical economic reform, the conservative political dictatorship and the bureaucratic apparatus resisted and obstructed all moves toward the purposeful introduction of new measures. This, in turn, converted the fight for economic reform into a political struggle aimed first at toppling Novotný and then at democratizing the entire political system. When Novotný fell (in January 1968), there followed the Czechoslovak "spring"—a start at consistent implementation of the reform program.

Whatever objections might be entertained against the Czechoslovak reforms, it should be remembered that they were the outcome of several years of highly intensive analytical work in all departments of social science by a large number of theoreticians as well as men active in practical affairs. People in Czechoslovakia came to perceive a need for fundamental economic and political changes, and they were confident that the reform would provide a cure for their economic distress, would engender successful economic development, and would foster genuine involvement and initiative by the great masses of the people.

The reform efforts were not an attempt to restore capitalist society, as is currently claimed by Soviet-inspired propaganda emanating from Czechoslovakia; on the contrary, they were directed toward building a more modern, humane and democratic socialism in forms better adapted to Czechoslovak conditions. The goal was to transcend the rigid dogmatism of Soviet communism and to devise flexible new institutions and forms for planning and administering the economy in a system which would afford the advantages of a macro-economically regulated market among socialist enterprises. Such a system would be conducive to the introduction of effective production programs oriented to the needs of society at large. It was looked upon as an open model capable of continuing change and development generated by new knowledge and experience, not as a closed, rigid system substituting new dogmas for old.

◆

TOWARD A DEMOCRATIC SOCIALISM

There was also general agreement that an essential requisite of economic and social development was the introduction of a modern, pluralist democratic system. Open criticism, free discussion, differences of opinion, and the peaceful competition of interest groups were envisaged as crucial to any progress, to any meaningful changes in society. Where political power is usurped and monopolized by a small group within the sole authorized political party, no opposing interest or dissenting idea has a chance to assert itself. Such a society will, of necessity, always be conservative, unchanging.

Thus, the Czechoslovak reformers recognized that socialist development in the CSSR could be saved only by true democratization of their society. It seemed quite conceivable to them that a political democracy could be built on the basis of a socialist economic system and that such a democracy could progress further than the Western democracies, avoiding the defects of the latter. Clearly, not all of Czechoslovakia's troubles could be blamed exclusively on the shortcomings of individual Communist leaders, despite the proclivity of successive leaderships to heap denunciation on their predecessors. The ultimate causes had to be sought in the undemocratic nature of the Communist system; hence the goal was more than the mere replacement of Novotný—what was sought was a fundamental change which would do away with the whole Stalinist monopolistic power system.

Tragically, this great and humane goal of the Czechoslovak reformers was perceived by the rulers of the Soviet Union and other Communist countries as a fatal threat to their own positions. The ultimate reason for their brutal intervention was not concern for socialism in Czechoslovakia, but rather fear that the democratic contagion might spread to their own countries. Once again, as in the days of Jan Hus, Czechoslovak heretics who threatened the power of neighboring princes by their progressive thought and example had to be crushed by overpowering military might. And once again, the foreign tyrants have since tried to persuade the Czechoslovak people that their freedom has been saved by the occupation of their country.

However, the Czechoslovak populace has been inured against such attempts by long historical experience—and it was too deeply convinced of the essential correctness and necessity of the reforms that were being launched to be cowed into total submission. A return to the Soviet-style Communist system has now been ruthlessly enforced against the will and interests of the majority of the people. But regardless of its hectic demagogic propaganda, the present collaborationist regime has been unable to enlist popular support or cooperation. The result is a simmering, all-pervasive crisis in the CSSR which is bound to have momentous consequences in time to come.

Before the Occupation:
The Political Crisis in Czechoslovakia

✦

Ivan Sviták

Sviták was one of two philosophers (Karel Kosík was the other) especially prominent in the intellectual ferment leading up to the Prague Spring. This essay is based on a lecture he gave at Ljubljana University, Yugoslavia, in July 1968, as events moved toward crisis in his country. He emigrated to the United States and has taught philosophy here as he once did at Charles University in Prague.

Czechoslovakia's democratization process of 1968 had its origin in the events of 1956, the year which began with the denunciation of Stalin at the twentieth Soviet party congress and ended with the Hungarian uprising. In the wake of the Moscow congress, the Czechoslovaks felt that the long night of Stalinism was ended, and that the communist party would lose some of its oppressive character. When, however, it became clear that the communist leaders were still guided by Stalin's democratic centralism and that the old methods would prevail, a deep-seated mood of disappointment set in, aggravated by a seemingly insoluble economic crisis. The explosion of 1968 arose out of these conditions.

With regard to the January–July events, it is possible to see three stages in the period. There were, of course, some preliminary indications of the impending storm. The voices of protest raised at the Writers' Congress in June 1967, the suppression of *Literární noviny,* the Strahov student demonstrations—these were obvious warning signals.

What might be called the winter period started with the January 1968 Central Committee meetings, at which Novotný was removed from the party leadership and the so-called democratization process was launched. During the same winter period, which lasted until early April, Novotný was forced to resign as president of the republic and some of the old leaders were replaced by reformers. During this period the process was limited to top communists and leading party intellectuals who had, during

Ivan Sviták, "Before the Occupation: The Political Crisis in Czechoslovakia," from *East Europe,* October 1968, pp. 13–16.

the first phase, contributed toward the diminution of the system of one-man control in the party. The defection of Major-General Jan Šejna and the suicide of General Vladimír Janko—accused of having been prepared to use the army to restore Novotný to power—was the catalyst which moved the party to further changes. Up to this point, the reformers in the party were interested primarily in making those personnel changes which would facilitate the implementation of the economic reforms.

The pressure for change was too great, however. The end of censorship, the widening attacks on Novotný, the purge of the state security organs, the demand for rehabilitation of former political prisoners—these went far beyond what the communist reformers had anticipated. A party crisis had become a total state crisis.

✦

THE SECOND STAGE BEGINS

The second, or spring stage, then began. Thousands of enthusiastic youths and most intellectuals, especially journalists, freed of the fetters of communist censorship, eagerly joined in the democratization process. The workers in the radio and television stations staged programs which breathtakingly discussed all the questions which had hitherto been talked about behind closed doors—not least of which was the free-wheeling debate on the nature of man under socialism. Equally sensational were the press and television revelations about the mysterious death of Jan Masaryk and the reports of the torture inflicted on political prisoners in the fifties. Although the communist party reacted to these developments with a program of democratization, rehabilitation and federalization, the Novotný group, still represented in the Central Committee, called for the suppression of debate through the employment of the People's Militia against the free press. They also made known that they would not be averse to seeking the support of Soviet tanks. In the background were the visits of Soviet statesmen and journalists, apparently seeking to support the conservatives, and to stop the democratization process.

The May 27 to June 1 plenum of the Central Committee, on the first day of which Novotny was expelled and some of his friends resigned, arrived at some sort of temporary accord. It was agreed that there would be no support for the formation of additional political parties, and that further decisions would be left to the extraordinary party congress scheduled for early in September. No action was taken against the operation of the People's Militia, considered the stronghold of conservatism. In this sense, the plenum could be considered a victory for the center group rather than for the reformers. Other factors in the compromise, which brought the progressives into combination with the center tendency, were the legalization of the abolition of the censorship, the rehabilitation program, and the purge of the state security apparatus. More problematic was the decision to rejuvenate the National Front.

It was at this stage that the great mass of citizens was drawn into the democratization process. Inspired by the open debates on television, the citizens were moved to civic commitment. They organized political clubs, set up committees in defense of a free press, founded an organization of former political prisoners and preparatory committees to organize new political parties and new cultural groups. This wave of democratic participation moved far beyond the control of the communist party. To stem the tide, it could only announce an embargo on legalization of such organizations.

✦

THE CONFLICT EMERGES

These moves were supported by a third, decisive impulse, which initiated what might be designated as the summer phase. If the writers and publicists were responsible for the breakthrough in the second phase, the intellectuals and scientists brought on the third stage. Implicit in their appeal—expressed in Ludvík Vaculík's now famous "2000 Words"—was a call for the elimination of the leading role of the party in favor of a program under which there would be an alliance of communists and nonparty members. It was, in effect, an appeal for the purification of political life. The response of the communist apparatus to this appeal verged on the hysterical. It was denounced as counterrevolutionary by the party hierarchy, while the condemnation of the National Assembly was somewhat more moderate. There was no doubt that it had wide popular support. The appeal was published at a moment when Warsaw Pact maneuvers were being conducted in Czechoslovakia and when district conferences were electing delegates to the projected extraordinary congress.

The third phase, then, can be characterized as a period when real and vital conflicts between the communist party and the nonparty groups emerged. It marked a process of change from the first period, when personal disputes were resolved, and the second stage, when the factions reached a compromise in advance of the party congress. Had the process continued into the fall, the country might have witnessed a fundamental political shift in which the people themselves would have become involved in the democratization process through free elections and the introduction of democracy in the realm of socialist production. It might have been the beginning of a significant experiment in democratic socialism.

What were some of the undercurrents that surfaced in the upheaval of January to July? First, one must point out the contradictory elements that appeared. These can be summarized as follows: the differences between the communist apparatus and the democratic aspirations of the citizenry; the differences between the party conservatives and the people; the tensions arising from the economics of socialism and individual freedom. These structural contradictions might have been solved through a democratic procedure, but they could not be mitigated by force. The party intelligentsia had come to recognize this fact, but the party apparatus had not.

The role of the party apparatus—whose power remained superior to that of parliament, government and the courts—was highly significant. It continued to disregard the opinions of the many millions of nonparty members, who remained under threat of personal abuse and of persecution by the People's Militia. The belief in party dictatorship was far from dead among the apparatchiks. The growth of the newly established clubs and organizations, while never numerically significant, posed a threat to both the state and party apparatus.

The problem of the new role of the communist party remained open. It sought to cling to its right to dictate change, and did not dissolve its military and bureaucratic structure. Could the party have transformed itself into an organization which would be responsive to the will of an electorate? This would have meant free elections and repudiation of the view that the party expressed the will of the people and the working class—though it never asked for their opinions.

The question of the economic role of socialism remained undefined in the discussion, although it was one of the most significant in the debate. What the communist party seemed to be tending toward was transforming the state into an "all people's state" (a formula which had been criticized by Marx) and disregarding its traditional class structure. The state was to be understood as having as its only goal—in a tacit agreement with the great majority of people—a rise in living standards. Yet the state had proved to be a most inefficient industrial entrepreneur. However, the idea was alive among the workers and the people generally that human freedom, and not living standards, was the true basis of socialism. Litanies about the inherent superior wisdom of the ruling power elite, whether called communist, Christian or socialist, were obviously reactionary, since the corollary was the limitation of personal freedom by the representatives of those who monopolize power.

◆

THE SPIRIT OF FREEDOM

What was unloosed among the mass of Czechoslovaks in 1968 was recognized even by Machiavelli as irrepressible: the spirit of freedom. This could not be tamed. Lenin himself paid tribute to it in the midst of a civil war in 1918: "The people must have the right to elect responsibly their leading workers. The people must have the right to change them. The people must have the right to know about and test every single step involving them. The people must have the right to authorize anyone from their ranks to represent them regardless of the leading functionaries."

Could these aims have been achieved? The contradictions between the power apparatus and the democratic rights of citizens could have been solved by submitting the power apparatus to democratic control. The contradictions between the conservative communists and the people could have been overcome by development of a real parliamentarianism, and not only an extraordinary party congress. The ideals of socialist humanism could have been infused into the economic structure of socialism.

Had these steps been taken, the country would have been on the road to solving some of its outstanding problems. If these contradictions remained unsolved, there would have been a clash between the opposing forces of the people and the elite who were in power. It was for this reason that every effort to introduce civil rights was met with the cry on the part of the communist apparatchiks at all levels that the political system of socialism was under attack. There was already evidence of the tendency of

Dubček and the Soviet Leadership. In August 1968, shortly before ordering the invasion of Czechoslovakia by Warsaw Pact forces, the Soviet leadership went to the Slovak capital, Bratislava, in a show of consulting with Alexander Dubček and other Czechoslovak reformers. Shown here, left to right in the front row, are Nikolai Podgorny, the Soviet president; Aleksy Kosygin, the Soviet premier; Leonid Brezhnev, the CPSU general secretary, Pyotr Shelest, the Ukrainian party leader; Dubček; and Mikhail Suslov, the CPSU's chief ideologist. (Tass/Sovfoto)

those who had favored the early changes to regard every argument for wider democracy as being directed at themselves. They seemed ready to enter a new claim for immunity from criticism. They were beginning to adopt the prerogatives of the elite groups whom they had replaced.

◆

THE LIMITATIONS OF CHANGE

What was involved basically in the democratization process was the attempt, which now characterizes society in both East and West, to introduce concern for human rights into modern technocratically manipulated civilization, to apply the findings of modern science and contemporary wisdom and humanity to the process of social change. It put back into the center of events the rights of man as against the dogma of ideology. In Czechoslovakia, this meant raising loftier goals than those of increased production to which both conservative communists and progressives were more than ready to pay homage.

There was little indication that leading communists went much beyond the recognition of the need for some political changes—if held to a minimum. They centered their hopes on the National Front despite its unsavory reputation in the past and the fact that it was not equipped to encompass modern democratic procedures. It is a mechanism for the alliance of institutions, and would have served basically to shroud the mechanics of manipulation which had been openly practiced in the past.

The intellectuals who stressed the necessity of putting humanity first in a system of socialist democracy were quickly condemned as counterrevolutionaries. Others were somewhat skeptical of the possibilities of Western-style democracy, and came to feel that the operation of an intelligent technocracy was the most realistic possibility. It cannot be said that theoretical programs of either politicians or intellectuals moved much beyond advocacy of national independence, a multiparty system, a consumer society or the formation of an effective technocratic government. Other alternatives were only occasionally raised for thorough discussion.

However, the fact that all ideas of this kind were in the air in the winter, spring and summer of 1968 indicated that in Czechoslovakia there was the hope of creating through peaceful means an experiment in socialist humanism which would have contributed to expanding the concepts of democratic socialism throughout Europe—East and West.

"2000 Words": A Statement on Democratization

✦

The novelist Ludvík Vaculík composed this statement which, with the signatures of some seventy workers and intellectuals, appeared in the Prague journal *Literární listy* on 27 June 1968. It provoked widespread discussion in Czechoslovakia and was denounced in the Soviet Union as a "counter-revolutionary program."

First, the life of our nation was threatened by the war. Then came blacker days, which threatened our spiritual and national character. Most of the nation accepted and had faith in the new program of socialism, which was taken over by the wrong people. It would not have mattered so much that they lacked the experience of statesmen, the knowledge of scholars or the training of philosophers, if they had allowed themselves to be replaced by more capable persons.

The communist party betrayed the great trust the people put in it after the war.

" '2000 Words': A Statement on Democratization," from *East Europe*, August 1968, pp. 25–28.

It preferred the glories of office, until it had those and nothing more. The disappointment was great among communists as well as noncommunists. The leadership of the party changed it from a political and ideological group into a power-hungry organization, attracting egotists, cowards and crooks.

They influenced the party's operations to such an extent that honest people could not gain a foothold without debasement, much less make it a modern political instrument. There were many communists who fought this deterioration but they could not prevent what happened.

The situation in the party led to a similar situation in the state, resulting in the linkage of party and state. There was no criticism of the state and economic organizations. Parliament forgot how to deliberate, the government forgot how to rule and managers how to manage. Elections had no significance and the laws lost their value. We could not trust any of our representatives, and when we could it was impossible to ask them for anything because they were powerless. What made things even worse was that we could not trust each other.

◆

THE DECLINE OF HONESTY

Personal and collective honor deteriorated. Honesty led nowhere, and it was useless to speak of rewards according to ability. As a result, most citizens lost interest in public affairs. They were concerned only with themselves and with accumulating money. The situation got so bad that now one cannot even rely on money. Relations among people were undermined and joy in work was lost. To sum up, the nation was in a morass that threatened its spiritual health and character.

We are all responsible for the present state of affairs, with the greater responsibility on the communists among us. But the prime responsibility lies with those who made up the component parts or were the instruments of uncontrolled power, the power of a dogmatic group placed everywhere by the party apparatus, from Prague to the smallest district and community. The apparatus decided what one could or could not do and directed the cooperatives for the cooperative members, the factories for the workers and the national committees for the citizens. No organization was run by its members, not even the communist party.

The greatest deception of these rulers was that they presented their arbitrariness as the will of the workers. If we believed this, we could now blame the workers for the decline of our economy, for the crimes against innocent people, for the introduction of censorship which made it impossible for all this to be described. The workers would have to be blamed for mistaken investments, for the losses in trade, for the shortage of apartments.

Naturally, no sensible person believes that the workers are guilty of these things. We all know—and each worker knows—that he did not decide anything. Someone else chose the union officials he elected. Power was executed by trained groups of officials loyal to the party and state apparatus. In effect, they took the place of the former ruling class and became the new authority.

In all justice, we can say that some of them did realize what was happening. We know that now because they are redressing wrongs, correcting mistakes, bringing decisions to the membership and the citizens, and limiting the authority and the size of the official apparatus. They no longer support the conservative viewpoint in the party. But there are still many officials opposed to change who exercise the instruments of power, particularly in the districts and in the communities.

Since the beginning of the year we have been in the process of reviving democratization. It began in the communist party. We must say this. And those noncommunists among us who, until recently, expected no good to come from the communists also know it. We must add, however, that this process could not have begun elsewhere. After twenty years, only the communists had an actual political life; only communist criticism was in a position to assess things as they were; only the opposition in the communist party had the privilege of being in contact with the enemy.

◆

THE BASIS OF DEMOCRATIZATION

The present effort of the democratic communists is only an installment in the repayment of the debt the entire party owes the people outside the party, who had no political rights. No gratitude is due to the communist party, although it should probably be acknowledged that it is honestly striving to use this last opportunity to save its own honor and the nation's.

The process of revival is not producing anything new. Many of its ideas and recommendations are older than the errors of socialism in our country. These errors should have been exposed long ago but they were suppressed. Let us not now cherish the illusion that these ideas prevail because truth won out. Their victory was decided by the weakness of the old leadership, aggravated by the accumulation of mistakes of 20 years of misrule. All the defects in the ideology of this system were nourished until they matured.

Therefore, let us not overestimate the significance of the criticism from the ranks of writers and students. The source of social change is in the economy. The right word is significant only if it is spoken under conditions which have been duly prepared. "Duly prepared conditions in our country"—unfortunately, this cliché means our general level of poverty and the complete disintegration of the old system of rule, under which certain types of politicians calmly and peacefully compromised themselves at our expense.

Truth does not prevail. It only remains when everything else fails. There is no cause for a national celebration of victory. But there is cause for new hope. We turn to you in this moment of hope, which is still under threat. It took several months for many of us to believe that they could speak out and many still do not believe it.

Yet, we have not spoken up. All we have to do is complete what we started out to do—humanize this regime. Otherwise the revenge of the old forces will be cruel. We turn to those who have been waiting. The days immediately ahead of us will determine our future course for many years to come.

✦

THE DANGER OF RELAXATION

Soon it will be summer, with its vacations and holidays, when we will want to relax. We can be certain, however, that our adversaries will not indulge in summer sports, that they will mobilize the people under obligation to them and that even now they are trying to arrange for calm Christmas holidays. Let us carefully observe what happens. Let us understand and respond to it. Let us deny the assumption that some higher-up will be on hand to give us the only possible interpretation of events and the simple conclusion that flows from them.

Each of us will have to take the responsibility for drawing his own conclusions. Consensus can only be found if freedom of expression, which happens to be the only democratic achievement of the year, is permitted. In the forthcoming days we will have to demonstrate our initiative and determination.

Above all, we will oppose views, should they arise, that it is possible to carry out some type of democratic revival without the communists—or possibly against them. This would be both unjust and unreasonable. The communists already have functioning organizations, and we should support their progressive wings. They have experienced functionaries and, last but not least, they hold in their hands the decisive levers of control.

The public has the party's action program before it. Above all, the program equalizes some of the greatest imbalances that exist today. No one else has a comparable program. We must demand that local action programs be submitted to each district and community. These long-awaited steps are routine enough, but they are what the situation calls for now.

The party is preparing for the congress that will elect a new Central Committee. Let us demand that it be better than the current one. If the party now says that in the future it wants to base its leading position on the confidence of the citizenry and not on force, let us believe this as long as we can believe in the people whom it is sending as delegates to district and regional conferences.

There are some who have recently become upset because they believe that the course of democratization has ended. This derives from the letdown following the first exciting developments—the surprising revelations, resignations from high places and speeches of unprecedented boldness. The struggle has merely become less evident. The battle is now over the formulation of laws and other practical measures. We must give the ministers, prosecutors, chairmen and secretaries time to prove themselves. Moreover, one cannot presently expect more of the central political organs, which have already shown, however unwillingly, surprising virtues.

✦

AN EXPLANATION FROM THE MANAGERS

The practical outcome of democracy in the future depends on what happens in the enterprises—it is the economists who hold the cards. We must seek out good managers and see to it that they are put into leading positions. Compared with the highly industrialized countries, we are all badly paid.

We could demand more money. It can be printed but it depreciates in the printing. Instead, let us demand that directors and chairmen explain to us what they want to produce at what price, to whom they want to sell their products and at what price, what the profits are and what part of them is invested in the modernization of production and how much can be distributed.

The newspaper headlines do not reveal the real struggle. On the one hand, the progressives are fighting for democracy and, on the other, the conservatives are fighting to keep their cushy jobs. The workers can intervene in this struggle in a businesslike way by choosing the right managers and councils of the enterprises. They will help themselves most if they elect trade union representatives who are capable and honest natural leaders, without regard to party membership.

The central political organs have done all they can up to this point. It is up to us to make new inroads in the districts and communities. Let us demand the resignation of those who have abused their power, who have harmed public property, who have acted dishonestly or cruelly. We must find ways to induce them to leave. Such steps include public criticism, resolutions, demonstrations, collecting funds for their retirement, strikes and boycotts. . . . But we must reject methods which are illegitimate, indecent or gross, since they might prejudice [First Secretary] Alexander Dubček. We must decry the writing of insulting letters, since they can be exploited by those that receive them.

◆

THE PROBLEM OF CZECHS AND SLOVAKS

Let us revive the activity of the National Front. Let us demand public meetings of national committees and, on questions which the officials refuse to consider, let us set up special citizens' committees and commissions to deal with the problems. It is a simple procedure: a few people convene; they elect a chairman; keep regular minutes; publish their findings; demand a solution. And they do not let themselves be intimidated.

Let us change the district and local press, which had degenerated into a mouthpiece for official views. Let us demand the establishment of editorial councils composed of representatives of the National Front, or let us start new newspapers. Let us establish committees for the defense of free speech. Let us have marshals to maintain order at our meetings.

If we hear of strange occurrences, let us check on them, send delegations to interview those involved and publish their replies on trees if we have to. Let us support the security organs when they prosecute genuine criminal activity. We do not want to cause anarchy and a state of general insecurity. Let us avoid disputes among neighbors and renounce spitefulness in political affairs. Let us unmask informers.

Many summer vacationers throughout the republic will be interested in learning about a constitutional solution to the Czech-Slovak question. We consider federation

The Prague Spring. Besides demanding political liberalization and "socialism with a human face," the students and intellectuals who spearheaded Czechoslovak reform in 1968 reached out toward the more relaxed, experimental cultural values of the sixties-era West. This photograph of young people informally grouped around posters and slogans extolling President Ludvík Svoboda captures both aspects of the Prague Spring spirit. (Goess/Sipa Press)

as one means of solving the nationality problem, but this is just one of the important steps toward democratization.

Federation itself will not secure better living conditions for either the Czechs or Slovaks or, for that matter, solve their other economic and social problems. The rule of the party-state bureaucracy may still survive, especially in Slovakia because, in its victorious fight, "it has gained greater freedom."

Recently there has been great apprehension that foreign forces may interfere with our internal development. Faced with their superior strength, the only thing we can do is humbly hold our own and not start trouble. We assure the government that we will back it, if necessary even with weapons, as long as the government does what we mandate and assures our allies that we will observe our alliance, friendship and trade agreements.

Excited reproaches and unfounded suspicions make the government's position more difficult, without being of any help to us. We can insure a new balance in our system only by improving internal conditions to such an extent that the revival can be carried to a point where we can elect statesmen who will have sufficient courage, honor and political wisdom to defend such conditions. This, by the way, is the problem of governments in all the small countries of the world.

As at the end of the war, we have been given a great chance once again. We have the opportunity to take up a common cause, which for all practical purposes we call socialism, and mold it so that it will correspond to the good reputation we once had and the high esteem in which we held ourselves.

The Invasion of Czechoslovakia, 1968

◆

Zdenek Suda

In this passage from his book, *The Czechoslovak Socialist Republic*, Suda describes the actual course of the Soviet invasion, which put an end to the Prague Spring and "socialism with a human face." Suda, a graduate of Charles University in Prague, is now professor of sociology at the University of Pittsburgh.

In the night of August 20 to August 21, 1968, more than half a million troops of the Warsaw Pact countries, with the exception of Rumania, invaded Czechoslovak territory. Only a historian who will have gained access to first-hand sources of information will be able to tell with certainty whether the feeling of relief, prevailing after the talks at Bratislava, was justified or not—that is, whether the Soviets actually had meant to give the Czechoslovak experiment a chance and changed their mind only later, or whether all negotiations from the very beginning had been a smoke screen and a treacherous game. It is easy to bring proofs in support of the opinion that the intervention had been planned since early spring 1968. The most convincing evidence would be the preparedness of the Soviet and allied troops, their incessant movements along Czechoslovak borders, as well as reluctance of some of them to evacuate Czechoslovakia after the summer military exercise. However, the alertness of the Warsaw-Pact armies might not have signified more than that the intervention had been considered as one serious *alternative* among several, with different courses kept open. On the other hand, it would not be difficult to argue that the invasion must

Zdenek Suda, "The Invasion," from *The Czechoslovak Socialist Republic,* Johns Hopkins University Press, 1969, pp. 139–148. Reprinted by permission of the Johns Hopkins University Press.

Wenceslas Square, August 1968. This was the scene in Prague, shortly after the Warsaw Pact's invasion of Czechoslovakia on August 21, 1968, which brought to an end the Prague Spring and ushered in twenty-one years of repression. Exactly twenty-three years later, on August 21, 1991, the people of Moscow would successfully resist a hard-line coup in the Soviet Union, initiating the downfall of communism in the USSR itself. (Eastfoto)

have been opted for on the spur of a moment—or, at least, that the actual order to the troops to move into Czechoslovakia was given on very short notice, under the influence of some precise event or fact. Many circumstances, in the first place the astoundingly poor preparation of the political, that is, the most important aspect of the intervention, would point in this direction.

If this was actually so, what could have been this definite event that tilted the scales in favor of the invasion? True enough, the political scene in Czechoslovakia remained lively after the talks at Cierna and in Bratislava. The long-postponed state visits of the two protagonists of national independence and sovereignty of the communist party states, Yugoslav President Tito and Rumanian Prime Minister Ceauşescu, were at last taking place. The response of the Czechoslovak public to them, especially to that of Marshal Tito, left no doubt what the country felt about the Moscow-style proletarian internationalism. However, it is likely that, far more than a possible resurrection of the Little Entente spirit, it was the internal development which provided the final impulse to the military action. On the assumption that some concrete event did alarm the Soviet leaders to the point when an armed intervention appeared as immediate necessity, it would seem that the formal constitution of the Social Democratic Party—or, more accurately, of its Preparatory Committee—in

Prague on August 15, 1968, might have triggered the action. However, on the other hand, the intensive press campaign in the U.S.S.R. and other Warsaw Pact countries immediately before the invasion which was an obvious propaganda build-up, paid little attention to this apparently significant fact. Another theory has it that, during a series of bilateral talks with the representatives of the smaller party states, such differences of opinion came up between the Czechoslovak communists and their comrades that these latter put whatever more pressure was necessary on the Kremlin to move it to intervene. A particularly active role in this connection is ascribed to the Chairman of the State Council of the G.D.R. Walter Ulbricht, who visited Czechoslovakia the week after the conclusion of the Bratislava conference.

✦

REACTION OF THE PARTY
AND THE POPULATION

No matter what the most immediate motives for the invasion might have been, the operation earned the respect of military experts on both sides of the Iron Curtain as an absolutely faultless strategic move. On the political side, however, the intervention was far from faultless; in fact, the history of world communism has hardly seen a politically more confused operation.

The invading units of the Soviet Union, Poland, East Germany, Hungary, and Bulgaria—in an estimated total number of 600,000—met with no military resistance but with a virtually unanimous passive resistance of the population. This unanimity did not have to bother the invaders any more than the nation-wide resistance of the Hungarian people did in November, 1956, but there were important new elements in the situation. It soon became evident that the occupant had no collaborators to rely upon; from this point of view the resistance was unprecedented. The usual "classical" measures of the Soviets—the arrest of the leaders and the seizure of the mass communications media—revealed themselves ineffective, as there was literally nobody to take the place of the silenced leadership and to put press, radio, and television at the occupant's service. On the contrary, the mass media personnel went underground in an admirably organized manner and, from hiding, continued to voice protests and to spoil the invaders' propaganda. A clandestine Party Congress was called to a Prague factory, where it was camouflaged as a staff meeting; it was held in lieu of the Fourteenth Congress which the invasion now made impossible. The Congress newly endorsed the reform program of the January Plenum, expelled dogmatist members, and expressed its full support for the jailed top officials. The Czechoslovak Trade Union Council proclaimed a general strike which was observed with impressive discipline all over the country. Students and members of youth organizations went into the streets and engaged the invading troops in discussions about the purpose and the justification of the invasion. Wall inscriptions in perfect Russian revealed to the hundreds of thousands of Red Army members the true feelings of the nation; here the twenty years of compulsory instruction in Russian language backfired on those who had imposed them. This picture did not agree with what the troops had heard in their ideological briefings for the operation: They had been told that a handful of counter-revolutionaries and Western agents oppressed the great majority of the Czechoslovak working people, who were anxious for their liberation by their "Soviet brothers."

Yet the most stunning experience for the invaders must have been the impossibility to find a group, however small, which would legalize the invasion by a formal request for "help," even issued *ex post,* and which could provide a basis for a quisling Party leadership and government. The curious fact that the Warsaw Pact armies marched into Czechoslovakia *prior* to the constitution of such a group permits two explanations: Either the Soviets were absolutely sure they would find sufficient response whenever they would come to "aid the imperiled Socialism," or the decision to carry out the operation was taken in such a precipitate way that there simply was no time to set up a new team—as, for instance, had been the case in Hungary, twelve years earlier. If the first surmise is correct, it would be interesting to know on what grounds and from what sources the Kremlin policy-makers gained the impression that the replacement of the reformist leadership would be a problem so easy to solve. Serious doubts about the validity of this theory arise if we ask why the same individuals or groups, who had succeeded in convincing the Soviets about a warm reception of the intervention by the great majority of the working people in Czechoslovakia, did not later co-operate in the Soviet efforts to establish new, Soviet-subservient Party and government organs. It is possible, of course, that these informants had the confidence of the Soviets but neither the popularity nor the record which would qualify them to succeed Alexander Dubček and his associates; such a description would fit, almost perfectly, the former First Party Secretary and the President of the Republic Antonín Novotný, who, all through the eight months of the new course, had been in a close contact with the Soviet Embassy in Prague and its top official, Ambassador Tchervonenko. The possibility cannot be ruled out, either, that the Soviets had obtained a promise of collaboration from certain personalities in the Communist Party of Czechoslovakia, but that these individuals revised their stand after the invasion, under the impression of the unanimity of popular support for the reformist leaders. However, many conservative Party officials later denied explicitly any collusion with the occupationists, before as well as after intervention.

Thus, the theory that, due to a very sudden decision to carry out the military operation, lack of time was responsible for the poor preparation of the invasion's political aspects remains the most probable. In this light, the Kremlin's action would appear to be a momentary alarm reaction of an irresolute and disoriented leadership, shaken by chronic internal dissensions rather than a "diabolic Asiatic ruse." The circumstance, for example, that the proclamation to the "Czech and Slovak working people" that had been waiting for twenty-four hours on the desks of the press agencies in the five party states participating in the invasion had to be finally withdrawn without publication because of the lack of signatures, or the fact that, three days later, the communication media controlled by the occupational forces made public a "Manifesto of Czechoslovak Communists, faithful to the ideas of Marxism-Leninism" but could not put one single name under it, seem to be very convincing indicators of the totally improvised character of the whole action.

✦
STRANGE COMPROMISE

At the height of the crisis, when the deadlock became patent and the passive resistance of the Czechoslovak population threatened to erupt any moment into a violent confrontation with the occupational forces, the President of the Republic Ludvík Svoboda, one of the few top leaders of the State present in the country and not under arrest, went to Moscow to negotiate a solution with the Soviets. In Prague, his travel to the Soviet capital was presented as an act taken on his own initiative; however, the pomp with which he was received upon his arrival there, showed that his step was most welcome to the Soviets. Maybe the CPSU [Communist Party of the Soviet Union] leadership hoped to make the same easy deal with President Svoboda as Stalin and Gottwald had made with President Beneš in 1948, or Hitler with President Hácha in 1939. Whatever their expectations might have been, the fact remains that the talks proved to be very difficult. After four days of negotiations, the Soviet Party and government leaders agreed to return the interned Czechoslovak politicians to power, in exchange for the promise that the situation in Czechoslovakia would be "normalized." There was little explanation given what was to be understood by "normalization," except that "anti-Socialist elements" were to be "rendered harmless" and anti-Soviet attacks and the criticism of the Soviet move in the Czechoslovak press was to be curbed. Until the satisfaction of this demand, the troops of the Warsaw Pact were to remain in Czechoslovakia. However, it could be guessed from various hints by the Soviet representatives that some contingents of the Red Army would stay in the country even after "normalization" would be achieved, in order to "protect the borders of the Socialist camp from the aggression by West German revanchists."

On August 26, 1968, Alexander Dubček and his group returned to Prague and resumed their offices in the Party and in the government. Though their personal experience must have been a serious shock and though they had to dampen many a naive hope pinned by the population and the Party rank-and-file members on their return, their comeback was an admission of failure by the Soviets. Moscow gave thus to understand that it did not see how Czechoslovakia and the Communist Party there could be led, at least at that time, by a team other than that of the hated "revisionists." This admission was all the more obvious, as hardly forty-eight hours earlier the official organ of the CPSU, "Pravda" of Moscow, had denounced Alexander Dubček as "a traitor to the Czechoslovak proletariat and to the cause of international Communism."

While the internal difficulties encountered in the occupied Czechoslovakia were probably the main motive of the Soviet retreat from the original plan to bring about a sweeping change, international complications ensuing from the invasion might have also played a certain role during the "four-day crisis." The indignation in the free world was great, and all the leading statesmen of the West condemned the Soviet action. However, judging from Soviet behavior at similar occasions in the past, it is not very likely that the Kremlin policy-makers were much impressed by these reactions. What might have weighed with them more seriously was going on in the framework of the United Nations, during the first days of the intervention. In contrast to what had happened in the wake of the Hungarian revolution in November, 1956, both the permanent Czechoslovak representative to the United Nations and the Czechoslovak Minister of Foreign Affairs denounced the invasion and flatly denied that anyone, either in the government or in the Party, would have ever invited the Warsaw Pact armies to enter Czechoslovakia. The Soviet move was thus deprived of even its most artificial formal basis.

Yet, by far the most effective means of pressure on the international level were probably those applied by several important centers of the world communist movement. The U.S.S.R. was not even able to rally on its side a convincing majority of the communist party states. Among the ruling communist parties outside the five who participated in the intervention, only the CP of North Vietnam approved the move without reservation; the rest voiced a very strong protest or took, at best, an ambiguous stand without hiding the fact that, in their opinion, the Soviet action could not be justified on any legal grounds. Among the parties in the remaining world, the response was even more crushing. The Soviet Union received support from a bare half-dozen of them, mostly negligible sects in the underground, and even these sometimes reached their decision only after serious internal conflicts. The two largest Western components of the international communist movement—the French and Italian communist parties—as well as a majority of the smaller parties, rejected the intervention in quite unmistakable terms. These consequences must have been particularly keenly resented by that part of the Soviet leadership which had been setting hopes on the International Communist Conference, slated for November, 1968, as a step towards greater cohesion of world communism. There is little doubt that the invasion dealt a serious blow to these hopes; some Western observers are even of the opinion that the conflict between Moscow and other communist parties over Czechoslovakia was "a death spasm of international communism."

Another important question is whether the decision to intervene actually put an end to the obvious differences of opinion among the Soviet leaders about the Czechoslovak issue, that had existed before August 21, 1968. It does not seem that it was so; on the contrary, there are signs that the policy of force adopted in this respect continues to meet with little enthusiasm on the part of at least some members of the top organs of the CPSU. It was probably no accident that the Central Committee of the Soviet Party, which had met shortly before the invasion, took another two months to meet again, obviously to endorse the principles of the strange compromise reached with the Czechoslovak representatives after the occupation. No points of agenda were mentioned in the final communiqué of this session, but the unusually emphatic assertion that the policy of the present leaders "enjoys wholesale and unreserved support of all Party members and of all Soviet people" would rather suggest that the team in control was in dire need of such assertions.

The Origin of the European Model of Socialism

✦

Radoslav Selucký

An adviser to Dubček's reform government in 1968, Selucký here reflects on the aims of the reform movement, connecting them to the non-Soviet socialist tradition. Formerly affiliated with the Czechoslovak Academy of Sciences, in emigration he became a professor of political science at Carleton University in Ottawa, Canada.

If I were asked to summarize the chief aims of the post-January social reform movement, I would say that we were trying to achieve a positive, humane and socialist victory over capitalism. We wanted not only to eliminate the bureaucratic *dirigisme* of Stalinism, but also to avoid the deformations of Western society. We had no desire to revive the acute social differences that exist in capitalist countries—and in some socialist countries. We naturally hoped to protect the social interests of all levels of the population. (Pensions and minimum wages were raised, and living standards improved, for the neediest groups *after* January.) At the same time we guided public sentiment to the realization that the purpose of life is not consumption, but life itself; and that consumption, like work, is only a means to the self-fulfilment of each individual, who needs to live his own unique existence in decent conditions, to have access to education, and to have opportunity for creative effort and for the satisfaction of his higher needs and interests. *To improve the destiny of individuals*—that was the supreme goal of our "socialism with a human face." For the first time in history we wanted to make the humanist creed an everyday reality, unfettered by class rivalries or bureaucratic tyranny.

It may be objected that the goal was utopian, and that, even if no outside hand had halted the new course, time would have exposed its ideals as too high-flown to be implemented in their pure form. I cannot disprove this, any more than I can claim that we should necessarily have achieved an earthly paradise. I am in any case doubtful whether a society *can* be created in which every individual, or even every social group, can find complete satisfaction. It is however, possible to create a system that would reduce to a minimum the defects of those social models familiar to us today, that

Radoslav Selucký, "The Origin of the European Model of Socialism," from *Czechoslovakia: The Plan That Failed,* Thomas Nelson Press, 1970, pp. 135–140.

would attempt a synthesis of rationalism and humanism, and come close to realizing the objective in great measure, if never completely. Our ambitions were naturally not to be secured in one year, or in a Five Year Plan. It was to be an unending process, bringing about an open-ended system with a capacity for self-perfection and adoption of every innovation beneficial to man's progress. The proclaimed programme and first achievements of this system had already won over almost the entire Czechoslovak public to the prospect of living no longer in a country shut off from the outside world, but in one able to withstand competition and comparison with any state and any system anywhere. It was a system whose theory and principles could be openly discussed with all comers; a system with values for present application, and with values for the distant future. Its outlook was no artificial construct but an attempt to express human longings, to improve the human lot and to develop in balanced synthesis every live and viable value of European civilization.

I do not think this project can be thought of as a Czechoslovak *national* model, even though it was created for us and none of us considered forcing it upon other countries. (Small nations are in any case disinclined to impose their ideas about life on others.) I regard our pattern of democratic socialism as a continuation of European thought and traditions, of Europe's cultural, popular and social ideals. To that extent it was a European socialist model, embarked upon by a small country in the heart of Europe which for centuries has been a meeting-place for all the currents of European thought, and which, on many occasions in her history, has spearheaded efforts to humanize society.

Does a concern for civic rights and freedoms suggest a narrowly national form of socialism? Or the call for pluralism, or the insistence that the government should be for the people, not the people for the government? These are scarcely national obsessions, in conflict with proletarian internationalism or prejudicial to the peaceful coexistence of nations. No country in the world, perhaps, has ever been so close to a practical fulfilment of the Universal Declaration of Human Rights as was socialist Czechoslovakia in the first half of 1968; none, perhaps, has ever in its history been so united, so active and so enthusiastically involved as was Czechoslovakia in both the first and second halves of that year. What state in modern times has displayed such a harmony of opinion between the public, the government and the ruling party as Czechoslovakia after January? Few nations could have done what the people of Czechoslovakia did in the days following 21 August 1968—defenceless as they were.

I have no wish to overlook the differences that existed within our society both in the period after January and in the days following 21 August. But if I consider the speed with which millions of people renewed their allegiance to socialism; the prudence with which they reacted to the revelations of crime and inhumanity committed in the 50s; the generosity displayed by the public towards the politicians who had led them to the edge of disaster; the dignity with which the public demonstrated its own will and hopes; and finally the mature and almost statesmanlike wisdom which simple, uninstructed and unorganized people showed in face of the external complications that attended the "Czechoslovak spring"—then I am far more impressed by the favourable traits in all this, guaranteeing favourable developments to come, than by any disruptive factors such as must accompany any process of social rebirth, and which in our own case grew weaker, not stronger, as time passed. It is significant that the whole course of events after January 1968 was marked, not by mere negation of the past, but by the creation of a positive programme. It is significant, again, that when the public learnt of the heavy economic losses for which the old leaders had been responsible, it decided of its own free will to offer sacrificial tributes. Simple folk brought in their jewellery, their gold rings and their savings for the Fund of the Republic; without thought of public recognition, people sacrificed their leisure to work extra shifts in order to give strength to their socialist government and their communist leaders. Does this not all testify to the fact that we were thinking of the future and not of the past; that we had begun to rid ourselves of inferiority complexes and to be proud, at long last again, not simply because we were Czechs and Slovaks, but because it was we who were taking the lead in rehabilitating socialism before the eyes of the world, and because we were in this way fulfilling our international duty to that working class movement in which we had never claimed any leading role or special right to determine what is socialist, and what not?

But good tactics, it seems, never pay in the end. If our publicists occasionally suggested that in creating a new socialist pattern we should be following our own specific traditions, this was not meant to imply undue pride in the Czechoslovak form of the model or an overestimation of the national features of socialism compared to the international. These claims were motivated rather by anxiety lest our allies suspect us of trying to give them advice, of intervening in their domestic affairs and claiming to teach them what true socialism should look like. Yet what we were aiming at was in truth a more general form of socialism, rather than a Czechoslovak speciality. If the Soviet form of socialism was not to be considered the only orthodox and authentic one then, as we saw it, neither should the Stalinist interpretation of Marxism and Leninism. Marxism has evolved not only in the country where the first socialist revolution saw victory, but in countries where that victory came later. It is evolving now in countries still belonging to the capitalist part of the world. We cannot, for example, overlook the contribution made to Marxist political science by such thinkers as the Italian communist Gramsci. We cannot exclude from the current of Marxism the minds of Labriola, Hilferding, or Plekhanov, people whose views on a number of questions differed from those which, in the 30s, became obligatory for all communists under the Stalinist system with its special Stalinist interpretation of Lenin. Nor indeed can we ignore the works of the young Marx, which Lenin did not know and in which today we find many a suggestive passage for anyone drawing up a programme of socialist construction.

We were aware that the Czechoslovak attempt to overcome the crisis of Stalinism was only one of several possible solutions, albeit one specially suited to a European state. Anyone who knows the process of differentiation now apparent not only in the international working-class movement, but in the approach to various theoretical questions and alternative models of socialism, will have noted that, like Christianity of old, Marxist socialism is now splitting up into numerous different schools and streams without any questioning of the common foundations. This pluralism of socialist systems and models is in accordance with natural law. Every known type of social structure has acquired different forms in differing countries. The institution of slavery looked quite different in ancient Greece and Rome from what it did in the despotic kingdoms of the Orient. The social forms that emerged from the ruins of European antiquity were quite different from those which followed the breakdown of older civilizations in Africa and Asia. Feudalism in Europe was different from feudalism in Russia or Asia. Swedish capitalism is considerably different in form not merely from American or Swiss capitalism, but from that of Spain, Japan or Brazil. This plurality of social forms is a natural occurrence; it is unrealistic to expect different countries to exhibit the same pattern in their progress from lower to higher forms of society. The contemporary world, after all, affords another example: in addition to the Soviet interpretation of socialism we can observe the interpretations of China, Yugoslavia, Cuba, Italy—and one could add many more.

The concept of national and international factors has also changed recently throughout the communist movement. As long as the U.S.S.R. was the only socialist country it was logical for all communists to see in her a prototype for the future of their own countries, too. But as soon as other socialist states came into being, the communists who lived and worked there were able to display their degree of internationalism not merely by their attitude to the Soviet Union, but by the examples they set in their own countries and the attraction they thereby exerted, or failed to exert. Of all the socialist countries Czechoslovakia was renowned for its sense of allegiance to the East European bloc and of the obligations involved in its membership of the Warsaw Pact and Comecon. From the start of the reform movement we were fully aware of the international factors limiting the abilities of small countries in either half of the divided world to follow their own courses. Our reform efforts were not directed to points outside, but only inside our society; our sole hope was to deal with the problems of domestic stability and dynamism while preserving the *status quo* in Europe. Without disturbing the balance of power in Europe or the world at large, we aimed to overcome the crisis of Stalinism in Czechoslovakia in a calm, constructive and democratic manner. We did not want to go back to capitalism, nor to see capitalism and socialism "converge." The only international implication of our reforms that we had in mind was that they might indicate, within the context of the existing world equilibrium, a *conceivable path* to international coexistence, to economic, cultural and scientific cooperation, and to the normalization of relations between the capitalist and socialist countries of Europe. But this we regarded as a possible secondary by-product of our efforts to solve purely Czechoslovak issues. Quite obviously it would have been better for us if changes in our own affairs had had no international implications at all, since we should then have enjoyed more peace and quiet to plan our course of action with due prudence. However, we behaved with almost obsessive circumspection to ensure that our experiment had no impact on the interests of our allies or of the international working-class movement.

Appeal and Declaration by a Group of Delegates to the Fourteenth Congress of the Czechoslovak Communist Party

✦

Eduard Goldstücker et al.

The five authors of this statement were elected delegates to the Fourteenth Party Congress of August 1968. The document is a protest against the Fourteenth Congress convened in 1971, in effect abrogating the original one. The protesters deny the legitimacy of the Congress called by a "sanitized" post-invasion Communist party.

✦

APPEAL

The undersigned, delegates to the Fourteenth Congress of the Czechoslovak Communist party, democratically elected in 1968, declare, in their own names and in the names of their comrades who cannot speak freely:

That they regard the only legal Fourteenth Party Congress as that which took place on August 22, 1968, at Prague-Vysočany;

That the meeting taking place on May 25, 1971, is not a Congress of the whole Communist party of Czechoslovakia, but solely of the "normalized" Party after the expulsion of half a million members. This Congress will thus make decisions only according to the will of the minority that, since April 1969, has seized control of the Party through an internal coup d'état imposed by foreign intervention. This Congress will be propped up by an artificial, falsified and essentially reactionary interpretation of the development of Czechoslovak society.

The signers consequently deny the legitimacy of this Congress, which will take place in an atmosphere of political and juridical persecutions, in the presence of foreign armed forces, the objective of which is to legalize the military intervention and the violation of sovereignty and to impose on the Party and the State a direction contrary to the will of the Communists and the people as a whole.

The signers reaffirm that, in the present circumstances, the democratic and socialist development of Czechoslovakia requires the following preconditions: the withdrawal of all foreign troops from Czechoslovak territory; the restoration of democratic and civil liberties; an end to political persecutions, to trials and confinement of dissidents, to attacks on the means of living and to all other forms of political repression; and freedom for scientific research and for artistic creation.

The signers appeal to the Communist and Workers parties invited to attend this Congress, that they state plainly their disagreement with the military intervention of August 21, 1968, and its consequences, in the interest of the common cause of socialism.

The signers appeal to progressive and democratic opinion to support the just struggle of the Czech and Slovak peoples for a free, democratic, and socialist Czechoslovakia. They hope that world opinion will not stay silent at the spectacle of "normalization" and persecution, and that the voices of protest and solidarity will be powerfully raised.

✦

DECLARATION

In May 1971, a Congress of the Czechoslovak Communist party was convened and presented as the Fourteenth Party Congress. We feel that it is necessary to remind Czechoslovak and world opinion that the only valid Fourteenth Congress was that which met on August 22, 1968, at Prague-Vysočany, which consisted of democratically elected delegates.

The annulment of the decisions of the legal Fourteenth Party Congress, the exclusion from the Party of the majority of its participants, along with half a million other Communists, have been imposed by a *diktat* from Moscow, under the threat of terror and military reprisals. The present leading committees of the Czechoslovak Communist party as well as of the state, have been installed by the will of the foreign occupying power and against the will of the Czechoslovak people.

The Congress which is now being organized will be forced to endorse the "normalization," of which the principal aim has been to deprive the Czechoslovak people of the possibility of deciding their own social development and their own destiny. The purges which have been carried out in the Czechoslovak Communist party and in the other political parties that formally exist, in the trade unions, in the youth organizations, as well as in the governmental and ideological institutions, have been aimed at eliminating and depriving of all political influence those who support the democratization and humanization of socialist society.

This regime, which claims to represent the working class, has crushed the seeds of a system of self-direction and workers' councils. Just as in the period of the Moscow Trials, every activity that tends to promote progressive and democratic reforms is called "counterrevolutionary," without the slightest proof. Every key position in the country has been filled by the most conservative and reactionary elements of the Czechoslovak Communist party. Thanks to a corrupt and bureaucratic apparatus, backed by the constant menace of reprisals and by the total ideological monopolization of communications and education, this little group holds the entire population under its fist.

The bureaucratic-centralist system, with all its insidious consequences for the country's development as a modern industrial state, has been reinstated. The basic civil rights and civil liberties have been trodden underfoot. Anyone who expresses dissatisfaction with the foreign occupation exposes himself to brutal economic and political reprisals.

Thousands of the most talented and courageous citizens have been driven from their jobs. The most capable intellectuals have been denied the chance to continue their work in science, education, journalism, the arts and all the other activities in which they formerly participated. The purge has also been widely extended in the ranks of the army. Whoever dares to protest and to speak the truth is tried and sentenced by rigged courts. Censorship, manipulated news and lying propaganda have reached dimensions that recall the decade of the fifties. All worthwhile artistic works—books, films, plays, etc.—are once again under the censor's thumb. Even national and world classics are censored and mutilated according to current political needs.

The economy is again dominated by the old system of centralized planning which has already proven its inability to carry on modern, efficient and competitive production able to meet the needs of the people. The losses that spring from wasted investments and materials, from abnormally long lags in construction, from the great number of useless goods manufactured, from the lack of promotion of foreign trade, from the inadequate services and commercial outlets at home, from the aging transportation system and from a grossly inflated administrative apparatus, lower the standard of living of the whole population.

Economic relations between the USSR and Czechoslovakia are not based on equality and mutual benefit. The economy of Czechoslovakia is more and more chained to that of the USSR and subordinated to its needs and objectives. Contrary to official propaganda, which presents the situation as advantageous to Czechoslovakia, a constantly increasing portion of Czechoslovak labor is thus drained off, in the form of merchandise shipments and long-term investments, into the Soviet Union, without obtaining the necessary quantities of consumer goods, housing and services. The result is a constant growth in hidden inflation.

Czechoslovakia is a developed industrial country whose people, by their capacity, their talent and their professional qualifications, are able to rival those of the advanced industrial countries. However, because of the inadequate economic and political system that has been imposed on the country, this state remains behind in technical development, in productivity and in the standard of living.

These "normalized" conditions, imposed by the foreign occupation, are in the first place symptoms of a limitation of the sovereignty of the Czechoslovak state. One of the fundamental preconditions for change is the departure of the foreign army from

Czechoslovak soil and the end of all foreign meddling in the internal affairs of the country. The leaders of the present regime, who not only conceal the loss of national sovereignty but even give thanks for the deed, do not represent the interests of the Czechoslovak people.

The Congress which is about to meet would like to give the impression—before world public opinion, and especially before the Communist parties of the world—that the Communists and the people of Czechoslovakia accept the present situation. At the same time, this Congress is bound to direct the Party toward even closer collaboration with the Great Power politics of the USSR. The fact that all the delegates to this Congress were chosen by the Party apparatus, the careful tailoring given all the speeches, resolutions and elections by the apparatus, make of this Congress a fraud and a swindle of the highest order. The only purpose of the Congress, and of the elections that will follow it, is to legitimize the status quo.

A regime which has deprived the people of its fundamental democratic liberties, which robs citizens of their work and persecutes them for their political opinions, which destroys every initiative of the people, which makes the standard of living depend on the whims of bureaucrats—such a regime must remain alien and hostile, and can maintain itself in power only by brute force. It is a mockery of all the great humanitarian ideals of socialism. The Czech and Slovak peoples will never be reconciled with this regime. They will fight to change it and will discover the appropriate forms for the struggle, which is waged in the interests of the peoples of all the socialist countries, including the Soviet Union.

As delegates to the Fourteenth Party Congress of the Czechoslovak Communist Party who are still able to express our opinions freely, we refuse to recognize the legality of either the Congress now being organized or the present regime. We see the only solution to the present crisis as the institution of fundamental democratic reforms that will open the way for our citizens to participate in the decisions that affect our society and to establish the democratic socialism toward which the "Prague Spring" of 1968 was leading. We shall continue, together with all democrats and all who espouse the ideals of socialism in Czechoslovakia and throughout the world, to struggle for these aims.

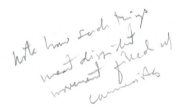

Charter 77

✦

This document, dated 1 January 1977, forms the keystone of Czechoslovak protest against the tractable, Soviet-sponsored regime of Gustav Husák that was installed after the invasion broke the back of the reform movement. It was signed by large numbers of Czechs and Slovaks from all walks of life and of diverse political persuasions. Signatories were routinely subjected to reprisal.

In the Czechoslovak Collection of Laws, no. 120 of 13 October 1976, texts were published of the International Covenant on Civil and Political Rights, and of the International Covenant on Economic, Social, and Cultural Rights, which were signed on behalf of our Republic in 1968, were confirmed at Helsinki in 1975 and came into force in our country on 23 March 1976. From that date our citizens have the right, and our state the duty, to abide by them.

The human rights and freedoms underwritten by these covenants constitute important assets of civilized life for which many progressive movements have striven throughout history and whose codification could greatly contribute to the development of a humane society.

We accordingly welcome the Czechoslovak Socialist Republic's accession to those agreements.

Their publication, however, serves as an urgent reminder of the extent to which basic human rights in our country exist, regrettably, on paper only.

The right to freedom of expression, for example, guaranteed by Article 19 of the first-mentioned covenant, is in our case purely illusory. Tens of thousands of our citizens are prevented from working in their own fields for the sole reason that they hold views differing from official ones and are discriminated against and harassed in all kinds of ways by the authorities and public organizations. Deprived as they are of any means to defend themselves, they become victims of a virtual apartheid.

Hundreds of thousands of other citizens are denied that "freedom from fear" mentioned in the preamble to the first covenant, being condemned to live in constant danger of unemployment or other penalties if they voice their own opinions.

In violation of Article 13 of the second-mentioned covenant, guaranteeing

"Charter 77," from H. Gordon Skilling, *Charter 77 and Human Rights in Czechoslovakia,* Allen & Unwin Press, 1981, pp. 209–212.

everyone the right to education, countless young people are prevented from studying because of their own views or even their parents'. Innumerable citizens live in fear that their own or their children's right to education may be withdrawn if they should ever speak up in accordance with their convictions. Any exercise of the right to "seek, receive, and impart information and ideas of all kinds, regardless of frontiers, either orally, in writing or in print" or "in the form of art," specified in Article 19, paragraph 2 of the first covenant, is punished by extrajudicial or even judicial sanctions, often in the form of criminal charges as in the recent trial of young musicians.

Freedom of public expression is repressed by the centralized control of all the communications media and of publishing and cultural institutions. No philosophical, political, or scientific view or artistic expression that departs ever so slightly from the narrow bounds of official ideology or aesthetics is allowed to be published; no open criticism can be made of abnormal social phenomena; no public defense is possible against false and insulting charges made in official propaganda; the legal protection against "attacks on honor and reputation" clearly guaranteed by Article 17 of the first covenant is in practice nonexistent; false accusations cannot be rebutted, and any attempt to secure compensation or correction through the courts is futile; no open debate is allowed in the domain of thought and art. Many scholars, writers, artists, and others are penalized for having legally published or expressed, years ago, opinions which are condemned by those who hold political power today.

Freedom of religious confession, emphatically guaranteed by Article 18 of the first covenant, is systematically curtailed by arbitrary official action; by interference with the activity of churchmen, who are constantly threatened by the refusal of the state to permit them the exercise of their functions or by the withdrawal of such permission; by financial or other measures against those who express their religious faith in word or action; by constraints on religious training; and so forth.

One instrument for the curtailment or, in many cases, complete elimination of many civic rights is the system by which all national institutions and organizations are in effect subject to political directives from the apparatus of the ruling party and to decisions made by powerful individuals. The constitution of the republic, its laws, and other legal norms do not regulate the form or content, the issuing or application of such decisions; they are often only given out verbally, unknown to the public at large and beyond its powers to check; their originators are responsible to no one but themselves and their own hierarchy; yet they have a decisive impact on the actions of the lawmaking and executive organs of government, and of justice, of the trade unions, interest groups and all other organizations, of the other political parties, enterprises, factories, institutions, offices, schools, and so on, for whom these instructions have precedence even before the law.

Where organizations or individual citizens, in the interpretation of their rights and duties, come into conflict with such directives, they cannot have recourse to any nonparty authority, since none such exists. This constitutes, of course, a serious limitation of the right ensuing from Articles 21 and 22 of the first-mentioned covenant, which provides for freedom of association and forbids any restriction on its exercise, from Article 25 on the equal right to take part in the conduct of public affairs, and from Article 26 stipulating equal protection by the law without discrimination. This state of affairs likewise prevents workers and others from exercising the unrestricted right to establish trade unions and other organizations to protect their economic and social interests and from freely enjoying the right to strike provided for in paragraph 1 of Article 8 in the second-mentioned covenant.

Further civic rights, including the explicit prohibition of "arbitrary interference with privacy, family, home, or correspondence" (Article 17 of the first covenant), are seriously vitiated by the various forms of interference in the private life of citizens exercised by the Ministry of the Interior, for example, by bugging telephones and houses, opening mail, following personal movements, searching homes, setting up networks of neighborhood informers (often recruited by illicit threats or promises), and in other ways. The ministry frequently interferes in employers' decisions, instigates acts of discrimination by authorities and organizations, brings weight to bear on the organs of justice, and even orchestrates propaganda campaigns in the media. This activity is governed by no law and, being clandestine, affords the citizen no chance to defend himself.

In cases of prosecution on political grounds the investigative and judicial organs violate the rights of those charged and of those defending them, as guaranteed by Article 14 of the first covenant and indeed by Czechoslovak law. The prison treatment of those sentenced in such cases is an affront to human dignity and a menace to their health, being aimed at breaking their morale.

Paragraph 2, Article 12 of the first covenant, guaranteeing every citizen the right to leave the country, is consistently violated, or under the pretense of "defense of national security" is subjected to various unjustifiable conditions (paragraph 3). The granting of entry visas to foreigners is also handled arbitrarily, and many are unable to visit Czechoslovakia merely because of professional or personal contacts with those of our citizens who are subject to discrimination.

Some of our people—either in private, at their places of work, or by the only feasible public channel, the foreign media—have drawn attention to the systematic violation of human rights and democratic freedoms and demanded amends in specific cases. But their pleas have remained largely ignored or been made grounds for police investigation.

Responsibility for the maintenance of civic rights in our country naturally devolves in the first place on the political and state authorities. Yet, not only on them: Everyone bears his share of responsibility for the conditions that prevail and accordingly also for the observance of legally enshrined agreements, binding upon all citizens as well as upon governments. It is this sense of coresponsibility, our belief in the meaning of voluntary citizens' involvement and the general need to give it new and more effective expression that led us to the idea of creating Charter 77, whose inception we today publicly announce.

Charter 77 is a free informal, open community of people of different convictions, different faiths, and different professions united by the will to strive, individually and collectively, for the respect of civic and human rights in our own country and throughout the world—rights accorded to all men by the two mentioned international covenants, by the Final Act of the Helsinki conference, and by numerous other international documents opposing war, violence, and social or spiritual oppression, and which are comprehensively laid down in the United Nations Universal Declaration of Human Rights.

Charter 77 springs from a background of friendship and solidarity among people who share our concern for those ideals that have inspired, and continue to inspire, their lives and their work.

Charter 77 is not an organization; it has no rules, permanent bodies, or formal membership. It embraces everyone who agrees with its ideas, participates in its work, and supports it. It does not form the basis for any oppositional political activity. Like many similar citizen initiatives in various countries, West and East, it seeks to promote the general public interest. It does not aim, then, to set out its own programs for political or social reforms or changes, but within its own sphere of activity it wishes to conduct a constructive dialogue with the political and state authorities, particularly by drawing attention to various individual cases where human and civil rights are violated, by preparing documentation and suggesting solutions, by submitting other proposals of a more general character aimed at reinforcing such rights and their guarantees, and by acting as a mediator in various conflict situations which may lead to injustice and so forth.

By its symbolic name Charter 77 denotes that it has come into being at the start of a year proclaimed as the Year of Political Prisoners—a year in which a conference in Belgrade is due to review the implementation of the obligations assumed at Helsinki.

As signatories, we hereby authorize Professor Dr Jan Patočka, Václav Havel, and Professor Jiří Hájek to act as the spokesmen for the charter. These spokesmen are endowed with full authority to represent it vis-à-vis state and other bodies, and the public at home and abroad, and their signatures attest the authenticity of documents issued by the charter. They will have us, and others who join us, as their coworkers, taking part in any needful negotiations, shouldering particular tasks and sharing every responsibility.

We believe that Charter 77 will help to enable all the citizens of Czechoslovakia to work and live as free human beings.

POLAND 1980–1981

◆ *Poland had a communist regime headed by Gomułka, a leader who had not undergone Moscow's special brand of "training." Rejecting the Soviet blueprint for Poland, Gomułka was the most outspoken advocate of a "national road" to socialism. Along with neighboring leaders of like mind, he was deposed when Stalin tightened the screws in the aftermath of the break with Tito. But in 1956, as Poland narrowly missed the fate of Hungary, Gomułka was reinstated. Even Stalinism had been relatively mild in Poland, but the Soviet accommodation in 1956 seemed like a vindication of Poland's independent inclinations.*

Gomułka's reign degenerated, however, and after a decade it was hard to distinguish it from a survival of Stalinism. Poland's participation in the Warsaw Pact invasion of Czechoslovakia in 1968, which shamed so many Polish citizens, was a low point in postwar experience. By the end of 1970 Gomułka had been replaced by Edward Gierek, a move precipitated in part by a wave of strikes and protests that set the tone for the ensuing two decades of public life in Poland.

With so much turmoil in postwar Polish history, it is not surprising that an independent trade union movement known as Solidarity unfolded there in 1980. The group presumed to negotiate with the government on its way to involving the whole Polish citizenry. The drama was so high and the implications—for Poland and the whole region—so far-reaching that the world's attention was riveted for the best part of two years until the Jaruzelski government declared martial law and repressed Solidarity.

The selections that follow offer brief illuminations of the crises of 1956 and 1968, the latter focusing on the ugly anti-Semitism that disfigured political rhetoric at the time; then come necessarily sketchy summaries of the prehistory of Solidarity and its two-year struggle against the government in the face of threatened Soviet intervention. The Solidarity program, lengthy but also unique in the postwar history of Eastern Europe, is included in full. And finally, Adam Michnik, one of the movement's intellectuals who put themselves in the service of a workers' program, reflects on the experience from the vantage point of the martial law period.

The "October Revolution" in Poland

✦

Władysław Gomułka

A workers' uprising in Poznań in June 1956 signaled that reform
sentiment, prominent in many places in Eastern Europe, would
challenge the Stalinists' grip on authority. Gomułka, deposed
earlier as a "national communist," was reinstated as party secretary in October, and only Soviet acceptance of this change
defused the crisis. This address to the Central Committee
sketched a more moderate and gradual path to socialism.

When I addressed the November Plenum of the Central Committee of the
Polish United Workers' Party seven years ago, I thought that it was my last speech to
the members of the Central Committee. Although only seven years have elapsed since
that time, or eight years since the August Plenum, where an abrupt change occurred in
the party's policy, these years constitute a closed historic period. I am deeply convinced that that period has gone into the irrevocable past. There has been much evil in
those years. The legacy that that period left the party, the working class, and the nation
is more than alarming in certain spheres of life. . . .

The working class recently gave a painful lesson to the party leadership and the
Government. When seizing the weapon of strike and going out to demonstrate in the
streets on the black Thursday last June, the Poznań workers shouted in a powerful
voice: Enough! This cannot go on any longer! Turn back from the false road. . . .

The Poznań workers did not protest against People's Poland, against socialism
when they went out into the streets of the city. They protested against the evil which
was widespread in our social system and which was painfully felt also by them, against
the distortions of the fundamental principles of socialism, which is their idea. . . .

The clumsy attempt to present the painful Poznań tragedy as the work of imperialist agents and provocateurs was very naïve politically. Agents and provocateurs can
be and act anywhere, but never and nowhere can they determine the attitude of the
working class. . . .

Among the charges which were raised against me in the past was that my attitude
in different matters stemmed from an alleged lack of faith in the working class. This is

Władysław Gomułka, "The 'October Revolution' in Poland," from Robert V. Daniels, ed., *A Documentary
History of Communism*, vol. 2, Vintage Press, 1962, pp. 235–240.

Gomułka in the "Polish October," 1956. Dramatically addressing a vast crowd in Warsaw, Władysław Gomułka pleaded for moderation. His determination to keep Polish resistance to communism within bounds may well have averted a Soviet invasion. (Eastfoto)

not true. I have never lost faith in the wisdom, common sense, selflessness, and revolutionary attitude of the working class. In these values of the working class I believe also today. I am convinced that the Poznań workers would not have gone on strike, that they would not have demonstrated in the streets, that no men would have been found among them who even resorted to arms, that our fraternal, workers' blood would not have been shed there had the party, that is the leadership of the party, presented the whole truth to them. It was necessary to recognize without any delays the just claims of the workers; it was necessary to say what can be done today and what cannot be done; it was necessary to tell them the truth about the past and the present. There is no escaping from truth. If you cover it up, it will rise as an awful specter, frightening, alarming, and madly raging. . . .

The loss of the credit of confidence of the working class means the loss of the moral basis of power.

It is possible to govern the country even in such conditions. But then this will be bad government, for it must be based on bureaucracy, on infringing the rule of law, on violence. The essence of the dictatorship of the proletariat, as the broadest democracy for the working class and the working masses, becomes in such conditions deprived of its meaning. . . .

. . . We must tell the working class the painful truth. We cannot afford at the present moment any considerable increase of wages, for the string has already been stretched so tight that it can break. . . .

The road to setting up a vast network of cooperative farms in Poland's country-side is a long one. A quantitative development of producer cooperation cannot be planned because, on the basis of voluntary entry in a cooperative, this would amount to planning the growth in human consciousness, and that cannot be planned. The consciousness of the masses is shaped by their experience in life. It is shaped by facts. There are not a few facts in our present state of cooperative farming which repel the peasant masses from the cooperative farms. Such facts must be liquidated. . . .

What is immutable in socialism can be reduced to the abolition of the exploita-tion of man by man. The roads of achieving this goal can be and are different. They are determined by various circumstances of time and place. The model of socialism can also vary. It can be such as that created in the Soviet Union; it can be shaped in a manner as we see it in Yugoslavia; it can be different still.

Only by way of the experience and achievements of various countries building socialism can the best model of socialism under given conditions arise. . . .

. . . The mapping out of the Russian road to socialism passed gradually from the hands of the Central Committee into the hands of an ever smaller group of people, and finally became the monopoly of Stalin. This monopoly also encompassed the theory of scientific socialism.

The cult of personality is a specific system of exercising power, a specific road of advancing in the direction of socialism, while applying methods contrary to socialist humanism, to the socialist conception of the freedom of man, to the socialist concep-tion of legality. . . .

The cult of personality cannot be confined solely to the person of Stalin. The cult of personality is a certain system which prevailed in the Soviet Union and which was grafted to probably all Communist Parties, as well as to a number of countries of the socialist camp, including Poland.

The essence of this system consisted in the fact that an individual, hierarchic ladder of cults was created. Each such cult comprised a given area in which it func-tioned. In the bloc of socialist states it was Stalin who stood at the top of this hierarchic ladder of cults. All those who stood on lower rungs of the ladder bowed their heads before him. Those who bowed their heads were not only the other leaders of the Communist Party of the Soviet Union and the leaders of the Soviet Union, but also the leaders of Communist and Workers Parties of the countries of the socialist camp. The latter, that is the First Secretaries of the Central Committees of the Parties of the various countries who sat on the second rung of the ladder of the cult of personality, in turn donned the robes of infallibility and wisdom. But their cult radiated only on the territory of the countries where they stood at the top of the national cult ladder. This cult could be called only a reflected brilliance, a borrowed light. It shone as the moon does. Nonetheless it was all-powerful in the sphere of its action. Thus in each country there was a ladder of cults from top to bottom. . . .

That system violated the democratic principles and the rule of law. Under that system, the characters and consciences of men were broken, people were trampled underfoot and their honor was besmirched. Slandering, falsehood, and lies, even provocations, served as instruments in the exercise of authority.

In Poland, too, tragic events occurred when innocent people were sent to their death. Many others were imprisoned, often for many years, although innocent, including Communists. Many people were submitted to bestial tortures. Terror and demoralization were spread. On the soil of the cult of personality, phenomena arose which violated and even nullified the most profound meaning of the people's power.

We have put an end to this system, or we are putting an end to it once and for all. Great appreciation should be expressed to the 20th Congress of the CPSU [Communist Party of the Soviet Union] which so greatly helped us in the liquidation of this system. . . .

The road of democratization is the only road leading to the construction of the best model of socialism in our conditions. We shall not deviate from this road and we shall defend ourselves with all our might not to be pushed off this road. And we shall not allow anyone to use the process of democratization to undermine socialism. Our party is taking its place at the head of the process of democratization and only the party, acting in conjunction with the other parties of the National Front, can guide this process in a way that will truly lead to the democratization of relations in all the spheres of our life, to the strengthening of the foundations of our system, and not to their weakening.

The party and all the people who saw the evil that existed in the past and who sincerely desire to remove all that is left of the past evil in our life today in order to strengthen the foundations of our system should give a determined rebuff to all persuasions and all voices which strive to weaken our friendship with the Soviet Union.

If in the past not everything in the relations between our party and the CPSU and between Poland and the Soviet Union shaped up in the manner it should have in our view, then today this belongs to the irrevocable past. . . .

Among the many ailments of the past period was also the fact that the Sejm [Parliament] did not fulfill its constitutional task in state life. We are now facing elections to the new Sejm which ought to occupy in our political and state life the place assigned to it by the Constitution. The elevation of the role of the Sejm to that of the supreme organ of state power will probably be of the greatest importance in our democratization program. . . .

Postulating the principle of the freedom of criticism in all its forms, including criticism in the press, we have the right to demand that each criticism should be creative and just, that it should help to overcome the difficulties of the present period instead of increasing them or sometimes even treating demagogically certain phenomena and problems.

We have the right to demand from our youth, especially from university students, that they should keep their ardor in the search for roads leading to the improvement of our present reality, within the framework of the decisions which will be adopted by the present Plenum. . . .

Our party should say clearly to the young people: march in the vanguard of this great and momentous process of democratization but always look up to your leadership, to the leadership of all People's Poland—to the party of the working class, to the Polish United Workers Party.

Disorder in Warsaw

◆

Witold Jedlicki

This article was written in 1968, a year of crisis in Poland. The Gomułka regime had departed from the more humane path charted in 1956, and student revolt in March was symptomatic of more widespread discontent. Ensuing turmoil produced a good deal of anti-Semitic rhetoric, an almost automatic reflex in politically troubled times. Jedlicki, a graduate of the University of Warsaw active in dissenting circles, focuses on this aspect of the crisis. He left Poland and became an Israeli citizen.

There are two aspects to the March 1968 student revolt in Poland: one is what actually happened and the other is what the Polish regime says happened. One is the story of a tough, desperate struggle; the other is an updating of the Protocols of the Elders of Zion. There is little relationship between the two, but neither story can be dismissed lightly.

The Polish government tried hard enough to link its story to the events themselves. So hard, in fact, that the arrested students were asked during their interrogation: "Why do you allow the kikes to dupe you?" (It is interesting to observe that the official claim of fighting "Zionists" instead of Jews—the Jews are just loved—gets lost soon as the multisyllable words of the official ideology get translated into the plain talk of policemen.) And the government went so far as to expel Richard Davy, the corre-spondent of the London *Times,* for failing to perceive a link between the rioting stu-dents and the "Zionist conspirators."

In the West, the government's campaign of Jew-baiting has tended to over-shadow the story of the student struggle. And that is unfortunate, for the student strug-gle had nothing to do with any Jewish question. Those students who were Jews acted not as Jews but as students; they fought for students' rights just as students in this country have done, and not in defense of Judaism. But with the government's anti-Semitism against them, the Polish students are in danger of respectability in the West, of being acclaimed nice anti-Communist fellows, at a time when respectable gentle-men in the West are becoming hostile to student rebellions everywhere else. The young Poles should be defended against such a respectable image.

The young Polish rebels face similar problems as their American counterparts, only from the opposite side, sort of upside down. Because the American Establishment calls itself democratic, student rebels, in order to fight it are forced either to call them-selves antidemocratic, Eastern-style, or to say that they are better democrats than LBJ. But the Polish government calls itself Communist, so Polish students opposing it are compelled either to be anti-Communist, Western-style, or say that they are better Communists than Gomułka.

The evidence indicates that the young Poles have chosen the latter alternative. In a recent editorial (March 24), the Warsaw *Kultura* (not to be confused with the Paris-based magazine bearing the same name) attacked and deplored the heavy influ-ence exercised upon students by what it called a "silly" piece of writing advocating (and here the reader is treated to the notion of a real horror) that the Polish army be dissolved and replaced by the "duty hours of workers serving the missile rockets." Of course the "silly" piece of writing that exercised so heavy an influence on the students was the Kurón-Modzelewski "Open Letter." . . . Similarly, an article in the daily newspaper, *Trybuna Ludu,* refers to a "not numerous but very mobile group of stu-dents around Modzelewski and Kurón." What such articles reveal is that the students were guided not by Western anti-communist slogans but by an ardently anticapitalist, Third Camp socialist ideological statement.

Not that all the resolutions, statements and programmatic documents produced by the students are very radical; some are surprisingly meek, such as the Zambrowski document, published in English in the London *Times* (March 22), which is reminis-cent of those noble outpourings in our mildly "left wing" journals, which praise dis-sent and civil liberty and fair trials but express disgust with violence and illegality. But even so, the Zambrowski document, whose author has been accused of being a "ring-leader" of the demonstrations, leaves no doubt that it has nothing in common with the Western Establishment's anti-Communism. And although Gomułka, in his speech of March 19, quoted some leaflet with slogans such as "down with Communism," the immense majority of pamphlets and resolutions published by the students stress devo-tion to Communism, to *true* Communism.

Like the rebelling American students, the Polish students press a demand for sensible, meaniful academic discourse, for scientific research unperverted by the vested interests of power-holders, for due process, for freedom of speech and freedom of association. Their methods of struggle are similar, most notably the sit-in. And like American students they even tend to yell "Gestapo" at the police and to adopt formal resolutions about the students' lack of personal access to his professor. These Polish students are quite plainly the allies and comrades of the New Left, not of the Polish emigres or of the United States troops fighting in Vietnam.

And they are allies of the Polish workers. By and large, the Polish working class stayed away from these recent demonstrations (in contrast to the struggles of 1956–1957). And the students, in their resolutions, made hardly any demands of direct concern to workers. But it is worth noting that the students received messages of solidarity from the crews of the two biggest industrial complexes in Poland: Nowa Huta near Cracow and Pafawag in Breslau. In the Danzig shipyard there was a solidarity demonstration. Moreover, some statistics provided by Gomułka in his speech of March 19 indicate that a substantial number of workers took part in the student demonstrations.

Gomułka's figures are as follows:

	Total	Students	Nonstudents
Persons arrested	1,208	367	841
Released for lack of evidence	687	194	493
Still under investigation	521	173	348

Mind you, there are very few idle people in Poland, and very few businessmen. Those who do not study work and the arrest statistics link students with those who work.

There is another statistic, one which tries to lump workers with the police: it is the casualty list. There exists in the Ministry of the Interior a department cynically entitled the Department of People's Wrath. It recruits thugs, pays them, arms them, teaches them to pose as workers and dispatches them to strikes and demonstrations. The thugs are of two kinds: those who receive some police training and those who receive none, or very little. The former are called "volunteer reservists of the citizens' militia" and the latter are called "working-class activists." (Neither are to be confused with American vigilante groups: they are simply police agents with no particular ideology.) Combining casualties from all three categories—the professional cops, the "reservists" and the "activists"—Gomułka tells us that 146 were injured during the disturbances. One hundred forty-six injured cops, "reservists" and plain thugs. It gives a notion of how tough the fight was.

There were widely reported factory meetings and demonstrations protesting against the students. These, of course, are not hard to arrange. It simply means assembling a factory crew on a square, giving them signs and ordering them to look indignant. It is surprising, however, when more than half the crew resists intimidation and goes home instead of joining the show. And that was precisely what is reported to have happened.

But perhaps most impressive about the response of nonstudents to the demonstrations is the total absence of any important name from any statement attacking the students. This writer has reviewed the Polish newspapers for the entire period of the student rebellion. There have been hundreds of letters, speeches and statements against the students. But there is not one that is signed by any known scholar or artist or writer—not even by any known sportsman. Not one faculty member in all of Poland appears to have come out against the students. With amazing clumsiness the press attempted to disguise that fact; an example is the following item: "The protest demonstration [against the students] took place in the school of cinematography famous for the fact that among its faculty are Messrs. so-and-so, such-and-such, etc." Not one of the persons mentioned was said to have signed his name to any antistudent statement.

It is not difficult to discover who "incited" the riots and the unrest leading up to them. Plainly, the students were "incited" to collect their 3,145 signatures protesting the ban against Mickiewicz's classic play, *Dziady,* written in 1832 and cherished as a treasury of Polish poetry and national freedom, by the ban itself. When the government demanded that the Writers' Association condemn the unruly behavior of onlookers in the theatre, as a means of justifying the ban, it only "incited" the writers to vote by a large majority a resolution condemning the ban and approving the subsequent demonstrations. The expulsion of Adam Michnik and Henryk Schleifer from the University for their role in collecting the 3,145 signatures undoubtedly incited the students to stage their demonstration of March 8, in which they protested against the expulsion of the two popular student leaders.

We have several interesting reports on the March 8 demonstration. The *New York Times* reports that the tear gas used against the demonstrators did not stop them but merely incited them against the police. The students, red-eyed and wet-eyed, with blurred vision, remained or re-emerged and continued to taunt the police. The *Christian Science Monitor* reports that the brutalization of female students by the police had an inciting effect. Gomułka himself admitted that rumors to the effect that two girls, one a student, and other a nonstudent, had been killed by the police had an inciting effect. He denied the rumor vehemently, and the student was put on TV to announce "Here I am, alive." But the nonstudent did not appear on TV, so we have only Gomułka's word as proof that she is alive.

But there was more incitement at the later stage of the riots. A Cracow newspaper reports, for example, that 112 people were admitted to the hospital, most of them bitten by dogs. Several days later the same newspaper apologized for "creating the wrong impression that the dogs were police dogs"—without the inciting effect of those dogs the apology would never have been necessary. Almost a month after the riots began, the University incited the students by ousting seven popular faculty members, including the world-famous philosopher, Leszek Kołakowski, for "spiritual instigation," and for advocating in their classes ideas which "stand in glaring discrepancy with the dominant developmental tendencies of the country and of the nation." These seven faculty members had committed an unforgivable sin: each of them had a long and honorable record of defending individual students victimized by the authorities, and these actions were cited along with "spiritual instigation" and discrepant ideas as a third reason for their ouster. And more recently, the scuttling of the University of

Warsaw—surely the right word for the closing of eight of its departments—must necessarily have had an inciting effect.

A reading of the Polish press gives a good idea of the regime's awareness of the inciting effects of its own actions. The official press endlessly and incessantly tries to convince the reader that whatever action the regime had taken was not responsible for further troubles. The ban against the play? A mere pretext for collecting signatures. The expulsion of Michnik and Schleifer? A mere pretext for staging the March 8 demonstration. And so on; the demonstrators, we are told, did not care about the play or about Michnik and Schleifer. This is said not once or twice or three times, but countless numbers of times, with stubborn obstinacy clumsily covering the incredibility of the government's argument.

But in a totalitarian country a newspaper article has the quality of law. The article may appear to state facts but, in reality, it spells out a rule under which anybody holding views contrary to those published becomes an "enemy of socialism." That is why the Polish students repeatedly demanded that the newspapers recant their slanderous accounts of demonstrations and street fighting; unlike the lies told in American papers about the FSM in Berkeley and the student strike at Columbia, the stories stridently repeated in the Polish newspapers have a normative force marking them as obligatory truths.

◆

EXPLANATIONS IN THE POLISH PRESS

The Polish press offers three explanations for the disturbances: it blames them on the Stalinists, the intellectuals and the Zionists.

The Stalinists and the students? The only evidence offered for that is the undeniable fact that many of the student leaders come from families in the Communist elite; they are sons or daughters of men who occupy high party and governmental posts. But that is all that the Polish press offers as evidence of Stalinist incitement: a guilt-by-association theory pure and simple.

Apparently the theory was needed for some account-settling within the Communist party leadership. We read in the Polish press how Mr. So-and-so oppressed the peasants in 1951 or how Mr. Such-and-such fraudulently pretended to be a liberal in 1956. The stories are true, but they are merely individual scapegoating intended to cover over the fact of the regime's *collective* responsibility for the crimes of the Stalin era. Interestingly enough, these press attacks are aimed at losers—at those who lost their power and their positions five or ten years ago. It is reminiscent of the Moscow trials, held eight years after their defendants lost all power, or of the 1961 campaign against an "anti-Party group" four years after that group was demoted to obscurity. Such scapegoating offers an outlet for daydreaming by winners about the absolute humiliation and annihilation of yesterday's foe.

With the intellectuals the matter is not so simple. They fall into two categories: writers and scholars. We are told that the writers are more guilty because they took a public stand in their speeches and in their Association's resolution. Stefan Kisielewski, one of the writers, described the Polish regime in his speech as a dictatorship of ignoramuses. This provoked "the wrath of the Polish working class" against Mr. Kisielewski: the night after his speech he was badly beaten up in the darkness of a secluded street by three unidentified wrathful "workers." It is undeniable that the writers cooperated with the student leaders and resisted the government together with them.

By comparison with such accused writers as Paweł Jasienica or Antoni Słonimski, the seven ousted faculty members accused of "spiritual instigation" are rather moderate. The writer knows six of them personally, five fairly well; not one was a fighter for a revolutionary cause. They were cautious men trying to protect scientific research from the government's political pressure, so far as possible—fine men and fair scholars, but without the temperament of revolutionaries. By antagonizing them, the government left itself short of people in a position to mediate between the authorities and the students.

Thus we are left with the Zionists. The campaign against them began with an article in the "progressive" Catholic daily, *Słowo Powszechne,* charging that Zionists had provoked the riots "in order to avenge Comrade Gomułka's correct appraisal of Israel's aggression against the Arab states last June." *Słowo Powszechne* is published by *Pax,* a Catholic association headed by Bolesław Piasecki, that has existed for over 30 years with substantially the same leadership. Before World War II its name was *Falanga,* in admiration for the movement of the same name in Spain. Its chief activity then was anti-Semitic propaganda and anti-Semitic violence; the actual extent of its activity is difficult to determine because its press claimed credit for every act of anti-Semitic violence that occurred. During the war it offered to form an auxiliary police force to help the Nazis fight "subversives," but the Nazis turned down the offer and the group turned against them. After the war, Piasecki was sentenced to death by the NKVD but made some deals with them and returned triumphantly to Warsaw, where he rallied his old followers and founded the new "progressive Catholic" movement. In 1956 he allied himself with the Natolin faction, which opposed any liberalizing change. Since then his association has proclaimed numerous moral-rearmament campaigns, none of which succeeded in morally shaking the nation. While Poland was still maintaining reasonably friendly relations with Israel, from 1953 to 1967, and the Polish press avoided anti-Zionism, Piasecki's press was busy warning about Zionist agents and Zionist infiltration. So now his group can claim to be the forerunner of the present policy.

As soon as the riots subsided, Piasecki was again in the news, providing ideological leadership for a purge of Jewish officials that had now stepped down from the top level to that of factory directors and the like. It is important to remember that the purge is not yet over.

Gomułka entered the scene with his speech of March 19, which the Western press incorrectly treated as an attack on anti-Semitism. His speech did differ from the line advanced by the Polish press in that (a) he was evidently opposed to the scapegoating of former Stalinists at that particular time and (b) he did not believe that Zionism constituted a real threat to the very existence of Poland. (Interestingly enough, when he said that in his speech, Gomułka was interrupted by voices shouting that Zionism does constitute such a threat. And there were cries of "Long live Gierek," referring to Gomułka's chief rival on the Politbureau, who had promised to "break the bones" of the students.)

But his speech contained its own version of anti-Semitism. Consider the following passage: "In the apartment of Jacek Kuroń, a group of young men, mostly of Jewish descent, convened a meeting. . . ." Twice in his speech he mentioned a certain Irena Lasota as a perpetrator of two major acts of sedition; he referred to her as Irena Lasota-Hirszowicz. Is Hirszowicz the name of her husband? No, she is not married. Hirszowicz is the former name of her father, who long ago changed it to Lasota. This is the familiar Soviet technique of indicating a person's Jewishness through a patronymic or some other bit of information which, to put it mildly, is non-essential. And here is how Gomułka handled the story of Paweł Jasienica, the actual leader of the oppositionist intellectuals. "His real name," said Gomułka, "is not Jasienica. It is Leon Lech Bejnar." That is true enough; Jasienica is actually a pen-name. The name "Benjar" is evidently non-Polish and, since Jasienica was the first to publicly condemn official anti-Semitism ("perfidiously," the Polish press said), the reader is likely to assume that it is a Jewish name. (After all, Lasota is only half-Jewish. . . .) The truth is that the name "Bejnar" is Tartar or Samogitian.

Gomułka's speech, of course, set the new pattern for the Polish press. As a result, one can now read, in an article dealing with a case of embezzlement involving a person with a familiar Polish name, some "subtle" hint like this: "His descent is irrelevant because, as everybody knows, embezzlements are committed by persons of all nationalities." The new style of the press is to distinguish "good" Jews from "bad" ones. A "good" Jew is one who considers Poland his homeland, is attached to Polish language and culture, is grateful to the Poles for his rescue during the war, loves the Communist party and government, and publicly condemns Israel. Any other Jew is a "bad" one. "Bad" Jews are Zionists, cosmopolitans, traitors, a "new fifth column," etc. Until recently, the Jewish danger was covered by a "cowardly silence," but now the press is "bravely" refusing to be intimidated by accusations of anti-Semitism.

"I am no anti-Semite," declares a certain Mr. Pietrzak, "because my father rescued five Jews during World War II." (Some of his father's best friends. . . .) Nobody is anti-Semitic. Not even Mr. Piasecki and his subordinates in *Pax*. Never. Anti-Semitism just disappeared, vanished; what is more, it never existed. There are only bad Jews.

◆

ANTI-SEMITISM AND CULTURAL CONFLICT

There is not enough data to explain or account for all this anti-Semitic hullabaloo. It may be explained as reflecting a conflict between political factions within the Communist party hierarchy. More likely, however, it reflects conflict not over issues but between cultures, in particular between the Party doctrinaires with a background in the intelligentsia and the *apparatchiki* from the lower classes. Life in the top leadership of the Communist party is one of constant paranoia concerning adversaries and rivals, and that paranoia begets corresponding delusions. The now-official Polish anti-Semitism seems to express the stereotyped view that *apparatchiki* hold of the intelligentsia. When the *apparatchiki* become dominant their delusions find public outlet; this is why we have recurrent waves of official anti-Semitism in Eastern Europe—now here, now there. It all depends upon the vicissitudes of never-ending struggles for posts, for succession, for power.

That the present wave of anti-Semitism in Poland should be so intense is, of course, related to events elsewhere in Eastern Europe, for whenever a dictator in any of the Eastern countries dies or is removed, and his death or removal gives rise to a struggle for his succession, the resulting popular excitement is apt to give rise to demands for democratization not only in that country but in surrounding countries as well. This is not true in those instances where the entire ruling clique stands together in opposition to the Russians and, at the same time, in opposition to their own people, as has happened in Yugoslavia, Rumania, Albania and China. But when a fight between rivals at the top breaks out, the rivals may start fighting each other openly and, in order to mobilize popular opinion, grant or at least promise some degree of democratization. This happened in Poland after the death of Bierut in 1956, in Hungary after the removal of Rákosi in July 1956, and in Czechoslovakia after the removal of Novotný. This may mean the opening of a genuine process of democratization—genuine, because the masses, thus encouraged, demand more and more democracy and, to get it, put pressure on the leadership. Eventually they have to be stopped, either by Russian tanks or by such complicated and tricky deals as took place in Poland in 1956–1957, or by a combination of the two as is now being practiced with regard to Czechoslovakia. But before they are stopped, their accomplishments provoke intense envy in the neighboring countries. Envy prompts the neighbors to act, even though such efforts are as a rule abortive—as was the case with Wolfgang Harich in East Germany in 1956.

That is why the recent Czechoslovak events pose a danger to the Polish regime—and why the Polish students shouted and displayed signs saying "Long live Czechoslovakia" and "We want a Polish Dubček!" It is why two Czechoslovak correspondents were expelled from Poland for taking the students' side in their reports. Mere nationalist opposition to the Russians—or opposition on the part of a unified Communist party hierarchy, such as the leadership of Ceauşescu in Rumania—raises no threat to the established order in neighboring countries. The substitution of the fist of Ceauşescu for the first of Brezhnev gives people in neighboring countries no reason for envy because it offers little or nothing in the way of democratization. Not even China's strenuous efforts to undermine Soviet might in Eastern Europe, by supporting underground groups of hard-core Stalinists, has caused any real disturbance. Gomułka has nothing to fear from Mao or Ceauşescu, but he has a great deal to fear from Dubček. The democratic turbulence next door in Czechoslovakia gives him reason to fear the Polish people.

KOR's Appeal to Society

✦

This document, dated 10 October 1978, emanated from the Workers' Defense Committee (KOR) as a critique of official lethargy in dealing with serious economic difficulties and the continuing resort to repression. It is a terse summary of the worsening conditions that led finally to the emergence of Solidarity, a movement that the KOR intellectuals served in an advisory capacity.

1. The increase in prices for foodstuffs that was rejected by the public in 1976 has been replaced by hidden price increases. There exists a widespread practice of introducing more expensive goods labeled with new names onto the market, while eliminating cheaper goods. This tactic has been used with a number of industrial goods and with most foodstuffs, even including bread. The increase of prices in the state trade is also reflected in private trade, causing a severalfold increase in the prices of fruits and vegetables. The scale of this phenomenon is difficult to determine, but there is no doubt that together with the official price changes, inflation is actually much higher than one would conclude on the basis of official data.

Difficulties with supplies are constantly increasing, both in the area of industrial goods and of foodstuffs. It is impossible to purchase many items in the stores without standing in lines, an enormous waste of time, or engaging in bribery or nepotism.

The problem of supplying the population with meat has not been solved. It is difficult to consider the extensive network of commercial stores as a solution, since in these stores the price of a kilogram of sausage equals the daily wages of an average worker (150–200 złotys per kilogram). Meat rationing has been introduced recently in several dozen industrial enterprises (e.g., the "Warszawa" Steel Mills and the Różza Luxemburg Enterprises). We do not know whether a system of meat rationing is necessary at this time. Until the state authorities publish full data on the availability of meat (production, export, and consumption), it will be impossible to adopt a position on this matter. It is certain, however, that any proposed rationing system should encompass the whole of society and be ratified by it. The hidden price increases and the supply difficulties have caused dramatic rises in the cost of living, and hit the poorest social strata particularly hard.

2. The state of health services is alarming. Chronic underinvestment over a period of years has recently been reflected in a decrease in the number of hospital beds (in psychiatry and obstetrics: *The Statistical Yearbook 1977*). The overcrowding and the technical conditions in a great many hospitals, which have never been renovated since the prewar period, create sanitary conditions that endanger the health of patients.

Insufficient nutrition and the lack of medications available in the hospitals and on the market are also obstacles to treatment.

The construction of a special modern government hospital for dignitaries in Międzylesie, and the special transport of medications, can be regarded in this context only as an expression of the full awareness on the part of the authorities insofar as the state of health services for the population as a whole is concerned; while the collection of contributions from the public for the Social Health Fund constitutes a cynical abuse.

3. The past several years have also brought about no improvement in the dramatic situation in housing. The number of people waiting for apartments grows larger every year, while the waiting period grows longer. This is coupled with a systematic increase in the cost of housing, which significantly burdens family budgets (monthly rent together with credit payments in housing cooperatives can run as high as three thousand złotys).

4. The authorities are attempting to make up for the disorganization of the economy through an increased exploitation of the workers. The average working day of many occupational groups has often been lengthened. Drivers, miners, construction workers, many other occupational groups now work ten to twelve hours a day.

The fact that miners were deprived of free days to compensate them for free Saturdays, that work is required on Sundays, and that a single day's absence even for the most valid of reasons (such as death in the family or illness) leads to a loss of approximately 20 percent of a monthly salary—all this can be compared only with early capitalist exploitation.

5. A comparison of the daily earnings of a worker with prices in a commercial store reveals yet another worrisome fact: a growing social inequality. Earnings are overly differentiated (without much regard for qualifications). There are enormous differences in retirement benefits. We have now in Poland families who are struggling under extremely difficult living conditions, and a small number of families who have no financial worries whatsoever. Another factor deepening social inequalities is the extensive system of privileges for groups associated with the authorities: privileged supplies, special health services, allocation of housing and building lots, foreign currency, and special recreational areas. These are only a few of the facilities available to small leadership groups. As a result, we are witnessing the growing social alienation of groups associated with the authorities, and their inability to notice the real social problems. When we learn that funds designated for the development of agriculture are being used to build a government center in Bieszczady and that in connection with this, local residents are being dislodged from the village of Wolosate, we are forced to view this fact as a proof that the authorities have lost all touch with reality.

More and more often, one can observe children inheriting the privileged position of their parents. The principle of equal opportunity for all young people is becoming illusory.

In a situation where the economic crisis threatens all of society, and especially the underprivileged groups, the assurance of special privileges to the governing groups provokes righteous anger and moral indignation.

6. The deepening crisis in agriculture is a fundamental factor in the economic, political, and social situation in the country. The consequences of a policy of discrimination and destruction of family farming, which has been conducted for thirty years, are now becoming visible. In spite of this, the production from one hectare of arable land in private hands is still higher than the production from one hectare of arable land in state agriculture. Still, gigantic investments are directed to the state agricultural farms and to production cooperatives despite the fact that the costs of maintaining state agricultural farms exceeds the value of their production.

Over the past several years, difficulties connected with the general state of the economy have been particularly evident: lack of coal, fertilizers, cattle feed, farming machinery, and building materials. This limits to a great extent the investment possibilities of peasant farms and leads to the exodus of young people to the cities.

Disorganization and corruption in the purchasing centers cause wastage of already produced farm goods.

At present, following the introduction of dues for retirement insurance for farmers, the financial responsibilities of the peasant farm to the state often exceed half of its income. The refusal by over 250,000 farmers throughout the country to pay retirement dues best illustrates the attitude of the peasants toward state agricultural policy.

7. The violations of the rule of law exhibited during the June events turned out to be a commonly used policy. Beatings of detainees by organs of the police are not isolated cases but constitute a form of police mob rule which is sanctioned by the higher authorities.

The materials gathered by the Intervention Bureau of the Social Self-Defense Committee "KOR" which have been published in the *Documents of Lawlessness* demonstrate the full impunity of the police and the security service. Even the most dramatic cases of murders of persons who were being detained does not result in any punishment of those functionaries guilty of such crimes. In the case of the murder of Jan Brożyna, the desire to protect the real murderers went so far that the investigation was entirely fabricated, as was the court trial.* All this ended in the death in prison of a major witness, and in long prison sentences for two other people whose guilt was never proven.

The activities of the sentencing boards for misdemeanors, which have been

---

*In June 1976 Jan Brożyna was beaten to death by the authorities in the industrial city of Radom, scene of the largest protests against the price rises instituted by the Gierek government in that month. His death became a cause célèbre and an important mobilizing event in the creation of KOR.

greatly extended at the expense of the court system, do not respect even the appearances of legality. The Office of the Prosecutor General, in disregard of the law, does not react to complaints that are filed; while the Council of State, the Diet, and the Ministry of Justice remain deaf to all information about the degeneration and anarchy that prevails in the investigative agencies and the justice system.

8. The usurpation by the party of the exclusive and totally arbitrary right to issue and impose judgments and decisions in all areas of life without exception has created a particular threat to Polish science and culture. Drastic limitations of the extent and freedom of scientific research and the publication of its results, especially in the humanities and social sciences such as philosophy, economy, sociology, and history; the stiff demands of the imposed doctrine, which has lost all the characteristics of an ideology and been transformed into a system of dogmas and unrestricted commands dictated by the authorities; the staffing of scientific positions with incompetent people who simply comply with the directives of the rulers—all of this brings harm to Polish culture and not only hinders its development but also the preservation and cultivation of its former achievements. Literature, theater, and film—those branches of culture dominated by language—are especially vulnerable to the arbitrary throttling of the freedom of thought and to the annihilation of creative activities. Under these conditions, culture is being deadened, while literature, an enormously important element in the spiritual life of the nation, though unmeasurable in its effectiveness, is either reduced to the role of an executor of the orders of the authorities or forced to divorce itself completely from expressing the truth about the surrounding reality, or else is simply tolerated as a harmless "flower on the sheepskin."

The preservation of culture has been reflected for several years now in initiatives in support of publications beyond the reach of state control and a science independent of official and distorting falsehoods.

The system of preventive censorship harms not only culture and science but the entire social and economic life of the country. Censorship stifles not only all signs of criticism but also all authentic information that could equip society with self-knowledge about its actual situation, which could prove undesirable for the authorities. *The Book of Prohibitions and Directives of the Main Office for Control of the Press, Publications, and Performances* published by KSS "KOR" demonstrates the extent of the censor's interference in all areas of life. Ever-greater regions of silence, made infertile by the discrimination against living contemporary culture, are invaded by monstrously inflated and omnipresent ersatz products privileged by cultural policy: Multifaceted entertainments and numerous pop song festivals are shabby substitutes for culture. This constitutes in fact the main object of such popularization and fulfills its role by blocking the deeper cultural aspirations of society and by systematically debasing its spiritual needs.

The most distinguished representatives of science and culture are subject to prohibitions against publication. The more ambitious films are not allowed to be shown. Entire periods of contemporary history are passed over in silence or falsified. The Polish Episcopate, the highest moral authority in the land, has warned against this phenomenon, seeing in it a threat to the national and cultural identity of society. The threat to culture and art posed by the censorship has been discussed at Congresses of the Polish Writers' Union and the Polish Sociological Association and is the subject of a pronouncement by the Polish PEN Club.

The system of disinformation constitutes a vicious circle that does not spare even the authorities who created it. According to *Życie Warszawy*, 65 percent of the data supplied by statistical units reporting to the Main Office of Statistics is falsified, and this estimate must be regarded as optimistic. It is impossible to make correct decisions on the basis of false information. Under these circumstances, paralysis must overwhelm the entire life of the country.

The authorities fear society and are therefore unable to provide it with the truth about the current situation. The so-called economic maneuver propounded as a solution to the crisis turned out to be only a set of immediate, arbitrary, and uncoordinated interferences into the economic life of the country. The result of this policy is only an increasing disorganization of the economy:

+ The freezing of investments has led to billions in losses because construction that had already started was never completed.

+ Drastic limitations in imports have led to weeks of idleness in factories across Poland.

+ The plunderous export of foodstuffs has increased shortages on the domestic market.

+ The dissolution of the planning system, together with the simultaneous denial of the market economy and the retention of an anachronistic system of directing enterprises by order and commands, has eliminated all regulatory mechanisms from the economy.

The system based on arbitrary and irrevocable decisions by state and party authorities who see themselves as infallible has caused immeasurable damage to the social consciousness of the nation. The persecution of independent views, together with the use of coercion to extort an unconditional compliance with all directives coming from above, has formed attitudes that lack all ideals and has fostered duplicity; the spread of conformism, servility, and careerism has been encouraged throughout society. These characteristics serve as recommendations in the staffing of leadership positions. Competent, enlightened, and independently minded people are deprived of the possibility of advancement, and often even of a job.

The total lack of consideration for public opinion means that an overwhelming majority of the citizens have ceased to identify themselves with the state, and feel no responsibility for it.

Radical economic reform is necessary. But even the most thoroughly developed and most consistent reforms will not be able to change anything if they run up against a barrier of public indifference and despair.

The economy will not be revived by Conferences of Workers' Self-Governments which blindly obey the PUWP [Polish United Workers' Party]. Committees of Social Control selected from among the authorities, and at their service, will not reach down to the sources of inefficiency, corruption, and illegality. The only result of such actions will be to increase the disorganization of life throughout the country.

The Twenty-one Demands

◆

This is the list of demands presented to the Polish government by the Interfactory Strike Committee (MKS) in Gdańsk on 23 August 1980. These demands were the basis for ensuing negotiations leading to the Gdańsk agreement.

1. Acceptance of Free Trade Unions independent of both the Party and employers, in accordance with the International Labor Organization's Convention number 87 on the freedom to form unions, which was ratified by the Polish government.

2. A guarantee of the right to strike and guarantees of security for strikers and their supporters.

3. Compliance with the freedoms of press and publishing guaranteed in the Polish constitution. A halt to repression of independent publications and access to the mass media for representatives of all faiths.

4. (*a*) Reinstatement to their former positions for: people fired for defending workers' rights, in particular those participating in the strikes of 1970 and 1976; students dismissed from school for their convictions.

(*b*) The release of all political prisoners (including: Edmund Zadrozynski, Jan Kozłowski, and Marek Kozłowski).

(*c*) A halt to repression for one's convictions.

5. The broadcasting on the mass media of information about the establishment of the Interfactory Strike Committee (MKS) and publication of the list of demands.

6. The undertaking of real measures to get the country out of its present crisis by:

(*a*) providing comprehensive, public information about the socio-economic situation;

(*b*) making it possible for people from every social class and stratum of society to participate in open discussions concerning the reform program.

7. Compensation of all workers taking part in the strike for its duration with holiday pay from the Central Council of Trade Unions.

8. Raise the base pay of every worker 2,000 złotys per month to compensate for price rises to date.

9. Guaranteed automatic pay raises indexed to price inflation and to decline in real income.

10. Meeting the requirements of the domestic market for food products: only surplus goods to be exported.

11. The rationing of meat and meat products through food coupons (until the market is stabilized).

12. Abolition of "commercial prices" and hard currency sales in so-called "internal export" shops.

13. A system of merit selection for management positions on the basis of qualifications rather than Party membership. Abolition of the privileged status of MO, SB [Internal Security Police], and the party apparatus through: equalizing all family subsidies; eliminating special stores, etc.

14. Reduction of retirement age for women to 50 and for men to 55. Anyone who has worked in the PRL for 30 years, for women, or 35 years for men, without regard to age, should be entitled to retirement benefits.

15. Bringing pensions and retirement benefits of the "old portfolio" to the level of those paid currently.

16. Improvement in the working conditions of the Health Service, which would assure full medical care to working people.

17. Provision for sufficient openings in daycare nurseries and preschools for the children of working people.

18. Establishment of three-year paid maternity leaves for the raising of children.

19. Reduce the waiting time for apartments.

20. Raise per diem [for work-related travel] from 40 złotys to 100 złotys and provide cost-of-living increases.

21. Saturdays to be days off from work. Those who work on round-the-clock jobs or three-shift systems should have the lack of free Saturdays compensated by increased holiday leaves or through other paid holidays off from work.

The Gdańsk Agreement

✦

This is the complete text of the agreement signed on 31 August 1980 by representatives of the strikers and the government. Recognition of the workers' right to form independent trade unions made this a milestone in the postwar history of resistance to state domination.

The governmental commission and the Inter-Factory Strike Committee (MKS), after studying the 21 demands of the workers on the Coast who are on strike, have reached the following conclusions:

On Point No. 1, which reads: "To accept trade unions as free and independent of the party, as laid down in Convention No. 87 of the ILO [International Labor Organization] and ratified by Poland, which refers to the matter of trade union rights," the following decision has been reached:

1. The activity of the trade unions of People's Poland has not lived up to the hopes and aspirations of the workers. We thus consider that it will be beneficial to create new union organizations, which will run themselves, and which will be authentic expressions of the working class. Workers will continue to have the right to join the old trade unions and we are looking at the possibility of the two union structures cooperating.

2. The MKS declares that it will respect the principles laid down in the Polish Constitution while creating the new independent and self-governing unions. These new unions are intended to defend the social and material interests of the workers, and not to play the role of a political party. They will be established on the basis of the socialization of the means of production and of the socialist system which exists in Poland today. They will recognize the leading role of the PUWP [Polish United Workers Party] in the state, and will not oppose the existing system of international alliances. Their aim is to ensure for the workers the necessary means for the determination, expression and defence of their interests. The governmental commission will guarantee full respect for the independence and self-governing character of the new unions in their organizational structures and their functioning at all levels. The government will ensure that the new unions have every possibility of carrying out their function of defending the interests of the workers and of seeking the satisfaction of their material, social and cultural needs. Equally it will guarantee that the new unions are not the objects of any discrimination.

3. The creation and the functioning of free and self-governing trade unions is in line with Convention 87 of the ILO relating to trade union rights and Convention 97 relating to the rights of free association and collective negotiation, both of which conventions have been ratified by Poland. The coming into being of more than one trade union organization requires changes in the law. The government, therefore, will make the necessary legal changes as regards trade unions, workers' councils and the labor code.

4. The strike committees must be able to turn themselves into institutions representing the workers at the level of the enterprise, whether in the fashion of workers' councils or as preparatory committees of the new trade unions. As a preparatory committee, the MKS is free to adopt the form of a trade union, or of an association of the coastal region. The preparatory committees will remain in existence until the new trade unions are able to organize proper elections to leading bodies. The government undertakes to create the conditions necessary for the recognition of unions outside of the existing Central Council of Trade Unions.

5. The new trade unions should be able to participate in decisions affecting the conditions of the workers in such matters as the division of the national assets between consumption and accumulation, the division of the social consumption fund (health, education, culture), the wages policy, in particular with regard to an automatic increase of wages in line with inflation, the economic plan, the direction of investment and prices policy. The government undertakes to ensure the conditions necessary for the carrying out of these functions.

6. The enterprise committee will set up a research centre whose aim will be to engage in an objective analysis of the situation of the workers and employees, and will attempt to determine the correct ways in which their interests can be represented. This centre will also provide the formation and expertise necessary for dealing with such questions as the prices and wages index and the forms of compensation required to deal with price rises. The new unions should have their own publications.

7. The government will enforce respect for Article I, paragraph 1 of the trade union law of 1949, which guarantees the workers the right to freely come together to form trade unions. The new trade union will not join the Central Council of Trade Unions (CRZZ). It is agreed that the new trade union law will respect these principles. The participation of members of the MKS and of the preparatory committee for the new trade unions in the elaboration of the new legislation is also guaranteed.

On Point No. 2, which reads: "To guarantee the right to strike, and the security of strikers and those who help them," it has been agreed that:

The right to strike will be guaranteed by the new trade union law. The law will have to define the circumstances in which strikes can be called and organized, the ways in which conflicts can be resolved, and the penalties for infringements of the law. Articles 52, 64 and 65 of the labor code (which outlaw strikes) will cease to have effect from now until the new law comes into practice. The government undertakes to protect the personal security of strikers and those who have helped them and to ensure against any deterioration in their conditions of work.

With regard to Point No. 3, which reads, "To respect freedom of expression and publication, as upheld by the Constitution of People's Poland, and to take no measures against independent publications, as well as to grant access to the mass media to representatives of all religions," it has been added that:

1. The government will bring before the *Sejm* [Parliament] within three months a proposal for a law on control of the press, of publications, and of other public manifestations, which will be based on the following principles: censorship must protect the interests of the state. This means the protection of state secrets, and of economic secrets in the sense that these will be defined in the new legislation, the protection of state interests and its international interests, the protection of religious convictions, as well as the rights of nonbelievers, as well as the suppression of publications which offend against morality. The proposals will include the right to make a complaint against the press control and similar institutions to a higher administrative code.

2. The access to the mass media by religious organizations in the course of their religious activities will be worked out through an agreement between the state institutions and the religious associations on matters of content and of organization. The government will ensure the transmission by radio of the Sunday mass through a specific agreement with the church hierarchy.

3. The radio and television as well as the press and publishing houses must offer expression to different points of view. They must be under the control of society.

4. The press as well as citizens and their organizations must have access to public documents, and above all to administrative instructions and socio-economic plans, in the form in which they are published by the government and by the administrative bodies which draw them up. Exceptions to the principle of open administration will be legally defined in agreement with Point No. 3, paragraph 1 (above).

With regard to Point No. 4 which reads: "(a) to re-establish the rights of people who were fired after the strikes in 1970 and 1976, and of students who have been excluded from institutions of higher education because of their opinions, (b) to free all political prisoners, including Edmund Zadrozynski, Jan Kozłowski and Marek Kozłowski; (c) to cease repression against people for their opinions," it has been agreed:

(a) To immediately investigate the reasons given for the firings after the strikes of 1970 and 1976. In every case where injustice is revealed, the person involved must be reinstated, taking into account any new qualifications that person may have acquired. The same principle will be applied in the case of students.

(b) The cases of persons mentioned in point (b) above should be put to the Ministry of Justice, which within two weeks will study their dossiers. In cases where those mentioned are already imprisoned, they must be released pending this investigation, and until a new decision on their case is reached.

(c) To launch an immediate investigation into the reasons for the arrests of those mentioned (the three named individuals).

(d) To institute full liberty of expression in public and professional life.

On Point No. 5, which reads: "To inform the public about the creation of the MKS and its demands, through the mass media," it has been decided that this demand shall be met through the publication in all the national mass media of the full text of this agreement.

On Point No. 6, which reads: "To implement the measures necessary for resolving the crisis, starting with the publication of all the relevant information on the socio-economic situation, and to allow all groups to participate in a discussion on a program of economic reforms," the following has been agreed:

We consider it essential to speed up the preparation of an economic reform. The authorities will work out and publish the basic principles of such a reform in the next few months. It is necessary to allow for wide participation in a public discussion of the reform. In particular the trade unions must take part in the working out of laws relating to the enterprises and to workers' self-management. The economic reform must be based on the strengthening, autonomous operation and participation of the workers' councils in management. Specific regulations will be drawn up in order to guarantee that the trade unions will be able to carry out their functions as set out in Point No. 1 of this agreement.

Only a society which has a firm grasp of reality can take the initiative in reforming the economy. The government will significantly increase the areas of socio-economic information to which society, the trade unions and other social and economic organizations have access.

The MKS also suggests, in order that a proper perspective be provided for the development of the family agricultural units, which are the basis of Polish agriculture, that the individual and collective sectors of agriculture have equal access to the means of production, including the land itself, and that the conditions should be created for the re-creation of self-governing cooperatives.

On Point No. 7, which reads: "To pay all the workers who have taken part in the strike for the period of the strike as if they were on paid holiday throughout the period, with payment to be made from the funds of the CRZZ," the following decision has been reached:

Workers and employees participating in the strike will receive, on their return to work, 40 per cent of their wages. The rest, which will add up to a full 100 per cent of the normal basic wage, will be calculated as would holiday pay, on the basis of an eight-hour working day. The MKS calls on workers who are members to work towards the increase of output, to improve the use of raw materials and energy, and to show greater work discipline, when the strike is over, and to do this in cooperation with the management of the factories and enterprises.

On Point No. 8, which reads: "To increase the minimum wage for every worker by 2,000 złotys a month to compensate for the increase in prices," the following has been decided:

These wage increases will be introduced gradually, and will apply to all types of workers and employees and in particular to those who receive the lowest wages. The increases will be worked out through agreements in individual factories and branches. The implementation of the increases will take into account the specific character of particular professions and sectors. The intention will be to increase wages through revising the wage scales or through increasing other elements of the wage.

White collar workers in the enterprises will receive salary increases on an individual basis. These increases will be put into effect between now and the end of September, 1980, on the basis of the agreements reached in each branch.

After reviewing the situation in all the branches, the government will present, by October 31, 1980, in agreement with the trade unions, a program of pay increases to come into effect from January 1, 1981, for those who get the least at the moment, paying particular attention to large families.

On Point No. 9, which reads: "To guarantee the sliding scale," the following decision has been reached: It is necessary to slow down the rate of inflation through stricter control over both the public and private sectors, and in particular through the suppression of hidden price increases.

Following on from a government decision, investigations will be carried out into the cost of living. These studies will be carried out both by the trade unions and by scientific institutions. By the end of 1980, the government will set out the principles of a system of compensation for inflation, and these principles will be open to discussion by the public. When they have been accepted they will come into effect. It will be necessary to deal with the question of the social minimum in elaborating these principles.

On Point No. 10, which reads: "To ensure the supply of products on the internal market, and to export only the surplus," and Point No. 11, which reads: "To suppress 'commercial prices' and the use of foreign currency in sales on the internal market," and Point No. 12, which reads: "To introduce ration cards for meat and meat-based products, until the market situation can be brought under control," the following agreement has been reached:

The supply of meat will be improved between now and December 31, 1980, through an increase in the profitability of agricultural production and the limitation of the export of meat to what is absolutely indispensable, as well as through the import of extra meat supplies. At the same time, during this period a program for the improvement of the meat supply will be drawn up, which will take into account the possibility of the introduction of a rationing system through the issue of cards. Products which are scarce on the national market for current consumption will not be sold in the "Pewex" shops; and between now and the end of the year, the population will be informed of all decisions which are taken concerning the problems of supply. The MKS has called for the abolition of special shops and the levelling out of the price of meat and related products.

On Point No. 13, which reads: "To introduce the principle of cadre selection on the basis of qualifications, not on the basis of membership in the party, and to abolish the privileges of the police (MO) and the security services (SB), and of the party apparatus, through the abolition of special sources of supply, through the equalization of family allowances, etc.," we have reached the following agreement:

The demand for cadres to be selected on the basis of qualifications and ability has been accepted. Cadres can be members of the PUWP, of the SD (Democratic Party), of ZSL (the Peasants Party)* or of no party. A program for the equalization of the family allowances of all the professional groups will be presented by the government before December 31, 1980. The governmental commission states that only employees' restaurants and canteens, such as those in other work establishments and offices, are operated.

On Point No. 14, which reads: "To allow workers to retire at 50 years for women and 55 for men, or after 30 years of work for women, and 35 years for men, regardless of age," it has been agreed that:

The governmental commission declares pensions will be increased each year taking into account the real economic possibilities and the rise in the lowest wages. Between now and December 1, 1981, the government will work out and present a program on these questions. The government will work out plans for the increase of old age and other pensions up to the social minimum as established through studies carried out by scientific institutions; these will be presented to the public and submitted to the control of the trade unions. The MKS stresses the great urgency of these matters and will continue to raise the demands for the increase of old age and other pensions taking into account the increase of the cost of living.

On Point No. 15, which reads: "To increase the old-style pensions to the level paid under the new system," it has been agreed:

The governmental commission states that the lowest pensions will be increased every year as a function of rises in the lowest wages. The government will present a program to this effect between now and December 1, 1981. The government will draft proposals for a rise in the lowest pensions to the level of the social minimum as defined in studies made by scientific institutes. These proposals will be presented to the public and subject to control by the unions.

On Point No. 16, which reads: "To improve working conditions and the health services so as to ensure better medical protection for the workers," it has been agreed that:

It is necessary to immediately increase the resources put into the sphere of the health services, to improve medical supplies through the import of basic materials where these are lacking, to increase the salaries of all health workers, and with the utmost urgency on the part of the government and the ministries, to prepare programs for improving the health of the population. Other measures to be taken in this area are put forward in the appendix.

On Point No. 17, which reads: "To ensure sufficient places in child care centres and kindergartens for the children of all working women," it has been agreed that:

The government commission is fully in agreement with this demand. The provincial authorities will present proposals on this question before November 30, 1980.

On Point No. 18, which reads: "To increase the length of maternity leave to three years to allow a mother to bring up her child," it has been decided that:

Before December 31, 1980, an analysis of the possibilities open to the national economy will be made in consultation with the trade unions, on the basis of which an

---

*The SD and ZSL were nominally independent political parties; in fact, creatures of the ruling PUWP.

increase in the monthly allowance for women who are on unpaid maternity leave will be worked out.

The MKS asks that this analysis should include an allowance which will provide 100 per cent of pay for the first year after birth, and 50 per cent for the second year, with a fixed minimum of 2,000 złotys a month. This goal should be gradually reached from the first half of 1981 onwards.

On Point No. 19, which reads: "To reduce the waiting period for the allocation of housing," the following agreement has been reached:

The district authorities will present a program of measures for improving the accommodation situation and for reducing the waiting list for receipts of accommodation before December 31, 1980. These proposals will be put forward for a wideranging discussion in the district, and competent organizations such as the Polish town planners association, the central association of technicians, etc., will be consulted. The proposals should refer both to ways of using the present building enterprises and prefabricated housing factories, and to a thoroughgoing development of the industry's productive base. Similar action will be taken throughout the country.

On Point No. 20, which reads: "To increase the travelling allowance from 40 to 100 złotys, and to introduce a cost-of-living bonus," it has been agreed that:

An agreement will be reached on the question of raising the travelling allowance and compensation, to take effect from January 1, 1981. The proposals for this to be ready by October 31, 1980.

On Point No. 21, which reads: "To make Saturday a holiday. In factories where there is continuous production, where there is a four-shift system, Saturday working must be compensated for by a commensurate increase in the number of holidays, or through the establishment or another free day in the week," it has been agreed that:

The principle that Saturday should be a free day should be put into effect, or another method of providing free time should be devised. This should be worked out by December 31, 1980. The measures should include the increase in the number of free Saturdays from the start of 1981.

After reaching the above agreements, it has also been decided that:

The government undertakes:

+ to ensure personal security and to allow both those who have taken part in the strike and those who have supported it to return to their previous work under the previous conditions;

+ to take up at the ministerial level the specific demands raised by the workers of all the enterprises represented in the MKS;

+ to immediately publish the complete text of this agreement in the press, radio, television and in the national mass media.

The strike committee undertakes to propose the ending of the strike from 5 p.m. on August 31, 1980.

Signed on behalf of the strikers by *Lech Wałęsa, Andrzej Kołodziej, Bogdan Lis, Mr. and Mrs. L. Badkowski, W. Gruszecki,*

A. Gwiazda, S. Izdebski, J. Kmiecik, Z. Kobylinski, H. Krzywonos, S. Lewandowski, A. Pieńkowska, Z. Pszybylski, J. Sikorski, L. Sobieszek, T. Stanny, A. Walentynowicz, F. Wiśniewski.

Signed for the government commission by *Deputy Prime Minister Mieczeslaw Jagielski, M. Zieliński, member of the secretariat of the central committee of the PUWP, T. Fiszbach, first secretary of the party committee of Gdańsk province, and the governor of Gdańsk province, J. Kołodzieski.*

August 31, 1980

Not to Lure the Wolves Out of the Woods:
An Interview with Jacek Kuroń

◆

Kuroń was a prominent figure in the Workers' Defense Committee (KOR) and an important adviser to Solidarity. This interview, conducted by the German magazine *Der Spiegel,* occurred against the backdrop of concern about a Soviet military intervention. Kuroń, imprisoned during the martial law period that saw the suppression of Solidarity, is now active once again in Polish politics.

Q: Mr. Kuroń, the Eastern bloc summit two weeks ago in Moscow eerily recalled the events of 1968 when the Soviet invasion of Czechoslovakia was decided upon. Have you already heard the sound of tanks in Poland?

Kuroń: The Russians know that an invasion would mean war and that it will be militarily and politically a very hard war. Therefore they do not want to invade us. However, the stakes are so high that under certain circumstances we must take such a possibility into account.

Q: What sort of circumstances are those?

Leaders of Solidarity. In this photograph from March 1981, Lech Wałesa (left) and Jacek Kuroń (right) urge impatient workers in the Polish city of Radom to give the government "time to solve its problems." As a result, a threatened strike was called off. (AP/Wide World Photos)

Kuroń: That is a matter for speculation. But one thing is certain: when the life of the nation is at stake, the greatest caution is required—whether we like it or not.

Q: Where does the boundary run that must not be crossed?

Kuroń: We must assume that the boundary—at least today—would be crossed if the government collapsed. But below this threshold of danger we cannot put the brakes on the people's expectations, even if we wanted to. What we are dealing with is a tremendous social democratization movement in all possible strata. The Independent Self-Governing Union Solidarity is just a part of this movement and at the same time its symbol. This movement can no longer be stopped.

Q: As a member of and spokesman for KOR, you surely feel a certain satisfaction.

Kuroń: I would prefer to answer your questions in my own name.

Q: Fine. Still it seems important to state that four years ago KOR predicted with astonishing accuracy both the current situation in Poland and the process that led to this situation. The new federation of unions, Solidarity, supported by yourself and your friends, was able to a large extent to impose its demands on the government. But relations between the state and the workers are still very tense. What is the cause for this?

Kuroń: One of the causes is repeated violations of the Gdańsk Agreement by the government. When, for example, the workers in Ursus responded to the arrest of a union member and co-worker of the independent press Nowa with a strike, that was just a natural consequence.

Q: You call that one of the causes. And the others?

Kuroń: The main difficulty is that of the people's attitude towards the government under which they have had to live for three-and-a-half decades is characterized by frustration and increasing antipathy in all areas. The result is that when any conflict arises between Solidarity and the government, no matter on what question, we always get tremendous support. On the other hand, any understanding, however favorable to the union it may be, arouses dissatisfaction or—to use perhaps a better word—disappointment, among the people.

Q: In past weeks, you and other KOR people have had to warn the workers at factory meetings several times against taking any rash steps. Why are workers so angry?

Kuroń: The frustration, tensions and aggressions are not clearly articulated. Even if the threshold of fear is increasingly lowered, certain taboos still apply. When people are fighting for wages, they are concerned for wages *also,* but not exclusively; they are also concerned with all those rights and freedoms which they do not have yet.

Q: So it is more a matter of symbolic conflict.

Kuroń: Every conflict here is partly symbolic.

Q: How would you describe current relations between workers and intellectuals in Poland?

Kuroń: A certain difference of attitudes has been emerging in the last few months; not an antagonism, not a conflict—just a difference of attitudes.

Q: How is this manifested?

Kuroń: On the one hand we have the already mentioned frustration, which is conditioned by the deteriorating economic situation and the authorities' incompetence, while the erosion of the threshold of fear has resulted in an increasingly open expression of the growing general aversion for the government. On the other hand, there is Poland's general situation, geopolitically and internally. Because of external factors, the government's fall is out of the question, and an improvement of people's living conditions is impossible because of the country's economic situation.

Q: So there is a contradiction between the people's expectations and the possibilities of social reforms?

Kuroń: Yes, and this contradiction is a result of the general situation. Workers are becoming increasingly radical, while intellectuals, who are more sensitive to the outside danger and who can more graphically picture the possible effects of the economic situation, are increasingly cautious and conciliatory.

Q: Do you believe that the government, i.e., the party, can reform itself?

Kuroń: If we start with the fact that we will have to live with this compromise for a long time—a society that is becoming more democratic, ruled by a communist party—then, of course, it would be better if the party mustered up enough strength for an inner reform. But I know too little about that and have no way of influencing it. I have to think in terms of my own categories. Thus I must start with the assumption that the party will not change. If it did, however, so much the better.

Q: How solid is Solidarity—as an institution and as a mass movement with considerable explosive potential and a charismatic leader?

Kuroń: Naturally the charisma of a labor leader plays a role, but it is not the most important factor. Solidarity is much more important. Cooperation with the government based on compromise will succeed only to the extent that the radical and the conciliatory wings within the movement agree.

Q: Are the differences of opinion of these wings limited to their different attitudes toward the government?

Kuroń: At the moment, yes. But we must expect tensions to develop between the various groups and centrifugal tendencies. These tensions have hitherto been pushed into the background because of the conflict with the government. After all, we are dealing with a movement that includes millions of people but has at its disposal neither tested forms of organization nor the necessary experience.

Q: Then, what chances are there for a co-existence between democratic, pluralist unions and a monolithic party?

Kuroń: I am not thinking just of pluralist unions. Developments have gone far beyond that. I am thinking of a democratic pluralistic society, i.e., pluralism on the level of corporations, cooperatives, consumer associations, economic self-managements; different cultural associations, sponsorships, etc.; an organized farmers' movement, a movement of citizens' initiatives, of discussion clubs designed to work out certain concepts, centres whose task would be to integrate individual programs. And, of course, also unions.

Q: And how should the interplay of these pluralist movements function in a state ruled by the communist party?

Kuroń: Institutional forms have to be created to enable these pluralistic movements to organize and cooperate. A system for society to function must be worked out.

Q: But how can that be reconciled with the leading role of the party?

Kuroń: It is a matter of a system in which the social structure can be established from below, while the decisions of principle are coordinated with the central authorities of the communist party.

Q: That presupposes the communists' readiness to cooperate. Does the party, which still calls itself Leninist, want and is it able to do that? Will it be able to accept so much pluralism?

Kuroń: It must. This country can no longer be governed in any other way. I repeat: this entire democratization movement comes from below, from the populace, which are increasingly well organized. Thus, it forces the government to give in. The government must, whether it likes it or not, meet the people's demand for more pluralism, more democracy—it must cooperate.

Q: Then you regard the party not only as your opponent, but also as a tactical ally?

Kuroń: Insofar as we—that's how I picture it—build up this pluralist structure in stages and gradually dismantle totalitarianism, step by step. Very slowly. The goals of the government and of the democratic movement are completely opposite. But the struggle between the two tendencies, the totalitarian one and the democratic one, are to be fought exclusively by peaceful means. The observation of this rule by the government will determine the degree of the partnership you mentioned.

Q: Everyone in Poland is talking about reforms. Are there any concrete models for this? Perhaps the Yugoslav one?

Kuroń: As far as the economic system and the structures connected with it are concerned, Yugoslavia's example could certainly be useful. But there is one fundamental difference. In Yugoslavia reforms came from above, from a strong communist party with great authority. Here, however, reforms are coming from below.

Q: Still, Yugoslavs are not completely happy with their system.

Kuroń: We are also aware of that system's serious disadvantages and we want to avoid them. But those are technical details. The macro-economic solutions are much more important. Since we are, as I said, dealing with a mass movement, reforms will have to be undertaken with the participation of society and decisions will have to be made more democratically than in Yugoslavia at that time.

Q: In your opinion, how far can Solidarity's collaboration with the government go, for instance, as far as common commissions?

Kuroń: If you had asked me this question a few weeks ago, the answer would have been: the union should be just a union. Responsibility for collaboration with the government in matters of reforms rests with the self-managements, the peasants' movement, the cooperatives, cultural associations, etc.

Q: You would have said that a few weeks ago. Are you now of a different opinion?

Kuroń: We are in a special situation today, because the country's situation is really tragic. Solidarity has tremendous power. It must no longer hesitate, it must show the way out of the crisis. It is no longer just a question of reforms, but of a solution.

Q: Not much can be seen yet of the separation you demand between the unions and self-management. Actually, self-management associations and similar movements that are springing up want to join Solidarity as soon as possible.

Kuroń: That is understandable. But I hope that in time we will succeed in separating these movements and making them independent of the union.

Q: Are the self-management organs supposed to be independent of unions even in the factories?

Kuroń: Absolutely. Solidarity must push through the concept of self-management, but as an institution it must be absolutely independent of unions.

Q: Why is self-management's independent from the unions so important?

Kuroń: Because it is impossible to occupy simultaneously the employer's and the employee's standpoint. A labor self-management will necessarily represent the enterprise's, i.e., the employer's, interests.

Q: Then, as in Western democracies, unions should represent only employees' interests?

Kuroń: There are very different views on this. On the one hand, it should represent only workers' interests. But at the same time unions are regarded as gains won from the state, i.e., as a kind of alternative force from which everything is now expected. Though this tendency is understandable, unions cannot fulfil all of the people's expectations. The establishment of other self-managed movements and institutions is thus all the more urgent.

Q: In your opinion, where should the communist party's monopoly of power be maintained?

Kuroń: In the police—which, of course, does not mean that they can stand above the law—in the military, in foreign policy. The communist party must also have a role in the central administration, which makes it possible for it to exercise its influence on domestic policy.

Q: That can mean very much or very little. Can you be more specific?

Kuroń: In this case, in a state whose basic factors are state power and society, to exercise influence means to understand oneself as just one of these two factors, and to act accordingly. Beyond that—and that is very important—the government must be able to implement everything agreed on in negotiations and compromises. It was agreed that censorship should be subject to strict controls. Its powers ought to be as narrowly circumscribed as possible, limited by the right of those affected to appeal in court, to challenge censors to publish newspapers with blank spaces instead of objectionable texts.

Q: What importance do you place on such guarantees?

Kuroń: They are significant only when they are connected with social organizations independent of the state. These organizations are the decisive thing, the key to it all.

Q: What role can and should the West play in view of the Polish changes?

Kuroń: I do not wish to evade this question, but I do not know. It is important that people in the West know and *understand* what is taking place in our country. The support of our movement by Western public opinion contributes to the stabilization of this movement.

Q: You stressed the word "understand." Are you saying that the events in and around Poland are not understood in the West?

Kuroń: The Poles are very upset by the hysterical manner in which some Western mass media, especially Polish-language radio broadcasts, report the danger of Soviet intervention. The tone of some Western publications may give the impression that the Poles are themselves to blame for the threat of a Soviet invasion.

Q: Is it just the reporting and not the danger itself that upsets the Poles?

Kuroń: A strange situation has arisen. We, who live in Poland and are directly exposed to the potential danger, believe we have the situation in our country under control and are able to democratize our social life without causing tanks to roll. The

West, however, which in the opinion of many Poles shares the blame for our present situation, screams and has the tanks already rolling. A Polish proverb says: "One should not lure the wolves out of the woods."

Q: If they want to stay in the woods! Don't you think that the communique from the Moscow summit two Fridays ago was intentionally formulated to sound like a last warning to Poland?

Kuroń: Not at all. I regard that communique as a further attempt to put pressure on the Polish people. They are supposed to restrain themselves because of this threat and not dare to continue in the direction of democracy.

Q: And how will the Poles act in view of this threat?

Kuroń: That is the main problem. We must not stop where we are now; that would be dangerous. The communist party's former power monopoly is already broken and the democratic reforms sought by society have not yet been realized. So, if all the institutions I mentioned in this interview are not quickly established so that the existing and ensuing conflicts can be solved peacefully through them, then—and only then—the worst could happen. Then the danger zone would actually be crossed—the fall of the communist government which is in charge of maintaining Soviet influence in Poland.

The Solidarity Program

◆

Although lengthy even in this slightly abridged version, the Solidarity Program is of such historic importance that it is presented here in an almost complete form. It was adopted formally in October 1981 at the national congress of Solidarity, just weeks before the Jaruzelski regime imposed martial law.

◆

I. WHO WE ARE AND WHAT WE WANT

The independent, self-governing union Solidarity, which was born out of the 1980 strike, is the most powerful mass movement in the history of Poland. The movement began among workers in large industrial enterprises in various regions of the country, reaching its peak in August, 1980, on the Baltic Coast. In the space of a year, it has won over all segments of the working population: workers, peasants, intellectuals, and craftsmen.

Our union sprang from the people's needs: from their suffering and disappointment, their hopes and desires. It is the product of a revolt by Polish society after three decades of political discrimination, economic exploitation, and the violation of human and civil rights. It is a protest against the existing form of power.

For none of us was it just a question of material conditions—although we did live badly, working hard, often for no purpose. History has taught us that there can be no bread without freedom. We also wanted justice, democracy, truth, freedom of opinion, a reconstructed republic—not just bread, butter and sausage. Since all the basic values had been trampled on, we could not hope to improve the situation unless they were restored. Economic protest was also social protest, and social protest was also moral protest. These movements did not appear out of the blue, but inherited the blood of the workers killed in Poznań in 1956 and the coastal towns in December, 1970. They also inherited the student revolt of 1968 and the suffering of the Radom and Ursus workers in 1976, as well as independent actions by workers, intellectuals and youth, the church's efforts to preserve values, and all Poland's struggles for human dignity. The union is the fruit of these struggles, and will remain faithful to them.

Our organization combines the features of a trade union and a broad social movement; it is this which gives us our strength and determines the importance of our role. Thanks to the existence of a powerful union organization, Polish society is no longer fragmented, disorganized and lost, but has recovered strength and hope. There is now the possibility of a real national renewal. Our union, representing the majority of workers in Poland, seeks to be and will become the driving force of this renewal.

Solidarity embraces many social currents, bringing together people of different political and religious views and different nationalities. What unites us is a revolt against injustice, abuses of power and monopolization of the right to speak and act in the name of the nation. What unites us is our protest against a state which treats the citizens as its own property. We reject the fact that, in conflicts with the state, the workers have no genuine means of defence against the "good will" of leaders who alone can decide the degree of freedom that should be accorded to their subjects. We are against the principle which consists in rewarding absolute political obedience instead of encouraging initiative and action. We are united in rejecting duplicity in public life and the squandering of the nation's hard work.

But we are not just a force of rejection. Our aim is to rebuild a just Poland.

Respect for the person must be the basis of action: the state must serve people instead of dominating them. The state organization must be at the service of society and not be monopolized by a single political party. The state must really belong to the whole nation. Labor is made for people and finds its meaning when it corresponds to human needs.

Our national renewal must be based upon a proper reordering of these objectives. In determining its activity, Solidarity turns to the values of Christian ethics, our national working-class tradition, and the democratic tradition of the labor world. John Paul II's encyclical on human labor is a fresh source of encouragement. As a mass organization of the working people, Solidarity is also a movement for the moral rebirth of the people.

We believe that people's power is a principle that we do not have the right to abandon. But it does not mean the power of a group which places itself above society, arrogating to itself the right to define and represent the interests of society. Society must have the right to speak aloud, to express the range of social and political views. Society must be able to organize itself in such a way as to ensure a just distribution of the nation's material and spiritual wealth and a blossoming of all creative forces. We seek a true socialization of our government and state administration. For this reason our objective is a self-governing Poland.

We hold dear the idea of freedom and total independence. We shall support everything which strengthens the sovereignty of our nation and state, everything which furthers the development of national culture and knowledge of our historical legacy. We believe that our national identity must be fully respected.

The union formed itself and acts under difficult conditions, following a path that has never been taken before. Those who join us are concerned to solve the great problems facing Poland. Our strength and authority is such that people expect us to help in every field of life. We are compelled to fight for the existence of our union, to organize at every level, and to learn, often through our own mistakes, how we should act and struggle in pursuit of our aims.

Our program reflects the desires and aspirations of Polish society. It seeks to fulfil distant objectives through the solution of present-day problems.

◆

II. THE UNION IN THE COUNTRY'S PRESENT SITUATION

The emergence of Solidarity as a mass movement has definitively changed the country's situation. It has become possible to set up new, independent social institutions, or to make independent those which have been subordinated to the state. The existence of independent organizations of power should be regarded as the most important factor in changing Poland's social and political relations.

There has been a change in the way power is exercised. The authorities should have come to terms with the will of society and accept its control, in conformity with the Gdańsk, Szczecin and Jastrzębie agreements. There should have been a reform of the economy, the state and its various institutions. We had the right to hope that the state would carry out these changes.

The present system of government, based on an all-powerful central party and state institutions, has brought the country to ruin. The brakes have been applied to change for more than just one year, although it is no longer possible to go on ruling in the old way. The situation is growing worse, and we are moving toward catastrophe with seven-league boots. Nowhere in Europe has the economic collapse reached such proportions since World War II. Tired and disappointed though it may be, society has shown a great deal of patience and determination during the last year. In the end, however, it is to be feared that exhaustion and impatience will become a blind, destructive force or plunge us into despair. We do not have the right, as a society, to lose hope in the possibility of overcoming the crisis.

Faced with this national tragedy, Solidarity can no longer confine itself to pressuring the government to keep its promises. Society looks on us as the only guarantors of the agreements that have been signed. This is why the union considers that its main task is to take every possible short- and long-term action to save the country from bankruptcy, and society from poverty, despondency and self-destruction. The only way forward is to renew both state and economy through democratic social initiatives in every field.

We are fully aware that Polish society expects actions from us that will allow people to live in peace. The nation will not forgive a betrayal of the ideals for which Solidarity was created. Nor will it forgive actions, even the best intentioned, which lead to the spilling of blood and the material and spiritual destruction of the country. This awareness compels us to carry out our objectives in a gradual manner, so that each consecutive action obtains the support of society.

Our sense of responsibility compels us to look with clear eyes at the relationship of forces in Europe which resulted from the Second World War. Our aim is to perform our great labor of renewal without damaging international alliances; indeed, we seek to provide more solid guarantees for those alliances. The Polish nation, animated by a sense of its dignity, patriotism and traditions, will become a valuable partner from the moment when it consciously assumes its own commitments.

The country's present situation necessitates a two-sided program: immediate actions to see us through the difficult winter period; and, at the same time, a program of economic reform, which can no longer be postponed, of social policies and reconstruction of public life—a program which points toward a self-governed republic.

◆

III. THE UNION, THE CRISIS AND ECONOMIC REFORM

The roots of the present crisis lie deep in the economic and political system, and the way in which the authorities, ignoring the needs of society, have blocked all reform projects and squandered huge foreign loans. The crisis began to worsen in the mid-seventies, reaching a climax last year as a result of the government's incapacity to promote major changes.

Faced with economic catastrophe, the government has announced a program to combat the crisis and restore economic stability. The union does not support this program, which only partially makes use of our economic resources and does not inspire the confidence of society. In our view, government decisions have to be made credible if there is to be a rapid solution to the crisis. This is why we demand social control over the government's anti-crisis measures. If they are to be credible, then people with some professional and social authority must be appointed to leadership positions in the national economy.

Thesis one: We demand that, at every level of leadership, a democratic, self-management reform should enable the new economic and social system to combine planning, autonomy and the market.

The union demands a reform that will abolish the privileges of the bureaucracy and make it impossible for them to reappear. The reform must encourage people to work and to show initiative, and not just remain a surface phenomenon. Since the reform will involve some social costs, the union must ensure that certain groups of the population are well protected.

1. The authoritarian direction of the economy, which makes rational development impossible, must be brought to an end. In this system, enormous economic power is concentrated in the party apparatus and the state bureaucracy. The structure of economic organization serving the command system must be broken up. It is necessary to separate the apparatus of economic administration from political power. Enterprise managers should no longer be dependent upon the ministry, and nor should important appointments fall under the party *nomenklatura*. The reform will only be successful if it results from the extensive activity of working groups, for which Solidarity's Network of Enterprise Commissions may serve as an example. The activity of this network signalled the start of a large-scale self-management movement.

2. A new economic structure must be built. In the organization of the economy, the basic unit will be a collectively managed social enterprise, represented by a workers' council and led by a director who shall be appointed with the council's help and subject to recall by the council. The social enterprise shall dispose of the national property entrusted to it, working in the interests of society and the enterprise itself. It shall apply economic calculation in the affairs of management. The state may influence enterprise activity through various regulations and economic instruments—prices, taxes, interest rates and so on.

3. It is necessary to sweep away the bureaucratic barriers which make it impossible for the market to operate. The central organs of economic administration should not limit enterprise activity or prescribe supplies and buyers for its output. Enterprises shall be able to operate freely on the internal market, except in fields where a licence is compulsory. International trade must be accessible to all enterprises. The union appreciates the importance of exports, which are of value to the country and the workers. Consumers' associations and anti-monopoly legislation should ensure that enterprises do not carve out a privileged place in the market. A special law must be introduced to protect consumers' rights. The relationship between supply and demand must determine price levels.

4. The reform must socialize planning so that the central plan reflects the aspirations of society and is freely accepted by it. Public debates are therefore indispensable. It should be possible to bring forward plans of every kind, including those drafted by social or civil organizations. Access to comprehensive economic information is therefore absolutely essential, requiring social control over the central statistics board.

Thesis two: The approach of winter necessitates immediate and energetic action; the union declares that people of good will are available.

In the present state of the economy, this winter may be a dangerous time for the population. It is to be feared that the authorities are not able to face up to this danger. Social aid must be organized. Our union declares that people of good will are available.

1. Immediate action on the economy:

(*a*) the union leadership will ask the government to communicate its program for the winter;

(*b*) the union will call for an assurance that adequate heating and lighting will be available in both town and country, and that the market will be supplied with essential consumer items (warm clothing, food);

(*c*) workers' organizations and their enterprise commissions should watch over the extra production of industrial and, above all, food products on free Saturdays; they should come to terms on the division of those commodities, directing them to the places most in need; and they should adjust production to the existing energy restrictions, reaching agreement with regional union leadership.

2. Social mutual aid:

The union should organize winter relief services, at both a local and enterprise level. Their aim should be: to assure, together with the scouts and the independent students association, supplies of food and coal to particularly vulnerable sections of the population; to organize housing-repair teams for such people and to protect them from the effects of winter; to use enterprise vehicles for school busing, doctors' calls, etc.; to help supply the town population with potatoes, vegetables and fruit; and to organize the distribution of aid from abroad. Enterprise relief services should help to solve supply problems, coordinating their activity at a district and regional level.

Thesis three: The defence of workers' living standards requires collective action against falling output.

The primary task facing us today is to halt the decline in output. It is necessary to improve supplies by using internal reserves and to increase the possibilities for importing raw materials and spare parts. This will depend on the effectiveness of our anti-crisis reform program, on an increase in exports, and on the securing of credits from both East and West.

In our view, the government should investigate the conditions under which Poland might join the International Monetary Fund and the International Bank for Reconstruction and Development, and present them to the public. At the same time, we should do everything possible to maximize output by using the country's existing resources.

1. New investment must be limited, and materials saved in this way should be used in existing enterprises.

2. It is necessary to use surplus stocks of materials, machinery and plant, making it easier for them to be sold abroad and selling them to private enterprises within Poland. Present restrictions on the activity of such enterprises must be lifted.

3. Given the particular importance of coal and other raw materials, it is essential to prioritize rapid growth in mining employment and technical equipment. The conditions must also be created for a future rise in output. Although the situation is very difficult in many regions of the country, priority must be given to food supplies for the mining areas. People should be encouraged to save coal, above all in the enterprises, but also at home.

4. In principle, the peasant economy must receive a large share of the means of production, especially agricultural tools and machinery, fertilizer and fodder (above all, of the high protein variety). This will permit higher food production, since the peasant economy is more efficient than the socialized sector.

5. Given the disastrous shortage of energy and raw materials, a number of factories will have to be closed in the coming months. Any decision must be based on the criteria of economic efficiency. Closures must be kept to the minimum necessary, and implemented only when there is no possibility of rationally altering production.

6. In several fields, the length of the working week does not at present crucially affect the volume of production. However, being aware of the requirements of this crisis situation, we may forgo demanding the introduction of more free Saturdays in 1982. If it is possible for overtime work to be performed on free Saturdays, any decision must depend on the wishes of the workforce.

7. During this crisis period, arms expenditures must be reduced to a strict minimum, and the resources made available should be used to increase output.

Thesis four: The union recognizes the need for a restored market equilibrium in the framework of an effective anti-crisis program that will involve a national reform and protect the weakest sections of the population.

The main way in which market equilibrium will be restored is through an increase in the production and supply of goods. However, this will not be enough to restore market equilibrium in the short run. It will also be necessary to reduce the demand for goods. This may be achieved by the following methods: a) a gradual rise in prices, together with the transitional retention of ration cards for major consumption items; b) a single round of price increases, together with the abolition of ration cards; c) a currency reform together with a reform of prices. A number of solutions and combinations are possible within this general framework. Some individual proposals have been presented by their authors for union members to consider (in an appendix); but other proposals are not ruled out.

Only if there is a simultaneous rise in production will these methods prove effective. If none of them is implemented, there will have to be a rationing system for all goods. But this would destroy the market equilibrium, inevitably leading to waste and artificial shortages, further swelling the bureaucracy and the black market, and removing the motivation for greater work-efficiency. Nor would it in any way protect the real purchasing power of the population.

After public discussion, society itself must choose one of these methods through a referendum. The union will demand that this happens. The sooner it takes place, the less will be the social costs of market stability.

Thesis five: The anti-crisis and the economic reform must be subject to the control of society.

A condition for the successful struggle against the crisis lies not only in drafting a program acceptable to society, but also in public control over the implementation of the program. The union hopes that such control will eventually be exercised by a new *Sejm*, [Parliament] national councils and workers' self-managing bodies.

However, public control institutions must be set up immediately. The experience of both the sixties and the seventies and of the most recent twelve months have taught us that the lack of public control leads to erroneous decisions and favors inaction and private interests. The union therefore proposes the creation of a Social Council for the National Economy, whose tasks would be to assess government economic policy, to examine the economic situation and relevant legislation, and to take initiatives in this field. The council must have the right to present draft legislation. Its deliberations should be made known to the public, and its members should be able to communicate with society through the mass media.

Thesis six: Although the union will protect everyone, it will take special care of the poorest sections.

We shall prioritize action to protect those whose lives are most seriously affected by the crisis. In conformity with the Gdańsk Agreement, we shall demand measures in 1982 to introduce a cost-of-living supplement, to generalize the system of educational grants, to raise family allowances, and to introduce a minimum subsistence threshold as the basis for an incomes policy.

The union considers that subsidies should guarantee the purchasing power of the least well off. It is essential: that subsidies should be given to workers (and pensioners), as well as to their dependents; that the level of prices should proportionately determine all social benefits; that there should be an income-ceiling for social benefits, and an increase in the budget of child-care institutions, asylums and hospitals; that the union should adopt the principle of relating benefits to income.

Compensation must be paid for any rise in the price of an established list of goods and services. Price increases, as well as the availability and amount of benefits, must be agreed upon by the union.

We demand a major increase in social welfare. The union will seek to moderate the effects of inevitable price rises on the cost of everyday life: a) by checking on the price index of basic items; b) by encouraging social initiatives to control the quality and price of goods; and c) by calling for a special fund to restrain retail price rises on certain goods and services (milk, schoolbooks, children's clothing, etc.).

Thesis seven: Food supply is now the most important problem; ration coupons must be honored in practice, and food should be distributed under social control.

Given the shortage of the most essential food items, the union is compelled to demand a system of regulation which ensures that every citizen has the minimum necessary. At present various rationed items, especially meat, are not available in sufficient quantity, particularly since there is also a lack of substitutes (fish, dairy products).

The union demands energetic government action to ensure that rationed items are available in sufficient quantity on the market, and above all that incentives are provided to encourage peasants to deliver livestock and increase animal rearing.

Rations must increase in step with rising production and deliveries. Trade and the rationing system must improve in such a way as to enable citizens to shop for their rations without waiting in line.

The nation's food supply is a priority issue.

The union will not remain inactive in the face of the present supply situation. It is essential to create a nation-wide network of union commissions, together with a central coordinating body, which will concern themselves with the market and food supply situation. These commissions will cooperate with Rural Solidarity, opposing the bartering practices of large enterprises, which undermine our solidarity.

Thesis eight: The union will resist growing social inequalities among enterprises and regions.

The economic reform will carry a danger of great social and income inequality among enterprises and regions. We must create the conditions in which such inequalities can be minimized.

Our efforts will be aimed at: a) bringing social action and enterprise welfare activity under the responsibility of regional self-governing bodies; and b) creating a socially controlled national fund to transfer capital from one region to another and thereby to reduce inequalities.

The union is currently seeking to change the method of financing enterprise welfare activity, so that the allocation of social funds to the enterprise will depend on the size of its workforce rather than its total wage bill; to ensure that the local population has access to the enterprise's social provisions (kindergartens, cultural activity, transportation); and to form local committees in districts and neighborhoods to decide on the operation and development of social services. . . .

[Sections IV and V of the Solidarity Program contain an extended discussion of labor protection and social service policy. The ten abridged points under these headings are:]

Thesis nine: The right to work must be guaranteed, and the wage system overhauled.

Thesis ten: Workers should have their health and safety ensured.

Thesis eleven: The right to work must be based on defence of the workers' common interests.

Thesis twelve: The union adopts all the initiatives contained in the constitution to satisfy the most pressing needs.

Thesis thirteen: The union defends the family's right to satisfy its needs and develop social awareness.

Thesis fourteen: The union will defend the rights of the elderly, disabled and severely ill.

Thesis fifteen: In view of the biological dangers to the nation, the protection of health is an area in which the union takes a special interest.

Thesis sixteen: The union fights for the effective protection of the natural environment.

Thesis seventeen: The union demands that the people's basic rights to housing are respected, and that an effort be made to improve habitation.

Thesis eighteen: The union should ensure that all workers have free time to raise their cultural level.

✦

VI. THE SELF-GOVERNED REPUBLIC

Thesis nineteen: Pluralism of social, political and cultural ideas must form the basis of democracy in the self-governed republic.

1. Public life in Poland requires deep reforms which should lead to the definitive establishment of self-government, democracy and pluralism. For this reason, we shall struggle both for a change in state structures and for the development of independent, self-governing institutions in every field of social life. Only such a course can guarantee that the institutions of public life are in harmony with human needs and the social and national aspirations of Poles. Such changes are also essential if the country is to find a way out of the economic crisis. We consider that pluralism, democracy and full enjoyment of constitutional rights provide the guarantee that the workers' efforts and sacrifices will not be wasted once again.

2. Our union is prepared to collaborate with the various social movements, particularly with other unions created since August, 1980, which belong to the broad Solidarity movement (the Union of Individual Farmers, the Artisans' Union, the Private Transport Drivers' Union), as well as with other independent, self-governed unions which current legislation prohibits from joining our movement. In fact, such legislation must also be changed. In Poland today, the freedom of trade union organization and the right to choose the union to which one belongs are of crucial importance to the workers. We therefore believe that the trade union law is our most precious asset: it must guarantee the freedoms mentioned above.

3. Our union maintains special links with the independent students' association and with independent youth movements like the Scouts. These organizations and associations are encountering many obstacles to their activity and registration. We believe it is necessary to pass a new law which will guarantee the complete freedom of association to citizens.

4. We hold that the principles of pluralism should apply to political life. Our union will assist and protect civil initiatives which seek to propose different sociopolitical and economic programs to society. But we will oppose any initiative by leaders of our union to set up political parties.

5. Faithful to the principles of pluralism, our union accepts the possibility of co-existence with other unions.

6. Unless there is a complete reform of penal law, and particularly of that part which can be used to repress civil rights, the principles of pluralism will always be threatened.

Thesis twenty: Genuine workers' self-management is the basis of the self-governing republic.

The system which ties political to economic power, based on continual party interference in the functioning of enterprises, is the main reason for the present crisis of the Polish economy. The so-called *nomenklatura* principle rules out any rational cadre promotion policy, rendering the millions of workers who do not belong to any party second-class citizens.

The only solution is to create workers' self-management committees which will give the real decision-making power to enterprise personnel. Our union demands that the self-management principle should be reintroduced into the cooperatives. It is essential to pass a new law protecting the cooperatives against interference by the state administration.

Thesis twenty-one: Regional self-government structures, legally and financially autonomous, should genuinely represent the interests of the local population.

The self-government of a regional structure is based on the principle of free elections. Everyone should be free to stand, with equal rights for all candidates. A wide election campaign should be organized, so that the various candidates can put forward their point of view. The forthcoming national council elections should be held in the same conditions.

Solidarity will insist on this point, drawing up by the end of December, 1981, a proposal for a new electoral system which will be presented to the *Sejm*, after consultation with our membership.

Regional self-government bodies should have the right to decide on all regional matters. They may be subject to control by the state administration, in conformity with the law. But such control should be confined to examination of the activity of such bodies in order to establish whether it is in conformity with the law. In the case of a dispute between a self-governing body and the state administration, the competent tribunal should issue a ruling. The regional self-government body should have the right to act on economic matters, and be able to collaborate with other self-governing bodies. In order that these aims may be fulfilled, the self-government bodies should have the status of a legal entity, with the right to acquire financial means through local taxation and so on.

The first congress of Solidarity instructs the national committee to draft a law on regional self-government along the above lines. This should be opened up for consultation and then presented to the *Sejm*. Solidarity will encourage any initiative by self-governing bodies which serves to resolve the problems bound up with the economic crisis.

Thesis twenty-two: The self-government bodies and structures must be represented at the highest level of state power.

1. It is essential to grant the unions the right to legislative initiative.

2. We shall fight to restore supreme power to the *Sejm*. The new election system must give it a genuinely representative character.

3. We consider it useful to examine the case for a self-governing body at the highest level of state power. Its task would be to supervise the implementation of the economic reform program, as well as the activity of regional self-government bodies.

Thesis twenty-three: The system must guarantee basic civic freedoms and respect the principles of equality before the law for all citizens and public institutions.

This necessitates:

1. Respect for the principles and commitments emanating from the international conventions ratified by Poland, and from the Universal Charter of Human Rights. In particular, ratification of the optional protocol to the Universal Charter of Human Rights—which provides for international supervision of the charter's practical application—will furnish in our eyes the necessary guarantee.

2. Explicit mention in the constitution of the principle of equality of all citizens, regardless of their convictions, ideas and political affiliation.

3. Subordinating all elements of public life, including political and social organizations, to the law. It is therefore necessary to change the constitutional enactments concerning the legal status of those organizations and to unambiguously define their legal position vis-à-vis the *Sejm* and other bodies of the state administration.

4. The creation of an independent Constitutional Court (or of an equivalent chamber within the Supreme Court), which will rule on the constitutionality of legislation and on the legality of other rights and decrees. The Constitutional Court should also check that Polish legislation is in conformity with the international rights of man.

5. A change in the law on public gatherings, associations and passports. (The passport law should express the right of everyone to freely choose their abode, even if it is abroad, and the right to freely return to Poland.) Any limitation of civil liberties must be subject to judicial control.

6. Abolition of secrecy in public life, and a guarantee that all citizens have access to state documents. Any decision which tends to introduce secrecy must be precisely defined by law.

Thesis twenty-four: The administration of justice must be independent, and the repressive apparatus must be subject to social control.

In order that this may be achieved, it is essential:

1. To conduct a thorough reform of the judicial system, and to ensure scrupulous respect for its independence.

This can be guaranteed by:

(a) Setting up completely self-governing bodies in the judiciary, which would have, *inter alia,* a decisive say in all judicial appointments and the appointment of the president of the court.

(b) Observing the principle that the function of judge must not be combined with any other public service, especially service in political organizations, and

that judges cannot be transferred or removed, except through disciplinary action or in case of illness.

These guarantees should be recorded in an amended Law on the System of General Courts and in the Law on the Supreme Court. These laws should also make it possible to recall a judge on the motion of the general assembly of judges within a transition period of one year of the law coming into force. Moreover, it is necessary for the Supreme Court to abolish the practice of appointing judges for a term.

(*c*) Appointing lay assessors and members of the college for offences by direct election in order to increase society's role in the administration of justice.

2. To do away with the state's arbitrary powers in the economy. Economic disputes should fall under the normal judicial competence.

3. To ensure correct functioning of the judicial apparatus through:

(*a*) The independence of the examining magistrate attached to a particular court, and the allocation to him of exclusive responsibility for pre-trial investigations and decisions on custody.

(*b*) A reform of the public prosecutor's office, limiting his role to penal law cases, bringing him under the ministry of justice, and ensuring his independence in carrying out his functions.

(*c*) The complete independence of lawyers, and measures to ensure that defence counsel has the right to attend preliminary hearings regardless of whether the body in charge of the case so approves.

(*d*) The removal from police tribunals to proper courts of all cases potentially involving a custodial sentence, and ministry of justice control over the functioning of such tribunals.

4. To pass a law on the militia, limiting its role to the defence of public order and citizens' safety, with no interference in the field of politics. By failing to distinguish political activities which threaten public order from other such activities, the militia has committed a number of abuses. There must be a new law on the secret services, precisely defining their area of competence and providing for social control over their activity.

5. Within the prison system, it is necessary to define the situation of political prisoners, to establish a charter of rights and obligations for all detainees, and to bring the prison system under social control. The social readjustment centres should be disbanded.

6. No one may be forced to act against their convictions. Another, non-military, form of public service should be allowed for conscientious objectors. The union will defend anyone persecuted for their trade union, political or social convictions.

Thesis twenty-five: In a Poland based on law, no one should be persecuted for their convictions, nor compelled to act against their conscience.

In conformity with the Gdańsk Agreement, our union is prepared to defend anyone persecuted for their political convictions. We shall insist on implementation of the Warsaw Agreement concerning the release of political prisoners and the cessation of judicial procedures against people who have expressed opposition to the existing regime. If repression is used against union militants, we shall use every means in our power to defend them.

It is absolutely essential to amend the penal code and the code of penal procedure—especially those paragraphs which allow for action against people who express different views from those propagated by the party and government.

No one should be held for more than 24 hours without charge. Decisions on this matter should be taken by the examining magistrate, so that it no longer has a repressive character.

Thesis twenty-six: The people responsible for the ruination of the country should be prosecuted.

We demand that the circumstances of shooting and persecution of workers in Poznań in 1956 and in the maritime region in 1970 be clarified and the guilty be revealed. We also demand clarification of the militia's brutal actions against students in 1968 and against the people of Radom and Ursus in 1976. This demand also applies to the perpetrators of the Bydgoszcz provocation. The persons guilty of violations of the rule of law should bear the penal and disciplinary consequences provided by the law.

The same procedure should be instituted against those who, by their actions between 1970 and 1980, have brought the country to economic ruin. It should spare no one, including those who occupy the highest functions in the party and government.

The principle of equality before the law, an elementary sense of justice, and the need to give concrete reality to the changes that have begun oblige the union to insist categorically on this point. If legal proceedings have not begun by December 1, the national committee will convoke a people's tribunal to hold a public trial and render a verdict.

Thesis twenty-seven: The younger generation ought to have favorable conditions for its physical, mental and moral development. . . .

Thesis twenty-eight: Culture and education should be accessible to all. . . .

Thesis twenty-nine: The union will assist and protect every independent initiative for self-management in culture and education. . . .

Thesis thirty: The union will support the freedom of scientific research and the self-management of scientific institutions. . . .

Thesis thirty-one: The union will fight against lies in every field of life, for our society wishes and has the right to live in truth.

To speak and write the truth is essential for the development of social awareness and the safeguarding of our national identity. To construct a better future, it is necessary to know the truth of the present.

1. We consider media censorship to be an evil which the present situation alone obliges us to accept temporarily. We do not accept censorship in science and art. Censorship cannot limit the people's right to know its own history and its literature. We will combat every abuse of censorship.

2. The most dangerous tool of falsehood is the language of propaganda, which debases the way we express our thoughts and feelings. The union will struggle for the purity of our language as a means of greater understanding among citizens.

3. The union will support the development of independent publications as one of the ways of struggling against censorship.

4. The effects of censorship on our culture and history are catastrophic. The union commits itself to struggle for the restoration of truth in these areas.

5. One means of propagating the truth is our own union literature. We will publish the news that is eliminated or falsified in state publications.

6. The union will support war veterans in their attempt to shed light on our history and to recognize the merits of those who consecrated their lives to the freedom and independence of Poland.

Thesis thirty-two: The media are the property of society. They ought therefore to serve it and be controlled by it.

Our union's struggle for access to the media is carried on in the interests of the whole population. The union demands respect for the freedom of the press and the freedom of speech expressed in the constitution. Hence:

1. The union considers as inadmissible the jamming of foreign broadcasts, the prohibition of literature which expresses a viewpoint other than the official one, the destruction of our posters, etc.

2. The union will participate in preparing the draft law on information, which should include all the means of social communication. The congress instructs the union's authorities to decisively support the socially accepted draft law.

3. The union demands respect for the right of citizens and their organizations to set up publishing houses and to have free access to radio and television. The allocation of paper, printing facilities and broadcasting time must be subject to social control.

4. The union is opposed to any form of information monopoly. The union demands an end to the state administration's unconstitutional monopoly over radio and television, as well as a change in the law of 1960 which established the radio and television committee. The union calls for an organ of social control over radio and television, comprising representatives of government, political parties, unions, religious and social organizations, intellectuals and radio and television staff. This organ should have the final say on programs.

5. So far, our efforts to obtain the right to broadcasting time have been inadequate. We therefore demand the fastest possible application of the agreement ratified by the national committee of Solidarity, and the creation of autonomous Solidarity editorial committees in the central and regional structures of radio and television.

6. The union will protect its members employed in radio, television and the press, supporting journalists who respect the principle of truthful information. The union recognizes the right of editorial staff to appoint their chief editor. The union will support the Association of Polish Journalists in its efforts to protect the ethics of their profession.

7. The union will create agencies for news, photos, cinema and press.

8. It will establish an information committee attached to the national committee.

9. In conformity with Article 33, Section 2, of the constitution, the union demands that it be able to open its own radio station.

10. In the struggle for access to the mass media, the union will use all the means provided for by its statutes.

◆

VII. OUR UNION

The union's life is based on the principle of democracy, which involves submission to the will of the majority, while maintaining respect for the ideas of the minority. Acceptance of decisions taken by union leaders in a democratic manner is a guarantee of unity in action.

The statutes are the basic document which determines the democratic functioning of the union. In practice, we recognize that an action not proscribed by the statutes is admissible—this allows union life to be enriched by new forms of action. In adopting a tolerant attitude towards different points of view, however, union leaders and all members should resolutely combat any breach of the statutes. Democracy in internal life, discipline in action, and the honesty of union members are the guarantees of the union's strength.

Thesis thirty-three: Members of our union have the right to express their views and wishes without constraint, and to organize freely for the achievement of common goals.

The effectiveness of union action depends on the various links between its members which augment the means and forms of struggle, ensuring the authenticity of our movement and its participation in the functioning of society. The creation of such links requires a free exchange of ideas and agreement on positions.

1. The Regions

Links between rank-and-file members are created at the level of enterprise branches; these branches then come together at the regional level, in accordance with the principles laid down in the statutes. The demarcation of regions should take place democratically under the control of the national committee, so that they coincide as far as possible with territorial administrative divisions. We must attempt to create regions that are strong enough to give structural and technical support to all the enterprise branches. We must avoid fragmentation of administrative units, because this restricts the union's effectiveness and influence vis-à-vis the authorities.

2. Intermediate Links

The practical life of the union has given rise to various intermediate links between enterprise branches and regional leaderships; the union leadership should assist such links by organizational, financial and technical means. The principal task of intermediate bodies is to assist enterprise commissions in the area of information and advice, and in the creation and development of centres of union life; they should also defend the interests of the population at the local level, and exert pressure on the administrative organs of power.

3. Occupational Branches, Occupational Sectors and Others

Union branches should assist one another and complement the actions of the union leadership in defending the interests of the different groups of workers and union members, without harming the interests of other groups.

The main tasks of the branch are: to initiate and coordinate activity dealing with the specific problems of their occupational sector, and especially to conclude common agreements; to represent the interests of a particular group in the union; to undertake actions at the level of the administration and the state, in agreement with the union.

The experience we have acquired demonstrates that broader representation of union members assists the leadership to resolve problems.

4. Agreements

Agreements between enterprise commissions and between different groups of union members take place outside the organizational forms prescribed in the statutes, thereby enlarging the scope for initiative and giving the opportunity to bring principles to life. In helping these different agreements to be concluded, union leaders should not assume the role of organizers.

5. The Means of Expression and the Formation of Opinion

The principal method is to use the union's information system in such a way as to popularize, without falsification, its goals and methods of action, as well as its position on social, economic and political problems. The union leadership must therefore pay particular attention to technical and material organization, the content of information, and working conditions in the information services. It is essential to improve our information network so that we can compete with the "party-state" broadcasting monopoly.

The most important tasks in this area are:

(*a*) to increase the print run of the weekly *Solidarność* to about a million;

(*b*) to create a national daily;

(*c*) to publish regional periodicals as far as possible;

(*d*) to publish an internal daily and weekly in each region;

(*e*) to create the necessary conditions for the development of a national news and publicity system (daily information service, collection of journalistic material) by relying on the existing centres and on the extension of regional information offices;

(*f*) to improve the information service in the regions;

(*g*) to build libraries attached to the regional and enterprise commissions.

At the moment, the news agencies of the press and of *Solidarność* tend to be self-financing. The union fights for the freedom of expression, and it ought to apply the same principle in its own information media. Thus the leading bodies of the union, to whom the editors of the dailies and periodicals are responsible, should not interfere in this work. They should give them the greatest liberty, except during periods of definite danger for the union (protest actions, strike mobilizations).

The teaching work carried out by the popular universities is indispensable to the union. The purpose of these universities is to spread knowledge without falsification, to develop the understanding of militants, to raise their civic consciousness, to promote social activity and self-education. The popular universities should diversify their methods to include courses, apprenticeships, seminars, initiation clubs, lectures and publications.

This should make it possible for them to reach all social groups, especially in the enterprises. While maintaining a diversity of programs and methods, the popular universities will maintain contact with one another for the exchange of experience and information. Their activities will be financed by the regional committees and enterprise commissions. Alongside the education of public opinion, the principal task of the education and information services is to link union members both with one another and with the leadership and union agencies. Such links will create a diversity of ideas in our organization, while maintaining unity in action.

Thesis thirty-four: The decisions and actions of union bodies should be based on a real knowledge of membership views and wishes.

The union's members should have a determining influence on leadership actions. This is achieved by means of elections and by the expression of opinion on all questions affecting the union. The free circulation of information and the transparency of union life are necessary in order to educate public opinion.

1. The Decisions and Actions of the Union Leadership

When the union leadership takes a decision, it should follow the position of the majority. To ensure the transparency of union life, the leaders and the commissions should, at every level, inform the members of their work by publishing all the documents and texts concerning all official discussions and negotiations.

National and regional leaders have a duty to work in common with the socio-occupational working groups and with the sectors and occupational branches. Leading members of the union have a duty to meet regularly with those who elected them.

2. The Organization of Work Around the Program

Union leaders should respect the regular functioning of democratic representation, which can be ensured by knowing the opinion of the greatest possible number of union members.

The circulation and synthesization of views can best be achieved by work around the program. Special groups, composed of union militants and experts, should be attached to national, regional and enterprise commissions for the study of a particular theme (e.g., wages, working conditions).

At the same time, it is essential to create and develop socio-occupational working groups with the task of preparing reports and programs for the union. These centres should function in an independent manner, under the control of the program council, and should be composed of militants with authority, scientists and other members designated by the leadership. Basing themselves on the demands and ideas communicated by each enterprise organization, and on the materials provided by the socio-occupational working groups, the program commissions should then formulate the questions to be addressed to the members of the union.

Having synthesized the results, these commissions should then: keep the union leadership informed about the strength of different opinions and the importance which union members give to different problems; formulate proposals concerning union information and propaganda; draw up a program to be discussed by the representative organs.

If it is organized in this way, work around the program should qualitatively improve the drafts and encourage enterprise branches to think about the program.

3. The Study of Membership Views in the Enterprise

It is also very important to conduct polls in order to find out what union members are thinking in the enterprises, the regions and the union as a whole. To carry out such surveys we must appeal to the socio-occupational working groups. This type of enquiry is indispensable for finding out correctly and in detail what union members think on the essential questions; this will determine the correctness and speed of decisions and strengthen the union's position in negotiations.

4. Direct Democracy

The union should adopt certain forms of direct democracy in addition to the forms of representative democracy prescribed in the statutes. The referendum merits special attention, not only because of its intrinsic importance, but above all because of the weight of the decisions or guidelines which come out of a referendum. The referendum can be used at different levels, but there must always be a great deal of thought before it is used at the national level. The national committee decides whether to organize a national referendum.

A referendum should be preceded by an information campaign presenting the different positions and allowing collective discussion around the questions posed. Union leaders who would like to ascertain members' views before taking a decision should always specify whose opinion they wish to know and how it should be discovered. One must proceed honestly in seeking the support of members' views.

Thesis thirty-five:
1. Negotiations and agreements are the principal means for defending the interests of the

workers and citizens belonging to the union. But if this method fails we must have recourse to forms of protest.

In seeking to achieve union demands, the leadership should first use means which do not have a negative effect on social peace. The first step is to present suggestions and proposals to the administrative, economic and state bodies. If there is disagreement, we must use discussion to try to find ground for agreement. But in the present situation, if no account is taken of the union's opinion in matters which concern it, then the leadership will be obliged to modify its tactics.

2. *The union leaders should negotiate with the competent economic, administrative and state bodies in serious situations of conflict.*

In carrying out discussions, the union leadership should convoke negotiating groups and clearly define their mission and competence. Negotiating teams have the power to sign agreements to be later ratified by leading union bodies. The preparations for negotiation should include among other things: consultation with the union members concerned, presentation of the subject, goal and tactics, and an analysis of what is at stake. The union must insist that the negotiations be conducted openly. Experts, whose role is defined by the negotiating team, may also take part in the discussions.

It is imperative that every agreement should specify the duration, method and conditions of implementation accepted by both parties.

3. *When attempts to negotiate fail, the union leadership may organize demonstrations and protest actions.*

The character of such actions (economic/political) depends on the causes that have provoked them, not on their object. Every action must have a clear and precise goal and be carefully organized; it is likewise essential to allow for circumstances under which the action may be called off.

Mass actions may also take the form of demonstrations to reaffirm certain positions (pressure to begin or continue negotiations, or a demand that signed agreements should be carried out); they may also have a protest character (against decisions that are harmful, or against the failure to carry out commitments). Such actions should set a deadline for acceptance of their demands, and fix a date for precise action in the future.

If the warning is not heeded, then our actions must prove the determination and mobilization of the population behind the demands which have been put forward. Strikes and boycotts form part of this type of action. Strikes are above all actions of protest. Because of the economic losses which they entail, they ought to be the ultimate form of protest.

The leading bodies of the union should carefully prepare the protocols and the conduct of negotiations, as well as the actions of protest. At every level, the leadership must also prepare short-term and long-term action for confronting certain dangers, such as a state of emergency or aggression.

4. *Decisions concerning the outcome of negotiations or protest actions, compromises and the terms of the final agreement should be taken only after an analysis of membership views.*

During the course of the negotiations and protest actions, the union members involved should be regularly consulted. Leaders should inform the membership about the positions taken by the union negotiators and about partial results achieved.

Information and propaganda actions should be addressed, especially during periods of tension, not only to union members but also to the entire population. Guided by the general interest, the union must strive to ensure that the goals which it seeks to attain are understood and accepted.

5. *All members of the union are united by fundamental common goals; internal conflicts should be resolved by discussion leading to unity and not by administrative or disciplinary decisions.*

Thesis thirty-six: Control and criticism of union bodies is the right and duty of every Solidarity member.

The activity of all union authorities is placed under permanent control. The reports of control commissions should be rapidly published and distributed in the union. All union members are free to criticize the leadership, either in the course of meetings or in the press. Those who are criticized have the right to reply.

Membership of representative bodies control the leadership by making use of the right of questioning and the vote of confidence. If there is a question, the answer must be given within a definite period. If it does not satisfy the questioner, then he or she may call for a vote of confidence. If the vote results in a decision of non-confidence then the leader or leading body must offer to resign. This may be refused—in which case a final solution may be found by appealing, if necessary, to a special commission. In conformity with the statutes, control over leadership activity is also exercised by the review commission. These bodies collect information, point out irregularities in procedure, indicate the means for remedying this type of situation, and prepare reports for the representative bodies.

◆

VIII. THE NEW SOCIAL CONTRACT

Solidarity is the guarantor of the social accords of 1980, and demands that they be consistently put into practice. The only way to save the country is to realize the constitutional principle of the sovereignty of the nation. Our union establishes its program at a moment when the nation is threatened with catastrophe. We cannot remain in crisis. A way out must be found.

The Anti-Crisis Agreement

The anti-crisis agreement should ensure the survival of society in the difficult winter months ahead. It must point out the direction to follow in order to emerge from the crisis. It should be the first text of collaboration between the state power and society.

Agreement on Economic Reform

Agreement on economic reform requires collaboration between the state power and society for a radical change in the existing economic order. The reform should give the leadership of enterprises to personnel within the economic system who will harmonize the laws of the market with planning. The hundreds of agreements signed by the government still remain only on paper. Promises made by the state to the working people should be honored.

Agreement for a Self-Governed Republic

The agreement for a self-governed republic should provide the direction and means for a democratization of public life, of the *Sejm,* the political, territorial and economic authorities, the courts, national education, etc. Realization of this agreement will establish a just relationship between citizens and the state. The road to a self-governed republic is the only one which will make Poland internally strong, an equal partner with other nations.

The union considers the new social contract to be an indissoluble unity. The action program of Solidarity is above all a commitment by the union to the nation. We are confident that it will meet with the approval of the entire nation. No partisan, individual or group can consider itself to be above the nation.

We do not pretend to have a monopoly on the truth. We are ready for an honest and loyal dialogue, an exchange of ideas with the state power, a quest for just decisions which will better serve the country and the interests of working people and citizens. May this accord unite us around what is national, democratic and human in Poland; around those things which do not divide us.

A Year Has Passed

✦

Adam Michnik

Michnik, another important figure in KOR and adviser to Solidarity, reflects in August 1981 on the year that has passed since
the signing of the Gdańsk agreement. He too was imprisoned—
for nearly three years—after martial law was imposed, and he
too is active in Polish politics again.

✦

THE PROMISE OF A CIVIL SOCIETY

On the last day of August 1980 the deputy premier of the government of the
Polish People's Republic, Mieczysław Jagielski, and the chairman of the Interfactory
Strike Committee, Lech Wałęsa, signed an agreement on the grounds of the Lenin
shipyard in Gdańsk; it was clear to all that a new chapter had opened in Poland's history. Much was said at the time about this being a "social agreement," although it was
only a preliminary one, merely a compromise that could temporarily satisfy both the
government and the people. For the first time organized authority was signing an
accord with an organized society. The agreement marked the creation of labor unions
independent of the state which vowed not to attempt to take over political power.

The essence of the spontaneously growing Independent and Self-governing
Labor Union Solidarity lay in the restoration of social ties, self-organization aimed at
guaranteeing the defense of labor, civil, and national rights. For the first time in the
history of communist rule in Poland "civil society" was being restored, and it was
reaching a compromise with the state.

✦

COMPROMISE OR A MARRIAGE OF CONVENIENCE

For both sides this compromise was a marriage of convenience, not of love. The
authorities did not for a minute abandon their attempts to minimize the importance of
the union, and society did not lose its justified distrust of the government. From the
very beginning attempts were made to block out information, create informational
confusion, cow the provincial unionists.

Later, the authorities tried to introduce new clauses into the union's statute.

Adam Michnik, "A Year Has Passed, 1981," from Maya Latynski, trans./ed., *Letters from Prison and Other Essays,* 1981, pp. 124–131. Copyright © 1986 The Regents of the University of California.

Their policy was guided by the desire to preserve the status quo. And yet public pressure was so powerful, the pressure of the working masses so great, that within two months a multimillion-strong labor union independent of the state was registered. The origins of these events were obvious: they lay in society's long resistance, that was marked by the tragic dates of spurts of national revolt. These dates—1956, 1968, 1970, 1976, which today are being engraved on monuments of national memory, are the dates of the stations of the Polish Via Dolorosa. The Church's opposition to atheistic policies, the villages' resistance to collectivization, the intelligentsia's defiance of censorship—all made up the "Polish syndrome" that bore fruit in the form of the August strikes and Solidarity. The actions of the intellectual groups that organized aid to the participants of the June 1976 strikes played a special role. It was then that a common denominator for the activities of different social groups, especially the intelligentsia and the workers, was successfully created.

◆

THE ORIGINALITY OF THE POLISH AUGUST

In contrasting the Polish events with the Budapest Rising or the Prague Spring, two essential differences, which define the originality of the Polish experiment need to be stressed. The first regards the direction of the changes; the second, their reach. The Hungarian case was characterized by the actual disintegration of the party apparatus and assumption of political initiative by the rebellious people in the streets.

In Poland the conflict took place inside factories that were being controlled by the workers' strike guard.

The Prague Spring occurred because of an impulse for change that came from above, from among the activists of the party apparatus. In Czechoslovakia a part of the communist power elite undertook to emancipate itself from Soviet tutelage. In Poland the centers that initiated the democratic movement lay outside the party and outside the power apparatus. The current claims by party notables that a guiding current within the party existed prior to August can only be considered the boasting of the propaganda machine. As a result, the Communist party was automatically driven into being the conservative defender of the existing institutions of power. This position has given it some credibility in the eyes of the Kremlin's leaders, though hardly any in the eyes of the Polish people.

◆

CONFLICT AND COEXISTENCE

This past year saw a perpetual conflict between the government and organized society, with the Church serving as mediator. It is also possible to see in this conflict the testing of various strategies for coexistence which are being formulated by either the authorities or Solidarity. They did have something in common: the authorities have not contested the existence of Solidarity. They have, however, contended that Solidarity is undertaking actions that lie outside its statute by interfering in politics, denouncing certain high-ranking officials, demanding that certain discredited politicians be recalled from their posts, calling for law and order, and seeking access to the mass media. The authorities have attacked the uncensored union press, the occupations of administration buildings, street demonstrations, and Solidarity's tactics for extorting concessions.

Solidarity has accused the government of not fulfilling agreements, of holding on for dear life to yesterday's realities, of creating a personnel merry-go-round, and of being completely deaf to all the public's demands that are not backed by the threat of strikes. It has been the conflict of two worlds, in which the ancien régime has found itself under the constant pressure of an awakened society. The pressure has been so spontaneous, the authorities so unadapted to the new situation, that their only response has been to attempt to break up the union from the inside. They started to attack the so-called antisocialist forces, to divide the union's activists into radicals and moderates. The purpose of this tactic has been transparent, its connection with reality rather loose, since it has been the young workers in the large factories who are the most radical. From them comes the greatest pressure for demands and change. Members of the MKZ [Interfactory Founding Committee]* by their very nature have been more moderate, more susceptible to the arguments of their fellow negotiators from the government and—what is more important—to the voice of the Church, which has been toning things down.

◆

THE REACTIONS OF THE CHURCH

The primate of Poland, Cardinal Stefan Wyszyński, has from the very beginning declared himself in favor of seeking compromise solutions. Such was the meaning of his homily on Jasna Góra in August, and later of his appeasement of the most drastic conflicts in Bielsko Biała, in Bydgoszcz, and in the case of rural Solidarity. His tactic was not always well understood by the public, and it revealed the differently accented approaches of individual representatives of the Church hierarchy. In the changed social situation cracks began to appear in the former unity of the clergy. The episcopate's documents provided a clamp for holding it together, but individual bishops stressed differently the needs for decisive action and for restraint.

◆

CHANGES IN THE POWER APPARATUS
AND MOVEMENT IN THE PARTY

The decomposition of the power apparatus and movement within the party are among the most interesting sociological phenomena. There, from the beginning, "operation scapegoat" has been conducted, throwing out more and more

---

*The committee that in August 1980 negotiated with the authorities for the legal existence of Solidarity. Lech Wałęsa was its chairman.

members of the elite to appease public opinion. Members of the party and state leaderships have become the target of brutal attacks, and have been accused of incompetence, lack of education, muzzling the people, and theft; they have been publicly abused, their villas and their not very properly obtained university diplomas written about with delight. When this whole scandalous spectacle did not bring the expected results, the quarrel about methods of defusing the crisis started. Some (Kania, Jaruzelski, Barcikowski, Rakowski) stressed the need to play for time and to conduct stationary warfare based on tolerating Solidarity; others (Olszowski, Grabski, Kociołek, Zabiński) defined Solidarity's actions as counterrevolutionary and demanded decisive action, pushing for confrontation by repeatedly organizing trouble that would erupt into conflicts. But no one formulated a program for emerging from the crisis. Then the lowest echelons of the party became active, demanding an immediate extraordinary party congress. This led the party apparatus to panic and launch a sudden attack on the horizontal structures—that is, the practice of establishing contacts between party organizations outside the existing party channels. These initiatives originated in the party organizations in Toruń, and especially from the secretary of the factory party committee in Towimor, Zbigniew Iwanow. The defeat of the horizontal structures, symbolized by the expulsion of Iwanow from the party, foreordained that the extraordinary congress, for all its stupefying democracy (secret voting for the delegates and members of the Central Committee, and even the first secretary), would bring the party no credibility among the people. For all the declarations about the pursuit of policies of "understanding," the election of Albin Siwak to the Politburo represented the highest party forum's homage to the idea of post-Stalinist populism, which defeated concepts of democratization. The social accords were understood as a tribute to exigencies of the moment, while the election of Siwak testified to the party's ideological orientation. Of course, the participants in the Katowice Party Forum and the Association Grunwald who support Siwak compose a tiny social margin, but in the party that is condemned to the specific form of communist Newspeak, this line can count on a certain popularity that grows with rank. But above all it represents the thinking of an apparatus that has been removed from power or is threatened with removal—it is from these circles that will originate the political initiatives of the Polish Bilaks.*

Movement in the party—the deformed reflection of activity throughout society—should be viewed against the background of the political revival of other institutions and organizations of the establishment. When we analyze the personnel and programmatic changes in SD [Democratic party], ZSL [United Peasant party], or even PAX [Catholic Association] it becomes clear that they are all searching for new institutional forms, although until now they have been content with purely decorative roles. The Diet debates also serve as proof that even this institution may take on a new meaning in the new situation.

---

*Vassili Bilak, a longtime Slovak party activist, was one of the signatories of the letter inviting the Warsaw Pact armies to end the Prague Spring.

✦

WHAT IS SOLIDARITY?

And yet it is Solidarity that has been playing the key role. In order to understand the meaning of this, it is worth recalling the contents and the reach of the Gdańsk accords, guaranteed in the eyes of the people by the existence of Solidarity. Claims that this labor union has gone outside the limits of its statute are ridiculous. Equally ridiculous were the assertions made by the official propagandists a year ago that the very idea of independent labor unions had been forced on the striking workers by antisocialist elements. Rather, this is an example of how the foul vocabulary used in propaganda clouds the picture of reality; instead of presenting the world as is, propaganda attempts to form it. Hence the dispute over language—the essence of the controversy over Judge Kościelniak's changes in Solidarity's statute—played an important role in Solidarity's strategy. To accept the wording used in the propaganda would have meant to acquiesce in lies in public life. The union had to speak a language that the people, whose trust is its strength and its weapon, could understand and agree with. It is also for this reason that the union has to fulfill public expectations, as broad as they are. And so the Solidarity union is everything at the same time: a labor union that defends the rights of the working people in their places of employment; an office that prosecutes lawbreakers in the power apparatus; a defender of political prisoners, law and order, and an independent culture—a true representative of the people in dealings with the authorities. But one thing it has not been: a political party aiming to take over power, even though it has been accused of precisely this.

Solidarity, a social movement with many functions, has for a year now been the guarantor of the growing Polish democracy. But it is still too soon to draw up a balance sheet of its bright and dark sides. It is still too soon to give a sociological profile of this movement—a movement that knows how to win but not how to retreat; that combines demands for market reform with the ethos of egalitarianism; that uses the language of national solidarity to formulate the traditionally leftist idea of social self-government; that is a cross between contradictory elements and a mélange of matter; that combines the cult of its leader with a democracy that reaches pathological proportions; and that joins an astounding wisdom with a rare naiveté. It is a democratic movement in the midst of antidemocracy, a movement of great hope—of self-limiting Polish revolution: a movement that strictly observes geopolitical realities but is forced to defend itself from the attacks of the press of neighboring countries.

Indeed, for the allies [Warsaw Pact] the very existence of Solidarity is proof that "something is rotten in the state of Denmark." Let us not go into complex and hypothetical reflection on the subject of a possible military intervention in Poland. The absence of basic information forces one to believe in prophecies. But one thing is certain: the Poles' determined stance shows that the consequences of such an intervention would be incalculable. And not just for Poland.

✦
WHICH WAY TO DEMOCRACY?

The history of the past twelve months again poses the question of whether the communist system can be reformed. Five years ago I had the opportunity to express the opinion that the experiences of the Spanish road to democracy might be applicable to Poland: a road of peace, which does not mean a road with no potholes. Today, one could say that those experiences, taking into account all the social, political, and geographic differences, have proved useful.

If dark clouds hang over Poland today, if the public mood is determined with increasing frequency by food shortages and not by a broad realm of freedom of speech, it is because the problem of a universal reform of the state, based on the implementation of the "social accords" and on a system of public compromise, has not been put on the agenda. Some voices in the official press seem to be starting to discuss these problems, but it is merely a beginning of a new stage.

The task that faces the Polish nation is to work out a plan for a realistic system of political democracy, even while consciously restraining ourselves in order not to impinge on the state interests of our powerful neighbor. I therefore declare myself for a compromise solution. Such is the demand of the moment. No reasonable person can promote a general confrontation today. Solidarity has a different perspective before it, a perspective of searching for solutions that lie—as it has been formulated in the independent press—between collaboration and evolution. The Bastille can be assaulted by an amorphous mob armed only with emotions and courage; a long-term policy of democratic evolution can only be conducted by a movement that is well-organized, that is aware of its goals, and that acts in solidarity.

Part IV

The Bloc Transformed

✦ *The processes of social and political change that are sufficiently profound and comprehensive to be considered transformations (and, hence, revolutions in the narrower and more precise sense) do not necessarily resemble each other from one time and place to another. More than a century ago, it was common among left-wing revolutionary groups to suppose that the outcomes of their respective strivings would be more or less identical in all the countries involved. These groups, however diverse they were in fact, proclaimed their loyalty to a common set of principles and maintained a close, if often uncomfortable, association with each other. Illusory as that expectation may have been then, there was at least some basis for it. In late twentieth-century Eastern Europe, the sole basis for any such expectation was the common experience of Soviet domination. When that factor was removed, the ensuing transformations displayed a diversity as great as the diversity of the societies undergoing transformation.*

Nevertheless, on the strength of observable developments so far, a rough grouping can be discovered amidst the diversity. The two countries most often thought of as exceptions to the regional pattern became even more exceptional: East Germany is being absorbed, willingly but with dwindling enthusiasm, into the neighboring Federal Republic, while Yugoslavia dissolves in bitter conflict among its constituent nationalities. Three others, never in the forefront of regional attempts at liberalization, are in a state of arrested transformation: Romania, Bulgaria, and Albania have used their new autonomy to introduce gradual reform measures without jettisoning the old order decisively. And the remaining three countries, precisely the three that had experienced dramatic revolts against Soviet-imposed social and political models, are engaged in wholesale reconstruction: Poland, Czechoslovakia, and Hungary are all searching for the distinctive paths that will lead each one to a market economy and a popularly-endorsed, that is, legitimate, system of governance.

Even the most sympathetic observers have to acknowledge that the regional outlook is, on the whole, rather bleak. Having rejoiced at the overthrow of a hated regime of domination, we recognize that it was only a first step, and probably not the most difficult one. Forty years of repression, corruption, and mismanagement leave all present efforts to reform and reconstruct heavily mortgaged. Only the foolhardy dare predict what path, what combination of policy and circumstance, will produce a beneficent outcome.

POLAND

◆ *Although Solidarity was outlawed and, the government hoped, replaced by a new set of trade unions, the movement simply took up an underground existence. Leaders were arrested or detained, but others took their places and continued to function. Above all, the Polish citizenry, instructed during Solidarity's time of strength in the task of overcoming fear, continued to behave like citizens in a system that had no room for citizenship. Even when it appeared, after some years of clandestine existence, that Solidarity was losing its grip on popular sentiment, the citizens persisted in their recalcitrance and their open scorn for party and government. Such passive resistance was disabling and contributed unmistakably to the downfall of the regime in 1989–1990.*

Solidarity survived, of course, but its role became entirely different in its second career. A social movement was transformed into an electoral coalition and contestant. Although this was appropriate to the changed circumstances, much of the original spirit disappeared, to be replaced by factionalism and political maneuvering. This is nothing more than the all but universal fate of opposition movements: as soon as the enemy is defeated, the unity required by the struggle dissolves into particularism. But this change also signaled the onset of confusion and rivalry in Poland's new politics.

The complexities of this process justify the lengthy opening selection by a thoughtful scholar from the Polish Academy of Sciences. The next selection simply illustrates the ferment that developed on the eve of the "new revolution" and was chosen because it manifests the central role played in this and all recent Polish developments by the church and groups animated by religious commitment. The remaining passages chronicle the major changes that occurred from 1989 into 1991 and afford some sense of the difficulties with which the country is trying to cope.

Transition from Authoritarianism to Democracy

◆

Włodzimierz Wesołowski

This essay comes from a symposium in which authors were encouraged to add postscripts to their original contributions. Thus, Wesołowski completed his text in November 1989 and appended additional comments in February 1990. Although his treatment of the problematical aspects of transition was not seriously modified, the pace of events in Eastern Europe in this period was such that any observations quickly became dated. Wesołowski is a member of the Institute of Philosophy and Sociology of the Polish Academy of Sciences.

There are two ways in which the relationship between the state and society is perceived in theoretical discussion. Both ways combine theoretical and axiological elements, so they can be called "philosophies of state power." One is authoritarian, the other democratic. These philosophies provide different answers to two questions: Which entity—the society or the state—should have the superior status? Where does the state's power originate?

The democratic philosophy asserts that the self-organizing propensity of society takes precedence over the organizing activity of the state, so that society is the ultimate source of power. The authoritarian philosophy argues for the supremacy of the state over society and sees the existence of a state as a precondition of any organized social activity. It claims that state power originates either in the structure of power itself or in a strong will to power that accumulates and erupts in particular individuals or organized groups. State power is never a product of social contract; it is always imposed.

Among the numerous philosophers of democracy, J. S. Mill and J. J. Rousseau proposed the most persuasive arguments on its behalf. Authoritarian arguments were developed by Pareto and Lenin, in spite of great differences between their theories in other respects.

The two contrasting philosophies evoke continuous debate. What is more important, however, is their implementation in actual political life. Philosophies have practitioners. In this paper I am more interested in practical implementation than in

Włodzimierz Wesołowski, "Transition from Authoritarianism to Democracy," from *Social Research*, Summer 1990, pp. 435–461.

theoretical debate. Theoretical exposition serves only an analytical purpose: it creates a framework for a historico-sociological analysis of the transformation of a real authoritarian system into a democratic one. Poland is the case.

One can enumerate four axioms of the authoritarian regime. They are:

1. The state's power (state) is the fundamental mechanism of social integration and regulation.

2. The state is an organism which stands above all other forms of social organization and exerts control over them; it uses violence when needed.

3. The state is always controlled by the minority; the rule of the majority is mere illusion.

4. The ruling minority is best prepared for governing the state. Its wisdom may manifest itself in various ways: through discovery of the laws governing historical processes, through competence, through experience in government, through a flair for leadership; usually through all of the above.

In opposition to the authoritarian axioms, the democratic axioms are:

1. The state is socially created, that is, it represents the will of society; hence the citizen's main attribute is the right to define norms and to establish government.

2. The state should be constitutional in its nature, that is, the first legislative act—the constitution—defines the competence of state organs. It is thus made clear which aspects of social life are to be controlled by the state and what procedures must be followed.

3. The state is linked to the society by intermediary bodies, such as parties and associations, organized by various groups of citizens wishing to protect their interests or promote their ideals.

4. Individual members of the state—the citizens—must be equipped with inalienable rights belonging to them as persons, both as "human beings" and as "members of society." The most important among these are freedom of thought, freedom of speech, the freedom to form associations.

The political system which existed in Poland from 1945 to 1989 displayed all the traits of an authoritarian regime. But it was not just authoritarian, as it was not merely a political system. It was intended and planned as a totalitarian system: based on authoritarian principles, but magnified and extended.* Such a system was imposed on Polish society by the Soviet army in 1945.

Even more than some other versions of totalitarianism, the communist version developed in the Soviet Union was characterized by these two traits: the complete subjugation of the economy to political power, accomplished through state ownership of the means of production and through global planning of production; and an exceptionally extensive, universalist ideology intended to explain all phenomena and to make social consciousness uniform and amenable to manipulation.

In books and slogans, communist totalitarianism presented itself as something

---

*Totalitarianism is an economic, social, and political system extending the principles of authoritarian rule into all spheres of life. It depends on detailed penetration and complete subjugation of all spheres of life by the central system of government, which shapes them according to a global plan. . . .

completely different—"socialism," the most humane system in history. There is no time here for analyzing why what happened could in fact have happened, but this image of the system as "socialism" contained seeds of self-destruction, as it invited a very high standard of evaluation, which the everyday reality could not meet.

◆

THE PROCESS OF CHANGE FROM 1956 TO 1989

As I already said, totalitarianism was imposed upon Poland by the Soviet army. This is why it could never be completely assimilated and did not develop its specific traits to the fullest scale. The people's resistance played an important part, and so did some reluctance of those who were implementing it. This was especially true of the cultural domain. However, it was the resistance of the people, the resistance of the "social texture" being "processed," that played the major role. Three well-known reasons for Poland's not conforming to the totalitarian pattern (even in the darkest years 1949–55) were (1) resistance of the church, which retained its integrity and autonomy; (2) resistance of farmers, who did not enter the agrarian cooperatives; and (3) survival of some intellectual circles which rejected the communist ideology and kept alive democratic ideals.

Thus, in order to understand the process of transition in its entirety and complexity, it is not enough to analyze the events that preceded the formation of Mazowiecki's government in 1989; one also has to keep in mind the preliminary processes that began as early as 1956, and prepared the ground for the breakthrough of 1989.

Many Poles perceived the system as oppressive as early as 1945, but they were muted and their influence was limited, especially on the young. The postwar generations recognize the system's real traits in their own experiences.

Very important in this respect was the "Polish October" of 1956. It released the process of systematic subversion of the authoritarian system based on Soviet patterns. First of all, it undermined the Stalinist ideology, that very foundation of the new social order. "Revisionism" requested better models of the socialistic future and ideas concerning how to reach it. At the same time, revisionism provoked another question: If other plans for the future were feasible, who was to decide what plan to adopt? Thus the former question resurrected democracy as the method of choosing both the path and the pattern, the road to and the model of socialism. The authoritarian form of government has since then been seriously questioned on the intellectual level.

Strikes and riots of 1970 and 1976 discredited the system politically. They totally eliminated the illusions that the Communist party represents the working class. The party and government could not represent the workers when using violence in dealing with protests against the malfunctioning of industrial management and against inhumane bureaucracy. In the years 1976–80 the system received another severe blow: the discreditation extended to its economic base. Despite Western credits, the logic of the economy resulted in increasing shortages of goods and in growing economic inefficiency.

Following those experiences, the years 1980 and 1981, the "times of Solidarity," were a period of eloquent criticism of the existing system in all its aspects, as well as the period in which down-to-earth attempts were made to oppose the system. Solidarity represented all social strata and became a counterforce to the authoritarian government. The power of this organization was formidable. That is why the reaction had to be adequate: the imposition of martial law. Even these drastic means, however, could not eliminate the society's resistance. The very next day after the imposition of martial law, the most active elements of society started to organize themselves for the next battle.

On the surface, authoritarianism remained strong until 1988. After that time, the official political elite started issuing signals of "reconciliation," because it knew that the system was getting weaker and weaker. Most likely as many as three separate factors convinced the authoritarian elite to change its mind. The first factor was the forbidding shape of the economy and a desire to make the opposition share in the responsibility for it (as well as a desire to use the opposition to obtain credits from the West). The second factor, revealed by martial law, was the political inefficiency of authoritarian communist rule despite its brutality. A third factor of great importance was the change in the Soviet Union.

However, the authoritarian way of thinking on the part of the official elite even as it initiated the first talks with the opposition was exemplified by the official announcements which did not admit of the possibility that Solidarity could be legalized. The government intended simply to place some opposition figures in its ranks. Many press articles proved this. The opposition was to be drawn into the political system, which itself would not be changed.

The social pressure, especially strikes, and the opposition's refusal to accept the co-optation strategy opened up the way to the Round Table talks. Real ground was gained: the authoritarian structure began to crumble.

The Round Table talks lasted two months, and they ended with an agreement (the "pact") which specified the program for the gradual change of the political system and the economic model. Among many paragraphs of the agreement two had paramount importance. The first concerned the legalization of Solidarity. The second: national elections. Although the Catholic church did not participate officially in the talks, it acted behind the scenes as a conciliatory force. Whenever the two sides at the Round Table (Solidarity and the Communist party) arrived at a stalemate, the church pressed hard to find a solution acceptable to both sides. At the same time, the church stressed that it stood for enlarging and strengthening the democratic forms of social life. This general position of the church was supportive of the Solidarity claims.

In return for its legalization, Solidarity promised to run in elections, which were expected to result in the victory of the "old coalition" of the Communist party (PUWP), the United Peasants' party, and the Democratic party. The election procedure was constructed in such a way as to ensure the coalition's winning 65 percent of all seats in the house of representatives (Sejm)—that is, 65 percent of the 460 deputies—while the results of the senate elections were in no way predetermined (but the political role of the senate was designed to be secondary).

This setup was intended to enable the Communist party to hold power and the opposition to express criticism. But the negotiated balance of power was destroyed by the electors, who decided not to ratify the pact. People decided that Solidarity should win, because it represented a countersystem, and its victory alone assured the electors that real economic and political reforms would take place. In the first round of elections, Solidarity won almost all seats (159 out of 161) in the house of representatives that it was allowed to contest, and almost all seats in the senate (99 percent).

The authoritarian structures of power proved arrogant as well as ignorant in recognizing the prevailing mood and in organizing the elections, which for the first time were to be partly competitive. Moreover, the opposition's tactics also helped to bring about the regime's defeat in the elections. Especially fruitful was Solidarity's decision to support some candidates of the Communist party, the United Peasants' party, and the Democratic party in the second vote. As a result of this, many non-Solidarity deputies elected in the second vote became actual supporters of Solidarity. This completed the electoral victory of Solidarity.*

Much happened in the two months between the second vote in June and August 21, when General Jaruzelski appointed the Solidarity candidate, T. Mazowiecki, the prime minister. It was a time of intensive talks and maneuvering on the part of the communist leaders. Mr. Kiszczak, the minister of the interior and the party's negotiator at the Round Table, was asked to form a government. He failed to do that because many politicians refused to cooperate. Resigning from his mission, General Kiszczak suggested publicly that Malinowski be nominated for the post of prime minister. This suggestion could not be followed because Malinowski, for many years the resident of the United Peasants' party, was losing support within his own party. He was seen as a compliant tool in the hands of the communists.

It was Wałęsa who suddenly proclaimed Solidarity's readiness to enter into coalition with the United Peasants' and the Democratic parties, despite his own and Solidarity's former opinions, which were the opposite. Though Adam Michnik published the prophetic article "Your President, Our Prime Minister" two weeks earlier, such an arrangement was not seen by the majority of Solidarity leaders as a feasible solution. Wałęsa's unexpected suggestion was instantly accepted by leaders of the United Peasants' party and the Democratic party. This led to a complete reorganization of political affiliations in the parliament and a major breakthrough. The Peasants' and the Democratic parties deserted the Communist party and supported the opposition. The new majority thus created was not anticipated by the Round Table pact. This way Poland entered a new phase in its political development.

◆

NEW PROBLEMS AFTER THE BREAKTHROUGH

The breakthrough took place in the legislative organ and was then extended to the executive organ. In a sense, the formation of Mazowiecki's cabinet can be seen as a

---

*The final results of elections to the house of representatives were the following: the Polish United Workers' party (the Communist party), 173 seats; Citizens' Committees of Solidarity, 161 seats; the United Peasants' party, 76 seats; the Democratic party, 23 seats; groups of lay Catholics, cooperating with communists, 23 seats.

victory of democracy at the top level of the state's structure. However, the erection of the requisite sociopolitical infrastructure necessary for the functioning of democracy has barely started. The structuralization of economic interests and the formation of real political parties and civic societies is at a very preliminary stage.

Thus there is a discrepancy between the achievements of democracy at the top level and the absence of organizational activity among the rank and file. This weakens the democratic representatives in the parliament. They cannot count on well-planned, balanced, and peaceful social support which would carry a predictable force. They lack information concerning the distribution of preferences among the population. On the whole, the political situation is extremely fluid. I will attempt to uncover some causes of its fluidity.

Economy: Neither the Old nor the New Structure of Interests

The Polish economy is confronted with the necessity of changing its mode of operation and ownership base. It is said that the transformation from a centrally planned, state-administered, and state-owned economy to one operating through market mechanisms and founded on a variety of forms of ownership is on its way. The ideas of marketization and of enlarging the share of private enterprises, whether big, medium-size, or small, are commonly accepted. The problems of "privatization" and destatization are appearing in everyday parlance as well as in official statements.

However, many ideas are debated rather than implemented. Not one clearly defined project has been adopted in any big enterprise in the metallurgy, machine, construction, chemical, or textile industries. The idea of privatization is put to work slowly, erratically, and on an exceedingly small scale, mostly in small enterprises. The idea of selling the large state-owned enterprises to the workers has not been conceptually clarified to a degree sufficient to use it in practice. It is quite astonishing that both the former communist government and the present democratic government lag behind the pressing need to provide specific, workable plans for reforming our economy in its complexity. Meanwhile, the economy has been disintegrating. A specific program limited to the aim of curbing inflation has recently been elaborated and implemented. But changes in the ownership structure are hindered by the absence of real banks and of real prices for investment goods, by the lack of a capital market, and by a deficiency of economic knowledge.

As a result of all the negative processes, the structure of group economic interests is disintegrating rather than crystallizing. There are no bearers of the process of economic reforms definitely interested in its success. Neither a group of "laborious Puritans" nor a group of devoted "captains of industry" is emerging. Almost all strata of the working class are very confused about the future, and they are silent.

The group interests that are visible are tied to the branches of industry. That is an old type of interest situation in a communist system. Miners, textile workers, and metallurgy workers fight for the survival of their industry and for the maintenance of the level of real wages. But even those structures seem weakened. The resulting phenomenon could be called the fragmentization of interests. Individual factories or mines go on strike, voicing their particular local demand, rather than fighting for the cause of industry or of the entire working class.

Because the new structure of the economy—whatever its shape may be—has not yet emerged, it is pointless to expect the structure of interests to yield impulses for a new structure in the political arena.

Political Fluidity

There is also great political fluidity. A definite constellation of political parties has not yet emerged. A clear party structure seems a prerequisite for the crystallization of political opinions and for unveiling the political preferences of the population. The Polish political scene, to the contrary, presents a mosaic of forces, in which one does not see clear contours of political actors with definite political orientations and specific, well-constructed programs. Within organized parties and groups there are signs of a continued disintegration into smaller fractions rather than integration into greater political entities. Prolongation of this situation may cause instability within the society and unproductive reshuffling of alliances within the parliament.

First and foremost, Solidarity won the election, but it still is a trade union. The trade union produced a political movement which has overgrown the mother-tree in its potential and popularity. This movement is composed, however, of a very loose federation of citizens' committees operating at the local level. It also has a large group of parliamentarians at the top level of the state political structure (in the Sejm and Senat). But there is no organization to produce a common program and no platform on which to discuss it. There is, in fact, no political program of Solidarity as a political movement.

Fortunately, the group of Solidarity representatives in parliament acts as a substitute for a normal party. They form the so-called Citizens' Parliamentary Club. This group sketches proposals for new laws and regulations. Moreover, in spite of great internal diversity, it displays coherence and consistency in parliamentary actions. This group forms the core of political supporters for Mazowiecki's government.

However, the laws that have been proposed and approved until now have been very specific. They aimed at putting some rudimentary order in the Polish economy (like a budgetary law, a law on indexation of wages), or they consisted of the implementation of widely accepted democratic ideas, like the separation of the judiciary system from the political authorities. The Polish parliament has not yet entered into the stage at which different political orientations, which are present in all democracies, will necessarily show up.

The discussion on the future development of the political movement associated with Solidarity seems unavoidable.

Theoretically, there are three possibilities. First, a mass centrist party could be formed. Its name could be "Centrum-Solidarity." It would encompass "moderate" liberals, Christian democrats, social democrats, and agrarists who are already within Solidarity. This project involves making a formal party structure out of what exists as a loose movement. A well-organized party may provide a strong basis for the present government. If it has a strong, charismatic leader, it can help in overcoming the social difficulties associated with necessary transformation of the economy. It could be a stabilizing factor. This solution may, however, lead to the "charismatization" of political life, if the leader is not immune to the "will to power."

The second solution is to divide the Solidarity political movement into two parties: Christian democratic and social democratic. To these two political orientations belong the most talented and the best known politicians of the former opposition, who are now within the Citizens' Parliamentary Club (of Solidarity provenance). Assuming that Christian-democratic attitudes and social-democratic attitudes (orientation) are widely represented in the population, one can infer that here is a ground for organizing two relatively strong parties, which are present in every stable modern democracy.

The third solution is to improve the internal organization of the Solidarity political movement as it is now, that is, as a loose federation of all social groups and forces that were involved in the process of liberalization. This solution has the strongest support among the Solidarity leadership, both in the trade-union branch and the political branch. This solution has tentatively been chosen. It is seen as the most practical solution for the coming year.

In the coming year there will be local elections in Poland. In light of this important event the third solution seems advantageous. It gives an adequate framework for the emotional unification of almost all people of all localities. They will unite in the battle against the vices of local authorities who are incompetent, nepotistic, and arrogant, and who were left intact by the revolution at the top of the state structure.

But the third solution, when looked at from a longer perspective, seems fraught with many uncertainties. One can develop the following argument. If Solidarity arrives late in the national political arena as a well-organized force with a definite program, it may suffer unexpected disintegration and defeat.

Political parties of the old authoritarian system are in a state of serious crisis. Some see it as a mortal crisis.

The PUWP (the Communist party) has lost its political and ideological identity. Its social base has dissolved or at least is hard to find and specify. However, the Communist party has not lost its newspapers, offices, cadres in ministries, and local administration. Using these resources, the leadership started its "long march" to the new democratic society. However, the remnants of the party are divided and confused, and the leadership is late in providing new thoughts and ideas.

The party congress will be held in February. The present leadership has not supplied members with a new program. Outside of the leadership several groups emerged proposing contrasting roads to the future. Some groups like "The Initiative of 8 July" suggest to change the ideology and political program of the party into a social-democratic one. They argue that this will improve the image of the party within society and, hence, increase the chances for survival. Other groups (like the Warsaw Workers' Forum) argue for the adoption of a more traditional program, pointing to the conservative inclinations of some strata of workers, and for certain, some groups of party activists. They are of the opinion that the marketization and privatization of the Polish economy will soon create an antigovernment mood among workers.

The leadership of the party is paralyzed by indecisiveness. It is wavering between the two options and selecting neither. Its main concern is how to secure unity, being afraid of either total dissolution if the split is announced or a drastic reduction of the membership if one ideological tendency is put above another.

If a somehow transformed Communist party survives at all, the major political dilemma for it will be whether to act as a stabilizing factor or a destabilizing one. There exists no single, good option for it. If it chooses to continue the present policy of a "responsible partner" in the Mazowiecki government (dominated by Solidarity), it accepts a secondary or even completely negligible role. If it chooses the role of the vigilant representative of "the working class," echoing some communist slogans, it may regain some territory, if the economic situation of the workers deteriorates.

However, by adopting such a policy it risks being completely smashed, if the workers follow the government and Solidarity in spite of the many hardships which the economic reform produces.

What is happening to the Communist party can be viewed as political irony. At the Round Table talks, the Communist party sought to include Solidarity as a part of the official government in order to compromise it and finally to diminish its political role. In fact, however, the opposite occurred. Its role, and not Solidarity's, has been diminished.

Extremely complicated is the situation among the political representatives of farmers. For decades, the United Peasants' party was the only officially recognized representative of the independent farmers. It was a very loyal satellite to the ruling Communist party until last summer. I have already referred to its dramatic change of allegiance from the Communist party to Solidarity. This paved the way for the formation of a democratic government. For the very same move—changing the allegiance—the United Peasants' party had to pay a very high price. It has lost its credibility and political identity.

Under the present, completely new circumstances this party leaves behind all its servility to the communist ideology and desperately tries to transform itself into a "new entity," the true representation of farmers' interests and desires. It goes back to the agrarian ideology which it abandoned in 1948 under the pressure of the communists. It prizes the market and free enterprise. Moreover, it claims to be transforming itself into the Polish Peasants' party. The PPP existed in Poland in 1945–48 and then was forcefully eliminated from political life.*

Today, however, not only the former satellite of the communists pretends to hold the legacy of the past agrarist and democratic party. Solidarity representatives in the parliament who come from agrarian regions do the same. They have declared themselves the true successors of PPP. There is still a third group aspiring to the same

---

*First it was decimated through various means of oppression and then, under the pressure of "friendly persuasion," "unified" with the procommunist Peasants' party, since then the United Peasants' party. Now this shameful act serves as the justification of the UPP's claim to be the heir of the PPP.

The reason for the attempted usurpation is clearly political. In the memory of the Polish people the PPP is kept as the major political opponent of the communists on their way to elimination of the remnants of parliamentary democracy in Poland in the period 1945–48.

political legacy. This group is composed of former members of PPP who are still alive and who attracted some young activists to join them. They consider themselves the only legitimate successors of the PPP.

The situation among the farmers' representatives may serve as an illustration for some general problems. Here I have described real actions in order to indicate that, first, the gradual transformation toward democracy may be combined with maneuvering and adjusting of discredited parties. Second, the democracy emerging out of authoritarianism may result in an excessive political differentiation. Today Polish farmers have three separate political parties that profess, at the moment, virtually the same ideology and stand for the same program. Too much representation for rather politically inactive farmers.

The Democratic party was the third organization in the former official procommunist alliance. In the summer it also reversed its course and turned to Solidarity. However, it has not been discredited to the same degree as the United Peasants' party and hence its political credentials look better. Since 1982, though grudgingly, it has distanced itself from the antidemocratic practices of the martial-law period, suggested some moves to make courts independent from the pressures of the party apparatus, and advocated a "constitutional, presidential political system."

In the past "political structure" it presumably represented the private sector (mostly independent craftsmen) and the "intelligentsia" stratum. In the near future the number of small and medium-size businesses will grow, therefore one could expect a growing role for this party within the new political system. However, the political appeals of the DP to join its ranks evoke very limited responses.

It seems that the case of the Democratic party illustrates a problem I have not mentioned until now. The first is the long-standing aversion of the Polish "old middle class" to politics. Paradoxically, the "old middle class" is today regaining economic strength and growing numerically, but does not seem to aspire to political power. The second problem consists of the "overpacking" of the political center (with the parties already existing as well as prospective ones). Solidarity is somehow in the center already. Besides, the Democratic party that wishes to represent the business and intelligentsia strata together looks to many Poles as a strange combination.

What I have described until now is the situation of parties which have their official representatives in the parliament. However, there is a growing number of parties which are not represented in the parliament at all, or whose leaders are members of Solidarity's citizens' clubs. Some of those parties were formed as underground parties at the end of the seventies, but the majority of them have evolved recently. Among those opposition parties, the most active is the Confederation for Independent Poland. The Confederation demands complete independence now, which would entail full autonomy from the Soviet Union. For instance, demonstrations protesting against Soviet troops stationed in Poland are being organized.

There is also the newly created Christian National Union with a liberal-conservative program, and there are numerous other political groups and small parties.

Nearly all parties and political movements are looking for members, creating political platforms, and establishing doctrines. It is characteristic for Poland that the smaller parties have worked out their programs to a greater extent than the larger ones. Will this situation cause the membership of particular parties to shift? To what final effect would such a shift lead? What relations will obtain between the party organizations and the social strata, the interests of the different branches of the economy, and finally the political issues generated not by material interests but by great ideals? No one today can answer these questions.

The matter is not merely academic. There is a need for stable political orientations both in social life in general and in the legislature in particular. Indefinite and fluid representation of interests by the parties may result in political instability in the land and may hamper the functioning of the parliament. This would undermine the process of democratization.

The Weakness of Associations

The fluidity of the parties is coupled with the underdeveloped structure of civic associations. In many countries the associations grouping scientists, teachers, lawyers, educators, consumers, religious organizations, and regional and cultural organizations are active. In Poland, however, contrary to some people's best hopes, the reactivation of associations is proceeding very slowly after the long period in which the whole of public life was dominated by authoritarian rule. The old-type associations of the authoritarian regime fail to provide the much-needed structure for interpersonal relations, for meeting group needs, for achieving goals and defending interests of the group. New associations exist rather on paper than in action. One might say that state-oriented society is only slowly becoming citizen-oriented. For the most part, it continues to be an anonymous mass.

The causes of such a situation are probably very simple: people focus first of all on fulfilling their elementary needs as far as nutrition, education of their children, and health of the family are concerned. This narrowness of everyday life has to be overcome if Poland is to become a real democratic society. A more advanced stage of activity of the associations might result in fulfillment of specific needs, creating stronger social bonds, and a more universal sense of participation. So far, only the ecological groups and the associations for the reestablishing of private schools, which were prohibited under the totalitarian system, have shown dynamic action.

Trade Unions and Social Instability

There are two trade-union organizations in Poland at present: the independent trade union Solidarity and the National League of Trade Unions (NLTU, in Polish OPZZ), created after the declaration of martial law (on Dec. 13, 1981).

Two fundamental questions asked today are: Which of these two organizations will exert greater influence on workers? Which of them will support the reforms, and which will organize protests and cause destabilization?

The Solidarity trade union has only 1.5 million members today, as compared with 10 million in 1980–81. Various explanations for this relatively small number of people who reentered the union are provided. The most simple proposition seems the most likely: most people are happy with the recent political changes, but they wonder if Solidarity as a trade union can be effective in the coming period of deep-reaching economic reforms. Workers will pay the cost of these reforms. Moreover, Solidarity is perceived as splitting into a trade union and a political movement: the two functions do not coincide. This division checks the inflow of new members and makes Solidarity less effective in many workplaces than it was in 1980–81.

Despite this weakness, the trade-union leaders today exert quite an influence on the deputies who form the Solidarity wing in the parliament because the union is a symbol of the former opposition's power and because Lech Wałęsa serves as a link between the union leaders and the parliament deputies. It is impossible to predict how long this can continue. It is difficult for members of the parliament to play the role of agents of the trade union. They were nominated deputies in general elections and they would like to serve the country, not the trade union. The rift between the two Solidarities, the union and the political movement, may cause instability within the former opposition. We have already witnessed some disagreements between the two wings of Solidarity.

The National League of Trade Unions evokes the politicians' concern, as it is a potential threat to stability within the country. It claims to have dissociated itself from the Communist party, even though its most active members are also party members. It also claims to have as many as 7 million members, which makes it much bigger than Solidarity. Until 1988 the League did not stage any protest actions in industry. After this date, in an attempt to change its image, it has transformed itself from a compliant tool of the Communist party into a militant protector of the "ordinary" people. It seems that its political line will continue to consist of slogans about protecting the workers' interests from the government, capitalists, and all other "profiteers." This could be a way of harnessing support at a time of inflation and declining real wages. In any case, they bide their time. One cannot exclude the possibility of anti-intelligentsia and anti-Semitic slogans. In short, the League may become an instigator of conflict and disorder. Another possibility is that the popularity of the League on the union front will decrease. Faced with such an alternative, the leadership may decide to revitalize its base by forming a populist party. Some leaders have already hinted at such a possibility.

The Inertia of the Old Bureaucracy

Shortly after Mazowiecki was appointed prime minister, the weekly *Polityka* published an article by Marek Henzler entitled "Wasz premier, nasz aparat" ("Your Prime Minister, Our Administration"). The article dealt with the state of central administration, 80 percent of which is composed of members of the Communist party. The title of the article was an allusion to a wider public debate in which many voiced the concern that the formation of a Solidarity cabinet will be ineffective, as many important decisions in industry as well as in culture, health, and education will be made by people nominated by the party, the *nomenklatura*. All cabinet decisions could be blocked by them as they could either refuse or procrastinate when directed to act.

I see another danger, however, that of the habits formed by the posttotalitarian bureaucracy. The bureaucracy of a totalitarian system is a bureaucracy *à rebours* if we take the Weberian model as the yardstick. It implements general regulations amended by phone calls "from above," it is incompetent, it is overloaded with the unnecessary production of many statistical reports, and it is cliquish and free from accountability and responsibility. Making it efficient requires a titanic effort. However, it is difficult to sack the entire administration. It must be used and worked with, even though it does not fit the new style and new tasks of the state. Contrary to some opinions, I do not believe that the bureaucracy will sabotage the implication of the new government's decisions. Most bureaucrats have been taught to shift this way and that, and they are ready for another shift. The question is whether good intentions can conquer bad job habits.

Of course, bureaucrats fired in the process of reducing the extended, parasitic apparatus may prove to be a dangerous element. Unable to hold any ordinary job, they may form a strong fraction of the Communist party, pressing for a political confrontation on all occasions. This is a more plausible development if the Communist party as a whole adopts a belligerent stand.

Remnants of Totalitarianism and Authoritarianism

I have argued that changes at the top of the state structure have got ahead of the formation of a normal, democratic sociopolitical infrastructure of democracy. I mentioned the weak articulation of interest groups, the fluidity of the political structure, obscure prospects for the relationship between the trade unions and the political parties. All these phenomena may cause great political instability, which could hinder the development of a democratic society and polity. However, the sociopolitical fluidity and instability is only one danger to the present transition from an authoritarian regime to a democratic one. The other danger is the survival of some elements of totalitarianism and authoritarianism within the public domain and within the state power structure. I will refer to three phenomena: the press, the military, and the presidency.

The Communist party has lost state power, but due to its previous political and economic position it runs the huge conglomerate of mass-media enterprises. They print and distribute newspapers and magazines. Profits made by this conglomerate subsidize the party. Moreover, in each region of the country the Communist party publishes its own newspaper that propagates its political line. As the monopolistic owner of printing shops and of chains of kiosks, the party now produces and distributes the opposition's press as well as its own. Thus everybody who buys a newspaper—even an opposition paper—gives money to the Communist party (to the said conglomerate owned by it). In the spring of 1989, under Rakowski's government, the National Bank of Poland gave the Communist party a loan at 3 percent interest, whereas the normal rate was 50–60 percent because of inflation. These are but a few examples of the widespread phenomenon that citizens of a totalitarian state supported with their own money and work the communist regime.

Another example of the survival of totalitarianism is the army and the police. All the highest positions in both ministries are held by members of the Communist party. Nearly all army and police officers are members of the Polish United Workers' party. Thus the instruments of violence are still controlled by the Communist party. For this reason the democratic parliament and the government are still endangered. They have no equivalent instrument of force. The imbalance in the "means of power" between the opposition, which established a cabinet, and the party, which distances itself from the present cabinet, is a serious factor in the macropolitical situation. All employees in the Ministry of the Interior have signed a pledge of loyalty to the Communist party (the Polish United Workers' party), and the documents are still kept in the personal portfolios. New employees no longer sign such a pledge, but all those who were hired before June 1989 should promptly respond to any call from the party. In a parliamentary discussion which took place quite recently, the vice-minister of the interior argued that law-abiding procedures make it impossible to remove these pledges from among the official documents.

Especially telling of authoritarian remnants is the office of the president, with its many prerogatives. The president was elected by a majority of a single vote, and some members of the opposition were consciously absent to make his election possible. However, once elected, only the president could appoint the prime minister. This prerogative, which the opposition accepted at the Round Table negotiations, gives the president the power to control the formation of the government. Furthermore, the president exerts control over the army, and he influences foreign policy. According to the terms of the pact signed at the Round Table, the president is to ensure a peaceful transition from authoritarianism to democracy. What has not been made explicit is that giving the president these prerogatives is itself a relic of authoritarianism, since these prerogatives are coupled with the party membership of General Jaruzelski, and party control over the army and police. To be sure, much depends on the president's future actions, and it is still unclear in which direction he will move.

Analyses to exemplify the remaining strongholds of authoritarian and post-totalitarian elements could be multiplied. For instance, the Polish United Workers' party has its offices in factories, and the party functionaries in large factories receive their salaries while they are exempted from doing actual work. Other parties do not have such privileges. Even if the democratic trend prevails in the near future, a lot of things will have to be modified or eliminated.

◆

INSTEAD OF A CONCLUSION

The withdrawal of authoritarianism is not a sign of a definite loss of strength. Postauthoritarian elements retained in the emerging democratic system still possess the state's highest office—that of the president—and institutions that dispose of the instruments of violence. The withdrawal of authoritarianism must then have a basis other than complete inability to act. One could hypothesize that the basis is the great political and moral attractiveness of the alternative solution: democracy. Its attractiveness captivates even those who held positions of power in the authoritarian system. They accept the democratization process, which deprives them of power.

This optimistic conclusion should be accompanied by one reservation, however.

The contemporary world is divided into "centers" and "peripheries." The processes taking place in Poland today cannot be analyzed in separation from the processes in the Soviet Union. Similarly, Latin America cannot be understood if one disregards the political orientation dominant in the United States. Latin America turns away from authoritarian rule just as does Poland.

The period has come when the Soviet Union has become a supporter of the idea of political pluralism. In this situation political elites of the satellite countries also opt for pluralism and democracy. The former practitioners of authoritarianism become converts to democracy either by conviction or by pragmatism. Their motivations need not be idealistic. Nevertheless, if one accepts the proposition that the center influences peripheries, the hope for the steady withdrawal of authoritarianism in the East bloc is strengthened. Recent developments in East Germany testify to that. However, the transition from authoritarian to democratic regimes must not be regarded as an historical necessity. Rather, it is the result of a number of factors, the net outcome of a specific constellation of conditions. We can only hope that this favorable constellation of conditions exists as long as possible.

◆

POSTSCRIPT

Since this essay was completed (in November 1989), the democratic processes have advanced in Poland, but the political structure has remained at the initial stage of its crystallization.

The anticommunist revolutions in Czechoslovakia and East Germany created a favorable international context for further changes in Poland. So did political developments in the Soviet Union. Under the present circumstances, Poland is in a position to concentrate on internal reforms, as it has been relieved from the threats of the conservative forces of international communism.

Poland's great domestic problems are two: the transformation of the economic structure, and the formation of a new sociopolitical structure.

On January 1, 1990, Poland entered an important stage of economic reform. Its aim is the stopping of inflation and the introduction of order into the country's financial system. The policy adopted is based on assumptions related to the concept of monetarism in economics. However, the changes in the structure of industry, such as transformation of the ownership base of big industry (privatization), demonopolization, increasing the share of medium-size and small businesses in the national economy, have not gained momentum yet. Therefore, the thesis developed in this paper about the weak structuralization of economic interests is still valid.

The parallel thesis on the weakness and fluidity of the party political structure also remains in force. The Solidarity movement is still a loose composition of social forces. The Communist party disintegrated after its congress in January. The peasant parties are unable to unify. The so-called extraparliamentary opposition parties (those which are not formally represented in the parliament) are numerous, but without a strong membership base.

Solidarity as a political movement decided to stay a loose federation of local citizens' committees, and a parliamentary club in the Sejm (the parliament). As a parliamentary force, Solidarity has strengthened its influence on the legislative process. The majority of members of other clubs follow Solidarity's lead. That means a strong parliamentary backing for Mazowiecki's government.

In spite of some uncertainty as to whether the workers will go on strike when confronted with the hardships caused by the anti-inflationary policy, there is social peace in the country. Neither Solidarity as a trade union nor the formerly official procommunist trade unions instigate strikes. They both declare support for the economic reform, despite its negative effects on almost all sections of the population. But still there is a threat of the former official unions taking advantage of the worsening economic situation; they haven't completely renounced their populist demagogery and their political ambitions.

On the whole, there still is a strong political, psychological bond tying together Solidarity as a political movement, the government, and the populace. It seems that the population at large has confidence in the guidance of the former opposition's elite, now in power under the Solidarity banner. This elite provided successful leadership in dismantling the communist regime. People are not so strongly confident about its success in reforming the country, but they still trust that this elite will provide the proper measures for leading the country out of crisis. No other social force is perceived as capable of performing this feat.

However, there is great uncertainty about how the Polish political-party structure will look and how it will function. Without crystallized group economic interests and without party structure, the parliament and the government today are in a comfortable position of enjoying unspecified support; it is doubtful that this situation can be a lasting one. Recently, Lech Wałęsa has said that Poland needs political parties and he has appealed to various sections of the population to form them. However, he has remained silent as to whether Solidarity itself will support the creation of any of them, or form a party of its own, or allow new parties to branch out from the Solidarity movement.

Solidarity as such has no economic or political program; the government formed under its auspices does. This creates a very peculiar situation. There is a gap between the articulation of tangible interests and various political orientations on the one hand and the government on the other. No well-defined party structure is helping to crystallize economic interests and the political goals of the various sections of the society. Civic associations, as mentioned in the article, are still in the initial stage of formation.

It would seem that the peasants are the closest to having a representation of their interests in the parliament, but their representatives are in disarray. There is grass-root pressure in villages and localities for the unification of all factions of peasant representation. Whether this pressure will produce a unified peasant party remains to be seen.

The former Communist party renamed itself the Social Democratic party at the congress held in January. Two weeks later it had only 5,000 members (as compared with its former 1.5 million). A small fraction of its activists and leaders formed a new party, called the Social Democratic Union, which also has very little following, though it is perceived as more truly democratic than the faction which has named itself the Social Democratic party. The leader of the Union, Fiszbach, received mild backing from Lech Wałęsa. What is most important, however, is the process of the vanishing of the former Communist party as an organization and a membership base. Its newspapers and printing shops are desperately looking for new sponsors in various regions of the country.

Except for Solidarity as a trade union, and for the former official trade unions, industrial workers have no sociopolitical representation of their own. It remains to be seen whether Solidarity as a nationwide movement can fill this political vacuum in the long run, once the workers' tangible interests are better crystallized and voiced.

The threat of conservative forces regaining political influence and blocking democratic changes has significantly diminished. In the army and in the police, the two strongholds of the former communist regime, there is much political ferment. In both formations, several groups have emerged aiming at creating independent trade unions. In the army, the nationalistic, "patriotic" spirit, which has always been present there, is helping to transform the attitudes of officers and the rank-and-file soldiers to progovernmental ones.

The president has been systematically striving to repair his public image. He is still hated in many circles as the man responsible for imposing martial law. Nevertheless, he himself attempts to change his unfavorable image, insisting that his decision was the lesser evil in comparison with the Soviet army's invasion. Simultaneously, he tries to remain in contact with several professional groups and social milieus, and he displays readiness to take part in the democratic transformation. It is not feasible that he will block any piece of legislation or any move by the government on the international arena.

The central state administration shows its loyalty to Mazowiecki's government. As a consequence of the coming elections to the local councils, which will almost certainly be won by Solidarity's citizens' committees, the personnel of the entire local administration will be changed. The process of replacing the lord mayors of several cities has already started, though not without some resistance from the old *nomenklatura* people still serving as representatives in local councils. This has been overcome with pressure from below (the population) and from above (the government). What remains a long-term aim is making the central and the local administrations competent and knowledgeable about how to act in a free-market economy and in accordance with democratic principles.

Freedom and Peace: Declaration of Principles

✦

The Freedom and Peace movement was one of several groups that emerged in Poland in the 1980s seeking to enunciate viable goals for the rebuilding of Polish society. This was one of those close to the Catholic church; others were entirely secular. Taken together, they spanned the whole political spectrum. Freedom and Peace issued its declaration in November 1985, indicating that it had branches in several Polish cities.

The "Freedom and Peace" movement was founded as an expression of the conviction that existing institutions and organizations fail to address issues and circumstances which people of good will should not ignore.

The struggle of human rights, for freedom of speech, press, and assembly, and for the freedom to organize associations is right and just. Right and just are the actions of the independent labor unions, which aim to protect workers from exploitation and injustice.

The Catholic Church, an institution of the highest authority, should be respected for its role as the representative and advocate of Polish national ideals and universal moral values. It is an indispensable part of the struggle for human rights to demand religious freedom, and to support the social and cultural initiatives connected with the Church.

The "Freedom and Peace" movement considers striving for national independence to be just. National oppression is an evil, and eliminating it will lead to freedom for nations and will bring about peace among them.

The "Freedom and Peace" movement takes as its first priority the struggle for human rights, religious freedom, and national independence.

At the present time, the world faces the imminent threat of war, the consequences of which may be irreversible for human civilization. Many Poles are not aware of the reality of this threat, and treat it as an invention of Communist propaganda. Many Poles are not aware of the seriousness of the threat of nuclear war, of the problem of militarism and of a militaristic education. The second priority of the "Freedom and Peace" movement is to change this situation.

Freedom and Peace, "Declaration of Principles," from *Across Frontiers*, Spring 1986, pp. 2–5. Reprinted by permission of the Across Frontiers Foundation.

Past experience indicates that political changes, though crucial, are unable to guarantee that love and truth will govern human relations.

The "Freedom and Peace" movement will disseminate knowledge which will enable man to understand human existence and man's place in the world. We will look to the attainments of Christian ethics, psychology, Eastern philosophies, and other branches of learning which treat man as a subject.

This is the third priority of the "Freedom and Peace" movement.

The "Freedom and Peace" movement takes non-violent resistance as its basic means of struggle against evil. Non-violence provides the most difficult, yet the most appropriate means for social struggle for human rights. It will be necessary to work out nonviolent tactics which will be effective in a communist totalitarian context.

We recognize that violence is morally justified in exceptional circumstances, for instance when life is endangered, particularly by mass extermination (e.g., the extermination of the Jews during World War II, or of the Cambodians under Pol Pot's regime).

✦

ISSUES
1. Human Rights

The attainment of basic human rights, such as the freedom to express one's own ideas and opinions, the freedom to organize labor unions and other associations, and full religious freedom provides the basis for deeper social change. The political system under which we live is characterized by perpetual violation and denial of these rights. Particularly important in this respect is the issue of prisoners' rights.

The "Freedom and Peace" movement wishes to concentrate on bringing about official recognition of the status of prisoners of conscience in Poland and throughout the world. The use of physical and psychological violence against prisoners is inadmissible. The "Freedom and Peace" movement will fight for the rights of prisoners, disseminate information about their situations, and organize relief action on their behalf.

We oppose capital punishment. Capital punishment is a disgrace of present-day legal systems.

In these matters, we wish to unite our efforts with those of organizations and institutions that have similar goals, such as "Amnesty International."

2. National Liberation

The "Freedom and Peace" movement will support the struggle of nations which have been the victims of the violence of foreign powers, be those powers national or ideological. It is unthinkable in the modern world that a nation which wishes to attain independence is politically prevented from doing so.

We support the efforts of ethnic groups and national minorities to achieve autonomy and greater control over their destiny.

The "Freedom and Peace" movement will demonstrate solidarity with those nations and minorities which demand their own rights.

We will support national minorities in Poland in their efforts to find an authentic institutional expression of their culture.

We will also take every opportunity to act on behalf of the rights of Poles who constitute a minority in other countries.

3. The Threat of War and the International Peace Movement

In view of the fact that the major threat to the modern world is nuclear annihilation, we will attempt to bring the enormity of this threat to the attention of Polish society. It is necessary to undo the currently militaristic character of education, both in the home and in the schools. It is time for the societies of East and West, which would find themselves adversaries in a future war, to undertake actions which would lead to dialogue and mutual understanding—especially in view of the failed attempts to do so made by their governments. Of particular importance to us is establishing closer relations with Germany, a nation separated from us by the catastrophes of recent history, yet bound so closely to us by a common danger.

The "Freedom and Peace" movement considers the demilitarization of Central Europe and the creation of a nuclear free zone there an absolute necessity. If accompanied by democratization of the East, this would decrease the danger of war.

At present, given the rift between the interests of the government and the aspirations of the Polish people, compulsory conscription violates people's consciences.

The oath of the Polish People's Army requires every soldier to pledge loyalty to the government as well as to the so-called "fraternal armies." Many individual soldiers find this text in conflict with their principles.

The "Freedom and Peace" movement plans to take action to change the text of the military oath, so that those who refuse to take it—such as Marek Adamkiewicz— would not face imprisonment for their beliefs.

Often military service is against an individual's moral, political, or religious beliefs. The "Freedom and Peace" movement seeks to win the right for draftees in Poland to perform alternative civilian service which is not threatening to life. Such an arrangement exists in many other countries.

We respect and appreciate the work of many organizations and institutions for world peace. The "Freedom and Peace" movement wants to become an integral part of these efforts. Therefore, the expressions of support and solidarity conveyed to us by Western Europe peace organizations such as **Comité pour le Désarmement Nucléaire en Europe** (CODENE), **Interkerkelijk Vredesberaad** (IKV), and **European Nuclear Disarmament** (END) are very valuable.

We wish to work together with the international peace movement. Of particular importance to us in this collaboration is recognition of the basic truth that we will not successfully oppose war if we do not overcome political systems based on state violence against citizens. For us—living in one such system—this is the first and most important step toward universal peace. We wish to proceed along this path together with all the independent peace movements in Europe and in the world.

4. Environmental Protection

In the face of the growing threat of destruction of the biosphere, the air, the water, and the soil, freedom should also mean this: the chance to live in an uncontaminated natural environment. At present, natural resources are being wasted, and the short-sighted policies of the authorities cause irreversible damage to the environment. Industry seeking to save on pollution-preventing devices is often the major cause of such damage. Poor management of natural resources leads to erosion of the soil, and the disappearance of forests and waters.

The "Freedom and Peace" movement will fight to make accessible information about the destruction of the natural environment.

Poland is not currently faced with the development of atomic energy plants. Nevertheless, industry's attempts to import nuclear technology—after the experiences of other countries—are a source of concern.

The "Freedom and Peace" movement will support those actions throughout the world whose aim is to safeguard the environment and ban nuclear testing.

5. World Hunger, Humanitarian Assistance

The "Freedom and Peace" movement considers hunger in the world today to be the greatest scandal of modern civilization. The demilitarization of Eastern Europe should serve not only to improve the fate of the Polish nation and her neighbors, but also to provide means of assistance to countries afflicted by poverty, famine, and death.

Although charity cannot substitute for structural social change, this does not absolve us from providing volunteer assistance to those who are in need of it.

This applies also to those suffering from poverty, sickness and loneliness in Poland.

The "Freedom and Peace" movement declares its willingness to cooperate with all organizations whose goal is to help the needy.

6. Human Development

Modern man faces several fundamental questions: What is the sense of human existence? How does one form and maintain relations with one's family and friends, as well as with people in general? How does one deal with personal and psychological problems?

The "Freedom and Peace" movement plans to organize and encourage lectures, publications, and other means of helping people to find their own direction in life.

7. Tolerance

Within our movement, the basis for cooperation by people of differing world views is tolerance and understanding of the fact that there are many possible approaches to solving the world's problems.

We will be united by our opposition to evil, to oppression, to intolerance, and to indifference to suffering.

The "Freedom and Peace" Movement, Gdańsk, Kraków, Warsaw, Wrocław

November 17, 1985
Machowa near Tarnów

The Demise of Solidarity and the Prospects for Democracy

✦

Janine R. Wedel

A veteran observer of the Polish scene since the formation of Solidarity examines the changes overtaking that movement as it began, in 1989, to shift from opposition to a positive effort to assist in Poland's reconstruction. She notes the inevitable loss of internal consensus and the reduced popular appeal as the organization began its second legalization and then entered into the government on the heels of its electoral landslide.

The West's euphoria over this year's news from Poland—the electoral triumph of Solidarity and its takeover of the prime ministership—is in many ways understandable. But it is evidence of a misperception about what Solidarity is and what it is likely to achieve. Factionalism, divisions, and authoritarian leadership within Solidarity are not what Americans, for example, want to hear about now. But it is important that the

Janine R. Wedel, "Lech's Labors Lost?" from *World Monitor,* November 1989, pp. 43–54. Reprinted by permission of Janine R. Wedel.

Anticommunism in Cracow, February 1990. By 1989–1990, dissent in Poland had turned into open, virulent anticommunism. Here, demonstrators protest an incident of police brutality. (Eric Miller/Impact Visuals)

problems be recognized, because the prospects for democracy in Poland are real, though more remote than many Americans imagine.

My information comes from visiting Poland seven times over 13 years—and spending about half the 1980s there—as an anthropologist studying the country. I was there under martial law working on my Ph.D. thesis. Like the Poles, I experienced the knock on the door at 5 in the morning, the strip searches, the tear gas in my apartment during demonstrations, the camaraderie, the arrests of close friends.

I got to know many Solidarity leaders, some of whom were fugitives or in jail, and some of whom are now elected members of the national legislature. Although I didn't know it at the time, Wojciech Arkuszewski, who was in hiding in a flat next to mine, is a close friend and adviser to the new prime minister, Tadeusz Mazowiecki.

A year ago I went back to Poland to do more research, and returned to the United States after the elections in June. Let me address Western misperceptions of Poland by first spelling out what has *not* been misperceived. The failure of the Communist government to serve the needs of Poland since World War II and the intense, and almost universal, resentment of this among Poles as reflected in their recent landslide vote against the Communists—these are real.

I traveled with candidates during campaigning for the June 4 election and heard one phrase again and again: "We don't want to be ruled by Communists." Even Communist Party candidates tried to position themselves as anti-Communist and avoided any rhetoric that might identify them with the traditional policies of their own party.

I sat for hours after the election with humiliated party apparatchiks as they lamented the sudden turn in their life's work. The party is bankrupt ideologically and has offered no credible new programs. The strongest campaign slogan it could muster in the recent election was "*Our* Faults Are Known." A political system that appeals to its people on such a platform has lowered its expectations virtually to ground level. Few new members, young or old, are joining the party. Many members use the term "disintegration" to describe the state of the party.

On the day after the election I dropped by the Communist Party club in the city of Kraków and found a demoralized lot. As party member and journalist Zbigniew Regucki told me, regretfully and humbly, recovery will be difficult and not only because party members are disheartened by the results. "My children don't even want to *hear* about the party," he admitted.

My doubt is not about who lost the election. My doubt is about who—or what—won.

◆

SOLIDARITY DIVIDED BY THREE

Americans envision Solidarity as two things: a labor union and a political party with nearly total public support. But the roles of a labor union and a political party are, at times, downright incompatible. Furthermore, in its early years Solidarity filled yet another role, perhaps the most important of all: a mass social movement, the source of national pride and unity for Poles.

As long as the Communists dominated the country and Solidarity's only task was opposing them, the natural inconsistency of these three roles wasn't evident. As the Communists weakened, Solidarity's innate problems rose to the surface.

Solidarity, in fact, had gone into marked decline when the Communists reinvigorated it last winter while looking for a way out of a political crisis. The economy was in shambles. Between 1980 and 1987, the purchasing power of most Polish working families, not great to begin with, fell by nearly 17%, according to the government's own statistics. And yet Poland, like other debtor nations, was under pressure from Western financial institutions to impose austerity measures to pay its debts. This would further tighten the belt on workers who believed they were backbone-against-bellybutton already.

The government saw only one way to impose further austerity without touching off massive strikes and possible civil violence. That was to seek the collaboration of Solidarity, which, ironically, was already in rather close agreement on the key issue of austerity economic planning.

Many other Poles, however, certainly many intellectual leaders, wanted to move more rapidly away from central economic planning. Many Solidarity activists, having emerged jobless from martial-law prisons, started businesses or other private organizations. They redirected their efforts from explicitly political to economic activity and preached a new philosophy: Form a club or lobby to do what needs doing and finance it yourself in the marketplace.

For Poles, "entrepreneurship" and private "organizing" have rapidly become tickets to influence in public life. Leaders in the Communist Party and Solidarity alike have been jumping on these bandwagons.

I recently talked with Mieczyslaw Wilczek, successful businessman and minister of industry until the Communist government collapsed, and Aleksander Paszynski, who resigned his position as editor in chief of the influential official weekly *Polityka* in protest against martial law. Communist and oppositionist echoed each other's positions: Both avidly supported the liquidation of state ownership and each formed an organization that lobbied the government to ease restrictions on private enterprise. (In September Paszynski was named minister of housing in the new Solidarity government and now presumably will be lobbied himself.)

Last spring, after much stalling and secret negotiation, the Communists decided to re-legalize Solidarity and to invite its leadership into talks—the so-called Round Table discussions. The Communists hoped that, with a united front, the two groups could implement the austerity program both supported. Clearly, the Communists got a lot more than they bargained for:

✦

AND THE COLLECTIVE KNEE JERKED

Solidarity insisted on open elections. The Communists acceded, believing they had rigged the rules so as to ensure their own continued domination of government. Solidarity would be allowed official minority representation, which would help legitimize the austerity program. Since even partially free elections were a novelty in Poland, hardly anyone—not even Solidarity's veteran leader Lech Wałęsa—expected that, with the first opportunity ever to kick at the Communists, the country's collective knee would jerk forward so forcefully.

The country kicked. And that is what led to this summer's dizzying leadership changes. But to believe that all this means a revolutionary change in Polish life is to confuse Solidarity now with Solidarity in 1981 and to ignore the bureaucratic infrastructure that the Communists built during nearly 45 years in power.

Following the Round Table, Solidarity rejuvenated itself in an organizational surge, creating local chapters, election bureaus, and campaigns almost overnight. According to one estimate, 49 committees sprang up in the course of 12 days. The campaign renewed enthusiasm among full-time activists and politicians, who had been starved of public forums during the previous eight years. But Solidarity failed to reawaken its former level of support.

Like the communism it came into being to resist, Solidarity faces an identity and generational crisis, and its backing over the long term is not clear. Both Solidarity and the Communist Party are undergoing extraordinary change in their constituencies and identities. The degree to which they are inspired, organized, and controlled from central supreme leaderships also is coming into question.

Organizational efforts are weaker than in Solidarity's heyday, and far fewer people are joining as full, steadily involved members.

+ Three weeks after Solidarity's legalization in 1980, the organization had 3 million members.

+ More than two months after its second legalization in 1989, Solidarity press spokesman Janusz Onyszkiewicz reported having half that membership.

+ In the region of Rzeszów, two months after legalization the union had barely 10% of the members it attracted during the corresponding period of 1980.

+ In the mining region of Katowice, once a Solidarity stronghold, only 10% of the workers in one large mine had signed up, compared with 70% eight years before.

+ Wałęsa's chief of staff, Leszek Kaczynski, predicts that 4 million Poles will sign up by year's end; 9 million did in 1981.

Many of those whose lives were so altered by Solidarity in 1980–81 are today cautious and weary. An elementary school teacher remembered how nine years ago almost all of her colleagues rallied to set up a chapter in her school the moment Solidarity arose. But now only 5 of 45 had joined by June.

✦

THE KITCHEN OF MARIA KRZYWONOS

What has made the difference? The most common answer from organizers is that, having seen the promises of earlier days dissolve, having lived through a decade of frustration and decline, people are skeptical about whether anything will effect meaningful improvements.

"People have distanced themselves—they simply don't believe," the teacher noted.

A decade ago, before it was broken apart by the martial-law government, Solidarity was a broad-based, populist movement, creating unprecedented ties among intellectuals, workers, and farmers that shattered the traditional barriers within Poland's class-bound society. The surge of revivalism that transformed these interpersonal relationships awakened an idealism and euphoria difficult to convey to those who did not experience it.

This time, in contrast with 1980–81, Solidarity is more successful in farming regions than in the cities, and many villages are more systematically organized than before. Maria Krzywonos, adviser to Rural Solidarity leader Józef Slisz, now a senator, is one reason. The mother of seven children, she nursed her youngest baby as we talked in her farmhouse kitchen. Krzywonos helped to bring villagers together for informal political teach-ins during martial law. Before such efforts, she explained, the countryside did not present a unified opposition. Now the objective of many country folk is simple—to get rid of government controls and bureaucracy, goals easily expressed in terms of "us" against "them."

In most of Poland, a once indivisible Solidarity is no longer united. It is divided within workplaces and between generations. A young generation of radicals—most of whom were barely in junior high school when Solidarity was born—won't have anything to do with Wałęsa's group. The still-underground "Fighting Solidarity," a small but burningly intense youthful faction, regards agreements with the authorities as corrupt bargains and refused to participate in the Round Table. Members of "Fighting Solidarity" often talk of "our lack of life prospects"—a quite moderate assessment of the average 15-year wait for an apartment, the unstable and rapidly declining living standards and morale.

There were other small, radical factions that boycotted the elections. A spokesman for one group not represented at the Round Table complained bitterly to me as he chain-smoked in his one-room apartment, which he shares with his mother. "We gained nothing from the Round Table," he said. "Solidarity has become a new establishment."

For many activists who lived and breathed Solidarity before and after it was forced underground in 1981 the name no longer speaks of hope and truth. Magda Nagorska's experience is typical of many. At the dawning of Solidarity, Nagorska, a journalist, felt she finally could pursue her profession with integrity, first for legal Solidarity publications and later underground. After nine years of secret, anonymous sacrifice without credit from any but her most trusted colleagues, she no longer devotes a majority of her time to the cause. Her disillusionment stems from years of intimate collaboration with a leadership that came to exploit the organization for patronage, self-promotion, and honor.

"Then Solidarity meant moral togetherness—mutual ethics and honor and sacrifice," said Nagorska. "Now it is only political business."

◆

WHY THEY BOOED WAŁĘSA

What groups legal Solidarity will draw on for its mass membership is an open question. Most members now are blue-collar veterans of 1981 Solidarity. In contrast with the formative years, young people and managers, engineers and professionals in industry are conspicuously absent.

Solidarity has always been more than a trade union, but even as a trade union it seems to be losing momentum. Like the Communist regime, it has its main support in large, outmoded, unproductive factories that the government is closing one by one. Even at enterprises that remain open, Solidarity—as a trade union called on to defend workers' rights—finds itself at odds with the most dynamic new doctrine that has swept through the educated Polish community in recent years: economic reform through free-market libertarianism.

Solidarity has not caught up with the economic reformers among its former supporters, who advocate closing unproductive enterprises even if this creates unemployment. Although such libertarian ideas find avid individual supporters within both Solidarity and the Communist Party, they challenge the purpose, indeed the raison d'être, of both organizations.

Poland's standard of living seems likely to sink further, and many expect this to trigger wildcat strikes not called by Solidarity. Under such circumstances, at both local and national levels Solidarity will face the uneasy choice to back or not to back the strikes. Solidarity members joined many of last year's walkouts, although Solidarity had not organized them. If its local units initiate or support such strikes, the center might try to face down the locals—but it cannot count on maintaining discipline and control.

Last fall, Wałęsa himself was called in to conciliate a strike in the Katowice mines but had to leave after being booed by striking miners and threatened with being chucked out in a wheelbarrow. Local Solidarity organizer Danuta Skorenko, who witnessed the event, could scarcely contain her apprehension about the coming months. As we talked in a dingy restaurant, she trembled.

"A mounting wave of strikes that cannot necessarily be controlled by Solidarity awaits us," she confided. "As a trade union, we have to defend workers. We'll have to join spontaneous strikes or risk being considered Reds. I think Solidarity as a trade union will fall apart. A third force is coming into play—the younger generation. They don't believe much in Solidarity, and they're more rigid and uncompromising."

While many in the West see Solidarity's entrance into the government as a long overdue triumph for the movement, Solidarity itself has reacted with cautious restraint. "We did too well," Wojciech Arkuszewski, a close aide to now-Prime Minister Mazowiecki, told me when he stopped by for dinner a few days after the election.

Prior to the election, Solidarity's legitimacy and success largely depended on the Communists' being permanently in power and permanently embarrassed. Now the movement has to share both the power and the embarrassment. Solidarity is in danger of being blamed for the country's next disasters without having had time to prevent them.

Even after Solidarity's June landslide, the movement's leaders resisted taking power, although the Communists repeatedly invited them into the government. But the country confronts such colossal problems that Solidarity's leaders have joined a coalition with their former jailers, not because they're fond of them but simply to prevent widespread anarchy. If Solidarity flees from responsibility at a time of such national crisis, it risks being discredited both at home and abroad. Thus, reluctantly— out of a sense of self-preservation, not achievement—Solidarity, moral watchdog and voice of protest, suddenly entered the political arena.

✦

REBELS WITH OLD SCHOOL TIES

Like the Communist Party, Solidarity has had very little experience that would prepare it to build consensus democratically within its own organization, to encourage broad-based grass-roots political participation, or to negotiate with other political groups. Many professional oppositionists, including the new prime minister, earned their status by devoting their lives to conspiracy and suffering the consequences dealt out by Communist authorities.

Solidarity and the preceding 15 years of opposition movements excelled in conspiracy, rhetoric, and symbolic protest, not in democratic processes like accommodation, consensus, and compromise. As one activist put it, "We haven't learned the culture of parliamentary democracy."

Being an oppositionist was a 24-hour-a-day occupation with many cult-like aspects: One spent hours every day with people who shared the same world view. Contacts outside the group became less important and eventually were cut off, and within these circles guru-type leaders arose who were revered and obeyed. The inner circle provided a family-like "normal" environment for people who felt lonely in Poland's atomized society. Loyalty to the group, of utmost significance, was enforced with vigor. For disloyalty, one risked losing friends as well as the economic support provided by the group's access to well-supplied informal markets in an economy beset with shortages of goods.

This was a very exclusive group. Most oppositionists came from intellectual families who had lived in Warsaw for generations. Many had parents who went to school together or fought in the wartime resistance together. Those who became leaders tended to be privileged enough not to have to worry about material needs. Well-known oppositionists Jacek Kuroń and Adam Michnik were unemployed most of their lives and thus could devote full time to their opposition activities.

There were people who resented the elitist nature of the opposition milieu. Veteran oppositionist Arkuszewski once confided to me exactly why he resisted leadership positions:

"People were imprisoned in the opposition circle because there was no life for them outside of it. They could not live any other life, and that is why they easily surrendered to the strong discipline and authorities of the opposition."

Arkuszewski noted that the hierarchy in opposition circles was more clearly defined than it was in other Polish settings:

"Everyone knew who was most important, whose opinion counted most, who was less important, and who didn't count at all."

In 1980–81, Solidarity's first free period, Poles publicly called for accountability, openness, and democratic process. The birth of Solidarity as a legalized organization created a structure of formal relations and groups within the movement, which thousands of new people joined.

But the old cliques still influenced who got what and who could sway whom. With the imposition of martial law and the outlawing of Solidarity in 1981, these long-established allegiances enabled Solidarity to survive through eight years of underground operation. And, with the re-legalization of Solidarity, some of these alliances have surfaced to carry out political activities openly. Throughout the recent campaign, election, and aftermath, Lech Wałęsa and his inner circle continued to operate from the old-style allegiances.

◆

A HANDFUL OF THE CHOSEN

Dissent from within the ranks stems from allegations that Wałęsa and those closest to him did not act democratically because of the highly structured choice presented to voters in the recent election: They could choose only between a slate put forward by the ruling Communists and another advanced by a non-institutional but very tightly knit inner circle of about ten seasoned oppositionists formed around Wałęsa.

I spent many hours in private apartments interviewing leaders close to the inner circle and hanging out at Solidarity headquarters. They behaved more like a handful of the chosen calling upon the nation to follow them than like the leaders of a broad-based de facto political party (noncommunist groups are not officially recognized as political parties in Poland). This was, at least in part, a conscious strategy: The inner circle's objective was to fill all possible seats and to maintain a central authority in choosing candidates.

Many candidates promoted by Wałęsa's group were enthusiastically endorsed in their assigned regions. But in several regions, local groups with their own candidates argued sharply with the powers in Warsaw. Disputes invariably were resolved in favor of Wałęsa's group.

Some activists outside the innermost circle—and even some inside it—denounced the lack of democracy in these procedures. They alleged, for example, that many of the movement's diverse elements were passed over—especially the more hot-headed, and several people who had been hand-picked by Cardinal Józef Glemp, primate of the Roman Catholic Church in Poland.

Some of those associated with the inner circle were open in acknowledging the validity of such allegations. During his Senate campaign, Józef Slisz was stridently challenged on the nomination procedures at a campaign meeting I attended in a town parish. "From the beginning it wasn't democratic," he replied. "You can create democracy if you aren't up against a system that has all the power. We have to be realists."

◆

THE WRONG COMMUNISTS WON

The spring campaign heightened expectations that the people actually could have a say in how they are governed. It was the first experience many Poles had with the idea that someone in legislative office could represent them. But people did not vote *for* reform programs or platforms, nor did they reflect on the differences in the merits or political positions of candidates.

Many candidates deliberately avoided discussing programs for the future. Thus, the election was not the culmination of a process designed to develop policies for the future but a vote against the past.

In the main election, Solidarity carried nearly half the seats in the Sejm (lower house) and newly formed Senate combined. The Communist coalition hung on to barely half the total seats it had occupied without challenge just weeks before. But the biggest blow—for both sides—was suffered when only two of those on the "national list," a bloc of 35 seats in the Sejm for which only Communists could present themselves, survived the initial election.

A successful grass-roots movement, *not* endorsed by Solidarity's leaders, had urged voters to "cross off the Communists" on the national ballot. Struck down were members of the Communist establishment—including heads of the three Communist alliance coalition parties, the premier, and the speaker of the Sejm—who were the very reformers who had made the election possible.

This forced a run-off in which the guaranteed Communist seats were won by more uncompromising candidates whom the party had substituted for the moderates. Many gained office with the support of only 2% to 3% of the votes cast. And this, in turn, led to a parliamentary standoff, the defection of two parties in the Communist coalition (the Peasants Party and the Democratic Party), and the stunning selection of a Solidarity man as prime minister.

Very different but almost equally powerful obstacles make it impossible for any one political force to govern Poland alone or with full authority. The three main political players—the Communists, Solidarity, and the Catholic Church—are cooperating with one another out of sheer desperation. None of the players is proposing a complete overhaul of the bureaucratic and economic system, and none has the resources to implement such change.

Solidarity is attempting to maintain stability, not foment revolution. This is why Wałęsa conceded on his own initiative that the Communists should retain their absolute authority over the army and the police.

Solidarity's ability to govern Poland is shackled: The Communist Party maintains a grip on executive and management positions in nearly all spheres of government and administration. Under this system of privilege, known as *nomenklatura,* a tangle of loyalties and favoritisms precludes broader political and social participation by noncommunist Poles. Moreover, the entire economy is without resources and without much likelihood of being bailed out by the West. For the time being, the impoverished, incompetent bureaucratic and economic system will remain in place; Solidarity doesn't have the wealth or the apparatus skills to replace it.

The country's almost insurmountable economic problems and this obstacle to real power are the main reasons that, until recently, Solidarity persistently refused to enter into a coalition with the Communists. Shortly after the election Solidarity press secretary Onyszkiewicz explained why. No Solidarity minister, he said, would be able to work efficiently with a *nomenklatura* staff selected during the past 40 years for loyalty to the party.

Although the Communists are not yet out the door, many Poles believe that, in the future, their bread will more likely be buttered by Solidarity than by the Communists. The Communist coalition, rock-solid for 40 years, has crumbled.

And we are also witnessing a true identity crisis in Solidarity. As it enters the corrupt world of Communist politics and attempts to deal with the country's entrenched problems, Solidarity is caught in a quandary.

The movement's legitimacy in the eyes of many of its supporters, not to mention its positive world image, largely depends on its ability to exercise a responsible role in the Polish government. Yet its reputation as an untainted and uncompromising moral force seems sure to become tarnished. The organization can expect factionalism, blame, and loss of its old integrity as it struggles with the tough choices of political office.

◆

DESPERATE TO SHARE THE BLAME

The latent drag of many Communist institutions that will survive even under a Solidarity government and the lack of a really democratic decision-making process within Solidarity itself will sorely inhibit the Solidarity administration's ability to make progress.

The economic crisis is what induced the Communists to invite Solidarity to dinner in the first place. Now the continuing crisis could work against the Solidarity administration and capsize it in a single dramatic moment. Things haven't been improving.

Steep inflation, 7% to 9% monthly, raised prices by 50% in the first six months of 1989. Food costs were increasing almost daily even before price controls on some goods were lifted, causing prices to jump as much as fourfold overnight. Sources in the Ministry of Finance say money is being printed day and night. Poles are on shaky ground when they budget in their own currency.

Publisher Lech Stefanski debated how to handle a tripling of his publication costs in two months' time. He paid 180,000 złotys to produce his independent magazine in June, compared to 58,000 złotys two months before and 30,000 złotys a year before that.

Both the Communists and Solidarity say that such unpopular austerities as wage freezes must be implemented. As a former Communist Party apparatchik told me after the rushed election schedule was announced: "The authorities are in such a hurry to hold elections not out of eagerness to share power with Solidarity, but because they are absolutely desperate to share the blame."

Ridiculous as this looked to some Westerners, that is exactly why Wałęsa and his group fidgeted for weeks, even summoning their former nemesis, Gen. Wojciech Jaruzelski, to be head of state, before finally offering up one of their own as prime minister.

◆

HANGING ON TO THE WELFARE STATE

Even under a Solidarity-led government, the potential for volatility is considerable. Wildcat strikes and protests might lead to police intervention and the suspension of trade unions. Newly chosen Sen. Krzysztof Kozłowski, deputy head of an influential Catholic weekly, cautioned shortly after the election celebrations had worn off:

"People are impatient because of the worsening economy. There are forces such as spontaneous strikes that can't be controlled by the Opposition, Solidarity, Church or Party. . . . We want very fast changes, but they may turn out to be too slow, given the state of people's nerves and their stamina."

And while Wałęsa and his team of advisers from the labor union core of Solidarity agree on an austerity program—only a quibble or two away from the Communist program—many who were part of the pro-Solidarity consensus at the polls disagree. Among Solidarity's strongest supporters are a burgeoning intellectual army of what are known in Poland as "liberals," for their 19th-century forebears, although the term might confuse some Americans. Their ultimate goal may be a free-market/government mix not unlike that favored by American liberals. But, given Poland's communist history, these activists are now fully bent on pushing capitalism.

The liberals are vocal and stir public discussion but have less chance to implement their policies than their outspoken proponents assert. Liberal spokesman Janusz Korwin-Mikke says that unemployment is not a problem and that the only concern of an enterprise should be profit. But as strong as is the reaction against communism, public opinion surveys show that meat-and-potatoes socialist values are widely endorsed by the population. Guaranteed jobs, housing, medical care, and social security benefits are generally favored.

Even Poles who choose lucrative private employment feel they should be entitled to the same social welfare benefits as state workers. Eighty percent surveyed in a 1989 University of Kraków study expected paid vacations, free health care, and nurseries at the workplace, and they viewed employment in the private sector as temporary and essentially insecure.

With everyone facing the same crises, the we/they divisions of the past are crumbling. New trends and interests cut across the three major organizations, dissolving divisions and creating new alliances. The Communist Party, Solidarity, and the Catholic Church all speak of economic and political reform, democracy, and pluralism. Powerful elements in both the party and Solidarity advocate socialist values. But almost everyone, including party officials, is anti-communist.

Solidarity's entrance into the government is the beginning of the end, but Poland cannot be transformed overnight. The forces of change may have generated political effects that astounded all participants, but the forces of continuity run deep. None of the leaders and very few of the followers want to press matters to an unresolvable extreme. The directions of Polish political and economic life—the redefining of communism, the evolution toward a competitive party system, and the struggle to displace an entrenched bureaucracy—make for an ambitious agenda and depend on the continued indulgence of the Soviet leaders.

By voting down the Communists, Poles have called for renewal. The challenge for the new coalition government is to keep that renewal from igniting into a full-fledged rebellion with possibly anarchic and international consequences. While the new government strives to maintain stability, it also will have to become more open and accountable as the party, Solidarity, and the Polish people learn constitutionalism and democracy.

Poland's March Toward Capitalism

✦

Jan B. de Weydenthal

A specialist on Poland for Radio Free Europe notes the obstacles that have appeared as the government pursues the transition from planned economy to a free market system. The early success of the program had begun to look questionable to some Poles and may have difficult political repercussions.

Nobody ever said it would be easy to bring capitalism to Poland. But with communist policies and practices publicly rejected and Western aid and advice proliferating, there has been a tendency to assume that the country is at least on the fast track toward reaching that goal. The Polish government has, after all, eliminated price controls and subsidies, embraced privatization, and taken a major step toward the convertibility of the złoty. All these actions have been lauded by economic experts everywhere and have received backing from the public at home. Now, six months after the introduction of these sweeping changes, major problems have surfaced that may endanger the government's program.

✦

THE PERILS OF SUCCESS

Some of those problems seem to have arisen in spite of and even because of the very success of government policies, which have been very successful, indeed. Following the implementation on January 1, 1990, of a series of economic changes designed to stabilize the economy, the monthly rate of inflation was reduced from about 78% in January to 5% in May; currency exchange rates stabilized (at about 9,500

Jan B. de Weydenthal, "Poland's March Toward Capitalism," from *Report on Eastern Europe,* July 20, 1990, pp. 32–34. Reprinted with the permission of Radio Free Europe/Radio Liberty.

złoty to the dollar); the country's current account in trade with Western countries showed a surplus of more than US $1,200,000 at the beginning of May; and, most important, once perennial shortages of consumer goods have largely been eliminated. All this has created the impression that a new economic system has already taken root in Poland.

Of course, the costs of this success were high. For example, as a result of the government's anti-inflation policy, industrial output by state-owned industries declined during the first five months of this year by more than 30%, a much larger drop than the government had anticipated. Considering that the state owns more than 80% of all industrial enterprises, the repercussions of this fall were serious in terms of unemployment. According to recent government figures, more than 500,000 people, or about 4% of the work force, were registered as unemployed by mid-June. The government also reported that if conditions did not change, the number of unemployed would exceed 1,300,000 by the end of the year. This development would certainly contribute to a major decline in the standard of living, which is already very low. Indeed, during the first five months of this year, the public's real income fell by almost 45% compared with last year, and six out of every 10 Poles are now said to be poor or very poor; this group includes most of the country's 7,000,000 or so pensioners.

The recession was, of course, anticipated by the authorities, although its magnitude is regarded as both serious and disappointing. The government recently said that it would "propose a set of measures that will focus on the supply side and reactivate the economy in a noninflationary way." These measures are to include budgetary adjustments to boost state spending in certain areas, such as housing; new rules liberalizing trade; and a major emphasis on the privatization of both industrial assets and services.

This is easier said than done, however. The government has already experienced serious problems in persuading ordinary citizens to become directly involved in the economy through private investment independent of government operations. Paradoxically, considering that privatization has received considerable attention from the government, people's apparent reluctance to help build up a capitalist economy is a result of the government's action, in that the authorities' policy of austerity has effectively depleted private financial resources. Although the total of cash in circulation plus bank savings remained virtually constant from the first quarter of 1989 to the first quarter of 1990, in the face of galloping inflation, the public's real purchasing power has declined sharply. Under these circumstances, with the great uncertainty about what is to come next, ordinary people cannot be expected to invest in industrial enterprises or to set up new businesses. This leaves the investing to people who might have gotten rich under the "old" system or who have ties abroad. But, in the eyes of many, letting some of these people buy industrial property undermines the very validity of the new system by opening it to charges of being no more than a means for the communist *nomenklatura* to legitimize its long-held privileges (justified in the past on the grounds of ideology and politics) within a new economic framework.

◆
POLITICAL CONSEQUENCES

Popular acceptance of economic policies has always been crucial to their success. This has been particularly so in the case of the Polish government's "march to capitalism," since its very viability depends on the public's ability to put up with austerity and its approval of the changes. And the public has been very supportive of the government. No major protests were registered during the first five months of the year, and there was no serious challenge to the concepts on which the government's economic policy rested. Popular acquiescence in the way the government conducts its affairs may weaken in the future, however.

The first warning that things were becoming difficult was a strike by railway workers, who succeeded in paralyzing the country's major transportation lines for more than a week in May. There have been numerous public protests against the growing economic difficulties since then, which have involved private farmers as well as workers in selected industries. Some of those protests were settled by negotiation between the government and the protesters, frequently with the help of Solidarity leader Lech Wałęsa. There is little doubt, however, that protests will continue, and it is likely that they will intensify.

The probability of such conflicts is enhanced by the government's stated determination to continue its policies of austerity and tightly controlled development. "The government does not intend to turn away from its program [of budgetary controls and fiscal restrictions], because that would endanger what has already been achieved," said Finance Minister Leszek Balcerowicz, a man widely regarded as the architect of the government's economic program, in a recent statement to the Sejm. The government believes that such determination is crucial for the continuation of its program; but could the government not be affected by public dissatisfaction with its policies?

The question is particularly relevant in a situation in which domestic politics have become increasingly turbulent and, as the recent local elections suggest, the public may be getting tired of and disillusioned with the current programs. (In the local government elections the turnout barely exceeded 40% of the electorate; the turnout in the 1989 parliamentary elections had been more than 62%.) In the opinion of some Polish politicians, the apparently growing alienation of the public from politics could well lead to sudden outbursts of dissatisfaction and protest.

The current political debates center largely on personalities: on Wałęsa, on the one hand, and Prime Minister Tadeusz Mazowiecki and several other established political figures, on the other. Underlying these personal conflicts, however, is a major controversy over the pace and scope of change within the newly established political system; Wałęsa advocates the speeding up and broadening of the changes, and his opponents insist on the need for a deliberate and controlled political evolution so as to preserve the stability of the government and the continuity of its operations. In this context, economic problems have a major political importance, because they affect the interests of the public as a whole.

Indeed, economic questions have featured prominently in the political debates, although no alternatives to the current program have been presented. The discussion has instead centered on the social consequences of the various decisions and measures. That concern over these matters is fully justified, and such debates are very much needed. The current program of economic change was devised largely by economic experts and government officials, with little or no input from the public. The program was conceived as an alternative to old communist policies and methods and was supported by the public basically for that reason. Now, after initial success in changing the basis for the economy as a whole, there is a growing feeling that major adjustments in the program should be made to satisfy immediate public interests. Some people believe that such adjustments should be a matter for political rather than narrowly economic debate. The results of this debate will determine the final success or failure of the Polish "march to capitalism."

The First Hundred Days of Wałęsa's Presidency

◆

Jan B. de Weydenthal

In a later *Report on Eastern Europe* the same author assesses the first three months of Wałęsa's handling of the presidency, noting the dominance he has given to the office and his flexibility in exercising power.

On December 9, 1990, Lech Wałęsa became Poland's first head of state to be elected by direct popular vote; he was inaugurated as President of the Republic of Poland on December 22. Over the ensuing three months, the Presidency emerged as the dominant institution within the Polish system of government, affecting not only the operations of the state's administrative and legislative bodies but also the style and character of the country's politics. Furthermore, the general public has increasingly come to regard the Presidency as the center of decision making. These developments may have a lasting influence on the nascent democratic political system as a whole, laying the foundations for a strong presidential authority.

Jan B. de Weydenthal, "The First Hundred Days of Wałęsa's Presidency," from *Report on Eastern Europe,* April 5, 1991, pp. 9–11. Reprinted with the permission of Radio Free Europe/Radio Liberty.

In many respects, this turn of events was predictable, considering Wałęsa's popularity and prestige as well as his leadership qualities. Being elected President by direct popular vote simply vested him with an institutional authority that could be neither challenged nor matched by any other political figure in the country. At the same time, Wałęsa's political ascendancy demonstrated anew the continuing weakness and fragility of other state institutions, particularly the national legislature, which has remained divided by internal differences and been rendered ineffective by a lack of public support.

Since his inauguration, Wałęsa has consciously sought to assert his decision-making authority, both by expanding his influence over the executive branch of the government and by providing members of his personal staff with the power to influence government operations in the areas of national defense, foreign affairs, local government, and the economy. After appointing as Prime Minister Jan Krzysztof Bielecki, a veteran Wałęsa supporter and activist from a small liberal party, the President played an active role in selecting the members of Bielecki's government, and he approved their candidacies before they became known to the public. Wałęsa also appointed several influential political activists to posts on his staff and set up a council of experts to advise him on political, administrative, and legislative matters.

Wałęsa's actions caused an uproar among his opponents and critics, many of whom read in them a threat of incipient authoritarianism. That criticism had little or no effect either on the public or on Wałęsa himself. The authority to make all those moves was derived from the current constitution, which provides the President with considerable latitude for action. Inasmuch as it was clear to the public that Wałęsa had neither broken nor circumvented any laws, his critics only succeeded in drawing still more attention to him, reinforcing the general impression that he had become the central figure in all political activities.

✦

A SENSE OF FAILURE

The President's success in expanding his political power base is especially significant in view of his apparent failure to fulfill his frequently repeated campaign promises. Wałęsa had vowed to speed up economic reform and to streamline government operations, but since the election there has been no noticeable improvement in those areas. Economic difficulties rather than receding have, in fact, intensified: productivity has declined, and inflation in January and February exceeded the projected rates. Moreover, attempts to accelerate the privatization of state enterprises have largely failed. In short, since Wałęsa took office, there has been little or no change in the economic system, which still operates in accordance with management practices developed under communist rule; this situation has severely restricted the growth of a market economy.

This situation could not but have a major impact on Wałęsa, who by now must realize that speeding up things, given the large, frequently cumbersome machinery of government, is very difficult. He must also be aware that economic change depends on factors (international financial institutions, for example) beyond the control of Poland's political leaders and that the current political conditions, characterized by a national legislature that is paralyzed by its own divisiveness, make rapid change unlikely. All this, though valid, does not alter the fact that no major changes have been introduced or are in the offing in the foreseeable future.

This point was not lost on the general public. According to a report on a recent public opinion poll that measured the popular approval rating of various politicians and other public figures, Wałęsa's popularity had slipped by 11 percentage points from December to February: from 63% to 52%. (In the same poll, Cardinal Józef Glemp rated 70% and Foreign Affairs Minister Krzysztof Skubiszewski 52%.)

Wałęsa's supporters and critics also sensed the atmosphere of failure. One of his most vocal supporters in the press recently admitted that "there is no speeding up. . . . Everything is at a standstill." Wałęsa's own Chief of Staff, Jarosław Kaczynski, bluntly commented in an interview, "Speeding up will [have to come] later." Wałęsa's critics went even further, deploring his manners and style, recalling his various "gaffes," and complaining about his allegedly "erratic behavior." For example, a former minister in Tadeusz Mazowiecki's cabinet scoffed at the style of the President's public pronouncements, suggesting that Wałęsa indulged in "populist" slogans instead of using rational arguments when discussing the country's economic and political problems.

In a particularly harsh criticism, two noted journalists claimed that some of the President's instructions had confused rather than streamlined the government's operations; that relations between the Presidency and the Sejm had been damaged repeatedly because of the clumsy treatment of the legislators by Wałęsa's aides and the contemptuous tone of the President's messages to the Sejm; that both Wałęsa and his staff had failed to understand or had ignored how some government institutions operated, resulting in administrative delays; and that Wałęsa's interference in the parliament had slowed down rather than facilitated the legislative process. Both journalists concluded that the "start of [Wałęsa's] term of office could hardly be regarded as successful."

Wałęsa's leadership style has hardly made his task any easier. His sending of Sławomir Siwek, a ranking member of his staff, to attend all meetings of the Council of Ministers and listen to its deliberations was constitutionally permissible but suggested an attempt to interfere in the council's work. His demand that the Sejm change its procedures for funding local governments, without, however, bothering to propose how the budget might be altered or how the necessary additional funds might be raised to implement the proposed change, only succeeded in antagonizing the deputies, who promptly vetoed the demand. His instruction that the government's main auditing body, the Supreme Chamber of Control, initiate an internal audit was rejected with a stern reminder from the chamber's director that the President had no legal authority to order such an audit. Finally, his attempt to force the Sejm to accept a constitutional amendment and new electoral rules for the forthcoming parliamentary elections (the purpose of both actions being to advance the date of the elections) backfired when the deputies voted to reject the amendment and to set a later date for the elections.

◆
THE GAME OF POLITICS

Clearly, Wałęsa's first three months in office were a time of learning. Accustomed to projecting the relaxed manner of a populist labor leader and to the organizational disarray so characteristic of Solidarity, he suddenly found himself constrained by regulations, laws, and the established practices of government. Wałęsa, apparently, also regarded these months as a learning period. In fact, the Warsaw weekly *Polityka* recently reported that in response to its earlier criticism of his style and performance, he had telephoned the newspaper's offices to defend himself. Although he admitted to difficulties in dealing with certain "problems" because of existing legal and institutional "obstacles," he said he had on many occasions purposely tried to draw the public's attention to specific issues and to use popular pressure to force the government and other state institutions to take action. In another interview, Wałęsa was even more explicit, commenting that the current problems would become more manageable once the political situation had stabilized, that is, following parliamentary elections in the fall. But he added confidently, "Some people think that I no longer control the game, but they are wrong."

That may be true. Wałęsa has long been regarded as having a particular talent for politics, for handling adeptly both opponents and supporters, critics and advisers, and, above all, the general public. Wałęsa could well end up neutralizing the negative impact of at least some of his "errors" by actually turning them to his political advantage.

In the meantime, the President has consciously remained above narrow political conflicts, avoiding identification with nascent political parties or direct involvement in their organizational affairs. The former Solidarity leader was careful not to take a decisive position on the internal organizational changes in the union necessitated by his departure. For example, in December 1990 Wałęsa had indicated his preference for the Gdańsk leader Bogdan Borusewicz as the next Solidarity Chairman; but when his choice was opposed, he backed down. Later, at the Solidarity congress in February 1991, he chose not to become involved in the election of the organization's new leader. (The congress elected Marian Krzaklewski, a relatively unknown activist from Katowice, on the third ballot.)

Similarly, the President has maintained a distance from several groups of political and electoral supporters, such as the Center Alliance and the national Citizens' Committee, refusing to appoint their leaders to top government positions (although some have found places on his staff or his advisory council). At the same time, the President has kept open the channels of communication with his opponents. He even supported a former Communist, Wiesława Ziółkowska, rather than the veteran Solidarity activist Zbigniew Romaszewski to head the Supreme Chamber of Control.

Wałęsa has repeatedly expressed his wish to be the President of Poland as a whole and of all Poles, irrespective of their political preferences and backgrounds. His first three months in office suggest his determination to achieve that end, but it will not be easy. Wałęsa clearly knows that. Speaking in February with a reporter for the Warsaw daily *Rzeczpospolita,* a former Wałęsa adviser turned critic remarked that the President was "a political realist." This sense of political realism will certainly be in great demand in the months and years to come.

The Plunge into Capitalism

✦

Jeffrey Sachs

The author, who is Galen L. Stone Professor of International Trade at Harvard University, has advised several Latin American countries on economic policy. Currently he is an adviser to the government of Poland. In this article Sachs defends the drastic economic measures that he has urged upon Poland. In Poland, Professor Sachs has numerous advocates, but there is also apparently growing opposition to the hardships associated with his recommendations.

To understand Poland today, it is important to start the story not in the middle of 1990 but in the fall of 1989.

Today much of the world is anxiously watching Warsaw's nine-month-old plunge into capitalism for signs of success. But in 1989, when Solidarity became the first noncommunist government of Eastern Europe, the situation was not merely unstable: It was collapsing at a terrifying rate. In October prices rose by more than 50% per month (meaning that annual inflation rates exceeded 10,000%).

Goods had disappeared from the shops and, when available at all, could be found only after hours of queuing, or by paying bribes, or by dealing in the black market. The system of central planning, long moribund, was no longer functioning at all. Production was collapsing.

✦

TRANSFORMING FISH SOUP

There was widespread desperation, a desperation that had provided much of the energy behind the revolutionary events of 1989. The economic crisis had been going

Jeffrey Sachs, "The Economist Heard Round the World," from *World Monitor,* October 1990, pp. 30–32.

on for 10 years, though the explosion of hyperinflation was new. Poland was bankrupt, owing $40 billion in unpayable debts to the West.

No one was sure how to change the economic system to a market economy—a maneuver that had never been accomplished before. As one quip had it, "Going from capitalism to socialism was like making an aquarium into fish soup. But could the fish soup be turned back into an aquarium?"

Then, at the beginning of 1990, the Solidarity-led government of Poland launched a bold and unprecedented economic policy to arrest hyperinflation and convert Poland's moribund communist economy into a working market economy.

After six months, the weight of the evidence strongly supports Poland's decision to "jump to a market economy." There is considerable progress in the conversion to a privately owned market economy, and in the integration of Poland into the world economy. The reforms give Poland a real chance to begin catching up economically with Western Europe.

✦

BLAMING THE CURE INSTEAD OF THE DISEASE

Of course, profound risks remain, as was evident when the shock waves of the Middle East crisis threatened to harm Poland's fragile start. There is also the chance that populists within Poland could derail the hard-won early gains. Shocks from the Soviet Union could also create new economic havoc. And one important safety valve—support from the West—has so far not been adequate. Despite lofty Western rhetoric, real support for Poland has so far fallen short of levels that could ensure the success of reform.

Ironically, the early successes of Poland's strategy have been obscured by many of the journalistic accounts coming from Poland this year. These reports speak correctly and sensitively of the profound economic hardships facing the Polish people, but then go on to make basic mistakes in interpreting the process of reform.

One frequent mistake is to attribute the hardships to the reforms themselves, rather than to the underlying economic disease that they are aimed at curing. Another common mistake is to rely on statistical data that experts know to be severely distorted. A third mistake has been to misunderstand the time scale of reforms, that reforms must be put in place fast but then must be given years to work their full effect.

✦

REJECTING PIECEMEAL REFORMS

Prime Minister Tadeusz Mazowiecki and his economic architect, Deputy Prime Minister Leszek Balcerowiez, recognized from the start of their plunge into reforms that they would have to move swiftly and comprehensively to have any chance of success. The Poles knew the Latin American experience of the 1980s, where several fragile democratic governments—in Argentina, Brazil, and Peru, among other places—had moved too slowly, too narrowly, and too timidly, to slay the inflationary beast and to undertake long-term reforms.

The lesson of those nations was taken to heart in Warsaw: Governments that waver because of doubts about the austerity that comes with reform soon regret their lack of staying power. They find it vastly harder to persuade their publics ever again to try reforms. It's better to see the program through to its promised rewards the first time.

One key aspect of reform was that there had to be progress on many fronts. The budget deficit had to be closed. Price controls had to be lifted. Private business had to be freed to operate. The currency had to be made convertible, and the economy opened to international trade. And preparations for returning the state enterprises to the private sector had to be made. One part of reform without the others would not work, since an economic system must hold together in all of its central elements.

Piecemeal reforms had been tried and failed in Poland as in the rest of Eastern Europe, and in the Soviet Union under perestroika. Gradualism promised incoherence, not less pain. It would be as if the British decided to shift from driving on the left to driving on the right but decided to do it "gradually"—first, by having just the trucks shift over to the other side!

◆

SEEING ENCOURAGING RESULTS

The results of the first half year of reforms have been very encouraging. The hyperinflation has been brought to a screeching halt. Prices are rising at around 3% per month, compared with the 50% per month of last fall (which had been threatening to accelerate!).

Goods returned to the shops, and the new free markets in goods did a brisk business. Reporters parroted the line that "the goods are available but the prices are too high for the Poles to buy anything," a piece of silliness that is both illogical (why would a seller, especially one of the tens of thousands of new private sellers, keep prices too high to sell?) and refuted by the direct observation of retail trade.

In the first six months of the year, 175,000 new businesses were established at official count. Many more unregistered firms have probably come into operation but are lying low to avoid taxes.

Exports to the West surged ahead. Dollar earnings on exports were 17% higher in January through July 1990 than in the comparable period in 1989.

The currency, which had been a joke—or tragedy, depending on your point of view—remained firmly stable against the dollar, and freely convertible into any Western currency.

The government established several new policies that will provide a framework for growth. These include: de-monopolization of key sectors (such as mining); a privatization law to turn enterprises over to private hands; new laws for competition in insurance, banking, and other services. Many of these laws have yet to be implemented, however. A failure to move fast on privatization could jeopardize the whole reform program.

Of course, the hardships have not gone away, and the dislocations of the policy changes have been real. Life remains very hard for many, indeed tragically so. But the fears of dislocation, and the reports of the pain, have overstated the costs of the policies and caused an underestimate of the benefits.

◆

SKEWING THE REALITIES

Three trends are regularly cited to measure the supposed costs of reform: the rise of unemployment; the fall of the real wage; and the drop in production. In each case, the superficial data present a skewed view of the Polish reality.

Unemployment has risen in Poland, up to around 600,000 workers. This sounds enormous, but it represents only 3.5% of the labor force (compared with a US unemployment rate of 5.8% of the labor force!). Moreover, only about one-third of the unemployed (just 1% of the labor force) are actually job losers. The rest are voluntary job leavers and new entrants to the labor force. Unemployment in Poland will continue to rise, perhaps to between 5% and 10% of the labor force in the next few months. But those are rates typical of Western European nations and are not surprising nor catastrophic for a country ending a hyperinflation and fundamentally transforming the economy (remember, the US unemployment rate temporarily reached 11% in 1982, when America stopped a 10% per year inflation and started the longest peacetime economic expansion in its history).

The catastrophic drop in the real wage is another misunderstanding. Reports from Poland speak incessantly of a "40% drop in living standards" since the beginning of the year. This is based on data showing that the monthly average wage has risen less rapidly than the official price index. But this measure, in fact, has almost nothing to do with living standards. Prices in the shops did go up sharply since 1989, but in most cases the goods were not available at the official prices in 1989, or were available only after waiting for hours in lines!

Consumer surveys show that households have cut back on food consumption by perhaps 5%. At the same time, there is much more leisure time because of the end of lines, as well as a vast increase in the quantity, quality, and diversity of goods. Whether consumer welfare on average has risen or declined is not clear, but a 40% drop has surely not occurred.

The third indicator frequently pointed to is the fall in industrial production. Here again, there is a mix-up of data, and a misunderstanding of the real economics at work. Officially, production is down by 28%, but the index covers only state production, completely ignoring the private sector, which is small but growing. Moreover, some of the production decline reflects a rise, not fall, of economic welfare (such as the cutback in coal production, following the introduction of the five-day workweek).

Another large part, perhaps up to 10%, reflects a collapse in trade with the Soviet Union, which has hurt industrial production throughout the region. The direct, properly measured output decline as a result of the stabilization program might be around 10%, of which a part is temporary.

The economic situation in Poland is very difficult, but the reforms are a solution, not the cause of the pain. The misunderstandings I have cited present real risks. If too many Polish politicians misunderstand the economic situation, they may lose the resolve to stick with the necessary measures. Real reforms take time and consistency of policies.

Contrary to a lot of mythology, the 1960s West German economic miracle under Chancellor Ludwig Erhard did not work in a day, when Erhard's currency reform was put in place. Erhard's free-market policies remained controversial for years, but fortunately he stuck by them, and a miracle in the end did ensue—one of the great international events of the past half-century.

There are signs of political difficulty in Poland, but the political situation is hard to judge. Lech Wałęsa's well-publicized attacks on the government he helped install have mostly called for a speed-up of reform, not a slowing down. Vital policy actions, such as privatization of industry, seem to be moving forward, but at a rate that still risks a costly stalemate of policy changes in the future.

◆

CALLING FOR WESTERN AID

In the West there has been much glorious rhetoric about support for Poland's efforts, and also rhetorical concern over the hardships now facing the Poles. But there has also been little real help to see the Poles through this difficult period. Under the Marshall Plan, US support for Europe amounted to about 2% of national income per year. Now, Washington's support of all of Eastern Europe doesn't reach *one-hundredth of 1%* of American national income! And even when it is recognized that Poland cannot possibly succeed without a significant reduction of its $40 billion of debt, senior US economic officials continue to temporize and fail to produce meaningful policies.

The efforts of the West have so far been miserly—too stingy for its own security interests. The lack of adequate support from the West could, tragically, prove to be the greatest danger to the Polish economic reform process.

CZECHOSLOVAKIA

✦ *So much in the developments of 1989–1990 in Czecho-*
slovakia reminds us of the heady atmosphere of preinvasion 1968 that it is difficult to
acknowledge that more than twenty years elapsed between the two dramas. Dub-
ček returned to prominence, to be sure, but a new generation actually took the helm,
in the main people like the new president, Václav Havel, who had earned the peo-
ple's respect by their fortitude during the restoration. Whether or not the new order
was any sort of socialism, it presented a decidedly human face.

That quality is abundantly evident in the selections below, including Hável's
charmingly candid New Year 1991 address to the citizenry. The later selections make
it clear, however, that problems are too intractable to be charmed out of existence. The
impulses are the correct ones, and there are many commendable achievements, such as
the laws on human rights. But there is also political turmoil, economic hardship, and
the seemingly permanent issue of balancing Czech and Slovak interests. Although
Šiklová's brilliant observations were directed at an earlier state of affairs, much of the
ambiguity she detected remains pertinent.

Although it has not been usual to analyze East European affairs with decency
as a reference point, that quality was so noticeable in 1968 and is so again that one
wants to give it transcendent importance, above and beyond grubby details. But
grubby details may not yield to decency, much as one might wish otherwise.

Czechoslovakia: An Abrupt Transition

✦

Jiří Pehe

This report from Radio Free Europe describes the dramatic changes that came toward the end of 1989 and the developments earlier in the year that led up to the "abrupt transition" that replaced the old order in what has been called the "velvet revolution."

Although for most of the year police repression prevented open opposition in Czechoslovakia, protest strikes and the largest demonstrations in 20 years erupted throughout the country after police had brutally suppressed a student demonstration on November 17. These massive displays of public sentiment led to a political crisis and demands by both official and unofficial organizations that the communist leadership resign. Both the communist party Presidium and Secretariat resigned on November 24, and Karel Urbánek, the communist party leader in the Czech Republic, emerged as the new Secretary-General.

In two emergency meetings of the Central Committee (CC), all the leaders associated with the neo-Stalinist policies of the past twenty years were forced to resign. An extraordinary party congress held on December 21 and 22 ended Urbánek's short tenure and replaced him with former Prime Minister Ladislav Adamec. The structure of the party's leadership was changed, and the membership of more than 30 senior officials associated with the Jakeš leadership was suspended. Jakeš himself had been expelled from the party earlier.

✦

THE GENTLE REVOLUTION

A nonviolent revolution spearheaded by students and artists took place in the weeks following the November 17 events. On November 29 the Federal Assembly abolished the constitutional principle of the leading role of the communist party. Government officials repeatedly met with the representatives of the opposition and, under

Jiří Pehe, "Czechoslovakia: An Abrupt Transition," from *Report on Eastern Europe*, January 5, 1990, pp. 11–14. Reprinted with the permission of Radio Free Europe/Radio Liberty.

mounting public pressure that culminated in a general strike on November 27, accepted virtually all the demands of the opposition. A new government, described by the leadership as a coalition, was named on December 3; but it was completely reshuffled after it had been criticized by the opposition. Prime Minister Ladislav Adamec resigned in protest against these demands. For the first time in 40 years, Communists did not hold a majority of seats in the new government when it was named on December 10. Four prominent dissidents were among the newly named ministers: Jan Čarnogurský, who became the First Deputy Prime Minister; Jiří Dienstbier, who was named the Minister of Foreign Affairs; Petr Miller, who was appointed the Minister of Labor and Social Affairs; and Miroslav Kusy, who was named the Chairman of the State Bureau for the Press and Information. Seven members of the new government were nominated by the opposition. New governments in the Czech and Slovak Republics were named at the beginning of December; in both, Communists were in a minority.

As demanded by the opposition, President Husák resigned on December 10, and a fierce political campaign over his successor followed. The playwright Václav Havel emerged as the candidate of the opposition. A new Chairman of the Federal Assembly, Stanislav Kukral, a non-Communist, was elected on December 12; but on December 28 he resigned to make place for Alexander Dubček, the party leader in 1968. Dubček's election was a result of an agreement reached by major political forces in the country on December 22, which also cleared way for the election of Václav Havel as President. Havel was elected on December 29. He took an oath from which the Federal Assembly had dropped references to socialism.

In the six weeks after November 17, all political prisoners were amnestied; and the government began working on draft laws that would liberalize the laws on assembly, association, and the press. The Czechoslovak media changed dramatically, carrying objective reports on political developments in the country and interviews with formerly proscribed figures. A number of new political parties, organizations, and artistic unions sprang up, filling up the political vacuum created by the political upheaval. Some 6,000 strike committees that were established prior to the general strike formed a nascent independent trade union and called a congress for January 1990. In the meantime, the official trade unions began disintegrating.

After November 17 a revolt erupted in many party organizations as members began calling for the resignation of unpopular leaders and for the re-evaluation of the Prague Spring. The communist party found itself in disarray. The extraordinary party congress, though approving a democratic program that called for political pluralism, the abolition of the People's Militia, and the rehabilitation of party members expelled in the aftermath of the Soviet-led invasion of Czechoslovakia in 1968, appeared unable to stem the tide of growing dissatisfaction within the party's ranks; and an extraordinary party congress was called for December 20. Factions, such as the Democratic Forum of Communists, that had appeared in the party prior to the congress expressed their dissatisfaction with the results of the congress. By the end of the year, thousands of individual party members had left the party and entire basic organizations had abolished themselves.

✦

THE POLITICAL SPHERE PRIOR TO THE REVOLUTION

At the beginning of 1989 the Czechoslovak leadership decided to neutralize the growing dissident community with an "ideological and political offensive." The new policy collapsed, however, when the leadership, reacting angrily to the demonstrations in Prague, returned to the use of openly repressive measures. A wave of political trials started in February and continued throughout 1989. At the same time the regime appropriated and twisted the opposition groups' demand for a dialogue between the authorities and the people. The party leaders repeatedly said that such a dialogue would not include the opposition. As a result, there were no negotiations until November when, in the face of mounting public pressure, Adamec met with representatives of the Civic Forum, an alliance of dissident and official organizations formed after the November 17 student demonstration had been suppressed.

The opening of negotiations with the opposition and the virtual breakdown of censorship after November 17 led to the collapse of the policy formulated earlier by party ideologist Jan Fojtik. In September Fojtik formulated a more extreme version of the policy the Czechoslovak leadership had pursued for almost two years, which called for instituting small and careful changes while maintaining an ideology free from the "excesses" of *glasnost*. His policy confirmed an apparent ideological hardening within a leadership faced with growing domestic dissatisfaction and international isolation.

This ideological hardening was also partly the result of the fact that in August and September both the Hungarian and Polish governments had repudiated their countries' participation in the Soviet-led invasion of Czechoslovakia in 1968. These reversals by two of Czechoslovakia's Warsaw Pact allies only increased the Czechoslovak leadership's ideological belligerency, as officials who based their legitimacy on the crushing of the Prague Spring still formed the nucleus of that leadership. Relations with Hungary and Poland—whose governments had not only condemned their predecessors' involvement in the 1968 invasion but had then begun instituting dramatic reforms—gradually worsened. Czechoslovakia repeatedly criticized political developments in the two countries and in November also began criticizing what was happening in the GDR. The Czechoslovak media were even critical of some aspects of the Soviet Union's reforms. Relations between Czechoslovakia and Hungary became especially bad after the Hungarian National Assembly had voted in October to discontinue participation in the Gabcikovo-Nagymaros dam project, which the two countries had undertaken together. Czechoslovakia announced that it would seek reparations for damages incurred as a result of Hungary's decision.

✦

THE PARTY PRIOR TO NOVEMBER 17

Despite repeated appeals by senior party officials for greater activism among party members, morale in the party remained low. The chief cause of this appeared to be party members' loss of faith in their leaders' ability to pull the country out of the deepening crisis. During the second half of 1989 party periodicals revealed that membership had dropped in all seven regions of the Czech Republic and that "negative trends [had] also appeared in Slovakia." The average age of party members was over 45 for the first time in the party's history.

◆

DISSENT AND RELIGION

Opposition to the regime grew significantly throughout the year. Older dissident groups broke out of their isolation and the total number of opposition groups grew to approximately 40. For the first time, many of the new groups were based outside Prague.

Three groups became almost as influential as Charter 77, the oldest of Czechoslovakia's dissident groups. They were *Obroda*—A Club for Socialist Restructuring; the Movement for Civil Liberties; and the Czechoslovak Democratic Initiative, which in November became an independent political party and applied for official registration. All three groups formulated their own political programs. Also in November, a number of both dissident and official groups reacted to the country's growing crisis by forming an umbrella group, the Civic Forum, to demand political changes. The Civic Forum organized mass demonstrations throughout the Czech provinces and published a program calling for free elections and democracy. The Civic Forum eventually established branches in virtually every part of Bohemia and Moravia and became a partner in negotiations with the government about changes. In December the forum announced that it would act as a unified political coalition in the elections planned for 1990. A similar role was played in Slovakia by a group called the Public Against Violence.

A number of demonstrations took place in 1989. A week of demonstrations in January clearly shook the Czechoslovak leadership. Other demonstrations followed in August on the 21st anniversary of the invasion of Czechoslovakia, and in October on the 71st anniversary of the founding of an independent Czechoslovakia. Smaller demonstrations organized by environmentalists also took place throughout the country.

Dissidents, leading cultural figures, and scientists signed petitions in February in behalf of those arrested during the January demonstrations. Thousands of people signed these petitions, especially the one demanding Václav Havel's release from prison. Later in 1989 Havel emerged as the Czechoslovak opposition's unofficial leader. He and other prominent cultural figures launched the June "Just a Few Sentences" petition, which called for democratization in Czechoslovakia and which, in 5 months, had almost 40,000 signatories. In October and November approximately 300 officially sanctioned Czechoslovak journalists signed a petition demanding their dissident colleagues' release from prison; in November more than 60 of them formed the Association of Independent Journalists.

Pressured by growing religious activism, in July the Czechoslovak authorities concluded an agreement with the Vatican to fill three vacant bishoprics in Czecho-slovakia, although seven of the country's thirteen bishoprics remained empty. In November the Czechoslovak media devoted a surprising degree of attention to the canonization of the Blessed Agnes of Bohemia. Czechoslovak Television broadcast the ceremony live—the first such religious broadcast in 20 years. The Czech Catholic Primate Cardinal František Tomášek became increasingly outspoken in 1989 and was one of the leading symbols of opposition to the regime. After a new coalition govern-ment had been named on December 10, an agreement with the Vatican on filling the vacant bishoprics was reached within a few days.

✦

OTHER POLITICAL PARTIES AND OFFICIAL ORGANIZATIONS

In May, Socialist Party leader Jan Škoda demanded more independence for non-communist parties. In November the Socialist Party leadership condemned the police brutality during the November 17 demonstration and accused the Jakeš leadership of avoiding a dialogue with the people. Some members of the People's Party openly revolted against that party's leadership during the second half of 1989, accusing it of betraying the party's Christian character, and formed a "Stream of Rebirth" within the party. The People's Party leadership resigned on November 26 and was replaced by a less conservative one. Members of both parties were present at the founding meeting of the Civic Forum on November 18. Dissatisfaction also appeared in the Union of Socialist Youth, as some members revolted against what they viewed as totalitarian practices by the union's officials. At the union's conference in November, some members pleaded for a dialogue with dissident groups; later in November the union's secretariat condemned the November 17 violence and demanded the govern-ment's resignation. In December a new union leadership was elected.

✦

CULTURE AND THE MEDIA

During the first half of 1989 the ferment within Czechoslovak society was most evident in the country's artistic and literary circles. Pressure from officially sanctioned artists resulted in the rehabilitation of a number of cultural figures banned after the 1968 invasion. The rebellion was strongest among actors, theater directors, and other performing artists, whose unions came to be dominated by previously ostracized artists. A number of leading artists signed petitions for democratization, and in August officially sanctioned and dissident writers together revived the Czech branch of the International PEN Club. In November the bulk of the Czechoslovak media revolted against the severe restrictions imposed by the Jakeš administration, and their reporting became increasingly open.

✦
THE ECONOMY

The Czechoslovak economy remained sluggish throughout 1989. Reports by the Federal Statistical Office indicated that most economic indicators were unsatisfactory. At the beginning of the year, 118 of the largest and most prestigious enterprises were declared bankrupt, although the state continued to bail them out. Despite its poor performance, the economy drew on its formerly formidable base to avoid a major crisis. Some reform-oriented economists have pointed out that such a crisis did not occur only because the leadership kept postponing radical measures that would have rapidly revealed the extent of Czechoslovakia's domestic indebtedness, particularly its long-term failure to invest in new technology. Despite the leadership's promises, environmental problems were not remedied during the year; and the ecological situation in parts of Czechoslovakia was described as catastrophic.

A new law on enterprises that introduced limited profit incentives produced mixed results in 1989. Although some enterprises showed signs of improvement, the reforms resulted primarily in a bureaucratic reshuffling of middle-level economic management. Late in the year the Federal Assembly passed a number of laws expanding economic reforms; but the new government named on December 10 announced that it would go even further and attempt to introduce a full-fledged market economy. More promising than the enterprise law was a new law governing joint ventures, which lifted restrictions on foreign investment in Czechoslovak companies. Even with the new law, however, the country's nonconvertible currency and a plethora of bureaucratic obstacles kept many potential foreign investors out of the Czechoslovak market.

This poor economic showing spurred an unusual public debate that centered on a report prepared by a group of reform-oriented economists at the Institute for Economic Forecasting of the Czechoslovak Academy of Sciences. The report proposed a radical restructuring of an economy currently overburdened with heavy industry. The report, which also recommended political reforms, reportedly became the subject of heated debate among the leadership and was temporarily suppressed. In November, Prime Minister Adamec reiterated some of the arguments made in the report in support of political changes, diverging from the leadership's current line and revealing rifts in its ranks. In November, in protest at the slow pace of reforms, Adamec resigned from the Presidium of the communist party. When a new coalition government was named on December 10, three economists from the forecasting institute, including its director Valtr Komarek, were named members of the government.

The "Gray Zone" and the Future of Dissent in Czechoslovakia

◆

Jiřina Šiklová

Although Dr. Šiklová, a sociologist at Charles University in Prague, was writing about the problems of dissent in the period before the changes of late 1989, her incisive observations also pertain, as her postscript makes clear, to the more recent period when the relative simplicities of opposition have given way to the ambiguities of social reconstruction.

Conversations with friends from abroad almost always reach the point where I have to explain how many expressions that sound identical to terms used in the West—and are even translated identically—convey an entirely different meaning here. Next comes the moment when my visitor asks, "And what do your Communists say? What about trade unionists' opinions?" I reply that they usually think the same as so-called dissidents, and that many Communist party officials tell the selfsame political jokes, and gripe just as much about the incompetence and corruption of our leadership.

In Czechoslovakia, experts, journalists, artists, authors, and, generally, people who are concerned about and with politics differ from one another not so much by how much they know or by how they assess the facts but mainly by their moral stance and the courage with which they voice their views. This stance distinguishes them from one another far more than whether they carry a party card. "Are these people reactionary or progressive? Do they belong to the right, or are they leftists?" my visitor asks, and I am near despair. I try to explain to my friends from the West that it is impossible to communicate today in Eastern Europe using the standard terminology inherited from France's National Convention, or Cromwell's Parliament, or the czar's Duma without clarifications or explanatory footnotes.

These expressions have been "depleted" here, "exhausted," by means of repeated revolutions, pseudorevolutions, state coups and their rationales, and the

Jiřina Šiklová, "The 'Gray Zone' and the Future of Dissent in Czechoslovakia," from *Social Research*, Summer 1990. Reprinted by permission of Jiřina Šiklová.

alternating stages of so-called revolution, reaction, rebirth, normalization, and the new reaction or opposition, followed by further normalization or reformation.

"Are you trying to tell us that critical members of the Communist party of Czechoslovakia hold the same political views as nonparty members or as people who have been expelled from the party? Then why are they in the party, why don't they just go ahead and join the dissidents?" my visitor insists, unsatisfied, perhaps even unsatisfiable by my explanation.

"All right, once more from the top," I say, and again (how many times already?) I explain that I know many members of the Communist party of Czechoslovakia, but personally I don't know a single one who is a communist by persuasion; I explain that today the absolute majority are not party members out of any conviction (they are neither Marxists nor revolutionaries) but rather for reasons of expedience or, at best, conformist and obedient by nature, they prefer to be "left alone"; they remained in the party precisely because they lacked clear-cut convictions, they let themselves be "screened" and, when invited to join the party, were reluctant to refuse. It is truly difficult to be a thoughtful and sanguine proponent of the communist ideology and Marx-Leninist philosophy today, following all the repeated reevaluations and the many different interpretations of that ideology and of the entire history of the movement. That is why rank-and-file members of the party differ from other members not by their views and their revolutionary convictions but by their personality traits: they want peace and quiet, and guaranteed, easy advancement on the job; they want to share the relative advantages of a preferred minority; they do not want to have complications in their lives; they are by conviction opportunists. That is why they are unhappy when the party "establishment" insists that they take a clear stand, or accept co-responsibility for a negative evaluation on a fellow worker. Party members would much prefer to leave that sort of decision to those who "are paid to do it," that is, party officials, members of the state police or the secret police, etc.

My visitor is once again confused. A sociologist querying me about our society, he expects my response to include more than just the political classification of parties and groups; he is also looking for their differentiation by social status, class affiliation, or some other, broadly acceptable stratification based on profession, or education, or income, etc. And I can't give him that, either!

When we differentiate in that way, we usually help ourselves with borrowed terms to which we assign our own, unique meanings, specific to contemporary reality.

Only two groups in our country can be clearly differentiated from the rest, on the basis of political stance and social classification: the first comprises those currently in power, or what we call "the socialist establishment," and the second consists of "the dissidents," or the opposition.

The socialist establishment is made up of party and government officials at the central and regional level, upper-level bureaucrats of the state police or the secret police, high-ranking military officers, ministers and their deputies, party secretaries, editors-in-chief, top executives of major enterprises, judges . . . such people are inseparably linked to—and severely compromised by—the contemporary political system, so much so that they cannot even change their position. They comprise the existing decision-making center, and rise and fall with it.

The other clearly differentiable group consists of the dissidents—the opposition: people who years ago made their position very clear in word and deed, rejecting the policy of the party establishment. These people also cannot change their position; they can neither retreat nor convert.

These two groups, although relatively small in numbers, are politically active, conscious of the risk they take by their unequivocal choice, and they don't need persuading or proselytizing. For them, everything is altogether clear. They are minorities, profiling the two poles of Czechoslovak political life. Between them, as in every country, there is a "silent majority," for the most part consumption-oriented and politically uninterested, and then there are the people in the so-called "gray zone," which I want to write about here.

The first use of the expression "gray zone" in this context in the field of historical science was probably in the article "Czech Historiography Yesterday, Today and Tomorrow," published in the *samizdat* periodical *Historical Studies* by authors writing under the pseudonyms R. Prokop, L. Sádecký, and K. Bína. It was used to describe historians who remained "within the structure," that is, inside the scientific institutions and universities, while also staying in touch with their former colleagues expelled during the post-1968 purges, remaining willing to associate with them, to debate with them, and, when needed, even to help them.

Today, the gray zone refers to a much broader group of people, a group that is—and more importantly, will be—of immense importance in the course of anticipated changes in this society in the future. This is because people in the gray zone are, and can be, partners to the dissidents, but also—in my opinion—they are the ones who will take over the leadership of this society. The gray zone consists for the most part of good workers, qualified, professionally erudite people. That is precisely why they perceived the errors of the socialist system early on, and also why they didn't have to buttress their careers by means of a party card or by taking on political functions. They knew it was possible for them to maintain a livelihood by means of honest effort alone, and so they found it easier to resist the lures and the pressures from the establishment. And because their political involvement was minimal, they also had a lot more time for their own education and training, both personally and professionally. And so today Czechoslovakia's very best experts in their fields fall inside the gray zone.

Why the color gray, and why call it a zone?

In this day and age, even colors have their clear and discernible symbology. In Stendhal's day, it was perfectly clear to everyone what "the red and the black" meant, just as today we know who the "greens" are, and the "reds" and the "browns." The color gray, however, is an uncertain one, neither white nor black, easily changing into one or the other. Gray can be viewed as being perhaps a little "dirty." Yes, dirty. That too determined, determines, and will determine the political stands of the people we slot into this group. If in fact there is a change in the political system and conditions in Czechoslovakia, the hands of these people will never by entirely clean, their moral credit entirely clear. Although hesitantly, reluctantly, they cooperated with the establishment all the same, and accepted certain benefits in exchange for their relative conformity. That is why, in spite of the fact that they agree with the views of the dissidents and are in favor of the relaxation of political conditions, those in the gray zone worry that, sooner or later, someone will hold their collaboration against them.

And why a zone? I'm not entirely sure, perhaps we were influenced by the motion picture that at one time was quite famous here, Tarkovsky's *Stalker,* in which the hero of the film was a guide, leading people into a mysterious, enigmatic "zone," a no-man's-land where "something went on" and where a perceptive visitor could encounter all kinds of things.

And in fact, while other partners in the political arena, that is, the establishment—the regime, "they," or, in young people's jargon, "the Bolshevik" (which globally encompasses the totalitarian state)—and the dissidents—the opposition—are clear and explicit, it is in the gray zone that something substantive is happening; the struggle between the establishment and the opposition is and will be over the gray zone.

Because the economic situation is deteriorating, and people are gradually getting less afraid, the population of the gray zone is increasing. Sometimes these people are much angrier with the current regime than the dissidents, because they encounter the establishment on a daily basis and partake directly and indirectly in the functioning of the totalitarian state. Because of this, and because they are aware of the manner and the degree to which the people are being manipulated, the arrogance of the establishment offends them even more. Those in the gray zone differ from the dissidents mainly in the sphere of courage, taking a stand, in their unwillingness or inability to confront power. They are spectators to what is happening, spectators who are clearly rooting for Charter 77 and other displays of independence, the way fans root for their favorite team. They are not players themselves; they aren't on the field, they are in the stands. Like fans, they occasionally cheer aloud and applaud visibly. And under the circumstances, that already is a lot: rooting, cheering, helping, applauding!

Dissidents, sometimes too focused on their own courage, often underrate this, and don't give these fans the credit they deserve. In my opinion, that is a pity and a mistake! After all, most of the people don't even bother to go to the stadium, and often don't even know where the game is and don't want to know.

By rights, I should also stratify the group I call the gray zone by social status, class affiliation, profession, political program, or at least by field of interest. But I can't do that either.

The gray zone exists within every defined social, professional, or interest group. I even know a few people in the gray zone around the editorial offices of official periodicals, institutes of economics, ministries, motion pictures, theater, and even among lawyers and judges. People in the gray zone have no single program of their own, no creed, or even any specific aims. They are frequently more open to the dissidents than they are among themselves. Formally, they are part of the "structure" and more or less fulfill the demands and criteria that the totalitarian state makes of its front lines. By political position, however, they stand behind the opposition, and perceive it as their point of reference.

Class criteria in Czechoslovakia—and apparently in other countries of Eastern Europe—have also been erased through repeated restructuring. Today, laborers may be former university professors, as well as former politicians and journalists, and vice versa. As for their standard of living, members of the gray zone belong to the upper middle; they don't receive the perks that high-level party functionaries do, which evoke envy and distaste, but neither are they living in poverty. They and their children generally slip through the various checks and screening processes, obtain a decent education, an acceptable job classification, a decent (if not exorbitant) measure of professional success. They do not aspire to the pinnacles of their fields. If that were their intention, they would have to leave the gray zone and join the Communist party, take on a more explicit commitment to "the Bolshevik," that is, to the regime. They are too honorable, and too timid, to do that. They have neither the positive nor the negative attributes required to be active in the opposition, or for that matter for careerist conformity. People in the gray zone are not indifferent, not cynical; it is more that they believe in traditional, historically tried-and-tested values introduced a couple of hundred years ago by the French Revolution. They hold various functions, adhere to formal political rituals, and then all the more do they rail at the totalitarian regime for this, their humiliation and their self-humiliation. They are employed within the structure, in jobs roughly in keeping with their qualifications; they are not ostracized, they want to retain the minor advantages that the regime grants those who stay within the norm. At the same time, they strive not to get "into" anything, not to damage anyone; they are often helpful to others persecuted by the political regime. On the other hand, they take no visible stands against the establishment and so to some degree compromise themselves. Thus they are endangered from "both sides," it is on their conscience, and they entertain covert fears that if there were to be another settling of accounts (and this nation has a broad experience with screening and almost masochistic soul-searching) they too will be accused of collaborating with the establishment.

In situations when they are not in danger, and not under too much pressure from the powers-that-be, they will take an unequivocal and fervent stand on the side of the dissidents, and then proceed to justify and call for economic reforms as well as human rights. Then the gray zone will start to turn away from the regime and become its highly erudite critic. But it will have to be the dissidents who win them the space for it.

The establishment has always vaguely sensed the danger of an expanding gray zone, and today it is very much aware of it. That is why from time to time it has conducted intimidation operations in the form of purges, screenings, interrogations, consolidated employee data files, party card exchanges, etc. Contemporary forms of intimidation campaigns also include the maligning of anyone who has signed any sort of manifesto publicly critical of the establishment, and the brutal disruption of demonstrations, as was the case in August 1988, in January 1989, and in August 1989. "The Bolshevik" is no longer able to browbeat the manifest dissidents, who have long since crossed the threshold of conformity, because they are counting on it. In its apathy, the silent majority is also immune. Those in the gray zone, however, are always intimidated for a while.

The reasons for these people being and remaining in the gray zone are varied, and not always morally reprehensible. The dissidents in particular should be able to understand them.

At the time of extreme political activity (say in the years 1967–69), they might have been in the middle of a divorce, or pregnant on maternity leave, or in traction with a broken leg; perhaps they were negotiating a complex apartment exchange in the extreme housing shortage, or immersed in their own personal mourning, or working abroad or for an enterprise that happened to escape the attention of the establishment. It wasn't always their own personal choice, then, but often just coincidence that allowed them to remain within the mainstream and conform for another twenty years. Certainly coincidence worked in the opposite direction too. The people in the gray zone, as well as the dissidents, can be the object of what Aldous Huxley wrote in his book *Point Counter Point:* "I doubt if anything is really irrelevant. Everything that happens is intrinsically like the man it happens to. . . . But in some indescribable way, the event's modified, qualitatively modified, so as to suit the character of each person involved in it. It's a great mystery and paradox." This "paradox" accuses, but also excuses.

Belonging to the gray zone inhibits these people, but it also radicalizes them; the establishment makes them party to maintaining totalitarian power by their own personal deeds. The establishment is always trying to draw people into being participants; where it succeeds, its power is reinforced, since that power is their only guarantee that people's participation won't be held against them. In an article quoted in 1989 in the *samizdat* philosophical periodical *Paraf,* Pavel Bratinka remarks that this feedback between the doers of minor deeds and the totalitarian state can even bring about the regeneration of power:

> Breaking with power means enduring not only its rage, but also the pangs of a reawakened personal conscience. That sort of transformation from Saul to Paul truly demands immense moral courage. On the other hand, staying on the side of power doesn't require any particular personal malice or enduring evil; all it calls for is a disinclination toward martyrdom, a very common human attribute indeed.

Citizens of the states of Eastern Europe have no difficulty understanding that. Up until the moment we crossed a certain line, every one of us was in the gray zone. It is only the youngest generation within the opposition who genuinely chose to join the dissent.

Mrs. Hana Jüptnerová used to teach in a secondary school in Vrchlabí, a small town in the border region. As a high-school teacher, she was "inside the structure" and willy-nilly was relatively answerable to the official requirements of the educational system. When in the spring of 1988 police brutality resulted in the death in prison of Pavel Wonka, whom she knew personally and held in high esteem, she spoke spontaneously and beautifully at his grave side. Totalitarian power settled with her! The school board immediately terminated her employment contract, and ever since she has been washing dishes in a confectionery shop. She wrote me about it in a personal letter: "I can't get other work. The regime is trying to punish me for my words, but wasn't my previous existence, down on my knees with my back bent, punishment itself?"

In June 1989, at a Prague meeting of publishing-house readers, we were addressed by a man who for years had worked for Odeon, a publisher of fiction and poetry. He said that in our country, in addition to officially published Czech literature, we have the literature of Czech exiles abroad, and we have *samizdat* literature, and that only these three together comprise Czech literature. I was tempted to get up and arrogantly ask him why he was saying that today, why he hadn't stood up earlier to the people who were banning and destroying books back then; I would have liked to tell him I thought he was just jumping onto a moving train. The rest of the audience applauded him enthusiastically, though. The idea he had voiced was not new to anyone, but they were glad to finally hear it from "one of them"; what they were applauding was that even one from that gray zone had been brave enough to take this kind of a stand. They seemed to be saying that his statements were "rehabilitating" them, as well. I did not speak out, and in the end I applauded too. I shouldn't be judging him, I should appreciate him; after all, each of us has his own limits where personal courage is concerned, a point where the burden is no longer acceptable or tolerable. It is our task to persuade people in the gray zone, to appreciate them and not turn them away by moralizing, attacking them, and poking around in their past.

If today's dissidents don't want to remain an exclusive minority, we must address those in the gray zone and challenge them to take on positions of leadership, now that the limits set by the rigid personnel selection process and the *nomenklatura* are being relaxed a little. That is why it will be inappropriate for us to remind them of their petty collaboration with the regime, or of our own merits, lost opportunities, careers, of how much we suffered and the years we spent behind bars.

It will be hard for both sides!

For many dissidents, their greatest competition will be from the gray zone. Its members are not as compromised, and besides, they have had far better conditions all along to nurture their own professional growth, to improve their qualifications, to gain experience in day-to-day, nondissident life. And of course, that is the life that will matter! The dissidents may have moral superiority, but they must also realize that they have lived, or survived, for twenty years outside "the structure," for the most part in isolation, out of touch with scientific institutions and institutes. By their enforced exclusion, they also lost—at least in part—their continuity in the context of "civil" life as well as up-to-date expertise in their original professions. As for the young people among the dissidents, they often refused to take places within the "structure" out of revulsion for the establishment's moral promiscuity, and hence also will lack much of their peers' experience with how normal society functions. The dissidents will still retain their moral superiority and moral credit, but their professional competence—for example, in the sphere of commerce or in administrative management—will at best be outdated. Although this handicap can easily be justified by citing difficult objective conditions, political persecution, job discrimination, barriers to education and travel abroad, the need to expend eight hours a day of exhausting physical labor to obtain a livelihood, and numerous other factors, the fact remains that this does not change the reality. With exceptions in the fields of pure politics, freelance art, journalism, political science, and perhaps even philosophy, most dissidents will be less qualified than people in the gray zone and their offspring. Recognizing that and accepting it will certainly be difficult. The life of every individual is contingent not only on his abilities but also on opportunities ensuing from historical events and where a person stands generationally.

I am thinking of my friend Jiří Ruml, once an editor for Czechoslovak Radio and on the editorial staff of the pre-1968 political weekly, *Reportér*. For the past two years, Jiří Ruml has been editing a very important and popular *samizdat* monthly, *Lidové noviny (People's News)*. Not long ago, when we were all praising "his" *People's News* to the skies, he shrugged his shoulders and said, "But what's the use of it all, I'm sixty-five years old, and nobody will ever give me back those twenty years of my life."

Not only will he not get them back, but he won't get anything for them, either. If the anticipated changes to the totalitarian regime do come about in Czechoslovakia, then the dissidents will also lose much that is valuable to them: some of the very things that led them to make their uncommon choice for how they will relate within society. Lost to them will be their unity, which up till now was considered a matter of course; their cohesiveness, their solidarity, their uniqueness, their moral superiority, their aura of being persecuted and ostracized, and along with these, a certain nonresponsibility for everything that is wrong in politics and society. The envisioned relaxation of the totalitarian regime will also intrude on the life they have become used to. When we try to open a sticky door, the moment it gives, we lose our balance for a moment. We may realize, for example, that we aren't as capable as we thought we were. Being isolated in the ghetto of dissent also meant a certain isolation from criticism. It is hard to disparage someone who is being kicked from all sides and who is generally recognized and understood to be having an exceptionally hard time. In Czechoslovakia, it will probably go the way every other political coup has gone: the most will be gained by those who stood aside, not manning either side of the barricades, those who just sat back and waited intelligently, that is, those in the gray zone. The space that will open out for them and the next generation will have been won by the efforts and the dedication of the dissidents. For purely tactical political reasons I think it will be expedient to enable even those who bordered on collaboration with the establishment to join the gray zone *ex post facto*. Better at that point that the gray zone grow and multiply than that our mutual denunciations grow and multiply.

My observations of the current, rather intolerant, recriminations for past accomplishments and past lapses among our fellow countrymen in exile lead me to fear that hard times are only just beginning for our dissidents at home. That we will discover how much of what we now refer to in facile terms as resulting from incompetence of the establishment is in fact a phenomenon common to every modern society. Ironically, it is decades of the incessant proclamation of the Communist party's leading role that led us to interpret many shortcomings, common also in democratic societies, as being the result of mistakes made by our own very concrete and ubiquitous party apparatus.

When today's dust in Europe settles, and we are able to confront the states of Western Europe, we will find that we are very poor. We will have to be able to adjust to this unfortunate heritage of forty years of socialism's experimental devastation of our land: to accept it as a fact, to realize that the widespread destitution we are faced with always presents fertile soil for new demagogues, new dictatorships.

It is common knowledge that if you know what to expect and how a certain process will unfold, the situation is easier to bear. That is why I have written this article now, perhaps prematurely, for myself, my close friends, and mainly for those in the gray zone. At the same time, I see it as a general problem that people in all the countries of Eastern Europe will have to come to terms with.

For the present, I only wish that this challenging situation would finally come to pass in Czechoslovakia. I hope I didn't write this study too prematurely.

Translated by Káča Poláčková-Henley

◆
POSTSCRIPT

Even these days I bump into ex-dissident colleagues fairly frequently. They have all lost weight, have colds, and are very weary. We embrace, say "Call me, drop by, come over some time," though knowing full well that it will be a good while before we'll see each other again—there isn't the time. We had time before, but it meant meeting clandestinely. Looking back on it, there was something to be said for it.

We all have so much to do, what with giving lectures, attending meetings, writing articles, answering invitations to hundreds of events, taking part in negotiations in various committees and associations, etc. People these days are seized with the urge to speak out, find themselves, voice their opinions, and in some instances to make excuses for decades of mute acquiescence. And we dissidents have to sit there and somehow affirm others' conversion by our very presence.

It's tiring!

Someone calls over to me from an adjacent escalator: "I need this like a pain in the head. . . . It was much easier to study in the boilerhouse." Someone else raises two fingers in a Churchillian victory gesture, but sheepishly puts them down again. Even V for Victory is weary.

"Where are you working?" I ask Ludek of the Original Videojournal, an independent project which earned him plenty of harassment on numerous occasions.

"I'm still in the boilerhouse. I don't feel like pushing myself in anywhere. Anyway, the things we used to film clandestinely in people's homes at enormous risk are now being done openly by professionals with whole film crews and a horde of lighting and sound technicians. So I'll go on stoking my boiler.

"Only yesterday I gave up my cleaner's job and I'm already beginning to regret it somewhat. I have no great wish to go and work somewhere where everyone else was hired according to the norms of the *nomenklatura*."

By chance, I hail a taxi and discover at the wheel an old acquaintance, a dissident who used to help us transport and distribute books, as well as take VONS people to court hearings.

"You'll all go back to your original professions," he laments, "while I'll be just a taxi driver and nothing else from now on." Will we go back to our professions? When no one wants us there? One employee who was given the job of dealing with cases of those dismissed for political reasons complained: "Those '68 people still want the top jobs. They were in the leading posts in 1968; when they left the faculty they were leading figures in the opposition, and now we're supposed to take them back into leading positions again." And it was not intended as a joke.

New structures are being formed. As always the running is being done chiefly by those who know how to assert themselves, even if it means disregarding others and their human problems. This is one capacity that the dissidents signally lacked, and why they became dissidents in the first place.

They were the creators and initiators of the drama, voicing the things that others feared to say. As recently as last year, they were Antigones in a silent Thebes.

The popular view in Thebes nowadays is that Polynices should be buried—and they always thought so anyway. The moral aspect of speaking the truth has already been toned down. The expression of truth is losing its ethical impact and becoming no more than a historical fact that arouses interest but not enthusiasm. And the experts are better informed and are able to quote facts more accurately than the dissidents.

I organized the official presentation of a gift for our patients. Representatives of various workplaces who wanted to accept the equipment indulged in mutual recriminations and I learned things I had no desire to hear. "This whole society is sick," I said to myself. "Wherever you prick it, the pus runs out." But it's only to be expected. Hungry people don't use silver cutlery—or damask table cloths, for that matter. That's why we became dissidents—so as not to dirty ourselves with such things.

In the past, the position was as clear as in a fairy tale. Evil was evil, good was good, and people in the opposition—unless they happened to be in prison—were the freest of all. We used to grumble and criticize, but by our actions we opted for a particular way of life just as much as those who said nothing, signed their agreement with the Soviet invasion or the Anti-Charter, and paid their tithes to the Communist party. Unlike them, we don't have a bad conscience, and maybe that's what annoys them about us. Yet again we're different! But it's not our fault!

There is even a contradiction in our "Havelite ideology" that asserts nonviolence and nonvengeance and proclaims the need to understand one's neighbor, while also guiding and leading society. Whereas the old power elite were totally unscrupulous and used to attack and imprison people for the merest Antigonean gesture, they now exploit our every single threatening gesture in order to denounce us, saying, "You see, they're no different!" And we are obliged—in order to distinguish ourselves from the old socialist establishment—to do everything in an ethical fashion and defer to a "higher principle." Morality has no weapons, and in fact it even serves to tie bare hands. And it ties our hands most of all. So yet again we retire into a corner and at most get on with some writing.

Those who joined us at the last minute in the name of the Velvet Revolution are settling their personal accounts in the nastiest way and act as if they were speaking on behalf of dissidents and all the victims of the previous regime, and fail to understand our misgivings about their conduct.

Unhappily, I was right. Hard times for the dissidents are only just beginning.

Postscript Translated by Gerald Turner

Czechoslovakia on Christmas Eve 1989

✦

Ivan Klíma

A novelist forbidden to publish in Czechoslovakia after 1968, Klíma has a following in the West, where several of his books have been published. His remarks for a *Granta* symposium on the state of Europe at Christmas 1989 follow very shortly the sudden transformation of his country toward the end of that year.

The first pictures of the Prague demonstration of 17 November were of young girls placing flowers on shields held by riot police. Later the police got rough, but their furious brutality failed to provoke a single violent response. Not one car was damaged, not one window smashed during daily demonstrations by hundreds of thousands of people. Posters stuck up on the walls of houses, in metro stations, on shop windows and in trams by the striking students called for peaceful protest. Flowers became the symbol of Civic Forum.

It is only recently that we have seen the fragility of totalitarian power. Is it really possible that a few days of protest—unique in the history of revolutions for their peacefulness—could topple a regime which had harassed our citizens for four decades?

Ivan Klíma, "The State of Europe," from *Granta*, 30, 1990, pp. 166–167.

Wenceslas Square, November 1989. Czechoslovakia's "Velvet Revolution" of November 1989 succeeded where the Prague Spring of 1968 had failed. Here, in the same square into which Soviet tanks had rolled in 1968 (see photograph, p. 218), students light candles in memory of those who had died resisting dictatorship. A few days later, the communist regime collapsed. (Donna Binder/Impact Visuals)

The rest of the world had all but forgotten the 1968 invasion of Czechoslovakia by the armies of five countries. Even now, our nation has barely recovered from that invasion; what did not recover was the leading force in the country, the Communist Party. By subsequently making approval of the invasion and the occupation a condition of membership, the Party deprived itself of almost all patriotic and worthy members, becoming for the rest of the nation a symbol of moral decay and betrayal. The government, then stripped of its authority and its intelligence, went on to devastate the country culturally, morally and materially. An economically mature country fell back among the developing countries, while achieving a notable success in atmospheric pollution, incidence of malignant tumours and short life expectancy.

Unrestrained power breeds arrogance. And arrogance threatens not only the subject but also the ruler. In Czechoslovakia the ruling party, deprived of an élite and of any outstanding personalities, combined arrogance with provocative stupidity. It persisted obstinately in defending the occupation of Czechoslovakia, indeed as an act of deliverance at a time when even the invaders themselves were re-examining their past. The government actually went so far as to suggest that the apologies offered by the Polish and Hungarian governments for their role in the invasion constituted interference in the internal affairs of the country. How could the nation consider such a government as its own?

The months leading up to the events of November, however static they may have seemed compared with the agitation in the neighbouring countries, were in fact a period of waiting for circumstances for change. The regime, unable to discern its utter isolation, in relation to both its own nation and the community of nations, reacted in its usual manner to a peaceful demonstration to commemorate the death of a student murdered by the Nazis fifty years ago. It could not have picked a worse moment—the patience of the silent nation had snapped; the circumstances had finally changed.

We, who had consistently tried to show the bankruptcy of the regime, were surprised at how quickly it collapsed under the blows of that one weapon, truth, voiced by demonstrators—students and actors who immediately went to the country to win over people—and then spread by a media no longer willing to serve a mendacious and brutal regime. As such non-violence was the only weapon we needed to use against violent power. Will those who were robbed, harassed and humiliated continue to be so magnanimous? As long as they can be, they have in their power to realize the idea of a democratic Europe, a Europe for the next millennium, a Europe of nations living in mutual domestic peace.

Translated from the Czech by Daphne Dorrell

Happiness in Czechoslovakia

✦

Abraham Brumberg

A veteran observer of Eastern Europe recounts his own visit to Prague at the end of 1989 as dramatic changes were taking place.

On the morning of August 28, 1968, I left my Washington home and headed by car for the seaside resort of Rehoboth, Maryland. I remember starting out in high spirits: there was not a cloud in the sky, and I was looking forward to sun and ocean.

Halfway, I switched on the radio for the news. It was grim: a Czechoslovak delegation, led by President Ludvík Svoboda and including the Soviet flunkeys Vasil Bílak and Miloš Jakeš had just returned from Moscow. With them were Aleksander

Abraham Brumberg, "Happiness in Czechoslovakia," from *Dissent,* Spring 1990, pp. 213–218.

Dubček and other leaders of the "Prague Spring," abducted and flown to the Soviet capital a few hours after Warsaw Pact troops occupied Czechoslovakia on August 20–21.

According to Tass, the Soviet Politburo and the Czechoslovak delegation, following discussions "in an open atmosphere of comradeliness and friendship," had signed a paper called the "Moscow Agreement." The agreement affirmed both governments' commitment to the "support, consolidation and defense of socialism and the implacable struggle with counterrevolutionary forces." It expressed the Kremlin's approval of the Czechoslovak government's policies and promised that the Warsaw troops would not interfere in Czechoslovakia's internal affairs.

There are events that in a flash illuminate the passing of one era and the birth of a new one. The sight of Neville Chamberlain waving a piece of paper that carried "Herr Hitler's" guarantee of "peace in our times" was one such event. Half a century later, Dubček et al.'s arrival at the Prague airport was another. As I sat in my car, I did not have to know precisely what had transpired in Moscow, later to be so chillingly depicted in Zdeněk Mlynář's *Nightfrost in Prague*. The fact that František Kriegel, chairman of the Czechoslovak National Front and the only Jew on the Czechoslovak side, failed to sign the "Agreement" was one straw in the wind.

But more. The document ignored the April Plenum of the Czechoslovak party's Central Committee, which adopted the "Action Program," the most important document of the "Prague Spring." It passed over in silence the party's Extraordinary Party Congress, held right after the invasion, which had repudiated the occupation and elected a new reformist Central Committee. It was full of the standard cant about "proletarian internationalism" and promised that all would be well once "normalization" had been achieved. In addition, the Tass communiqué referred to the Czech diehards by their old titles, even though they had been shorn of them a few days earlier. So I knew the jig was up.

In 1968 I was editor of the journal *Problems of Communism*. For reasons professional and personal, I was swept up by the events rocking the communist bloc at that time—the emergence of a dissident movement in the Soviet Union, the student unrest followed by the foul anti-Semitic campaign in Poland, the Prague Spring. In June I had spent two weeks in the Czechoslovak capital, talking to numerous people and wondering whether their dream of "socialism with a human face" would ever come about. I remember asking them whether they thought it safe to see me and whether the secret police wasn't monitoring our encounters. They shrugged off my question with a laugh: One of them, I think it was Antonín Liehm, blithely assured me that "those policemen are sitting in their barracks, guzzling beer and playing checkers."

Somehow, it was all too good to be true. More than a year later, on the first anniversary of the Warsaw Pact invasion, I went to Moscow. On that day, *Pravda's* lead article, reprinted from the Czech party paper, *Rudé pravo,* detailed all my movements in June 1968 and fingered me, with two or three others, as one of the main instigators of the 1968 "counterrevolution." I learned then, and in later issues of *Pravda,* that I was a known "agent," a tool of world imperialism and international Zionism, and a "long-time operative of the Israeli secret service."

But all this was to come later. On that fateful day in August 1968, I decided that I must ask somebody with inside knowledge of the Czech and Soviet apparatus to write an article on the "Moscow Agreement" and its aftermath. During the months that followed, as things took their inevitable turn (a stepped-up offensive by Moscow in tandem with its Czech and Slovak allies, successive capitulations by Dubček, ending with his ouster in April 1969), I cast about for a suitable candidate, finally finding not one but two: Jiří Dienstbier, Prague Radio's man in Washington, and Radomir Selucký, a colleague of the Czech economist Ota Šik, who had left his native country a few months earlier.

It was an audacious idea: to get an article, written pseudonymously by two Czech participants in the "Prague Spring," one of whom—Dienstbier—was contemplating returning to his native country (he did, and I took him to the airport in November 1969), and to publish the piece in what the Soviet press referred to as "a leading organ of anti-Sovietism." I knew both men and was very fond of them. And so at one of those interminable Washington parties, I sprung the question and obtained an instantaneous response: "Yes, happily."

The article, called "The Politics of Retrenchment," appeared in the July–August *Problems of Communism* as part of a series titled "Czechoslovakia: Agony of a Nation." It was signed by "Jan Provazhnik," identified as "the pseudonym of a well-known Czech writer and former member of the Czechoslovak Communist Party," who "has personally participated in some of the events described in his article."

Twenty years after "Jan Provazhnik's" piece, on Christmas 1989, I returned to Prague to meet my old friend Jiří Dienstbier, now Czechoslovakia's Foreign Minister. I had been aware during those two decades of Jiří's role in the Charter 77 movement, of his many arrests, and of his work—literally until the day he reported to the Ministry—as a stoker in a Prague apartment building. (Being a stoker was a choice job among those held by dissidents: it merely involved looking after the building's heating system, and it allowed plenty of time for reading, writing, and conspiring.)

Jiří had grown older—who hadn't? A tall man, he retained his striking good looks and his faintly Schweikian sense of humor. "I recall," I told him after we embraced in the empty palace that houses the Foreign Ministry, "that you seemed undecided, until you stepped on the plane, whether you were doing the right thing to return to Czechoslovakia." He smiled. "Not at all. We had a crazy party that day, remember? And I was too drunk to think straight about anything."

◆

FROM MY DIARY

December 26, 1989: Prague is redolent with the "Spring of Nations," wintry breezes notwithstanding. Groups of people gather to gaze at television sets in front of shops and office buildings. Some programs highlight the violent goings-on in Romania; others report preparations for Havel's inauguration. The atmosphere is peaceful, in turn somber and cheerful, but unfailingly good-natured. The young men and women working at the offices of the Občauske Forum (Civic Forum), while visibly overworked, are polite and helpful.

Every inch of wall space seems covered by placards, slogans, bulletins, proclamations, some stenciled, some typewritten, some in print. Havel is everywhere, but I find only one picture of Dubček. It was different in early December, I learn, when Dubček was, next to Havel, the most revered symbol of resistance to Moscow and its local henchmen. But the "Prague Spring" was becoming increasingly irrelevant. The stores are packed, but with virtually no queues.

And the food, the food! Let a horde of Soviet and Polish tourists loose and there would be mayhem. Tempting cuts of beef, all sorts of sausages, cheeses, canned goods, fruits, vegetables. Similarly with clothing, especially footwear: boots, boots. I buy a pair, for the black-market equivalent of $12. The official rate is nine kronen per dollar, and the unofficial (obtained everywhere) is thirty-five. Every other man who approaches me on Va clavike namesti with an offer to buy dollars speaks Italian. Why? Is Italian the lingua franca of the country's second economy?

December 27: A brief telephone conversation with Dienstbier. I can almost see his smile as he says, "Well, Abe, so you are here!" "A bit of a delay," I say, "twenty years to be exact." He asks me to come to the Ministry the following day, and in the meantime to look up Marlin Paloš, a spokesman of the Civic Forum and a good friend of his. In the crowded anteroom there I run into the son of the writer Arnošt Lustig, whom I first met in June 1968, and who has been teaching at the American University in Washington. "My father and I," says the young Lustig, "are here for *Life* magazine." I wish him luck and proceed to find Dienstbier's friend.

Paloš turns out to be an amiable man in his early thirties, formerly a philosophy student, with an excellent command of English. He too, he says, had worked as a stoker. We walk—or rather run—to a university student and faculty meeting several blocks away, to discuss the expansion of academic exchanges with Western countries. Luckily the meeting, attended by about two dozen serious-looking men and women of different ages, is soon over. Luckily, because even though as I discovered later I can understand Dubček's speech delivered in Slovak and most of Havel's Czech address, I find it almost impossible to follow spoken conversation in Czech.

Paloš gives me various names and addresses and says with a sigh: "You can't imagine what a crazy life I lead. I am absolutely exhausted." "It's not an easy thing to make a revolution," I say. He beams, and when we see each other several hours later, he repeats the phrase.

Back in my hotel that evening, I watch Ceauşescu's "trial" on television, with a voiceover in Czech. A hideous spectacle. If there was no way to submit him to a more or less decent judicial proceeding, then he and his wife (whom, in peasant fashion, he orders to keep silent whenever she tries to say something), should have been shot on the spot. Instead, his former military associates sit in judgment over the two miserable creatures, firing questions at them. "Bring me before the Romanian works," says Ceauşescu with icy contempt, "and you will hear them cheering after I have explained everything."

When the interrogation is over, the "court" meets for a brief time, and then orders the culprits into the courtyard to be executed. The two bodies tumble onto the ground. Sic transit gloria Conducatorul and Romania's "greatest woman scientist." I reflect on how lucky the Czechs are with their "velvet revolution": no sign of vindictiveness, no body counts, and a good chance to endow "normalization" with its normal meaning.

December 28: Dienstbier introduces me to two friends—Michal ("Misha") Reinmann, a one-time member of the Czech CP [Communist party] and for the past twenty years a professor at Berlin's Free University, and his Russian-born wife. We chat about the outlook for the future. I ask Dienstbier whether the new government can count on support from the workers. After all, their role had been in question until they laid down their tools on November 27, in solidarity with the intellectuals and students.

Dienstbier is quietly optimistic: the only problems that might arise, he says, would be among the workers in the industrial towns of Ostrova and coal mines of Slovakia. When some of the huge inefficient and pollution-breeding plants as well as some of the coal mines are closed—as they are bound to be—the thousands of unemployed will have to be retained for new jobs, and care will have to be taken to avoid the emergence of right-wing Slovak (which is to say anti-Czech) nationalism, still a potent force in that area.

Czech workers, too, will find themselves without work, but whereas in Bohemia and Moravia the traditions of industriousness have flourished for more than a century, the Slovak workers, many of them barely out of their peasant huts, will find it more difficult to adjust to the new conditions. "But we can manage," says Dienstbier, "the nation is behind us."

Michal Reinmann is less sanguine. "You are not sufficiently aware," he says to Dienstbier, "of the enormous difficulties that lie ahead. Unemployment and increased social differentiation will eventually replace today's euphoria." Among the unemployed will be hundreds of thousands of members of the "working intelligentsia," formerly employed in party establishments, who will become a serious source of discontent.

In addition, there is the danger of German industrial might. Once reunified, Germany, with its economic preeminence, will flood the Czech markets with cheap goods that the Czech economy will not be able to compete with. Furthermore, with living standards relatively low (high in comparison with, say, Poland but low in comparison with Austria or Germany) Czechoslovakia may lose thousands, if not hundreds of thousands, of workers to the West. I am doubtful about the latter (and even more doubtful two weeks later, after a visit to Berlin), what with the problems West Germany will face in absorbing the East German economy. But Reinmann's cautionary attitude makes perfectly good sense.

Later that day, I meet with Tomáš Jezek, an economist working at the Institute of Forecasting of the Czechoslovak Academy of Sciences, and just about to join his colleague Václav Klaus, recently appointed Minister of Finance, as his right-hand man. Like so many East European economists and politicians these days, Jezek believes in the "liberal" theories of Friedrich von Hayek. But his commitment to a market economy, I note, is hedged with more qualifications than that of his Polish colleague, Leszek Balcerowicz. In fact, he says that his country can "learn from the mistakes of other East European countries, say Poland"—a clear reference to Balcerowicz's headlong plunge into unrestrained laissez-faire.

Czechoslovakia's situation is incomparably better than Poland's: its industrial potential, despite the obsolete equipment, lack of spare parts, and dearth of even old generation computers, is still in working order; its enterprises ("which of course will have to be cut from the sway of the central ministries") are productive; its rate of inflation hovers at most between 6 and 8 percent, wages have not been rising more than 3 to 4 percent annually, and its foreign debt stands at $6 billion (compared with Poland's $40 [billion]).

In addition, rather than owing money to the Soviet Union, the latter is in debt to Czechoslovakia to the tune of 6 billion roubles. "We compare ourselves to Austria," says Jezek—a statement that would sound bizarre if uttered by any other East European official. "I am for the complete dismantlement of all government planning," he says, "but of course there are many economists who have different views on what a market economy should be like." He mentions a few names, but I doubt whether I'll be able to see them—time is short. Mr. Jezek, it occurs to me, is the Czech equivalent of a "wet Tory."

December 29: A brief meeting with an official of the National Socialist party—no relation to the German namesake—whose most famous member had been Edvard Beneš. Our conversation leads nowhere, probably because his English and German are as bad as my Czech. There is one amusing moment, however. When I ask him what was his party's definition of "socialism," he replies with a mock-anguished smile: "Perhaps you can suggest one?"

Lunch with Miroslav Gáluska, a man in his late sixties, an old (now ex-) CP member, who had held an impressive number of posts both in the diplomatic service and in the party apparatus. Like Reinmann, he is worried about possible workers' discontent and the power of the *nomenklatura*—especially since in Czechoslovakia "the Communist Party had a genuine base in the working class." Go to the Slovak mines and steel towns, he says, and you will see that the workers have "very little enthusiasm for Havel and what he stands for."

Galuska provides me with startling information about Czech agriculture: it is totally collectivized, it works, and the peasants are not in the least interested in a return to private farming. They produce enough food even for export. Their yields are on the average three to four times higher than before the war, and the peasants retain a vivid memory of prewar poverty.

Not a professional economist, Galuska is nevertheless well informed on the state of the country's economy and is dead set against immediate deregulation of prices and letting the market alone dictate production and distribution. Like Reinmann, he thinks the new government is counting too much on the long-range impact of the current euphoria. (Good politicians, these former Marxists.)

December 30: A loud, joyous, feverish party in the offices of *Ludové noviny,* until recently a *samizdat* publication, now on the way to becoming a weekly and, perhaps eventually, a daily. I meet the other half of "Jan Provazhnik": Radek Selucký, in his native country for the first time since 1968. "This is mad, mad!" he shouts, glass in hand. He plans to divide his time between Carlton University, where he has been teaching for the past eighteen years, and Charles University. I leave *Ludové noviny* a bit tipsy, bolstered in my conviction that Czechoslovakia will make it.

My wife and I spent the last two days in December watching Havel's formal election as president of the republic—solemn, elegant, and welcomed by hundreds of thousands of happy citizens who had massed in front of the presidential *Hrad* (castle)— and later in the magnificent Old Town Square, rubbing shoulders with beaming Czechs, Slovaks, and foreign tourists. We climbed to the third floor of a palace over-looking the temporary stage and watched dances performed by a string of folkdance groups—Gypsies, Slovaks, Moravians, Hungarians, Bohemians. The atmosphere was intoxicating.

On December 31, after another telephone conversation with Dienstbier, we went to the apartment of Rita Klimová, a high-spirited and wise woman in her late fifties, a long-time activist in Charter 77 and later in the Civic Forum. She had just received word from Dienstbier that she was appointed Czechoslovak Ambassador to the United States. She was fussing about the lack of any long dresses and total igno-rance of diplomatic protocol. My wife told her that if she doesn't have time to shop in Europe, she will take her on an all-day shopping spree in Washington. There were only a few people in Klimová's apartment, among them the elderly Jiří Hajek, former Minister of Foreign Affairs, and a towering figure in the Charter 77 movement.

A quiet but delightful evening. At midnight, we all raised our glasses to the future of Czechoslovakia and of all the countries in Eastern Europe. And thus the last remarkable week in the remarkable year that was.

New Year in Prague

✦

Václav Havel

This is President Havel's New Year address to his people at the beginning of 1991.

Dear Fellow Citizens,

There was a time when each New Year the president could deliver the same speech as he had the year before and no one would know the difference. Fortunately, that time is past. Time and history have come back into our lives. The gloomy skies of boredom and stultifying inaction have cleared, and we can only marvel at the vast range of possibilities a truly free political climate can offer, and at how it continues to astonish us, in both the good and the bad sense of the word.

Let me first talk about the unpleasant surprises the last year has brought us. In the first place, the heritage of the past few decades has proven worse than we could possibly have anticipated in the joyous atmosphere of those first few weeks of freedom. Each day brings new problems, and each day we realize how interrelated they are, how long they will take to solve, and how difficult it is to establish the proper order in which to deal with them.

We knew that the house we had inherited was not in order: the plaster was cracking and falling off, the roof looked as though it might leak, and we had doubts about other parts of it as well. After a year of careful inspection, we are shocked to discover that all the pipes are rusting, the beams are rotten, the wiring is in terrible shape, and the reconstruction we had planned for and looked forward to will take longer and cost far more than we first thought. What a year ago appeared to be a rundown house is in fact a ruin. This is not a pleasant discovery, and not surprisingly it has made us all feel disappointed and out of sorts.

Many of you are asking why we have settled so few accounts with the past, why we have failed to rehabilitate all its victims, right all the wrongs, and justly punish all the guilty ones. Many of you are asking why the "aristocracy" of the former regime, who grew rich at the society's expense, are still the aristocracy and why they have been able to find their feet so quickly in the new conditions. Many of you are surprised that

Václav Havel. Playwright, political dissident, and now president of Czechoslovakia, Havel epitomized the spirit of Czechoslovakia's "Velvet Revolution."
As a public figure, he belongs to the Czechoslovak tradition of the politically
committed intellectual and moral leader that stretches from the fifteenth-
century martyr Jan Hus to the founder of the first Czechoslovak republic,
Tomáš Garrigue Masaryk. (Sovfoto)

the broad transformation of our economy is still only being talked about, and that you
cannot see any changes for the better in your everyday lives. People are anxious
because all that planned reforms have brought so far are higher prices and the threat of
a loss of social security and jobs. We are all upset by the serious increase in crime. Our
hopes for a better future are increasingly mixed with a feeling of the opposite kind: fear
of the future.

In this atmosphere of general impatience, anxiety, disappointment, and doubt,
elements of spitefulness, suspicion, mistrust, and mutual recrimination are creeping

into public life. Surprisingly, freedom has opened the door to many of our negative qualities and has revealed the depth of the moral decline infecting our souls. We have clearly defeated the monolithic, visible, and easily identifiable enemy and now— driven by our discontent and our need to find a living culprit—we are seeking the enemy in each other. Each of us feels let down, even cheated by the other.

A year ago we were all united by the joy of having liberated ourselves from the totalitarian system; today we have all become somewhat neurotic from the burden of freedom. Our society is still in a state of shock. It could have been predicted, but no one predicted that the shock would be so profound. The old system has collapsed, the new one is not yet built, and our life together is marked by a subconscious uncertainty about what kind of system we want, how to build it, and whether we have the know-how to build it in the first place. The distance, the vagueness, and the uncertainty of the new order leads many of us to seek substitute, partial solutions and to forget that our success as individuals or groups is only possible with the general success of our whole community.

The unpleasant surprise of 1990, then, is this rather uncertain, if not stultifying, atmosphere that surrounds us at the end of the year.

This atmosphere may have caused us to forget some of the large, pleasant surprises of this first year following our uprising against the totalitarian regime. I have a duty to remind you of the good things that have happened, things that we could scarcely have imagined accomplishing a year ago.

+ The last units of the Soviet Army that invaded us twenty-two years ago are leaving the country.

+ The first free elections in forty-two years, in which we elected representatives of our choice to all levels of government, were successful.

+ Our parliaments have passed dozens of new laws that form the primary foundations of a genuine rule of law in a democratic and decentralized state.

+ The whole world, after many decades, now views us again as an independent democratic state which enjoys international respect. Prominent world statesmen have visited us, and they think highly of our foreign policy initiatives directed toward the creation of a new, peaceful Europe.

+ There is complete freedom of speech and expression in this country, and freedom of assembly and association is guaranteed.

+ We have torn down the barbed-wire fences surrounding our country that made us one big concentration camp. We can all travel anywhere we wish, and anyone may enter our country.

+ Freedom of religion has been renewed; all Catholic dioceses are represented by bishops; the Pope has visited our country, and we have established diplomatic relations with the Vatican.

✦ After difficult discussions, we have worked out a scenario for economic reform, and have passed several important economic laws that will establish the legal basis for these reforms. These reforms come into effect today.

✦ We have begun to create a genuine and workable federation [of the Czech and Slovak republics]. The first, and probably most dramatic, phase of this process culminated with the recent passing of the constitutional law that creates a new division of executive powers between the two republics and the federation.

Clearly, we have accomplished more in the past year than in all the preceding forty-one years. I know this is still far too little, and that the main task still lies ahead. What we have just completed constitutes the groundwork for the future. We have created a new environment. In the year ahead of us, we shall begin to fill this environment with its proper content. On this new groundwork, we shall begin to build our new democratic state and its new economic system. We shall move from the planning stage to actual reconstruction.

I make no secret of the fact that 1991 will be a year of great challenges. We will learn how good we are at facing them and whether we are capable of making the sacrifices that so far we have only talked about, and without which the great transformation of our country we have decided on will not take place.

None of the new representatives of our state is calling for these sacrifices in order to bring suffering to his fellow citizens. All of them are seeking ways to keep these sacrifices to a minimum. But they all know too that sacrifices are unavoidable. The former system has collapsed, not only in this country but in the whole former Soviet bloc. The old system of foreign economic relations has collapsed along with it. Even if we had wanted to keep the disastrous centralist economic system alive, we could simply not do so because the very environment in which it could have survived, and without which it would have been unthinkable, has vanished.

Dear fellow citizens, dear friends,

Let me now, in conclusion, try to summarize the basic tasks that lie before us in the coming year.

✦ By the end of this year, at the very latest, our parliaments should have passed three new constitutions: one federal and two for each of the republics. These constitutions are to form a logical triangle that will provide a stable and lasting foundation for the new legal order. If our legislatures succeed in this, they will have accomplished the main task that you, their electors, gave them to do over their two-year mandate. Until these new constitutions come into effect, several provisional laws should be passed to establish a constitutional means of settling any disputes that might arise during this difficult period.

✦ This month, auction sales should begin according to the law on the privatization of small business. This so-called small-scale privatization, as well the restitution of illegally confiscated property, could also, in my opinion, be completed by the end of this coming year. The large, inflexible, and bureaucratic organizations in the area of services, trade, and light industry, should be broken up and replaced by an extensive network of private and fully independent businesses.

+ At the same time, large-scale privatization of large factories and enterprises should begin as well. This process will probably require several years, and when it is completed, all ownership—that is, ownership of the land, of real estate, and the means of production—should be in the hands of specific, clearly defined, and fully independent owners.

+ Today, as you know, marks the beginning of a period in which prices can be set with relative freedom. This is one of the conditions of a genuine market environment. The deregulation of prices is also related to the domestic convertibility of the crown, which is intended to be the first step on the long and difficult road to a full and genuine convertibility. In the first half of the year, despite countermeasures, we can expect an increase in inflation. This too is one of the costs of economic reform. We will also have to pass laws governing trade and commerce so that foreign investors will regain confidence in doing business in our country. So far, what has held them back has been the lack of clear ownership policies and a legal framework for foreign involvement in the economy.

+ Along with these initial economic measures, the government should develop a clear strategy in two areas. First, in the social sphere where, in cooperation with the trade unions, it will be necessary to accelerate the creation of a system of legislative and administrative safety nets to alleviate any unjust and inhumane impact the economic reforms might have; and second, in determining the structure and aims of the energy resources and heavy industry sectors. So far, we are not clear about which course to take, and in the given situation, we cannot rely on the emerging market environment to settle the matter for us. The new strategies must also take into account the basic requirements of ecological well-being. . . .

+ Next year, we will once again start preparations for new parliamentary elections. During this year, the spectrum of political forces in our society should stabilize, and I believe that by the next elections a better electoral law will be in place, and that the representative assemblies will be smaller and more practical, as defined by our new constitutions.

+ In our foreign policy, we should continue to take new initiatives. As soon as possible—perhaps in January—the Political Advisory Committee of the Warsaw Pact should meet in order to dismantle all its military structures, including the joint command system, as member countries have already agreed to do in preliminary meetings. In the spirit of the Paris Charter, we will try to bring a new quality into the Helsinki process; in this regard the fact that the permanent secretariat of the CSCE [Conference on Security and Cooperation in Europe] will be located in Prague should inspire us. As for our inclusion in the existing and newly emerging structures in Europe, we intend to coordinate our approach on all fronts chiefly with Poland and Hungary, our closest neighbors. We believe that in January or February, Czechoslovakia will be accepted as a full member of the Council of Europe. At the same time, we expect to conclude mutually advantageous treaties of association with the European Community. We make no secret of our wish to become a full member. At the same time, we would like to work in closer cooperation with NATO, even though we have no intention, for the time being, of joining it.

Dear fellow citizens,

I am saying nothing new if I tell you that a difficult time lies ahead, and that the year which begins today will be the most difficult. It is most important that we not lose hope, no matter how difficult the trials we face may be. Were we to become dispirited, these trials would no longer be a test of our mettle, but merely the occasion for suffering and want. We will meet these challenges, I believe, and pass the test with flying colors. It all depends on the degree of hope we can keep alive in our souls. We must safeguard this hope both in ourselves, and in those around us. . . .

After so many years, we have got rid of the evil landlord, and no matter how desolate the state of our house after so many years of his rule, it now belongs to us, and what we do with it is up to us alone. Therefore I ask you all, Czechs, Slovaks, and people of other nationalities, to respect our new state, to treat it as your own, and to make a contribution to its overall success. We have already undergone the first difficult test of our ability to coexist as different nations in the same state, and the Czechs and Slovaks have passed that test.

I wish all Slovaks success in building an autonomous and economically independent republic. I believe that it will be a republic of love and pride for all its citizens. I wish the same to all Czechs. I believe that their republic will be a republic of wisdom and tolerance for all its citizens. . . .

I appeal to all who, through their work, create things of value for the whole society. Once again you will be creating these things for yourselves and those close to you, not for those who rule over you or for the abstract future of a utopian ideology. I appeal to all those who quickly find their feet in the new economic system to be mindful of those who do not find immediate success, to use their skills to help them. . . . I ask them not to forget that the profit they create is not an end in itself, but a means to enhance the common wealth of society, and to create conditions for a genuinely dignified and full human life.

Dear fellow citizens, dear friends,

The time when New Year's addresses were the same each year has definitely come to an end. I firmly believe that the coming year will contain more pleasant surprises than unpleasant ones. I believe that I will be able to announce to you that the reconstruction of our house has been successfully begun, and that its foundations once more rest firmly in this land and its best traditions.

A year ago I finished my New Year's address by paraphrasing a well-known quotation from Comenius: "People, your government has been returned to you!" Today, I would add: "And it is up to you to show that the return of your government into your own hands has not been in vain."

Translated by Paul Wilson

Václav Havel's First Term

✦

Vladimír V. Kusin

As Havel was being elected to a two-year term as president in July 1990, this report from Radio Free Europe offered an assessment of his first six-month term as president.

Václav Havel's first term as President of Czechoslovakia lasted a little over six months, from December 29 to July 5. It was a momentous half year in the country's history and Havel had an indelible impact on it.

After the brutal suppression of the student demonstration on November 17, 1989, Havel was quickly recognized as the embodiment of Czechoslovakia's "velvet" revolution. He took the lead in founding the Civic Forum only two days after the revolution had begun and steered the organization to the head of an emerging coalition of opposition groups. During the first weeks of the revolution, Havel appeared as the main speaker at most of the large demonstrations in Prague and was instantly recognized, not least because both his ideas and his voice were known to the public from Western radio broadcasts to Czechoslovakia. His only conceivable rival, Alexander Dubček, another symbol of opposition to neo-Stalinism, quickly acknowledged Havel's superiority, agreed to join forces with him, and ceded to him the leadership of the opposition movement. The old regime also acknowledged Havel's singular

Vladimír V. Kusin, "Václav Havel's First Term," from *Report on Eastern Europe,* July 20, 1990, pp. 11–13. Reprinted with the permission of Radio Free Europe/Radio Liberty.

position, and the Prime Minister at the time, Ladislav Adamec, was compelled to sit down at a negotiating table with him. Havel became synonymous with the revolution and was the obvious choice for the Presidency.

◆

REFORMER BECOMES REVOLUTIONARY

Under the pressure of events over which he had only limited control, Havel developed a conceptual framework for the revolution within a matter of days, if not hours. Broad concepts that are able to start influencing developments immediately, without gestation or the need to educate the public, are notoriously more difficult to engender than frameworks erected by theorists or politicians who are part of a regular political process. Until November 1989 most people (including foreign observers of Czechoslovak communism) believed that change would come about through a gradual loosening by reformists of the communist leadership's rigid rule, not unlike the processes that were seen under former party leader Antonín Novotný in the latter part of the 1960s, under János Kádár in Hungary, and under Mikhail Gorbachev in the USSR.

When, contrary to expectations, hundreds of thousands of Czechs and Slovaks appeared on the streets (where modest concessions are not best negotiated but where more ambitious goals stand a chance of being achieved), Havel readily responded by persuading the opposition to relinquish the idea of reforming the Communists and to pursue instead their ouster. At the same time, he succeeded in making the popular uprising retain the advantages of a gradual change, such as continuity, the coalescence of divergent opposition groups, and, above all, the absence of violence. Havel was the principal force that telescoped reform into revolution, without abandoning the former.

◆

PHILOSOPHER OF TRANSITION

The Civic Forum was at the heart of the plans for a transition from communism to democracy that Havel and his friends conceived during December 1989 and later fine-tuned. The movement became the guiding force of the revolution; a rallying point for diverse anticommunist interests; and a harbinger of the party-political landscape that emerged from the turmoil.

From the start of the revolution, and throughout the six months of Havel's first term of office, the Civic Forum and its Slovak sister group, the Public against Violence, sought to conquer the old regime by making use of revolutionary power (enforcing dismissals and appointments) and taking advantage of existing "legal" institutions and processes. Havel advocated a broad coalition of prodemocracy forces. Aware of the support he had among former dissidents, intellectuals, and young people, he took pains to establish good relations with three groups without whose backing, he believed, democracy could not evolve: the Slovaks, religious believers (especially Catholics), and those who had worked with the old regime but had not been responsible for its crimes. The last group included not only members of the former satellite parties but also Communists who had joined the revolution, such as Prime Minister Marian Čalfa and, perhaps above all, Minister of Defense Miloslav Vacek. Indeed, the success of the revolution can be attributed in part to the fact that the military did not attempt to stand in democracy's way.

Havel consistently advocated the continued existence of the Civic Forum as an umbrella movement of groups and individuals rather than a fully organized political party. In his opinion (shared by many former dissidents), the future of Czechoslovak politics would be determined by the pressure the citizen was encouraged to bring to bear on the state. Havel favored elections in which individuals rather than parties would compete for seats in parliament; but he eventually let himself be swayed by those who argued that the enormous tasks in hand would be better tackled by a more homogeneous parliament, such as only a contest between parties could produce. The Civic Forum won the elections overwhelmingly; but, no doubt under Havel's influence, it has remained a movement embracing many beliefs and persuasions. The profile of the Civic Forum may, however, change during the process of political consolidation.

◆

MORALIST

There is little doubt that the "velvet" nature of the Czechoslovak revolution was primarily the result of the influence exercised by Havel, who has always displayed a tolerant attitude toward his fellow men. Havel realized that a dangerous situation might arise if the revolution were to turn into a violent tumult. Furthermore, he had before his eyes the political upheavals in Poland, Hungary, and East Germany, during which violence had been avoided. After the suppression of the student demonstration on November 17, no one was injured for political reasons or as the result of acts of revenge or retribution. Thanks to Havel, the understandable excitement over the issue of collaboration with the secret police, fueled as it was by the passion of electioneering, remained within manageable proportions. He repeatedly pleaded for national reconciliation, and, long before the revolution, had said that all who had lived under the old regime were marked by it, as either victims or victimizers. After the revolution, in his celebrated New Year's speech, he emphasized this once more. And in his address to the new parliament after the June elections, Havel pleaded for the broadest possible moral regeneration, stressing that morality was in the last instance more important than economic reform and certainly more desirable than party-political gains.

An unexpected revolution, the heat of the first competitive election campaign after more than four decades, the legacy of communist rule, and the knowledge that economic change will make life tough do not form the most propitious backdrop to a moral rebirth. Not even Havel's towering morality has been able, nor will it be able, to prevent strife in which less than pristine methods are used. It is, nonetheless, generally recognized that he has already done a great deal to promote fair play in Czechoslovakia and to help the country cope with its problems calmly and in a humane manner.

◆

ADVOCATE OF A UNITED EUROPE

Thanks to both Havel and his friend Foreign Minister Jiří Dienstbier, the new image of Czechoslovakia as a democratic and cooperative country was projected into the international arena swiftly and forcefully. The foreign policies of Havel and Dienstbier correspond on the whole to what one would expect of a country that has the history and geopolitical position of Czechoslovakia and is now governed by a liberal-democratic coalition. Havel and Dienstbier have placed strong emphasis on a rapprochement involving all European countries, on the removal of barriers deriving from the earlier rifts between blocs, and on the nonconfrontational handling of problems arising from the legacy of communist expansionism. Havel has addressed the delicate issue of Czech-German relations; opened up the country to foreign contacts and cooperation; proposed a collective security system under the aegis of the Helsinki process; started regular consultation with Poland, Hungary, Austria, Yugoslavia, and Italy; and pushed for a reconstruction of the Warsaw Pact that would negate its military influence but retain its links with the USSR. Dienstbier has argued that the Soviet Union should not be isolated further, since this could pose a threat to European stability.

◆

DEMURRALS

Most people find it difficult to criticize Havel, perhaps because it is not easy to decide which of his more controversial undertakings were necessary to propel the democratic revolution further and which were not. Moreover, there seems to be a genuine consensus that the country has needed Havel, will continue to need him for some time to come, and is generally fortunate to have him.

Observers have noted what they call the amateurish way in which Havel makes decisions and launches initiatives. Until quite recently, almost all Havel's advisors were intellectuals, somewhat bohemian and well meaning but not well versed in the art of government. The sheer magnitude of the tasks in hand suggests that a professional underpinning would have been required; but the necessary experts were simply not available, most professionals in Czechoslovakia being communist bureaucrats. Some observers have said that Havel interferes too much in the day-to-day running of the state and has usurped more power than becomes a President. According to some people, he has developed a taste for the authority that has accrued to him so quickly and so unavoidably. One might, however, argue that vesting an arbiter of Havel's moral standing with temporary suzerainty is just what the country needs, if it is not to linger too long in the grips of its communist legacy. But there remains the fact that some of Havel's decisions have been questioned. Did he have to release so many prisoners, many of whom were common criminals, in his amnesty, without securing adequate police protection for the public? And did he campaign too blatantly for the Civic Forum and, in Slovakia, for the Public against Violence when presidential nonpartisanship would have been more appropriate? These, and other, questions remain open to debate.

Be that as it may, the public's endorsement of Havel is overwhelming. As for the politicians, before the vote on July 5, all parliamentary factions had agreed tentatively to vote for Havel's re-election, but in the end 50 of the 300 deputies cast their votes against him. Indeed, politics in a democracy are not about assent alone.

Relations Between the Czechs and the Slovaks

✦

Peter Martin

The long-standing tension between Czechs and Slovaks has resurfaced to plague efforts to fashion a new order in Czechoslovakia. This report examines the problem in general and the particular negotiation undertaken in August 1990 to resolve matters in dispute.

There has been no lack of polemics recently on the issue of relations between the Czechs and the Slovaks. First, the Czechoslovak Federal Assembly's decision to adopt a dual name for the country without incorporating a hyphen between "Czecho" and "Slovak" met with strong resistance in Slovakia. The Slovaks then expressed concern about the future federal and Slovak Constitutions and the Slovak Republic's right to greater autonomy. In April several thousand Slovaks demonstrated in Bratislava for Slovak independence. The leaders of the movement that organized the demonstration, the National Council for the Liberation of Slovakia, presented a program whose primary goal was said to be "the proclamation of an independent

Peter Martin, "Relations Between the Czechs and the Slovaks," from *Report on Eastern Europe*, September 7, 1990, pp. 1–6. Reprinted with the permission of Radio Free Europe/Radio Liberty.

Slovak state." The proposal also called for a nationwide referendum on Slovak independence.

In May, writing in the Czech literary weekly *Literání Noviny,* the Czech writer Ludvík Vaculík sharply criticized the Slovaks and their separatist tendencies. His article "Our Slovak Question" provoked the Slovak writer Vladimír Mináč to respond just as caustically. Mináč's article, "Our Czecho-Slovak Question," appeared in the Slovak literary weekly *Nove Slovo.* Reactions to Vaculík's article showed that the topic of future relations between the Czechs and the Slovaks had developed into an intense controversy in both republics.

Two recent events have fueled the controversy. On July 8 alumni of the Teachers' Training College at Banovce nad Bebravou attempted to display a commemorative plaque for Monsignor Jozef Tiso, President of the pro-German Slovak Republic during World War II and the college's founder in 1934. But the plaque sparked so many protests that it was removed. Local government officials also asked the Slovak National Council to establish an independent commission to evaluate and clarify, "in their full historical context," the roles of both Tiso and the Slovak state. The Slovak National Democratic Movement in turn demanded the removal of all "plaques, statues, and names associated with the former President, Edvard Beneš."

Tension mounted after the Czechoslovak Socialist Party daily *Svobodné Slovo* published an article falsely accusing one of the most prominent prewar Slovak leaders, Andrej Hlinka, of being a "fascist murderer." The party's leadership said that the article had "undoubtedly caused serious consequences for relations between the Czechs and the Slovaks and [had] contributed to making national problems more acute."

✦

VACULÍK'S CHALLENGE

The exchange of views between Vaculík and Mináč provides a good example of the current discussion about relations between the Czechs and the Slovaks. In his article, Vaculík claimed that the Czechs owed much to the Slovaks. The Czechs, he claimed, had taken possession of the Slovaks' territory but had given nothing in return, failing to understand the Slovaks' feelings and thoughts. Vaculík observed that the Czechs were at fault for not having absorbed "Slovakism" into their collective conscience and for not trying to understand the Slovaks. Vaculík then abandoned his conciliatory tone, becoming increasingly critical of the Slovaks. They had, he said, no genuine history of their own and could only be supported with the assistance of other nations. After the defeat of fascism, the Slovaks should have taken a critical look at their "fascist experience." Instead, they had renewed their adherence to "good Czechoslovakia," erasing the fascist experience from their minds. Having commented that Slovak complaints about the Czechs were "sociopsychological," Vaculík observed, without elaboration, that the Slovaks had not been prepared to interact with other nations as equals.

Vaculík criticized the Slovaks' lack of political activism, maintaining that they had left the most difficult issues for the Czechs to resolve. He noted, for example, that during the 1968 Prague Spring the Slovaks had seemed to think it was primarily the Czechs' responsibility to oust the Communists. The Slovaks seemed to be saying, "You, the Czechs, imported communism into Slovakia, so you will have to remove it." While the Czechs had been severely punished for rebelling in 1968, the Slovaks had not been, and they had continued to push for autonomy:

> Misled by their history, spoiled by Czech intervention in their behalf, the Slovaks do not know how an autonomous and proud nation should act. In the future they will continue to seek excuses for their own failures, blaming them on the Czechs.

Vaculík then asked whether the Czechs really needed a coexistence of this kind. The Slovaks, he maintained, had not had to suffer the way the Czechs had in the past; someone else had always been available to solve their problems for them. Not even the Slovak national uprising, he said, had managed to force them to confront the basic existential and moral question "Who are you and what do you want?" Having no yardstick they could use to test their maturity, the Slovaks had always used the Czechs to that end. Again Vaculík asked, "Do we need such a coexistence?"

It indeed appeared that this outspoken criticism of the Slovaks was designed to offend Slovak readers. Vaculík rejected the notion of giving the "adult Slovak brother a bed in a common house," dismissing the hypothetical Slovak with "No bed for you, my brother: you have your own house." Vaculík then asked why the Slovaks should try to get anything (specifically their independence) from the Czechs "by centimeters" when they could have it all immediately. He enumerated the advantages the Czechs would enjoy if they separated from the Slovaks. First, the Czechs would eliminate many of their economic losses as well as numerous ethnic problems connected with the Hungarian and Ruthenian minorities. With only one government, the Czechs would be able to live relatively peacefully, using the opportunity to catch up with the West. With regard to relations between the Czechs and the Slovaks, Vaculík suggested that all questions, economic and otherwise, could be solved through agreements similar to those that exist between the Czechoslovak Federal Republic and, for example, Denmark or Sweden. The Slovaks' demands for autonomy provided the Czechs with a "genuine opportunity" to begin a new life, Vaculík concluded. Everything had changed; people only needed to recognize this fact.

Czech and Slovak reactions to Vaculík's article varied. Most Czechs appeared to agree with Vaculík and reportedly considered Czechoslovakia mature enough to separate into two nations. The Slovaks, reacting somewhat more mildly, suggested that the article provided an impetus for re-evaluating relations between the republics.

◆
MINÁČ'S RESPONSE

While Vaculík did not leave any room for compromise, the prominent Slovak writer Vladimír Mináč took a somewhat milder approach to the problem, suggesting that decisions about Czech-Slovak relations be made properly and peacefully. The Slovaks regretted not having a feudal history of their own, he said, but it was not easy to "cobble together a history that past political administrators [Czechs and Hungarians] [had] torn to pieces, trodden under foot, and concealed."

Mináč first declared that the call for an autonomous Slovak state was a legitimate demand that had not originated with the Slovak Fascists. He firmly maintained that Slovakia, which had always been a political nation, did not have to ask for an identity card from any Czech "gendarme"—or from Vaculík. He dismissed the idea that the Czechs were the Slovaks' "older brothers," commenting, "We have no older brother." This notion, which revealed Czech political thinking in its most outdated form, was a new myth that had become central to the "Czechoslavak legend," Mináč asserted. According to this view of things, the Czechs were the lords and the Slovaks their servants, and the Czechs would have to teach the Slovaks how to act decently. Mináč continued:

> For more than 100 years, Slovak politics has deserved to be reproached often. Slovakia was not free: it flattered Vienna, then Budapest, and repeatedly Prague. It was more rhapsodic than realistic; it was more tearful than energetic. More than once did the Slovaks demonstrate their determination to become autonomous, but they could never achieve their goal because of Prague's economic and administrative centralism, its armed and violent police. It was Prague's centralist thinking that would have made a "social group" of our nation.

Mináč emphasized that the Slovaks had examined their fascist experience during fascism's "powerful existence" rather than after its defeat. The Slovaks had kicked "a well-armed Fascist and not a dying horse," he said, and their national uprising had been the second largest antifascist revolt in Europe. Mináč said his nation's rebellion against Hitler's Germany had been an "instinctive" reaction, a response to a need to keep what Mináč referred to as the country's "national conscience" clean, and not an attempt to restore the Czechoslovak Republic:

> The Slovak does not want to be a Czechoslovak. He does not want to be forced to live behind an alien facade. He wants to be independent and sovereign. Like the National Socialists in 1947, Vaculík frightens the Slovaks with Hungarians and Ruthenians, with economic consequences, with Czecho-Austrian unity. But we are not so easily frightened anymore.

Mináč concluded that all major Slovak political forces were convinced that some form of official coexistence with the Czechs could be "useful, advantageous, and reasonable." But he added that, during the next two years, the Slovaks would have time "to debate issues freely . . . , to agree or disagree on the basis of arguments rather than resentments." It should be noted that some Slovaks disagreed with parts of Mináč's assessment.

✦
TRENDS

The roots of this latest conflict run deep. The disputes are taking place in a country plagued by economic uncertainties, threatened with falling living standards, and governed by a leadership divided on many issues—the pace of economic reform, for example. But the most difficult political problems lie ahead, when the Federal Assembly and the Czech and Slovak National Councils will have to draft and adopt new constitutions.

Against this background, both the Czechs and the Slovaks have reached a new level of national awareness. The Czech government's program emphasizes the creation of a "new Czech statehood" and a civil society. In addition, two regions of the Czech Republic, Moravia and Silesia, have been demanding more autonomy, although none of the movements in either region has ever questioned the country's federal status. In an interview exploring ways in which Moravia and Silesia might "detach themselves from Prague's centralism," the secretary of the Ostrava local administration, Karel Baron, suggested two methods of attaining autonomy. One called for the establishment of a Moravian-Silesian government in Brno, the other for the creation of self-governing towns and communities. Baron favors a gradual transition to regional autonomy in accordance with the future constitution.

Evidence of this new national awareness appeared in Slovakia soon after the November 1989 events, manifesting itself in three separate political trends. First, Slovakia's major political force, the Public against Violence, together with some minor parties such as the Democrats and the Greens, has defended Czechoslovakia's federal system while calling for more autonomy for both republics. The second major political group, the Christian Democratic Movement, advocates establishing a Czecho-Slovak confederation and allowing Slovakia to enter Europe "as a sovereign and equal entity." The Slovak Freedom Party has issued a statement supporting the Christian Democrats' program. The third political group, represented by the Slovak National Party and the Movement for an Independent Slovakia, has called for a "sovereign, autonomous, and independent" Slovak Republic; these groups do not seem to want to look back to the days of the pro-German Slovak state of 1939–1945, however.

✦
GOVERNMENTAL INITIATIVES

The continuing dispute over future relations between the Czech and the Slovak Republics prompted federal, Czech, and Slovak government leaders to meet behind closed doors in Trencianské Teplice on August 8 and 9. There, guidelines were drawn up for the experts who will draft the governments' new constitutions. It was also decided that decision-making power would be shifted from the federal to the Czech and the Slovak governments as of January 1, 1991. The federal government itself is to become a coordinating agency that will help the two independent states to work harmoniously together. It will retain control of defense and border security, establish legal standards, maintain a standard currency, fight crime, and assume responsibility for taxation, price controls, and foreign policy. The proposals from the meeting will be submitted to the political parties that make up the three governments and to the legislatures themselves.

Slovak Prime Minister Vladimír Meciar said that the meeting's participants, rejecting the idea of confederation, had decided to preserve the current state alliance between the Czech and Slovak Republics. The decision was sure to offend some Slovaks, he added, and might, in fact, have drawn the lines for a confrontation between certain Slovak groups and the governments. In fact, the proposal agreed to in Trencianské Teplice incorporates elements of both a federation and confederation.

On August 14 the Slovak National Party and the Independent Party of Slovaks organized a meeting of nine Slovak political parties. The result of the meeting was a joint statement demanding that a fully independent and sovereign Slovak state be established and rejecting the proposal agreed to in Trencianské Teplice. On August 15 the Slovak Christian Democrats distanced themselves from the statement and expressed support for the governments' proposal.

The varying attitudes of Czechs and Slovaks toward the Roman Catholic Church also play an important role in contemporary Czechoslovak politics. The former prominent dissident and Catholic priest Václav Malý has said that Czech intellectuals have an anticlerical tradition, particularly in the more secularized regions of Bohemia and Moravia, which he called an "atheistic zone." In his opinion, this non-religious atmosphere might also exacerbate relations with Slovakia. His friends in the Civic Forum had often failed to understand Slovak religious feelings, he observed. For instance, they were enthusiastically replacing the statues and pictures of discredited communist leaders with images of Tomáš Masaryk, who had helped found Czechoslovakia in 1918. Rightly or wrongly, Malý noted, many religious Slovaks suspected Masaryk of having been anti-Catholic.

◆

ASSESSMENT

Just ten months after the November revolution and two months after the elections, the biggest political question in Czechoslovakia is whether a satisfactory alliance can be established between the Czechs and the Slovaks. It remains to be seen whether the increasingly divided country can devise constitutions that recognize the Czech and the Slovak states' political rights, satisfy their nationalistic feelings, and at the same time maintain a viable federal arrangement.

Even though the Czechoslovak federation is troubled by serious economic problems, all aspects of the country's life will be increasingly filtered through the prism of "national" interests. In June the Institute for Public Opinion Research in Prague published the results of a poll on relations between the Czechs and the Slovaks. The survey showed that 39% of the respondents considered that these relations were "friendly"; 41% found them to be "hostile"; and 20% thought relations were neither "friendly" nor "hostile." The percentage of people who believed relations were "hostile" was considerably higher than the 32% in last February's poll. Thus, there seems to be little time left to resolve the "division of power" issue in Czechoslovakia. Federal Deputy Prime Minister Pavel Rychetský commented, "It is impossible to wait another two years for the new constitutions in order to arrange the division of power." In his opinion, the republics' constitutions needed to be completed in one year and the federal constitution in two.

Four major factors will affect the country's future. The first is the Federal Assembly, whose strength and authority will be tested by sensitive national, economic, and social issues within the next few months. The leading political forces, the Civic Forum in the Czech Republic and Public against Violence in Slovakia, whose cohesion is also being tested, constitute the second factor. Their popularity has decreased as smaller political parties, such as the Slovak National Party, become more dynamic and successful. The success of these smaller parties is the direct result of the national issues now included in their programs. The third factor involves the transition to a free market economy. Should the three governments fail to achieve their free-market goals, social tension and national awareness in both the Czech Republic and Slovakia may increase. Finally, national issues in the Soviet Union and especially Yugoslavia might encourage the Czechs and Slovaks to seek a quick solution to their own national problems.

The Civic Forum Splits into Two Groups

✦

Jiří Pehe

In February 1991, the Civic Forum, which had presided over the radical transformation of the country, met in a congress that authorized formation of two distinct wings of the organization, one conservative and the other liberal. This report analyzes the split and the prospect that the electoral coalition will survive.

On February 23 the Civic Forum, the movement that led the anticommunist revolt in Czechoslovakia in late 1989 and emerged victorious from the parliamentary and local government elections in 1990, held a congress at which the formal division

Jiří Pehe, "The Civic Forum Splits into Two Groups," from *Report on Eastern Europe,* March 8, 1991, pp. 11–14. Reprinted with the permission of Radio Free Europe/Radio Liberty.

A New Threat in Czechoslovakia. Environmental deterioration, often caused by the belching smoke of such old-fashioned blast furnaces as these in the city of "black" Ostrava, presents an acute ecological and economic challenge that the nation's democratic leadership must meet. Much the same scene could be found in every other East European nation. (Eastfoto)

of the forum into two groups was approved. One group plans to function as a right-of-center party with a well-defined internal structure; the other wants to establish itself as a loosely organized civic movement with a liberal political agenda. The proposal to split the forum had been approved by the leaders of the forum's two rival factions on February 8. It was also decided at the congress that, at least until the next parliamentary elections, the two new political organizations would remain in a coalition bearing the name of the Civic Forum.

WHY A SPLIT?

The rapid polarization of the Civic Forum started in the fall of 1990, when Finance Minister Václav Klaus was elected chairman of the movement. Criticizing the loose organizational structure of the forum and what he thought was its nebulous political program, Klaus had vowed to transform the movement into a political party with a well-defined structure and a registered membership. At about the same time, some deputies of the Civic Forum in the Federal Assembly and the Czech National

Council formed the Interparliamentary Club of the Democratic Right, which also expressed strong support for transforming the forum into a right-of-center political party and for Klaus's concept of the radical privatization of the Czechoslovak economy.

Opposition to the idea of transforming the Civic Forum into a political party with a clearly defined political philosophy, as well as to some of Klaus's economic policies, was expressed by forum deputies and ministers with centrist and left-of-center political views. In early December they formed the Liberal Club of the Civic Forum, whose initial statement was signed by eight of the forum's ten ministers in the federal government. The program of the group was vague; its main objective seemed to be to prevent Klaus and his followers from transforming the Civic Forum into a right-wing political party.

In December 1990 and early January 1991 representatives of the two groups clashed repeatedly over the future of the forum. The growing conflict was seen as a danger to the forum's unity as well as to the stability of the Civic Forum–led government. At the forum's congress on January 12 and 13, delegates voted to transform the Civic Forum into a political party with a solid internal structure and a clear-cut political program and to require all members of the forum to register. It decided against any form of collective membership, effectively forcing various political groups that have used the forum as a political umbrella to leave.

Although the congress was a clear victory for Klaus and his followers, members of the Liberal Club said that they would remain in the forum to prevent a split. Like the Interparliamentary Club of the Democratic Right, the Liberal Club was given three seats on the forum's newly created seventeen-member Executive Council, which was to be headed by Klaus. The congress elected Klaus chairman of the revamped forum. Although it was expected that some individual members of the Liberal Club would leave the forum after the congress, the majority of the forum's membership appeared ready to accept the results of the congress. The Republican Council, which after the congress was to be replaced by the Executive Council, was asked to implement the decisions reached at the congress.

◆

AFTER THE JANUARY CONGRESS

On January 18 Klaus asserted that "the political situation within the Civic Forum was clarified after the congress." However, conflicts between the two rival factions continued. These took the form of charges, publicized in the media, that some right-wing deputies of the forum were ready to demand a vote of no confidence in the government. The purpose of this move, according to the press and some politicians associated with the Liberal Club, was to replace some of Klaus's opponents in the government with his supporters. Some reports even alleged that a shadow cabinet had already been formed.

Klaus described these reports as "an act by forces within the Civic Forum that do not want to support its present development." He denied any plans for personnel changes in the government. Zdenek Jičinský, the Deputy Chairman of the Federal Assembly and one of the leading representatives of the Liberal Club, contested Klaus's denial. He said he had "certain, quite specific information" that some members of the Interparliamentary Club of the Democratic Right had discussed the question of "whether the ministerial posts they should take over were the right ones." He added he did not doubt that attempts to enforce personnel changes in the government would have serious consequences and warned that the "existing political coalition would disintegrate."

On January 31 the Liberal Club issued a statement in which it contested the results of the congress, stating that the club wanted the Civic Forum to continue "to span a broad political spectrum." The club also maintained that "political parties should come into existence in a natural way" and their development should not cast doubt on "the results of the elections." Charges that the transformation of the Civic Forum into a political party would invalidate the Civic Forum's electoral mandate were also made by other groups and parties outside the forum. Some parties even saw a need for early parliamentary elections.

◆

THE AGREEMENT ON AN OFFICIAL DIVISION

On February 8 the leaders of the two factions held a meeting at the presidential retreat in Lany. President Václav Havel, who had helped found the Civic Forum in late 1989 and had led it during the first weeks of its existence, chaired the meeting. The leaders agreed that the Civic Forum be officially split into two groups: one would be a right-of-center political party led by Klaus and founded on the principles approved by the Civic Forum congress in January, the other would keep the looser internal structure of a political movement and be formed around the Liberal Club of the Civic Forum. Neither group was to be allowed to use the name of the Civic Forum.

The agreement further stipulated that both groups form a coalition that would remain in place at least until the next parliamentary elections, scheduled for 1992. Both would support the current program for economic reform and would continue to cooperate with the groups for which the Civic Forum had served as a political umbrella. The Civic Forum itself would be transformed into a nonpolitical umbrella organization, represented by a committee whose purpose would be to coordinate the work of the two coalition partners. The main partners of the coordinating committee would be the chairmen of the Civic Forum's Caucuses in the Federal Assembly and the Czech National Council, both of which would continue to function until the next elections.

Commenting on the agreement, Klaus said that the "dividing line would be between those who respected the conclusions of the January congress and those who, for whatever reason, did not respect them." In fact, the dividing line appeared to run deeper: most of the members of the Liberal Club are former dissidents associated with Charter 77, whereas many of Klaus's supporters, like Klaus himself, have no dissident past. Klaus tried to define this division when he said that the current conflict was between the original task of the forum, "which was the abolition of the communist regime," and its present task, "which is the construction" of a new society. In Klaus's view, those "who did not belong to the former regime" found it easy to carry out the first task, but adopting "a constructive attitude" was something quite different. While Klaus's definition was perhaps somewhat simplistic, it indicated what kind of political ammunition the two groups might use against each other in the future. The nondissident past of Klaus's supporters could serve as a point of reference in future debates as often as the past of those members of the Liberal Club who became dissidents only after their expulsion from the communist party in the wake of the Soviet-led invasion of Czechoslovakia in 1968.

Klaus said on February 8 that Havel supported the division of the Civic Forum. Responding to the proposal by some forum leaders that he lead the coordinating committee, which would keep the forum's name, Havel said that such proposals might be premature, because "currently my participation in the work of the Civic Forum is not necessary." However, he added that if he was needed, he would "accept a role in the coordinating committee."

On February 12 Klaus observed that after the extraordinary congress of the Civic Forum on February 23, the two groups would probably hold their own constituent congresses. He argued that both groups, but especially the Liberal Club, should use the congresses "to define themselves more precisely."

✦

BEFORE THE CONGRESS

Some Civic Forum members protested the agreement reached at Lany on February 8 to divide the forum. A group called the Initiative for Preserving the Civic Forum as a Movement, which was formed on February 9, issued several statements criticizing the decision. Some individual members of the Liberal Club also expressed misgivings about the possibility of a formal split and complained that February 23 was too early a date for the forum's extraordinary congress. The Interparliamentary Club of the Democratic Right, on the other hand, issued a statement on February 14 emphasizing that the club's deputies "intend to observe the legitimate results of the Civic Forum's congress of January 12 and 13." But they also expressed doubts about the agreement reached at Lany and said the creation of a coordinating body was "unnecessary."

Deputy Prime Minister Pavel Rychetský, one of the leaders of the Liberal Club, stated that if the February 23 congress were to uphold the results of the January congress and insist on the transformation of the entire forum into a right-of-center political party, his group would "have to constitute itself as an independent political entity" and might even initiate a law suit. Rychetský did not specify whether the law suit would cite Czechoslovak law, which does not permit political movements to be transformed into political parties, or focus on the Liberal Club's legal right to the Civic Forum's name and assets.

The Republican Council of the Civic Forum, meeting on February 19 in an attempt to interpret the agreement reached at Lany, was initially unable to decide whether the forum should be divided into two groups, which would then form a coordinating committee, or whether it should be kept alive and the two groups constitute its sole collective members. The latter option was seen as enabling the forum to continue as a "legal entity" with its own property and legal rights, which would gradually be transferred to the two groups. Had the council chosen the former option, the forum would have had to forfeit immediately all legal and property rights to the two new groups. The council also decided that the delegates to the next congress would be nominated in accordance with the system used in nominating delegates for the January congress. (At that congress, the majority of the delegates had been supporters of Klaus.)

On the eve of the February 23 congress, members of the Republican Council finally reached a consensus on their interpretation of the decision made at the Lany meeting. They agreed that the council would propose to the congress that the two new political groups constitute the collective members of the Civic Forum, thereby enabling it to continue to act as an umbrella organization with its own property and other legal rights.

◆

THE SPLIT AUTHORIZED BY THE CONGRESS

In his speech to the congress, Klaus urged the delegates to approve the proposal for the forum's division. He emphasized that the main objective of the congress should not be to define the two new political entities. That, in Klaus's opinion, had to be done by the congresses of the groups themselves. He added that one of the groups would become "a modern democratic party similar to West European parties" with a right-of-center agenda. The second group would probably, in Klaus's words, remain a "broad political movement that did not intend to adopt firm organizational principles." Klaus also recalled that one of the concrete reasons for the split was the refusal of part of the forum's membership to accept "the democratically adopted conclusions of the last congress"; he added, however, that the split had, in any case, been unavoidable. In his opinion, the Civic Forum had become an unpredictable political entity and had begun "to stand in the way of solving the fundamental problems of our country."

The congress approved the Lany agreement by a vote of 161 to three, with three abstentions. It approved new statutes stipulating that the forum henceforth comprise two collective members, the one an association of forum followers who respected the decisions reached at the forum's January congress, the other an association of forum members who wanted to constitute a loose political movement. Both groups would abide by their own programs and organizational principles and have their own names. The name of the Civic Forum would be used until the next elections only by the clubs of the Civic Forum's deputies in the Federal Assembly and the Czech National Council, as well as by the forum's newly formed coordinating committee.

The statutes also stipulated that the coordinating committee consist of ten members, each of the two collective members having five representatives. Besides coordinating the work of the coalition partners, the committee would supervise the division between them of the Civic Forum's property. All decisions of the committee would have to be approved by the majority of its members. The Civic Forum's agencies established at the district level in September 1990 would cease to exist as of April 30, 1991, or be abolished prior to that date by the appropriate district congress. Furthermore, the Civic Forum in its present form could be abolished by means of a joint resolution of the top bodies of its two new collective members. Failing such a resolution, it would cease to exist automatically on the first day of the next election campaign.

Immediately after the congress, the leaders of the new groups outlined some of their plans for the future. Klaus emphasized that his group, tentatively called the Civic Democratic Party intended to abide by the program approved at the Civic Forum congress in January. That program emphasized the need for radical economic reform and advocated building a modern democratic society based on Western traditions and democratic values. It explicitly rejected "any form of socialism" and called for the introduction of "what is usually referred to as capitalism." The program also stated that Czechoslovakia's foreign policy should be aimed at defending its borders and gaining membership in the European Community. It described the North Atlantic Treaty Organization as "the guarantor of peace and freedom." Klaus also emphasized that his party intended to be active in both the Czech and the Slovak Republics but was not seeking to undermine the Public against Violence, the Civic Forum's coalition partner in Slovakia.

The group organized around the Liberal Club made a tentative decision to name itself the Civic Movement. One of its chief spokesmen, Deputy Prime Minister Rychetský, argued that the movement should stay "in the political center." Since, according to the law on political parties, political groups have to register with the Ministry of Internal Affairs to be officially recognized, the Civic Movement has begun collecting signatures (a minimum of 1,000 are required by law to register). The Civic Movement also planned to draft its statutes and political program and scheduled its first constituent congress for early April.

◆

ASSESSMENT

The process of polarization within the Civic Forum was inevitable. Keeping the forum intact would have been a temporary solution only. On the other hand, the decision to uphold the results of the January congress, at which it had been decided to transform the entire forum into a right-of-center party, could have led to protracted legal and political conflicts between the two groups over the right to keep the forum's name and assets. Thus, the official division of the forum appeared the most rational solution.

Both groups may face problems. Klaus's party may be handicapped by the fact that many people in Czechoslovakia still do not seem to trust political parties with registered memberships, well-defined structures, and "ideological discipline." Referring to these features of the new party, one of the leading members of the Liberal Club, the deputy Miloš Zeman, called Klaus's group a "right-wing party of the Leninist type." The Civic Movement, on the other hand, is likely to be plagued by many of the problems experienced in the past by the Civic Forum, such as a lack of internal discipline and of a hierarchy.

The Civic Forum's coalition partner in Slovakia, the Public against Violence, recently said it was prepared to work with both new groups and strive for the stability of the government. However, Klaus's intention to expand his party's activities to Slovakia may well alienate the Public against Violence. At its February 23–24 congress, the Public against Violence decided against transforming itself into a political party and emphasized its liberal political leanings. It may, therefore, find it easier to communicate with the Civic Movement, with its loose structure and liberal program, than with the right-of-center political party led by Klaus.

Critics of the official division of the Civic Forum have argued that, despite the pledge of the two groups to remain together in a coalition, the formal split will probably destabilize the government. The Liberal Club currently holds eight and Klaus's group only two posts in the government. Although Klaus promised not to seek more government posts for his party, some observers suggested that a dispute over the composition of the government might erupt soon. At any rate, the coalition of the two groups will probably become increasingly vulnerable as the next parliamentary elections, in which the two political forces will run independently, draw nearer.

EAST GERMANY

✦ *The exceptional status of the German Democratic Republic at its birth was that it had been a zone of military occupation and hence necessarily subservient to the occupation power. This feature changed rapidly, however, as the GDR became a full-fledged member of the bloc, important because of its economic strength and its continuing obedience to Soviet influence. The notion of "reunification" surfaced only in political speeches and then virtually disappeared. The Wall, so often reviled in Western political discourse, signaled the end of any hope that East Germany would simply collapse (or perhaps become depopulated) and opened a period in which the regime even seemed to have some success in generating a degree of civic pride in the population.*

The newer version of the GDR's exceptional status was an opening to the West by way of the GDR's special relationship to the Federal Republic of Germany (in part at least a reward for good behavior, akin to the latitude accorded Romania). This opening negated in part the isolation implicit in the erection of the Wall, while also securing decided economic benefits. It is hard to assess how much stimulus was thereby given to any urge to rejoin the West. There is some truth to the political anecdote that, when a significant Western migration was authorized in 1984, a disproportionate fraction of the migrants came from Dresden, the only part of the GDR unreached by West German television.

At any rate, Romania comes to mind again when one contemplates the sudden and tumultuous outburst of civic independence that swept away the communist regime and opened the way to coalescence with West Germany. Plainly, the emergence of vigorous opposition, noted in the first selection below, owed something to the pressure built up through years of effective repression. But, as the following selections show, the course of reunification (absorption is perhaps a better word for it) was anything but smooth. There can be no doubt that East Germany has opted out of Eastern Europe, albeit with Soviet acquiescence, but the ensuing difficulties show that the legacy, however fully repudiated, of "real existing socialism" cannot disappear by decree. It is certainly too soon to say that reunification has failed, but it is also impossible to call it a success.

Democratic Opposition in East Germany

◆

This letter was addressed by twenty-one leading activists to the 11th Congress of the Socialist Unity Party in April 1986. It shows the way in which the diverse concerns of pacifists, feminists, environmentalists, and democratic socialists could be fused in a reasoned appeal for needed change.

The 11th Party Congress of the SED [Sozialistische Einheitspartei Deutschlands] will be taking stock of 5 years of social development in the GDR. The discussions and resolutions will outline the shape of future policies in every area of society. The Party's claim to leadership makes these decisions far more important than those of the state apparatus or of the People's Chamber (*Volkskammer*). From the welcoming speeches, commitments to competition and "spontaneous" statements by workers one can guess what kind of success it will be and how much satisfaction it will provide. . . .

"The Party, the Party, the Party is always right." This song, performed so often now by FDJ [Freie Deutsche Jugend, or Free German Youth]-song groups in honour of the 11th Party Congress, clearly indicates the Party's claim to rule and control every aspect of state, social and public life. The Party determines the shape of the economy, and of ideological, domestic and foreign policy, as well as the forms of the internal and external defence of the state (police and army).

Increased official contact abroad at party and government level does not, however, mean that the GDR is open to the world. This apparent openness often goes hand-in-hand with increased internal repression.

Its hierarchical structure means that the SED is able to use Party discipline to push the correct line down from the centre, where state leadership and Politburo are almost indistinguishable, to its smallest units (group and neighbourhood party organisations). Party discipline means that orders must be obeyed. For a comrade there is nothing worse than to infringe this command structure.

In the period covered by the Central Committee's report the basic organisations "for the preservation of the unity, purity and the integrity of the Party—as the most important precondition of its fighting power and strength—excluded and expelled

"Democratic Opposition in East Germany," from *Across Frontiers*, Spring 1987, pp. 16–20. Reprinted by permission of the Across Frontiers Foundation.

approximately 63,000 people from the party on the basis of the party constitution. In addition, about 25,000 resigned from the party."

Exclusions for the preservation of unity and purity: this pseudo-religious phrase deliberately serves to marginalise, to criminalise and to render "anti-social" those comrades who, in the course of their Party membership, learn to question the Party mechanism and social structures, to point out errors, to address them publicly and to express opinions which differ from the current Party line.

Where is the unity of the Party, how questionable is its unity, when it is not even able to debate with these comrades and, in critical debate, to resolve these contradictions positively?

The Party's constitution demands free objective discussion within the framework of inner-party democracy on questions of party/state policy. But such discussions rarely take place. They are nipped in the bud and dismissed as opportunist-revisionist, as dogmatic or sectarian. There is no openness in the party, no public debate, and there are no publications on these subjects. The official Party line must be carried out "everywhere" by each comrade, for "where the comrade is, there is the Party" and "the Party is always right!"—and this when only one citizen in six over 18, and of these every 5th working person, is a member.

All of this has very little to do with the everyday problems most people face. The contradictions and conflicts which they experience and which form their social consciousness seem to belong to another world, and are excluded from official discussion. Yet a realistic policy must address these questions publicly; they occupy large sections of the population and cannot be solved over their heads.

In recent years the GDR's traditional economic strength and its special role as invisible partner of the EEC have served it well—by comparison with the fraternal socialist countries—in relation to export earnings and Western debts. But when, in 1982/83, there was a clear drop in the economic growth rate, a growing need for foreign currency and a complete orientation toward Western technology led to a series of risky maneuvers in foreign economic and trade policy. At the end of 1983 this was manifested in an acute disruption of the supply of goods and meant that for a short period everything available was exported at give-away prices. Cheap GDR workers are a particularly macabre export success story.

Even economists have difficulty in estimating the extent and the consequences of such a dependence on exports; the population has no chance at all to figure out what's going on. In the following years a series of politically often questionable credit loans from the West were arranged (in the billions), the conditions and the political economic value of which remained ambiguous.

This situation is typical not only for foreign trade, but for the whole of the economy. Decisions about particular branches of the economy, about the distribution of investment, about the nature of production, about variations on and alternatives to the plan, are not up for discussion, neither inside nor outside the enterprises. Even economic functionaries, planners, designers and technicians are left with only the details of execution; at best, they can make only cosmetic corrections.

The problem of ecological damage, both now and in the future, arises from the highly energy- and pollution-intensive nature of many branches of industry in the GDR. Though needs are satisfied, the need for a clean and undamaged environment is not met: the GDR is Europe's leader in air and water pollution and in destruction of the soil. This is another process about which those who are affected are deliberately deceived. They are confronted with the consequences and comforted with the argument that developed technology can repair the damage. The truism that nature can be damaged irreparably hardly exists for the official mind; possible alternatives to industrialisation and the automobile—both environmentally destructive—are suppressed. Discussion of the danger associated with a hurried adoption of nuclear energy is also absolutely taboo.

The SED regards economic growth not as an end in itself but as something which, as part of the unity of economic and social policy, serves the "constantly improving satisfaction of the material and of the spiritual and cultural needs of the workers." The simple phrase "everything for the good of the people" blocks discussion about who decides about whose good and how they might know what is good for others. It is not the people's consumer greed which makes the Party build hotels which accept only foreign currency, delicatessen chains stocking expensive Western goods, and show palaces, but rather the Party's own notion that the way to keep the population quiet and assume its political control is to increase the amount the individual consumes. An unspoken consumer treaty functions as long as enough falls into open hands and there is enough to go around.

This no longer has anything to do with social responsibility or even "socialist perspective," for the problems of bleak satellite towns, of a countryside ruined by settlement and of broken family relationships will affect the next generation. Such shortsightedness becomes particularly obvious in the social policy of which the GDR is particularly proud.

It is clear that efforts are being made to build flats, but concentration on the renovation of old buildings and on the preservation of intact living spaces in cities and in the country began much too late and remained inconsistent. Independent initiatives in these areas are more often blocked and obstructed than supported. Berlin's development as showpiece of the republic is taking place at the expense of many neglected cities and regions. Despite all their petitions and protests Berliners were presented with the worst examples of socialist realist monumental art: the Thalmann "park" and the Marx Engels forum. When it comes to managing our heritage, political aggrandizement and the possibility of economic exploitation are still the decisive factors.

The advancement of the family in our society should create conditions in which different forms of partnership, of co-habitation and of relationships between the generations can develop. A fixation on the stereotypical nuclear family in determining the size of flats, of relevant social policies and of the relevant regulations [*Erlaubniswesen*] hardly allows for the development of equality of the sexes, the emancipation of the socially disadvantaged and of new forms of social contact and communication. One-sided criteria of achievement and conformist thinking are the only sort of encouragement and support provided. The dual burden on women and pressure to achieve within the family could be reduced by the introduction of flexible work schedules and of part-time work for men and women and by a reduction, rather than an increase, in shift work.

Despite all quantitative developments medical care is still unsatisfactory. There is a stark contrast between the equipment in and working conditions of many outpatient departments and small doctors' practices, between waiting times and the availability of medicines on the one hand and the equipment in special hospitals and wards for rich or privileged patients on the other. The maintenance of the work force is given priority over general health care for the population, in particular for pensioners, who appear at best to be a marginal concern for medical care and social policy as a whole.

The role of science, both a basic stimulus of progress and as a productive force in our society, remains problematic. . . .

The fact both that the decision-making processes in the Party and state leadership remain concealed from the public and that it is only the results of decisions which have already been made which are ever made known means that the theoretical basis of such decisions is hard to gauge. At best one can say that certain privileged scientists have an influence on Party policy. It is impossible to create a scientific basis for policy making if the policies themselves are excluded from scientific criticism. At the same time science in our society will remain incapable of criticism for as long as access to scientific public life is controlled and the people dominant in this area do not expose themselves to scientific discussion.

When it comes to filling academic places, to allocating grants or research materials, to scientific contacts, etc., the criteria of cadre politics usually replace those of competence. For most scientists elementary requirements, like access to international literature, availability of technical equipment and opportunities to publish, are quite insufficiently met. Universities and academic institutes persist in becoming increasingly school-like, despite the supposed unity of teaching, research and study. The requirement, in the natural sciences and technology, that planned projects correspond to international trends has two consequences: first, that new projects must be tailored to suit existing trends and, second, that research and development in the GDR is, at best, carried out on the coat-tails of globally important projects.

Often, however, it is too late, because of the sluggish bureaucratic decision-making process which affects research projects. Many of those working in applied research and development have been aware for a long time that while it is generally possible to meet the Party's correct demand that projects should reach production stage within two years, the necessary decision about the investment required for production will hardly have been considered, let alone taken, in that period. The results of numerous research and development projects already contracted simply disappear into the archives. The frustration of many researchers, development engineers and industrial designers grows as they face the mountain of useful products which have not been produced and techniques which have not been not applied. This frustration itself becomes an obstacle to research or diverts creative energy into a search for substitute satisfaction.

The demand that the social sciences meet the highest international standards is simply not raised seriously. Hardly any notice is taken of progressive trends or of critical discussions of traditional viewpoints, which in the last 20 years have increased enormously, particularly in the democratic and anti-imperialist movements in the developed capitalist countries. New questions and insights in the international communist and workers' movement are not taken up. Even official views, for instance of the PCF, the PCI, the Hungarian SWP, and of the Polish PUWP are, as requirements dictate, dismissed as "revisionist deviations." Occasionally the slogan "to learn from the Soviet Union means to learn victory" paves the way for censorship in GDR publications of speeches by the General Secretary of the CPSU.

Cultural needs are not determined by the people, but are created and artificially manipulated by the Party according to pragmatic criteria. Cultural policy, shaped by the Party, is a channel for ideological infiltration into every area of art and culture and hinders a release of artistic creativity.

Financial means are provided according to political criteria. We condemn particularly the orientation of cultural policy towards economic profit, which is evident in the selling off of irreplaceable cultural artifacts (antiques, museum objects and whole collections of antiquarian books).

It is incomprehensible, in view of the global problems of the 80s, that our cultural policy is oriented towards the creation of an optimistic and idealised picture of social relationships. The ever increasing tendency of art and culture to satisfy the public's desire for amusement and distraction fulfills at the same time both the population's need for relief and the ideological requirement that reality be embellished. There is an increasing tendency to revert to trivial culture and cheap pseudo-art when the schema of socialist realism are no longer adequate. Classical kitsch and neo-kitsch both block critical consciousness and function as safety valves.

The constrictions which cultural policy places on artists and those active in the cultural sphere have driven many—even those with privileges (e.g., material goods, opportunities to work and to travel)—to emigrate and leave behind them a barren cultural landscape in the GDR.

An educational system should aim at bringing up fully developed, mature citizens capable of living in a democracy. This is claimed to be the function of the GDR's youth and education policy, but in practice it cannot do justice to this claim, as its basis is the inculcation of modes of good behaviour which destroy the personality.

In the GDR, social criteria have been replaced by political criteria in determining who receives educational privileges, i.e., careers or further education are heavily dependent on political good conduct.

This is assessed already in school reports under the rubric "social work." In this way pressure to conform—which goes beyond pressure to achieve at school—is created. Membership and assumption of functions in certain mass organisations (JP [Junge Pionere, Young Pioneers], FDJ, GST [Gesellschaft für Sport und Technik, Society for Sport and Technology]) counts as "social work." In this way these organisations, particularly the FDJ, assume the role of political-educational authorities. Membership is a "voluntary obligation," as a result of which these cannot function as real youth organisations. This pressure to conform increases as one's education continues.

The militarisation of the educational system begins in early childhood, in kindergarten. It continues with "defence studies," at school, with the increased importance of the GST and with pre-military instruction. Membership in the Civil Defence is of great importance in further education and in one's career. It is almost impossible to take one's school-leaving examination, to finish one's apprenticeship or to go to university if one does not take part in pre-military instruction. This is particularly obvious in the allocation of university places where a voluntary commitment to a longer period of army service is a criterion by which one is assessed.

By contrast there is almost a complete absence of education in democratic attitudes. The shortcomings in this sphere are horrifying. Many people have difficulty in formulating their needs and demands, or even in some cases in recognising them at all. Instruction in individual rights and in the means by which one can sue for them plays hardly any role in the education process. International pedagogic findings are seldom drawn on and there is no opportunity for experimentation with new methods. Even discussions about the content of education are stilted. Individual teachers have almost no opportunities to set their own tone in the education process.

The opportunities for young people to evolve and develop freely outside education and work are also severely limited. This is the result of the curtailment of basic rights, such as freedom of movement, freedom of speech and writing, freedom of information, and free access to the products of culture and the spirit.

The monopoly of the FDJ is also evident in the realm of leisure pursuits. There are, apart from the FDJ, hardly any youth clubs and institutions set up specifically for young people. The very restrictive legislation makes it impossible both to set up, outside the existing mass organisations, independent and autonomously organised leisure areas and to form one's own interest groups. Participation in organised trips to the West, or even in large part to foreign socialist countries, is only possible through the FDJ and is bestowed as an honour and privilege.

All these practices restrict creativity and activity. One can see that many young people retreat, at an early age, into petit-bourgeois family life and turn to consumerism.

The youth and educational policy of the GDR patronizes young people. All these experiences lead many young people to adopt an attitude of resignation. This is evident in the number of those who apply for an exit visa [to the West] or attempt to escape; it is evident in the increase in alcohol abuse, in suicide attempts and in the growing level of juvenile crime. Not least, there is a worrying increase in neo-Nazi activity. Statistics on these facts are withheld from the public and, it seems, ignored by those responsible. Up until now all official statements by the Party and government, and also by the FDJ, on youth policy, have created the false impression that there are no problems.

The GDR's peace and security policy indicates a serious desire on the part of the government to end the arms race. Evidence of this are the numerous disarmament proposals which the GDR has submitted jointly with the other alliance partners. All such proclamations are empty, however, if at the same time the GDR continues to participate in the arms race. We consider that the present threatening situation makes it necessary to point out clearly, on the basis of an objective analysis, the causes of the arms race and of the threats to external and internal peace.

One of these causes is the existence of military blocs. Many leading politicians of the Warsaw Pact states apparently understand that, in a world bristling with nuclear weapons, security cannot be achieved by deploying yet more weapons. Yet they remain attached to the—now questionable—concept of balance and thus are unable to reject clearly the spirit and logic of deterrence.

The threat posed by NATO and its superpower the USA is used as a reason for increasing internal pressure in our camp, both by our own superpower, the USSR, on the alliance partners, and within the Warsaw Pact states themselves. One form which this internal pressure takes is of a permanent militarisation of society, which, among other things, has the aim of creating discipline in order to maintain the political status quo. In the relationship between domestic and foreign policy another peculiar process—to be found also in the Western hemisphere—is noticeable: the greater the number of bi- and multilateral contacts at state level (which are to be welcomed), the more vigorously are politically important contacts below this level obstructed. Thus it appears that Mr. Honecker can meet Mr. Strauss, Mr. Bangermann, the manager of Krupp Mr. Beiz and many others, but that members of the West German Greens or representatives of other significant peace organisations in Western countries are to be prevented from entering the GDR and thus from talking with members of the GDR peace movement. Thus peace movement concepts which are discussed around the world—for instance, unilateral disarmament, alternative defence, the dissolution of the blocs and the withdrawal of foreign troops—are ignored at the official level in the GDR. We believe that it is absolutely necessary to discuss such concepts publicly, particularly since in the West prominent politicians support similar political ideas—for instance, Oskar Lafontaine, who demands the withdrawal of the FRG from NATO.

A policy aimed at the medium-term withdrawal of the GDR from the Warsaw Pact would be precisely what is necessary to encourage the process of military disengagement in Central Europe. This applies also to the withdrawal from our territory of foreign troops together with their weapons of mass destruction. The long overdue settlement of the related questions of legal status arising from the still existing rights of the victors of WWII would then also have to be achieved. If the complete sovereignty of the GDR is to be established the question of the outstanding peace treaties with both German states can no longer remain a taboo subject.

Within its obligations to the Warsaw Pact alliance the GDR has demonstrably not realised the possibilities it has to set a peaceful tone. Thus numerous suggestions of the peace movement have either been ignored or rejected as being unsuitable for discussion such as—to name but a few—a ban on war toys; the abolition of "defence studies" at school; and a halt to canvassing young people to serve longer in the army and the preference—connected to this practice—shown in the allocation of college places.

Many problems related to military service have until now met with no response;

for example: the rejection of call-up for women in the preparations for mobilisation; the demand for a change in the military service law which would make it possible for reservists to withdraw their military oath; and the use of Construction Soldiers exclusively in the civilian sector.

In the nuclear age the question of maintaining a standing army must be posed and answered in a completely new way. In this area calculable disarmament steps are conceivable—such as, for instance, a staged reduction of the compulsory and voluntary periods of military service.

The peace and security policy of the GDR cannot simply be left to the party and government. Peace is a human right and thus each member of society must be able to discuss and help determine everything which affects this right. There is thus a need for a forum which would allow all ideas and suggestions related to peace to be expressed publicly. On the basis of this a peace policy could be constructed which corresponded to the actual interests of society and the state. The Peace Council could be such a forum, but its present structure and function make it inappropriate for this task. Its dependence on the foreign information department of the Central Committee of the SED means that its sole function is to be a mouthpiece of the peace policy of the state.

At present there are in the GDR about 200 peace groups with a few thousand members who are active on peace issues inside and outside the church. The discussions in these groups largely reflect the opinions of broader social circles. The spectrum of political approaches is correspondingly broad. In order that this potential is used, we suggest that an independent peace council be created. This council would coordinate theoretical and practical initiatives on the theme of peace with the aim of harmonising the interests of state and society.

There are no ready-made solutions to the problems referred to so far. They are not insoluble, yet we can overcome them only through open discussion in which many participants both have equal status and can participate in social processes in a creative way. The independent peace movement is an expression of the growing commitment of recent years. Yet along with this commitment there has been an increase, from Party congress to Party congress, in state pressure on activists. They are constantly accused of drawing attention to unsolved problems in order to weaken and discredit the GDR. Representatives of the state thereby avoid open discussion while on the other hand activists are harassed. Unfortunately these repressive measures often affect "irreproachable" citizens and family members, who, frightened by these efforts to teach them "a lesson," lose all courage to think and act for themselves.

[The authors here chronicle three years of repression against peace activists.] What are the reactions of those affected in this way?

+ They lose all courage to become involved in social matters;

+ They flee into private life;

+ They leave the GDR

Or else they become so involved with the problems in our country that they are even prepared to accept criminalisation and imprisonment.

If the SED wants to fulfill its claim that it does everything "For the good of the people," then those who identify our problems must not be criminalised.

We therefore await the beginning of a constructive dialogue in our country.

Life in the Unpromised Land

✦

This 1988 article, translated from the German news magazine *Der Spiegel*, describes the readiness of East German citizens to vote with their feet in the face of stagnation in the country's leadership and a complacent disinclination to respond to Soviet promotion of reform measures in Eastern Europe.

*N*eues *Deutschland*, the official organ of the East German Communist Party, recently assured its readers that "every citizen . . . has, under socialism, a place and all the opportunities for a good job and democratic participation in our system." The rub is that several hundred thousand citizens of the German Democratic Republic would like to abandon their places tomorrow.

East Germany is being overwhelmed by a wave of applications for exit visas. Church sources say that at least a quarter of a million people have lost interest in the Communist Party's conception of democracy—to the point of giving notice that they desire to leave the GDR.

The number of people willing to take considerable risks to emigrate has gone up, too. Not long ago, for example, six citizens of the GDR managed to enter the quarters of the West German delegation in East Berlin and stayed, demanding that they be allowed to leave the country. At the same time, 16 others were staying in the British embassy. Meanwhile, three people tried in vain to break through the Berlin Wall with a truck.

East German discontent with socialism is due mainly to the efforts of a prominent communist: Comrade Mikhail Gorbachev of the Soviet Union. The news about the reconstruction of Soviet society has awakened expectations of reform in the GDR—for political participation, social openness, and tolerance for dissident ideas.

But in East Germany, nothing is moving. The old men in its Politburo have dug in their heels. They believe, as always, that they can wait out their enemies. "This stagnation," says a Western diplomat with long experience in the GDR, "cripples everything. It causes widespread frustration and hopelessness—doubt that reasonable conditions will ever come to East Germany."

Economic conditions have certainly made more and more people desire to leave the socialist nest. In such fields as chemicals and machine tools, where East German products used to compete well on the world market, a recent failure to invest has cut exports. Alternative investment strategies aimed at giving the country economic autonomy have been less successful than the leadership had hoped. In computers, for example, East German products have little chance to sell in the West, because they are too expensive and do not measure up to international standards of competition.

The funds that went into computers were missed elsewhere in the economy, especially by the country's consumers, who cannot understand how a major industrial power like East Germany is not able to fill their needs. Dissatisfaction with East Germany's living standard [higher than that of Britain or Italy] has grown, especially among the more than 2 million East Germans who have visited West Germany in the past two years and compared the sad shops at home with the full supermarkets across the border.

Experts say that the number of consumer-refugees is still modest. More of the recent applicants for exit visas have no opportunities for advancement in East Germany, despite their qualifications. These managerial types are the very people the GDR can least afford to lose. Yet in a socialist society, they are the most frustrated. In the East, where every inhabitant is put on a conveyor belt that takes care of everything from cradle to grave, creativity and initiative are neither demanded nor rewarded. Wages are decided by collective criteria, and above-average performers get small bonuses at best. Promotions depend more on political reliability, good behavior, and loyalty than on the quality of work.

No wonder doctors, managers, technicians, and scientists lead the list of professionals applying for visas. Church sources estimate that the number of people with few strong ties to East Germany—the reservoir of new applicants—is about 5 million to 6 million strong, meaning a third of East Germany's population. But the communist leaders have not realized the seriousness of the situation. "Those at the top," says a party member, "have no idea why the people really want to leave."

New Forum Seeks Its Own Road to Socialism

✦

D. Dose and H. R. Karutz

This article from the newspaper *Die Welt* of Bonn focuses attention on the leading opposition group in the GDR, New Forum, with an estimated 10,000 members. The group stood for progressive change within the GDR rather than migration or making the country an appendage of West Germany.

Considerable surprise has been expressed in the West, particularly in Bonn, at the critical statements made about the refugees from Prague and Warsaw by a GDR reform group which has become an opinion leader among Opposition circles in East Germany.

In a television interview Bärbel Bohley, speaking for the East German Opposition movement New Forum, said it had been misunderstood.

She said: "We are not of the view we should pass judgment on the refugees who get to the West, but we want to say that that is not a political solution, but simply a solution which is enforced by the facts.

"There is only one solution for the GDR and that is political reform." When she was asked if New Forum approved of the refugees leaving the GDR she replied unequivocally: "But yes."

These queries and amendments are both typical of problems of intra-German understanding and confirm the dilemma which faces New Forum.

There was no question that the first people to sign the appeal entitled "Departure 89"—more than 10,000 signed this petition—did not consider themselves to be the mouthpiece for the refugees or as a sounding-board for the majority of the people.

A vital sentence in the appeal made at New Forum's foundation said: "We want to hold on to the tried and tested and still create a place for new ideas."

The Forum wants to think beyond the immediate future, wants to overcome the speechlessness and hopelessness of the thousands in the embassies "and those who will follow them," but not turn its back on the GDR.

The call of the 20,000 in Leipzig, "We want to stay" as a reply to the chorus "We

D. Dose and H. R. Karutz, "New Forum Seeks Its Own Road to Socialism," from *Die Welt,* November 14, 1989.

want to get out," indicates the deep gap between the moral-intellectual aims of the Forum and the real opinions of broad sectors of society in the GDR.

New Forum has not been able to impress on people that it is a solution, an aim or an alternative to leaving the country.

The founding members included pastors, students, doctors, music teachers, physicists and prominent microbiologists. They are striving plainly for changes within the GDR system.

The group's first document was quickly branded as "anti-state" by the GDR Interior Ministry. The document called for reflection "together and in the whole country."

One of the most important reform thinkers in the GDR was asked why the refugees in Prague and Warsaw did not believe the undertakings made by Honecker's intimate friend Wolfgang Vogel.

"I'm not concerned with that," he said. "It isn't a matter that interests me."

The question of leaving the country is, indeed, neither a matter of importance to him and others, nor is the analysis of the reasons people leave the GDR a matter of great concern.

If New Forum is to be placed in the stereotype view of the parties in the Federal Republic then it can be described in these terms.

It is to the right of the Socialist Unity Party (SED) as the party of the working class, ready to work together with comrades from the SED, but recognisably left of the SPD, basically democratically organised and "green," making its own "way to socialism."

Obviously not a party after the SED example, as lawyer Rolf Heinrich, expelled from the Honecker party, emphasised.

The five most important headings in the appeal New Forum made on its establishment included a "desire for justice, democracy, freedom, and protection and safeguards for nature."

These illustrate its political approach. It is a mixture of the Prague Spring, Gorbachov, Hungary's "revolution from above" and Green ways of thought.

Until now the national question has not been important either with New Forum or with other critical groups. Bärbel Bohley has nothing to do with words such as "reunification."

Reinhard Schult, who is a cement worker and is a founder-member of New Forum, said: "We are not interested in reunification. This CDU tootling about 'our brothers and sisters in the East' is irritating and disgusting."

This is one voice among many in the range of opinions included in New Forum, and the majority of founders take up this posture.

On the other hand an experienced man such as Pastor Hans-Jochen Tschiche has thought the matter through further. He is head of the Protestant Academy in Magdeburg and a founding member of New Forum.

He said: "The continued political existence of the GDR is dependent on how the country itself determines its function in central and eastern Europe. The country cannot be an appendage of the Federal Republic."

The sovereignty of the GDR is not questioned, but its role in connection with the European dimension of the German Question is.

It is to be noted that members of New Forum have so far, for example, not openly gone along with the frank statements made by Otto Reinhold. He is one of the most important SED ideologists who thinks about the GDR as being in principle moulded by Marxist-style socialism.

He says that if the GDR did not ideologically hold contrary views to the Federal Republic, then the country would have no justification for its existence.

Where would the GDR be if "Germans here were the same as Germans over there," all brought into a similar system?

Bärbel Bohley has to do battle on several fronts at the same time. While the Free German Youth's daily *Junge Welt* reproaches her for doing nothing more than strive for a "platform against the present socialist circumstances," the majority of people, for a long time tired of politics, reject every kind of activity with political "models" or gradual, positive steps towards development.

Since signals for reform, which the SED leadership should have sent out at the latest in summer 1988, are lacking, domestic estrangement progresses.

How East Germany Got to the Brink of Ruin

✦

Hermann von Berg

A professor of economics from Humboldt University in East Berlin until he left for West Germany in 1986 describes here, in a 1989 article in *Die Welt*, the failures of the GDR leadership in economic policy.

The Socialist Unity Party (SED) [Sozialistische Einheits partes Deutschlands] has so far given the lead in the GDR. But where has it led it? To the brink of disaster.

It has reduced what used to be the most creative, the most productive part of Germany to the level of a developing country only half as productive, in per capita terms, as the Federal Republic of Germany.

A party that has done the people such lasting damage must step down. The

Hermann von Berg, "How East Germany Got to the Brink of Ruin," from *Die Welt*, November 1989.

Opposition, which as yet lacks an economic concept of any kind, must insist on the resignation of the SED's chief economic ideologist, Otto Reinhold.

Professor Reinhold has upheld his clumsy economic policy concept to the last. Only now has he suddenly, flexibly, discovered "market-oriented economic planning."

What is it? Political democracy and an effective, social market economy coupled with a party-political monopoly and a "democratised" system of socialist mismanagement?

Will bureaucrats continue to fix prices arbitrarily, or will that be left to the pressure of genuine competition?

Can one define as a market a system in which prices and subsidies amount to officially organised chaos and there is no objective yardstick by which efficacy can be measured on the basis of the ominous principle of socialist performance?

The true reformers—the democrats and not the "democratisers"—must arrive at a decision. There is no third road midway between the capitalist market and the socialist plan.

The elimination of the market brought about by the abolition of money took Russia to the brink of ruin between 1917 and 1921.

In 1921 Lenin's New Economic Policy reintroduced money and the market yet retained planning, even planned prices.

This is the third road that combines communist and capitalist features. Neither capitalism nor communism, it is socialism.

The principle of economic accountancy was introduced at the same time, envisaged as profit-oriented production on a performance basis subject to financial control, but it never worked.

It is a hybrid that can but vegetate. Prices can only be either bona fide market prices or bureaucratic sham prices.

Seven reform waves of this system have failed in the Soviet Union, three in Comecon, the East Bloc Council for Mutual Economic Assistance.

The Yugoslav alternative has failed too, as has socialism all over the world. Socialism has transformed the richest part of the world into the poorest of the industrialised countries.

Terror, exploitation, mass pauperisation and, in effect, ecocide practised against one's own people were and are socialism as practised, regardless of the nameplate, whether "real," i.e. East Bloc, or democratic.

No economy can get by without a combination of state and market economy mechanisms, but the crucial question is which decides the issue. Does the market mechanism prevail over the state mechanism or vice-versa?

Where the world market prevails, the economy flourishes. Where bureaucrats practise a system of state control monopolised by one political party they destroy both freedom and affluence.

Each system has its own objective inner logic.

In the GDR the decline of socialism has hitherto been braked for traditional and national reasons.

According to estimates by Professor Dieter Voigt of the Ruhr University, Bochum, the GDR benefits to the tune of between DM6bn and DM7bn a year from the planning reserve fund administered by the Chancellor's Office in Bonn—in exchange for about DM800m in actual returns.

The Russians subsidise the GDR's economy to a similar extent. Yet the East German mark is worth only about 10 pfennigs in trade with the West—according to the latest official SED figures.

The more loans have been granted to the East as a whole, the feebler the system has grown, degenerating to the point of insolvency.

The GDR is ruined and can solve neither present nor future tasks without productive assistance from the Federal Republic of Germany.

What is the solution? In political terms, a pluralistic democracy that reactivates the devastated desire to perform and offsets the demotivation and passive resistance of the producers.

In economic terms, in a social market economy that minimises losses, makes profits possible and thus raises funds to meet the cost of social, economic and ecological needs.

The reactionary monopoly on power held by the SED must be broken and a democratic government elected. It must start, without delay, to set about safeguarding energy supplies.

In 30 years the GDR has succeeded in installing nuclear power capacity sufficient to meet about 10 per cent of its needs. Where is the rest to come from when open-cast brown coal reserves are exhausted 20 to 30 years hence?

Who is to ensure the GDR's economic survival? Can the present policy be continued, given the shorter life expectancy and the highest increase in serious respiratory complaints in Europe (the GDR can't afford to instal smokestack desulphurisation plant either)?

How is the chemical industry to be restructured? How are the cities and the GDR's technical and social infrastructure to be streamlined and renewed?

These are not, by any stretch of the imagination, all the questions that arise. But what is the Opposition in the GDR to do?

First, it must ensure that free elections are held and that it comes to power to save country and people.

Second, a new system of commercial law must be introduced, with mixed intra-German joint stock companies that pay part of their wage and tax bills in (Western) deutschemarks.

Companies of this kind must be set up and extended to include enterprises in the commercial, services, trades and health sectors.

Third, goods and services must be made fully convertible, failing which the currency cannot be made convertible. Fourth, this progress toward full convertibility can be completed within five years, including a uniform economic and monetary system. It can be done, given West German technology, joint management and a free flow of manpower, capital and equipment within Germany.

Ludwig Erhard, Bonn Economic Affairs Minister from 1949 to 1963 and Chancellor from 1963 to 1966, accomplished this transition in the decade between currency reform in 1948 and full convertibility of the deutschemark. Fifth, patronising welfare and unproductive loan facilities must be scrapped and replaced by a productive, cooperative community of economic performance. That is how to earn and accumulate the funds needed to pay for urgently needed structural change. What is more, this process will eliminate unemployment and trigger a fresh economic miracle from which neighbouring countries, European Community and non-EC, will benefit.

East Germany in 1989

✦

Barbara Donovan

In this report from Radio Free Europe, the author summarizes the course of events leading up to the more dramatic changes of 1990. The people's action in unseating a calcified party and state leadership and launching peaceful processes of constructive change began, by the year's end, to be overshadowed by economic weakness and the harbingers of reunification.

For East Germany, the most important development in 1989 was the flight of hundreds of thousands of its citizens to the West. This exodus was the catalyst for the series of events that dramatically changed the East German political landscape. At year's end, the country that was one of the vestiges of orthodox socialism in Eastern Europe until just a few months ago found itself immersed in transition from totalitarianism to democracy. The Socialist Unity Party of Germany (SED) was unable to reassemble the power and authority that had been the basis of its control over society in the past. In the resulting vacuum, new political groups and parties coalesced, pushing the country toward the first free elections in its history.

✦

A CHAIN OF EVENTS

The first six months of 1989 were bleak, as the Honecker leadership distanced itself from reforms by increasingly desperate means. In June, for example, the SED was

Barbara Donovan, "East Germany in 1989," from *Report on Eastern Europe,* January 5, 1990, pp. 15–18. Reprinted with the permission of Radio Free Europe/Radio Liberty.

The Wall Opens. No event more vividly symbolized the end of communist domination in Eastern Europe than the opening of the Berlin Wall in November 1989. A desperate attempt by the GDR leadership to conciliate its own people, the opening of the wall instead accelerated the collapse of the East German regime. (AP/Wide World Photos)

the only East European communist party to welcome enthusiastically the Chinese authorities' bloody suppression—in order to restore "order and security"—of the student pro-democracy movement. It soon became evident, however, that the party leadership's efforts to isolate the GDR from the reforms that had taken hold elsewhere in Eastern Europe would fail. In May 1989 the Hungarian government decided to begin dismantling the Iron Curtain, thus opening up a possible escape route for East Germans to the West. That single act resulted in reforms that reached even East Germany.

In August a few hundred East Germans began to cross the Hungarian border to Austria illegally. Within a few weeks the exodus had grown to staggering proportions, and by early November 120,000 East Germans, the majority of them young, highly skilled workers, had managed to make their way to the West by slipping out the back door—via Hungary, Czechoslovakia, or Poland. The exodus was proof that 40 years of East German socialism had failed to secure for the regime either legitimacy or public approval. Moreover, it brought the facade of political stability and economic well-being that had sustained the Honecker regime crumbling down. Yet the SED leadership itself first ignored the crisis, as if oblivious to the possible implications.

Gradually, pressure on the party leadership to heed the message inherent in the exodus of East Germans and to introduce reforms grew on all fronts. The opposition, seeing the country being drained of its potential and hoping that reforms would encourage people to remain and work for change in East Germany, began to organize itself on a nation-wide scale. Numerous opposition groups formed overnight. Members of the SED rank and file became aware of the demoralizing effect that the leadership's policies were having on the party and the extent to which the SED's authority was declining. These members began to pressure the party leadership into taking action to reverse these trends.

The final push came in early October, at the commemoration of the 40th anniversary of the founding of the GDR. Thousands of people took to the streets in Berlin, Leipzig, and Dresden in what became at times violent protest. The demonstrations reached a climax on October 9, when 70,000 people marched through the streets of Leipzig. Although it was not known then, Leipzig came close to being the scene of another Tiananmen Square. Top SED officials have since acknowledged that Honecker had signed an order for the police in Leipzig to use force against demonstrators that evening. Only the intervention of other Politburo members prevented a bloody confrontation between the police and the protesters. Honecker's successor, Egon Krenz, claimed that he personally had been responsible for reversing the decision.

The presence of Soviet leader Mikhail Gorbachev in East Berlin during the 40th anniversary celebrations almost certainly helped to shift the balance in favor of those members of the SED Politburo who sought leadership and policy changes that would help defuse the political situation. Even so, persuading Honecker to leave appeared to take some time. Only after another week of continued public protests did Honecker consent to abdicate, making way for Krenz, who promised a "turning point" in the SED's policies.

◆

THE PARTY AND REFORM

Within weeks the East German political scene became unrecognizable. The only way for the communist party to keep up with developments was to begin dismantling its monopoly on power. Krenz gave the media an astonishing degree of independence; on November 9 he opened the East German borders to the West, including the Berlin Wall, allowing unlimited travel for East Germans; and he embarked on major political reforms, recognizing the opposition and promising free and democratic elections. On December 1 the SED joined in the parliament's unanimous vote to abolish from the constitution the provision guaranteeing the leading role of the communist party in society.

Despite its efforts, however, the party leadership was not able to survive the situation intact, let alone re-establish its authority. Krenz never managed to convince the public that he was an ardent reformist, and the party was unable to control the pace and direction of change. When a detailed investigation initiated by the state-run media revealed an extensive corruption scandal involving a number of former senior SED officials, the party rank and file turned against Krenz and, together with prominent SED reformers, organized its own revolt against the leadership. The entire Politburo and Central Committee were unseated; and a working group, established to manage party affairs until a new SED leadership could be elected, set itself the task of transforming the SED into "a new, modern socialist party governed from below."

The first installment of a special party congress, held on December 8 and 9, brought dramatic changes in the shape of a completely new party leadership under the 41-year-old reformist lawyer Gregor Gysi. The congress as a whole was not able to achieve the kind of break with the past that the reformers had hoped for. Although there was universal criticism of the corruption and misrule that had characterized the Honecker era, there was less certainty and agreement among the delegates about how to define the SED's role anew.

The party was not given a new name, as had been expected. Instead, it was given the designation "Socialist Unity Party—Party of Democratic Socialism," a compromise until a new name could be agreed upon at the next regular party congress in the spring. Similarly, the final formulation of new program statutes was deferred until the next congress.

◆

INDEPENDENT GROUPS AND POLITICAL PARTIES

Both the opposition groups that emerged in the fall and the established political parties that had been subordinated to the SED were instrumental in pushing the East German Communists toward reform. The opposition kept up the pressure on the streets and other parties persistently outpaced the SED leadership in their demands for reform and political change. But the political vacuum left behind as the SED gave up its control over society began to be filled only slowly.

Four major new independent groups emerged in the course of the emigration crisis: New Forum, the largest of the new groups; Democratic Awakening; Democracy Now; and the Social Democratic Party (SDP). The groups expressed similar political ideals combining the hope that a second German state would continue to exist with plans for a more humane and democratic form of socialism. The groups rallied substantial support in just a few weeks and began to exert an important influence on political developments. Although initially reluctant to do so, the SED was forced to recognize these groups as legitimate and to accept their input into plans for East Germany's political future. In late November the communist party leadership announced that it would hold round-table talks with the opposition to discuss a new electoral law and other political reforms. The round-table discussions would also include the four established political parties, which, after some hesitation, released themselves from their ties with the SED and began to pursue independent political programs. By early December the Christian Democratic Union (CDU), the Liberal

Democratic Party (LDPD), and the Democratic Peasants' Party had all announced that they would take part in the round-table talks as "independent" parties.

The round-table discussions got under way on December 7. At this first session, the participants agreed that free elections should be held on May 16. They also proposed to draft a new constitution and set up a working group for this purpose. The round-table will continue to meet until free elections are held to serve as a type of control instrument.

Internal divisions, the absence of effective organizational structures, and the lack of competent leadership hindered opposition groups, such as New Forum, from assuming a leading role in developments in East Germany. Similarly, the established political parties found that in view of their past loyalties they lacked the credibility needed to command wide-spread political support. By the end of 1989 there was little indication of which, if any, of these political forces, could fill the vacuum left by the SED.

The Evangelical Church in East Germany, for years the mouthpiece of opposition to the regime, stepped into the background as reforms got under way. The Church gave its full backing to the democratic opposition and continued to provide the independent groups with places to meet. Moreover, leading figures in the opposition movement, such as Pastor Rainer Eppelmann, are officially associated with the Church. Yet the Church's earlier importance, generated by its role as the only dissident voice in the country, had obviously diminished. It was probably not without a touch of satisfaction and pride, however, that the Church's leaders listened to Prime Minister Hans Modrow's words that the SED and the government should be grateful to the Church for "keeping alive the idea of democracy through all these years."

◆

ECONOMIC AFFAIRS

The new reformist East German government put economic reform aside for the moment as it struggled to get the political crisis under control, postponing a full overhaul and restructuring of the economy until the new year. It did, however, admit that the economy was in dire need of reform. The last few months of 1989 saw many features of the command economy long held sacred in East Germany come under attack from the new leaders, including the planning system, price and wage mechanisms, subsidies, and the emphasis on developing technology independently of other countries. For the time being, the government introduced short-term measures to stabilize the faltering economy, which, the new leadership acknowledged, had reached a crisis state. As the year approached its end, it became clear that West Germany would be playing a central role in bringing the East German economy back on its feet.

In the course of the move toward close economic cooperation, the political relationship between the two German states improved significantly as well. Prime Minister Hans Modrow himself proposed setting up a "community of treaties" between the two Germanies. On December 19 West German Chancellor Helmut Kohl visited Dresden to meet with Modrow.

The economy suffered heavily from the exodus to the West in 1989, as the loss of so many young, highly skilled workers exacerbated already severe labor shortages in important industrial sectors. East German factory workers reported having to work double overtime. Army draftees and former state security officials were sent to work in factories, power plants, and health care facilities to make up for the shortage. East Berlin reported acute shortages of doctors and nurses. On November 7, in the wake of a mass exodus to the West via Czechoslovakia that within just 5 days had cost East Germany over 50,000 citizens, the new government's spokesman, Wolfgang Meyer, was forced to appeal to the population "to ensure that all functions vital to people, to society, and to the economy are maintained." He listed "the smooth functioning of industry, construction, transportation, agriculture and the food economy, trade, and health and social services" as vital to the country's well-being.

◆

A ROCKY ROAD AHEAD

Emigration will remain one of the most serious problems confronting the new East German leadership in 1990. The decision on November 9 to open the border to the West, intended to stem the tide of émigrés, did not halt emigration. In the next week, however, of the 5,000,000 East Germans who visited West Germany, less than 1% decided to stay. Another related problem that looms on the horizon is that of German reunification. The communist party and a majority of the independent groups have rejected reunification. There are, however, indications that at least some East Germans think differently, as demands for reunification have begun to surface at protest rallies. While there is as yet no evidence that a majority of East Germans would be in favor of uniting with West Germany, the issue promises to be a significant one in the period preceding free election. The GDR has begun the transition to democracy; but that transition promises to be more complicated and with greater implications for the rest of Europe than it has been elsewhere in Eastern Europe.

The Division of Germany Ends After 45 Years

♦

This was the front page of the Berlin newspaper *Tagespiegel* on 3 October 1990 as the former GDR became five new *Länder* of the Federal Republic: Mecklenburg, Brandenburg, Saxony, Saxony-Anhalt, and Thuringia. This was the culmination of months of effort, precipitated by growing awareness that the new leadership in the GDR could not overcome its economic crisis and did not command the allegiance of East German citizens.

The Federal Republic of Germany no longer ends in the east where the Elbe and Werra rivers flow. Today, Leipzig and Dresden, Rostock and Brandenburg are as much part of the nation as Munich, Cologne and Hamburg. Berlin is also a part—but now the whole of Berlin and not just half.

The division of Germany, the political inheritance of Europe after the Second World War, has been overcome in a process lasting barely a year. The firmly rooted idea that Europe had to settle for two German states and, indeed, could do so easily, has disappeared from people's thoughts with breath-taking speed; so much so that no one looks back, but also so much so that, with the aim now having been reached and unification achieved, there is also a mood of contemplation. The Germans can be happy but they also must be thankful.

Thankful that unification took place in peace. It was the call for freedom which, in the then East Germany, preceded the call for unity. It was an echo reflected from a process of emancipation which had taken shape much earlier in Eastern Europe. It could march on because the Soviet Union under Gorbachov not only did not block the way but saw it as a chance for its own reforms.

So we come to the second point. The completion of German unity did not take place against the will of Germany's neighbours. It has not been imposed, nor has it been bullied into place. The four victorious allies of the Second World War worked together in unique fashion to make it possible in a spirit of goodwill. Fears of a bigger and stronger Germany could be dispelled. A by no means minor factor was that the Federal Republic of Germany, which East Germany decided it wanted to join, was

---

"The Division of Germany Ends After 45 Years," from *Der Tagespiegel*, October 3, 1990.

demonstrating as a loyal partner its place within and its role as a pacemaker in a united Europe.

The Federal Republic at no stage saw the realisation of a national state as a sort of German self-fulfilment but as a type of preliminary stage towards becoming an integral part of a larger federated Europe. In keeping with the spirit of the times German unity goes hand in hand with closer cooperation in Europe. First and foremost, the new Federal Republic is entrusted with the task of giving its citizens the freedom in whose name the people of the former GDR sought unity.

Freedom, of course, always involves risks. No matter how long it has been yearned for, the actual experience is a challenge, since familiar ground is missing. Yet freedom is also always a prerequisite for social peace and prosperity within a society. It ensures that these are not just distant and unattainable objectives.

Our aim must be to help the people in the new federal states to social peace and prosperity as soon as possible. This can only be successful if a new motivation among the people there meets with our willingness to devote our attention to their problems.

We must do our utmost to prevent fear on the one side meeting with heartlessness on the other. The organisational unity of state which now exists must be turned into a humanitarian unity in our relations with one another.

The new Germany will also have to prove its worth in the international community. The Germans may initially be mainly preoccupied with their own problems. This will gradually change. Growing together into a larger political entity gives us a new responsibility. Our achievements during this process must also benefit others. Furthermore, we can invite our neighbours to give us a helping hand to shape this new Germany. It should not become narrowly isolationist or nationalist, but should stand freely by its international commitments.

The new Germany can only find its fulfilment on the basis of international cooperation, new friendships and new trust. It was this cooperation which enables unity in the first place.

Our own history should have taught us that sheer size and power alone do not guarantee a country's happiness. In the hour of unity we should consider with sobriety that a country can only have one paramount goal: to guarantee human rights for all its citizens and to make sure that they can live in peace with their neighbours.

Economic Divide Between East and West Deepens As Adjustment Causes Dislocation

◆

Gerda Niemeier

Although the Berlin Wall had fallen and despite the heralded treaty on economic union that took effect in July 1990, this news report from near the end of the year makes clear that union will be achieved only gradually, and that severe problems stand in the way.

On 14 October, state election day in the five new *Länder* in the former GDR, 192,123 fewer persons were entitled to vote than on 18 March, the East German general election day.

The Statistics Office in Berlin says this means that 192,123 people headed West in the intervening seven months, a rate of almost 30,000 a month.

They no longer left for political reasons, but simply to earn a living. And, researchers at the Deutsches Institut für Wirtschaftsforschung (DIW) [German Institute for Economic Research] in Berlin say, this trend will continue.

Whereas there were just under 16.5 million GDR citizens at the end of 1989 the figure will probably have fallen to 16 million by the end of this year, and drop to 15 million by the end of 1995. A population loss of a further 500,000 is expected by the turn of the century. The motto of the new "West Germans" is: let's get out now.

In its latest joint report on the economic situation in Germany the Association of German Economic Research Institutes predicts that, after decreasing by a sixth in 1990, the gross national product in the territory of the former GDR will decline by a further tenth next year. So far the crash has only been slowed down and delayed by emergency financial assistance. Ailing companies are artificially kept alive by liquidity loans, even though they are in fact "lifeless."

The sight of too many former state-owned firms going to the wall just doesn't fit in with the picture of a prosperous future for all Germans being painted in the run-up period to the first all-German general election on 2 December. The peak of eastern

Gerda Niemeier, "Economic Divide Between East and West Deepens As Adjustment Causes Dislocation," from *Deutsches Allgemeines Sonntagsblatt,* November 2, 1990. Reprinted with permission from the publisher.

East German Housing. This photograph of a housing project under construction in Cottbus, taken in February 1990, testifies to the quality of life in the former GDR. In the foreground, a totally uninsulated prefabricated concrete wall is being erected, over which wallpaper will be pasted. The uniformly gray monotony of the finished apartment houses is evident in the background. (Marvin Collins/Impact Visuals)

German unemployment is not even visible on the horizon. After the winter months the situation is unlikely to improve.

To put it in researcher German: "The eastern recession outweighs by far any seasonal effects." The worst, therefore, is yet to come.

The DIW expects an annual average unemployment figure of 1.8 million in 1991 (the autumn report of the Association of German Economic Research Institutes even refers to a figure of 3.4 million) and 1.7 million short-time workers. This would mean an unemployment rate of 21 per cent and a share of 20 per cent of workers on short time.

Experience has shown, however, that well over half of all short-time workers in fact work "zero hours"—in other words, not at all. Experts call this hidden unemployment.

The same ratio next year would produce an increase in the real jobless figure, including persons allegedly working on short time, to 2.8 million or 33 per cent. This is the annual average with the peak (3.2 million unemployed) in early summer.

Calculations, however, are based on a figure of 8.6 million gainfully employable persons in the territory of the former GDR. Some experts feel that this figure is now too high. Pensioners still working and many older people eligible for early retirement will be the first to be sent home in the wake of attempts to reconstruct former state-owned firms.

Many women will "voluntarily" quit their jobs to return to hearth and home and escape the threefold burden of working, running the household and looking after the children. Then there are the 192,123 people who left eastern Germany during the past seven months to make a fresh start in Mannheim, Hamburg or Castrop-Rauxel.

As the base reference figure of gainfully employable persons decreases, the corresponding unemployment and short-time percentages become even more alarming. The situation is completely different in the eleven "old" *Länder*. The five leading German economic research institutes expect a growth figure of 2.5 per cent in real terms in 1991 in this area.

Unemployment is expected to remain at this year's level of roughly seven per cent. Germany has a divided economy. Hardly surprising that more and more people living in the poorer East move to the West to improve their lot.

The mayoress of a small village in the former border area between the two Germanys, for example, claimed that "half the village now works in the West. The first to go are the qualified workers, young people and people with initiative"—and these are not isolated cases.

Almost one in two who begin work subject to social insurance contributions in West Berlin are officially resident in the former "capital of the GDR" (East Berlin) or nearby. Some even commute to Nuremberg in Bavaria every day. A large mail-order company handed out leaflets advertising jobs—over 2,000 people came from Plauen, Gera and even Suhl, which means two hours travel time.

After the Berlin Wall was breached in November last year temporary jobs were the appetiser to "real" money (deutschemarks). Waiters and supermarket workers followed, and now skilled building workers, electricians and craftsmen from the East are much sought-after in the West.

According to the Munich-based Ifo Institut für Wirtschaftsforschung about 100,000 people are working on this basis in the old *Länder* and a further 200,000 are ready to make a move. As the chairman of the Berlin section of the German Trade Unions Association (DGB), Michael Pagels, points out: "this leads to growing competition on the labour market."

Despite a booming economy in Berlin, the unemployment figure is not decreasing. The number of job vacancies in September was 40 per cent down on the previous month's figure. The chances that persons who lack qualifications or whose health is in a poor condition and the elderly will find a job are melting away like the snow of the cold war in the warm sun of unification.

The socialist model in the former GDR had, at least on paper, an extensive social "safety net." Overnight, it's goodbye to guaranteed employment, social rights and the host of protective regulations, for example, for mothers.

This approach is not entirely new in Eastern Europe. For years Communist officials, at a loss as to how to handle the problems they faced, called for a basic percentage of disciplining unemployment. In the GDR there were calls for better pay for more qualified work.

Thanks to stable prices for essential products, however, everyone was able to "manage." The belts may have been tighter, but the self-confidence was often greater than imaginable for corresponding groups in the former Federal Republic of Germany.

Single women with children in the former GDR, for example, were able, thanks to the extensive kindergarten system, to go out to work despite the "burden" of motherhood. Now it's like falling into an abyss. Above all, women bringing up their children on their own are hit by poverty.

A study by the DGB and the Deutscher Paritätischer Wohlfahrtsverband [German Equal Welfare Alliance] shows that the number of people receiving welfare assistance has doubled since 1978 to a figure of roughly 4 million.

Whereas wages have increased during this period thanks to a thriving economy, approximately one-tenth of the population lives on or below the poverty line. A vicious circle appears: a lack of professional qualifications means poor job market prospects, which in turn leads to low income.

At work, Ernst-Ulrich Huster, the co-editor of the survey, explains, these people are exposed to greater strain. Chronic illnesses increase and access to better medical services deteriorates. As a result, unskilled and semi-skilled workers have a poorer life expectancy than better qualified persons.

The trend towards the "divided two-thirds society," in which two-thirds of the population are the "haves" and the other third the "have-nots," will increase.

Kohl Blamed for Perceived Failure of Reunification

◆

David Gow

In the April 1991 dispatch to the *Guardian Weekly*, its Bonn correspondent describes the disillusionment already apparent concerning the recent unification of East and West Germany. By failing to appreciate the enormity of the task and planning inadequately for the process, the West German leadership appears to have left Germans in the east profoundly dissatisfied and those in the west apprehensive about the costs they will have to assume.

$\mathbf{M}$anfred leans forward in his chair and expostulates. "There hasn't been any real change at all. People took risks, they went on the streets, they brought down the old guard; but they haven't gained anything, only lost their jobs."

At the demo earlier on the Augustusplatz in Leipzig, known for 40 years as the Karl-Marx-Platz, a homemade banner—"The big bosses of yesterday. The winners of today?"—summed up the bitter disappointment and sense of betrayal felt by many east Germans.

Like countless others, Manfred and his colleagues from a petrochemicals plant simply believe that the old guard, the Stasi officers who held them down, have regained all the power they should have lost, and occupy the top managerial posts. It is these people, they say, who are now throwing the lot of them on to the dole, especially the ones who challenged them in the past. The workforce in their firm of nearly 10,000 in January is due to be cut to 2,200 by the end of the year in a strategy for survival that few, if any, believe in. The German Chancellor, Helmut Kohl, and his government are in grave danger of failing to grasp the scale of social and economic crisis enveloping east Germany nine months after monetary union and six months after state unification. It can be measured in terms of a collective-psychological breakdown among 16 million people who, naively, placed a quasi-messianic faith in the ability of the Chancellor and the market economy to deliver well-being, and a fully rounded identity, after 40 years of repression.

The collapse of self-confidence is tangible. According to Pastor Christian Führer

David Gow, "Kohl Blamed for Perceived Failure of Reunification," from Manchester *Guardian Weekly,* April 7, 1991.

of the Leipzig Nikolaikirche, which was a leading centre of resistance to the old communist regime, the number of registered births has fallen by 50 per cent, a decline unknown outside wartime. Suicides, particularly among older people, are rising, and Lothar Beuermann, who runs the local office of the Association of the Unemployed, says many of the jobless are suffering from acute depression and other illnesses.

The Federal Criminal Office (BKA) in Wiesbaden reported last month that the crime rate in east Germany rose 30 per cent last year, with especially sharp increases in threatened use of violence, robbery, blackmail, arson, and theft. Research for the BKA indicates that 90 per cent of east Germans fear they will be victims of crime this year, much of it carried out by west German gangs. Organised crime, it appears, is setting up the usual panoply of sex shops, brothels, and amusement arcades, while drugs and, with them, addicts are increasingly visible.

Even an optimist like Hubertus von Wulffen, a senior official in the Magdeburg office of the Treuhand, the trust agency set up to privatise, rationalise, or close down some 9,000 former state-owned firms, is worried about social unrest. He had been so seized by the vista German unification opened up that he sold his half-share in a Californian vineyard and returned home after 13 years. "People put out of work will have much more money than they would have had a year ago," he says. "But what I fear is that dissatisfaction could lead to symptoms of social unrest such as excessive drinking, drug-taking, and the like." Others, like Pastor Führer, fear that without a great display of sympathy and solidarity from the west, the unrest could take on violent forms, such as the random attacks by young people on foreigners.

The short-term crisis is exacerbated by the medium- to long-term lack of secure employment. Horrifying estimates of up to 50 per cent unemployment by the end of the year have become commonplace. In a report for the federal Economics Ministry, two leading forecasting institutes said that overall industrial output in east Germany, which fell by 50 per cent in the second half of last year, would on average be 20 per cent lower again this year, largely because of the collapse in trade with eastern Europe, including the Soviet Union. This would push the jobless and those on short-time work to at least three million in 1991; and the employed labour force would fall from 8.73 million in 1990 to 6.5 million this year, with 500,000 either commuting or moving permanently to jobs in west Germany.

Other people, the saying goes, work in order to live; Germans live in order to work. "For our people, unemployment is a totally new experience," Mr Beuermann says. "The very thought of it was inconceivable. . . . People are suddenly confronted with a new psychological situation which they find it very hard to come to terms with, especially as they tend to lose contact with their colleagues."

Belatedly, Dr Kohl and his ministers have realised that they do indeed face what Karl Otto Pöhl, the Bundesbank president, had called the inevitable disaster of monetary union. But they are still tending to look for scapegoats, blaming others for the crisis in the east, rather than facing up to an angry populace. Western trade unions are being blamed for stirring up fear and anxiety with their spate of demonstrations, when it is clear that the unions are desperately trying to contain the protests as well as to exploit the government's difficulties.

Dr Köhl, who is due to visit east Germany for the first time in months on an unspecified date after Easter, has responded to widespread accusations that he has broken pre-election pledges: he insists that he never promised it would be easy to move from a planned to a market economy. But, probably foolishly, he is still holding out the prospect of equal living standards between west and east in three or five years' time, when the growing evidence is that the German economy as a whole is entering choppy waters.

With the Deutschmark weakening on the foreign exchanges and trade surpluses about to become a thing of the past, many forecasters are predicting slower growth and a rise in inflation later this year. Dresdner Bank suggests growth could be down to 1.8 per cent in the second half of 1991, and to 1.7 per cent in 1992, as a whole.

This, accompanied by rises in unit labour costs as employees try to recoup the loss of purchasing power caused by increased direct and indirect taxes, suggests that Bonn will hardly be in a position to meet any extra demands from the east. It has already stretched the budget deficit to the limit by committing £35 billion, over 18 months to the end of this year, to east German economic recovery.

The government's credibility problems in the east are beginning to be matched by mounting dissatisfaction among voters and taxpayers in the west, who view the daily protests in the east as unjustified. Without a stronger political lead from the Chancellor, the whole experiment of unification could rebound badly on the once-hero of the hour.

HUNGARY

◆ *Developments of 1989–1990 in Hungary belied the earlier appearance of relative liberalization under Kádár and underscored the unforgettable status of 1956 in civic memory. Hungary had, to be sure, witnessed some highly significant innovations in the 1980s. Samizdat not only was a lively pursuit but was carried on almost openly. Certain kinds of social services were conducted privately, offsetting the deformities of the official system. Such activities are not just mechanisms for the expression of dissident sentiment but are also infringements of the state monopoly of public affairs. This is the significance of the common East European striving recently for the so-called revival of civil society and an early expression of the demand for "privatization." And by the mid-1980s Hungary was arguably in the vanguard of such efforts, Solidarity having been suppressed in Poland.*

The dramatic events at the end of the decade had thus been clearly foreshadowed, much more than in, say, Romania or East Germany. But, once set in motion, changes proceeded at a great pace and produced the turnaround described by the following selections. As the later entries suggest, the dizzying tempo has abated and the Hungarians now in charge seem to be groping for an appropriate course. Like its neighbors, Hungary must pay a high price for the calamitous mistakes of the old regime, and palliatives are often more appealing than stern measures.

Bloc Buster

✦

William Echikson

A seasoned observer of Eastern Europe describes the quiet processes of change proceeding in Hungary toward the end of the 1980s: change that promises to alter the Soviet pattern of domination quite fundamentally.

The Jurta Theater is no typical Communist establishment. When the 1,000-seat structure opened in 1987 on the outskirts of Budapest, it became the first privately owned theater in Eastern Europe. Its architects avoided erecting a soulless glass and steel socialist structure; instead, they drew from national traditions to construct a building that evokes a cowboy tent out on the Hungarian *puszta*. Without any state control, independent groups could rent out the attractive premises.

That freedom didn't make much of a difference at first—the few dissidents who existed in 1987 Hungary found it hard to fill a private coffeehouse.

Everything now has changed. On visits to Budapest during the past year, I found myself almost every evening squeezed into a packed house at the Jurta. One night I heard the speakers from the populist Democratic Forum lament the plight of Hungarians under Romanian rule. Another evening there was a passionate meeting of the Network of Free Initiatives, a group bringing together various opposition factions. A new student union called the Federation of Young Democrats (FIDESZ) used the Jurta for its inaugural congress. Even András Hegedüs, the officially disgraced prime minister during the bloody 1956 Hungarian Revolution, gave a lecture on the tragic events three decades ago that left the country so demoralized and dispirited. "The political process has speeded up," says László Rosorholyi, the Jurta's jeans-clad director with shoulder-length hair. "We've started to come out of a 30-year-long coma."

The Jurta's varied activities convinced me that Hungary is the country to watch in the Soviet Union's volatile European Empire. Despite the decision to re-legalize Solidarity and hold partially free elections, Poland lives in the ever present shadow of a potential social explosion. Romania wins awards for misery. East Germany, Czechoslovakia, and Bulgaria detest perestroika and glasnost. Yugoslavia, outside the Warsaw Pact, is torn apart by ethnic rivalries and economic difficulties. While these countries

William Echikson, "Bloc Buster," from *World Monitor,* June 1989, pp. 29–35.

go backward—or at most grope forward—small, open Hungary proceeds at break-neck speed with a quiet democratic revolution. The Hungarians now have arrived at a decisive moment. What they envision goes far beyond anything reform-minded Mikhail Gorbachev himself imagines for the Soviet Union. If carried to their logical conclusion, the changes could result in a new democratic model that would close Europe's present divide.

Just consider how the boundaries of debate have expanded. A year ago only the most radical of dissidents dared imagine establishing democracy in Hungary. I laughed at them. "Micky," I asked my dissident friend Miklós Haraszti, "don't you think you should be a little more realistic?" Publisher of an underground journal and a blacklisted writer, Haraszti has spent countless hours in police interrogations. A nervous, emotionally explosive man, he clenched his fist and answered defiantly, "Why not dream the impossible?"

When I returned to Budapest six months later, top-ranking Communists had endorsed the idea of a Western-style democracy.

"I think a multi-party system is unavoidable," said Imre Pozsgay, a leading Politburo member, at his spacious office in Budapest. "It should be realized within two years."

I thought I had misunderstood.

"Mr. Pozsgay, Poland also has several political parties in addition to the Communists," I said. "Are you thinking of creating a Polish-type situation or something closer to Austria?"

"Much more like Austria," Pozsgay answered without hesitation. "When I think of a multi-party system, it's not like Poland."

Parliament acted soon afterwards on these stunning words. It voted a new law on "association" that permits new non-Communist political parties to establish themselves legally.

Within a few months dozens of new political parties had sprouted. The old prewar Smallholders and Social Democrat parties were revived, and new organizations such as the Independence Party emerged to challenge them. The press law was amended to permit anyone—Hungarian or foreign—to start his own newspaper. As dozens of new publications appeared, underground publishers predicted their own demise. There are almost no taboos left. The press regularly covers the anti-Communist opposition. It now openly discusses the trauma of 1956, which after a fierce Central Committee debate in February, Mr. Pozsgay and other Politburo radicals no longer speak of as a "counterrevolution," but as a "popular insurrection." As for the present reforms, an important party official, Gyula Horn, has said their goal is genuine democracy, with an end result that "must be of a revolutionary nature."

The huge wedding cake of a Parliament building—full of Gothic spires and domes and measuring precisely one meter longer and one meter wider than the British Houses of Parliament—has taken on more than a physical resemblance to the combatively democratic British Parliament. Deputies send back legislation for revision. At a session late last year they rejected a proposed new tax, while approving the creation of a full-fledged stock market open for business and legislation vastly expanding the rights of private entrepreneurs and foreign investors.

Private businesses now may employ up to 500 workers, instead of the former limit of 30. Western companies are permitted to buy 100% of Hungarian firms. Officials say a third of the economy should be in private hands within a few years.

"Call our reforms capitalistic, socialistic, whatever you want," says István Ipper, a reform-minded official at the Hungarian National Bank. "We don't like labels. We want something that works."

This can-do optimism admittedly is not universal. Pessimists point out that the tough economic reforms mean slashing state subsidies on inefficient industries. As many as 200,000 people will lose their jobs by 1990—Hungary now officially acknowledges unemployment—and prices for food, housing, and fuel will be pushed higher. Skeptics question whether these cuts in living standards, capping almost a decade of painful austerity, could create political unrest.

"The atmosphere is delicate and dangerous," worries Miklós Vásárhelyi, Prime Minister Imre Nagy's spokesman back in the 1956 Revolution. "Just like then, a malaise lies just under the surface."

Other doubters wonder whether a Communist Party, if defeated in a free election, would stand aside. Soviet officials have made conciliatory statements about Hungary's move towards democracy, but will Moscow tolerate a multi-party system? If calls, now subdued, mount for pulling out of the Warsaw Pact and declaring neutrality, would there be a repeat of 1956's nightmare when Soviet tanks rolled into Budapest to crush Hungary's first postwar flirtation with democracy?

All the answers are unclear. Many party conservatives, probably including party leader Károly Grósz, have expressed doubts about democracy. Pozsgay and his fellow radical reformers may not be able to implement their radical words. "I just don't see a real commitment to democracy," one Western diplomat says. "Pozsgay and the other people who talk about it don't have all the power."

But I think these qualms miss the most important fact. The mere fact that a Communist Party is considering the possibility of holding such free elections represents an unprecedented development in Soviet-dominated Eastern Europe. It shows just how far Gorbachev's example is expanding the frontiers of the possible. Ever since the cold war erupted four decades ago, West Europeans and Americans have assumed that the division of Europe was settled, the unfortunate if inescapable result of the advance of Soviet troops into Eastern Europe. Few considered what might happen if Soviet control were loosened. The prospect seemed too theoretical, unrealistic.

Now the Soviets have announced plans to withdraw some of their forces from Eastern Europe, including an entire division from Hungary. East-West negotiations appear to be on the threshold of larger cutbacks in conventional weapons on both sides. These talks are bound to affect Moscow's relations with its Warsaw Pact allies.

"The crucial issue," says Finnish commentator Max Jakobson, "will be how to manage the emancipation of these countries without upsetting stability in Europe." American columnist William Pfaff draws a similar conclusion. "The problem is what to do about the politically obsolescent, intellectually discredited, economically unworkable structure that has linked this part of Europe to the Soviet Union since the war," Pfaff writes in the New Yorker. "The structure of relations is becoming increasingly dangerous just because it doesn't work. It is the most serious problem in international affairs at the present time."

Hungary appears the best place to begin preparing a solution. East Germany and Czechoslovakia border NATO linchpin West Germany. Poland lies along the main Soviet transport route to the Central European front. In contrast, Hungary stands next to neutral Austria. Moscow could withdraw its troops without hurting its overall presence on the Continent. A full-scale Soviet pullback would open the way to German unification. That prospect frightens Europeans on both sides of the Iron Curtain, the French as much as the Poles, the Dutch as much as the Czechs. But positive change in Hungary could come without raising this vexing question of ending Germany's partition.

If external conditions make Hungary a good laboratory, so does its internal progress. Hungarian leaders themselves say they would like to see all Soviet troops withdrawn—in contrast with the more reserved attitude toward too dramatic troop withdrawals in conservative East Germany and Czechoslovakia. Rulers in both East Berlin and Prague fear change could undermine their tenuous legitimacy. Only one other country in Eastern Europe has a pro-reform leadership: Poland. But despite its recent reforms, compromise remains a dirty word for many in Warsaw. Poles don't address their government in civil terms. They use the labels "us" and "them."

In Hungary this deep split between the rulers and ruled does not exist. The majority of the opposition and the party are on speaking terms. When I visited Sándor Csoóri, a poet and founder of the country's largest opposition group, the Democratic Forum, he offered compliments to Communist reformers.

"We can work with men like Mr. Pozsgay," he said, sitting in the salon of a villa in the hills of Buda across the Danube from the city center of the capital. "Our idea is a sort of coalition."

Politburo member Pozsgay in turn praises Csoóri and his colleagues, and has even attended their meetings. "It is a responsible group," he said. "We must open the party up to dialogue, new opinions, and new associations."

The emerging model for Hungary's future may be nothing less than Finland, another border country that combines Western democracy and prosperity with friendly relations with the Soviet Union. Given the volatility of his European empire, Gorbachev might sooner or later rethink the fundamentals of his position. In return for guarantees of his vital security interests, he could let East European states enjoy complete internal, political, social, and economic freedom, to the point of allowing democratic elections and capitalist economies.

The Soviets would discover that they are better off this way. Instead of subsidizing their allies, they would profit from them, just as they do in their trade with Finland. And, instead of worrying about unrest, as they now do with their communist allies, they would finally have stability on their frontiers, just as with Finland.

As former US Secretary of State Henry Kissinger recently asked, "In the long run, aren't arrangements in Finland more useful to Soviet security than those in Eastern Europe?"

Logical as it may sound, "Finlandization" will not be simple to achieve. In contrast with the prewar authoritarian regimes that ruled all of Eastern Europe except Czechoslovakia, Finland enjoys deep democratic traditions. The Finns fought bravely for their independence against both the Soviet Union and Germany in World War II. Their country never was occupied; its social fabric emerged intact from the war.

"The political structure of postwar Finland was not hammered together in a deal between the victorious powers to be imposed from the outside," comments Max Jakobson. "Free and unfettered elections were an integral part" of this system.

Does Finlandization "mean that the East Europeans should first give the Russians a bloody nose in a winter war?" asks Timothy Garton-Ash, an Oxford University lecturer. "Obviously it cannot mean that; but would the Finns enjoy even their present measure of autonomy had it not been for their brave military resistance in 1939–1940? Does it mean achieving a new status in the context of an international settlement, a 'new Yalta'? In all the Soviet 'new thinking' about foreign policy—a fundamental reexamination of Soviet positions in many parts of the world—there has been no hint of Soviet interest in such a renegotiation of the status quo in Europe. The vagueness of the metaphor is amply illustrated by the fact that when applied to Western Europe it means the precise opposite of its putative meaning in Eastern Europe. For Western Europe it means a process of increasing dependence on the Soviet Union, for Eastern Europe, a process of diminishing dependence."

To Hungarians, however, the comparison with Finland doesn't look so outrageous. The two peoples are cousins. Both came from somewhere beyond the Ural Mountains. Their complex languages form the Finno-Ugric linguistic group. If a student majors in Hungarian at the University of Budapest, he must study Finnish. Finnish tourists swarm over Budapest.

"When I arrived at the airport, the guards greeted me in Finnish," says Finnish student Anu Ristola. "I could hardly believe it."

Like the Finns, the Hungarians hold a strong feeling of being "different," of not being Slavs, of being between the East and West. Both made a tradition of adapting to their more powerful neighbors; the Finns carved out a position of significant autonomy within the czars' empire, the Hungarians did the same within the Austrian Hapsburgs' domain. And perhaps because they cherish their sense of belonging to a unique people, both are homogeneous, consensus-minded nations, which have avoided the ethnic strife of multi-ethnic countries such as Yugoslavia.

"I went to Finland and found something special, unique about the people," says poet Csoóri of the Democratic Forum. "Just like them, we are thinking of a 'Third Way,' some way of ensuring the survival of a little nation caught in the unfortunate situation of being between the Russians and the Germans."

This "Third Way" is not new. The idea first was raised back before World War II for the purpose of carving out a neutral path between the blocs. It failed. Hungary joined with Germany against the Soviet Union. The idea resurfaced in 1956 with the revolution and withdrawal from the Warsaw Pact. Soviet tanks ended this dream.

In an ironic twist, the "Third Way" finally was rescued by the man who crushed that revolution, crafty Communist leader János Kádár. After a period of repression, Kádár formulated a recipe that has become known as "goulash communism." Without challenging the policies of Moscow, a series of economic reforms freed the country from many of the stifling restrictions built into other Soviet-style economies. Collectivization of land was ended and a limited amount of private enterprise encouraged.

Hungarians began to enjoy broad personal freedoms—as long as they didn't cross the line into outright dissent. The government stopped jamming Western radio broadcasts, relaxed restrictions on travel, and loosened direct control over the press. Stalin once said, "He who is not with us is against us." Kádár reversed the doctrine. He proclaimed "He who is not against us is with us."

Budapest became the East bloc's "fun" city. Hungarians and visitors strolled along the elegant renovated pedestrian mall on Vaci Street, past boutiques stuffed with designer fashions and electronics stores filled with imported stereos and personal computers. Relaxing in glossy Vörösmarty Square, they paused for coffee and pastry at the classy Gerbaud café. And for dinner they visited well-appointed restaurants, enjoying tempting meals from a menu including foie gras and caviar, wild game spiced with paprika, and groaning pastry carts.

Because he had managed to achieve the best possible compromise for the nation, Kádár earned genuine popularity unique among East-bloc Communist leaders. Hungarians fondly nicknamed him "The Old Man."

The bargain frayed in the mid-1980s. The economy, which grew at a robust 4.5% annual rate in the previous decade, slumped. Today, Hungary suffers from 20% inflation, Europe's highest per capita foreign debt, and steadily falling living standards. The average monthly wage of $140 does not go far, considering that a pair of women's boots costs $64 and a color television $700. While a fortunate few have managed to prosper, the vast majority have a hard time making ends meet. It is usual for Hungarians to work two, even three jobs. Pal, a taxi driver, is actually a university-trained engineer. "Driving a taxi is much more profitable," he says. "This country is crazy, crazy."

The human cost is appalling. Hungary traditionally had a high suicide rate; now it leads the world, with 45.1 per 100,000, about one-and-a-half times more than in runner-up Denmark. Alcoholism and drug abuse also are soaring. Poverty is becoming a national tragedy. In a small park in central Budapest, pensioners such as Mrs. István Marasz sit alone. She is 77 years old, white-haired, widowed, retired since 1968. Her monthly pension is half the national average. "You have to really pay attention," she says. "If I buy a chicken, I make it last through three days of meals."

Along with the elderly, youngsters are the other hardest-hit group. Peter Molnár is 25 years old and still lives with his parents. So do his brother and his sister-in-law, married three years ago but without an apartment of their own. The couple has delayed having children.

"Young people are frustrated with their futures," Molnár says. "After we look at the situation around us, the lack of apartments, the lack of good paying jobs, it's no wonder that none of us grew up believing in Marxism."

This disillusionment is being channeled into hard-line opposition. Since last spring, new independent student associations have formed. Molnár and 36 of his friends from law school founded the illegal independent student association, FIDESZ, mentioned earlier. FIDESZ's program can be summed up in two words: liberal democracy.

"Democracy worked in Western Europe and in the United States," Molnár says. "Why shouldn't it work here?"

Molnár and his colleagues accept no compromises. They want Hungary to pull out of the Soviet-led trading bloc Comecon and join the Common Market, to withdraw from the Warsaw Pact and proclaim its neutrality.

"People are fed up," says Peter Veress, a 27-year-old former spike-haired punk turned political activist. "We want change."

"Old Man" Kádár didn't know how to respond to the mounting public disgust. His cautious, paternalistic ruling style became more and more out of touch with this generation that had come of age after 1956. In comparison to the youthful, energetic Mikhail Gorbachev, Kádár appeared stodgy and immobile, a relic like bygone Soviet leader Leonid Brezhnev.

"During the Brezhnev period, other socialist countries were telling us that we were going too far, so it was easy to be cautious and limit ourselves to a type of enlightened absolutism," admits József Bognár, director of the Institute for World Economies. "In the Gorbachev period, the psychological situation is different and we need to make radical changes."

At a special Communist Party conference in May 1987, one young delegate after another mounted the podium to denounce his elders for incompetence. A public vote was held. Kádár, then 76 years old, lost his post as party chief to 57-year-old Prime Minister Károly Grósz. In all, eight septuagenarians were removed from the 13-member ruling Politburo to make room for radical reformers, including economist Rezsö Nyers and Imre Pozsgay.

Grósz himself enjoyed a reputation as a centrist pragmatist. He won power by making an alliance with the reformers. Before the shakeup, police had called in Molnár and his friends for interrogations and threatened to have them expelled from the university. Afterwards the atmosphere changed completely. FIDESZ held its first conference at the Jurta and more than 1,000 students showed up. Nothing happened. The new leader Grósz told his economists to go ahead and prepare a new reform plan.

"All of a sudden, the orders came, 'The sky's the limit, do what is necessary,' " recalls banker Ipper. "There no longer were any taboos."

Events took off. Within a month plans for a stock market, delayed for years, had been approved. "In the past, stocks were considered a capitalist invention," explained Zsigmond Jarai, chairman of the Stock Exchange Council. "The whole political situation changed: Rationality became more important than ideology." Official newspapers and magazines began publishing interviews with opposition figures.

"When the journalist called," says Ferenc Mislovecz, a leader of the Free Democratic Alliance, "I couldn't believe it." Over the summer Grósz made the first trip ever to the United States by a Hungarian Communist leader, shaking then President Reagan's hand at the White House and even embracing Mickey Mouse in Disneyland. Average Hungarians now have Western-style passports that let them travel wherever they want, whenever they want. On holidays, Hungarian shoppers overwhelm nearby Vienna, and in May, Hungarian troops began pulling down the electronic barbed-wire warning fence on the Austrian border. Earlier, Pozsgay had announced that the fence, a symbol of the Iron Curtain, was outdated.

US Ambassador Mark Palmer has been a regular tennis partner of the new Harvard-trained Prime Minister Miklós Németh, and, largely thanks to Palmer's energetic efforts, a new American-style business school held its first courses this March in Budapest.

"We can be really active here," says a Western diplomat. "There're so many new things we can do."

The new Hungarian revolution is approaching a point of no return. On June 15, the body of former Prime Minister Imre Nagy, executed for his role in the 1956 Revolution, will be reburied with honors in Budapest. It was Nagy who more than three decades ago made the momentous decision to declare neutrality.

Calls for similar radical measures once again are mounting. Not long ago, Grósz issued a warning that "anarchy, chaos, and white terror" would result unless the authorities resisted new "counterrevolutionary enemies." Free elections might provoke a crackdown, not lead to freedom.

"We envisage some sort of transition period," Pozsgay says. "We can't destabilize the country, we have to find a consensus solution." To soothe Soviet fears, one possibility is that the party would accept after the next election a popularly elected non-Communist government to deal with economic and social issues, while insisting that the party maintain its "leading role" over defense, internal security, and foreign affairs.

"I could see an opposition leader as prime minister," says János Barabas, Budapest first secretary. "But if he were wise, he would name a Communist as his secretary of defense."

Neither Pozsgay nor Barabas offers a more exact solution. The opposition groups meeting at the Jurta Theater also offer only imprecise ideas. Everyone knows that Hungary faces an unknown, totally new situation. It must feel its way forward. Both sides must compromise.

"Hungary has a great chance to show the path towards a New Europe," concludes one Western diplomat. "It is not an easy path. It is not a clear path. Let's just hope that they show themselves to be great statesmen."

Budapest: The Last Funeral

✦

Timothy Garton Ash

Few if any writers have done as much as Timothy Garton Ash to interpret developments in Eastern Europe to the West since 1980. This chapter of his recent book on the events of 1989–1990 is a particularly poignant account of the way in which Hungarians recalled and paid tribute to 1956, even as they were facing the dramatic changes of the present.

In Poland it was an election. In Hungary it was a funeral: the funeral of Imre Nagy, just thirty-one years after his death. Exactly a year earlier, when opposition activists held a demonstration to mark the anniversary of Nagy's execution on 16 June, they had been violently dispersed by the police. Now those same police assisted opposition activists in preparing an extraordinary, ceremonial reburial of the hero of 1956.

Everyone knows that Russian tanks crushed that revolution, setting the pattern of Soviet responses (and Western non-responses) to East European revolutions for the next thirty years. But Hungarians recalled the special perfidy of Nagy's execution: how he and his closest associates were lured out of their refuge in the Yugoslav embassy by a solemn, written undertaking from János Kádár, only to be carried off by Soviet security forces, deported to Romania, returned to Hungary, kept in solitary confinement, subjected to a gross parody of a trial, and then hanged. They also remembered how, for thirty years, the man directly responsible for Nagy's execution, János Kádár, the state and party he led, the newspapers and the school-books, just lied, lied, lied about it all. It was a popular memory all the more potent for being so long repressed.

One of the few defendants who survived the Nagy trial and lived on in Budapest to see this day was Miklós Vásárhelyi. A quiet-spoken, smiling, slightly crumpled figure, Vásárhelyi had been Nagy's adviser and press spokesman during the revolution. In the 1980s he became a sort of elder statesman to the fledgling democratic opposition, well-known to Western visitors but also keeping in touch with senior Party members. Together with the relatives of the executed men, and other insurgents and activists who had survived their time in prison, he watched and waited. By befriending a prison guard he eventually found out that the mortal remains of Nagy and his comrades had been buried in an unmarked grave on Plot 301, the remotest corner of an outlying cemetery. So long as János Kádár was in full control, there was no chance of justice, even retrospectively: to clear Nagy would be to indict Kádár. Indeed, according to an account by one usually reliable source, when two of Kádár's protégés had tried to persuade him to resign, he shouted at them: "You know what would happen! Within months they would rehabilitate László Rajk, and within a year, Imre Nagy!" Although the West sung his praises, and the world had long forgotten that ancient history, Kádár remembered. He was Macbeth, and Nagy was Banquo.

In the spring of 1988, with Kádár very clearly on the way out, the relatives and survivors established a Committee for Historical Justice. On the thirtieth anniversary of the murder, they held a small, dignified ceremony at Plot 301, but the subsequent demonstration in the centre of town was broken up by the police. Yet the new Party leaders saw the imperative of rehabilitating Nagy if they were ever to gain lasting credibility. If they did not, the shadow of '56 would always be upon them. So in January the government announced that it had decided to allow the exhumation, identification and decent reburial of the remains. Two days later, Imre Pozsgay again forced the pace of political change by trailing the results of a Central Committee sub-committee established to re-evaluate the last forty years (!), and pronouncing 1956 to have been not, as previously maintained, a "counter-revolution," but rather a "popular uprising against an oligarchic rule that had debased the nation."

It was, however, not the Party or government leadership who organized the reburial. It was the Committee for Historical Justice, in association with the main opposition groups (but also in private consultation with Pozsgay and other leading reformist politicians). The Committee declared this to be the day of Imre Nagy's "ceremonial burial and political resurrection." It appealed emphatically for calm and dignity. No political banners should be carried, only flags in the national colours or in black. The occasion should not be exploited for disturbances of any kind.

In the days before there was none the less great nervousness among officials of the Hungarian People's Republic. They were afraid of the people.

Heroes' Square, 16 June 1989. The great neo-classical columns are wrapped in black cloth. From the colonnades hang huge red, green and white national flags, but each with a hole in the middle, a reminder of how the insurgents of 1956 cut out the hammer and sickle from their flags. Ceremonial flames burn beside the six coffins ranged on the steps of the temple-like Gallery of Art: five named coffins for Imre Nagy and his closest associates, the sixth, a symbolic coffin of the Unknown Insurgent. A varnished wooden structure shaped like the prow of a schooner juts out from one side. The whole setting has been designed by the opposition activist and architect László Rajk, son of the victim of one of the most notorious Stalinist show trials— another piece of hidden symbolism. Just off one corner of the square is the Yugoslav embassy where Nagy vainly took refuge.

Funeral music sounds from the loudspeakers as people queue under the burning

The Reinternment of Imre Nagy. On June 16, 1989, Imre Nagy and the other executed leaders of the insurgent government of 1956 were buried as national heroes in Budapest. This was one of a series of dramatic events in the year that saw the downfall of communism throughout most of Eastern Europe. (S. Julienne/Sipa Press)

sun to lay flowers in tribute to their martyrs. First come ordinary citizens, quietly placing one or two carnations. They are followed by the official delegations with large, formal wreaths: local councils, churchmen, diplomats, a delegation from Warsaw for Polish-Hungarian Solidarity and senior reformist Hungarian Party politicians, formally representing the government and the parliament, but not—emphatically not—the Party as such.

Then the speeches, including an ancient recording of one of Nagy's wireless appeals from 1956. "You have just heard the words of Imre Nagy," says Miklós Vásárhelyi, a remote figure on the pulpit shaped like a schooner's prow, and then he recalls the magic moment before the second and final Soviet intervention (on 4 November), when "the weapons became silent, no more brotherly blood was shed, and the process of reconciliation and democratic transformation began." He pleads for "mutual tolerance and indulgence towards those who are thinking and acting in different ways, for only thus can we . . . secure the peaceful transition to a European, modern, free and democratic society."

"Will freedom for Hungary grow from the blood of these heroes?" asks Sándor Rácz, head of the Budapest Workers' Councils in 1956. There are, he says, three obstacles. The first obstacle is the presence of Soviet troops on Hungarian soil. Then there is the communist party, clinging to power. The third obstacle is the fragmentation of society. Another survivor invites everyone to join hands and declaim the words of Sándor Petöfi, the poet of 1848: "No more shall we be slaves!" "No more shall we be slaves!" they intone.

Yet the crowd, perhaps some 200,000 strong, is still quiet, subdued, when the last speaker takes the stand. "Citizens!" cries the raven-haired Viktor Orbán of the Young Democrats, "Forty years ago, although starting from Russian occupation and communist dictatorship, the Hungarian nation just once had a chance, and the strength and courage to try to realize the aims of 1848. . . ." "We young people," he went on, "fail to understand a lot of things about the older generation. . . . We do not understand that the very same party and government leaders who told us to learn from books falsifying the history of the revolution now vie with each other to touch these coffins as if they were lucky charms. We do not think there is any reason for us to be grateful for being allowed to bury our martyred dead. We do not owe thanks to anyone for the fact that our political organizations can work today." People applaud, as if this is what they have been waiting for. "If we can trust our souls and strength, we can put an end to the communist dictatorship; if we are determined enough we can force the Party to submit itself to free elections; and if we do not lose sight of the ideals of 1956, then we will be able to elect a government that will start immediate negotiations for the swift withdrawal of Russian troops." The crowd is finally roused to fierce and prolonged applause. Everything is shown live on national television.

Later, a smaller group travels by bus to the outlying cemetery, where, at the wish of the relatives, the martyrs are to be reburied in the same place where they had lain unidentified for nearly thirty years. I go in company with some Young Democrats, and Adam Michnik, who is here to represent Polish-Hungarian Solidarity. The incorrigible Michnik cheerfully makes the V-for-Victory sign out of the bus window, and a couple of Young Democrats rather self-consciously follow his example. Most of the passers-by look bewildered, but a few do wave back, grinning furtively.

I visited the now legendary Plot 301 just after last year's ceremony. I still have my amateur photographs of the large rubbish dump which then occupied the ground that is now at last prepared for decent burial. They have laid a new road to Plot 301, and lined it with a guard of honour. Along the dusty bulldozed verges, the men in their brown and red uniforms stand incongruously on concrete blocks, like tin soldiers complete with their bases. Around the plot, in the places where a corpse could be identified, they have erected rough-hewn wooden grave-posts, with the tops carved not into crosses but into traditional Hungarian forms. There is a curious atmosphere here, partly because people stand around having ordinary, political conversations while the speakers go on and on, but also due to the almost complete lack of Christian symbolism, ritual or language.

Nagy is often quoted as having declared at his trial: "I wonder if the people who now sentence me to death won't be the ones who will rehabilitate me later." Miklós Vásárhelyi testifies that this is a myth. What Nagy did say was that the final words in the case would be spoken by the Hungarian people, history and the international workers' movement. Well, the international workers' movement no longer exists, but the Hungarian people and history have spoken. According to the account Vásárhelyi subsequently pieced together from fellow prisoners and former gaolers, Imre Nagy spent most of his last night writing. "His letter or notes were never forwarded to his wife. All she got back from the prison was a wedding-ring, which turned out to be a fake."

One name is not mentioned in any of the speeches, although it is in everyone's mind. It is that of János Kádár, and Kádár remembered not as the leader of the West's favourite "liberal" communist country in the 1970s, but as the traitor who took over from Nagy on the back of Soviet tanks, the man who was directly responsible for the murder of Imre Nagy. Where is he today, that sick old king? Is he watching on television? Does he see Banquo's ghost lying in state on Heroes' Square? This is not the funeral of Imre Nagy. It is his resurrection, and the funeral of János Kádár.

That is what I thought at the time. Next day, there were rumours that Kádár and his wife had committed suicide as Imre Nagy was finally laid to rest. In fact Kádár died three weeks later, on the very day that the Hungarian Supreme Court announced Imre Nagy's full legal rehabilitation. Shakespeare would not have risked such a crude tragic irony. Kádár was buried in the Kerepesi cemetery, in a "pantheon of the workers' movement." Nearby lie the bodies of communists who died fighting against the insurrection of 1956.

The Hungarian funeral was, like the Polish elections, a landmark in the post-war history of Eastern Europe. It clearly marked the end of the post-1956 period which is inextricably associated with the name of János Kádár. Kádár died with his time. But of what it marked the beginning was less clear.

Reactions to the funeral were mixed. Some in the more radical part of the opposition felt that the Committee for Historical Justice had made too many concessions to the reform communists. Although relatives and friends of Nagy had actually organized the event, it acquired the character almost of a state funeral. Leading Party reformers such as Imre Pozsgay, the prime minister Miklós Németh, and the president of the parliament, Mátyás Szűrös, had been allowed to take their turn at standing guard beside the coffin of Imre Nagy. It almost seemed that the authorities had managed to reclaim the revolution for themselves.

Those who had an unquestionable claim to the legacy of Imre Nagy were less offended. "Try to be happy with us," the writer Árpád Göncz gently admonished me. And the most moving experience of all was not the grand ceremony or the internment, but a party at Miklós Vásárhelyi's flat with a small circle of relatives, survivors and friends, some on their first visit to Budapest for more than thirty years. Outwardly, it was just a quiet drinks party. But the deep, inward glow of satisfaction was like nothing, except, perhaps, the feeling of having just voted Solidarity into parliament. They had lived to see the day. And if, politically, it helped Imre Pozsgay to force the pace of reform inside the Party, well, that was all to the good too. For they were less ready than angry Young Democrats to say that even a radically reformed Party had no part to play in the transformation of Hungary. Imre Nagy was, after all, a communist.

An historian friend, by contrast, described the Heroes' Square event as a "masquerade." She compared it with the ceremonies of almost a century before, when the hero of 1848, Lajos Kossuth, was buried in state by a regime he abhorred. There was something in this, too. Thus it was curious to watch, for example, the historian and President of the Hungarian Academy of Sciences, Professor Iván T. Berend, prominently paying his respects before the coffins. To be sure, he was a clever man who had tried to get as near the truth as was compatible with making an impressive career within the official Kádárite establishment. He chaired the Party subcommittee which began the official rehabilitation of Nagy. There were many worse. But what would he have said just a few years before to a member of the Academy who proposed to say publicly what everyone was now saying? "The time is not yet ripe"? Of course the fortunate Westerner is in no position to sit in judgement, for who knows how you or I would behave in such circumstances? But this is no reason to ignore all differences. Historical justice, like treason, is a matter of date:

> *Then to side with Truth is noble when we share her wretched crust,*
> *Ere her cause bring fame and profit, and 'tis prosperous to be just.*

The largest questions concerned the response in the country at large. Here some feared—or hoped, according to viewpoint—that the very subdued outward manifestation of popular feeling indicated a deep, sluggish residue of scepticism, apathy and suspicion of all politics. Others said that the longer-term impact of the event, and above all of the nationwide televising of the event, could not be overestimated. It would, they suggested, break through a crucial barrier of fear. And then the emotions and memories that people had inwardly repressed for half a lifetime would re-emerge with a vengeance. The most optimistic assessment came from the controversial Young Democrat, Viktor Orbán. The funeral of Imre Nagy would be to Hungary, he said, what the first visit of Pope John Paul II had been to Poland. Clear the decks for a Hungarian Solidarity?

In fact, neither the greatest hopes nor the greatest fears were realized. There was no massive social mobilization. Active participation in politics remained largely confined to the intelligentsia. But nor did things simply go the Party reformers' way. To be sure, that was the immediate political result. At a Central Committee plenum one week after the Nagy funeral, they effectively toppled Károly Grósz (hailed by Mrs Thatcher just a year before as a man in her own image), replacing him with a presidium of four, in which he was a minority of one, beside Pozsgay, Németh and the veteran economic reformer Rezső Nyers. It was then Nyers, not Grósz, who represented Hungary at a Warsaw Pact summit in Bucharest. The plenum also announced the date for an extraordinary Party conference: 7 October. But the story of the next few months was not just that of the battle within the party. Beside the external struggles fought mainly in the media, and a series of by-elections won by opposition candidates, this was above all the story of immensely complex and Byzantine negotiations between the Party (insofar as you could still talk of one Party) and the very diverse opposition groups.

These negotiations might loosely be compared with the Polish Round Table. But whereas the Polish Party negotiated with Solidarity *at* a Round Table, the Hun-

garian Party was negotiating *with* a Round Table. The Opposition Round Table was
an umbrella organization that brought together the most important opposition parties
and groups. It was founded shortly after the 15 March anniversary demonstration,
which had shown how effective joint actions could be, and co-ordinated by a small
independent group acceptable to all, the Independent Lawyers' Forum. For some
time, they argued with the authorities just about the shape of the table. The authorities
wanted a Polish-style round one. The Opposition Round Table, being itself round,
wanted a regular two-sided one: us and them. They compromised on a three-sided
table, with the third side seating representatives of what in Britain have been called
"quangos"—quasi non-governmental organizations—although in the Hungarian
case they should perhaps rather be called "quapos," that is, quasi non-Party organizations. The talks were chaired by the President of Parliament, Mátyás Szűrös, who sat
alone on the fourth side.

They began on 13 June, three days before the Nagy funeral. Opening for the
opposition, the lawyer Imre Konya said: "We must now carry out peacefully the task
of three unfulfilled Hungarian revolutions." By the calendar these talks lasted just over
three months, a month longer than Poland's. However that included a month's time
out in August, partly because the talks had reached a stalemate, but perhaps also
because it was, well, holiday time. As in Poland, for this period the table was effectively the highest political instance in the land.

An agreement was finally signed on 18 September. Like the Polish Round Table
agreement this was a complex document, including a series of draft laws and constitutional amendments on issues ranging from election procedures and the status of political parties to changes in the penal code. Unlike the Polish agreement, it envisaged a
fully free parliamentary election. Before that free election, however, the president was
to be elected by the old, compromised and still largely conformist parliament. Rather
as in Poland where there was a nod-and-wink understanding that the job would go to
Jaruzelski, so here there was a certain understanding that the job would probably go to
Imre Pozsgay. But the most clearly anti-communist opposition groups, the Free Democrats (heirs to the earlier democratic opposition), the Young Democrats, and the
Independent Trade Unions, broke that consensus before the ink was dry. These three
groups refused to sign the agreement at all.

In order to press their point, the Free Democrats then swiftly organized a street-
corner campaign which succeeded in obtaining some 200,000 signatures for a petition
requesting a referendum on four issues, of which the most important was the proposal
to delay the presidential election until after the free election to parliament. The Party
then provided a nice diversion by proposing that the president should be elected not
by parliament but by a direct vote, which they believed that Pozsgay would still have a
chance of winning. The Free Democrats were having none of that. Yet while the Free
Democrats' campaign might at first glance seem to have been directed mainly against
the communists, it was in fact almost as much directed against their chief opposition
rivals, the Hungarian Democratic Forum. In the course of it, the Free Democrats both
boosted their own membership and established their anti-communist credentials with
a wider public. Altogether, the opposition parties were somewhat busier fighting each
other than they were fighting the communists.

This might seem foolish, when, unlike in Poland, the communists still formed the government. But it was based on a fair estimate of the real power relations in the country. And after 7 October, people could very well ask: "What communists?" For on the first evening of its congress, the Hungarian Socialist Workers' Party dissolved itself, dropped the Workers, and resumed its deliberations as the Hungarian Socialist Party. This seemed to be a triumph for the reformers. But the old–new party's membership grew only very slowly, reaching little more than 50,000 by the end of the year. Meanwhile a new–old communist party re-emerged, calling itself, defiantly, the Hungarian Socialist Workers' Party, and led by none other than Károly Grósz.

On 18 October the parliament went ahead and passed the constitutional amendments supposedly agreed at the talks with the Opposition Round Table. The most dramatic of these dropped the People from the name of the state, and changed the preamble to the constitution so it now declared that "the Hungarian Republic is an independent, democratic state based on the rule of law, in which the values of bourgeois democracy and democratic socialism are equally recognized." (So here socialism did scrape in.)

At noon on 23 October, the thirty-third anniversary of the outbreak of the 1956 revolution, Mátyás Szűrös then formally proclaimed the new Hungarian Republic from the balcony of the magnificent parliament building on the banks of the Danube. He started by saying, to loud applause, that the new constitution was "motivated by the historic lessons of the historic uprising and national independence movement of October 1956." But then he made a terrible misjudgement, declaring, "We continue to regard the undisturbed and balanced development of our relationship with our great neighbour, the Soviet Union, as being in our country's national interest." True enough, perhaps, but hardly the words for this occasion. The crowd whistled and booed. In the evening, three separate memorial marches met up in front of the parliament, for a genuinely free and independent celebration, with speeches from old men who had served long prison terms, and young men clambering on statues.

Then it was back to politics as usual. The Free Democrats got their referendum, won it by a narrow margin, and therefore had the presidential election postponed until after the free general election, which was scheduled for 25 March 1990. So confusing was the political scene that when pollsters included in one of their surveys the name of a wholly fictitious party, the Hungarian Democratic Party, twelve per cent of those asked said they supported it.

Hungary thus took things in a different order from Poland. In effect, it had multi-party politics before it had democracy. The government was still largely composed of members of the old–new Party. Poland, by contrast, had a largely non-communist government, but limited, popular front, coalition politics. In the months and years ahead the two countries would surely play leap-frog, each trying to get ahead of the other and keep the attention of the West. But two things they had in common. In both, the relatively long drawn-out politics of "revolution" had deepened the economic crisis that was a major factor in precipitating the changes in the first place. But equally, in both the political breakthrough had unmistakably come. In Hungary, there was perhaps no single moment in 1989 quite so decisive as the election of 4 June in Poland. But for symbolism and emotion, the funeral of 16 June ran it very close.

On the day before the funeral, I met one of the survivors, the wry and charming old Árpád Göncz. "You know," he said, "I'm happy to have lived to see the end of this disaster, but I want to die before the beginning of the next one." Hungarian pessimism is as incurable as Polish optimism, yet both are as richly endowed with Central Europe's greatest natural resource: irony.

Hungary in 1989: A Country in Transition

◆

Alfred Reisch

This summary of the events of 1989, a Radio Free Europe report, notes in particular the transformation of the ruling party into the Hungarian Socialist Party, the preparations for free parliamentary elections early in 1990, and the severe economic strains that beset the country.

In 1989 Hungary underwent a number of remarkable changes in almost every area of political and economic life and moved closer to achieving democracy and freedom. The country is still in a period of uneasy transition, however, and the changes are taking place more rapidly, stimulated by social and political forces that the former ruling communist party can no longer control. By now it is almost certain that the communist party has lost its monopoly on power and that Hungary is likely to have a coalition government after the first free national elections in the spring of 1990.

◆

NEW LEADERS, NEW PARTY

Following the ouster of János Kádár and his leadership in May 1988, the HSWP [Hungarian Socialist Workers' Party] was forced to move increasingly faster to counter

---

Alfred Reisch, "Hungary in 1989: A Country in Transition," from *Report on Eastern Europe*, January 5, 1990, pp. 19–23. Reprinted with the permission of Radio Free Europe/Radio Liberty.

the pressure of both the deteriorating economic situation and the independent political and social forces that had been organizing and rallying support for democratic reforms. By the spring of 1989, the party's so-called reform circles had, in fact, accepted the ideas of Hungary's opposition and were in the forefront of the transition of the Hungarian Socialist Workers' Party to a social-democratic political party. During most of 1989, however, the process of change was painstakingly slow, and conservative elements remained intransigent.

The HSWP, torn between its pragmatic but ideologically more conservative Secretary-General Károly Grósz and wholehearted reformist leaders such as Imre Pozsgay, Rezső Nyers, Prime Minister Miklós Németh, and Foreign Minister Gyula Horn, temporarily managed to prevent a split in the party. The four-man party Presidium agreed on in June and composed of Nyers, Grósz, Pozsgay, and Németh, with Nyers as party chairman, lasted only until the October party congress. The expected clash between advocates of radical and of moderate reforms ended with a compromise that excluded conservative elements. On October 9 the overwhelming majority of the delegates voted to put an end to the HSWP as a ruling state party and to set up as its legal but not political successor the new Hungarian Socialist Party (HSP). The HSP quickly drafted a new program in order to be able to survive the challenge of the forthcoming free elections. By the end of November, the new party had more than 51,000 members but was still in serious disarray. As for the old HSWP, which called itself a Marxist party and claimed to have close to 100,000 members, it held its 14th congress on December 17 under the organizational guidance of Grósz and former HSWP Central Committee Secretary for ideology János Berecz, and it elected Grósz's former foreign policy adviser as its chairman.

◆

INCREASINGLY ASSERTIVE PARLIAMENT AND OPPOSITION

In the framework of institutional reform, Hungary's National Assembly slowly but surely shed its former role as a "rubber stamp" organization for party decisions. Throughout 1989 it debated and approved key pieces of legislation designed to usher in parliamentary democracy based on a multiparty system. By the end of October, in keeping with an agreement reached in September between the HSWP and the opposition, the National Assembly approved a modified democratic constitution and a new electoral law that would be followed by free multiparty national elections. The most recent opinion survey indicated that, should such elections be held today, the new HSP would get 16% of the vote, forcing it into a coalition government with other political parties. The communist party's monolithic rule appears to have ended, since Pozsgay, Nemeth (who resigned on December 17 from the HSP Presidium), and other advocates of reform among the leadership seem to be willing to accept the verdict of the people.

Other political groups in Hungary also became increasingly active in 1989,

organizing and drafting alternative programs of their own. The outcome was a proliferation of political parties, groups, and movements (some 40 at the latest count), all
preparing for the electoral battle to win over the previously "silent majority" of Hungarian voters—a battle that had already begun in the summer of 1989.

Parliamentary by-elections in four localities, including the large university town
of Szeged—the first free multiparty elections since 1947—were held in July, August,
and September. Opposition parties formed *ad hoc* coalitions; and four candidates of the
Democratic Forum were elected, apparently making it the leading independent political group even before it was officially registered as a political party. A fifth by-election
in a Budapest district in early December was declared invalid and will have to be
repeated because less than the required 50% of the voters turned out to vote. The
Communists' very poor showing at the by-elections indicated that voters were rejecting the HSWP even more firmly than had been anticipated, making the idea of a
future coalition between Communists and non-Communists questionable.

A dry run for the parliamentary elections in 1990 took place on November 26 in
the form of Hungary's first national referendum, following an initiative by the Association of Free Democrats and three other opposition parties. The main issues were
the timing of and the manner in which Hungary's new state president was to be
elected. After more than three months of arduous negotiations, the HSWP and Hungary's opposition parties reached an agreement in September on new fundamental
laws in preparation for a constitutional state with a multiparty system. The legislation
was subsequently passed by the National Assembly. The Free Democrats (SZDSZ),
who did not sign the accord, collected some 200,000 signatures calling for a referendum demanding that the state president be elected after the next free elections by the
new democratic assembly, rather than by popular vote beforehand.

The referendum gave the SZDSZ a marginal victory by some 6,000 out of the
almost 4,300,000 votes cast, postponing the presidential election scheduled for early
January 1990 until after the 1990 parliamentary elections. This was a setback for the
HSP, whose presidential candidate Pozsgay had been considered a sure winner. The
government and all parties subsequently agreed that the parliamentary elections
should take place as soon as possible in order not to destabilize the country, and the
National Assembly voted on December 21 to end its original five-year term (until
June 1990), dissolving itself on 16 March 1990 in order to make it possible to hold
national elections on 25 March 1990. The 58% turnout at the polls confounded those
concerned that Hungarian voters might be politically apathetic; this response may
indicate greater popular political activism in the future.

◆

ECONOMIC PROBLEMS REMAIN

On the economic front, progress has been slow and painful. Inflation, unemployment, and the foreign debt ($20 billion gross, $14 billion net) have been growing
steadily; the budget deficit for 1989 will reach 49 billion forint rather than the planned
21 billion forint. Hungary is paying the price for some 15 years of postponed decisions

Capitalism Returns to Budapest. By the late 1980s, even before the communists surrendered power, enterprising Hungarians were busy setting up small-scale private businesses like this boutique in Budapest. (Eastfoto)

on, for instance, the radical restructuring of its aging and inefficient industries; the subsidizing of unprofitable enterprises, which has strained the national budget; and restrictive economic policies that hurt more than they helped. The government now seems more determined than ever to create a real and not just a simulated market economy, to stimulate rather than hinder private enterprise, to increase private ownership, and to try to attract both domestic and foreign capital. Since Hungary's resources are heavily depleted, the authorities hope that the West will come to the rescue and support the economy as a means of ensuring the success of the political reforms.

There is a vast difference, however, between these self-proclaimed objectives and day-to-day practice. With a few exceptions, an entrenched conservative and professionally inept bureaucracy is keeping a paralyzing hold on Hungary's huge state-controlled industrial and agricultural sector. Various ministries and the country's National Bank retain the same power. Long overdue and now urgently needed reforms in areas such as private ownership, wages, social welfare policy, and taxation have yet to be carried out. With production falling and the threat of foreign insolvency growing, many experts are now convinced that only substantial privatization and quick, extensive economic and financial aid in the form of working capital rather than loans from the West can save Hungary from economic disaster. To enable Hungary to obtain much-needed new international loans, in late December the National Assembly passed a drastic austerity budget that will bring hardship to many Hungarians but seems to be the country's last chance of preventing economic collapse.

◆

FINANCIAL RESCUE OPERATION

Thanks to the actions of the US Congress, President George Bush's visit to Hungary in July 1989 yielded $81,000,000 instead of the originally promised $25,000,000 over the next 3 years. In September the USA granted unrestricted most-favored-nation (MFN) trade status to Hungary, which also turned for assistance to the wealthy European Economic Community (EEC) and Organization for Economic Cooperation and Development (OECD) member states. By the end of the year, the EEC had guaranteed a loan from the European Investment Bank of one billion ecu to Hungary and Poland for the period 1990–1992; it had provided 10 billion ecu in capital for setting up an East European investment bank; and it had given its support for a $1 billion loan from the International Monetary Fund. Hungary also received a DM 500,000 loan package from the FRG to set up joint enterprises with West German firms; and the Hungarian National Bank and Deutsche Bank signed a credit agreement worth another DM 500,000. Other major and minor loans and credits were obtained from Japan, the United Kingdom, Switzerland, Italy, Belgium, Denmark, Finland, Holland, Norway, and Canada.

◆

EVOLVING FOREIGN POLICY

Hungary has become increasingly open to the West and has also received support from Soviet leader Mikhail Gorbachev and his advisers. In line with policy followed during the last years of Kádár's rule, the Hungarian government has continued to make a special effort to develop relations with other countries. The most visible signs of this policy in 1989 were the establishment of full diplomatic relations with Israel and South Korea (formal relations with the Vatican will be established in February 1990); the introduction of liberalized travel and emigration policies; the removal of the barbed wire and other obstacles from the Hungarian-Austrian border; the invitation to US President George Bush to visit Hungary in July; and the permission granted Radio Free Europe to open a bureau in Budapest. Also, the President of South Korea and West German Chancellor Helmut Kohl visited Hungary in November and December, respectively.

This emphasis on national interests in foreign policy has been accompanied by the conviction that, while Hungary should remain in the Warsaw Pact, it will in the future become a neutral nation, much like Finland and Austria. To this end, and also under the pressure of budgetary constraints, Hungary has adopted a new defensive military position and has reduced its armed forces, while the partial withdrawal of Soviet troops stationed on Hungarian territory, begun in 1989, will be completed by the end of 1990 and perhaps even earlier. There is a growing demand that should an agreement on conventional troop reductions be reached in Vienna in 1990, all Soviet troops should leave Hungary by the end of 1990. Other new elements of Hungarian foreign policy include a comprehensive trade agreement with the EEC, a formal request for admission as a regular member of the Council of Europe, and the special economic treatment Hungary has received from the USA and the other advanced industrial nations, primarily Japan.

Within the Warsaw Pact, Hungary's political and economic reforms aroused the suspicion and disapproval of orthodox Czechoslovak, East German, and Romanian leaders, who feared that these reforms would threaten their hold on their own people. Relations with Czechoslovakia were also disturbed by Hungary's recent decision to suspend construction on its section of the joint hydroelectric project on the Danube and by the open discussion in the Hungarian media of the 1968 invasion of Czechoslovakia, which the Hungarian National Assembly and the new HSP formally condemned in the fall. Relations with the GDR were seriously strained by Hungary's decision in September to open its western border, allowing tens of thousands of East German refugees to enter the West. This decision did, however, contribute to the triumph of reform forces in the GDR. Relations with both Czechoslovakia and the GDR have already begun to improve following the recent political changes in these countries. The main beneficiaries are likely to be the members of the Magyar minority in Slovakia and the Czech, Slovak, and Hungarian ecologists opposed to the Danube dam project. Relations with China, which had improved as a result of the two countries' joint interest in economic reform, cooled off after June following the bloody crushing of the Chinese students' democratic movement, which both the Hungarian government and communist party condemned.

Relations with neighboring Romania reached a new low level following party leader Nicolae Ceauşescu's refusal to discuss the mistreatment of the Magyar minority in Transylvania. Since 1988 some 40,000 individuals, most of them of Hungarian origin, have sought refuge in Hungary, placing an additional strain on the already-troubled Hungarian economy. Hungary has raised the issue of this national minority in a variety of international forums, but has only received verbal support from the West. In February Hungary became the first Warsaw Pact member to sign the 1951 Geneva Convention on the treatment of refugees, and the United Nations High Commissioner for Refugees opened an office in Budapest in September, relieving the Hungarian authorities of at least part of the burden of the refugees. The persecution and then forcible arrest of an ethnic Hungarian clergyman in Timişoara and the bloody police and army repression that followed in that city led to massive, constant demonstrations against Ceauşescu in Budapest and prompted the HSP to break all relations with the Romanian Communist Party. The Hungarian media gave continuous and heavy coverage to the subsequent revolutionary events unfolding in Bucharest and throughout Romania, which ultimately led to the downfall of Ceauşescu on December 22. Through Foreign Minister Horn, Hungary was quick to welcome the victory of the Romanian revolution. For Hungary, he said, the democratization process in Romania offered a historical possibility to re-evaluate and restore good relations between the two countries and peoples and to ensure the individual and collective rights of the Magyar minority in Transylvania. Horn went to Bucharest on December 29 to discuss both issues with members of Romania's new government.

◆

CONCLUSION

Social tension resulting from rising prices, poor housing conditions, and falling standards of living is now threatening to produce a dire economic and political situation. There is also a growing gap between those who can afford to buy everything available in the country and in the West and those whose daily struggle to make ends meet is becoming increasingly difficult.

Uncertainty continues about the extent and timing of reforms before the next national elections, now probably only four months away. The HSWP's re-evaluation in February of the events of 1956 and the full rehabilitation in June of former Prime Minister Imre Nagy—on the same day Kádár died—and the proclamation of the Republic of Hungary on the 33rd anniversary of the October 1956 Revolution were milestones in Hungary's rapid and peaceful, if somewhat chaotic, transition to a new political and economic model. The changes will not be easy or painless; but the further the reforms progress, the more difficult it will be to reverse them.

The population at large remains somber, skeptical, and at times anxious; it has already heard too many unkept promises, suffered too many disappointments, and seen too many failures on the part of the authorities. Should the economic situation continue to deteriorate and the average working person's standard of living drop even further (unemployment is expected to rise to more than 50,000 because of the closure of large loss-making factories), social unrest in the form of demonstrations and strikes remains a possibility. Unless the situation improves soon, and unless Hungarians have more faith in themselves and their opportunities, they will find it harder to believe that, as a result of political reforms, better days under a truly democratic system may be ahead at last.

The Hungarian Democratic Forum Wins National Elections Decisively

✦

Zoltan D. Barany

In this 1990 *Report on Eastern Europe,* Hungary's first free elections are described and analyzed, emphasizing both the unexpected margin of victory for the Democratic Forum and the difficulties that will face the government and parliament thereafter.

The result of the second and final round of Hungary's first free elections since 1947 did not come as a total surprise to close observers of Hungarian politics. The Hungarian Democratic Forum (HDF), which had won the first round of the elections on March 25 by a small margin only, finished the run-off elections held in 171 individual districts with a clear and impressive victory.

✦

THE RESULTS

The computer and communications network, which had proved inefficient and unreliable during the first round of the elections (results only became available two days after polling), functioned more efficiently in the second round. In the late evening of April 8, only a few hours after the last ballots had been cast, the first, unofficial results were announced by the Hungarian media.

Voters were able to elect representatives to the Hungarian National Assembly from three different lists: individual, regional, and national. The seats were distributed as shown in the accompanying table. Six independent candidates and four others jointly endorsed by parties not listed above also gained seats in the assembly, for a total of 386 deputies, and a further eight deputies representing ethnic minorities will be appointed in due course. Only 45.5% of the eligible voters in Hungary (3,556,881

Zoltan D. Barany, "The Hungarian Democratic Forum Wins National Elections Decisively," from *Report on Eastern Europe,* April 27, 1990, pp. 11–13. Reprinted with the permission of Radio Free Europe/Radio Liberty.

DISTRIBUTION OF SEATS IN THE NATIONAL ASSEMBLY

Parties	Lists			Total Seats	Percent of Votes
	Individual	Regional	National		
Hungarian Democratic Forum	14	40	10	164	42.29
Alliance of Free Democrats	35	34	23	92	23.83
Independent Smallholders' Party	11	16	17	44	11.40
Hungarian Socialist Party	1	14	18	33	8.55
Alliance of Young Democrats	1	8	12	21	5.44
Christian Democratic Party	3	8	10	21	5.44
Agrarian Alliance	1	—	—	1	0.26

Source: Radio Budapest, April 9, 1990, 1:00 A.M.; *Magyar Hirlap,* April 10, 1990.

valid ballots were cast) participated in the second round of the elections, as opposed to almost 65% in the first two weeks earlier.

Although the electoral victory of the HDF came as no surprise, the margin by which it won the elections was truly unexpected. It appears that the HDF benefited from the so-called 4% rule, which stipulates that only those parties receiving at least 4% of the vote be represented in parliament. In the first round of the elections, several parties, including the Social Democratic Party, did not achieve this bench mark, and some of their supporters may well have transferred their votes to the HDF.

The forum's leader, József Antall, could hardly have received a better 58th birthday present than his party's landslide victory. In a speech after the elections he said that he was "a patriotic, liberal Christian Democrat." Antall, who only became a prominent member of the forum during the roundtable discussions last summer, was courted by the Independent Smallholders' Party and the Christian Democratic Party before he became active in the forum. His contacts with these parties should prove very useful, since these are the very organizations with which the forum must now form a coalition.

The forum is certain to dominate Hungary's future government. Antall, Hungary's next Prime Minister, categorically rejected the possibility of a "grand coalition" with the forum's main rival, the Alliance of Free Democrats. If it joins forces with the Independent Smallholders and the Christian Democrats, which seems likely, there will be a ruling coalition with a comfortable 60% of the seats in parliament, that is, a majority of 229 to 157 seats. Several of the independent candidates can also be expected to support the coalition. The Independent Smallholders and the Christian Democrats appear to have a political orientation and agenda relatively close to those of the forum. Both have described themselves as Christian and patriotic parties, topped with a large dose of anticommunist sentiment.

The forum's leaders have been speaking out in support of Hungarian minorities abroad, and with coalition partners such as the Smallholders and the Christian Democrats, it can be expected that the forum will continue to publicize their cause. Political rivals have accused the HDF of nationalistic and chauvinistic tendencies and even anti-Semitism—accusations that the forum's spokesmen have rejected as slanderous. After the elections Antall said that "this day means . . . that we must send a message to every member of the worldwide community of 15,000,000 Hungarians." He added that the "Hungarian nation stands united regardless of the citizenship that some [Hungarians] may have acquired in the tempest of history."

◆

BAD DAY FOR RADICALS

Perhaps one of the most important features of the elections was the failure of a large number of individuals considered the most radical within their parties to win on the individual lists. Most of these radicals will have seats in the new parliament, however, since they also appeared on their parties' national lists. But the fact that they were not elected on the individual lists clearly indicates that the Hungarian voters preferred candidates offering more substantial arguments and less rhetoric. Radicals who failed to win on the individual lists include Viktor Orbán and Gabor Fodor (the Alliance of Young Democrats); István Csurka and Denes Csengey (Democratic Forum); Gáspár Miklós Tamás, Ferenc Koszeg, and Peter Tolgyessy (the Alliance of Free Democrats); and József Torgyan (the Independent Smallholders' Party). Some of the losers had been in the lead during the first round on March 25, and their defeat, at times by a very small margin, may also indicate that in the second round electors voted more for parties than for individuals, thereby giving a nearly 3 to 1 advantage to the Democratic Forum over the Free Democrats.

Acting President Mátyás Szűrös, a member of the Hungarian Socialist Party (HSP), won his party's only electoral district seat; both Minister of Foreign Affairs Gyula Horn and Minister of State Imre Pozsgay, also members of the HSP, lost in their districts. Horn's defeat was somewhat surprising considering his relative popularity and constant exposure as Foreign Minister. A year ago Pozsgay was perhaps the country's most popular politician, but his failure at the polls confirms reports of his decreasing popularity. He withdrew from the contest after the first round when he came third in the town of Sopron. Both Horn and Pozsgay, however, will have seats in the new parliament. The victory of Béla Kiraly, an independent candidate and a hero of the 1956 Revolution who only recently moved back permanently from the USA to Hungary, shows that a proven anticommunist track record is of great political value in the country.

◆

AN UNGENTLEMANLY CAMPAIGN

The electoral campaign, which lasted only from mid-January to mid-March and two weeks after the first round of the elections, had its share of charges, countercharges, mudslinging, and blows below the belt. The resulting tension is unlikely to be defused soon, and parliamentary life may well be rather stormy.

The two weeks of campaigning prior to the second round of the elections were especially heated. Although János Kis accused the forum of conducting an aggressive campaign, Kis's own party did not refrain from using similar tactics. For instance, Gáspár Miklós Tamás recently wrote in *Beszélö,* an organ of the Free Democrats, that Hungarians had to choose between "*Mucsa* and fear [on the one hand], and a Free Democrat majority [on the other]; there is simply no third road." (*Mucsa,* a Hungarian word roughly equivalent to "Podunk," clearly refers to the forum's small-town roots.) The forum responded by publishing a half-page advertisement in *Magyar Hirlap* accusing the Free Democrats of dogmatism and arrogance and of being either former Communists or members of communist families.

✦

ASSESSMENT

Hungary's newly elected parliament can be expected to convene for the first time at the end of this month (as Antall has suggested) or in early May. Although a future coalition of the forum, the Independent Smallholders, and the Christian Democrats would have a clear majority in the National Assembly, it would certainly have little opportunity to rest on its laurels. The government will face severe economic and social problems, not to mention a vocal and intelligent opposition. Perhaps the most important task of the new government will be to unite the country, forgetting about the recent electoral squabbles and asking for the cooperation of all representatives in the National Assembly. Antall's government will have to convince the Hungarian people that it wants social, economic, and cultural progress for all Hungarian citizens, regardless of religion, social origin, race, and gender. The losers may find comfort in the fact that the new government is bound to make mistakes and draw criticism. But even they cannot fail to recognize the historic significance of the new political era in Hungary: having peacefully elected a legislative body of their own choice for the first time in 43 years, Hungarians are once again masters of their own fate.

Lean Times Ahead in Hungary

✦

Girard C. Steichen

This dispatch of 8 March 1991 in the *Christian Science Monitor* describes Hungary's worsening economic situation and the danger that hardships will cause people to develop nostalgia for the old system.

In Budapest's sprawling Central Market, shoppers jostle past vending counters heaped with fine cuts of meat, fresh vegetables, canned goods, and imported luxury products.

But for many Hungarians, these first fruits of democracy and a free-market economy are still out of reach.

"I just come here to look," says Juliana Szántó, a retired shop clerk. "That's about all I can afford on my pension."

János Tamás, another elderly shopper, agreed. "The cheapest of the cheap is what I always buy," Mr. Tamás said, holding up a plastic bag containing two packages of margarine.

Although Hungary leads most of its East European neighbors in dismantling its communist economy, the changes have not come without considerable hardship.

Hungary's $2.1 billion foreign debt, now the highest per capita in Eastern Europe, continues to slow economic reforms. Interest alone on the debt amounts to $1.2 billion a year, or about 10 percent of the national budget.

Austerity measures imposed in exchange for International Monetary Fund (IMF) support this year have left the government with few resources to help the needy. The measures made Hungary eligible for a crucial $2 billion aid package from the IMF.

The magnitude of the problems accompanying the economic transition prompted Prime Minister József Antall to warn Hungarians that 1991 would "be a year of grave tribulation."

Pensioners and others on fixed incomes suffer the most, because benefit increases have not kept pace with inflation, which peaked at 30 percent last year. Economists predict the rate could surpass 35 percent or 40 percent this year.

Girard C. Steichen, "Lean Times Ahead in Hungary," from *Christian Science Monitor,* March 8, 1991. Reprinted by permission of the author.

Following a decisive victory in the 1990 elections, Mr. Antall's government is being held increasingly to blame for the hardships caused by its economic reform policies.

Although some sectors are booming and a wealthy class of entrepreneurs is slowly emerging, government statistics describe an economy that is shrinking as the reforms take hold. The dissolution of Comecon, the Soviet-led trading bloc, and the war in the Gulf have also made Hungary increasingly vulnerable.

Hungarian products must now compete in an unprotected market. Even slight increases in the price of oil can mean whopping growth in costs. The Hungarian government estimates that each dollar increase in the price of oil costs it an additional $100 million in expenditures.

According to recently released Finance Ministry figures, the nation's gross domestic product dropped 5 percent last year. Real wages declined by nearly 9 percent, dropping to levels of the early 1970s, while retail trade turnover fell 16 percent compared to 1989.

But there are bright sides to the reforms. While big industry is having a terrible time, studies indicate that output of companies with fewer than 50 people has increased by nearly 200 percent, a good indicator of entrepreneurship taking hold. Exports to hard currency markets also grew by 17 percent, slowly replacing crumbling trade with troubled Comecon partners.

Antall's government has also approved an ambitious privatization program. Under the plan, more than 150 big state industries are to be sold over the next year. The government predicts that within four years private enterprise should account for more than half the economy, compared to barely 20 percent now.

But the next few years are certain to be difficult for thousands of Hungarians struggling to make the adjustment. So far, 90,000 people have lost their jobs. That figure is expected to swell to well over 300,000 of the 4.6 million work force as inefficient and insolvent industries are shut down, unable to continue without generous subsidies. Government officials have predicted a sharp increase in the nation's homeless, estimated at 50,000.

Loss of government subsidies and a major drought last summer have also hurt Hungary's agricultural sector and helped to drive up prices.

That means frugal times for Mrs. Szántó, who together with her husband receives retirement benefits of 11,000 forints ($150) a month. While that sum is nearly 2,000 forints more than the average net income of 9,300 forints, it doesn't go far at many booths at the Central Market. At most meat vendors, one kilo (2.2. pounds) of sausage sells for 700 forints. A kilo of good coffee costs 400 forints.

Such prices are beginning to make Szántó wonder whether it's all been worth it. "If this keeps up much longer, I'm going to start missing the old system."

Government officials plead for patience. Says one high-ranking Trade Ministry official: "We need to perform a miracle. But for a miracle to happen, people have to believe in it."

ROMANIA

✦ *Because Romania did not experience the kind of upheaval that occurred in some of its neighboring countries, it has not appeared in earlier chapters. What distinguished Romania instead was a unique combination of unrelieved repression and defiance of Soviet dictate. If one compares Romania with, say, Hungary or Czechoslovakia, it becomes evident that the latter was purchased at the price of the former. By maintaining a rigidly disciplined, party-dominated social order, Romania appeared singularly secure in Soviet eyes and, accordingly, was able to get away with accents of independence, especially in foreign policy, that were too threatening when they arose in less securely disciplined client states. Under prevailing conditions, Soviet judgment has been decisive in establishing what counts as a revolt against its wishes; but the Romanian tendency to self-assertion was nevertheless sufficiently impressive in the West to obtain a certain favor so long as bipolar perspectives reigned.*

Romania became the home of a singular phenomenon, a kind of dynastic socialism, as Anneli Maier indicates. She and Tira Shubart explore the extent of repression that undergirded Ceauşescu's peculiar style of rule, leading to the explosiveness that characterized his overthrow, as described in the next two selections. The final entry suggests the degree of confusion and uncertainty that has obtained since. Whether or not responsibility can be assigned directly to the deposed dictator, Romania appears to be very far from a constructive and complete replacement of the old order.

Ceauşescu Family Succession?

✦

Anneli Maier

This report on Ceauşescu's style of rule, combining nepotism
with repression, sheds some light on the desperate conditions
afflicting the Romanian people in the 1980s.

With rumors about President Nicolae Ceauşescu's alleged health problems
becoming more insistent in Romania, any period of his absence was observed with
some suspicion. Moreover, the Romanian media were taking pains to efface any traces
that might arouse suspicion.

Ceauşescu dropped out of sight after July 26, 1985, and did not reappear in
public until August 2, when he visited military units in the Black Sea port of Mangalia.
His address to a rally in Galaţi on August 8 was broadcast several hours after the fact. It
was brief and seemed to have been cut into shape by the Bucharest broadcasters, his
voice was tiring very quickly and becoming hoarse toward the end.

The photographs published in the newspaper showing Ceauşescu during the
first days of his reappearance on the scene showed a man who had lost a lot of weight,
with his eyes half-closed, the corners of his mouth pointing downward, his face drawn
and haggard. Most of the photographs published on August 8 of Ceauşescu's visit to
the Constanţa area were so heavily retouched that they raised doubts as to their
authenticity altogether; the suspicion arose that the head of a healthier-looking
Ceauşescu from an older photograph had been superimposed over his face. In these
pictures his face and sometimes even his entire body are lit by a kind of halo, and his
wrinkles and dark spots are spirited away. In one case, one and the same photograph
was published in two different newspapers in two different ways: on August 9 *Scînteia
Tineretului* presented Ceauşescu with a strained, painful expression on his face,
whereas the same picture put out one day later in *Neuer Weg* changed the downward-
pointing corners of his mouth into a smile.

Ceauşescu's visit of the Constanţa area on August 7 was used as an opportunity
to feature other members of the Ceauşescu clan, too: his wife Elena, his son Nicu
(who was in charge of the work performed by the youth brigades at the construction

Anneli Maier, "Ceausescu Family Succession?" from Vojtech Mastny, ed., *Soviet/East European Survey,
1985–1986,* Duke University Press, Durham, 1987, pp. 317–22. Reprinted with the permission of the
publisher.

Ceauşescu in Power. Top: President Nicolae Ceauşescu ruled Romania with an iron hand, demanding and receiving public adulation akin to Stalin's a generation earlier. (Eastfoto) **Bottom:** His flamboyantly grotesque presidential palace arose on the rubble of an entire neighborhood demolished for his benefit. (Teun Voeten/Impact Visuals)

site in his capacity as UTC [a union for working youth] first secretary and minister of youth) and even—for the first time—Poliana Cristescu, the chairman of the Pioneers' organization, who was rumored to be Nicu's wife. There were, however, differences in the way both Nicu and Poliana were put forward by the various newspapers. The party daily *Scînteia* showed three photographs on its front page; two of them featured Ceauşescu and Elena, and the third included their son Nicu. This last picture stretched over half the width of the page and showed Nicu in profile on the far right, standing to his father's left. *Scînteia Tineretului* (the daily put out by the Young Communist League headed by Nicu) and two dailies put out by the Front for Socialist Unity and Democracy, *România Liberă* and *Neuer Weg,* had only one Nicolae and Elena picture on their front page. In the second photograph, stretching over the entire width of the page, Nicu figured prominently, next to his father, with Elena not in the picture at all.

Scînteia was the only newspaper to run a picture of the three most prominent members of the Ceauşescu clan that seemed to illustrate the hierarchical order established between them. In front, standing on a carpet in front of a microphone and saluting, is Nicolae. Several steps behind him and off the carpet is Nicu, his hands folded behind his back, and farther back, standing on the carpet, is Elena Ceauşescu. In iconographical terms, it would appear that she was being groomed as Ceauşescu's immediate successor; Nicu's bid, however, still maintained credibility.

Following his elevation to alternate member of the CC Political Executive Committee at the Thirteenth RCP [Romanian Communist Party] Congress in November 1984, Nicu Ceauşescu continued to enhance his domestic prestige and his stature abroad. The main goal of the Ceauşescus seemed to be to achieve support for the family succession from other communist countries, primarily the Soviet Union. On the eve of the RCP congress, Nicu spent a week in the Soviet Union in the course of which he was received by Boris Ponomarev, an alternate member of the CPSU Politburo and CC secretary in charge of relations with foreign ruling communist parties. In January 1985 Nicu went to East Berlin where he met with Egon Krenz, SED [Socialist Unity Party] CC secretary for security and Erich Honecker's heir apparent. In June Nicu again stopped over in Moscow on his way to North Korea and China. In reporting about the meeting between Nicu Ceauşescu and the general secretary of the Chinese CP Central Committee, Hu Yaobang, the Chinese news agency Xinhua reported that Hu had told Nicu and his delegation that "friendship between China and Romania would continue from generation to generation."

On November 28 and 29 Romania's first Congress of Science and Instruction was held in Bucharest. It was opened with a brief speech by Elena Ceauşescu, wife of the head of state, a member of the Standing Bureau of the Political Executive Committee, first deputy prime minister, and chairman (since June 1979) of the National Council for Science and Technology. Before the agenda of the congress was presented and even before her husband spoke, she made the following surprising announcement: "In the context of the efforts to improve the guidelines for all areas of activity and to develop a revolutionary workers' democracy, the leadership of our party and state deems it necessary to merge the two bodies of science and instruction and to set up a single body of democratic leadership, the National Council of Science and Instruction of the Socialist Republic of Romania."

On the second day of the proceedings Elena Ceauşescu was "appointed unanimously" (not elected) as chairman of the newly founded Council for Science and Instruction. Her takeover of this new supercouncil—one of the party and state bodies characteristic of Romania's leadership model—boosted her power and prestige.

The protocol and press coverage, including the pictures published, clearly pointed to a new, considerably higher status for Elena. The newspapers printed her portrait on the front page thus giving her equal treatment with her husband. At the conference itself delegates praised each of the Ceauşescus equally: however, whereas Nicolae Ceauşescu was said to be the strategist of Romania's overall economic policy, Elena was presented as the chief executor of this policy and as the guarantor of its implementation in the future.

This seemed in accordance with Ceauşescu's reply to a Western correspondent's question about whether he planned to establish a "hereditary monarchy" in Romania in favor of his son Nicu: "Neither the Constitution nor the party congress provide for such a move. Only competence and the people's will can decide on a person's future," he is said to have replied.

By having Elena Ceauşescu publicly acclaimed as a highly powerful political leader, the Ceauşescus may have been trying to fend off criticism by other possible contenders for power. This assumption was strengthened by an article published on the eve of the congress by the party paper *Scînteia* rejecting the claims made by "some people" that "competent groups" selected on the basis of their "professionalism" were entitled to occupy leading functions in the political sphere, too. According to *Scînteia*, these claims were said to have been backed up by the argument that "transforming professional elites into political elites would safeguard impartiality and competence and would result in the optimum functioning of the entire sociopolitical system," something that *Scînteia* would not tolerate.

The protocol observed in January 1986 for the birthday of Elena Ceauşescu abounded in praise of her merits. Among the usual epithets pegged to her virtues as the "great leader's" wife, the "mother of the fatherland," and the guiding spirit behind science and culture, however, there were some new elements.

Elena was being credited with almost all the virtues that had hitherto been the sole preserve of her husband. Like him, Elena was praised as a providential personality whose birthday was "a crucial date in Romanian history, by which the nation, glorifying its chosen ones, is glorifying itself. . . ." Elena was said to be the "perfect personification of the traditional values of the Romanian people" and to have been reserved a place "in the golden gallery of the great personalities of national history." She was described as "the party's torch," "the woman-hero," "the hero of the fatherland," and "our tricolor." The poet Ion Gheorghe's allusions to the "trinity" and the "three dimensions" formed by Nicolae Ceauşescu, Elena Ceauşescu, and the fatherland were almost religious in connotation.

In the interval that had passed since she was made chairman of the National Council for Science and Instruction, Elena's political profile and influence were considerably enhanced. When Bulgarian party and state leader Todor Zhivkov was in Romania for a "friendly visit" from December 20 to 21, 1985, she participated in the second round of talks. Moreover, during Ceauşescu's visit to Yugoslavia on December 13 and 14, Elena's active participation in the talks was drawn to the attention of Western correspondents by the Yugoslavs. Photographs published in the Romanian but not in the Yugoslav press in connection with the visit to Belgrade showed a rather placid Nicolae Ceauşescu seated alongside his energetic-looking wife. At the close of the visit, two communiqués were published in Romania only: a joint communiqué signed by Nicolae Ceauşescu and the Yugoslav party and state leaders, and one signed by Nicolae and Elena Ceauşescu for the RCP and Vidoje Jarković for the LCY [League of Communist Yugoslavia]. The attempts to found a communist dynasty in Romania were being carefully observed and somewhat critically commented on for some time in Yugoslavia. Already in 1984 there had been references in the Yugoslav press to countries such as Romania, where the "family of the ruling leader supplies more than one capable member occupying top offices."

"I feel bound to praise you and kiss your temple" wrote the poet Dumitru Brădescu in the Timişoara cultural weekly *Orizont* on the occasion of Ceauşescu's sixty-eighth birthday, and there was much more. But although there was the annual outpouring of laudatory books, movies, and broadcasts rained down on Ceauşescu, and although busts, paintings, and drawings of him (some also featuring his wife, Elena, and some his son Nicu, too) went on show at Bucharest's major exhibition center, there was no disguising of a certain shortfall in the output of nationwide rejoicing.

The pattern contained a new angle that placed increased stress on Ceauşescu's past role and legacy to the future rather than present triumphs. The party and state leadership's official letter of congratulations emphasized less Ceauşescu's alleged role as the initiator of Romania's overall postwar policies and more the role of the RCP as a whole: "never in the history of Romania has there existed a political party that has served the interests of the homeland, of its independence and sovereignty, and of the well-being and happiness of the whole people with so much devotion, firmness, and abnegation."

By extending the praise to include the role of the party at large, the document had the effect—intentional or not—of freeing the party from Ceauşescu's personal wheel of fortune. In addition, whereas in 1985 the customary congratulatory telegram had concluded by conveying heartfelt wishes to both Ceauşescu *and* his "comrade in life and combat, that highly esteemed comrade and outstanding militant of our party and state, Elena Ceauşescu," the 1986 telegram made reference to Elena only in conveying greetings to Ceauşescu's family. In the contex of the advances in Elena Ceauşescu's political career, this omission could be construed as an indication that any succession bid by her did not command full support among the country's leadership. The omission was rendered all the more striking by the ardent support that at least one prominent member of the Ceauşescu elite, PEC [Political Executive Committee] member and Vice Chairman of the State Council Mănea Mănescu, did bestow upon her on the occasion of her husband's birthday. According to Mănescu, Nicolae and Elena had "always been united in their thoughts and deeds on the brilliant road of revolution," and he paid "warm homage to the titanic activity they have carried on together both domestically and internationally."

To judge from the tone of his birthday speech, the omission of Ceauşescu's wife from his birthday greetings was not all that had annoyed him. The speech seemed to be written against a wider background of estrangement between Ceauşescu and elements within the leadership. By expressing a determination to use "all my strength and my entire being" in continuing to fulfill his duties, Ceauşescu, intentionally or not, struck the valedictory note of a man determined to go down fighting. It was an angry speech full of criticism of party members, and suggested disagreements on a number of organizational and ideological matters, such as whether the RCP represented a "vanguard of the proletariat" (and was therefore an elite, "class" organization) or whether it was "the vital center of the nation" (in which case national interests would take precedence over internationalist duties). Ceauşescu criticized unnamed members of the party for supporting a greater degree of autonomy for industrial enterprises, which he labeled "anarchosocialism." He made a point of calling for more party discipline on all levels and expressed hope for support from "the entire Central Committee and its Political Executive Committee."

The fact that two earlier speeches by Ceauşescu before the Political Executive Committee had been published, which was not a usual practice, also suggested divisions within the leadership. The second of these, on February 6, 1986, was made during the Political Executive Committee's rather positive evaluation of the 1981–85 plan results; Ceauşescu, however, used unusually sharp language in criticizing the party and government for having failed to implement their tasks. In 1981 minister for oil, Virgil Trofin, was reprimanded at a party plenum not only for the failure of Romania's crude output to have increased but also for his refusal to indulge in self-criticism and to offer himself up as a scapegoat for errors that had originated with Ceauşescu personally. In 1986 the number of those refusing to take on the blame for policies originating elsewhere seems to have grown.

Arrested in Romania

✦

Tira Shubart

This eyewitness report from a freelance writer and expert on human rights further underscores the uniquely repressive Romanian system at a time when liberalization was in evidence almost everywhere else in Eastern Europe.

The butcher's shop was empty. The trays in the glass-topped display stands contained nothing but dried bloodstains from the time when meat had last been on sale. The two shop attendants in their white coats leaned against the counter, bored and surly. On the wall, hanging from meat hooks, were a dozen pigs' feet; the Romanians call them "patriots," because they are the only part of the animal that doesn't leave the country.

The herds of cattle and sheep that graze in the breathtakingly beautiful Romanian countryside are almost all exported as well. Meat has become a memory to most

Tira Shubart, "Arrested in Romania," from *World Monitor,* October 1989, pp. 59–62. Reprinted with the permission of the author.

households, and other staples of life are in equally short supply. Eggs, a valuable commodity, are a form of currency, sometimes changing hands a dozen times before they're actually eaten.

Western journalists and visiting businessmen who stay in the foreign currency hotels of Bucharest describe how ordinary Romanians in the dead of winter watch hungrily through the street-level windows of the dining room while people with dollars and Deutsche marks eat their heavy meals. The country that was once known as the breadbasket of the Balkans now exports 90% of its food produce, and its citizens have to plan their day around the food queues, which start before dawn.

The free market in the dismal town of Deva offers a limited opportunity for people to supplement their meager state rations—at a price. In an empty lot behind rows of shabbily built apartment blocks, peasants sell vegetables brought in from the nearby countryside. The range of food on offer is not great: a few heads of lettuce, some spices, bunches of garlic cloves, and a wealth of radishes. The radishes seem startlingly red and appealing, the only color in a gray town.

Nearby, from the back of a pickup truck, a man displays a live sheep for sale. A crowd has gathered to watch the animal being exhibited: It represents a rare feast for some rich person. After furious bidding, an unlikely, slightly dubious-looking man claims his prize and slings the unhappy, bleating sheep over his shoulders. Perhaps he's a black marketeer, or has relatives abroad who have sent him ground coffee worth the official equivalent of $100 per pound, or cartons of Kent cigarettes which have assumed an almost mythic monetary power in Romanian society. He walks off proudly, carrying the struggling animal, and envious glances follow him down the street as the bleating grows fainter.

There is a sudden movement around the vegetable stands, and a man, not quite running, deliberately brushes past us. "Securitate, Securitate!" he whispers urgently, and slips down a side street just as the police appear. The truck that delivered the fat sheep vanishes as well. The peasant women studiously examine their vegetables, but free market radishes aren't as serious a matter as black market sheep.

The police are interested in a far rarer species: foreigners. They escort us to the police station: the first of several such arrests during our visit to Romania. Our crime is to be in possession of a video camera. We are journalists who, having been denied entry in the usual way, have taken the drastic step of entering the country as tourists. The authorities are nervous about the hostile press Romania habitually receives, and do their best to stop anyone who they think may be trespassing across the line that separates ordinary tourism from reporting.

Our big disadvantage is that so few genuine tourists come to a place like Deva nowadays. At the police station we are ordered about roughly but not actually manhandled, and we undergo the usual few hours of police procrastination and routine intimidation before being allowed to leave. For us, as journalists, it is part of our job; what a genuine tourist would make of it is difficult to say.

Ordinary Romanians are terrified of the vast powers which the police have over their lives. Romania is believed to have the highest proportion of secret police to population in Eastern Europe, which is saying something. Even the man who discreetly warned us in the market was breaking the law: Every Romanian who talks to a foreigner is required to report the conversation to the Securitate within 24 hours.

Police can enter people's houses under any number of pretexts and confiscate "illegal" possessions. The Illicit Goods Law of 1974 declares the ownership of rare metals and precious stones a state monopoly; retaining family heirlooms is therefore difficult. Almost everything has to be registered with the police: fruit trees, vineyards, animals, typewriters. Duplicating machines are banned altogether. A typewriter, of course, may well be the most potent instrument any individual can possess, and so a sample of the typeface from every machine in the country is kept on file by the police, in order to discourage underground or *samizdat* literature.

Romanian law says that the freedom of the press cannot be used for goals opposed to the socialist order. An officially announced shortage of paper means that writers are not allowed to publish more than one book a year. The only exception is the most prolific author in Romania, President Nicolae Ceauşescu, whose 31-volume series is enticingly titled "On the Way of Building Up the Multilaterally-Developed Socialist Society." Every volume has been a best seller.

The US State Department, like the foreign ministries of most Western European countries, regards Romania as the most repressive and dictatorial nation in the Communist bloc. It operates a cult of personality that is consciously modeled on that of Stalin, though Romania's ruler has taken the example even further.

Nicolae Ceauşescu, who became his country's leader in 1965, is the first Communist leader to appear in public carrying a scepter. A slow, reverential handclapping, accompanied by the slow chanting of his name, "Cea-u-şes-cu," greets his appearance at a Communist Party Congress. The official media have a hundred epithets for him, including "The Great Conductor" and "The Polyvalent Genius." Every town and city is dominated by portraits of him each dating from the years when his hair was dark and his face young and handsome. A vast art gallery in Bucharest is entirely devoted to canvas after canvas of Nicolae and his designated successor, his wife, Elena.

Their son, Nicu, who used to be the chosen heir, has recently disappeared from public view: the victim, diplomats say, of his mother's ambition. The front page of every newspaper, every day, carries a prominent story on Ceauşescu; and Romanian state television, which broadcasts only three hours a night because of the shortage of electricity, devotes much of its allotted time to the activities of the President and his wife.

There are no statues to Ceauşescu in Romania; but he intends to leave a concrete legacy. In Bucharest his chosen project is the Boulevard of the Victory of Socialism, three miles long and as wide as a football field. Its construction has ripped the heart out of a city that was once called, somewhat exaggeratedly, "the Paris of the East." A dozen churches and synagogues have been demolished; so has any building, regardless of historical value, that is above a specified height.

Only the vast House of the Republic, at the head of the boulevard, is allowed to dominate the skyline. It is still under construction, and so far each time Ceauşescu has visited the site he has ordered a new wing or a new floor to be added to what is intended to be his future home. I asked our hotel porter about it: "It's like the Kremlin and the White House put together," he said. The hotel receptionist, however, was less helpful. He was unable to provide a map of the city because, he explained, there had been some building work. "Anyway, everybody can direct you back to the hotel."

But it is another project, Ceauşescu's most ambitious one, an attempt at human engineering on a grand scale, that has aroused most international protest. As long ago as 1967, to eliminate the differences between town and country, Ceauşescu ordered the destruction of 6,000 traditional villages. Peasants, who watched their homes bulldozed under, were housed in hastily built concrete apartment blocks, some without plumbing or electricity. Although some wooden sheds for chickens and geese have appeared behind the apartments, the uprooted peasants who once had household gardens are no longer self-sufficient.

Even the party faithful have found it hard to accept the demolition of ancestral villages, and so far only a dozen communities have been destroyed. Significantly, four of the "systematized" villages are along the road out of Bucharest that Ceauşescu takes when he is driven to his summer residence. The shortage of cement to build alternative accommodation for displaced villagers and intense dissatisfaction with the policy may have stopped the bulldozers. Instead, subtle pressure has begun to encourage villagers to leave voluntarily. Public transport, health facilities, and permits to run food shops and even schools are being withdrawn from villages in a heavy-handed effort to force peasants to move to one of the approved "agro-industrial complexes."

Romania has always been different. The Roman emperor Trajan ensured this by colonizing the territory with his troops in the second century A.D. To this day, Romania is a Latin island in a sea of Slavs, and feels itself to be different from its neighbors in almost every way. Even under communism it has acted independently.

For 25 years, Ceauşescu has maintained an independent stance from the Soviet Union. He was courageous in his opposition to Leonid Brezhnev's invasion of Czechoslovakia in 1968, and he refused to allow Warsaw Pact troops to be stationed on Romanian territory. The United States and other Western countries saw Ceauşescu's Romania as a Trojan horse inside the East bloc—a nation that managed to maintain relations with both Israel and China. Ceauşescu was rewarded by the US with "Most Favored Nation" status and loans from Manufacturers Hanover and the Bank of America. In Britain Queen Elizabeth II gave him an honorary knighthood; in California he received the freedom of Disneyland.

But during the 1970s Ceauşescu's independence of mind became more and more like totalitarianism, and Stalin was his chosen model. By 1988 increasing human rights abuses in Romania, such as the widespread taking of political prisoners and kidnappings of intellectuals, prompted Washington to finally withdraw its MFN status.

Nowadays it is the Soviet Union under Mikhail Gorbachev that is increasingly liberal, and Ceauşescu's Romania that is a reminder of the bad old days in Moscow. Outside the offices of the Soviet airline Aeroflot on the Boulevard Bălcescu, one of the main streets of Bucharest, I watched as a small crowd took turns examining and copying down the schedule of radio programs from Radio Moscow, which broadcasts in Romanian six hours a day. It is almost the only legal source of independent information for Romanians. Other broadcasts for Eastern Europeans—Radio Free Europe, the BBC, and West Germany's Deutsche Welle—are forbidden to them by law, though many people take the risk of listening even so.

One night I managed to give the slip to the security policemen who were assigned to follow me and visited the apartment of a family with friends in the West. I brought the usual gifts, but it was clear immediately that I was not a welcome visitor. The two-room apartment was dark—just one 40-watt light bulb is allowed per household. The only other light was generated by the flickering images of Ceauşescu on the nightly television broadcast. Though I was welcomed with great hospitality, it was obvious that the people I was visiting were terrified of the consequences of inviting me into their living room. We spoke in whispers, our voices covered by the sound of President Ceauşescu's doings on television. It was pure George Orwell.

The woman I had come to see confirmed that she, like every woman of her age, was subject to the official policies designed to counteract the decline in the birthrate. Married women are urged to have five children to bolster the population, which appears to have been declining at a faster rate than in any other country in Europe, East or West. There are tax penalties for childless couples, and birth control is denied to those who haven't fulfilled their "quota." Abortion is illegal except in narrowly defined medical circumstances. As a further inducement to procreate, all women of childbearing age are subjected to compulsory gynecological tests. The office where this particular woman worked was visited by a doctor every month. The doctor disliked the task she had been ordered to carry out, but anyone who was found to have broken the law was liable to a fine or imprisonment.

The door of the apartment closed after me, and I felt my way down an unlit staircase and stumbled across broken pavement in search of my car with not even the moonlight to guide me. I knew I hadn't been followed. There were no cars around, and at this time of night the streets were entirely empty. Time and again on my trip to Romania I found that the secret police worked office hours: After five o'clock the unmarked cars and the young men in leather jackets who stood around on street corners tended to melt away. The evening shift was much fewer in number. But that night the hotel receptionist was very agitated when I returned so late. Somebody would obviously be blamed for my unexplained absence.

The next day my colleagues and I were arrested once more and again wasted several hours in a police station. It seemed clear to us that the woman I had visited must have spent a sleepless night and decided that she must inform the proper authorities of our conversation, just in case I had after all been followed to her apartment.

Later in the week as we approached the border to leave Romania, the security men left us to travel the last miles unsupervised. We were now the responsibility of the border militia. There was the usual period of waiting in line while the guards ostentatiously did nothing. Then much of our car was expertly dismantled and all possible hiding places were searched. Our luggage got an equally professional going over. The polite men in the customs office exposed every roll of film they found, and tried to erase every videotape cassette with a magnet—though fortunately their technology wasn't up to the task. After six hours they let us go, and we crossed the bridge over the Danube into Yugoslavia.

In front of us, in the evening light, the river passed through the spectacular ravine known as the Iron Gates. A weight that had hung around us since we entered Romania, more than a week before, was lifted. As the sun went down over the Iron Gates, we looked back at the sweeping hills and forests of the country we had just left. From the vantage point of freedom, Romania at last looked extraordinarily beautiful, and extraordinarily sad.

In Romania: Between Euphoria and Rage

✦

Vladimir Tismaneanu

In this selection a political scientist who has published widely on Eastern Europe seeks to explain the exceptional violence accompanying the overthrow of Ceauşescu's regime at the end of 1989 and, in doing so, also calls attention to the frailty of the government that succeeded Ceauşescu.

Unlike the other East European revolutions, the Romanian one was extremely violent. It resulted not only in the replacement of a despised ruling family but in the dissolution of all party and government structures. But the drastic nature of these events is sadly consistent. The magnitude of the collective decompression has been directly proportional to the amount of repression accumulated in more than forty years of "proletarian dictatorship." Bereft of power and authority, the Communist party simply collapsed, ingloriously. The party had essentially disappeared the moment Ceauşescu and his wife fled from the roof of the Central Committee building in Bucharest's Palace Square on December 22, 1989.

The dictator's flight signified the end of more than four decades of brutal Stalinism. Did it also mean the end of communism in any form? Did it usher in full-fledged pluralism? How can one save a spontaneous revolution from below from being co-opted by those adept in the Leninist techniques of manipulation? How can

Vladimir Tismaneanu, "In Romania: Between Euphoria and Rage," from *Dissent,* Spring 1990, 219–223.

one explain both the tremendous amplitude of the Romanian revolution and also its failure to engender political forms that would guarantee a break with the past?

Romania was different from the others because it had never undergone de-Stalinization. It had never passed through the process of moving from the absolute rule of one man to the (slightly less absolute) rule of a Communist Politburo. To Westerners the distinction between these two forms of oppression may seem irrelevant, but it is very large to people who live under them. A single absolute ruler, in the mold of Stalin, Mao, Kim Il-sung, Castro, or Ceaușescu, means a rule unchecked and unmoderated in its arbitrariness, ignorance, and cruelty. The autocrat enters with impunity upon the most erratic actions. A Politburo, even one made up of cruel individuals, provides a moderating check against the worst depravities of any one member. Compare, for example, Stalin's rule to that of Khrushchev. The former terrorized not only the whole of society but also his closest collaborators. The latter returned to the alleged "Leninist norms of party life" precisely because the party bureaucracy could no longer tolerate Stalinist methods of intimidation and persecution. In the same vein, with all his sins, Erich Honecker was only the *primus inter pares* within a Mafia-like Politburo in East Germany. Ceaușescu not only monopolized power, he also dynasticized the Romanian party by appointing members of his clan to top party and government positions. The degree of hatred oppressed people feel toward their masters is bound to be quite different in the two cases.

Some historical background is indispensable here. Nicolae Ceaușescu did not emerge out of the blue. He was the product of Romanian Communist political culture, and his extravaganzas did nothing but carry to an extreme its never-abandoned Stalinist features. He climbed the career ladder within the Romanian Communist party (RCP) under the protection of Gheorghe Gheorghiu-Dej, the party's general secretary between 1944 and 1965. It was Gheorghiu-Dej who avoided the de-Stalinization process initiated by Khrushchev in 1956. Ceaușescu, who became a Politburo member in 1954, helped Gheorghiu-Dej to forcibly collectivize agriculture and organize repeated anti-intellectual witchhunts. The Romanian Communists, who before the arrival of the Soviet troops in August 1944 numbered no more than one thousand members, preserved an uncompromising commitment to hard-line Stalinism. Both under Gheorghiu-Dej and Ceaușescu, the party suffered a painful inferiority complex: since its leaders were perfectly aware that their coming to power was the result of the Soviet diktat, they could not arrive at a genuine source of legitimacy. This was indeed their Achilles' heel: a total alienation from the Romanian nation. Scared by Khrushchev's anti-Stalin campaign, Gheorghiu-Dej simulated Romanian patriotism and defied Moscow's plans for economic integration within the Comecon. Instead of de-Stalinizing Romania, Gheorghiu-Dej de-Sovietized her. But by the end of his life, Romania had the potential to become a second Yugoslavia: an impressive economic growth and encouraging links with the West could have been used for a gradual dissolution of Stalinism. Even the national intelligentsia, viscerally anticommunist, was ready to credit the party leadership for the break with Moscow.

Ironically, when Nicolae Ceaușescu took power in March 1965, it appeared he would de-Stalinize the party. He condemned the holding of political prisoners, deplored the abuses of the past, and instructed the *Securitate* (secret police) to abide by the law. In April 1968, he rehabilitated Lucreţiu Patrascănu, a former Politburo member and Marxist thinker executed in 1954 under trumped-up charges of espionage. He also reinstated into the party many victims of Gheorghiu-Dej's terror and proclaimed the need to write a true history of both the party and the country. It was *glasnost avant la lettre,* with Ceauşescu championing a self-styled version of reform communism. At the same time, the general secretary continued to de-Sovietize through his independent line in foreign policy—he distanced his country from the Soviet Union by maintaining diplomatic relations with Israel after 1967 and by vehemently condemning the Soviet invasion of Czechoslovakia in 1968.

This stance won Ceauşescu plaudits and even aid from Western governments. In April 1968, Charles de Gaulle visited Romania and congratulated Ceauşescu for his alleged independence. In August 1969, Richard Nixon went to Bucharest, where he was triumphantly received by an increasingly self-enamored Ceauşescu. The myth of the maverick diplomat, the super-negotiator and the only trustworthy communist leader, was naively bought by many Western analysts, who glossed over Ceauşescu's growing dictatorial propensities. This image also strengthened Ceauşescu by allowing him to portray dissidents as traitors.

The president's Stalinist inclinations were catalyzed by a trip he made in May 1971 to China and North Korea. He appears then to have considered the possibility of importing into Romania the methods of indoctrination used during the Cultural Revolution. This was not just a matter of personal preference: Ceauşescu was trying to contain the liberalization movement in Romania, curb intellectual unrest, and deter students from emulating their rebellious peers in other communist states. He was also trying to consolidate his personal power and get rid of those in the apparatus who might have nourished dreams of "socialism with a human face." Thus in June 1971 he published his "proposal for the improvement of ideological activity," a monument of Zhdanovist obscurantism. What followed was a radical re-Stalinization and the emergence of an unprecedented cult of personality surrounding, first, himself and then, after 1974, his "evil genius" wife, Elena.

Several thousand people in Romania—the hard core of followers—came to believe the myth that Ceauşescu was the demiurge of national dignity and sovereignty. Above all, the myth was believed by Elena, who after 1979 was his second-in-command. Her influence catalyzed Nicolae's Hitlerian personality, expunging the impulses that had prompted his regime's early promises of liberalization. Many of Ceauşescu's initial supporters, party apparatchiks like Virgil Trofin, Ion Iliescu, and János Fazekas; the prime minister, Ion Gheorghe Maurer; and the defense minister-general, Ion Ioniţa, were marginalized or sacked.

The only criterion for political success in Ceauşescu's Romania was unconditional loyalty to the president. A permanent encomiastic deluge was engineered by agitprop hacks: making Ceauşescu's name synonymous with communism, the sycophants heaped hagiographic epithets on him. A victim of the mechanism he had created, Ceauşescu himself came to believe in his providential role as the "savior of the nation," the "hero of peace," and the "most brilliant revolutionary thinker of all times." In an attempt to ensure his political immortality, he promoted his youngest

The Ceauşescus on Trial. Arrested and tried before a secret military tribunal after a bloody revolt had toppled his regime, Nicolae Ceauşescu attempts to defend himself while his wife Elena watches. This footage appeared on Romanian television on December 26, 1989, along with a view of their bodies after the Ceauşescus had been executed by a firing squad. (AP/Wide World Photos)

son, Nicu, to high party positions. The dictator dreamed of leaving his imprint on the Romanian soul. He submitted Romanians to incredible humiliations by forcing them to simulate joy in times of utter poverty and despondency. He presided over the bulldozing of old Bucharest and imposed the building of a giant palace, an apogee of "socialist realist" kitsch. Possessed by an overweening hubris, hypnotized by a self-image magnified to grotesque proportions by the corrupt scribes of the presidential court, Ceauşescu completely lost touch with reality.

Obsessed with Hitler, while believing passionately in orthodox Stalinism, Ceauşescu merged these two horrifying legacies into a personalized tyranny that ranked with any of this century. Its principal underpinning, and sole explanation for its longevity, was the *Securitate*. Like Stalin, Ceauşescu managed to annihilate the party by converting it into a passive body of almost four million members whose sole duty was to worship him. Not only the party, but all sources of independent social life were suppressed. In 1977, when coal workers in the Jiu Valley organized a massive strike, their leaders were captured by the *Securitate* and made to disappear. Ten years later, in November 1987, when street demonstrations took place in Braşov, the *Securitate* intervened, order was restored, and the organizers vanished. Prominent intellectual dissidents were forced into either external or internal exile. There was no possibility of engaging in anything similar to Czechoslovakia's Charter 77 or Poland's Committee for Workers' Defense. An all-pervasive police terror thwarted any attempt to launch democratic initiatives from below. Romania's civil society was almost completely paralyzed.

Under these circumstances, it is understandable that Ceauşescu could not be removed so easily as the other East European leaders. There was no institution that could ensure a nonviolent transition from this terrorist dictatorship to a softer version of communism. As a tyrant, Ceauşescu had to be removed by tyrannicide—a method with a long and honorable tradition.

Those who organized his execution are themselves former Communists. It is not at all clear why the leaders of the National Salvation Front (NSF)—the ruling body that emerged immediately after the revolution claiming to be a spontaneous popular organization—organized Ceauşescu's trial in a manner disturbingly reminiscent of Stalinist frame-ups. Furthermore, there are indications that former leaders of the *Securitate* were among the first to lend their support to the new authorities.

With Ceauşescu dead and most of his main acolytes in jail waiting for open trials, the question now is how deeply the process of uprooting his regime will reach. Because the Romanian revolution was a violent one, it is also likely to be thoroughgoing: with its martyrs, it also has its momentum. So far, the signals from Bucharest are mixed.

The Council of the NSF was initially led by a foursome made up of old Communists. Its chairman, Ion Iliescu, studied in Moscow in the early 1950s and was Ceauşescu's protege until 1971, when he fell in disgrace for "intellectualism." Presumably anti-Stalinist, he is far from being anticommunist. His model is Gorbachev and his ideal a reformed version of the one-party system. Since his advent to power, Iliescu has not kept these convictions secret. On the contrary, in a conversation with student leaders on January 21, 1990, Iliescu described political pluralism as "an obsolete ideology of the nineteenth century." In his speech, which was not published in the still state-controlled Romanian media but publicized by the Soviet press agency TASS, Iliescu claimed that the NSF advocated a "democratic model without pluralism." In this he was echoing not only Gorbachev's opposition to a multiparty system, but also the political philosophy of the NSF's principal ideologue, communist veteran Silviu Brucan.

With surprising candor, Brucan has expressed his deep contempt for Western-type democracy. He is the author of the concept that the recent Romanian revolution is so original that its aftermath must essentially be different from those of other countries. For Brucan, as for Iliescu, terms like socialism, communism, Marxism, Leninism, capitalism, and fascism have lost any sense. They consider the NSF to be a supra-ideological body, a mass party movement, a corporation of diverging but not necessarily incompatible interests. In the light of this outlook, there is no need for other parties to exist and compete for power with the "truly national exponent," that is, the NSF ruled by Iliescu, Brucan and Prime Minister Petre Roman.

The fourth member of the initial ruling quartet, Dumitru Mazilu, resigned on

January 26, 1990, in protest against the "Stalinist methods of the new leadership." Mazilu knows something about Stalinism: a former *Securitate* colonel, he taught international law at the University of Bucharest and served as a government-appointed United Nations expert on human rights. In 1987 he smuggled out of Romania a report on human rights violations there. Harassed by the *Securitate,* Mazilu refused to recant and reemerged on December 22, 1989, as one of the leaders of the revolutionary movement.

Is the conflict between Iliescu and Mazilu a simple clash of ambitions? Or are we witnessing an obscure struggle between two groups that secretly conspired to take over power on the day Ceaușescu would be deposed? This is only one of the many mysteries surrounding Romania's new government.

In the meantime, taking advantage of the new laws on associations, political parties have started to form. Among them, one can identify such "parties of nostalgia" linked to Romania's fragile interwar democracy as the National Peasant party and the Liberal party. For the time being, the Communists have refrained from trying to reestablish their party, but it is likely that some of their activists will try to emulate the Hungarian strategy and propose the formation of a "Socialist party." Their handicap, however, is that there is little constituency for a group that is in any way responsible for the historical tragedy of the last forty years. As for the Romanian Social Democrats, they have formed their own party, and it is probable that they will attract votes among blue-collar workers.

Learning the democratic process will be difficult in a country with very few democratic traditions. But there are also some encouraging signals: the students, who spearheaded the overthrow of the dictatorship, have created a Student League, which may become a rallying point for Romania's democratic youth. Critical intellectuals of various persuasions have organized a Group for Social Dialogue, whose tasks are to reflect on the country's problems, monitor the government's observance of democratic procedures, and, most important, help the development of a civil society in Romania.

During the first days of the revolution, Romanians engaged in romantic dreams of national redemption. Students and intellectuals were ready to trust the new leaders' pledges of commitment to pluralism. Things changed quickly: the NSF announced that it would field its own candidates in the forthcoming elections; former *Securitate* officers were suddenly released from prison without explanation; criticism of communism (and not only of Ceaușescuism) was toned down. More ominously, instead of disbanding the hated *Securitate,* the NSF decided to subordinate it to the Ministry of Defense. Correspondence is still censored and telephone conversations are reportedly tapped.

Mass meetings have been organized to protest what many Romanians perceive as the hijacking of their revolution. During the first stage of the upheaval, the people showed remarkable moderation as the *Securitate* murdered and tortured thousands of unarmed civilians. But if the NSF continues to trample the democratic aspirations of the population, and if the logic of postrevolutionary bureaucracy prevails over that of a genuine renewal, then one can expect more turmoil. To date, the NSF Council has failed to establish its democratic bona fides. It has committed a number of immense blunders and alienated many of those who could have fostered its authority. Although intellectuals may succumb to a state of resigned malaise, students will not capitulate as easily. After all, without their sacrifices, Ceauşescu might have retained power. They will not accept the spilling of their blood to see the replacement of a clique of illiterate Stalinists with one of neo–Bolshevik reformers.

At this critical juncture, with an overcharged political atmosphere and with only a precariously legitimate government, one cannot rule out the danger of a military coup. To prevent such an outcome, independent social forces will have to coordinate their actions in a broad democratic movement. If they fail, frustrated ardor and betrayed ideals may beget a state of collective despair, which, in turn, could generate new waves of popular rage.

The Timişoara Declaration

✦

Timişoara was the birthplace of Romania's 1989 revolution, and the town's civic and intellectual groups drew on this fact in issuing this declaration at a public rally there on March 11, 1990. The declaration stresses the inadequacies of the successor regime and had a noticeable echo elsewhere in Romania.

The citizens of Timişoara initiated the Romanian Revolution. From December 16 through 20, 1989, they alone waged a fierce war against one of the world's strongest and most hatefully repressive systems. It was a ferocious struggle whose true proportions only we, the inhabitants of Timişoara, understand. On the one side was the unarmed population; on the other were the *Securitate,* the militia, the army, and the zealous troops of party activists. But all the methods and means of repression proved futile against the people of Timişoara's desire for freedom and determination to win. The arrests, the violence, even the mass murders could not stop them. Each bullet that was fired brought scores of new fighters onto the barricades of the revolution. And we carried the day! On December 20, 1989, the people ruled Timişoara, turning it into a free city within the prison of Romania. From that day on, the Romanian Democratic Front, in the name of the Timişoara Revolution, coordinated the entire city's activities from Opera Square. The same day, the soldiers fraternized with the demonstrators; side by side the people and the army would defend the people's victory. On December 21, more than 100,000 voices chanted in Opera Square: "We are ready to die!"

The events that have occurred in Romania, especially after January 28, 1990, contradict the ideals of the Timişoara Revolution. Only a few of these ideals have, in a very confused way, been brought before the people by the Romanian media. Under these circumstances, we who participated directly in the events that took place from December 16 through 22, 1989, feel it is our duty to explain to the entire nation why Timişoara's citizens triggered the revolution, what was fought for, what so many of them gave their lives for, and why we shall resolutely continue to fight against any one, at any cost, until full victory is attained.

1. From its first hours, the Timişoara Revolution was not directed only against the Ceauşescus: it was categorically directed against communism. Every day during the revolution, people chanted hundreds of times: "Down with communism!" In keeping with the aspirations of hundreds of millions of East Europeans, we also called for the immediate abolition of this totalitarian and bankrupt social system. The ideal of our revolution has been and remains a return to the genuine values of democracy and European civilization.

2. All social sections of the population took part in the Timişoara Revolution. Blue-collar workers, white-collar workers, intellectuals, university students, secondary-school pupils, children, and even village-dwellers who had come to support the revolution fell side by side, killed by bullets on the streets of Timişoara. We categorically oppose the typical communist technique of dominating the people by provoking feuds among the social classes and groups. In 1917 the Bolsheviks took power, basing their claim on the ideology of the class struggle; similarly, after 1944 Romanian Communists acting as instigators set one social class against another and tore apart society in order to terrorize it more easily. We warn against the danger of repeating such a sad historical event and call on workers, intellectuals, students, peasants, and all social groups of the Romanian population to begin a civilized and constructive dialogue with a view to rebuilding without delay the unity created during the revolution. One must start from the reality that all these social groups have been oppressed under the communist regime, and today none of them means any harm to the others.

3. People of all ages took part in the Timişoara Revolution. Even if young people predominated, it is fair to say that those of other ages fought just as unflinchingly for the revolution's cause. The casualty list, although incomplete, bears testimony to this.

4. Together with the Romanians, Hungarians, Germans, Serbs, and members of other ethnic groups that have for centuries peacefully and as good neighbors shared our city sacrificed their lives for the victory of the revolution. Timişoara is a European city whose nationalities have refused and are still refusing to accept nationalism. We invite all the country's chauvinists—whether Romanian, Hungarian, or German—to come to Timişoara and take a course in tolerance and mutual respect, the only principles that will rule in the future European house.

5. As far back as December 16, 1989, in the first hours of the revolution, one of the most frequently chanted slogans was "We want free elections!" The idea of political pluralism has been and still is one of the ideals closest to the hearts of Timişoara's inhabitants. We are persuaded that without strong political parties there can be no genuine European-style democracy. With the exception of the extreme left-wing and right-wing parties, all parties have the right to exist in the city of Timişoara. In our town, no party headquarters were attacked or devastated; no party members were threatened, insulted, or slandered. Party members are our fellow citizens, colleagues at our work places, friends with political opinions. European democracy means that political opinions can be freely expressed and that a civilized dialogue can be carried on by candidates in honest competition trying to win public support and, implicitly, state power.

We would have accepted the Romanian Communist Party (RCP) within the ranks of Romanian democracy as well had it not completely and irrevocably compromised itself by degenerating into red fascism. In those East European countries where communist parties have preserved a minimal decency, society is contesting the party in principle but tolerating it in practice. In our country, however, the communist party has gone so far as to commit genocide; as a result, it has excluded itself definitively from society. We shall not tolerate it either in principle or in practice, regardless of the name under which it tries to resurrect itself.

6. After four decades of exclusively communist education and propaganda, prejudices symptomatic of communist ideology still persist in the consciousness of all Romanians. The people are not to blame for this. But when groups keen on reinstating communist power try to manipulate them, it is a counterrevolutionary act. Slogans 45 years old were included in the list of chants distributed on January 28, 1990, to the demonstrators in Banu Manta Square in Bucharest. One of these slanderous slogans, for instance, identified the "historical" parties with parties that betrayed their country, when in fact the Communists of 45 years ago—some of whom are still holding major positions in the country's leadership—are guilty of betraying Romania and subjugating it to the Soviet Union. It was not the members of the "historical" parties but these people who used to chant "Stalin and the Russian people brought us Freedom!" The "historical" parties in fact opposed the transformation of Romania into a satellite of Moscow, and some members of these parties paid with their life for this daring. It is imperative that a brief but correct history of the 1944–1950 period be prepared, printed for mass circulation, and distributed as soon as possible.

7. Timişoara initiated a revolution against the communist regime and its entire *nomenklatura,* and by no means in order to create the opportunity for a group of anti-Ceauşescu dissidents from within the RCP to gain power. Their presence at the head of the country makes it seem that the Timişoara heroes died in vain. We might have accepted these leaders 10 years ago, if at the 12th RCP Congress they had joined Constantin Parvulescu and overthrown the dictator's clique. But they did not do so, although they had the opportunity, holding as they did major positions that allowed them certain prerogatives. Instead, some of them even obeyed the dictator's order to abuse the dissident Parvulescu. Their cowardice in 1979 meant 10 more years of dictatorship, the hardest of the entire era and, moreover, terrible genocide.

8. As a consequence of this point, we suggest that the electoral law forbid former communist activists and *Securitate* officers from running as candidates on any electoral list during the first three consecutive legislatures. Their presence in the country's political life is the main source of the tension and suspicions that currently plague Romanian society. Until the political situation stabilizes and the nation is reconciled, it is absolutely necessary that they stay away from public life.

We also demand that the electoral law include a special paragraph forbidding former communist activists from standing as candidates for the position of President of Romania. The President of Romania should be one of the symbols of our parting from communism. To have been a party member is not a fault in itself. We all know to what extent the individual's life—from professional achievement to the allotment of a flat—was governed by the red party card and how grave the consequences of handing it over would have been. But the most active Communists were those people who gave up their professions in order to serve the communist party and benefit from the material privileges it provided. Someone who has made such a choice does not present the moral guarantees a President should offer. We suggest that the powers of this office be reduced in keeping with the model of many civilized countries throughout the world. Furthermore, prominent cultural and scientific figures without any particular political experience might become candidates for the high office of President of Romania.

Along the same line, we suggest that the first legislature should exist only for two years, as it is necessary to strengthen our democratic institutions and clarify the ideological position of each of the numerous political parties that have sprung up. Only at that time would we choose a permanent legislature, for then we would have the knowledge necessary to organize open and honest elections.

9. The citizens of Timişoara did not create the revolution in order to obtain higher salaries or other material advantages. If such had been their object, a strike would have been enough. We are all dissatisfied with the wage system; in Timişoara some workers must perform under extremely hard conditions, and they are badly paid (the foundry workers, for example, or those in the detergent industry). Nevertheless, no plant has ever gone on strike for a wage increase; no delegation has ever tried to negotiate exclusive material claims with the government. The majority of Timişoara's citizens are aware of what economists are currently trying to bring to people's attention: the fact that any wage increases at the moment would automatically trigger inflation, as has already happened in some East European countries. And once inflation started, years of effort would be required in order to stop it. Only an increase in production (that is, an increase in the goods available on the market) would allow salaries to increase at the same time. Because of Romania's small budget, from now on priority must be given to expenses that will help us to re-establish a minimum level of civilization. For instance, immediate investments must be made in medical care and public sanitation.

10. Although we are militating for a re-Europeanization of Romania, we do not wish to copy Western capitalist systems, which have their own deficiencies and inequities. However, we categorically favor the concept of private initiative. The economic foundation of totalitarianism has been the absolute power derived from the monopoly on property. We shall never have political pluralism without economic pluralism. But some of those who still have communist leanings try to equate private initiative with "exploitation" and maintain that the emergence of rich entrepreneurs would be a catastrophe. In the same way they try to play on the feelings of those who are lazy and would therefore envy the wealthy, and those who—having once enjoyed the privileges of the communist system—are afraid of the effort of working.

The fact that several enterprises have already announced their intention of becoming joint stock companies testifies to the fact that Timişoara's inhabitants are not afraid of privatization. But in order for this stock to be bought with honestly earned money, commissions should be set up in each town to inventory the property of the former powerful and privileged, who built up their wealth through corruption and the penury of others. It would be fitting for the stock of an enterprise to be offered first of all to its workers.

We also consider constructive the more radical idea of privatizing by offering an equal number of shares to each worker in an enterprise, with the state keeping only the percentage necessary to maintain control of the management. In this way, all workers would have the same chance to become prosperous. And if some lazy people did not take advantage of this opportunity, they could not complain that they had been discriminated against.

11. Timişoara has decided to take seriously and put into action the principle of economic and administrative decentralization. A suggestion has been made to establish as an experiment in Timiş County a model of a market economy because of the area's strong economic capacity and the skill of available specialists. In order to attract foreign capital—especially technology and certain raw materials—quickly and more easily, and to set up joint stock companies, we request that a branch office of the Bank of Foreign Trade be opened in Timişoara. Some of the Romanian earnings (in convertible currency) of these joint ventures will be added to workers' wages; the percentage will be negotiated on a case-by-case basis with trade union leaders. Paying a share of the wages in convertible currency will ensure workers a sound material incentive. Then passports will no longer be just pieces of paper good for nothing but keeping in a drawer. Another positive consequence of this suggestion would be the drop in the exchange rate on the free market, which would result in an immediate increase in the population's living standards.

12. After the dictatorship collapsed, all Romanians in exile were invited to return to Romania to help in the country's reconstruction. Some have already come back, and others have announced their intention of doing so. Unfortunately, instigated by dark forces, some people began abusing those exiled compatriots who returned home, calling them traitors and asking them devious questions about what they had eaten over the last 10 years. This is an attitude that does us no credit. During those 40 years when despair held us in its grip, perhaps there was no Romanian to whom it did not occur at least once to go into exile in order to escape the misery. Many of the Romanians now far from their fatherland left after being persecuted for their political beliefs; some had spent years in prison. It is shameful to abuse them by throwing at them the calumny of former communist activists. Romanian exiles include hundreds of outstanding professors teaching at the biggest universities in the world, thousands of specialists appreciated by the most prominent Western companies, tens of thousands of skilled workers specializing in the most advanced technologies. We should be proud of them. Let us convert the evil into good by turning the sad and painful Romanian Diaspora into a renovating force for the country. Timişoara is waiting for all Romanian exiles with open arms. They are our compatriots and we need their skills, their European thinking, and even their material support more than ever. Romanian culture will be whole only if it is integrated with the culture of its exiles.

13. We do not agree with making December 22 Romania's national day. Using this date means that the dictator's memory will be perpetuated, for each year will celebrate the number of years since his downfall. Most countries that have linked their national day to a revolution have selected the day when the revolutionary movement was triggered, thus glorifying the courage of the people in taking up arms and fighting. Just one example: France's national day is July 14, the day in 1789 when the Great National Revolution began destroying the Bastille. Consequently, we are asking that December 16 be set as Romania's national day. Thus, our children, grandchildren, and great-grandchildren will celebrate the courage of the people in defying oppression and not the downfall of an infamous tyrant.

Except for the daily *România Liberă,* the Bucharest press, radio, and television have almost buried the Timişoara Revolution in oblivion. In their commentaries, the only revolutionary events are those of December 21 and 22, 1989. We pay homage to the Bucharest heroes, as well as to the heroes of Lugoj, Sibiu, Braşov, Tîrgu-Mareş, Cluj, Arad, Reşiţa, and all the other towns that needed martyrs in order to win freedom. But we are distressed and angered by this policy of playing down our revolution, a policy that is also obvious in the media's efforts to reduce the number of Timişoara's casualties. We were in the streets of Timişoara during the days of the revolution and know that the number of deaths was higher than that officially reported. And we are assuring those who conceal the truth that we shall not cease our struggle until they are brought to court as accomplices in genocide.

This declaration was born of the necessity to bring before the Romanian nation the true ideals of the Timişoara Revolution. This revolution was made by the people and by the people alone, without communist activists and the *Securitate.* This has been a genuine revolution, and not a *coup d'état.* It was directed against communism and not only against Ceauşescu. People did not die in Timisoara so that second- or third-rate communist activists could move to the front or so one of the participants in the genocide could even be appointed Minister of Internal Affairs.

People did not die so that social and national discord, personality cults, media censorship, disinformation, telephoned and written threats, and all the other communist methods of constraint should be practiced in full sight of everybody, while we in Timişoara are being asked to keep quiet in the name of social stability. This declaration is addressed first of all to those who have received the revolution as if it were a Christmas gift and are wondering why we are displeased, since the dictatorship has fallen, a number of bad laws have been abolished, and a few goods have appeared in the shops. Now they know why we are discontented. For these were not the ideals of the Timişoara Revolution.

We, the authors of this declaration, the participants in the events that occurred from December 16 through 22, 1989, do not consider that the revolution has been concluded. We shall continue it peacefully but firmly. After defying and defeating without anybody's help one of the strongest repressive systems in the world, no one and nothing can intimidate us any more.

As of Sunday, March 11, 1990, the following have joined in signing the Timişoara Proclamation:

> *The Timişoara Society* (of writers and journalists who have directly participated in the Timişoara Revolution), *Europe Society* (of Timişoara journalism students), *The December 16 Confederation*—an independent organization of the young people from Timiş County, *The Democratic Union of Banat Hungarians*, *"The Banat Is Still Up Front" Association*, *The Romanian-Hungarian Friendship Association*, *Timsez*—an organization of young Hungarians from Timişoara, *The Society of Young Journalists*, *The League for the Defense of Human Rights*, *The Timişoara Municipal Council.*

The Communist Party Re-emerges Under a New Name

◆

Dan Ionescu

The formation of the Socialist Labor Party in Romania late in 1990 affords a glimpse, according to this article from *Report on Eastern Europe,* of the way in which the old communist appa-ratus is seeking to retain a role under a new name within the governing framework of the National Salvation Front.

On November 17 the media announced that a new party, the Socialist Labor Party (SLP), had been created the previous day by merging the Democratic Labor Party (DLP) and the Socialist Party. The Socialist Party, which had never formally registered with the authorities, was described as "the result of the reorganization, on a new basis, of the former Romanian Communist Party" (RCP). The SLP's founders pledged to take into account "the socialist and workers' movements' traditions in Romania and the experience of West European left-wing, socialist, and democratic parties." They elected Constantin Pîrvulescu honorary President and established a steering committee headed by Ilie Verdet, a former high-ranking official of the RCP and Romania's Prime Minister from 1979 to 1982.

Pîrvulescu, who was born in 1895, is the only surviving founder of the RCP, which was formed in 1921. He is known for having publicly criticized former Roma-nian leader Nicolae Ceaușescu at the RCP's 12th Congress in 1979, as well as for having cosigned the so-called Letter of the Six, a document blaming Ceaușescu for Romania's disastrous economic, political, and social situation (first published in the West in March 1989). Verdet, who was born in 1925, is the "strong man" of the new party. He was re-elected Chairman of the RCP's Central Auditing Commission at the 14th RCP Congress (its last) in November 1989, only a month before the uprising that marked the end of the Ceaușescu regime. He was probably not tried later along with the other leading RCP figures because he had not been a member of the Political Executive Committee of the RCP's Central Committee, which had approved Ceaușescu's orders to crush the popular revolts in Timișoara and Bucharest.

Dan Ionescu, "The Communist Party Re-emerges Under a New Name," from *Report on Eastern Europe,* December 21, 1990, pp. 22–26. Reprinted with the permission of Radio Free Europe/Radio Liberty.

◆

NO DEATH CERTIFICATE FOR THE RCP

The announcement of the RCP's re-emergence on the political scene hardly came as a surprise; legally, the party had never ceased to exist. The day Ceauşescu was toppled, the RCP (with a membership of no fewer than 3,800,000) seemed to vanish into thin air, together with such pillars of the old regime as Ceauşescu's last government led by Prime Minister Constantin Dáscálescu. Immediately after Ceauşescu had fled from Bucharest, Verdet desperately tried to form a provisional government able to ensure a certain amount of political continuity. It was reportedly the protest by a group of young people who had forced their way into the Central Committee building that put an end to Verdet's "ghost cabinet" only 22 minutes after its formation.

On December 30, 1989, an "initiative group" within the party launched a television appeal to all RCP members to support the convening of an extraordinary congress in order to proclaim their party's dissolution, owing to the fact that the RCP had been "definitively compromised in the people's and history's eyes by the dictatorship of the Ceauşescus and their acolytes." The appeal also raised the delicate issue of the party's assets, recommending that they be handed over to the people "through the agency of the National Salvation Front [NSF] Council." In a conversation with a foreign journalist, a young scientist summed up the public's generally apprehensive mood in a rather prophetic comment on the RCP's future: "They will change the name of the [communist] party, but it will be the same. It must be dissolved or it will reorganize."

On January 11, *România Liberă* reported that Verdet had paid a visit to the former Ştefan Gheorghiu Party Academy, claiming that he needed a base from which a working team could prepare the dissolution of the communist party. But another daily, *Libertatea* (the NSF Council's mouthpiece during the first days of the NSF's existence), appears to have been better informed, observing that Verdet was, in fact, looking for "suitable headquarters for the Socialist Party." (A party with this name had never been officially registered in Romania.)

On January 12, the day after the teaching staff of the former party cadre school had firmly rejected Verdet's attempt to take possession of its premises, Verdet and some of his communist followers made their initial attempt to take over the Democratic Labor Party, a satellite of the NSF that provided a haven for old-guard Communists such as 81-year-old Eduard Mezincescu, Minister of the Arts in the early 1950s, who fell out of favor with Ceauşescu in the 1970s. At the time of the attempted takeover by Verdet, the DLP had not yet officially registered with the authorities. (On February 6 the DLP was registered as Romania's 26th party and the NSF as its 27th.) Although Verdet boasted that he could bring some "800 members and 6,000,000 lei" with him, his offer was turned down. With memories of the Ceauşescu era still fresh in Romania, the DLP leaders were hardly in a position "to enter into an alliance with [former] *nomenklatura* members whose faces were turned only toward the past."

✦

OUTLAWED FOR ONE DAY

One of the key moments in the history of communism in Romania occurred on January 12. During a relatively small but turbulent rally of several thousand people, Ion Iliescu, at that time President of the NSF Council, bowed to public pressure and announced that the NSF Council would issue a decree-law stipulating that "the RCP is outlawed, as this party goes against [Romania's] national spirit and our ancestors' law," a rather populist description of Romania's political tradition. The move resulted in Romania's being the first and only country thus far in Eastern Europe to have banned its communist party. The decision was reversed, however, only one day later. On the evening of January 13, Iliescu announced on Radio Bucharest that he had received many letters criticizing his weakness in yielding to the pressure of the crowd. He announced that the decision to ban the RCP would be submitted to a referendum on January 28, but the idea of the referendum was subsequently abandoned.

Probably the most influential person behind the decision to annul the ban on the RCP was Silviu Brucan, at that time the chief ideologist of the NSF. In an interview published several days later, Brucan declared the communist party "terminated" for its failure to oppose Ceauşescu's dictatorship; but he rejected the idea of banning it by a decree-law as "antidemocratic." By the same token, he suggested that such a measure would "offend [the communist parties in Romania's neighboring countries] and create difficulties for them." In the days following the events of January 12, the pro-NSF press was flooded with letters to the editors describing the ban on the RCP as contrary to Western democratic principles. Some young intellectuals, however, hailed the short-lived decision to outlaw the RCP, insisting that this party was by no means less extremist than the extreme right-wing parties, whose registration was forbidden by the law. A group of young writers from Timişoara (the so-called cradle of the December revolt) published their opinions on the January 12 rallies in both their town and in Bucharest in the local cultural magazine *Orizont;* one of them wrote:

> I want to congratulate the people of Timişoara and Bucharest for having demonstrated on the day of national mourning [January 12 had been proclaimed a day of mourning for the victims of the December uprising]; they have succeeded in bringing the most precious offering to the dead of the revolution: namely, the outlawing of the Romanian Communist Party. One could hardly imagine a more splendid victory to be presented at the heroes' graves.

✦

BEHIND THE SCENES

With anticommunist sentiments running high in the wake of the January 12 demonstration, members of Ceauşescu's *nomenklatura* preferred to keep a low profile for a time. Many rank-and-file Communists, however, opted to dissolve their local party organizations and eventually burned their membership cards publicly. But time and again, rumors about the communist party's resurrection circulated in the media. In March, for instance, *România Liberă* denied a rumor that the RCP had been registered at Bucharest's Municipal Court by Verdet. As the May 20 elections approached, the rumors intensified, fostering the impression that the party planned to compete in the elections. With such rumors in the air, it was easy for the NSF to present itself as a much more palatable alternative to the Communists. In an interview in April 1990 with a Western journalist, for instance, Prime Minister Petre Roman obliquely admitted that the Communists' participation in the elections would make it easier for the NSF to distance itself from its "neocommunist" image. He added that the only problem was the impossibility of finding a single person willing openly to declare himself a Communist in post-Ceauşescu Romania.

A certain amount of camouflaged procommunist agitation continued throughout the summer and fall of 1990. An appeal from a "truly communist" organization was sent to various media for publication in August, but the appeal was denounced as a fake by a clandestine group calling itself the Communist (Marxist-Leninist) Party of Romania Organization No. 1/Craiova. In another, more serious development, Verdet renewed his advances to the DLP leadership in mid-August in an attempt to persuade that party to become a communist organization. At the beginning of November, the pro-NSF daily *Dimineaţa* announced that a group of "inveterate Russophiles" and "pro-Soviet fossils" was about to restore the defunct RCP in a new formation that would include some smaller parties. Finally, the very day the SLP was founded (November 16), the independent daily *România Liberă* published a photograph of a document resembling an application for membership in the RCP and bearing the heading "Romanian Communist Party 1990" and the country's emblem from the communist era; the daily warned of a possible "communist counterrevolution."

◆

MORE ON THE SLP

More details are currently emerging on the circumstances under which the new communist party was formed, together with information on its leaders, membership, political program, and ideological profile. Several leading figures of the former DLP complained that their national conference had in fact been hijacked by a group of between 100 and 120 Communists who had been invited as "guests." A group of seven leading DLP figures released a communiqué denouncing the conference as "a masquerade . . . [in which] maneuvers, forgeries, and intimidations prevailed," apparently along with some old-style communist secrecy. After only one night of membership in the new SLP, one of its vice chairmen, George Serban, formerly of the DLP, resigned "in bitterness" to protest Verdet's failure "to dissociate himself from the ideology of the former RCP." The entire editorial board of the DLP's mouthpiece *Fapţa* also resigned. Despite this internal struggle, the new party registered with Bucharest's

Municipal Court on November 22, 1990. A group of former DLP leaders protested the registration, describing the way in which the merging had taken place as "a typical case of communist forgery."

Various newspapers published Verdet's *curriculum vitae,* not neglecting to mention the monthly pension of 8,549 lei Verdet receives for his activities as a communist *apparatchik.* They also disclosed details about other former high-ranking officials of the RCP (some of whom had fallen into disgrace during Ceauşescu's last years in power) who now hold key positions in the newly created SLP, including Traian Dudas, Vasile Vilcu, Ion Stanescu, and Gheorghe Pele. SLP leaders claim that their party already has a membership of up to 123,000. As for the party's political program, Verdet maintained in a series of interviews that it focused on the rights of "large social strata," including blue- and white-collar workers. He described the SLP as "a left-wing, moderate, socialist-type party," whose intention is to ask for membership in the Socialist International. Such claims could raise problems for the ruling NSF, which describes itself as a social democratic party that aspires to membership in the same international organization. At the last annual council meeting of the Socialist International in New York in October, a Danish Social Democrat dismissed similar claims from former communist parties in Eastern Europe: "The irony is that the old communist parties in Eastern Europe are now trying to grab the social democratic label as their own . . . they're all social democrats [now]."

✦

CUI BONO?

The reappearance of the RCP under a new name will provide former members and activists of the *nomenklatura* with few, if any, benefits. Some of these activists seem to realize that re-entering the political limelight at a moment when the Ceauşescu era is still a vivid memory in the country may be dangerous. That may be why some old-guard Communists have refused to join the new party. One of them, Cornel Burtica, denied any connection with the SLP, stating, "I have no reason to be nostalgic about the former RCP or to wish its rebirth in any form."

Members of the opposition, as well as independent critics of the current regime, have tended to identify the NSF as the true winner of this political game. The word most frequently used to describe the sequence of events is "diversion." The daily of the National Peasants' Party spoke of the "Verdet diversion." The NSF, it said, "can have a more peaceful life now," since the revived communist party's role seems to be that of "diverting public attention from the ruling political formation, whose leadership is a regrouping of the most important figures of the old regime, with the exception of those directly involved in the last years of the Ceauşescu tyranny." The small National Democratic Party issued a communiqué claiming that "the diversion of creating the so-called Socialist Labor Party . . . [was a way] to distract public attention from current problems . . . [such as] the clarification of the ideological position of the NSF."

România Liberă described the new SLP as "the puppet of the NSF," alleging that a kind of division of labor existed between the NSF and the SLP: "The SLP was invented as a scarecrow: look, you should be afraid of this new-born [party], not of us!" In fact, the daily added, "We are now blessed with two communist parties. . . . What is the NSF, with its scores of notorious Communists and [former communist party] activists, but just another communist movement?" According to the daily, it could be assumed that "the two parties [would] fling mud at each other just for show" in the future. In its following issue, *România Liberă* spoke of a double diversion, aimed both at discouraging those who tend to equate the NSF with the former RCP and at creating " 'phony targets' for the opposition, which has concentrated its fire in a threatening way on the NSF and those in power, including the country's President." It is, indeed, difficult to gloss over the fact that the resurrection of the communist party took place only one day after the large anticommunist demonstrations marking the third anniversary of the Brașov revolt against the Ceaușescu regime. The rallies, organized in many Romanian towns, turned into the largest antigovernment protest to date and were a clear sign of the erosion of the NSF's popularity.

The timing of the Communists' reactivation is favorable to the NSF in at least one other sense. "The NSF's [national] convention is drawing nearer," wrote the political weekly *Lumea Azi,* adding that

> many true promoters of economic and political reforms from the NSF's ranks are probably not ready to accept being labeled "neo-Communists" any more, the more so that they feel more like Social Democrats, or even Liberals. The communist party could be their salvation!

The weekly concluded by observing that the NSF could now shift to the SLP the burden of responsibility for the past, as well as the current accusations that it was neocommunist.

◆

REACTIONS

The outcry over the re-emergence of the Communists has been almost universal. One of the first organizations to react to the creation of the SLP was the Association of Former Political Detainees from Romania; it staged a silent protest march on November 19 in which between 3,000 and 15,000 people reportedly took part. It also released a communiqué recalling the "hundreds of thousands of people killed on direct orders from this abhorred party." The same day, the National Liberal Party–The Young Wing stated that "the NSF in fact bears the moral responsibility for the new Romanian Communist Party." The ruling NSF reacted within hours to those accusations, rejecting any hint of alleged links between the NSF and the new SLP as "tendentious and provocative." In the evening, the NSF's political leader, Prime Minister Roman, said in a televised interview that the founders of the new SLP had "committed an act of irresponsible bravura"; but he insisted that communist parties could not be banned in a democratic state. Two days later, the NSF's mouthpiece *Azi* tried to play down the issue, stating that the re-emergence of the Communists was "nothing but a tempest in a teapot" and claiming that the real danger came from ultraleftist groups such as the rather mysterious Communist (Marxist-Leninist) Party of Romania.

The controversy over the SLP also reached the parliament's two houses. During the debates, a deputy for the National Liberal Party repeated accusations that the ruling NSF was "responsible for the rebirth of the 'monster.' " Ion Raţiu, a parliamentary deputy representing the National Peasants' Party and a presidential candidate in the May 20 elections, said that he hailed the new party's creation "as an important moment in our national history," suggesting that the Communists would thus have a chance to compromise themselves in an open democratic contest and would consequently "be vanquished for ever." Another deputy from Raţiu's own faction strongly disagreed with him, however, insisting that the communist party had already sufficiently compromised itself and that its leading figures should be put on trial for their past activity.

Numerous institutions, organizations, parties, trade unions, and professional groups as diverse as the Orthodox Church, the Jiu Valley miners (well-known to the public for their expedition to Bucharest on June 14 and 15), the Romanian Journalists' Association, and the small Liberal Monarchist Party joined in the protest. In a twist of historical irony, the miners even threatened to return to Bucharest to help get rid of the SLP. But a journalist from *România Liberă* appeared less than sanguine about these reactions, warning that this wave of quasi-universal protests could be misused by the NSF:

> Do not be surprised if the NSF joins us from now on every time we shout "Down with communism!" It will probably shout even louder than we do. In this way a national consensus can be reached. For, when the issue is communism, we stop thinking about hunger, cold, bad government, or the events of June 13 to 15.

BULGARIA

◆ *Starting the postwar period with quite minimal historical rea-*
sons for resenting its Russian neighbor, Bulgaria was for a long time the most willing
and obedient satellite. That fact, coupled with its remoteness from European concerns
and its relative backwardness, allowed it to be ignored by Western observers almost as
fully as Albania was. Although the country had its share of internal frictions in the
early years, it never offered any serious challenge to Soviet tutelage and was for the
most part a tractable participant in the regional economic division of labor sponsored
by the Soviet Union.

In light of its relative quiescence and despite some unpleasantness, barely
noticed abroad, with its Turkish population, Bulgaria's participation in the drastic
changes of 1989–1990 was somewhat unexpected (though it might not have been
had we been paying closer attention). In the first selection, John Bell skillfully sums
up the course of events leading to radical change. The ensuing reports from Radio
Free Europe document the events of early 1990, and press reports cover developments
of the next twelve months which, as the last two entries indicate, allow some room for
both optimism and pessimism.

"Post-Communist" Bulgaria

✦

John D. Bell

One of this country's closest observers of Bulgaria, Professor
Bell of the University of Maryland, details the processes leading up to the emergence of a new leadership after the departure
of Zhivkov in November 1989. In recounting the political turmoil
that ensued in 1990, Bell emphasizes the promise contained in
the rise of an able group of new leaders who must grapple with
Bulgaria's reconstruction.

It is a commonplace that Bulgaria has had little experience with democracy.
Indeed, since 1878, when the country was liberated from five centuries of Ottoman
domination, it has usually been governed by royal-military or Communist dictatorships that explicitly rejected democratic institutions as "anarchic" or "bourgeois." Yet
the struggle for democracy is one of the central and recurring themes of Bulgaria's
modern history. Democratic values motivated many of Bulgaria's political actors and
were a cause to which the Bulgarian people contributed more than their share of
martyrs.

During the nineteenth century those Bulgarians (often educated in West
Europe) who tried to revive their people's sense of national identity hoped to create an
independent and democratic state. At the constitutional convention held in Veliko
Turnovo in 1879, they adopted one of the most advanced constitutions in Europe,
providing for a unicameral legislature elected on the basis of universal male suffrage, a
strictly limited monarchy and a broad array of civil rights. This attempt to transplant a
Western constitutional system into Balkan soil foundered because of a weak middle
class and a low level of political consciousness among the rural masses.

Nor did Bulgaria's imported monarchs have sympathy for democratic values,
preferring to recreate the absolutist system in which they were raised. Outside powers
also intervened in Bulgarian politics by supporting particular parties or making deals
with the monarchy.

Despite these obstacles, Bulgaria still nurtured forces committed to democracy.
The Democratic and Radical parties, drawing their support from the country's intel-

ligentsia and professional classes, were usually loyal to the constitution, and the Social Democratic party (or "Broad Socialists") advocated gradual reforms within a democratic context and attracted the support of much of the country's civil service and part of the working class. The Bulgarian Agrarian National Union (BANU) became Bulgaria's party of mass democracy, aiming to bring Bulgaria's peasant majority into full participation in the country's political life. After World War I, the BANU government led by Alexander Stamboliski promised a rebirth of genuine constitutional government. But Stamboliski was murdered in 1923 and his government was overthrown by monarchists. When the People's Bloc, a coalition of the Democratic and Radical parties and the BANU, won a stunning election victory in 1931, it was followed by the military coup of 1934 that turned the country into a royal-military dictatorship.

During World War II, some members of the democratic opposition joined the Communists in the Fatherland Front directed against the government's alliance with Germany's Führer, Adolf Hitler. When the Bulgarian government collapsed and the Front took power, it soon became apparent that the Communists viewed the coalition as a stepping stone to their achievement of complete power. Resistance to communization was led by the BANU, which organized an Opposition Bloc under Nikola Petkov to compete with the Communist party internally and to seek Western support. In the elections for a Grand National Assembly to write a new constitution, held on October 27, 1946, the Bloc polled nearly one-third of the votes in the face of a brutal campaign of intimidation. Western indifference to Bulgaria gave the Communists a free hand. Petkov was charged with treason, arrested and condemned to death, and the Opposition Bloc was made illegal. Petkov's execution by hanging marked the end of the democratic resistance to communism in Bulgaria.

During the Communist era, Bulgaria developed a reputation for passivity. Alone among the states of East Europe, it experienced no crisis in its relations with the Soviet Union, and the long tenure of Todor Zhivkov, who became party leader in 1954, suggested almost complete political immobility. But although Bulgaria was politically stable, it experienced fundamental economic and social changes that provided the foundation for the dramatic political events of the late 1980's. In his study of totalitarian regimes, Zhelyu Zhelev, leader of the opposition and now President of Bulgaria, wrote:

> Moreover, the fascist state that on the one hand destroys free-thinkers, on the other is forced to encourage thinkers in order to keep in step with the progress of democratic societies, at the very least in the military sphere. But thinkers easily become free-thinkers able to criticize what exists. It is precisely this that gives rise to opposition to the regime.

At the end of World War II, three-fourths of Bulgaria's population lived in villages and the overwhelming majority of these villagers were engaged in small-scale, primitive farming. The Communist regime was committed to transforming Bulgaria by developing industry and educating the population to include it in the "scientific-technological revolution of the twentieth century." Today about two-thirds of the population is urban, and only about one-fifth is still directly involved in farming. Bulgaria ranks among the most advanced nations in terms of the proportion of its eligible population that receives secondary and higher education.

For the first time, Bulgaria possesses the equivalent of a Western middle class. It is not a bourgeoisie in the classical Marxist sense of owning the means of production. But in terms of psychology and outlook, skepticism toward inherited dogmas, desire for material success and personal autonomy, it resembles its Western contemporaries more than the generation of its parents and grandparents. Signs of the growing influence of this social group have been mainly cultural: the development of Sofia's Vitosha Boulevard as a Bulgarian Via Veneto of shops devoted to luxury goods; the opening of an aerobic dance studio; the growing popularity of tennis; the building of the country's first golf course; and the many pet dogs being walked in the country's parks. But there has also been a political dimension; this group proved receptive to the new currents that have been set in motion in the Communist world by Soviet President Mikhail Gorbachev.

Because Zhivkov always stressed Bulgaria's fidelity to the Soviet Union, stating that the two countries had "a single circulatory system," it was inevitable that he would have to introduce his own version of Gorbachev's "new thinking," even though he had little appetite for it. In 1987 he inaugurated the "July concept," apparently embracing the cause of reform wholeheartedly. Along with a wave of administrative and economic reorganization, the July concept called for several steps toward political democratization, including an expansion of press freedom and experiments with multicandidate elections. Both of the latter proved short-lived. Following its exposure of several cases of official corruption, the press was again subjected to more stringent controls, and uncompliant editors and reporters were fired.

In the elections for mayors and regional and municipal councillors (held on February 28, 1988), local electoral commissions disqualified all but the officially approved candidates in 80 percent of the electoral districts. In those districts where "outsider" candidates managed to find places on the ballot, the authorities ensured their defeat by trucking in absentee voters from districts where there was no challenge to the official list and by changing the results on forms submitted by the election precincts.

Despite government persecution, dissidence in Bulgaria continued to build in several quarters. On the one hand, many members of the country's intelligentsia, particularly in the Sofia region, joined Clubs for the Support of Glasnost and Perestroika, which developed an organization independent of the government and kept a critical spirit alive. Podkrepa (Support), an independent trade union, was organized in February, 1989, and quickly began to enroll thousands of members. In the city of Russe, which was being slowly poisoned by chlorine gas emissions from a Romanian chemical combine across the Danube River, an organized ecological movement openly challenged the government's indifference to the destruction of the Bulgarian environment. In various parts of the country, groups were formed to promote human rights and religious freedom or to revive old political parties.

Zhivkov's regime turned to the measures that had been effective in stamping out dissent. Party members affiliated with dissident groups received sanctions or were

Shopping in Sofia. This line of shoppers anxiously waiting outside a vegetable store in Sofia, Bulgaria, could have been photographed anywhere in Eastern Europe. Cumbersome and wasteful food distribution systems were endemic in all communist states, causing shortages despite these countries' rich agricultural potential. (AP/Wide World Photos)

expelled from the Bulgarian Communist party (BCP). Many of them (along with nonparty members) were dismissed from their jobs and subjected to vicious slander in the press. In February, 1989, Zhivkov met with "representatives of the intelligentsia," warning them that Bulgaria would not tolerate "national nihilism" or "negative attitudes toward our country or toward socialism." But this time the opposition did not retreat into passivity. Bulgarian dissidents carried on their activities in defiance of threats and actual persecution. During the year, most of the usually docile cultural unions turned out their old leaders in favor of critics of the regime.

During the spring, the protest movement also spread among Bulgaria's ethnic Turks, who had been relatively quiet since the brutal assimilation campaign of 1984–1985. Hunger strikes initiated by individuals escalated to clashes with the authorities that resulted in several deaths. By the end of May, 1989, there were demonstrations with thousands of participants.

Zhivkov appeared on national television to quell rumors of massive unrest. Denying that Bulgaria had a substantial Turkish minority, he repeated the fiction that most of the ethnic Turks were really Bulgarians who had been forcibly converted to Islam and a Turkish identity during the Ottoman period. He attributed disturbances among Bulgaria's Muslims to confusion over the terms of a new passport law and to an anti-Bulgarian campaign carried on by Turkey; he challenged the Turkish government to open its borders to Bulgarian Muslims so that it would be clear how few were discontented with life in Bulgaria. When Turkey responded to Zhivkov's challenge by declaring that it would accept refugees from Bulgaria, the authorities launched a broad reign of terror against the ethnic Turks, forcing thousands to cross the border, where they were placed in hastily organized camps. Before the Turkish government again closed the border, more than 300,000 ethnic Turks had abandoned Bulgaria, an exodus that focused worldwide attention on Bulgaria's human rights record and disrupted an already shaky economy.

Zhivkov's increasingly erratic leadership, compounded by his efforts to promote his wastrel son's career, caused an erosion of support among the party leadership. The details surrounding his actual removal are still not clear, but the key figures were Petar Mladenov, in charge of foreign affairs since 1971, and Dobri Dzhurov, the minister of defense. Mladenov may have stopped in Moscow for discussions with Soviet leaders on his return from a visit to China.

On November 10, 1989, the day after East Germany opened the Berlin Wall, a meeting of the BCP's Politburo and Secretariat accepted Zhivkov's "resignation." The fiction that Zhivkov had resigned voluntarily lasted only days. He was soon under intense attack for personal corruption and for establishing a "totalitarian" regime. His relatives and closest supporters were quickly purged from their posts in the party and state. Many other "dinosaurs" of the Zhivkov generation went quietly into retirement; others found themselves the targets of popular demonstrations that began to play an increasingly large role in putting pressure on the leadership to speed the pace of reform.

Mladenov and the rest of the new leadership pledged to welcome and promote the development of pluralism in the country and to respect the rule of law. To this end, they halted the persecution of the ethnic Turks and invited those who had fled to return to Bulgaria, allowed opposition groups to register as legal entities, and promised to eliminate the domestic role of the state security forces. Bowing to widespread demonstrations, the party also amended Article One of the constitution, which recognized the party as the guiding force in society.

At an extraordinary congress that began at the end of January, 1990, the party carried through a number of structural and personnel changes and took the first steps to separate the party from the state. Mladenov resigned the party leadership while remaining titular head of state. Andrei Lukanov, widely regarded as the party's ablest statesman, became Prime Minister. And Alexander Lilov was elected chairman of a restructured BCP supreme council. Lilov had been purged from the leadership in 1983 by Zhivkov and was long known to favor liberalization. In a 1986 work on imagination and creativity, he offered an analysis that, though couched in a Marxist framework, was remarkably similar to the passage by Zhelev quoted previously.

Lilov and the new leadership continued to push for changes in personnel that favored younger and better educated leaders, denounced the "totalitarian" practices of the past and even conducted a party referendum to change the name from "Communist" to "Socialist." In the following months Lilov advocated making the party more open to a diversity of views and spoke of its development in a "Euro-socialist" direction, taking as a model the Democratic Socialist parties of West Europe. Some former dissidents responded to these changes with enthusiasm. For example, Stefan Prodev, who had abandoned the party, returned to it to become editor of the party newspaper, making it as diverse and interesting as the opposition press.

For others, the reforms did not go far enough, and a number of divisions began to appear. One was the Alternative Socialist party, which broke away to form its own organization. A faction, "Road to Europe," was formed within the party to promote more rapid democratization and to pursue a policy of reconciliation with the West. A conservative opposition to the party's new course also surfaced, objecting to the change in the party's name and all that that implied.

In addition to the changes that took place within the party after Zhivkov's fall, a number of the party's auxiliary organizations collapsed or ceased to function. The Central Council of Trade Unions declared its independence and elected a new leadership. Some unions dropped out altogether, while alternative unions, especially the independent Podkrepa, recruited thousands of new members. The Komsomol (Communist Youth League) disintegrated at its congress early in the year and was replaced by a new organization that declared itself independent of party control, and by a number of rival youth organizations, some of which were affiliated with the political opposition. The puppet Agrarian Union purged itself of its old leadership and declared its independence. Party cells in the workplace were dissolved or disbanded.

While the Communist party was dealing with the legacy of the Zhivkov era, opposition political groups were also being organized. Discussion clubs transformed themselves into a political party, as did the environmental movement, renamed Ecoglasnost. The number of parties and movements mushroomed—approximately 50 were formed—but at the end of 1989 the most important groups entered into a coalition, the Union of Democratic Forces (UDF), with Zhelyu Zhelev as president.

The UDF quickly showed its ability to stage mass demonstrations in the capital, and its leaders gained the agreement of the Communists to enter into roundtable discussions on the future of the country. The roundtable, whose sessions were televised, came to function almost as a substitute Parliament. After dramatic negotiations, it reached decisions on three basic issues. The first provided for the election of a Grand National Assembly (GNA) to be composed of 400 deputies, half elected in single-member districts and half selected by proportional representation. Over a period of 18 months, the GNA would function both as a Parliament and as a constitutional assembly to design a new political structure for Bulgaria. A neutral commission whose membership was approved by both sides was set up to implement the election agreement.

The agreement on political parties was extremely generous, granting recognition to parties on the basis of little more than an individual declaration. It did, however, ban the formation of parties on an ethnic or religious basis, a measure aimed at preventing the organization of a separate, and perhaps separatist, party to represent the country's ethnic Turks and Muslims. Despite this provision, the party of Rights and Freedoms, organized by Akhmed Dugan, became the de facto "Turkish party," although its charter proclaimed general goals.

There was an obvious imbalance of resources between the opposition and the newly renamed Bulgarian Socialist party (BSP). Reflecting its 45 years in power, the BSP possessed a developed political organization with local headquarters and clubs in every populated area, the country's largest newspaper (with a circulation of 700,000), and the advantage of holding national and local power. The roundtable agreement on the conduct of the election required the government to provide basic resources to the opposition and to allow it equal access to the media. While some local authorities resisted implementing this agreement, it was adhered to on the national level. Newsprint was made available to the opposition press, and time on television was assigned to the individual parties and was made available for debates between representatives of both parties.

The UDF entered the campaign with a high level of confidence. Assuming that if the populace were given the opportunity to vote freely it would automatically reject the BSP, the UDF sought to make the election a referendum on the past 45 years of Communist rule. Consequently, much of the UDF campaign focused on the past, particularly on the atrocities committed by the BCP during the Stalinist era. By its very nature, the UDF coalition had difficulty speaking with a single voice or advancing specific measures to deal with Bulgaria's problems.

This was particularly evident with regard to the future of the Socialists. Some UDF leaders, particularly Petur Dertliev of the Social Democratic party, spoke with some sympathy of the BSP's efforts to reform itself, advocated an eventual reconciliation and opposed the idea of reprisals against BSP officials. In this vein, Zhelyu Zhelev and other UDF spokesmen advocated what they called a "Spanish policy," following the example of Spain's transition from fascism. Others, however, adopted a far more strident tone, frequently referring to the BSP as "murderers" and a "Mafia," giving the impression that the UDF would conduct a wholesale purge of the government if it won. Both the BSP and some members of the UDF referred to this as a policy of "McCarthyism."

The UDF economic program called for shock therapy—an immediate and complete transition to a market economy—but did not make clear how this would be effected or how the most vulnerable elements in the population would be protected.

In their overconfidence, the UDF leaders rejected BSP offers to participate in a coalition government and vowed that under no circumstances would they cooperate with the Socialists. In the last days of the campaign, they even turned down a BSP proposal to sign a pledge of mutual nonviolence, a decision that was portrayed as proof of their extremism.

✦

THE SOCIALIST CAMPAIGN

Striving to distance itself from its past record, the BSP ran a campaign that was devoid of Marxist ideology. Indeed, BSP spokesmen rivaled the UDF in their denunciations of "totalitarianism" and stressed that they had brought down Zhivkov's regime. The party's new symbols—a red rose and a cartoon boy who somewhat resembled Pinocchio—its thumbs-up gesture, and "good luck for Bulgaria" slogan replaced the heavy-handed mottoes and portraits of party leaders characteristic of past campaigns. BSP supporters waved the Bulgarian flag rather than the red banner.

The BSP presented itself as the party of "responsible, conservative change," stressing the experience of its leaders and minimizing its policy differences with the UDF. It denied seeking a monopoly of power and called for the formation of a coalition with the opposition either before or after the elections. The BSP also turned to "voodoo economics," pledging a gradual transition to a market economy in which no one would suffer. The party's claim that old-age pensions would be endangered by a UDF victory was particularly effective.

While cultivating a new image designed to appeal particularly to Bulgaria's middle class urban voters, the BSP apparently conducted a more traditional campaign in the countryside. There, local party and government officials put heavy pressure on the village population, whose habits of subordination, developed over the past 45 years, were not easily broken. This pressure was admitted by BSP leaders, who attributed it to overzealousness on the part of local activists while denying that it was a tactic promoted by the national party leadership.

The election results [see table] came as a shocking disappointment to the opposition, whose expectations had been unrealistically high, but they were hardly the "overwhelming Socialist victory" that was reported in the Western press. The BSP failed to get a majority of the popular vote, and some of its leading figures, like Prime Minister Andrei Lukanov, were forced into embarrassing run-offs or, like Defense Minister Dobri Dzhurov, were actually defeated. The opposition dominated Bulgaria's cities, especially the capital, and enjoyed a commanding level of support from professionals and the young. And because decisions of the Grand National Assembly required a two-thirds majority, the opposition could exercise a veto on any Socialist proposals.

RESULTS OF ELECTIONS HELD JUNE 10–17, 1990

Party	Votes	Percent	Seats
BSP (Bulgarian Socialist party)	2,886,363	47.15	211
UDF (Union of Democratic Forces)	2,216,127	36.20	144
BANU (Bulgarian Agrarian National Union)	491,500	8.03	16
Rights and Freedoms	368,929	6.03	23
Others	158,279	2.59	6
Total	6,121,198	100.00	400

Source: *Duma,* June 15, 1990, and John D. Bell, Ronald A. Gould and Richard G. Smolka, *An Orderly Rebellion & Bulgaria's Transition from Dictatorship to Democracy* (Washington, D.C.: International Foundation for Electoral Systems, 1990).

◆

A BULGARIAN WATERGATE

Political tension continued to run high after the elections because the UDF and other parties rejected all proposals to join the BSP in a coalition government. In the streets of major towns, protesters established "Communist-free zones" in tent cities and demanded full investigations of past Communist crimes. A student strike at the University of Sofia spread to the provinces. Increasingly, protests focused on a statement made by President Mladenov the preceding December when, unable to gain a hearing from a hostile demonstration, he had told the defense minister that "the best thing is to let the tanks come." Although this statement was not acted on, it was captured on a videotape that was made available to the opposition and broadcast during the election campaign.

Mladenov's immediate response was to charge that the tape had been fabricated by the opposition. When its authenticity was upheld by a panel of experts, he maintained that his remark was "being taken out of context." Finally, he admitted having made the statement, but pleaded that it was due to the passion of the moment and that in fact he had never authorized the use of force against his opponents. Although this last argument was valid, the opposition focused on Mladenov's long effort to cover up the truth and called for his resignation. Even the BSP newspaper suggested that presidential dignity required Mladenov to leave office. With support eroding even in his own party, Mladenov resigned on the evening of July 6, 1990, stating that he had no wish to be "a cause of tension."

The question of Mladenov's successor led to the first breakthrough in Bulgaria's political stalemate. After several votes in the Grand National Assembly, no candidate gained the required two-thirds majority. At this point the various nominees withdrew in favor of the candidacy of UDF leader Zhelyu Zhelev, who was elected with the support of a majority of the BSP's parliamentary group. Zhelev immediately nominated General Atanas Semerdzhiev of the BSP as Vice President. Semerdzhiev, who as minister of the interior was responsible for depoliticizing the police and ending censorship, was elected with the support of the opposition. The Grand National Assembly was still far from creating an effective government, not to speak of undertaking constitutional reform, but the compromise on the presidency demonstrated that some degree of cooperation between the major political forces was possible.

◆

THE TASKS AHEAD

Whatever the composition of the new Bulgarian government, it faces an enormous array of immediate and long-term problems. In the political sphere it must dismantle the legacy of communism by carrying through a program of "secularization," the separation of the party from the state. Much has already been done to eliminate compulsory education in Marxism-Leninism and to remove party symbols from public buildings. The BSP has supported this change, taking the initiative by removing the mummy of Georgi Dimitrov (the first Communist Prime Minister and the leader of the BCP until 1949) from its mausoleum and cremating it. Its hesitation in removing the illuminated red star from party headquarters in Sofia, however, provoked an attack from protesters who burned part of the building.

The 1990 elections will raise again the ethnic question, for in some regions local majorities of ethnic Turks and Muslims will oust ethnic Bulgarians from office. While both the BSP and the opposition parties claim to reject policies of ethnic repression, there is a genuine fear of Turkish separatism and a growing hostility among ethnic Bulgarians in regions where they are the minority. The potential for ethnic conflict similar to the violence in Kosovo in Yugoslavia is real.

When Zhivkov was removed, his successors stated that Bulgaria's economic situation was catastrophic. It has since worsened. The government has been forced to halt interest payments on its $10-billion foreign debt; basic commodities are being rationed or are unavailable; and the embargo against Iraq has cut off a major source of energy. The Bulgarian environment also suffers from 45 years of industrialization that took no heed of ecological concerns. Although the BSP endorsed the idea of a free market and the privatization of enterprises, it took no actual steps in this direction. Even if the BSP and the opposition could agree on an economic program, it is unlikely that a significant economic upturn could be achieved without substantial support from the West. And this help is problematic at best. What aggravates the situation even further is the fact that Bulgaria's economic crisis is leading many citizens, particularly those with critical skills, to emigrate. It would be a great tragedy for the country if, of all the rights won in the last year, the right to leave becomes the most valued.

Bulgaria must also search for a new foreign policy. The end of Pax Sovietica in the Balkans requires Bulgaria's leaders to consider carefully how to provide for national security in a region of historic instability and violence. The rebirth of democracy carries with it the danger that political opportunists will seek to gain popularity by reviving such issues as the treatment of Bulgarians in Yugoslavia's Macedonian Republic.

Bulgaria's crisis has led to the emergence of a new "post-Communist" generation that includes men and women of exceptional intelligence and accomplishment who have already overseen a nonviolent transition from a bureaucratic Communist dictatorship toward multiparty democracy. It is an auspicious beginning for the work that lies ahead.

A Year of Crucial Change in Bulgaria

◆

Rada Nikolaev

This report on the year 1989 in Bulgaria, besides noting the growth of independent associations of citizens, gives prominence to the repression of ethnic Turks and an ensuing exodus to Turkey, merely the latest phase of Bulgaria's long-standing ethnic problem.

Several politically significant developments made 1989 a crucial year for Bulgaria. Three events, which by themselves justify applying the term "historic" to 1989, decisively influenced the political scene: the surge in number, size, and activity of independent groups; the mass exodus of ethnic Turks; and the ouster of party and state leader Todor Zhivkov.

◆

ZHIVKOV'S FALL

On November 10 Zhivkov's fall from power put an end to 35 years of undisputed rule by the now 78-year-old dictator, who had appeared to believe more and more in his own everlasting power and irreplaceability. His ouster provided both a way out of the prevailing stalemate and the possibility of real reform. Television viewers at home and abroad were shown a shot from the November 10 Central Committee (CC) plenum of a stunned Zhivkov listening to his own "resignation" as it was presented by Politburo member and Prime Minister Georgi Atanasov. Observers tended to agree that the move had been a coup, carefully prepared by the man who succeeded him, Petar Mladenov. Having received the blessing of Moscow, Mladenov had also gained a majority in the Politburo, where Defense Minister Dobri Dzhurov is believed to have played a crucial role.

It soon became clear that the "sincere gratitude" Atanasov and Mladenov expressed to Zhivkov had been but a polite formality, a lame attempt to sweeten the bitter pill and a short-lived pretense that the "resignation" had been voluntary. Less than a week later, on November 16, the CC held another plenum and ousted five

Rada Nikolaev, "A Year of Crucial Change in Bulgaria," from *Report on Eastern Europe,* January 5, 1990, pp. 7–10. Reprinted with the permission of Radio Free Europe/Radio Liberty.

Politburo members and candidate members, as well as two of the CC Secretaries. All seven had been among the people most closely associated with Zhivkov and most hated by the population, and all had been linked to either Zhivkov's personal rule, to political repression, or to economic setbacks and delays in *perestroika*. Three other CC members, one of them Zhivkov's son Vladimir and another his late wife's nephew, Hristo Maleev, were also ousted. Subsequent developments showed that these first purges were cautious in order not to upset the party; more victims were to follow very soon. On December 8 a plenum revoked the gratitude expressed to Zhivkov. Another five people were ousted from the Politburo and no less than twenty-six from the CC; and a prominent party figure, Aleksandar Lilov, purged by Zhivkov in 1983, was fully rehabilitated and became both a Politburo member and a CC Secretary. On December 13 Zhivkov and his son, as well as the ousted Politburo member Milko Balev, were expelled from the party.

The second CC plenum after Zhivkov's ouster gave the green light for attacks on the former leader who, with his son, had disappeared from public sight. Attacks on both Zhivkov and the other ousted officials continued in the National Assembly on November 17 and at numerous official and independent mass rallies, which began in Sofia on November 17 and 18 and then spread to the provinces. Zhivkov was criticized for his shortcomings as a leader and for encouraging his personality cult; the political line pursued by the party under his leadership was also criticized, though still somewhat reluctantly. The main emphasis, however, was placed on the corruption and nepotism prevalent under his regime and his misuse of power for his own benefit. His son was also accused of corruption and misuse of public funds, among other things, and protesters called for the trial of both father and son.

◆

MLADENOV AND REFORM

The choice of 53-year-old Petar Mladenov as Zhivkov's successor came as a surprise to most observers. A familiar figure abroad after having served as Foreign Minister for the last 18 years, Mladenov was believed to have been little involved in internal party life and apparently had taken no firm position on political and economic reform. His status as a member of "Gorbachev's generation" was one of the few confidence-producing credentials granted him abroad, while most observers believed that he would be only a transitional figure.

Mladenov's coup appeared to have been a well-timed and carefully calculated tactic. After the ouster of Erich Honecker in the GDR and the uncontrollable surge of public mass demonstrations in that country and before similar developments had occurred in Czechoslovakia, Mladenov took over, presented himself as a reformer, and managed to control the mass rallies that were already in the offing, skillfully directing them to express support for himself and protest against the ousted Zhivkov.

During his first month in power, Mladenov had hardly anything concrete to say about economic reform but concentrated his efforts on political liberalization by small but impressive steps that were novelties in Bulgaria. His first two speeches centered on

The Revolution Reaches Bulgaria. In November 1989 Eastern Europe's anticommunist revolt swept into Bulgaria, energizing that country's hitherto small dissident movement to lead massive public demonstrations for change. Here, a protester calls for jailing the country's longtime communist leader, Todor Zhivkov. (AP/Wide World Photos)

building "a democratic, civil, socialist society," instituting *glasnost* and pluralism of opinions, separating party and state functions, and strengthening the role of the National Assembly—all targets that more than once had been set but never implemented by Zhivkov.

Mladenov declared that all reform would have to stay within the framework of socialism, but he almost at once began implementing at least some of the declared goals. He started by restoring party membership to 11 people who had been expelled in the course of the last 2 years for dissident activities; and he implicitly recognized the right of previously persecuted independent groups and movements to exist legally by allowing them to hold public meetings, permitting the media to cover their activities, and meeting himself with some of their activists. He abolished the controversial Article 273 of the Penal Code, which made a crime of almost every form of unauthorized political activity, granted an amnesty to those sentenced under this article, and decided to close down a department of the Ministry of Internal Affairs that dealt with ideological subversion. On December 15 other similarly controversial provisions of the Penal Code were abolished. He gave permission for the Komsomol and the trade unions to take the first steps toward becoming independent from the party and allowed the Bulgarian Agrarian Union to begin redefining itself as a political party. The media were given a freedom unknown for the last 45 years and began publishing audaciously outspoken statements, including some by blacklisted writers and journalists. Good will was also apparent in the abolition of privileges such as special shops for the *nomenklatura* and state and party residences, which were turned over for use as children's homes and for other social purposes.

Mladenov's reforms remained far removed from real political reform of the kind taking place in, for example, East Germany. He did, however, announce free elections for the second quarter of 1990, although without defining what exactly was meant by this term. He also promised the abolition of the controversial Article 1 of the constitution on the leading role of the party by January 1990. Party and state functions have not been separated as promised, and after November 10 the majority of decisions on reform were made by the Politburo rather than the government or the National Assembly. Mladenov himself combined in his person the posts of party leader and head of state, but this might have been a necessary step in order to consolidate his authority and free him for action.

◆

INDEPENDENT GROUPS

In the first months of 1989 the few independent groups that had begun to emerge the previous year were severely persecuted. The intellectual Club for the Support of *Perestroika* and *Glasnost* was prevented from holding its meetings and several of its activists who had been party members were expelled from the Bulgarian Communist Party (BCP). Activists belonging to the Independent Association for the Defense of Human Rights and the more recent trade union *Podkrepa* (Support), as well as to the Committee for Religious Rights, Freedom of Conscience, and Spiritual Values, were harassed and arrested and their homes were searched. Some activists were expelled from the country, others defamed in press campaigns.

The first shift in the regime's attitude toward these groups emerged in October during the Conference on Security and Cooperation in Europe (CSCE) Eco-forum, which was held in Sofia from October 16 to November 3 and was used by the regime to polish up its image in the presence of foreign delegates and journalists. The independent environmentalist group Eco-*Glasnost*, although occasionally harassed by the police, was for the most part allowed to collect signatures to a petition on ecological issues, enroll new members, and even organize a march to the National Assembly to deliver its petition. The march was joined by a crowd of some 5,000 people. Both Eco-*Glasnost* and the Club for the Support of *Perestroika* and *Glasnost* were allocated halls where they held large meetings. The Southern Park in Sofia became a "free zone" where existing and newly emerging independent groups held rallies, earning it the nickname of "the Bulgarian Hyde Park."

Despite this apparent openness, the media prior to November 10 continued to attack these groups and their contacts with the first Radio Free Europe correspondent ever allowed in Sofia. This lack of a clear-cut policy toward independent groups was perhaps one of the first signs of weakness in Zhivkov's regime, while the immense popular support for these movements might have contributed to his fall and Mladenov's subsequent takeover.

The weeks that followed the change of regime on November 10 saw a further shift in the official attitude toward these movements. At the same time, numerous new and often very small organizations began to emerge—everything from independent students' societies to resurrections of old political parties.

In a development related to the dissident movement, the first real *samizdat* publications in Bulgaria, the literary and journalistic magazines *Glas* and *Most,* appeared in the spring of 1989. They were followed in the fall by other publications, such as *Promyana* and *Alternativa.* During the first month after the change in power, the new regime indicated that it might concede to these magazines the right to legal existence.

✦

THE TURKISH EXODUS

A very dark spot in Zhivkov's last months in power was his handling of the Turkish ethnic minority, whose Moslem members constitute more than 10% of the total population. Encouraged by the growing dissent, members of the minority held demonstrations and hunger strikes in May to protest their forced assimilation, which began in the winter of 1984 to 1985. Clashes with the police resulted in several deaths, and a number of ethnic activists were expelled from the country. On May 29 Zhivkov made a televised statement in which he reiterated the hard-line position adopted in 1984 that people professing to be ethnic Turks were ethnic Bulgarians descended from ancestors who had been forced to become Moslems during the 500 years of Ottoman rule. Asserting that these people had no reason for discontent, he nonetheless appealed to Turkey to open its frontier and receive those wishing to emigrate.

In June the Bulgarian authorities applied to the Turkish minority only a law enacted on May 9 that would not affect other Bulgarian citizens until September 1. This new law guaranteed the right of Bulgarian citizens to obtain passports for travel abroad; as a result, between the first days of June and August 22, when Turkey introduced visa requirements, more than 300,000 ethnic Turks crossed the frontier and had to be accommodated by the Turkish authorities. After August 22 only a few thousand Turks left the country, while more than 50,000 returned to Bulgaria because they were disappointed with conditions in Turkey, had been separated from family members, or had left simply to visit relatives without intending to stay.

The Zhivkov regime's handling of the issue of the Moslem minority badly damaged Bulgarian-Turkish relations, Bulgaria's human rights record, and the country's image abroad. At home it brought unprecedented conflicts between the ethnic groups and a division of opinion among the ethnic Bulgarian majority. Zhivkov, up to his last day in power, continued to assert that, on the contrary, his handling of the Turkish minority problem had united the nation. While there can hardly be any doubt that the Turkish issue was one of the matters that helped cause Zhivkov's fall from power, Mladenov failed during his first weeks of tenure to express any concrete position on it.

◆

THE ECONOMY AND *PERESTROIKA*

The mass exodus of ethnic Turks, most of whom were engaged in agriculture, livestock breeding, transport, and construction, caused serious economic problems, especially as it coincided with a harvest season that promised exceptionally good yields after several years of setbacks. To cope with the situation, the regime issued a special decree on "civil mobilization in times of peace"; this decree was repealed on December 15. Official claims that the difficulties had been overcome were not substantiated and preliminary statistics showed very unequal performance in the various economic sectors. The domestic market was upset and, in the last months of 1989, many food items and other consumer goods were unavailable. After Zhivkov's fall information was released showing that mismanagement had led to a grave economic crisis.

Zhivkov, meanwhile, continued to announce big reforms in the economic sector that, as in the past, consisted mainly of reorganizing the management, a practice much criticized even before and especially after his fall. The main manifestation of Zhivkovian-style *perestroika* in 1989 was the notorious Decree No. 56, issued in January. This decree stipulated that enterprises of all sizes and on all levels "might" be transformed into "firms" of several types, including joint-stock companies. An important aim of this decree was, in view of the soaring foreign debt, to attract foreign capital to Bulgaria. As had often happened in the past, however, the "might" provision was soon interpreted to mean "must," and a wave of reorganization produced giant new firms, depriving numerous enterprises of their self-managing status. At the same time, however, hundreds of private and cooperative firms were authorized. In agricultural management, a new type of collective farm was introduced, which in practice revived the "labor-cooperative farms" of the 1950s that had been quietly abolished in the early 1970s.

The flood of opinions expressed at rallies and in the media after Zhivkov's fall indicated that many of these "reforms" might be repealed, just as references to "the July concept," which predicated that the July 1987 CC plenum was the foundation of Bulgarian *perestroika,* were tacitly dropped.

Round-Table Talks on Economic Reform: Gradual Approach or Shock Therapy?

✦

Kjell Engelbrekt

In the following selection, an analyst from Radio Free Europe discusses the controversy that surfaced in March 1990 over the pace of those economic measures designed to introduce a market economy in Bulgaria.

On March 15 the round-table discussions between the Bulgarian government and the Union of Democratic Forces (UDF), a coalition of the main opposition groups, turned to the crucial economic sector. The five-hour session, held at the National Palace of Culture, was broadcast live and in full by Radio Sofia. In addition to discussing the country's economic crisis, the round table held the first debate on the government's new program for tackling this crisis.

The government's economic proposals had been made available to the participants in the round table but had not been published. They had only been hinted at in the press in the weeks preceding the meeting. It had been reported that the government was consulting economists and politicians from several Western countries, including a French ministerial delegation, on issues related to a radical economic reform. The party daily had recently published some details of a draft proposal by the Ministry for Trade and Services suggesting that a large part of the state sector would be sold to the highest bidder and that restrictions on foreign business activity in Bulgaria would be abolished.

✦

THE GOVERNMENT'S PROPOSALS

The government's program, however, turned out to be less drastic than had been indicated by the suggestions of the Ministry of Trade and Services. Minister Without Portfolio Professor Stefan Stoilov, who was the first to speak at the March 15 meeting, said that the present government saw no reasonable alternative to a market

Kjell Engelbrekt, "Noncommunist Opposition Tries to Overcome Disunity," from *Report on Eastern Europe*, March 30, 1990, pp. 4–5. Reprinted with the permission of Radio Free Europe/Radio Liberty.

economy. The question was how and at what pace the reforms should proceed. He outlined the proposed program, stressing the importance of some parts of it, such as the encouragement of private initiative, the liberalization of prices (40% of prices should be freed from government control during 1990), and the control of inflation.

Stoilov urged that Bulgaria be integrated into the world economy, but he expressed doubts about whether the transformation should be of a "shock" type. What he chose to call a "sufficiently fast transition" would, he said, ensure a higher degree of both social and economic stability. Nonetheless, he admitted that, even using this approach, the proposals might result in social problems and an increase in unemployment; it was therefore planned to introduce guarantees for a minimum standard of living beginning in the second half of 1990.

◆

THE OPPOSITION'S OBJECTIONS

The next speaker, UDF Chairman Zhelyu Zhelev, strongly criticized the government's proposals. He implied that the Bulgarian Communist Party (BCP) was unfit to carry out the necessary changes by recalling that the present economic system, which he described as an "anti-economy," had been built up by the Communists. "The planned economy," he said, "in which our ideologists saw the supremacy of socialism, in practice turned out to be the most horrifying economic anarchy and mismanagement." According to Zhelev, the government had only presented a superficial analysis that failed to admit the economic collapse.

The debate was then largely taken over by various specialists, many of whom took the opportunity to present their own proposals for economic reform as well as commenting on those of the government. Ivan Pushkarov of the Bulgarian Social Democratic Party and Ventseslav Dimitrov, both of whom are prominent economists, and Professor Georgi Petrov, all of whom spoke on behalf of the UDF, agreed that the proposed program was inadequate to meet Bulgaria's economic crisis. Pushkarov said it was essential that any recovery program be accompanied by strong financial measures, particularly for coping with the country's foreign debts (which now exceed $11 billion). Petrov advocated a law protecting the rights of private producers.

A representative of the Bulgarian Agrarian National Union (which was formerly allied to the BCP), presented as a specialist in international trade, described the BCP's vision as "a socially oriented market economy" and pointed out that it would give priority to agricultural and light-industrial production. He did not agree that there was a need for further investment in the energy sector, since the problems in this area, he said, arose from the uneconomic use of, rather than a lack of, resources.

◆

A SHOCK THERAPY CONCEPT

It seems to have been UDF Chairman Zhelyu Zhelev who first introduced the term "shock therapy" in the context of the Bulgarian economy, at a meeting with

Latin American diplomats on March 13. He now compared the country's economy to a broken engine and said that instead of trying another type of gasoline, the engine itself had to be changed. The economist Dimitrov cited a number of measures that should accompany such a radical approach. He demanded an immediate halt to the authorities' interference in the economy, the privatization of state companies, the reintroduction of private ownership in industry and agriculture, and financial measures to keep down inflation.

Even if nobody in the UDF openly opposed the "shock version" of reform, it was noted by Dimitrov that the opposition had not shown a united front on the issue. While Zhelev, Dimitrov, and Petrov unequivocally demanded a thorough transformation of the economic system, the leader of the Bulgarian Social Democratic Party, Petar Dertliev, warned of "the social consequences" of radical economic reform. Speaking of the prospect of increasing unemployment, he said that the state must take responsibility for those affected by the reforms and that "people should not be dismissed because of an administrative procedure."

◆

WORKING GROUP SET UP

The two sides eventually agreed to try to reach a compromise through a special working group. Despite considerable confusion at the end at the meeting about when the next session of the round table would take place (which introduced a more heated note to the generally restrained proceedings), no one opposed the idea of cooperation. It was at last agreed that the next meeting should be scheduled for March 19 and would cover pending legislation on elections, parties, and a new constitution. Talks on economic reform would resume on March 26.

◆

CONCLUSION

The March 15 negotiations suggest that the round-table discussions have entered a new phase. Apparently, the agreement of March 12 that all major decisions be approved by both sides resolved the previous deadlock between the UDF and the communist government. As a Radio Sofia reporter noted in the first commentary on the meeting, one got the impression that the differences between the UDF and the communist government on economic issues were more over the means than the ends. There was certainly some irritation on the UDF's part, however, that the National Assembly had been allowed by the government to go ahead and pass the 1990 budget, thus impeding quick and radical policy changes.

The talks also demonstrated that the UDF's unity and readiness to compromise are likely to be put to the test. In the new game being played there are fewer points to be collected from public speeches and more from negotiating skills. Much will depend on whether the opposition has enough political talent to devise a successful strategy.

Judging from the concluding statements by both sides, there seems to be a reasonably good prospect of some kind of compromise. It remains to be seen, however, whether an accelerated economic reform program will be sufficient to attract the badly needed foreign economic assistance or whether investors would not rather await the outcome of the elections in June before committing themselves and their money.

The Bulgarian Communist Party After Its "Congress of Renewal"

✦

Rada Nikolaev

This report covers the 14th Congress of the Bulgarian Communist Party early in 1990 at which the party was reorganized and the way was paved for adopting a new name, the Bulgarian Socialist Party. At the same time, a party faction split off to form the Alternative Socialist Party.

The 14th Congress of the Bulgarian Communist Party (BCP) was described as extraordinary because, as a result of the political and internal upheaval caused by Todor Zhivkov's ouster, it was convoked more than a year ahead of schedule. The gathering has been termed a "congress of renewal," a label that seems only partly justified. The congress itself witnessed events that differed vastly from the usual formal and sterile party congress procedures. The work of the congress lasted for three days, one whole night, and another half-day, rather than the scheduled three days. Delegates made unusually open statements, and stormy discussions bordering on disputes developed. The statements revealed that a strong conservative element still existed among the 2,793 candidates, although more radical party factions and ideological currents were also represented. The professed reformist leaders, who have been heading the party since November 10, 1989, were forced into considerable maneuvering and compromising in order to maintain their power and avoid an open split.

The BCP emerged from its congress still the leading force in the Bulgarian state, despite the fact that the constitutional provision guaranteeing its leading role had been abolished two weeks earlier. The party was even strengthened, if only superficially, by the refusal of its former ally, the Bulgarian Agrarian National Union, to continue and

Rada Nikolaev, "The Bulgarian Communist Party After Its 'Congress of Renewal,' " from *Report on Eastern Europe*, April 20, 1990, pp. 4–9. Reprinted with the permission of Radio Free Europe/Radio Liberty.

of the opposition to join in a coalition government. On February 8, after the congress, an all-communist Council of Ministers was formed for the first time.

Bulgaria is admittedly a country in deep economic and political crisis. The BCP's power is limited by its commitment to hold free elections in June and by the opposition. In addition, the splintering that was formally avoided at the congress became a reality after it. The Alternative Socialist Association, which took part in the congress first as a faction of the BCP, split off on February 11 and part of it became the Alternative Socialist Party (ASP). The diverse ideological currents in the BCP and the surviving conservative Zhivkovite trends in many party organizations (especially those in the provinces) make the BCP far from monolithic, a quality it once exemplified.

♦

NEW PARTY STRUCTURES

The BCP emerged from its congress with both new statutes and a new Manifesto for Democratic Socialism, which is to serve as a temporary party program. Some aspects of these documents were the subject of particularly heated discussion at the congress, and numerous written suggestions that were incorporated into the drafts were made to the respective commissions. Meanwhile the party has already departed from at least one provision, the most controversial of the statutes, which concerns party organizations at work places. Abolishing these organizations was one of the opposition's most adamant demands, and on February 12 opposition forces refused to continue the round-table talks until it had been met. At the congress approximately the same number of speakers spoke for and against the provision. But the statute preserved its initial text, which stipulates that "every member has the right to choose the basic organization of which he wants to be a member: according to place of work, place of residence, or place of study."

Even before the congress the party had made a concession on this point by deciding, on January 24, to abolish basic organizations in one of the most sensitive areas, the armed forces. These organizations were to be replaced by "organs for educational work." Reportedly, by February 15 all party and Komsomol organizations in the armed forces had been disbanded. Another concession came in the party leadership's February 25 "package of political initiatives," which suggested that political parties be legally banned from work places. It also reiterated a provision of the new statutes that allows members to form professional and interest-oriented party clubs outside the work place. Party press reports have given examples of both disbanded basic organizations and newly formed party clubs, many of them still workplace-oriented. The opposition has criticized these new clubs on the grounds that they are nothing but camouflaged party organizations.

♦

THE PARTY'S NAME

The question of changing the BCP's name was also discussed at the congress. Almost all the speakers, whatever the ostensible subject of their speeches, offered widely differing opinions on the matter. The name should be changed, supporters argued, to distance the BCP from the discredit it had earned during Zhivkov's "totalitarian" regime and the admissions of collective guilt. Additionally, they said, the new name should reflect the party's newly formulated commitment to renewal based on the principles of democratic socialism.

The manifesto's first draft, published on January 19 before the congress, mentioned the proposed change and suggested several alternative names. The manifesto's final version, as approved by the congress, reiterated that the name change was "not a formal but an essential political issue" and urged that it be submitted to the party for discussion and voted on in a referendum. On February 24 the leadership called for a March referendum by secret ballot in basic party organizations, offering as a new name the Bulgarian Socialist Party. Finally, on March 21, *Rabotnichesko Delo* announced the beginning of the formal referendum, submitting the single officially proposed new name to a "yes" or "no" vote.

The BCP clearly faces some difficulties in changing its name. The February 24 decision pointed out that not all party members were ready to accept a new name and, in fact, some letters to *Rabotnichesko Delo* expressed such opposition (as did many speakers at the congress). The results of a poll of party members in Sofia reported in the same paper on March 21, 1990, showed that 67% favored a change. Conservative party members obviously felt strongly about preserving the BCP's name, and the party might have suffered a real split after the new name was officially announced. On the eve of the referendum, party Presidency member Filip Bokov only expressed the "hope" that this would not happen. Another difficulty emerged in connection with the proposed name: a Bulgarian Socialist Party already exists. It was set up on December 31, 1989, and has protested the "attempts of certain groups to usurp our name." On March 31 it held a press conference, at which it declared that it would "use all legal means" to protect its name. A clash over the name seems inevitable.

The results of the referendum were announced on April 3. The new name, the Bulgarian Socialist Party, was approved by only 64% of the total party membership, or 86% of those who participated. Nearly 20% of all Communists did not vote.

✦

THE NEW PARTY LEADERSHIP

Some of the most striking if not the most important innovations introduced in the party statutes by the 14th congress concerned its top leadership. The party's top decision-making body has until now been the party congress, held every five years. From now on it will convene every four years (a two-year timetable was rejected). The statutes now allow congressional delegates to keep their mandates until delegates to the next congress are elected and to meet for annual sessions if necessary.

The new statutes replaced the BCP Central Committee (CC) with a Supreme Party Council and the Central Control Revision Commission with two new agencies: a Central Financial Revision Commission, which will control party funds, and a Commission on Party Ethics, which will assume responsibility for penalizing and rehabilitating party members and considering complaints and appeals. These three agencies, as well as the chief editors of the central party publications, are to be elected by the congresses. The 14th congress, for the first time, elected a new editor in chief for the daily *Rabotnichesko Delo*. Stefan Prodev won by a large margin over the incumbent Radoslav Radev.

In the same way the CC used to elect a Politburo, the Supreme Party Council is to elect a Presidency consisting of a chairman, deputy chairmen, a secretary, and five members. There will no longer be any body corresponding to the former CC Secretariat. The statutes do not stipulate the number of members of any of the new bodies; their size was fixed by the congress during an overnight session after heated disputes over candidates and several attempts at compromise.

✦

THE SUPREME PARTY COUNCIL

In its efforts to streamline the party apparatus, the congress proposed that the Supreme Party Council consist of 131 members, replacing a CC of 190 members and 121 candidate-members. It took 19 hours to fill the 131 seats, for which 158 candidates were proposed, because each candidate had to be voted on individually. BTA announced on the morning of February 2 that those not elected included Prime Minister Georgi Atanasov, one of the three members of the old Politburo who survived the November and December purges but presented his government's resignation on February 1 after heavy criticism from the party. Other top party figures not elected included Politburo candidate members Petar Dyulgerov, who had already been dismissed from his post as Chairman of the Bulgarian Trade Unions, and Dimitar Stanishev, who had only recently been promoted after many years as CC Secretary in charge of international relations. It was no surprise that Petko Danev, the party secretary from Varna promoted after Zhivkov's fall to candidate membership in the Politburo, failed to be elected, since at the congress Mladenov had described his promotion as a mistake. Rather more surprising was the fact that two of Mladenov's Politburo members elected last November, Mincho Yovchev and Panteley Pachov, as well as former Prosecutor-General Vasil Mrachkov (now Deputy Chairman of the State Council), were not elected.

Two or three hours after announcing these results, BTA revealed that they were not final and described a procedure that sounded very much like a manipulation of the list. Andrey Lukanov, who had presided over the session, suggested that the Supreme Party Council be expanded from 131 to 153 members in order to include all candidates who had received more than 50% of the votes; this would have left out only five of the 158 candidates. Despite strong opposition, BTA reported, the proposal was approved "by a large majority." Lukanov's argument was that the Supreme Council should include "people from all ideological currents and platforms, veterans of the party, and people who can be useful in helping solve the country's vital socioeconomic problems." Among the 22 additional members, BTA said, were three members of the

Alternative Socialist Association; the popular artist Svetlin Rusev, repressed for participation in Bulgaria's first ecological group in 1988; and the retired Generals Tsvyatko Anev and Lyuben Dinov, dismissed and persecuted for participation in the 1965 "April plot" against Zhivkov.

Together with these anti-Zhivkov members, the addition brought into the Supreme Party Council the rather unpopular Yovchev and Pachov, Vasil Mrachkov, and the party and administrative heads from Sofia, Georgi Grigorov and Stefan Ninov. Grigorov and more particularly Ninov had been openly criticized; Ninov was accused of actively opposing mass demonstrations. It may be significant that all these were among those receiving the fewest votes in the first ballot.

◆

NEW NAMES

The new Supreme Party Council's makeup to a surprising extent reflects the congress's intention to restructure the BCP's leading bodies. According to BTA, only 10% of the old CC has been retained in the new Council. A preliminary analysis identified 20 people as former CC members and four as former candidate members. Seven members can be identified as belonging to particular ideological factions within the party. There is, of course, no guarantee that among those newly elected members, a large number of whom are "unknowns" and not readily identifiable, there are not people who support Zhivkov's old regime.

Soon after the congress, four of the new members of the Supreme Party Council, in a surprising move not seen before at that level, handed in their resignations. In two separate statements, Koprinka Chervenkova (a prominent intellectual dissident, an active member of the Club for *Glasnost'* and Democracy, and a member of the Alternative Socialist Association) and Hristo Ganev (a well-known film director and dissident) gave the same reason for their action. Neither had been delegates to the congress (Chervenkova had been there as a guest) and had thus not been able to take part in the voting. Chervenkova also objected to being included in the Supreme Council as one of the additional list of 22 candidates who had received more than 50% of the vote, while Ganev pointed out that, at the age of 66, he had never even been a secretary of a basic party organization.

The two others, Academician Kiril Vasilev and Professor Ivan Nikolov, both of whom represented the Alternative Socialist Association, issued a joint statement implying that they, too, objected to having been elected as members of the additional list. They expressed support for the BCP's new top leaders but objected to the composition of the Supreme Party Council. A compromise had been made, they pointed out, that resulted in the election of people with questionable political reputations who represented "the old way of thinking and acting." Vasilev and Nikolov called on all 22 members on the additional list to resign from the Supreme Council. Apparently no one did, but the loss of these four prominent members who refused to be co-opted and the accompanying protest is a serious blow to the BCP.

◆

THE BCP PRESIDENT

After Petar Mladenov, who had headed both the party and the State Council since November, firmly declared that he wanted to separate the two posts and remain only head of state, Aleksandar Lilov became party chairman, while Mladenov became a member of the Presidency. Later on April 3, when Mladenov was elected to the new post of President of the Republic, he also resigned from the Presidency. The 56-year-old Lilov made a remarkable comeback last December after having lost his position as chief ideologist and his posts of Politburo member and CC Secretary in 1983. He has been regarded as one of Zhivkov's victims, although like Mladenov and other party members who now condemn Zhivkov, he was a long-time adherent of the former leader and faithfully carried out his policies (on the nationality issue, for example). His very close relationship with Zhivkov's daughter Lyudmila, who died in 1981, was also regarded by some as evidence of his opportunism. When a congressional delegate rather indiscreetly asked him about these aspects of his past, Lilov gave a dignified but angry response.

During the six years Lilov was in disfavor he served as Director of the Institute for Contemporary Social Theories at the Bulgarian Academy of Sciences; he also traveled abroad and kept in touch with foreign scholars. There can be no doubt that he is highly qualified intellectually for his new post. Lilov would like to be seen as a reformer. In an interview with the West German weekly *Der Spiegel* he said that he would count himself "in the center of the reformers, a bit further left than the center."

◆

THE PRESIDENCY

After the all-night session of the Congress, the Supreme Party Council elected only Lilov and what was described as the "nucleus" of the future 11-member Presidency. It consisted of the three top BCP figures: head of state Petar Mladenov, Minister of National Defense Dobri Dzhurov, and Andrey Lukanov. Lukanov, the party's nominee to replace Georgi Atanasov as Prime Minister, was confirmed in this post by the National Assembly the next day, February 3. Later that evening, when the Supreme Council reconvened, yet more discussion ended in a compromise similar to that involving the Supreme Council: instead of 11 members, the Presidency has 17 members including the chairman.

The two deputy chairmen and the secretary were rather surprising choices, as they had never been in the party's top hierarchy but had held government offices. A common denominator for them all was their involvement in diplomacy or foreign trade, activities that connected them directly with Petar Mladenov, Minister of Foreign Affairs from 1971 to 1989. They all speak English, Russian, and a third foreign language.

Georgi Pirinski (born in 1948), one of the two deputy chairmen, emerged as a top candidate immediately after Zhivkov's fall. From having been a candidate member of the BCP CC and a Deputy Minister of Foreign Economic Relations, in November 1989 he became a full CC member and Deputy Prime Minister. The second deputy chairman, Aleksandar Strezov (born in 1935), spent his entire career in the diplomatic service and in late 1987 became First Deputy Minister of Foreign Affairs and permanent Bulgarian representative at the United Nations in New York. In December 1988 he became for the first time a candidate member of the BCP CC and was promoted to full membership after Zhivkov's fall in November 1989. Finally, the Secretary of the Presidency, Rumen Serbezov (born in 1939), has also been a diplomat (from 1974 to 1978 he was Ambassador to Japan) but later served as Minister of Light Industry. His latest post was as an adviser to the Council of Ministers, probably thanks to his reputation as an expert on Japanese economic affairs and technology. He was a candidate member of the BCP CC and, like Pirinski and Strezov, was promoted to full membership in November 1989.

Among the Presidency's 17 members are two representatives of the opposition within the BCP: Professor Chavdar Kyuranov, a sociologist and well-known dissident, who at the congress confirmed his nonaffiliation with any ideological current, and Professor Petar-Emil Mitev, another sociologist and Chairman of the Bulgarian Road to Europe faction in the BCP. Ivan Stanev, who after Zhivkov's fall was made a candidate member of the Politburo, is the sole remaining workers' representative. The Bulgarized Turkish minority is represented by Nadya Asparuhova, formerly Nayde Ferhadova.

◆

A TRIUMVIRATE PLUS ONE

Since the party's 14th congress and the personnel changes made immediately after it, three men have managed Bulgaria's political affairs: head of state Petar Mladenov, Prime Minister Andrey Lukanov, and party President Aleksandar Lilov. While on the one hand they try to make at least a pretense of strictly separating offices and Mladenov even tries to appear free of any party commitments, there are many indications that the three men work together as a kind of "collective leadership" firmly in charge of the "ruling party." The man behind them, however, seems to be General Dobri Dzhurov. Aged 74, Dzhurov has been Minister of Defense since 1962 and a BCP Politburo member since 1977. It is generally and increasingly believed but not openly admitted that he played the crucial role in the November 10, 1989, coup by keeping control of the armed forces. With the appointment of his long-time deputy General Atanas Semerdzhiev as Minister of Internal Affairs on December 27, 1989, Dzhurov has extended his indirect control over that sensitive ministry. Meanwhile, something not unlike a personality cult is building up around the old general. During the congress, *Rabotnichesko Delo* published a picture of him walking past applauding delegates. The caption read, "A place of honor in the Presidium—a homage to Army General Dobri Dzhurov for his honest, valiant, and steadfast position." And, reporting on a mass meeting organized by the BCP on March 1, the paper said that, when taking the floor, Dzhurov had been received "with unconcealed love." In recent opinion polls on political leaders' popularity, he has invariably been rated first.

◆

PARTY MEMBERSHIP

While there has been a considerable drop in membership in a number of other East European parties as a result of recent changes, the BCP, both before and even more so after its congress, has experienced a steady influx of new members. Numerous reports about ceremonies welcoming the new Communists have been published, yet no explanation of the party's growing attractiveness has been proffered. At the congress the official membership figure was put at 983,899, almost exactly 10% of the country's population. Some reports on newly recruited members from individual towns have given figures for those who left the party; these are, as a rule, much lower than the number of new members, leaving a net increase in the BCP's ranks.

Separating the ASP from the BCP, at least initially, did not result in a drastic drop in membership. The new party was said to number 2,400 people. But larger losses can be expected if the ASP expands and if the renaming of the BCP results in a further split, as is feared.

Although purges among rank-and-file party members and the lower echelon apparatus were admitted to be necessary immediately after Zhivkov's ouster, the present BCP leaders seem reluctant to begin these purges in the light of the forthcoming elections. These leaders will need all the support they can get not only to compete with the opposition but also to carry out the unpopular measures necessary to overcome the economic crisis. Filip Bokov, a member of the Presidency, said in connection with the referendum on the new name that party members' registrations would be "renewed" but stated that the timing of such a move would have to be considered.

◆

A DEAD PARTY?

More than once Zhivkov's successors have shown their flexibility and surprising ability to cope with new situations and urgent problems in ways that have allowed them to maintain their own and their party's leading role. The fact that the BCP, unlike other East European communist parties, has survived and was able to "renew" itself is evidence of the party's strength. But the increasingly open media have not spared the party harsh criticism. Such criticism can be found not only in emergent opposition publications but also in the party press. The film director Ducho Mundrov, a pre-1944 resistance fighter, severely criticized the present party leadership for having rehabilitated all Stalinists repressed by Zhivkov, which meant that many of them could be nominated as delegates to the congress. Many others who had criticized Zhivkov from progressive, antidogmatic, and anti-Stalinist positions had not even been invited as guests to the congress, Mundrov maintained. He objected to the current Supreme

Party Council members and advocated holding another congress soon. In his opinion it was not enough to declare the party "renewed," as the 14th congress had done; it would have to be "reborn."

A political scientist, Andrey Ivanov, went even further with his criticism, maintaining that the BCP would have to split in order to regain the image of a political party. He said that organizationally and ideologically the BCP was dead and added that this could hardly be considered a misfortune for the country. Even if the first half of this statement is a little exaggerated, there are certainly many people—perhaps the large majority of Bulgarians—who would certainly agree with the second half.

Struggling to Be Born

✦

Slavenka Drakulić

A Yugoslav journalist offers here an eyewitness report from Bulgaria as of early 1990, conveying the flavor of political life there as the country attempted to create a new order, but one still led by the heirs of the ruling Communist Party.

I was in Sofia in mid–February when the first issue of the opposition newspaper *Demokratia* was published. "Look," my friend said excitedly, holding the thin paper in his hands, as if he didn't really believe it. "It's the first sign of freedom." From that day on, he woke up at 5:30 in the morning and waited about half an hour in line in front of his local kiosk to get it. Once home, he would go back to sleep: It was important to have the newspaper, one of the very few alternative sources of news. But people like my friend who welcomed political change and democracy were, he explained, not the only ones waiting for *Demokratia* at dawn. There were also a lot of retired people, Communist Party members who, following instructions from the party, bought copies, brought them to the square in front of the National Assembly building and burned them. Later, on the TV news, this was explained as a "people's protest" against the opposition.

This is in a way a symbol of the new situation in Bulgaria. On one hand, there is the enthusiasm and hope of the people who are hungry for uncensored information and prepared to wait in line for *Demokratia,* the newspaper of the Union of Democratic Forces (U.D.F.), or the social democratic paper, *Svoboden Narod* ("Free People"). On the other hand, there is the Bulgarian Communist Party (B.C.P.), fighting to stay in power and trying to keep its hands clean at the same time, in part by its recent name change to the Bulgarian Socialist Party. The battle is raging; the winner is uncertain. In this highly politicized society, every move by the government or Communist Party is watched with suspicion. The process of change can't be stopped, but the obstacles are great and visible.

The process began last October, with an international meeting on ecology attended by representatives from thirty-five countries and by many foreign journalists. Because of the foreign media presence, some 150 human rights activists and members of unofficial Bulgarian opposition organizations such as Eco-glasnost and the independent trade union Podkrepa took a chance and turned out for the meeting, the first that had not been broken up by the police. They voiced their criticisms of the party openly, capturing the attention and the sympathy of Western reporters and governments. Afterward, they did not face the usual punishment of the state—imprisonment—a sign that this last bastion of Communism (apart from Albania) was giving up.

Bulgaria was for a long time such a devoted and peaceful satellite of the Soviet Union that Todor Zhivkov, General Secretary of the B.C.P., even proposed that the country become one of the Soviet republics. Fortunately this did not materialize. But the party, like its Soviet counterpart, did not leave the initiative for democratic change to the "streets." It started the reform of the party and the state at once, perhaps under the influence of changes in other Eastern European countries. On November 10 the 78-year-old Zhivkov was removed from his position. For thirty-five years he had been Bulgaria's undisputed leader, the longest-ruling figure in the Eastern bloc. Zhivkov was a symbol of the totalitarian state. The purge of "Zhivkovists" after November 10 was not easy, and it split the party organization first in two, and later into at least four fractions. Many would say that even today the "Zhivkovist" mafia continues to rule the party. In January Andrei Lukanov, who is considered to be the author of the new reforms, became Prime Minister. Alexander Lilov was named head of the Supreme Council, the party's newly created Presidium.

"Ludmila's lover," the crowd shouted the night Lilov was elected. It was widely known that he had indeed been the lover of Zhivkov's daughter Ludmila, who was one of the most important persons in the country—a member of Parliament, Minister of Culture and obviously intended to be her father's successor. Despised because of nepotism, she died after a car accident in 1981, at the age of 39. But my friend, a well-known Bulgarian journalist, told me another story: "She had cancer. Before death she was eating only macrobiotic food and doing yoga all day long." Stories about the Zhivkov family circulate so freely that one wonders if they are disseminated on purpose by the party. There is one about the enormous Zhivkov fortune, another about his killing a television reporter. Then there are the tales of his son Vladimir, who spent vast sums of money gambling in casinos. The latest joke asks the definition of zero: Zero is Vlatko (Vladimir) without his *tatko* (father). "They won't bring Todor Zhivkov to court even though he has been arrested," says another well-connected friend. "They will keep him in the hospital and pretend he is sick until he dies. They are too afraid to put him on trial." The Communists, meanwhile, are trying to draw a line between the past and the present. We are different, the line goes: Zhivkov, Ceauşescu or Stalin were to blame, not the party. But as they say in Bulgaria, not even children believe this.

In the meantime, about a hundred opposition groups and parties have formed, and the strongest twenty or so have united in the U.D.F. coalition. Their president is Zheliu Zhelev, "the Bulgarian Sakharov," a professor of philosophy and a well-known dissident. He was barred from teaching at the university and spent years in prison. His books have been banned in Bulgaria; in one on the totalitarian state he draws a parallel between Communism and fascism. In early January the U.D.F. forced the government into round-table negotiations, threatening it with a general strike. The U.D.F. felt confident enough to do this because in November and December it had drawn more than 100,000 people to its meetings in Sofia. Among its demands were political democracy and a state governed by law, a multiparty system, free elections, a market economy, depoliticization of the military and constitutional reform. As a result, Article One of the Constitution, which had guaranteed the leading role of the Communist Party, was soon changed. New parties were then allowed to register, and in that sense Bulgaria went further with its reforms than the Soviet Union, especially after abolishing party organizations in the army.

The Bulgarian Communists call it "a peaceful revolution," proud that no blood was shed. But the government proved unable to undertake economic reform. Faced with more than 300 strikes in January alone (with at least 200,000 participants) demanding better living conditions, it responded with nothing more than clichéd declarations and appeals.

Social tensions are growing. Bulgaria's foreign debt stands at $12 billion, and the decay of the economy is evident in the shops: only one kind of cheese, no vegetables except cabbage and potatoes, one kind of salami, no milk, no fruit, no chocolate or candy . . . nor much of anything else. I imagine a Western visitor would feel desperately hungry at this display of poverty. But Bulgarian cheese, peppers, tomatoes and succulent peaches can easily be found in Sweden, Germany or the United States, and one wonders what kind of economy this is, starving its own people. You learn fast to buy whatever is available, so I joined a line in front of a grocery store without knowing what people were waiting for. It turned out they were waiting for eggs, and I bought a dozen. But when I brought them home to my host, she was desperate. "Only a dozen!" she exclaimed. "What can I do with a dozen eggs? When you were so lucky to spot them, you should have bought at least five dozen, because God knows when they will come again." If one has the patience to traipse around the city and wait in lines, it's possible to scrounge all the bare necessities. However, refrigerators or TV sets or washing machines or any other appliances are much harder to find. There is a waiting list of 600,000 for cars, which are imported from the Soviet Union. Not only are they prohibitively expensive but delivery can take up to ten years!

The dream of democracy among ordinary Bulgarians is more and more identified with a vision of higher living standards. Therefore one may conclude that the planned June 10 elections will be won by those who offer the better economic program. But things are not so simple. Whoever comes to power (most likely a Communist-U.D.F. coalition) can hardly change the chaotic economy overnight.

According to recent public opinion polls, the Communists will receive an extraordinarily high 40 percent of the vote. This is hard to explain: Perhaps people still act out of fear. But there are also arguments in favor of the party. For one, it is credited with starting the process of change. Also, there is the egalitarian mentality of people brought up with the notion that everyone should have the same—even if what they have is nothing. The Communists could decide to manipulate this, stressing the opposition's demand for a free market and its consequences, such as unemployment and greater social inequality.

The party's other potential argument is the upsurge of ethnic nationalism against Turks. Since 1984 the Turkish minority of 1.5 million has been forcibly assimilated. Turks were obliged to register themselves as Bulgarians and adopt Bulgarian names. Because their elementary human rights were denied, about 300,000 of them left for Turkey. Bulgaria's new leaders have restored their rights, and some have returned. But now those Bulgarians who benefited from the Turks' absence (by taking possession of their vacant apartments) are holding violent protest meetings against Turks. Potentially dangerous ethnic nationalist tensions bring with them the danger that the Communists' option of "saving the country" from chaos may be reinforced.

The opposition is very weak, fragmented and lacking funds to mount a proper election campaign. "We operate under impossible conditions," says Elka Konstantinova, a famous literary critic and leader of the Radical Democratic Party. Konstantinova was the only woman at the round-table talks. "You see, there are hardly any typewriters or Xerox machines, or even paper. The typing and distribution of our program is enormously difficult for us. And how do you suppose we'll go into the country and hold meetings, inform the people there? We have no money and our access to the media is controlled by the B.C.P."

Paradoxically enough, the current social tensions may also work to the opposition's advantage, since they could escalate into antigovernment riots. But the time factor is definitely not in the opposition's favor. The government wants elections as soon as possible because for the time being the Communists are Bulgaria's strongest and best-organized political force. Postponing elections until the autumn would give the opposition more time to organize. Well aware of this, the opposition has demanded a postponement. But if the elections go ahead on schedule, this could mean that the Eastern European "domino theory" will not work in Bulgaria and that the Communists, with strong opposition, will continue to rule. They are fast learners: As Alexander Lilov said recently, "Yes, we have an opposition and you should congratulate us on that. A democratic society is not possible without political opposition."

The U.D.F. is not just sitting around and waiting for things to happen. Apart from holding meetings and round-table talks, they have started to work on political marketing. Recently, the biggest name in French advertising, Jacques Ségela, visited Sofia to help the U.D.F. His track record includes helping to create the image of the

Hungarian Democratic Forum, Poland's Solidarity, French President François Mitterrand and George Bush. At the same time, British publishing magnate Robert Maxwell has promised a thousand tons of printing paper, to be distributed equally among the opposition parties.

But U.D.F. leader Zhelev has something else in mind: the possible role of the Soviet Union in the democratization of Bulgaria. "If it comes to a civil war there," he says, "if the Gorbachev position becomes weak or if he falls, this will destabilize the U.S.S.R., which may have bloody repercussions here as well. That is why we are asking for quick changes, so that we can cross the Rubicon and make it impossible to turn back."

Bulgaria Slips Deeper into Economic Crisis

◆

Girard C. Steichen

A journalist reports on the worsening economic situation as of early 1991.

In an outdoor park cafe near Sofijska Komuna Street, a dozen patrons huddle in the freezing late-night fog, drinking coffee under flickering green neon lights. Around them, the streets and buildings that bound the park in downtown Sofia are deserted and dark.

"They've turned off the electricity again," says Valentin Stoyanov, pointing to a gloomy bank of row houses and apartment buildings. "There's no heat either."

Bulgaria is slipping deeper into its worst economic crisis ever, bringing increasing hardship. Once self-sufficient in agriculture, Bulgaria has had to plead for foreign food aid this year.

Basic foodstuffs are scarce or have disappeared altogether from Sofia's store shelves. Sugar, cheese, flour, eggs, and cooking oil are rationed, along with fuel oil and gasoline. Lines at Sofia's few gas stations snake for miles through city neighborhoods and the wait for a tank of gasoline can be more than 12 hours. Electricity is shut off for

Girard C. Steichen, "Bulgaria Slips Deeper into Economic Crisis," from *Christian Science Monitor,* March 5, 1991. Reprinted by permission of the author.

long periods each day in many neighborhoods. Only a fraction of the city's street lamps are switched on at night.

The situation is so dire that Prime Minister Dimitar Popov has warned that Bulgaria faces "a hard and decisive fight for survival" in the coming months.

The collapse of the Soviet-led Comecon trading bloc and the Gulf crisis have put increasing pressure on the country's fledgling efforts to overcome four decades of communist mismanagement. Supplies of Soviet crude oil have dwindled, and Moscow is now demanding payment in hard currency for future shipments, an almost impossible task for the nation's bankrupt treasury. Worse, Iraqi oil deliveries were halted by the United Nations trade embargo against Baghdad.

Iraq owes Sofia more than $1.2 billion from previous trade deals and had agreed before the invasion of Kuwait and the imposition of sanctions to repay the debt in oil. As a result of the loss, Sofia has been forced to increase the export of precious meat and livestock reserves to pay for oil.

Reformers blame former communist leader Todor Zhivkov for shattering Bulgaria's economy. Mr. Zhivkov, who was ousted in 1989 after 35 years of rule, went on trial last week in Sofia on charges of corruption and misappropriating millions of dollars.

Zhivkov's policies, economic reformers say, ruined Bulgaria's once successful agricultural sector and polluted the nation. A chronic shortage of spare parts and raw material has seriously hurt heavy industry.

Agricultural production was further damaged by the exodus of hundreds of thousands of ethnic Turks, many of them farmers, who fled the country in 1989 to escape growing persecution under Zhivkov. Few have returned since Zhivkov's fall.

Bulgaria's communist government also left the nation saddled with $11 billion in foreign debt. The cash-strapped new government last March froze payments on the debt, but unpaid interest on it is mounting, more than $367 million so far.

Economic reforms are also beginning to bite. Prices have jumped tenfold in recent weeks, with an inflation rate nudging 200 percent. More increases are expected as further government controls are removed.

In 1990, production dropped by 10 percent and more than 70,000 workers lost their jobs. That number is expected to increase to 300,000 this year as more and more factories fail without the support of generous government subsidies.

But government leaders express optimism that foreign help will increase as the nation turns to a market economy. There are also plans to lure more Western cash by promoting tourism at the country's Black Sea beach resorts.

To speed the process, Central Bank officials want to make Bulgaria's lev convertible soon. Like other reforming East European nations, currency convertibility is a key component in Bulgaria's shift to a market economy.

Sofia wants a $380 million standby loan from the International Monetary Fund to help with currency convertibility.

As the government haggles over reforms, many Bulgarians have become small entrepreneurs out of necessity. Near the Sheraton Balkan Hotel, where foreigners with hard currency can stay and dine in luxury, vendors offer everything from hand-carved trinkets to silver and gold family heirlooms.

Raiko Bodurov, a factory worker, sells hand-painted decorative plates after his 12-hour shift. He says he earns about 500 leva a month at his factory job, about $16 at the market rate likely to be used after convertibility is established.

"We need this money just to get by," he says.

Bulgarians See Glimpses of Better Days to Come

✦

José-Alain Fralon

This correspondent reports from Sofia with a somewhat more positive assessment. Without denying the country's economic difficulties, he finds that Bulgarians are seeing signs of a better future as the market economy begins to take hold.

While things are not quite looking up yet, people here seem slightly less desperate than they were last December: "Things are improving, of course. But they could have hardly been worse." Yet a small difference has apparently eased the expressions on the faces of all those who enthusiastically took part in the peaceful revolution that ended 40 years of communist dictatorship only to start having misgivings about their country's future.

Could Bulgaria have sunk lower than it did in December? Like most of the cities in this country, the capital was provided with electricity only every other hour, shelves in most stores were desperately bare and petrol was drastically rationed. "It was worse than in wartime," said those Bulgarians who lived through the shortages of the '40s. The political crisis prevented Andrei Lukhanov's "post-communist" government from taking even small decisions. Victorious in the June 1990 general election, the former Communist Party, renamed the Socialist Party, did not want to govern alone in spite of its imposing majority in the assembly.

But the opposition refused to share responsibility for an unpopular policy with the former communists whom it held responsible for all the ills plaguing the country.

José-Alain Fralon, "Bulgarians See Glimpses of Better Days to Come," *Guardian Weekly,* April 7, 1991.

In January, demonstrations and increasingly violent strikes finally swept away Lukhanov's government and made room for Dimitar Popov, a judge without political affiliations. Popov finally managed to cobble together a coalition government and all the political groups and labour unions in the country proclaimed 200 days of "civil peace" during which there would be no demonstrations, protests or strikes.

Born 63 years ago in Kula, a small town near the Yugoslav border, to a family of churchmen and intellectuals, Dimitar Popov did not take long to prove that he wanted to make full use of the unexpected political honeymoon he was being offered. By his political line, or rather by the absence of one, this man, well known as a tough judge, stands out sharply from the mass of Bulgarian politicians who are so much at ease in tortuous discussions.

Though he belongs to no party, Popov insists he is not apolitical and considers that his democratic convictions are logical. This needs to be read as: he has no affinity at all with communism. A vigorous speaker, the new prime minister says he has made "no decision concerning my political future." If he continues this way when the next general election comes round, doubtless next autumn, he will be able to point to a more than satisfactory record.

Opposition parties, which polls place comfortably ahead of the former communists, want the elections brought forward to the spring. Breaking the undertaking not to engage in public demonstrations, almost 50,000 Sofia citizens took to the streets on March 17 to demand elections in June.

The February 1 decision to dispense with price controls at first sent a tremor through the country. Meat today is ten times the price of two months ago: 45 levs a kilo whereas the average wage is around 300 levs. Cooked pork products have also risen similarly, while bread is nine times its previous price.

As a result of the price increases, food stocks hoarded by peasants and middlemen are reappearing in shops. Noted a Sofia girl student ironically: "Previously, things didn't cost much, but there were none available. Today, there are goods, but we can't afford them." The Bulgarians seem to be blunderingly learning the hard way to behave like "real" consumers: learning to look carefully at what they buy, compare prices and buy in small quantities instead of snatching everything that appears on the shelves.

The semblance of a market economy appears to be emerging also with difficulty and somewhat haphazardly. After all, recent reports show that meat prices—clearly too prohibitive—are falling in Sofia. One must also remember that strict wage controls—for every lev paid out in wage increases, the employer has to give the state one lev—encourage the Bulgarians to go to great lengths to limit themselves to the barest necessities. But the conclusion is unanimous: "Things are improving."

Another encouraging sign is the agrarian bill, adopted at the end of February which should enable former landowners to recover their property and thus shake Bulgaria's agriculture out of its torpor. The government has also promised that a new trade code and a bill on foreign investment will be adopted very soon.

The foreigner arriving in Sofia today is surprised to see that there is no black market in foreign currency. True, there will always be some taxi driver to offer the visitor an advantageous rate of exchange. It is also true that the dollar is still the required offering to obtain certain services, but the visitor will be rarely accosted in the street by scores of furtive "money changers": for the excellent reason that, on the advice of international monetary authorities, the government has quite simply decided—like the Hungarians—to bring the local currency's exchange rate into line with the prevailing black market rates.

Early in February, for example, an event took place unthinkable a few months earlier: Bulgarians rushed to the National Bank to change wads of dollars carefully collected over the years into levs. The advantageous rate offered—28 levs to the dollar instead of the previous 3 levs—justified the Bulgarians' sudden yearning for their national currency, but there again it was an indication of the new economic outlook starting to emerge.

Svetlin Statkov, chairman of Bulgaria's first private bank, said that at the time his bank bought a million dollars for levs in a few hours. Established on April 28, 1990 at the Union of Private Producers' initiative for helping the non-nationalised sector, the institution wants to become a "real" bank.

Another happy man is a wily trader who has been taking his road tankers into Greece and filling them with petrol which he sells at premium prices to Sofia residents too impatient to wait for hours at filling stations. The Bulgarian authorities are trying to put a stop to the operation. On March 17, police raided a Sofia immigrant workers' hostel allegedly the centre of an illegal trade in goods carried on by Vietnamese workers whose contracts have run out and who are waiting to be sent back to their country.

"There are plenty of spivs," said a Western expert, "and their numbers are growing. Especially, among members of the former communist establishment taking advantage of their contacts with the world outside and the nest-eggs they have made to bring off lucrative deals. On the other hand, there are still no signs of real producers emerging, people who want to start their own businesses." It is as if, in discovering the liberal economy, the Bulgarians—like most citizens of the former people's democracies—had totally overlooked what constitutes this economy's driving force, production. And it is precisely when the authorities get down to tackling this problem that Bulgaria is likely to be shaken by the most violent convulsions.

It is when drastic cuts are made in an overmanned administration and tens of thousands of surplus workers begin to be laid off in obsolete and inefficient enterprises that the former communist structures will show how well they can resist change. All you need is to see a minister being forced to attend to his files alone, given the little confidence he has in his administration, to realise the strength of this nomenklatura, which is decidedly hard to root out.

ALBANIA

✦ At best Albania has occupied a marginal position in Eastern Europe throughout the postwar period. It was anything but a modern society to start with, and it still resembles Third World countries more than it does its neighbors. It remained stubbornly Stalinist well beyond Stalin's lifetime, and when its posture became entirely unsuitable in the context of the Soviet bloc it proclaimed its loyalty to a Maoist model instead. In its version of socialism, archaic habits survived and even party affairs were conducted according to distinctly unmodern practices. But processes of change were unleashed in Albania as it became slightly open to outside influence in response to its own economic needs.

Because of its marginal status, Western observers have been able to ignore Albania in large measure, fortified by the country's unreceptivity to outsiders. Fortunately that pattern is not universal, and the J. F. Brown selection provides a good summary of the country's past. Fortunately too, Radio Free Europe continues to monitor developments there. The selections below offer insight but cannot of course tell us yet where Albania is heading.

Albania

✦

J. F. Brown

This specialist on Eastern Europe, long associated with Radio Free Europe, is among the few who have kept abreast of developments in Albania. This chapter from his book *Eastern Europe and Communist Rule* is all but unique in its coverage and analysis as Brown brings the story down to the eve of important changes in a hitherto isolated country.

In the West only experts or eccentrics have been interested in Albania as a subject. As an object, however, Albania has attracted a wider interest. Its not inconsiderable energy and mineral resources have drawn geologists and enquirers. But it has been Albania's strategic significance, attracting soldiers and diplomats alike, that has made it important. Situated at the entrance to the Adriatic, just over forty miles from Italy, it has held a key position in southeastern Europe. As a partial wedge between Greece and Yugoslavia it has also beckoned any power wishing to control the western half of the Balkan peninsula.

Small wonder, therefore, that Albania has brought out the acquisitive or the competitive instincts in others. In fact, it only owed its establishment as a sovereign principality in 1913 to the Austrian determination to deny Serbia access to the Adriatic. It emerged as a frail but fully independent state only after World War I in 1920. It was a client state almost by definition, being neither militarily nor economically strong enough to be viable. Yugoslavia, Italy, and Greece vied with one another in efforts to occupy, control, or dismember it. First, it fell under Yugoslav influence, but then, under the northern Albanian chieftain Ahmed Zogu, first president and later king, it became increasingly dominated by fascist Italy. In the 1930s Albania became Mussolini's first satellite, dominated to a degree greater than ever in its history. It was a fatal embrace that culminated in the Italian military occupation of the country in 1939.

During World War II Albania was occupied first by the Italians and then by the Germans. Of the three serious resistance groups it was the least likely communist-dominated movement that, through its exertions, support from Tito and the British,

J. F. Brown, "Albania," from *Eastern Europe and Communist Rule,* Duke University Press, Durham, N.C., 1988, pp. 371–383. Reprinted with the permission of the publisher.

and the necessary slice of luck, became the most powerful force. But it was completely under Yugoslav tutelage. Thus, though the actors were different, the situation remained the same as before the war. Albania remained a satellite. Yugoslav Tito was the patron and the communist Enver Hoxha the client.

◆

ENVER HOXHA AND HIS LEGACY

Enver Hoxha, therefore, began his career as Albanian leader as a Yugoslav client. He was to end it forty years later as pater patriae and the deadly enemy of Yugoslavia. He had become Albanian party leader in 1941 at the age of thirty-three. Before that, in the 1930s, he had spent six years in Western Europe as did many scions of wealthy prewar Albanian families, including several of his later party associates.

No assessment of Hoxha can begin without reference to his inhumanity, his ruthless elimination of political opponents. Yet he cannot just be moralistically written off as a monster. For one thing he seemed to have been spared that element of personal evil that dogged some of his contemporaries, Mátyás Rákosi, for example, in Hungary; and for sheer ferocity he was nothing compared with Mehmet Shehu, Albanian premier for twenty-seven years till 1981. As for his political crimes, he was the creature of both his environment and his time. He had less blood on his hands than Tito or, probably, Milovan Djilas. The difference, though, was that while Djilas repented and Tito mellowed, Hoxha's paranoia continued unabated, and his personal reputation has duly suffered.

But he was more than just the last Stalinist paranoid. He became an Albanian nationalist who secured and assured his country's independence with extraordinary skill and audacity. Albanian independence may have seemed fairly self-evident by the end of the 1980s, but it had been far from such forty years earlier. Hoxha changed all this. By the time he died, Albania was an accepted fact of international life. Over one hundred countries recognized it, and none threatened it.

It was an extraordinary feat. But Hoxha should not be seen primarily or originally as a nationalist or even as a communist. He was above all a survivor, bent on keeping his own power and his own life. He could have lost both in 1948 had not the Tito-Stalin break intervened. He could have lost both in 1956 when Tito, supported by Khrushchev, tried to get rid of him.

It was the survival instinct that inspired both his political philosophy and his strategy. By inclination he may have tended toward left-wing extremism, as many Balkan communists originally did. But what made him embrace it as a fighting creed for life was Tito's policy as it emerged after 1948. Tito, though he remained at least a Leninist, adopted a radically new "revisionist" policy. With his archenemy doing this, therefore, and being denounced by his new protector Stalin, the only tactical path for Hoxha was the one that led to the opposite end of the communist spectrum. And there he remained, showing his real political mettle a few years later when Stalin's successor, Khrushchev, must have seemed to him seduced by Tito, with both bent on his destruction. Other earmarked victims might try accommodation. But realizing that such a course would signify weakness Hoxha insisted both on the correctness of his course and on the baseness of his enemies. His boldness was rewarded by survival, and this was soon to be guaranteed by the emergence of China as a challenger to the Soviet Union.

It was by 1961, when the open break came with Khrushchev, that Hoxha's metamorphosis from formidable opportunist to national savior was completed and publicly acclaimed. But he and Albania had survived through the parading and manipulation of a hard-line Stalinist dogmatism. And this hard-line dogmatism was to remain policy for the next quarter of a century—the second most important part of the Hoxha legacy after the securing of his country's independence.

But it is probably only in retrospect that both Albania and Hoxha seemed safe after 1961. For the next twenty years many things happened that could have disturbed any Albanian leader, even one without the paranoid tendencies Hoxha was increasingly to display. Khrushchev fell in 1964, a matter of satisfaction till his successors more clearly emerged. In any case, his prime enemy, Tito, was still flourishing. In 1968 the invasion of Czechoslovakia must have given cause for genuine alarm: at last Albania took the legalistic precaution of formally leaving the Warsaw Pact, feeling safer outside than inside it. The decade of East-West détente opened up unsettling possibilities; even more the transformation of the Chinese leadership and policy. The death of Tito in 1980, itself the occasion of ungracious jubilation in Tirana, made Yugoslavia less predictable than before. Finally, there was the death, debility, and disarray in the Kremlin itself between 1982 and 1984. All Albania's points of reference were changing radically.

The continued uncertainty abroad probably reinforced Hoxha's determination to maintain tight personal or centralized control over political and economic life at home. Albania was doomed to the hard line—with occasional flurries of Mao-like militancy, it is true, but these too were closely supervised. There was no Red Guard spontaneity in Albania. Toward the end of his life Hoxha even introduced changes in agriculture that destroyed whatever vestiges of material incentive had remained. China may have become prostituted along with the rest, but Albania would preserve its communist virginity.

It is intriguing—and may be instructive—to compare Hoxha's personality and practices with those of Nicolae Ceaușescu in Romania. . . . Hoxha, of course, predated Ceaușescu in power by a good twenty years, and with Gheorghe Gheorghiu-Dej, the Romanian leader till 1965, he had precious little in common. But with Ceaușescu the similarities are tantalizing: the megalomania; the paranoia; the personality cult; the highly personalized rule; the rigid centralism and hard-line domestic policy. There have been enough similarities to pose the question whether they represent just personal coincidences, whether they could partly derive from the circumstances where, *toutes proportions gardées,* both leaders have pursued a policy of independence from the Soviet Union and isolation from the Soviet bloc, or whether they also derive from historic aspects of Balkan ruling practice.

◆

HOXHA AS NATION-BUILDER?

Stavro Skendi, probably Albania's greatest historian, saw King Zog in the role of nation-builder. "Whatever his flaws," Skendi wrote, "he made a nation and a government where there had been a people and anarchy." Obviously Zog, who dominated Albanian public life for a decade and a half, gave his country an international profile and a degree of internal unity it had never had. It is reasonable to question, though, how much the Albanians had acquired a feeling of nationhood in the modern sense by the spring of 1939 when Zog and his entourage left the country, never to return. Albanians, it should be stressed, had always had a sense of their identity, their "Albanianism." They were proud of their descent from the ancient Illyrians, of their Skanderbeg heritage, and their differences from Slavs, Turks, and Greeks. They have also had a sense of racial superiority over these nations (and have known that these nations have looked down on them).

This was the inchoate legacy Zog inherited, and he molded it into something firmer and more definite. But he hardly finished the job of nation-building. During the wartime occupation, first by Italians and then by Germans, there had been hardly any united resistance. Such resistance as there was came from three distinct groups who, like the Chetniks and Partisans in Yugoslavia, tended to fight each other as well as the foreigner. (There was also some active and much passive cooperation with the occupier.) However, one development of great historic and symbolic significance did occur during the wartime occupation. That was the incorporation of the Kosovo area of Yugoslavia as well as the predominantly Albanian parts of Macedonia and Montenegro into greater Albania. Albania, therefore, though not free, was historically whole for the first time since 1912, and this gave something of the same stimulus to Albanian national sentiment as the wartime existence of the Slovak republic did for the Slovaks. . . .

After World War II the Albanian communists seemed to present the poorest credentials possible for nation-building. They were part of a movement ostensibly transcending nationality but which had become firmly identified with Russian national interests as determined by Stalin. Within Albania itself the communist party was largely a Tosk movement originating in the southern part of the country. The Tosks of Albania spoke a different dialect from the other tribal composite, the Gegs, of the northern part. These two tribes also had different social structures, and their members are often of different appearance. The Tosks have tended to be quieter farming people. The Gegs (of whom King Zog had been a spectacular example) were more flamboyant mountaineers with a social organization reminiscent of the medieval Highlands of Scotland and the custom of the blood feud that militated against even the crudest type of civic organization. Traditionally the Gegs had despised the Tosks, and it has been plausibly argued that one reason for the relative communist strength in the Tosk areas was their identification with ethnic equality. Numerically Gegs outnumbered Tosks by nearly two to one.

Just as the Geg clan chiefs dominated Albanian politics during the Zog era, after

1945 it was Tosk communists who largely took over, and, though proclaiming a break from the past, they too brought some traditional characteristics with them, notably the familiar system. The wives of Enver Hoxha, Mehmet Shehu, and Hysni Kapo, who were to become the three top men in the regime, were prominent central committee members, and Shehu, in particular, was to flank himself with several powerful family members.

Hoxha, after he had consolidated his domestic power, appears to have tried to reduce the strong Geg fears that a communist Albania would mean discrimination against them by the victorious Tosks. Many Gegs assumed powerful positions in the party, state, and economic bureaucracy. His eventual designated successor, Ramiz Alia, is a Geg. But the perceived differences have continued to be very much part of the popular psyche, as has the Geg sense of victimization. One of the most widespread of Geg suspicions against Hoxha was that he neglected to press Albania's irredenta regarding Kosovo because the Albanians in Yugoslavia (Kosovars) are Gegs and their incorporation would mean an overwhelming Geg preponderance in a new greater Albania.

But if Hoxha could never bridge a chasm that still preoccupied many Albanians, the adventures of his long period of rule gave them a sense of identity as never before. The perils they faced together were themselves a unifying factor, especially when skillfully dramatized. And, like all demagogues, Hoxha could project dangers to himself as mortal dangers to his country. What was good (or bad) for Enver Hoxha was good (or bad) for Albania. His own survival in 1948 and 1956, for example, became matters of survival for his country.

In domestic affairs the centrifugal forces that previously dominated Albanian public life were smashed and replaced by a forced multifaceted centralism in political, social, economic, and cultural life. Society also became heavily militarized. A rigid ideological doctrine was the only one tolerated. Hoxha saw organized religion in Albania, in its three varieties of Islam, Orthodox [Christianity], and Catholicism, not only as an alternative domestic source of power and ideology but also as an actual or potential foreign fifth column. He therefore suppressed it in 1967. The personality cult was also a cohesive force. Finally, the spectacular purges of the late 1950s and then the 1970s, with the victims denounced as foreign agents, helped to increase that sense of threat and the need to unite against it.

Thus Hoxha's predilections and idiosyncrasies, combined with his remarkable political perceptiveness, helped build Albanian nationhood. A momentous phase in the history of a tiny nation produced a man whose virtues as well as his vices helped it through from near-extinction to relative safety. One may assume Hoxha seldom worked from a conscious program of action. No leader consciously sets out on a policy of nation-building. This, after all, is the historical by-product as well as the climax of a whole series of everyday actions that are both the stuff of leadership and the preoccupation of those engaged in it. Hoxha in this context should be seen as a pragmatist using hard-line policies for specific short-term purposes. Much of his policy took on an ideological coloration. But the motives behind it were severely practical.

In his choice of successor, however, Hoxha obviously did make a longer-term calculation. In doing so he brought on one of the most dramatic episodes in his long, action-packed rule.

On 18 December 1981 the Albanian media announced that Mehmet Shehu, prime minister for twenty-seven years, had killed himself in a "state of agitation." It was later claimed by Hoxha that the man who had been his closest political associate for forty years and had always been regarded as the nation's number two man had in reality been, from his earliest youth, an agent working for *four* enemy secret services: the American, British, Soviet, and Yugoslav. Hoxha also revealed what he claimed had been the final abortive efforts of Shehu to assassinate him and take his place. The whole concoction was so bizarre that the only possible recipients of sympathy were the Albanian people, whose intelligence was so grievously insulted. More than anything it revealed Hoxha's Stalinist paranoia: his version matches, even exceeds, anything from the Soviet show trials of the 1930s or the Soviet and East European show trials of the late 1940s and early 1950s. It also reveals the continuing clan nature of Albanian politics. (Shehu's family following has already been mentioned.) With both the interior and defense ministers as supporters through kin, Shehu may well have felt strong enough to pressure even Hoxha into giving a commitment that he would be recommended to succeed him. Alternatively, knowing Hoxha had settled for Ramiz Alia, the Shehu clan may have tried not to oust Hoxha totally but to kick him upstairs to the state presidency on the grounds of ill health. At any rate, the Shehu group failed and paid dearly for their temerity with either their lives or their liberties. Hoxha had his way and died peacefully, mourned with massive sincerity and succeeded by Ramiz Alia.

Hoxha bequeathed Alia a totally different land from the one he had begun to lead forty years before. It was now a nation-state that had asserted its identity and independence. The question, though, was whether Albania could achieve a stable viability with the legacy he had left behind him.

◆

THE END OF THE CHINA CONNECTION

In China, Albania had found the ideal patron. This patronage would pay in several ways. Yet China was far away and only asked for what Hoxha was ready to give anyway: unstinting support against the Soviet Union. True, China could not defend Albania militarily, but there seemed little danger of this being needed. The Chinese turned out to be the longest-standing patrons in Albanian history—for seventeen years, taking 1961 as the beginning and 1978 as the end of its patronage, longer even than Italian patronage between the two world wars.

Estimates of Chinese economic and financial aid vary. In a study for the Joint Economic Committee of the U.S. Congress Michael Kaser has put total Chinese financial aid at about $885 million between 1959 and 1975, well over half of this coming in the five-year plan period of 1971 to 1975. But Albania's reliance on Chinese aid after 1961 was measurable not only in dollars. For example, thousands of Albanian specialists and students went to China, for varying periods, for study and training. Hundreds of Chinese experts came to Albania to help build industrial projects, including the radio-television center and the powerful broadcasting transmitters that have made Radio Tirana's somewhat single-minded foreign language services so boringly audible. There was a Sino-Albanian shipping company and a weekly Tirana-Peking flight connection. Finally, Albania became dependent on Chinese military hardware. It is impossible to put a price on this, but, taking into account Tirana's incessant propaganda about military preparedness, it must have been considerable. In 1986 Albania's total armed forces numbered about 40,400, and, while most of their heavy armament was originally of Soviet provenance, the Chinese themselves had made much of the Albanians' lighter armament and equipment.

But on 11 July 1978, a date that might turn out to be the most fateful in the whole of Albanian history, the Chinese announced they had cut off all aid to Albania. Vitriolic polemics between China and Albania (together with its "true," splinter-party Marxist-Leninist allies) had been waged for more than a year before, ostensibly over Peking's "Three Worlds Theory." This theory, originally conceived by Mao himself, was based on the division of the world into three groups of states—the two superpowers, the developed countries, and the developing countries. It was bitterly attacked by the Albanians as "revisionist," but, as usual, communist theory was simply the thin cover for differences involving national interest. From the Albanian point of view the militant support of the Chinese had been useful in its anti-Soviet and especially its anti-Yugoslav phase. But now that post-Mao China was in the process of drastically revising both its foreign and domestic policy and drawing what must have seemed dangerously close to Yugoslavia, it was necessary for the Albanians to renounce their alliance of convenience.

It was time for Albania to move on. But, unlike twenty years before, there was now nowhere to go. Moreover, Albania had painted itself into a tight corner by a constitutional law of 1976 that forbade any present or future regime to raise international loans. Such a self-disbarment was yet another factor making Albania unique among the world's states. It was also the culminating point in the mythology of self-reliance that Hoxha had been developing since the break with Khrushchev in 1961.

But mythology never makes good policy. "Going it alone," taken literally, was always impossible. What Hoxha appears to have had in mind was a policy that, taking "self-reliance" as the cornerstone, would add to it three other components: (1) a further intensification of economic relations with the Third World; (2) a partial restoration of economic relations with China; (3) a greater development of economic relations with the West.

This seemed the best combination of alternatives over the short run, and before Hoxha died all three of these external possibilities were being implemented. The picking up of trade relations with China might be surprising after the bitterness of the polemics such a short time before. But it was another small example of Hoxha's pragmatism, and, in any case, the scale of relations was very much lower than in the days of Chinese patronage.

There were two other alternatives that were indignantly dismissed by the Albanian leadership. These were rapprochements with Yugoslavia and the Soviet Union.

Despite the political enmity, Yugoslavia remained Albania's biggest single trading partner, whereas direct economic relations with the Soviet Union were completely discontinued after 1961. But the trade with Yugoslavia was "mutually beneficial" and was on a strictly commercial basis. It could be increased, but any basic improvement in the relations between the two countries that would have a major impact on the Albanian economy was rejected by Tirana on the grounds of the concessions it might involve. Thus, the completion of the railway between Shkodër and Titograd in Montenegro, which connected Albania with the European rail system for the first time, had nothing but symbolic significance. As for the Soviet Union, it continually held out the olive branch, which just as continually was spurned by the Albanians.

But what most intrigued Albania watchers even before Hoxha died, but especially after, was the possibility of a general rapprochement with the West. Albania enjoyed full diplomatic relations with several economically advanced West European countries, notably Italy, France, and Austria. When Hoxha was still alive the first signs of an Albanian Westpolitik became discernible.

Perhaps the most striking development was the remarkable improvement of relations with Greece, culminating in 1987 with the formal ending of the state of war between the two countries, which had technically lasted more than forty years. Previous attempts to improve relations had been vitiated not just by Albanian obduracy: Greece had territorial claims on parts of southern Albania, which it referred to as "Northern Epirus." But even when these claims had been quietly dropped Greek resentment continued at alleged persecution of members of the Greek minority in this territory. This minority probably numbered about 50,000, but some Greek sources claimed it was over 300,000. Despite this important bone of contention, however, intergovernment relations at a high level had developed and flourished.

Relations with Italy had always been better than with any other Western country. They took a step further when a three-times-a-month ferry service between Durrës and Trieste was inaugurated in 1983—a small financial disaster for the Italians who were paying for it, but worth the loss for its diplomatic and political potential. Visits by Italian officials and businessmen increased, as did important visits from France. With Great Britain there had been contacts to try to break the deadlock arising from the Corfu channel incident in 1946 when two British destroyers were struck by mines with considerable loss of life. As a result, Britain had impounded some Albanian gold. There was a steady optimism that a solution could be found. Informal contacts had also been made with Washington. But the key role in any broader Albanian Westpolitik would necessarily be played by the Federal Republic of Germany. Contacts between the two countries began apparently in the late 1970s. Some of these were well publicized like the visit of the Bavarian premier, Dr. Franz-Josef Strauss, in 1984. Others were secret and more meaningful, like the visit of the Albanian Academy of Sciences chairman, Professor Aleks Buda, to Bonn in 1983. The Albanians were at first insisting on a West German payment of a "war reparations" bill for DM 4 million as an earnest of good intentions, but this appeared to have been considerably modified after Ramiz Alia took power. So much so that in 1987 the two countries agreed to assume diplomatic relations. The breakthrough had been made.

✦

THE NEED FOR A NEW LOOK

The future of relations with the West would, of course, depend on how literally the Albanians took Hoxha's self-reliance principle. The real crux lay in the 1976 self-disbarment from credits. How long would it be before this needed to be modified? The resolutions and the tenor of the ninth congress of the Albanian (communist) Party of Labor in November 1986 were hardly encouraging. But Ramiz Alia has subsequently given some reason to believe that this was a hurdle that could eventually be vaulted or circumvented.

As expected, the congress was dominated by the dead Hoxha. No one expected anything else. Nor need anyone expect any public "de-Enverization" for a long time—if ever. But, assuming Alia is not just an interim leader and shows enough strength to assert his control, it might be expected that, under the rubric of "creatively applying" the Hoxha tradition, new policies will gradually be introduced and some old taboos lifted, especially in the economy. Already in the first year after Hoxha's death there was talk in Albania of a general relaxation of the atmosphere, which inevitably caused complaints about the "erosion of discipline." Whether this was the prelude to significant changes was difficult to say. But if Albania were not just to survive but also prosper in the twenty-first century, some veritable revolutions in policy would be needed. And no matter how these were presented they would involve shedding the Hoxha legacy.

The first essential was a slowdown in the population growth, which was the fastest in Europe. In 1961 when Albania broke with the Soviet Union the population was 1.6 million. In 1986 it was over 2.9 million. By the end of the century it was expected to be 4 million. One of the main planks in Hoxha's policy had been rapid population growth. Large families were actively encouraged. Abortion was forbidden, other forms of birth control discouraged. Emigration was impossible.

Albania simply could not sustain such a growth. Most of the country is mountainous, uninhabitable, and/or infertile. It was estimated to have only about 600,000 hectares of arable land, and even if the population were to be considerably lower in A.D. 2000 than the estimated 4 million, a revolutionary change would in any case have to be made in agricultural policy. It would involve the introduction of material incentives. Private plots needed enlarging and encouraging. Private animal breeding needed to be reintroduced and a free market in agricultural produce permitted.

But if it were not just a case of avoiding the worst, but getting the best, then a new economic strategy would be needed. This would involve discontinuing much of Albania's heavy manufacturing industry. True, a complete change would be virtually impossible, since heavy industry in Eastern Europe and the Soviet Union had become synonymous with socialism. But for Albania especially the products of this obsession with industrialization were almost totally unsalable. A much simpler economy based on natural resources and agriculture might facilitate real viability.

With an annual oil production of about 2.5 million tons in 1985 Albania supplied its own needs and exported to Italy, Greece, and Yugoslavia. It also had considerable reserves of natural gas. It was the third largest producer in the world of chrome

Albanian Life. This tailor's shop in Scutari, photographed in 1984, suggests the economic backwardness of this tiny nation. Looming behind the tailor is an obligatory photograph of Enver Hoxha. (Ferdinando Scianna/Magnum)

and the second largest chrome exporter, mainly to the West. It also had large reserves of copper and nickel, exporting large quantities of the latter. Its own energy requirements were mainly supplied by hydroelectric power, which it also exported to Yugoslavia and Greece. These reserves were not infinite, and the existing oil deposits could well run out by the end of this century. After 1984 in any case the international price of oil slumped badly. But there would still be time for an intelligent and profitable exploitation of these natural resources to be made the basis of a modest and appropriate industry. As it stood, the Albanian economy was dominated by a bizarre gigantomania expressed in a few large metallurgical and light industrial combines, grossly overmanned and totally unprofitable.

Albania's fully collectivized agriculture, too, was chronically overmanned and inefficient. But still, in the first half of the 1980s agriculture accounted for about 30 percent of the country's total exports. Albanian tomatoes, for example, were known in many parts of Western Europe. What was needed was the encouragement of greater personal incentive, already mentioned, and greater financial support for those branches with an export potential. Khrushchev, during his visit to Tirana in the summer of 1959, urged the Albanians to make their country a "flourishing garden." It was part of his campaign to induce the Southern Tier to cast aside comprehensive industrialization, and it foundered on both the nationalist and socialist aspirations of his audiences. Some thirty years later some may have been begun timorously acknowledging that he had a point.

Eventually Albania also needed to begin fully participating in international trade. (Indeed this should be the prelude to change rather than the climax of it.) But to participate in international trade it would need credits—and this brings the argument back once again to the 1976 provision. If it remained untouchable for long, this culminating gesture of Hoxha's isolationism could become a sentence of death on Albania as a nation-state. The East European experience with credits in the 1970s may have been unfortunate. But any long-term Albanian existence without them could be fatal.

Albania's future, therefore, looked woeful but not hopeless if the country were served by strong and imaginative leadership. What was needed, if public "de-Enverization" was not possible, was a partial, creeping "de-Enverization." If the essence of Hoxha's legacy—the building of the Albanian nation-state—was to be preserved and built upon, then the errors of that legacy would have to be discarded.

Albania's New Path

✦

Louis Zanga

This report describes the onset of significant change in Albania in the first half of 1990 as the country abandoned its self-imposed isolation and initiated a set of economic reforms.

Although Albania still seems determined to go its own socialist way, a number of significant events in early May indicate that the country's image as Europe's last Stalinist bastion is rapidly changing. The upheavals in Eastern Europe, which caused Albanians to pressure their government to introduce reforms, set in motion a process

Louis Zanga, "Albania's New Path," from *Report on Eastern Europe,* June 15, 1990, pp. 1–5. Reprinted with the permission of Radio Free Europe/Radio Liberty.

of political and economic change. And while Albania's leaders are carefully controlling the pace of change, they have apparently realized that they are dealing with a new situation and that there is also a need to break with the Stalinist past and institute reforms.

Like other East European countries, Albania did away with the traditional mass parades, orchestrated by the authorities, that have always marked May Day. Instead, in an apparent attempt to make the country's democratization process more credible, the Albanian authorities announced that the May Day celebrations should have a "popular" character and be celebrated with, for example, picnics. The leadership possibly feared that antigovernment demonstrations might occur during a traditional May Day parade and, to avoid embarrassment, decided to introduce a more democratic way of marking the day. First Party Secretary and State President Ramiz Alia, touring a number of southern cities, was shown picnicking with the people. In the capital other leaders, including Enver Hoxha's widow Nexhmije smiling alongside Prime Minister Adil Carcani, were shown taking part in popular festive activities. These images seemed designed to discourage rumors that a power struggle is taking place within the Albanian leadership between the pro-Alia liberal faction and pro-Hoxha hard-line elements.

The People's Assembly session of May 7 and 8 was a major event, producing a package of economic and human rights reforms that received much publicity both in Albania and abroad. The human rights reforms, which included a liberalization of travel restrictions, were especially well publicized and somewhat eclipsed other important issues the assembly dealt with. The Albanian authorities were quick to announce only a few days after the law had been approved that 3,000 passports had already been issued. The government also announced that passports would be granted within two hours for special emergency medical travel and official business trips. In addition, foreigners wishing to visit Albania would be granted visas promptly, even at border crossings.

◆

ECONOMIC ISSUES

The economic reforms Prime Minister Adil Carcani announced at this session, though quite extensive by Albanian standards, are not as far-reaching as those being introduced in other East European countries. The reforms give enterprises a degree of financial autonomy. They will now be able to set their own pay levels and establish bonuses for production levels exceeding those stipulated in the plan. These reforms should be firmly in place by 1992, at which time the government would introduce further reforms.

Some of the deputies' reports to the People's Assembly, such as Farudin Hoxha's on economic cooperation with foreign countries, were also significant. Hoxha, who is a young professor of engineering, has in recent months been extremely active in representing Albania's interests abroad. Although specializing in hydroelectric dam construction, Hoxha holds two governmental posts: Minister to the Presidium of the

Council of Ministers and Chairman of the People's Assembly's recently created Foreign Economic Cooperation Committee. Hoxha pointed out that Albania would have to increase its economic and industrial cooperation with other countries in order to procure the modern technology necessary to many proposed projects, including the remodeling of existing industrial complexes. He also noted that Albania has rich mineral resources, an optimal climate for agricultural production, and the natural conditions favorable to building a tourist industry.

In the past Albania has remained immune to suggestions that it exploit its vast tourism potential, but the authorities have evidently reversed their policy on this matter as well. Tirana is now trying to make up for lost time by launching a tourism campaign. The authorities have told the foreign press that Albania's first resort, consisting of five villages, will be opened to Western tourists this summer. Negotiations with foreign companies interested in constructing other tourist centers along the country's southern Riviera have also begun. In addition, the recently started superhighway between the Yugoslav border to the north and the Greek border to the south will be completed by 1995. Moreover, the Yugoslav luxury liner *Dalmacija,* carrying 240 Italian tourists, recently stopped for the first time in the port city of Durrës.

Although Hoxha's report was a blueprint for Albania's new economic priorities, it was also an admission of what foreign experts have repeatedly stressed: that Albania's woefully retarded economy can only be improved with the help of modern foreign technology. Hoxha seemed to imply that Albania would begin seeking foreign economic aid in order to acquire needed Western technology. According to the constitution, Albania cannot accept foreign credits; but Hoxha's report hinted that the authorities might be considering scrapping the 20-year-old taboo on foreign credits, loans, and investments. Hoxha noted that

> We are trying to cooperate with others for our common benefit in accordance with both known and new ways, but without violating the great principles of the sovereignty, freedom, and independence of our socialist country.

The key word in this passage is "new," suggesting as it does a reversal of the economic policy that for so long has kept Albania from cooperating more closely with other countries.

Hoxha disclosed that Tirana has, in fact, signed agreements on economic, industrial, and technical cooperation with Algeria, Bulgaria, China, Cuba, East and West Germany, France, Greece, Italy, Romania, Turkey, and Yugoslavia. Similar agreements are being negotiated with Austria, Belgium, Denmark, Finland, Norway, Tunisia, and other countries. Hoxha admitted, however, that the country had taken only the first steps toward international economic cooperation and that the results had been "modest because of a lack of experience, fear, resistance, and the difficulty of doing away with old ways and practices." On the positive side, added Hoxha, replacing the "classic form of commerce" with new forms of economic cooperation "had substantially increased other countries' interest in cooperating with Albania." Cooperation with the European Community (EC), especially after 1992, would not be merely a procedural matter, Hoxha said, but one requiring "serious and thorough preparation."

Hoxha's subsequent lengthy article in *Zeri i Popullit,* which appeared shortly after the parliamentary session, shows that Hoxha is Albania's leading promoter of economic cooperation with other countries. In the article Hoxha discussed Albania's coal-mining industry (2,400,000 tons of coal are mined there annually) and concluded that in its present form, the industry was losing money and harming the environment. He said that it was unacceptable and irresponsible for Albania to allow the industry to carry on as it had been and that "the generation at the end of this century will not forgive us for such primitiveness."

Minister of Foreign Affairs Reis Malile, a leading architect of Albania's new foreign policy, said in his report on foreign relations that Albania already has diplomatic relations with 113 states and planned to start talks on normalizing relations with the USA and the USSR. Discussing Albania's "good-neighbor policy," he said that "the internal problems of one state or another, of whatever nature, should not influence or determine its level of cooperation with others." He also said that, given regional conditions, "where many family ties straddle the borders, mutual visits also have a humanitarian character." This suggests that Tirana no longer objects to allowing families to visit relatives living in neighboring countries.

This new liberal policy could have a major impact on the internal situation in the Autonomous Province of Kosovo if the Yugoslav government also decides to lift its restrictions on border crossings. The Kosovars have not shown any particular inclination to unite with Albania, but they are closely following developments there. In the past, the repressive nature of Albania's brand of communism had acted as a barrier between the two sides. But a more liberal and democratic Albanian society might have a considerable impact on the unruly Kosovars, and Belgrade will undoubtedly be giving serious thought to the implications of the changes across the border.

Although not directly related to the same issue, a two-day visit by US Congressman Tom Lantos (D-California) and former Republican Congressman from New York Joseph Dioguardi (a leading Albanian lobbyist in Washington) made to Albania after talks in Pristina with ethnic Albanian leaders has already become a controversial issue that might affect US-Yugoslav relations. Yugoslavia and the Yugoslav Republic of Serbia protested the visit; Serbia charged that it was "a serious blow to US-Yugoslav relations." Aside from the obvious significance of their talks with senior Albanian officials in Tirana, the sight of a US Embassy car carrying the US visitors was surely cause for more than a little curiosity among the Albanian public, who are hungry for information and alert to new developments.

An important step that could lead to better relations with neighboring Italy was Tirana's decision to end the Popa family's four-and-a-half-year ordeal. The four brothers and two sisters, aged between 57 and 64 and all seriously ill, had managed to enter the Italian Embassy on December 12, 1985, and immediately requested political asylum. The Albanian authorities accused the Popas of "antistate activities" and demanded that Italy turn them over to Albania, which the Italians steadfastly refused to do on humanitarian grounds. The Albanian government has now allowed the six Popas to leave the country (Italy provided a special military plane to fly them to

Rome). Humanitarian implications aside, the asylum drama had strained Italian-Albanian relations, and resolving the case will undoubtedly benefit Albania more than Italy.

Many foreign commentators have noted that Albania's current foreign policy is a departure from its previous dogmatic positions on many issues. Albania refused, for example, to join the 35-nation Conference on Security and Cooperation in Europe (CSCE) or to establish diplomatic relations with the superpowers. Albanian representatives accordingly only attended the current Copenhagen human rights conference as observers. Albanian Ambassador to Stockholm Petrit Bushati told journalists that Albania aimed to "adopt all the rules of the conference" and "accept what has been accepted" by other participating countries. But asked if Albania would allow opposition parties, another Albanian delegate, Bejo Saza, said that there was no history of opposition and there was "no need to artificially create opposition." The more pragmatic Albanians are apparently not bothered by such comments these days. Shaban Murati, the chief foreign affairs editor of the party daily *Zeri i Popullit,* made this point very clear in his recent editorial "Great Changes in Europe." He wrote:

> Today's Europe is not the same as yesterday's in many ways. The great changes taking place on the continent create new movements and relations that cannot be understood by *a priori* schemes. There is a well-known saying: "Foreign policy cannot be based on the ideas of the past." It takes national interests into consideration, and the basis of the policy and diplomacy that the Albanian people have pursued throughout their modern history has been the national ideal, national criterion as a guide for international relations.

The total absence of ideological jargon in this passage is worth noting. In citing the proverb, Murati implied that Albania's national interests were dictating its new foreign policy in the face of the changed conditions in Europe. Yet former Albanian leader Enver Hoxha's teachings on foreign policy have not been abandoned, at least officially, and are still being published.

◆

UN SECRETARY-GENERAL'S VISIT

One of May's political highlights was UN Secretary-General Javier Pérez de Cuéllar's visit to Albania, which was intended to encourage the Albanian leadership to continue to improve its human rights record. For Albania the visit was a major step toward opening up to the world and improving its international image. In [Pérez de] Cuéllar's talks with Albanian leaders during his visit from May 11 to 14, Alia admitted that Albania had been rigidly ruled in the past. It was the first such admission by any Albanian leader. Alia did attempt, however, to justify the leadership's past behavior:

> Those who do not know Albania and criticize its development forget that to arrive where we are now, we have had to make many sacrifices and accept

great privation, tightening our belts. . . . Under Albania's current conditions, these changes could not have taken place without a centralized leadership and tight discipline. It was unavoidable that some privations accompany these conditions.

Now, Alia said, democratic tendencies in Albania had gradually been strengthened and "disciplinary centralism" relaxed. But he stressed that the country needed unity and could "not tolerate divisions in the same way that a larger country could." He emphatically rejected Western-style democracy and declared that it would be "absurd to recommend the French or English pattern," since the British parliament was hundreds of years old and Albania's had been established less than 50 years ago.

[Pérez de] Cuéllar took a firm stand on the question of human rights. Recalling that Albanian Minister of Foreign Affairs Malile had delivered an address to the UN in which he had mentioned the close links between economic and political relations, [Pérez de] Cuéllar said:

> Experience shows that human rights are inseparable and that economic and social rights cannot be separated from the enjoyment of individual rights. . . . Being convinced that such a thing is valuable for both the peace and progress of nations, the United Nations would be failing to carry out its mission if it had not attempted to have its members share the same conviction. Hence, the Albanian government's recent decision to orient itself in a new way and to undertake reforms—the importance of which has been noticed by everyone—is welcomed by the community of nations.

[Pérez de] Cuéllar seemed to have done his best during his short but successful visit to encourage the Albanian leadership to speed up democratization, which still has a long way to go.

Other surprising aspects of this visit were the presence of about 18 foreign journalists in Tirana and the interview Alia granted them. In fact, more foreign journalists, including two Soviet reporters, visited Albania in May than ever before. This is another indication of Albania's improved communications with the world beyond its borders. The journalists' reaction was unanimously positive, and they gave Alia high marks for the ease he displayed in dealing with the foreign press. There were also a number of interviews in the Albanian press with foreign journalists, including reporters from *The New York Times,* Voice of America, and the BBC.

Albanian newspapers have begun sending their own editors abroad for on-the-spot reporting. Two *Zeri i Popullit* reporters, for example, recently returned from a meeting of Balkan journalists in Sofia to report their colleagues' curiosity about the current developments in Albania, specifically the speed with which the country is trying to adjust to the changed situation in Europe. They were asked, among other things, about "young people's demands" and Albania's policies on the EC, the CSCE, the United States, and the Soviet Union. The Albanians told their fellow journalists that the new airline route between Sofia and Tirana would enable Albania to cooperate more closely with Bulgaria. Radio Sofia's Albanian language service also interviewed the *Zeri i Popullit* reporters.

Although the recent developments in Albania are revolutionary by the country's own standards, it is unlikely that the Albanian leadership intends to discard all elements of traditional communism at the moment. It is clear that it is not contemplating the introduction of a multiparty system—at least, not in the near future.

A Watershed Year

✦

Louis Zanga

The year 1990 brought Albania almost abreast of its neighbors in Eastern Europe as it underwent far-reaching political change: development of a multiparty system, a new constitution, and a free electoral system. But, as this account from Radio Free Europe indicates, economic deterioration and popular unrest threatened the stability that the ruling party had sought to maintain.

For Albania, the sole East European country still under traditional—but rapidly eroding—communist rule, 1990 was a watershed in its 46-year communist history. The fundamental political transformations that took place were as radical and at times as dramatic as those that had occurred in the other countries of Eastern Europe in 1989. The events of the second half of 1990 in particular indicate that the country is finally emerging from its repressive system and moving toward democracy, but the road may still prove to be very long.

Judging from the number and the speed of the decisions and reforms that were made in 1990, it would appear that the race for change has truly begun. Despite the repeated official denials early in the year that the changes occurring in Albania had been influenced by the political developments in Eastern Europe, the new policies launched almost single-handedly by Albanian leader Ramiz Alia were clearly designed to help Albania adapt to the dawning of a new era in Eastern Europe. Alia had little choice but to try to accomplish the near-impossible feat of leading the country out of almost half a century of Stalinist isolation and helping it join a new, undivided Europe that had just closed the chapter on the Cold War. The use of force as a means to

Louis Zanga, "A Watershed Year," from *Report on Eastern Europe,* February 8, 1991, pp. 1–6. Reprinted with the permission of Radio Free Europe/Radio Liberty.

perpetuate single-party rule was the other alternative, but as the dramatic events unfolded, it became increasingly clear that Alia was opposed to that approach. Moreover, the steadily deteriorating economic situation and the desperately needed cooperation with and assistance from the once-feared and mistrusted outside world forced the Albanian leadership to abandon its bankrupt policy of self-imposed isolation.

As developments throughout the year demonstrated, every new step in the direction of liberalization and democracy or concession to opposition forces that Alia made merely led to demands for still more changes, and by the end of the year he had come to realize that the process he had unleashed threatened to become uncontrollable. By December the political and economic situation had become so complex that it was difficult to foretell even the immediate future. So rapidly did one significant reform follow the next during the year that each was almost outdated by the time the deadline for its implementation or completion arrived. A record five communist party Central Committee plenums were held (two alone within the space of 30 days in late 1990), in addition to a specially convened meeting of party activists on December 26.

◆

INITIAL REFORMS

The ninth plenum of the Central Committee, held on January 22 and 23, 1990, led the way toward major reform with a 25-point program that was clearly in response to the transformations and dramatic events in Eastern Europe; and Alia the reformer set out to achieve the impossible. He was clearly on the defensive when he rejected international speculation that, in accordance with the domino theory, Albania would be the next country where the Communists lost their hold on power. The reforms he announced in early 1990, for example, only remotely resembled those being implemented in Hungary or Czechoslovakia. Yet, by Albanian standards, some of the proposals were regarded as radical deviations from the country's postwar practices. For Albanians and Westerners alike, they signaled a significantly positive trend in the last bastion of Marxist-Leninist orthodoxy in Europe, since in general terms they called for greater decentralization of the economy and for more democracy in political and social institutions. Although the new program constituted a continuation of the reforms initiated by the eighth plenum in September 1989, there was still widespread dissatisfaction over the government's failure to implement some of the decisions and over their limited scope.

Never had an Albanian leader been as defensive as Alia seemed to be in the early days of 1990, as he tried desperately to convince the world that Albania should be seen in a different light from the other East European societies. He argued that because of the country's specific conditions, traditions, and even "national psychology," its future would be different from that of its former socialist allies. He was later proved wrong in his claim that the country did not have any democratic traditions and did not require a Western-style multiparty system. Yet, he did seem to sense that the pressure for political change would increase with time, observing, "Of course, we are not complacent about the existing situation." Ever the pragmatist, Alia, when actually confronted with pressure for democratic change, proposed multicandidate parliamentary elections and the democratization of electoral procedures, contradicting his earlier pronouncements. His proposals were at first rather limited, for he insisted that all candidates were to be drawn from the conservative Democratic Front, a communist umbrella front group headed by Nexhmije Hoxha, the widow of the former Albanian leader Enver Hoxha.

In his report to the ninth plenum, Alia presented a number of limited economic reforms, the same ones he had been discussing since 1985 and that had received particular emphasis at the eighth party plenum in September 1989. Limiting centralized management, the subdivision of enterprises, improvements in wage and price regulations, changes in some retail prices, and the introduction of supply-and-demand mechanisms were some of the proposed limited economic reforms.

Alia told the ninth plenum that the country had no democratic traditions and did not need a Western-style multiparty system. He noted that during King Zog's regime no political parties had existed and added that both the Nationalist Party and the Monarchist Party, which were founded during World War II, had turned into "collaborationist" parties in the service of the Italian and German occupiers. Moreover, he said, the demands from the international bourgeoisie for political pluralism would result in the revival of *Balli Kombetar* (the Nationalist party) and *Ligaliteti* (the Monarchist party) or the creation of similar antisocialist and antinational political parties. In what appeared to be an attempt to compensate somewhat for the party's rejection of a multiparty system, the ninth plenum report called for the "enrichment of the principle of elections" and for reducing the term of office of various senior government officials, including deputies. Significant legislative changes were also included, suggesting that in the future citizens would enjoy more and better legal rights. Measures were to be adopted guaranteeing legal defense for citizens not only during police investigations and trials but whenever requested by the citizen under investigation. Another important change was the restoration of the Ministry of Justice, which had been abolished at the height of Albania's cultural revolution in 1966.

◆

SHIFT IN FOREIGN POLICY

The plenum document was the first hint that Albania was preparing to make a radical change in foreign policy. It displayed, for example, a more receptive attitude toward such organizations as the Conference on Security and Cooperation in Europe (CSCE) and the European Community. Also, for the first time the plenum conspicuously omitted any hostile reference either to the United States or the Soviet Union, an indication that a major policy shift vis-à-vis the two superpowers was in the offing.

Hardly had the ink dried on the ninth plenum document than Alia announced a major shift in Albania's foreign policy at the tenth plenum in April. He declared that, for the good of the country, Albania would no longer object to the re-establishment of diplomatic relations with the United States and the Soviet Union and also signaled Tirana's intention to join the CSCE. Alia argued that this 180-degree turn in the country's foreign policy from dogmatic, ideological positions to more realistic ones was necessitated by the changed political equilibrium in Europe and that a new approach to Albania's diplomacy was now required to protect the country's interests.

Alia, however, badly miscalculated in thinking that Albania would find it easy to rejoin the mainstream of international politics. The country lacked a credible human-rights record and the democratic credentials necessary to qualify for membership in a democratic Europe. As it turned out, only Moscow was willing to re-establish diplomatic relations; and in July the two countries renewed the diplomatic relations broken in 1961 as a result of the ideological conflict that had so shaken the communist world at the time. Although Washington welcomed Albania's conciliatory overtures, it seemed that it did not consider its efforts to date sufficient to warrant diplomatic recognition, much to Alia's obvious disappointment; instead, it adopted a wait-and-see attitude.

◆

REFORM OF THE LEGAL SYSTEM

The leadership took another big step toward breaking with its past by introducing sweeping changes in the legal system. The Albanian People's Assembly passed new laws on human rights, travel, religion, foreign credits, and other matters on May 7 and 8. These measures showed Albania's determination to step up democratization and to improve its poor human-rights record. It had become quite clear that the Albanian leadership had no choice but to abandon its Stalinist form of rigid, internal rule and respect human rights, a prerequisite for membership in the CSCE. It is also quite likely that the Albanian leadership was caught off guard by the rapid developments in Eastern Europe and had come to the conclusion that something had to be done to prevent Albania from going through the kind of violent upheavals that other former socialist countries had experienced. But, although the possibility of averting bloodshed and upheaval was very real, the Alia leadership had again misjudged the mood of the country. Albania was ripe for change and the people were impatient for reform.

The reforms gave Albanians the right to apply for and obtain passports for travel abroad. The new law on penal reform also stated that defection was no longer to be considered an act of treason but simply "illegal border trespassing," a lesser offense. Agitation and propaganda against the state were also reclassified, and only acts aimed at "overthrowing the social and state order" were to be considered crimes. Another important innovation for the formally atheistic state was striking "religious propaganda" as a crime from the penal code. Henceforth, the question of religious belief was to be "a matter of conscience for every individual." Although the wording was rather ambiguous, the parliament also appeared to signal the abandonment of the 20-year policy of refusing foreign credits, loans, and investments. These reforms set in motion a process of political and economic change whose snowball effect no one could have foreseen.

One of the year's political highlights was the visit to Albania in May of United Nations Secretary-General Javier Pérez de Cuéllar. The visit was apparently intended to encourage the Albanian leadership to continue to improve its human rights record.

For the hard-pressed Albanian leadership, the visit was a major step toward opening to the world and improving its image abroad. During the short visit, the secretary-general encouraged Tirana to speed up democratization, which at the time was still in the early stages.

✦

REFUGEE CRISIS

As in other East European countries, Albania learned that deliberate bureaucratic delays or inefficiency could have unpleasant consequences, especially at a time when the popular appetite for change was accelerating with the implementation of each new reform. Alia's fear that hasty or sudden changes to the system might be dangerous was unexpectedly realized in the first week of July, which will no doubt be remembered as the moment in Albanian history when the complexion of the country's own peculiar brand of communism began to change. On July 2 a group of young people demonstrated in Tirana; events quickly took a dramatic turn when thousands of people sought refuge in embassies in the capital, and Albania suddenly found itself facing a stampede of refugees reminiscent of that in East Germany a few months earlier (which, as it turned out, sealed the fate of that socialist state). Never before had the world seen an exodus of such proportions from Albania. According to an estimate by the United Nations, which organized the orderly departure, 4,786 people, for the most part young, were allowed to leave the country under dramatic conditions that received heavy international news coverage. The mass emigration, although quite unexpected, was caused by the government's decision to issue passports to all Albanian citizens upon request. Once the mass hysteria to leave the country began, the regime was unable to stop it without bloodshed, which it wanted to avoid at any cost.

✦

PERSONNEL CHANGES IN THE GOVERNMENT AND THE PARTY

These events, which shook the foundations of Albania's communist regime, clearly took Alia by surprise and brought about the gravest crisis of his long political career. His ability to control the smoldering internal situation and, in fact, his ability to survive at all in the long run became the topic of debate. He opted for a conciliatory approach rather than a show of force in dealing with the situation, hoping to avoid, if at all possible, a repetition of the bloody Romanian scenario. He convened the 11th plenum of the communist party on July 6 and 7, at which new measures to stabilize the country's political, social, and economic situation were presented. In the same month, Alia made major personnel changes on three separate occasions, retiring a number of Politburo members and promoting others. The most significant promotion was that of Xhelil Gjoni, who became a full member of the Politburo and a Central Committee Secretary and was subsequently appointed First Party Secretary of the district of Tirana.

The leading hard-liner Simon Stefani lost his post as Minister of Internal Affairs (and in December his Politburo membership). He was replaced by Hekuran Isai, reputed to be a moderate, who had previously occupied the post before Stefani from 1982 to 1989. In late 1990, it was reported that Isai had moved out of his state-owned villa and into an ordinary apartment of the type available to other Albanian citizens. Other unpopular members of the old guard, such as Minister of Defense Prokop Murra, Rita Marko, Manush Myftiu, and the sole woman in the Politburo, Lenka Cuko, were also relieved of their high positions. Kico Mustaqi, the Chief of the Army General Staff since 1982, was promoted to full Politburo membership and appointed Minister of Defense. Vangjel Cerrava, the economist Xhemal Dymylja, and Niko Gjyzari were also promoted to full membership in the Politburo. (Gjyzari was later also appointed Director of the Albanian State Bank.) A number of ministerial changes were also made. Through these major personnel changes in the party and the government, Alia consolidated his leadership position after the refugee crisis, replacing several old-guard, hard-line Politburo members with younger technocrats. More such changes were to be made throughout the year.

◆

ECONOMIC REFORMS

The introduction of private enterprise was another significant measure designed to placate the discontented populace. The Politburo passed a law giving agricultural workers larger plots of land to farm individually. On the whole, however, the economic situation deteriorated with each passing day, and the summer's severe drought only darkened the picture. A *Zeri i Popullit* editorial in November estimated the damage done to the economy by the drought, the breakdown in work discipline, and absenteeism (in the industrial and mining sectors, it had reached disastrous levels) at 1.3 billion lek, roughly $250,000,000. Alia was forced to admit that the implementation of measures to reorganize cottage industry, to increase the availability of consumer goods, and to attract foreign investment was not proceeding at all smoothly. He observed that a lack of raw materials and a reduction in the import of spare parts, equipment, and various kinds of machinery had resulted in a decline in the production of petroleum and minerals, Albania's major exports. As a result, Albania had suffered hard-currency losses amounting to one-third of the value of its total annual exports.

Toward the end of 1990, the Albanian leadership began issuing alarming statements about the country's economic plight. In early November Prime Minister Adil Carcani made the frankest admission to date about the serious economic problems, characterized by unemployment and shortages of food, raw materials, and energy; he announced that Tirana would start importing a number of food items. In fact, according to some observers, the food shortage was Albania's most pressing problem.

◆

BALKAN MINISTERS' CONFERENCE

Dramatic events continued to unfold in the fall, culminating in December in the most critical moments of Albania's postwar history. In late October, during the Balkan

Hoxha Comes Down. In March 1991, a crowd of demonstrators tore down the statue of Enver Hoxha, Albania's communist leader from 1945 to his death in 1985, showing the extent to which resistance to communism had reached even distant, seemingly isolated Albania. (Eastfoto)

Foreign Ministers' conference in Tirana, the first international meeting at this level to be held in Albania, the country's most prominent writer, Ismail Kadare, defected to France. The defection dealt yet another devastating blow to Albania's image at home and abroad, just at a time when the Albanian leaders were desperately seeking to improve their country's international standing. Kadare's explanation for his defection was his disillusionment over the slow pace of democratic change, which he maintained was shared by the "overwhelming majority" of the Albanian people.

The conference yielded few immediate results, and the final document simply reiterated the fundamental principles of cooperation in the Balkans that had been adopted in Belgrade some two-and-a-half years previously. The participants tried to outdo one another in their demands for greater regional cooperation and concerted efforts to achieve integration with the rest of Europe. Although the declaration adopted by the conference was on the whole perhaps overly ambitious and vaguely phrased, it did include a few specific proposals, such as the establishment of a permanent body with its own secretariat, which the Bulgarians suggested be located in Sofia. Of the six Balkan states attending the conference, the host country was generally thought to be the one that would benefit most from the meeting. It afforded Albania an opportunity to increase its prestige, end its protracted isolation, boost its international image, and improve its chances of becoming a full member of the CSCE.

✦

EFFORTS TO JOIN CSCE FAIL

Yet, the slow process of democratic change destroyed Tirana's dreams of quickly achieving full integration with Europe. Within a few months of having changed its long-standing policy of self-imposed isolation from the community of European nations, full membership in the CSCE had become the Albanian government's most important foreign-policy objective. As it turned out, Alia and the Albanian leadership had set their sights too high. Although Albania was allowed to attend the CSCE summit meeting in Paris on November 19 and 20 as an observer, it was refused full membership. Tirana's reaction to the decision was "surprise and disbelief." Albania had no other course but to comply with the international decision; it declared that it would continue to act in accordance with the spirit of European developments by speeding up the pace of democratization and would try to meet the criteria for CSCE membership in 1991.

✦

STUDENT PROTESTS

By December, the domestic situation had reached such a critical point that extraordinary measures were needed to cope with it. On the night of December 8, what seemed at first a harmless student protest over poor student dormitory conditions produced some of the most dramatic developments in Albania's postwar history. Within less than a month, Albania had undergone a political metamorphosis. On December 9 the protests intensified then somewhat calmed down again. On December 12, following a decision by the Central Committee at its 13th plenum on December 11, the government announced that an opposition party would be established. Political pluralism, doggedly opposed by Alia and the leadership throughout the year, had finally won the day. Permitting a multiparty system, the government believed, would erase the consequences of Albania's years of isolation, accelerate its integration into the European process, and appease the population. In the short run, this was not to happen. Instead, the student unrest that had begun a few days earlier resulted in riots in four of the largest cities in northern Albania, further evidence that the more Alia gave in to demands for change, the greater became the mood of tension and confrontation in the country. Given the unrest, it is remarkable that not one fatality was officially reported. Alia was prepared to go to great lengths to avoid bloodshed, which would have sealed the fate of communist rule. The French daily *Le Monde* accurately described the developments in Albania as "the revolution with no name." But it would have been still more accurate to refer to it as the "bloodless revolution."

✦
MORE DEMOCRATIC REFORMS

The success of the student protest set off a chain reaction of important developments. Following the introduction of a multiparty system on December 12 (in time for the general elections scheduled for March 31, 1991), the Albanian Democratic Party was founded. On December 18 the Presidium of the People's Assembly formally approved a government decree that provided for a multiparty system in Albania, and on the following day the Ministry of Justice formally recognized the first alternative party to be founded in communist Albania. On December 28 Albania's Council of Ministers set up a state commission to draft a law on the press, radio, television, and publishing and formally defined the jurisdiction of the directors of the various media. The council also legalized the first opposition newspaper, *Rilindja Demokratike,* the organ of the Democratic Party of Albania. (The first issue of the newspaper appeared on January 5.) For the first time in postwar history Christmas was celebrated in Albania with well-attended Catholic and Orthodox services.

Perhaps the clearest sign that democratization was well under way was the publication on December 31 of the complete text of Albania's new draft constitution, which was to replace that of 1976. The 129-article draft constitution is free of communist dogma and steers clear of the totalitarian practices sanctioned in the past. One important change is the complete omission of both the name and the role of the Albanian Workers' Party. The constitution lifts the ban on religion and permits foreign investment. It also introduces a system in many ways similar to a parliamentary democracy and considerably broadens the President's rights and powers. The constitution would suggest that Albania, at least in theory, is ready to break with its Stalinist past. It is expected to be approved by the new parliament at its first session, probably two months after the elections.

✦
CONCLUSION

In his traditional New Year's message broadcast on television and radio, Alia described 1990 as a special year for Albania and said that 1991 would be a turning point. Considering the revolutionary developments that took place last year, it would perhaps have been more accurate to say that the turning point was 1990. What Alia actually fears the most in 1991 and is desperately trying to avoid is a bloody revolution. So far, he has skillfully maneuvered the country toward joining, albeit belatedly, the wave of democracy that has swept across most of Eastern Europe. Whether he will be able to lead the country through a peaceful transition to a democratic society and prevent the transformation from becoming a blazing conflict is uncertain.

Albania—the Domino That Didn't Quite Fall

◆

Janusz Bugajski

The author, an East European analyst at the Center for Strategic and International Studies in Washington, D.C., describes Albania's first multiparty election in March 1991 in terms of a split between town and countryside. The communists retained power by focusing on rural areas and leaving urban areas to the opposition Democratic Party.

The unstable aftermath of the recent Albania elections demonstrates that democracy does not necessarily arrive with the ballot box. At the end of March, Albania staged its first multiparty elections since the communist takeover at the close of World War II. The result, a clear communist victory, may have stunned the outside world, which has watched consecutive communist dominoes fall in Eastern Europe during the past two years. But it comes as no surprise to many Balkan watchers.

Communist control and manipulation in the Balkan states of Albania, Romania, Bulgaria, and parts of Yugoslavia has not collapsed overnight, as it did in East Germany and Czechoslovakia. An entrenched party leadership has clung to as many instruments of power as possible, including nationalism, populism, and public anxiety about change.

In Albania a xenophobic leadership has steered the country out of Eastern Europe and placed it somewhere between China and North Korea—ideologically, politically, and for all intents and purposes, geographically. Albania's isolation was reinforced by official paranoia about foreign invasions. This paranoia is still on display in a bizarre network of concrete bunkers that litter the countryside. They were to protect against allegedly imminent attacks by Yugoslavs, Americans, Russians, among others.

The system was petrified by a doctrinaire Stalinism, in which "Little Stalin" Enver Hoxha ruled the country for over 40 years as a virtual labor-camp commandant. Hoxha died in 1985, but the system survived him, and his chosen successor, Ramiz Alia, took the minimal reformist steps necessary to pacify Western public opinion and prevent a bloody revolution. At the end of last year, the Albanian Party of Labor

Janusz Bugajski, "Albania—the Domino That Didn't Quite Fall," from *Christian Science Monitor*, April 25, 1991. Reprinted by permission of the author.

(APL) decided to retain power in the guise of democracy, using every trick in its Leninist arsenal to limit the effectiveness of newly formed opposition groups.

The election campaign in Albania was in many respects more important than the elections themselves. Unfortunately, observers from several West European parliaments issued superficial reports on the polling based on a few days' stay and the appearance of technically correct election procedures in urban districts. They seemed to ignore the APL's overwhelming advantage in terms of funds, staff, assets, and control of the mass media.

The party leadership decided to sacrifice the cities, where the opposition is strong. It focused instead on rural areas, which could return a clear majority to the national assembly and where the opposition had little access to the collectivized peasantry.

The elections therefore created urban islands of democracy in a rural Red Sea. Riots and shootings in Shkodër on the day after the ballot, and warnings of a strike, reflected the frustrations of a city population that wanted to bury communism and rejoin the European order, but saw the opportunity slipping away. The party authorities reacted with violent repression, and blamed the opposition for the unrest.

Albania's immediate future looks chaotic, not only because of the widening gulf between town and country, and the seething public anger with party manipulation, but also because the economy is collapsing. The country's dilapidated infrastructure is crumbling, food output has slumped, and increasing industrial stoppages have contributed to the general malaise in production and distribution.

If the Democratic Party opposition, which won nearly one-third of the vote, is excluded from parliamentary decisionmaking, and if the new government only implements slow and partial reforms, the streets and factories may well decide Albania's future. The Democrats may find themselves in the unenviable position of defending the government from popular discontent, by urging self-restraint on embittered workers and students.

The West is not powerless vis-à-vis the Albanian turmoil. Aside from humanitarian assistance, a two-track policy must be undertaken to democratize Albania and improve its people's well-being. Democratic parties (Democrats, Republicans, Greens, Agrarians) must be helped to expand their organizational reach, to educate the public in democratic processes, and guarantee pluralism and open competition for the next elections.

Conversely, communist leaders must be pressed firmly against the wall and told that the free world demands civilized treatment of their citizens, otherwise no major credits will be forthcoming and no international institutions will open their doors to Tirana. The victory signs that greet all foreign visitors to Albania will then symbolize the successful construction of democracy, and not just popular yearnings for freedom.

YUGOSLAVIA

◆ *Having been outside the Soviet bloc since the very beginning of the postwar period, Yugoslavia cannot in any sense be lumped together with the states adhering to the Soviet model. The continuation of socialism has long been modified by the distinctly Yugoslav system of self-management, which, however imperfect in its implementation, embodied quite different organizing principles. Tito's foreign policy was also distinctive, with its emphasis on nonalignment in the cold war period, and the Yugoslavs were not shy about offering encouragement when various of the East European states posed challenges to Soviet domination.*

On the other hand, the hostility of 1948 did soften, and relations between Yugoslavia and the whole Warsaw Pact system were kept, for the most part, on a polite basis. Yugoslavia remained an East European state, not just geographically but also, and preeminently, in the ethnic mixture that linked its problems with similar ones in Romania, Bulgaria, and Czechoslovakia, not to mention the Soviet Union. Tito's strong position, whatever disadvantages it had for the democratization desired by many internal critics, had managed to keep the lid on the nationality conflict, but the collective presidency he left behind as an intended counterpoise to latent antagonisms among the republics of the federation proved less than effective. So where Bulgaria could expel Turks, Romanians could discriminate against Hungarians, and Czechs and Slovaks could maintain an uneasy balance, Yugoslavia was threatened by outright dissolution.

Hence the focus, in the selections that follow, is on the one central Yugoslav issue. Democratization has not been achieved and the self-management system is far from realizing its promise, although the worst cases of earlier violations of the rights of citizens have been largely repaired. For the moment, nothing looms as large as the animosity dividing the constituent republics. It appears that this issue will have to run its course and be settled one way or another before the country can give serious attention to its other problems.

The Federal Dilemma in Yugoslavia

✦

Robin Alison Remington

Professor Remington, a political scientist at the University of Missouri, surveys the country's condition in 1990 as the conflict among its constituent nationalities became so acute as to drown out the other issues that needed to be faced.

The popular revolutions of 1989 that swept Communist politicians from power in East Europe did not stop at the borders of Yugoslavia. Communist regimes in East Germany, Bulgaria and Czechoslovakia toppled off the Berlin Wall like so many humpty-dumpties. The violent collapse of Romanian dictator Nicolae Ceauşescu's "socialism in one family" was graphically serialized on Yugoslav television. Thus the specter of multiparty democracy haunted the January, 1990, congress of the League of Communists of Yugoslavia (LCY).

Prophetically, this was the "extraordinary" fourteenth congress of the LCY. Indeed, the congress was extraordinary in more than name. The ruling party gave up its 45-year monopoly of power, admitting that "the first condition of our social reform is to rid the political system of anyone's monopoly, even that of the LCY . . . in a democratic society, nobody can be the exponent of exclusive political truth."

These concessions were too little and came too late. Consistently outvoted in their demands for still more radical change—including the demand that the LCY reconstitute itself as a confederation of independent, republican organizations that are "freely united"—the reform-minded Slovene delegation walked out. Congress delegates then rejected Serbian president Slobodan Milosević's demands that the congress should continue and went home. Officially, the congress was "suspended." Morning-after assessments in the Yugoslav media were divided as to whether the LCY was "definitely dead," "the departing political party" or "the only true Yugoslav-oriented party in Yugoslavia."

Whatever the result of the aborted congress for the federal party, Prime Minister Ante Marković stated flatly that Yugoslavia would continue to function with or without the League of Communists. His government went forward with the reform agendas of the anti-inflation program adopted at the end of the year. Meanwhile, the LCY staggered behind the march of events while opposition candidates upstaged regional Communist politicians in the spring, 1990, elections. To sort signal from noise in the subsequent sound and fury of Yugoslav political drama, one must review the script inherited by the collective leadership after Josip Broz Tito. Who were these political actors? How did they relate to each other and to their constituencies?

◆

THE ROAD TO MARKET SOCIALISM

For some three decades, Yugoslavs had lived relatively comfortably with the inconsistency implicit in a society that was devoted to participatory, self-managing socialism and dependent on charismatic authority. Before he died in 1980, Marshal Josip Broz Tito tried to resolve this "contradiction" (as a Marxist might say) by spelling out an elaborate power-sharing arrangement in the constitution of 1974. This complex quota system further changed the rules of the political game in which the federal government's powers were already limited to foreign policy, defense and an ambiguously defined united market.

Post-Tito politicians replaced one another with dizzying speed on a merry-go-round of party and state collective leaderships. There were three federal players: the party, the government and the armed forces. On the regional level, eight parties and governments vied with one another and the federal center. In this contest, decision making by consensus gave regional party leaders virtual veto power, while the quotas applied to most political jobs undermined any sense of national Yugoslav unity.

Known as the Titoist solution, this highly decentralized federalism came under Serbian attack as a "parcelization" of power. Conversely, the constitution of 1974 was seen as protection for the northern republics of Slovenia and Croatia, which were fearful of Serbian hegemonic ambitions, and for the Albanians who make up 90 percent of the autonomous province of Kosovo within Serbia.

In short, Tito's successors had inherited a cumbersome political machine that had the unintended consequence of decreasing the federal government's ability to broker solutions among regional politicians who were always tempted to put regional needs above national needs. The situation was exacerbated by the fact that Tito, like his East European neighbors and much of the developing world, had fallen into the hard-currency debt trap of the 1970's. With debt-servicing obligations on some $20-billion worth of Western debts, there was no way that post-Tito politicians could stand on their records of economic performance.

The 1983 Krajger Commission on Economic Stabilization established official priorities under International Monetary Fund (IMF) supervision. Whether Prime Minister Milka Planinc's attempt to turn market socialism into an instrument of economic reform failed because of interference from the federal party (as rumored in Belgrade) or because of popular unwillingness to accept the unequal distribution of benefits and burdens of a market-regulated economy, the result was the same. The federal party lost public confidence, and regional politicians became more nationalist.

The economy had done well enough to be released from IMF supervision when Plan-inc's successor, Branko Mikulić, took over as Prime Minister in 1986; but this fact went largely unnoticed.

Mikulić resigned from what he had come to consider a thankless job in Decem-ber, 1988, amid charges of corruption and mismanagement. Whatever his weaknesses, the former Prime Minister had a point when he complained that his government had taken the heat for crises that were the product "of decades during which others made decisions" and that regional politicians infected with economic nationalism had sabo-taged his efforts.

Thus Yugoslavia began 1989 without a government, with an increasingly fac-tionalized party at the federal level, and with the then Serbian party chief Slobodan Milošević refusing to give priority to economic reform until the autonomous prov-ince of Kosovo was reintegrated into Serbia on Serbian terms. The road to Yugoslav market socialism had detoured down the alley of national and ethnic strife.

✦

SEARCH FOR LEGITIMACY

Unable to match Tito's charisma or resolve the country's economic crisis to the satisfaction of Yugoslav workers and housewives suffering under cyclical IMF auster-ity programs, provincial politicians tried to become champions of national or ethnic constituencies. The "nation" became the source of legitimacy. Regional party leader-ships played populist politics as if they were playing soccer. The federal League of Communists became an increasingly ineffective referee; it was attacked by players and fans who were obsessed with short-range, often symbolic, goals.

For Serbia, the coveted trophy was to regain control over the autonomous prov-ince of Kosovo, where the Serbs had been defeated by the Turks in 1389. Unfor-tunately, Kosovo is also the cradle of modern Albanian nationalism. In post-Tito Yugoslavia, Albanian demands for self-determination challenge Serbian territorial integrity. The rapidly growing population of the province is overwhelmingly Alba-nian. By the year 2000, Albanians are expected to replace the Slovenes as the third largest ethnic group in Yugoslavia. From the Kosovar Albanian point of view, their numbers justify upgrading Kosovo to republic status. To Serbs such a suggestion is separatist heresy, a dagger pointed at Serbia's heart.

Serbs feared for the physical safety and human rights of some 200,000 Kosovar Serbs and Montenegrins who, Serbian scholars claim, face genocide at the hands of Albanian separatists intent on an ethnically pure Kosovo. These fears give Serbian strongman Slobodan Milošević a visceral issue in his role as protector of the Serbs in Kosovo.

At the elite level this has translated into a confrontation with Albanian provincial leaders intent on retaining the de facto independence granted under the constitution of 1974. Serbian party leaders charged their Albanian comrades with fostering Alba-nian nationalism and harboring separatists. Albanian politicians objected to what they saw as Serbian chauvinism. In their eyes, the Serbian leadership was blowing isolated incidents out of proportion, creating provocations to satisfy Serbia's hegemonic ambitions.

These conflicting views became personified in the clash between Milošević and the former president of the provincial party, Azem Vllasi, who was arrested for his role in the Gandhi-style hunger strike of Albanian miners. The miners were protesting the March, 1989, amendments to the Serbian constitution that reduced provincial autonomy in the areas of foreign policy, security and defense.

Western and Yugoslav media alike chalked up a victory for Milošević. However, his success in pressuring federal and provincial bodies into accepting the Serbian reintegration of Kosovo came at the cost of increased opposition. In Slovenia, there was popular sympathy for Kosovar Albanians and concern over what was seen as a double standard in responding to Serbian and Albanian national aspirations. The Slovene party leadership expressed reservations about Milošević's street politics. His use of mass meetings to bring down the governments of Montenegro and Vojvodina raised fears in Zagreb with regard to the Serbian minority in Croatia and multinational Bosnia-Hercegovina. The hero of Belgrade became controversial in Sarajevo and a villain in Ljubljana and Zagreb.

The confrontation between the Slovene and the Serbian leaderships came to a head in December, 1989, when the Slovenes banned a rally in Ljubljana at which an estimated 40,000 uninvited Serbs had intended to tell Slovenia the truth about Kosovo as they saw it. The Serbian Socialist Alliance, a mass organization generally considered to be in Milošević's pocket, retaliated by calling for breaking political and economic relations with Slovenia. This once unthinkable scenario was personified as a standoff between Milošević and the then leader of the Slovene League of Communists, Milan Kucan.

To whatever degree the Serbian strongman benefited in Serbia and among Serbs in other provinces, he lost through the union against him of federal and regional politicians who were worried about the negative repercussions for an already staggering Yugoslav economy. Even among Serbs who had followed him blindly on Kosovo, there was concern that this economic strategy amounted to shooting the Serbian economy in the foot. Never had Serbia been so isolated. Given the fact that Kučan subsequently won his election as president of Slovenia, the challenge in itself positioned him to score.

By the end of 1989, many Yugoslavs were fed up with the game. They were tired of political circuses that did nothing to come to grips with the 2,000 percent inflation strangling the Yugoslav economy and did not slow their own slide into poverty. Prime Minister Ante Marković's anti-inflation program was seen as a narrowing window of opportunity; indeed, perhaps the country's last chance.

When 64-year-old Ante Marković (a Croatian) took over as Prime Minister, he brought to the job an entrepreneurial spirit, substantial economic experience and a reputation as a supporter of a market economy. He inherited an economic policy on probation; he was dependent on temporary measures adopted by the state presidency in the absence of an agreement between provincial delegates in the Federal Assembly (Parliament). During the Mikulić government's 18 months in office, inflation had galloped from 90 to 250 percent. The $20-billion foreign debt had grown to an estimated $23 billion. The internal debt (what enterprises owed to one another) was officially put at $14 billion but unofficially it was $20 billion, and some economists said it might be twice that figure. Unemployment had increased to 15 percent officially; many observers thought it was actually closer to 20 percent. Personal income had fallen 25 percent since 1980; personal income fell 7.8 percent during 1988.

According to the Yugoslav Institute for Market Research, inflation moved faster than the new Prime Minister's ability to put together a government; it had reached 346.3 percent by the time he had a working team and presented his program to the Assembly. There was widespread support for Marković's agenda of tackling the economic crisis by striking at root causes. However, as inflation continued to gallop, so demands grew from the underdeveloped parts of the country for concrete anti-inflation measures. Striking farmers joined striking workers. The government promised an anti-inflation package. Everyone agreed that the officially recognized 800 percent inflation rate of 1989 could not be endured, yet there was no agreement on what to do about it.

Marković continued to defend his long-term policy. Piece by piece he presented the Federal Assembly with the laws necessary to establish the legal infrastructure of market socialism. The essence of these reforms—independence of enterprises without strong state influence, market criteria, equal status of enterprises under all forms of ownership, and "profit as the ultimate objective"—remained acceptable. Calls for market socialism were combined with the contradictory demand that the instruments of economic reform should have an equal impact on all economic sectors.

A Croatian daily newspaper summed up the government's dilemma: "there is no economic policy measure that equally hits and benefits everybody." Disagreement centered on who would pay the cost of change. Once again these splits reflected varied regional levels of economic development.

Not surprisingly, there was more willingness to live by the rules of the market in Slovenia, where some 10 percent of Slovene enterprises would face bankruptcy, than in Montenegro, where an estimated 80 percent of the enterprises might not survive. In Bosnia, the Prime Minister's program was attacked as a sellout to capitalism; his government was considered doomed.

Notwithstanding his detractors, Marković stayed the course, insisting that anti-inflation measures required the creation of a legal foundation for a market economy and "material conditions" for the reforms. Proposals were made to the Assembly to amend existing laws on enterprises, banks and other financial institutions, and on accounting; and to pass new laws on labor relations, foreign trade, commodity reserves, securities, and the money and capital markets. When inflation climbed to 2,000 percent, Marković ducked the ongoing battle on foreign currency laws, prices and taxation in the Federal Assembly and announced that the time had come to move forward.

The preconditions were as good as they would ever be. Exports were up. There was a $2.3-billion balance of payments surplus. Foreign exchange reserves had reached $5.8 billion. The hard currency debt had dropped to $16.6 billion. Only 16 percent of the foreign currency went to debt servicing, compared with 45 percent "in the most difficult periods." Industrial production was up 1.9 percent; agricultural production, 6 percent.

Marković presented the Assembly with a program for shock treatment worked out with the IMF along the lines of Harvard economist Jeffrey Sachs's cold-turkey capitalism. The dinar was pegged to the deutsche mark at a ratio of seven to one (to the United States dollar at twelve to one) and was not to change until June, 1990. Yugoslavs would have the right to exchange dinars freely for foreign currency at the official rate.

The convertible dinar was to be combined with a tight monetary policy, a balanced budget, a floating interest rate and, for the most part, market-determined prices. Some exceptions were made for "infrastructural services" like energy and utilities, where prices would be frozen until June, 1990. Wages were to be frozen at the November, 1989, rate until June.

The Serbian leadership condemned the program as it came off the press. Slovenes would not agree to the taxation measures. Others had their complaints as well. However, none of the opponents fielded an alternative strategy. Sachs was the golden boy of international financial circles. The Marković program had international credibility. It would facilitate debt rescheduling and tap whatever resources there were.

With the population and the Federal Assembly frustrated, the Federal Assembly settled for temporary, emergency measures. Within three months, inflation had been slowed to a crawl. As compared with the rate of nearly 65 percent in December, 1989, prices went up 2.6 percent in March and actually fell .2 percent in April; annual estimates ranged from 15 to 20 percent. In July, monthly inflation was zero; however, by September, there were fears that summer pay raises would ignite another inflationary cycle.

Prime Minister Marković has made good on his promise to deliver economic reform with or without the League of Communists. In the process, he has become the most popular Yugoslav politician. Marković has a record to stand on and has declared his intention to organize an Alliance of Reformist Forces to run in the promised first postwar federal multiparty elections, thereby defending his national program amid proliferating national, ethnic and regional political agendas.

◆

THE ROAD TO MULTIPARTY DEMOCRACY

Even before the League of Communists abolished the legal fiction of its monopoly of political power in January, 1990, the handwriting was on the wall. Political parties, associations and movements were openly organizing. In multiparty assembly elections in Slovenia and Croatia in April and May, center-right coalitions defeated reform Communists by substantial margins. The presidency of Slovenia went to the leader of the Slovene Communist party of Democratic Renewal, Milan Kučan. In Croatia, the leader of the nationalist Croatian Democratic Community (also referred to as the Croatian Democratic Union), 68-year-old wartime partisan Franjo Tudjman, became the first non-Communist president of a Yugoslav republic.

A "hundred flowers" have bloomed on the Yugoslav political landscape. There are socialist, radical, liberal, democratic, regional, nationalist, religious and environmental movements and parties. Which of these parties, alliances or coalitions will be prepared to compete seriously in federal elections before the end of 1990 is an open question.

Among political players, the LCY is a ghost of its former self. The party is further weakened by the decision of Serbian president Slobodan Milošević to jump ship. In July, this once staunch opponent of multiparty politics became the president of the Socialist party of Serbia (SPS); thus the Serbian League of Communists disappeared in a merger with its own mass organization, the Socialist Alliance of Serbia. In Serbia, opposition parties were officially registered only on August 27.

When the much disputed Serbian elections take place at the end of 1990, the SPS may well face a coalition of opposition parties: the Liberals, the Democrats, the Social Democrats, the Radicals, the Peasant party and the Serbian Renewal Movement. Meanwhile, ruling center-right coalitions in Slovenia and Croatia will be defending their records against regional reform Communists and other left-oriented challengers. In Bosnia-Hercegovina, where the population is 43 percent Muslim, 38 percent Serb and 18 percent Croatian, serious contenders were weeded out from some 40 parties registered in the republic elections set for November 18.

There is a visible shortage of viable national, all-Yugoslav parties. In this regard, Prime Minister Marković's Alliance of Reform Forces undoubtedly will benefit from a lack of competition as well as from his successful anti-inflation program. According to a *Borba* midsummer public opinion poll, the Prime Minister received a 72 percent vote of confidence as compared with 21 percent for Milošević and 7 percent for the new Croatian president, Franjo Tudjman. Marković has name recognition and national standing. At the same time, however popular the government's bankruptcy policy may be with the IMF, if the 8,608 enterprises that are in serious trouble go out of business (putting some 3.2 million Yugoslav workers out of work), it will not help the government party at the polls.

Moreover, in view of the fact that Serbs in the predominantly Serbian city of Knin have taken up arms to conduct what Croatian authorities view as an illegal referendum on Serbian autonomy within the republic, with Kosovo under what many Kosovar Albanians consider martial law, there are fears that there is no time to waste. The army has warned of "the unforeseeable consequences" of Yugoslav disintegration. In and outside Yugoslavia, there is talk of civil war.

◆

YUGOSLAVIA: TO BE OR NOT TO BE?

This is not the first time that serious questions have been raised about Yugoslavia's ability to pull together instead of pulling apart. For at least ten years before Tito died in 1980, there was speculation that without his charismatic authority, the country faced civil war, an army coup or a return to the Soviet bloc. In these days of post-Communist East Europe we can rule out the third scenario; however, the first two are still possible. Ethnic tensions could escalate into armed conflict either in Croatia or Kosovo. Yugoslav soldiers in politics could lose patience with the chaotic process leading to elections and could move to protect the existing constitutional order.

Evaluating worst-case scenarios is particularly difficult because post-Tito Yugoslav politics has an operatic quality. This combination of verbal sectarianism and negotiated solutions makes it difficult to determine whether the voices of doom and disaster are prophetic or are crying wolf in the choreography of an ongoing political struggle.

Neither these dangers on the Yugoslav road to multiparty democracy nor the legitimate fears of the 600,000 Serbs (as of the 1981 census) in Croatia should be minimized. How can this Serbian minority remain immune to the rising nationalist ferment or the contradictory signals coming from the repercussion of midsummer declarations of sovereignty by Slovenia and Kosovo? For the moment—notwithstanding the warning from the armed forces that the Yugoslav military is prepared to defend Yugoslav territorial integrity—the Slovenes appear to have suffered few consequences. Conversely, Serbian authorities suspended the provincial government following the proclamation by the Albanian-dominated provincial assembly that Kosovo was an "independent unit in Yugoslavia, equal to other republics." With the shape of the future Yugoslav federation or confederation at stake, jockeying for political advantage involves high-risk tactics, including the threat of force.

The Slovene leadership has stressed that sovereignty for Slovenia does not necessarily mean withdrawing from Yugoslavia. Policymakers in Ljubljana see themselves as positioning the republic to take part in a "flexible federation" that would leave Slovenes with an independent legal system, expanded foreign policy powers and control over units of the Yugoslav army stationed on Slovene territory. The Kosovo assembly did not vote to separate; it voted to change its status. The Serbian response was predictable. The leadership drew its own political "line in the sand." In the Serbian view, Kosovo will remain part of Serbia, no matter what federal relationship is negotiated between Yugoslav republics.

Thus, after more than four decades of diverging from the Soviet model of political development, the federal dilemmas in Yugoslavia more closely resemble the problems facing Soviet leaders than the problems of politicians in other post-Communist East European countries. In both the Soviet Union and Yugoslavia, the search for national and ethnic identity creates pressures for political autonomy, fragmentation and decentralization. These pressures are countered by economic realities. The transition to a viable market economy that can survive in the political economy of a common European home requires cooperation, economic integration and substantially less than complete economic sovereignty for the Baltic republics, Slovenia and Croatia. Without the power of taxation, any federal government is hamstrung.

These days the most effective advocate for a federal Yugoslavia with enough power to reform the Yugoslav economy so that it can join the march to a united Europe in 1992 is not Serbia but the European Community (EC). Slovene politicians are well aware that the EC does not want to confront the collapse of Yugoslavia.

Notwithstanding the aggressive tone of the Serbian secretary of state, Aleksandar Prlja, the Serbian leadership knows that prolonged repression in Kosovo risks isolating Serbia in Europe and seriously damaging relations with Washington. There is no Yugoslav equivalent to Soviet President Mikhail Gorbachev to praise or blame; Ante Marković is not Peter Sampras.

Whatever the outcome of the scheduled republic elections, the federal election originally projected for the end of 1990 will take place only when the Yugoslav republics can agree on how to conduct them. Then Yugoslav voters can weigh the issues of economic performance, political autonomy and national identity. Some will vote their pocketbooks or their prejudice. The struggle to strike a compromise between economic reform and national self-determination will continue into 1991.

Living in a Le Carré Novel

✦

Slavenka Drakulić

A Yugoslav writer reports from her home city of Zagreb on the intensifying animosity between Serbs and Croats in early 1991.

I feel dizzy. I suffer from nausea. I have a headache as soon as I open my eyes in the morning. My heart beats too quickly. I perspire and choke—sometimes I think I'll suffocate, since there is not enough air. I am afraid to open newspapers, watch TV or listen to the radio. I don't dare go outside at night. I have bad dreams. And yet I don't visit my doctor. I know there is no cure for my disease, because I simply suffer from the *symptoms of living here,* in a country where even mother's milk is poisoned by politics.

On the surface, everything seems normal. Streetcars are running, people go to work, schools and hospitals are open. But ominous events have been taking place. The Republic of Slovenia passed a referendum declaring its right to secede. Croatia adopted a new Constitution proclaiming its sovereignty. And most recently, the army has threatened a coup.

It seems clear to me now that the symptoms I describe are closely connected

---

with a dangerous and contagious disease that has been developing for some time and spreading in the past couple of years, until no part of this land is spared: It is nationalism, a very specific illness, perhaps characteristic of the Balkans. The disease is shaking the whole country so hard that with every passing day we are further from a remedy, if there is any. For thirty-five years Tito, the Communist Party and the army held Yugoslavia together. Crushed and melted in their iron embrace, Serbs, Croats, Slovenians, Macedonians, Montenegrins, Bosnians, Herzegovinians, Albanians, etc. were ready to recognize the "truth" that in this Arcadia there is no nationalism, only brotherhood and unity. When Tito died eleven years ago, *The Economist* predicted that Yugoslavia would split apart within a year. It was wrong. It took a good ten years, because after Tito died, the Communist Party was still alive. God knows what would have happened if the revolutions of 1989 in Eastern Europe hadn't helped the process along (although they didn't in Serbia). But the third leg of the "iron triangle," the Yugoslav People's Army, is still alive and well. Until now, it was only a wicked presumption of the Croats and the Serbs that the army favored a "Serbian solution" because 80 percent of the commanding cadre are Serbs—that is, retaining the federal and centralized structure of the country as opposed to a confederation of republic-states decentralized to the point of secession, the solution preferred by Croatia and Slovenia. In this country the army has always played an important political role, and no one doubted it would try to continue to play one, despite its proclaimed depoliticization. But not until January did it become apparent that the army is the joker in the federalists' pack—a very dangerous card.

On January 9, the federal presidency announced a ten-day deadline for all illegally armed paramilitary groups and individuals in Yugoslavia to turn in their weapons. However, it was clear that this ultimatum was aimed primarily at the Croatian police reserve, which has been accused by the federal presidency of being armed illegally. The Croatian government rejected this accusation, saying that every sovereign state has the right to arm its police, that it had done so according to the Constitution and that the terrorist groups in Knin, if anyone, should be disarmed first. (Last August, Serbs in Croatia, under the influence of nationalists in Serbia, claimed that their minority rights were imperiled after the election of the new Croatian government, and in protest committed a series of terrorist actions around the town of Knin and proclaimed their autonomy.) On the other hand, the Croatian authorities' intention to constitute the Croatian police as a parallel, republican army was evident. Everyone knew that underlying this ultimatum of the federal presidency was a more important and more dangerous dispute about the legality of the new Croatian non-Communist government, installed after the first free elections were held last April, which the Serbian Communist leader Slobodan Milošević and the army regarded as a threat to the centralized federal system.

Most Yugoslavs, accustomed to political games at the top, didn't pay much attention to the ultimatum. They started to pay attention to it only recently, when salt, sugar and flour couldn't be found in any of the stores here, not even for pancakes. I admit that this frightened me more than the rumors about tanks being sent in—it was more real. And while I could understand why people were hoarding flour, oil and sugar, salt I didn't understand. When a friend's grandmother bought twenty-five kilos of salt, I asked her, Why so much? "Because you can sell it later, or trade it for food," answered the 87-year-old lady, who had survived two world wars. My God, are we coming to this? I thought, opening a kitchen closet and staring at my one-pound store of salt (because salted food is unhealthy!), no sugar and no flour (because they make you fat!), and a little vegetable oil.

Before the deadline, some 200 rifles were returned to the police station—peanuts compared with the automatic rifles, variously estimated at from 20,000 to 80,000, that supposedly have been imported illegally, mainly from Hungary (Hungary admitted the export of 10,000 weapons). The presidency (or I should say the army, because by then it was clear that this decision was made under very strong army pressure) thought so too. The government angrily extended the deadline two more days. The army started rattling its tanks and helicopters, threatening to confiscate the illegal arms directly, which sounded like a threat of a military coup. Still the arms were not turned in.

Croat leaders made speeches psychologically preparing their people for resistance to the army, for civil war. On January 22 and 23, army maneuvers in Croatia were reported. Buses, trains and trucks were posted as barricades at the bridges and entrances to the city of Zagreb. On the evening of January 24, tensions were at a peak. Nobody could be sure that the political games wouldn't involve bloodshed. Nobody slept, the streets were empty, the president of Parliament called an extraordinary session for the next day. Television and radio broadcast news bulletins all night.

But as the longest night in recent history passed, the tension eased and it became clear that the army wouldn't attack, at least not that night. In the morning, after attending the stormy session of Parliament where deputies unanimously called people to arms to defend the sovereignty of Croatia, President Franjo Tudjman, who had previously decided not to attend a scheduled meeting with Serbian leader Milošević "because in this situation it doesn't make any sense," changed his mind and went to Belgrade, realizing that talks were the only way to overcome the biggest crisis yet in relations between the two republics.

In the meantime, the collective federal presidency was in session, and the federal Prime Minister held a Cabinet meeting. In the late evening Tudjman issued a statement announcing a "historic decision": The federal presidency, including the representative of the army, had recognized the Croatian government for the first time in its eight months of existence. The representatives of the republics agreed that the talks at the top about the future of Yugoslavia should continue. The army took the troops off the highest state of alert. We were relieved—but not for long. Everything that followed was not politics but a first-rate spy novel. The day after a cheerful President Tudjman returned from Belgrade, the whole country found itself in the middle of a John le Carré novel. And while it is a very interesting position to be in, it gives one an extremely uneasy feeling.

That Saturday evening, the 26th, Croatian TV broadcast a supposed documentary on the "illegal armament of Croatia." The forty-minute movie was produced by Zastava Film, the army film company. It showed Croatian Defense Minister Martin

Spegelj explaining the illegal importation of arms from Hungary and tactics for attacking army officers and soldiers in the event of civil war. What shook the TV audience, and then the entire country—apart from the question of whether the documentary was true—was the words the Minister used. He talked about execution of army officers in their apartments, along with their wives and children; extermination of Serbs in Knin; assassination of unreliable people; secret lists of people to be killed; liquidation squads. The movie was murky, without close-ups and with a soundtrack so poor that certain words and phrases were unintelligible. (The text was transcribed and run as subtitles.)

Minister Spegelj immediately released a statement saying that phrases and words had been inserted into his speech. He accused the army of manipulating public opinion because the documentary had been broadcast on Serbian TV while talks between Tudjman and Milošević were still going on.

But the top Croat politicians and their advisers apparently didn't coordinate their statements, because President Tudjman's security adviser said that same evening, in a discussion after the movie, that Spegelj was aware that he was being filmed and said what he did on purpose, to send disinformation to army headquarters. To add a dramatic note to the already surreal plot, that same night, after recognizing himself in the movie, a man who had collaborated, perhaps unwillingly, with army intelligence killed himself in front of his wife and friends.

The Croatian media were silent for two days, publishing only Spegelj's statements and waiting for a decision by the Croatian government on his guilt or innocence. The Serbian media had already proclaimed him guilty and called not only for his resignation but for his arrest. The point is that the Croatian and Serbian media took the sides of their governments, and, unlike the press in a democratic country, they didn't show even a minimum of professionalism or investigative spirit. Rather than being journalists, they acted like parrots.

As the story progressed, the people realized that they were only extras in the movie of le Carré's novel, directed by Francis Ford Coppola. The next scene took place at the Zagreb airport on Monday, January 28: We saw President Tudjman on his way to Vienna, saying a joyful farewell to his beleaguered Minister Spegelj. So it seemed that nothing more needed to be said. However, on Tuesday evening Croatian TV broadcast an interview with Spegelj so he could defend himself publicly. But the interviewer didn't dare ask him what should have been asked, so the key questions were left hanging in the air and the Minister departed, leaving the impression that he had handled an extremely difficult and sensitive political situation with too much self-assurance, almost with arrogance.

And then, while Croatian TV was preparing "smashing" proof that the movie was falsified, the army prosecutor issued a warrant to arrest Spegelj for "armed mutiny." The Croatian government and a civil prosecutor answered that the army had no authority to issue such a warrant, and, besides, Spegelj was innocent; he was only performing his duties as Defense Minister. The next day the Croatian delegation walked out of a meeting of the federal presidency. The day after that, Croatian TV broadcast another episode in the drama, showing another person from the incriminating movie who claimed that he was forced to collaborate with army espionage and that in the movie he was saying what he was told to say. The federal presidency said that the army will go to the end. A week later there was another failed attempt to settle the problem peacefully.

As I write this, we are totally victimized by homogenization. There is no possibility anymore of acting or speaking publicly or privately as anything but a Croat or a Serb. All differences—political, ideological, individual—are swept away by the danger of "outside enemies." In a truly democratic country, in spite of pressures and dangers, it would be normal for the opposition to jump on the Spegelj case in an attempt to gain some points for itself in future elections. Not in Croatia. Here the parliamentary opposition (ex-Communists, liberals, social democrats) is giving its support to the central government, i.e., the ruling party, proving that the totalitarian mentality lasts longer than the totalitarian system.

Another consequence of the crisis is the suspension of democracy on all levels. The two most important questions about the controversial movie are: Where did money for importing the arms, legal or illegal, come from? And did the Croatian Parliament know about and approve such an expenditure? These two questions haven't even been asked—not by the opposition, not by journalists, not by the general public. This silence, more than anything, shows where we are and how far the pollution of fear, hate, nationalism and war has advanced. Because the harm has been done already; the ground for civil war has been prepared. We are not only poisoned by politics; it is now our only and ultimate reality. This country is playing a game of Russian roulette, but while the pistol is in the hands of those in power, it is aimed at our heads.

The Yugoslav Crisis: No Solution in Sight

✦

Milan Andrejevich

This Radio Free Europe report summarizes the several ethnic conflicts that threatened, as of early 1991, to tear the country apart, whether or not the central government resorted to military countermeasures.

During the third round of negotiations between federal and republican leaders, on February 8, no headway was made in resolving the long-standing, steadily deteriorating economic and political crisis in Yugoslavia, which in its present form consists of a multinational, loosely knit federation of six republics and two provinces. The Croatian delegation, headed by federal Vice President Stipe Mesić and Croatia's State President Franjo Tudjman, boycotted the meeting, objecting that a planned demonstration of anti-Croatian protesters outside the Palace of the Federation in Belgrade (the seat of the federal government and the State Presidency) would not be conducive to "a calm and peaceful dialogue." In reaction to the Croats' boycott, Slovenian State President Milan Kučan charged that no discussion on Yugoslavia's political future had been opened; it was fruitless to hold talks without Croatia; and protests had created "impossible conditions" for peaceful discussions. He said that Slovenia would begin the process of secession and walked out of the meeting. (The protests in question, involving some 5,000 women, had been organized by the Council of Women–Movement for the Preservation of Yugoslavia in support of the State Presidency and the Yugoslav armed forces. Croatia and Slovenia had also walked out of the second summit meeting on January 31 to protest the armed forces' involvement in politics.) Shortly after Kučan's walkout, which coincided with the start of the women's protest rally, a fourth round of talks was scheduled for February 13 and the meeting was adjourned.

✦

SLOVENIAN SECESSIONIST MOVES

Meanwhile, Slovenian Prime Minister Lojze Peterle, making good earlier threats, announced on February 8 that the republic would take its first concrete step

---

Milan Andrejevich, "What Future for the League of Communists of Yugoslavia?" from *Report on Eastern Europe*, March 2, 1990, pp. 32–36. Reprinted with the permission of Radio Free Europe/Radio Liberty.

toward secession. Peterle said that Slovenia would concentrate its efforts on seceding peacefully rather than on seeking ways to stop Yugoslavia's disintegration. He affirmed that the next Slovenian parliamentary session on February 20 would adopt legislation annulling obligations between the northwestern republic and the rest of Yugoslavia, a move that would, in effect, make Slovenia independent of the Yugoslav federation. Since September 1989, Slovenia has been taking steps toward independence, and the results of a December 1990 referendum in the republic showed overwhelming support for autonomy. On February 7 both Tudjman and Kučan announced that their republics were ready to break with the Yugoslav federation. Tudjman told reporters in Zagreb that his republic was large enough to exist independently, much like Luxembourg, Norway, Denmark, and other European states that are, in fact, smaller in terms both of population and territory. He was expected to announce officially at the February 13 meeting that Croatia would follow Slovenia's suit if the latter seceded. Kučan reiterated the Slovenian position, saying that "if a common road is not possible for a majority in Yugoslavia, which is regrettably more than likely at this point, Slovenia will accept the challenge of life as an autonomous state."

✦

WHAT HAVE TODAY'S LEADERS INHERITED?

The fact that no solution is in sight should come as no surprise. For the past decade, politicians and intellectuals have been saying that Yugoslavia's political paralysis is the principal obstacle to much-needed economic and political change. The paralysis is largely a result of the country's decentralized political structure, within which the leaders of the six republics and the two autonomous provinces defend their own interests at the expense of those of the country as a whole. Yugoslavia's political system has failed to provide a common ground where the diverse interests of Yugoslavia's multinational population could be addressed over the long term, within a constitutional framework. Since 1945, periods of reform have been succeeded by periods of opposition to reform. The reforms undertaken have largely resulted from and been influenced by regional interests and the constitutional controversy, which has dogged Yugoslav leaders from Josip Broz Tito to the current federal and republican leaders. The present trend seems to be toward economic and constitutional reform, but an escalation of regional particularism and nationalism is likely to prevent (as it has in the past) major improvements in the near term.

✦

THE CURRENT DILEMMA

This latest in Yugoslavia's long series of crises appears to have brought the country closer to total disintegration. It is not yet clear how serious the Slovenian and the Croatian secessionist initiatives are, or how determined the federal State Presidency, the federal government, and the Yugoslav People's Army (the YPA, whose

Yugoslavia Breaks Up. This photograph of a Slovene guard on the Austrian border, taken on June 26, 1991, illustrates the collapse of Tito's Yugoslavia and its replacement by a series of nationalist regimes. Slovenia, the smallest, most prosperous, and ethnically most homogeneous of the successor republics, seemed to have the best chance of emerging relatively unscathed. (AP/Wide World Photos)

commander in chief is the State Presidency) are to maintain the federation's fragile unity. There has been much speculation on these points, as well as many dramatic descriptions of what has taken place and what lies in store for the country. But, since the death in 1980 of Tito, communist Yugoslavia's founder, the problem of distinguishing between fact and mere rumor has become increasingly difficult, degenerating into what the Sarajevo daily *Oslobodjenje* described as the "theater of the absurd."

For the past decade, Yugoslavia has been burdened with a multitude of problems, collectively referred to as "the Yugoslav crisis" by many Yugoslav and foreign analysts. It is undeniable that these economic, constitutional, political, and social problems, exacerbated by ethnic tension, have now dramatically come to a head. During the last three years, politicians, intellectuals, and the majority of the media observed numerous developments that, in their estimation, were leading the multinational country to the very brink of civil war. But none of the events during that period were as dramatic as those in the past month. In many respects, Yugoslavia is confronting its worst political crisis since the end of World War II. An increasing number of politicians and journalists believe that civil war and subsequent disintegration are unavoidable, since the country's leaders appear unable—indeed, at times unwilling—to reach a workable compromise. According to the Belgrade daily *Borba,* which is financed by the federal government and the Federal Assembly, "In order to have the politicians open a quiet and reasonable dialogue on the country's future order, it seems that the Yugoslav nations need to start a war."

Radio Belgrade commented recently that "the crisis we are going through at the moment unfortunately seems to confirm the idea that Yugoslavia can choose between only two possibilities: reform or dictatorship." Uncertainty over the country's future is as frightening as the seemingly uncompromising political stances of federal and republican leaders. Yet, 1990 ended with the prospect of a resolution of the conflict: on December 26 and 27, for the first time in two years, the country's leaders (with the exception of Tudjman) sat down together at the negotiating table. They decided to continue meeting until a solution to Yugoslavia's political and economic crises had been found; however, their discussions thus far seem to have confused matters further rather than to have brought the country closer to some sort of a compromise. The meetings, widely referred to as the "YU[goslav] Summit," officially began on January 10; a second meeting was held on January 31 and a third on February 8; a fourth session was scheduled for February 13.

The major bone of contention at present is between those who want strong federal control over the economy (but nominally affirm the sovereignty of the republics) and those who advocate a much looser confederal arrangement that would allow the republics to form an alliance of sovereign states and further decentralize economic and political power in the country. The former position is shared by the majority of the eight-member State Presidency, the YPA (70% of whose noncommissioned and commissioned officers are ethnic Serbs), numerous federal officials, and the Serbian and Montenegrin leaderships. The Croatian and Slovenian leaderships, on the other hand, support the latter, confederal arrangement. This conflict has been exacerbated by long-standing animosities that have their origins in Serbia's historic domination of the state and the armed forces. Since early February, several Slovenian leaders have said that the republic would give up the idea of creating a confederal Yugoslav state as "entirely unrealistic" in view of Serbia's opposition. Kučan said that the failure of the talks meant that "next year the Slovenes would surely live in an independent state": and Joze Pucnik, the President of the Democratic United Opposition of Slovenia, the ruling coalition, said that Slovenian independence would be achieved by June 1991.

Although the leaderships of Yugoslavia's other republics (Bosnia and Herzegovina and Macedonia), as well as federal Prime Minister Ante Marković, have not, during the past two months, explicitly expressed their views on the feasibility of trying to maintain the current federal system, they appear to favor strong federal control over economic matters only, leaving responsibility for the day-to-day business of politics to the republics. Marković seeks the support of all the republics for his "11 conditions," the minimum framework required, in his view, to ensure the continuation of economic and political reforms during a transitional period. The conditions include common defense and monetary policies, respect for federal laws, the continued financing of the federal government, and the convertibility of the dinar.

◆

FAINT GLIMMER OF HOPE

The secessionist trends in Croatia and Slovenia and the threat of a possible military intervention in the two republics have dashed hopes of resolving the crisis in the near future. Yet, the possibility of preventing the country's dissolution through nonviolent means should not be completely discounted. The latest series of meetings is cause for guarded optimism. First, the mere fact that they were held is an achievement: nearly two years had already elapsed since all the important political players had come together (with the exception of the final congress of the League of Communists of Yugoslavia [LCY] in January 1990). Second, the latest meetings were the first to include republican leaders who came to office through democratic, multiparty elections. Since the last LCY congress, multiparty elections brought to power noncommunist governments in four republics: in Croatia and in Bosnia and Herzegovina, non-Communists predominate; and in Slovenia and Macedonia the reform Communists, while playing an important role, no longer hold the monopoly on political power. (The majority of those in power today were at one time either influential Communists or party regulars. In Serbia and Montenegro, the Socialists—formerly the Communists—and the Montenegrin League of Communists are still in power.) Thus, the recent negotiations for a "new" Yugoslavia (which, in fact, began with the First Conference of the LCY in May 1988) involved both old and new political players for the first time. These leaders brought to the summit meeting a blend of realism and optimism that the situation requires: they have admitted that a solution is far from sight but stress that their promise to continue negotiations until a solution is found is itself an important victory.

◆

PRESIDENTIAL DECREE PROVOKES CRISIS

On January 9, as the country's leaders prepared for the January 10 YU Summit meeting, the Yugoslav State Presidency issued a decree calling for the disarmament of all "illegal paramilitary units" in the country within 10 days. The decree stipulated that maintaining the internal stability and security of Yugoslavia was to be the exclusive domain of the YPA and the federal and regional state security agencies. Croatia and Slovenia refused to comply with the order. In contrast to the prevailing situation during the past three years, it was Croatia, rather than Slovenia, that was on the verge of clashing with the YPA when the decree was published, and leaders throughout the country scrambled to defuse the conflict. The members of the State Presidency (with the exception of the Slovenian representative Janez Drnovsek and the Croatian representative Mesić) and the federal government supported the decree; but all those involved, whether opposed or in favor, advocated a peaceful, negotiated settlement of the issue.

The nine-point decree was published in reaction to reports from the Secretariat for National Defense, which, together with Croatia's obstinacy, almost caused an open clash between the YPA and Croatia. The decree claimed that "in certain parts of the country weapons from neighboring and other countries are being secretly imported and distributed to citizens depending on their national and political affiliations." This accusation did not appear to be explicitly aimed at a particular republic or ethnic group, but it was obvious that the decree was an attempt by the federal leadership to assert its influence over Croatia and Slovenia. In rejecting the decree, both republics implied that they would deal themselves with the issue of "illegal paramilitary units" through their respective security forces and laws.

The reference to unidentified "illegal paramilitary units" in the decree was believed to target Tudjman's party, the Croatian Democratic Community. The order that all weapons seized by citizens be returned within 10 days was in accordance with a law established under the 1974 federal constitution. Even Tudjman conceded that "the decree was acceptable in the formal sense, because it concerned the disarmament of illegal groups"; but he stressed the Croats' view that it "was essentially aimed at disarming the Republic of Croatia."

At the time of the decree's issuance, the media were already quoting "confidential" sources who claimed that both Slovenia and Croatia had purchased weapons from Italy and Hungary, needed for a new wave of recruitments for the republican internal security forces. (Most of the new recruits were destined for the newly formed police reserve units.) On the basis of federal laws stating that such purchases are legal only when the territorial defense commander and the republican Ministry of Internal Affairs coordinate them with the appropriate federal ministries and that republican territorial defense systems are under the jurisdiction of the federal Secretariat of Defense, federal officials judged the Croatian and Slovenian purchases to be illegal. Croatia and Slovenia challenged the federal government's interpretation of the law, angering the State Presidency and the YPA, and claimed the decree was specifically directed against their laws that transferred command of the territorial defense system to their respective republics. Croatia took its objections one step further, insisting that the decree was an attempt to undermine the democratically elected Croatian government.

The decree was also directed at those Serbs in Croatia who had raided police and territorial defense armories last August, jeopardizing not only Croatia's stability but also Serb-Croat relations in general and Serb-Croat-Moslem relations in neighboring Bosnia and Herzegovina. The Serbs in Croatia, who account for some 12% of the republic's population of 4,600,000, have repeatedly claimed that the Tudjman government is genocidal and that Croatia's policies are aimed at the elimination of Serbian cultural and historic rights. On December 22 a new Croatian Constitution was promulgated, opening the way for Croatia's declaration of independence and possible secession by a plebiscite. Croat leaders, like the Slovenes, had stated prior to the issuance of the presidential decree that Croatia would secede if a peaceful solution to the political and constitutional crisis could not be found within six months. On December 21, the eve of the promulgation of the new constitution, Croatia's Serbian activists declared the predominantly Serb-populated Krajina region of Croatia autonomous. On January 10 the leaders of Croatia's Serbian community appealed to their constituents to return all weapons they had "borrowed" to the local police and republican militia storage areas. Milan Babić, a leader of the self-designated Serbian Autonomous Region of Krajina, made the announcement. On January 16, Serbs began to return some, but not all, of the weapons they had seized last summer. On January 30 Tudjman acknowledged that the Croatian government had ordered weapons following disturbances last summer in the Croatian city of Knin and the region surrounding it, where the majority of the inhabitants are Serbs.

On January 13 Mesić tried to reassure the Croats, saying that the Croatian government was "so strong that it [could] defend itself"; he added that it feared "no repressive action of the sort just demonstrated in [the Lithuanian capital of] Vilnius." Following a statement released on January 15 by the federal Secretariat of Defense warning that it was "determined to carry out the presidential decree," Slaven Letica, a chief adviser to Tudjman, said he thought the statement was timed to coincide with the events in the Baltic republics and the Gulf crisis, which, he said, provided "cover for the military to implement a bloody resolution of the Yugoslav crisis." YPA leaders repeatedly declared that the references to a pending putsch were ridiculous and unfounded. Indeed, as the developments continued to unfold and rumors of a planned military coup became increasingly widespread, key political leaders such as Mesić, Tudjman, and the State Presidency's representative from Bosnia and Herzegovina, Bogić Bogicević, stressed that negotiations were the only way to settle disputes. Mesić declared confidently, "Yugoslavia, despite everything, is entering a more peaceful period"; and Bogicević remarked that the "insinuations about the YPA's plans for a coup do not hold water. The YPA has never overstepped its legal powers."

One day prior to its expiration, on January 19, the State Presidency extended for two more days the decree's ten-day deadline for turning in all weapons in order to give Croatia time to comply with the order. Tudjman told the Croatian National Assembly on January 25 that the battle against Croatia was "not being waged by legal and political argument but by special warfare and military pressure." He added that the YPA was attempting to take the crisis into its own hands, bypassing its own commander in chief (the State Presidency). The situation was temporarily defused the same day when Tudjman, the State Presidency, and the military agreed that the YPA would call off its full state of combat readiness in Croatia and that the republic, in turn, would comply with the decree by disarming its paramilitary reserve police forces.

◆

THE SPEGELJ AFFAIR

While the agreement was being negotiated, Belgrade Television broadcast a 40-minute, black-and-white video tape that had been produced over a four-month period by the YPA's Counterintelligence Service. It showed Croatian government officials discussing both arms purchases from Hungary, the USA, and other countries, as well as how to wage civil war in Croatia. Although the tape sent shock waves through the country, its authenticity was the subject of much controversy: the sound was not clear, and Serbo-Croatian subtitles were required to understand the muffled conversations. The film's narrator said that Croatia's Ministers of Defense, retired Colonel General Martin Spegelj, and of Internal Affairs, Josip Bojkovać, had discussed arms imports and drawn up plans for "subversive terrorist actions." During two segments filmed on October 14 and 19, 1990, Spegelj purportedly told two officers that "each member of the army will be slaughtered. We have to kill everyone so that not a single soldier reaches his barracks alive." Spegelj allegedly went on to say, "There will be a civil war in which there will be no mercy toward anyone, not even women and children." This gruesome conversation reportedly took place in Spegelj's kitchen; the video showed a bottle on the table, and Spegelj seemed inebriated.

Spegelj himself said the film was a fake and promised to prove his innocence. On January 30 the federal military prosecutor's office in Zagreb ordered the Croatian police to arrest and turn over Spegelj to the federal authorities. The charges against him were arming paramilitary groups and planning attacks on YPA personnel, their families, and military installations. Croatian officials refused to comply with the order. Tudjman said that Spegelj had not been and would not be detained, and his aide Mario Nobilo stated that "Croatian police do not arrest Croatian ministers."

Some interesting questions were raised by the Yugoslav press concerning the Spegelj affair. The Belgrade news magazine *Intervju* quoted Dragisa Vukasinvić, a respected Belgrade lawyer, as asking if Spegelj had actually been filmed planning to incite civil war, terrorism, and murder, "why he was not immediately arrested, as would have been the case in all other countries?" On January 27, Mesić told Sarajevo Television that Spegelj was "bluffing" by having "intentionally planted misinformation, knowing that it would be fed to the other side." The Belgrade daily *Politika* pointed out that Spegelj and Tudjman's staff had failed to coordinate their respective versions of the incident, with the result that Spegelj was

> saying the video tape was fabricated, while Tudjman's adviser Ante Barisić said it was authentic but that Spegelj, knowing he was being taped, played the game perfectly with the intention of showing that Croatia was stronger than had been assumed.

The Belgrade daily *Borba* commented that "if the tape were authentic, it showed a horrifying terrorism of a kind not advocated even by profascist and racist organizations in democratic societies." The daily added that if Barisić's "most naive explanation . . . that Spegelj was playing games were true, [then] the democratically elected authorities were playing Russian roulette with the people."

Spegelj, a member of the Party for Democratic Changes (formerly the League of Communists of Croatia), was appointed Croatia's Defense Minister on August 24, 1990, following a conflict between Tudjman's government and Serbian activists in the Croatian town of Knin over the minority rights of Serbs in Croatia. From the mid-1970s to 1982 Spegelj was in Serbia, where he worked for the General Staff of the YPA and as Chief of Staff of the First Military District headquartered in Belgrade; thus, he is thought to have been the commander of the current YPA Chief of Staff, Colonel General Blagoje Adzić, a Serb who has quarreled with Yugoslav Vice President Mesić. In 1979 he was sentenced by a military court in Split to a two-month prison term, which he never served, for having criticized the party and the military hierarchy for tolerating Serbian nationalism. From 1982 to 1985 Spegelj served as Territorial Defense Commander for Croatia; and from 1985 until early 1990 he was Commander of the Fifth Army District, which comprises Croatia and Slovenia and has its head-quarters in Zagreb. The 63-year-old Spegelj is widely regarded as "the liberal general" and was one of the first high-ranking military officials to advocate multiparty elections. In an interview in July 1990, he emphasized that the YPA would not engage in armed intervention anywhere in Yugoslavia, because "the multiparty system has been developing in a relatively peaceful manner." In November he told reporters that the threat of YPA intervention did not exist; at the same time, he warned that the YPA was "not capable of democratizing." Spegelj, whom the Croatian government has steadfastly refused to turn over to the federal military authorities, is reportedly being kept in a Croatian government building under heavy guard.

Spegelj's appointment was one of several major personnel changes in the Croatian government and ministries, made not merely as a concession to the other Croatian parties but also with the aim of persuading the Croatian government and the Croatian National Assembly to band together to support Tudjman. The changes demonstrated the government's ability to react quickly in crisis situations. Moreover, through the appointments of Spegelj and Mesić (who will take over as head of the State Presidency on May 16, 1991), the Croatian government strengthened its bargaining position, not only within the republic but with the federal State Presidency and the YPA.

◆

THE MILITARY FACTOR

Meanwhile, as federal and republican leaders were holding their round-table meetings on the future of Yugoslavia, the military was becoming more in evidence than at any time since World War II. It took no direct action to break the stalemate between the federal authorities and the independent-minded republics of Croatia and Slovenia; yet, it still emerged at the forefront of the political scene. Although the YPA had officially begun to depoliticize itself on December 13, 1990, with the disbanding of its organization in the LCY, it followed the example of several republican communist parties by simply retaining the organization under the party's new name. With the assistance of senior military officers, including retired generals and admirals, the conservatives in the former LCY formed the League of Communists—Movement for Yugoslavia (LC–MY). The LC–MY, which was organized in mid-November, held its founding convention on December 21. The YPA, however, stressed that its personnel were not required to join the LC–MY and that membership was based solely on individual preference.

But the YPA is more active than ever before thanks to its commander in chief: the State Presidency has underscored the military's importance, not through the tough words and warnings used in the past, but through ultimatums. For the first time, the State Presidency gave the YPA free rein to implement a presidential decree. Thus far, the YPA has arrested some 20 individuals in Croatia who either failed to comply with the terms of the decree or were charged with engaging in activities against the state. The military's higher profile has sparked a debate throughout Yugoslavia about the role the YPA should play in Yugoslav politics. The majority of Croatian and Slovenian leaders believe that the YPA should be depoliticized; leaders in Bosnia and Herzegovina and in Macedonia also share this view in principle. The YPA, they argue, should remain "Yugoslav in character, completely devoid of politics." On February 10 the federal government submitted to the Federal Assembly draft legislation that would ban all political organizations in the armed forces. This move may defuse tension between the federal authorities and the republics of Slovenia and Croatia.

A document (whose authenticity is not confirmed), reportedly originating from the YPA's Political Directorate and published in several Yugoslav newspapers on January 31, sparked more controversy and rumors. Released by Slovenia's Information Secretariat, the document pledged that the YPA would defend the country against "anti-communist hysteria" and stated that "the functioning of the federal system must be assured." The document concluded that proposals for a Yugoslav confederation ignored the fact that "such a state cannot exist."

◆

SUMMIT ASSESSMENTS

The first YU Summit meeting on January 10 did not resolve the current crisis, but at least it ended with an agreement to hold extensive bilateral talks between federal and republican leaders that would continue until a peaceful solution was found. And, in fact, thanks to that meeting, bilateral talks were held from January 14 to 25, at which most of the participants expressed optimism that within six months a new constitutional order would be established. In the interim, however, the talks have merely resulted in a further deterioration of the situation and exasperated Slovenia's and Croatia's leaders, who believe the federal leadership incapable of resolving the crisis.

A few days prior to the January 10 summit meeting, a major financial scandal erupted that undoubtedly cast a shadow over the critical proceedings. On January 7 the federal government revealed that Serbia had issued $1.4 billion in unauthorized loans to the republic by printing money without federal approval. The Serbian National Assembly voted in a closed session on December 27 to authorize the printing of the money without the permission of the Yugoslav National Bank. Serbia needed the money to pay for pensions, subsidies to the agricultural sector, and the bailing out of failing Serbian enterprises. The federal government claimed the move threatened economic reform, and the Republics of Croatia and Slovenia condemned the action. Yugoslav federal Secretary for Finance Branimir Zekan announced on January 10 that Serbia had returned about $250,000,000 of the unauthorized loans. This scandal on the eve of the January 10 meeting, not to mention the State Presidency's decree, exacerbated the already tense situation and unleashed a flood of accusations and rumors. Many Yugoslav and foreign journalists gloomily predicted Yugoslavia's imminent demise.

Surprisingly, not much was said during the bilateral discussions about the status and future of Serbia's province of Kosovo, where more than 90% of the population are ethnic Albanians. In July 1990, Serbia suspended Kosovo's government and in September it completed its 18-month drive to annul the autonomous governments of Kosovo and Yugoslavia's other self-governing province, Vojvodina, through the promulgation of a new constitution. During the January 10 summit meeting, Hisen Kajdomcaj, Kosovo's State President, warned that future negotiations must not neglect the interests of the Albanian population; Albanian leaders throughout the country expressed similar views. In the past two months, the situation in Kosovo has reportedly become so tense that ethnic Albanian opposition leaders fear they cannot appeal much longer to the population to remain peaceful. Last year, the federal authorities expressed concern over the rapid pace at which ethnic Albanians and the minority Serbs in Kosovo were arming themselves. The State Presidency's decree was also aimed at groups in Kosovo and western Macedonia who illegally armed themselves with the assistance of local political movements. Fearing unrest at home and anticipating a possible need for reinforcements, Macedonian officials announced on February 8 they were ordering the withdrawal of the Macedonian contingent of the federal militia units stationed in Kosovo.

By and large, however, the summit meetings have thus far produced no surprises. Serbian State President Slobodan Milošević's announcement at the January 10 meeting that Serbia would seek to unite all Serbs in Yugoslavia into a single state if the country became a confederation of independent states was hardly novel. His pronouncement was widely interpreted as meaning that Serbia would attempt to absorb large sections of the neighboring republics of Croatia, Bosnia and Herzegovina, and Macedonia. The leaders attending the summit meetings in Belgrade were well acquainted with Milosevic's ideas for protecting Serbian national interests, and his statements were by no means their main focus of concern. Nor were Croatia's January 31 walkout and February 8 boycott and Slovenia's secessionist moves surprising. Yugoslav Prime Minister Marković's stand remains for the most part unaltered. The Republic of Montenegro remains steadfastly on Serbia's side. Bosnia and Herzegovina recently offered a third model for Yugoslavia to follow, a compromise between the federal and confederal models. Although Macedonia has not yet clearly committed itself to a particular form of government for a "new" Yugoslavia, it seems to be leaning toward a less extreme version of confederation. (On January 25 Macedonia's multiparty National Assembly did adopt a declaration of sovereignty, including a clause on the right to secede, which would be determined by a plebiscite.) The provinces of Vojvodina and Kosovo also made their views heard, although their specific concerns were not addressed at the meetings. The Belgrade daily *Borba* strongly criticized the State Presidency prior to the third round of talks on February 8, commenting:

> It would be best if the two bristling republics of Serbia and Croatia were to agree on how to settle the Yugoslav problem first, before the federal State Presidency organizes an all-Yugoslav consultation on the country's future. It has become clear that the State Presidency is not the place where the conflicting sides will reconcile or come to any solution whatsoever in the present "Kalashnikov" phase of negotiations. The State Presidency has failed to formulate a single common stand that would be reliable proof that there is a point to the negotiations. Instead [the negotiations] now seem to be closer to a definitive end than ever before. As it turns out, it would appear that the talks have progressed from dispute to separation rather than to agreement.

Press commentaries on the failed February 8 session and Croatia's boycott were harsh. *Oslobodjenje* wrote that the women's rally had obviously suited Tudjman, giving him a pretext to demonstrate his sovereignty and to drop out of the talks. *Borba* noted that the anti-Croatian rally had not been a strong enough reason—and had probably not been the real reason—for the Croatian representatives' absence. The daily criticized the action as a "drastic move that again placed Croatia in a provocative and isolated position in relation to other parts of Yugoslavia." It also questioned whether the boycotts had been only an excuse for radical separatist moves, observing that "the unconstructive behavior of some republican leaders might be pushed into the background by an alliance of others who are more constructive." The daily may have had Bosnia and Herzegovina and Macedonia in mind, and possibly Serbia, which has maintained a low profile over the past two weeks. The Ljubljana daily *Delo* commented on the situation in Yugoslavia as "a spontaneous and uncontrolled dying of the state," adding that the situation was characterized by "a fragile and even forced balance of fear."

◆

WHAT NEXT?

The Zagreb daily *Vjesnik* recently commented that none of the participants in the talks on Yugoslavia's future political order was showing any flexibility in its position and warned that the republican leaders' participation in the talks was only a cover for the preparations for war that had been made. *Borba* observed that many people were still not aware of all of the passions and political irresponsibility involved in the latest developments, which had made the danger of a clash with the Croatian paramilitary forces and the YPA and the outbreak of civil war very real. The daily commented that "politicians first mobilize the people as privates and then promise dialogue and a new historic accord" on Yugoslavia's future. The newspaper suggested that the politicians were following the logic that "the greater the hysteria among the people, the better the atmosphere for a democratic dialogue." *Borba* warned that arming the people was more likely to lead to a 100-year civil war than to dialogue and that the dangerous game the politicians seemed to be playing could easily get out of hand.

Probably the most damning statement made during the latest summit meeting was by federal State President Borislav Jović: "We have achieved both the complete collapse of the country and the impossibility of reaching a political agreement." He went on to say that the country's leaders should take whatever measures they could; if they did not, he said, they deserved to be replaced for their lack of responsibility. His pessimistic assessment is bound to generate much discussion. It is altogether likely, however, that Jović was expressing the view of many federal and republican leaders that Yugoslavia is on the verge of a violent breakup and that, in an emergency, the State Presidency would have no choice but to mobilize the military, a measure that is strongly opposed in most parts of Yugoslavia. Tito once threatened to use military force at the height of the Croatian crisis in 1971. The army was also used to quell rioting in Kosovo in 1945, 1968, and 1981 and has been called in to assist the federal militia and the local police in the province several times since 1987. But it would be the first time in Yugoslavia's postwar history that the military were called in to settle a constitutional and political crisis.

Nevertheless, all the leaders agree, at least formally, that Yugoslavia has no chance of surviving unless it creates a system that provides some common ground for all the republics: in Marković's words, "a minimum agreement" that would at least establish an integrated market economy. The greatest fear is that Yugoslavia will simply continue to move from one constitutional crisis to the next, smoothing over differences with vaguely worded legislation and constitutions. The danger now, as tension escalates, particularly among the various ethnic groups, with the threat of labor unrest mounting and as secessionist forces gain momentum, is that nationalist fervor or political exigencies might cause the crisis to take a different, more violent course. And recent events, according to the assessments of many observers within Yugoslavia, may justify those fears.

THE REGION

✦ *The East European members of the Soviet bloc have always been distinctive, even when their individuality seemed to be obscured by the uniformities of the so-called Soviet model to which they were subject. The processes of change initiated by Gorbachev after 1985 eventuated in a veritable orgy of individuality as, for the first time, it became clear that the Soviet Union would no longer enforce its alliance system in the region. Each country responded in its own way, united it seemed only by a loathing of alien domination and the ideology that was its apologia.*

But after so many years of operating according to a single socioeconomic scheme and a common political order, it would be surprising if no shared traits survived. In fact, of course, there are such, and they are all vexatious problems, most notably the search for adequate mechanisms for registering the preferences of citizens against the backdrop of profound economic inefficiency and the crushing burden of environmental damage. These region-wide problems are sampled in the selections that follow.

The New Eastern Europe

✦

Ronald Linden

An analyst for *Report on Eastern Europe* surveys here, as of mid-1990, the major problems shared by the East European states after the initial phase of reform had definitely dethroned the old order throughout the region.

Even when the states of Eastern Europe were all covered by the appellation "communist," there were often stark differences in the way that ideology and politics were applied from state to state. The endurance of private agriculture and the Church in Poland, for example, contrasted sharply with the virtually total collectivization of agriculture and suppression of civil liberties in Romania.

Thus, it should not be surprising that in mid-1990 Eastern Europe is displaying a divergence rather than a uniformity of developments now that revolution has become evolution. In some countries, such as Hungary, the formerly dominant communist party has all but disappeared as a national political actor, while in others, such as Bulgaria, the renamed and purportedly reformed party still heads the government and holds a majority in parliament. In Poland the former "outs" are now firmly "in" and, like many movements that have made such a transition, Solidarity finds the struggle to maintain unity while in power at least as challenging as the struggle to achieve power in the first place. On the other hand, in Romania some of those at the very pinnacle of power are people who held it once before, though not at the same level, and they have shown a disturbing tendency to imitate the behavior of their predecessors when it comes to dealing with the opposition.

As for economic reform, "shock therapy" has been tried only in Poland, perhaps because its situation was the most dire, while still vigorous but less dramatic changes have begun in Hungary and Czechoslovakia. The moves toward reform in Bulgaria and Romania have been the least rapid, perhaps because the new governments there feel less secure about the impact of reform on their political support. All these states have eagerly begun to seek Western investment and even assistance, but only East Germany was in a position to take this to its logical conclusion and be economically absorbed by the Federal Republic, preparatory to full political union.

Ronald Linden, "The New Eastern Europe," from *Report on Eastern Europe*, July 13, 1990, pp. 1–5. Reprinted with the permission of Radio Free Europe/Radio Liberty.

✦
DEVELOPMENT OF THE DEMOCRATIC PROCESS

Recognition of these differences should not cloud our vision of the common dynamics of political development, which are occurring in varying degrees through the region and which allow a certain assessment of the progress of the states of East Europe on the road to becoming simply another part of Europe.

Most important of these has been the development of the democratic process. In this respect, as we gauge the movement of the East European states away from state-directed socialism, it is the processes by which this takes place that are more important than the specific results. Thus, the fact that the Bulgarian Socialist Party (BSP), formerly the Bulgarian Communist Party, won a majority in the recent elections does not by itself disqualify that country for consideration as democratic, since the election and run-off were judged by independent observers to have been free of large-scale manipulation and fraud. The electorate's long-standing and well-grounded apprehension and the impression left by some instances of fear and smear campaigns against opponents will, however, take time to eliminate, underlining the central importance of the electoral process itself in the movement toward what is commonly recognized as a democratic system.

In this respect the institutionalization of the democratic process is key. And the first act for virtually all the new legislatures in Eastern Europe will be the framing of new constitutions. Although these will not by themselves guarantee the continuation of democratic governments, they will answer important questions about the commitment of the new governments and the opposition to the new system and should establish a legal, institutional base from which both government and opposition alike can offer their choices to the public. Crucial cases to watch in this respect will be Bulgaria and Romania; especially the latter where the National Salvation Front's overwhelming majority in the legislature could lead to the re-establishment of one-party rule if a legitimate role is not created for opposing political forces.

✦
GROWING PLURALISM

The existence of such forces throughout Eastern Europe signifies the pluralization of politics throughout the region. In some of the East European states opposition forces did, of course, exist before the revolutions; but their politics had to be underground, unofficial, and usually unrecognized. None of the new governments in the region, not even the Romanian, has that luxury anymore. The range of voices and forces that appeared during and after the revolution has become part of the political process. There are parties, papers, and people representing the entire spectrum of political views and starting from the principle that they have a right to a role in formulating policy or in the government that makes policy.

Hand in hand with this development has come the pluralization of the media. This is one of the most uneven developments in the region. In some countries (Poland

and Hungary, for example) the press and even the broadcast media have become privately owned. But in Bulgaria the central government's predominance within the media threatens to become media dominance, especially outside the capital; and in Romania vigilante actions such as the unleashing of the miners on the opposition had the immediate effect of crippling the independent press.

✦

OTHER INDICATORS

There are other markers of the progress being made in these East European states. In reviewing the past six months it is worth noting where and to what extent the people of the past have been replaced by those of the future, or at least the present. There have been some spectacular cases of this, such as in Czechoslovakia where virtually the whole government and, of course, the presidency have been replaced by people with perspectives diametrically opposite to their predecessors'. This is also the case, to say the least, in East Germany where parties in the election vied with each other to demonstrate their commitment to unification and thus to their own political demotion, if not demise.

But Wojciech Jaruzelski, the person who declared martial law on Solidarity in 1981, is still president in Poland; and Ion Iliescu, once close enough to Nicolae Ceaușescu to be seen as his heir, is now president in Romania. More broadly, in most of the countries, the national *nomenklatura,* which brought each ruling party's reach and power to all areas of the country and sectors of the economy, is still in place and, as seen in Bulgaria and Romania, capable of asserting its political will or blocking the will of others.

Probably the most important of the party's instruments, the security apparatus, has still to be effectively dispersed or controlled. The various new governments are pursuing this project at a relatively slack pace, with East Germany again being the exception. The actual degree of power retained by the secret police in any of the countries is uncertain but in the worst instances, such as Romania, the public perception is that they remain in force and in power. And it is after all this perception that gives such forces their power and which acts to slow or block progress toward the creation of an open and competitive political system. Even where the leadership is committed to their dissolution, such as in East Germany and Czechoslovakia, the security forces played a role in determining the public's choice of candidates simply by having their names associated with past security activities.

Some benchmarks for assessing democratic developments in Eastern Europe cannot be evaluated yet. For example, a key element in a democracy is that governments can not only be voted in but can also be voted out. Though democratically elected, a government not vulnerable to rejection by the electorate could proceed to use its mandate, especially a strong one, to govern autocratically. It could deny the opposition the platform and resources needed to function and could determine its policies without regard for the opposition's views, doing so without fear of being removed because of its policies.

This was perhaps the central common feature of communist rule in East Europe during the past four decades—the relative absence of political vulnerability. Leaders at the top could be removed by each other or with the interference of powerful neighbors. Sometimes, only very occasionally, a public action would precipitate a change. But the leadership, much less the party as a whole, did not have to present its program for public approval either directly or indirectly. Neither its policies nor its people had to undergo any public scrutiny that might, even in theory, result in their removal.

The revolutions of 1989 changed that, most dramatically, as evidenced by the rapidity with which once dominant communist parties changed their leaders, their official principles, and their names as the prospect of elections loomed. In those elections the once unchallengeable communist parties of Czechoslovakia, Hungary, and East Germany were forced to yield their control, a development that marked the beginning of a transition to democracy. In Poland a fully open national election has yet to be held and in Bulgaria the party once known as communist won a majority under the label "socialist." These elections essentially ratified the results of the different revolutions that had pushed the parties to the brink. They were thus both a culmination and an important first step on a path that will, if the experience of the democratic states holds, see many future turnovers occasioned by ballots rather than bullets.

✦

MASS POLITICS

The question of a government's political vulnerability points to other interrelated phenomena that have been evident in East European politics since the revolution. One is the rise—and perhaps fall—of mass politics. Not since the end of World War II had the populations of the East European states found themselves engaged in determining the future of their countries, whether by referendum on its form of government, as occurred when Hungarians voted on how to vote for the new presidency, or through involvement in any of the hundreds of new political parties or public action groups tied to issues rather than parties. It was the revolutions that catalyzed this new public involvement. Then the campaigns and elections and the prospect of an uncertain but now malleable future sustained it.

But there is growing evidence of the exhaustion of political participation. Voter turnouts in successive run-off elections in Hungary and Poland became smaller, which had been foreshadowed by reports of lower turnouts at rallies and campaign meetings. It may be that the intense period of revolutionary upheaval, the creation almost from scratch of a participatory electoral system, and the almost constant politicking since then has run its course. With the basis laid and the system now given a push, there will be a strong temptation, based on real need, for people to devote their energies to the more individualist aspects of their lives. Indeed, the economic reforms either in place or in mind throughout the region will require them to do so as the state's heavy but supporting hand disappears. High voter turnouts and broad participation in policy making are not absolute requisites for democracy, as seen by the case of the United States, but in the absence of a century or two of democratic experience, such involvement may be a more critical factor.

✦

THE SEARCH FOR LEGITIMACY

Hoping to keep that involvement, at least on their side, most of the governments of the new Eastern Europe are engaging in a new search for legitimacy. At first it was enough for the new leaders and parties of Czechoslovakia, Poland, and Hungary to base their right to govern on the replacement of discredited predecessors. That appeal actually allowed them to carry through the revolution and set up the new institutions. But their role atop these new institutions will depend to some extent on the degree to which they accurately assess and respond to newly active populations.

Most of the governments will have a hard time securing public support with economic gifts; the cupboard is bare. Most will have to rely on creating a firm public perception that they are the rightful rulers, as shown by their responsiveness to national aspirations. In some cases simply reversing the policies of the past will gain them this credibility and legitimacy. Witness the support for the National Salvation Front in Romania based in large part on the undoing of Ceauşescu's policies on food and energy. In several cases returning to the population national symbols, such as the flag or place and street names, gains the government good will. Even better is to have a person of symbolic stature in a place of prominence and power, for example, President Havel.

The temptation when such actions are not enough or are unavailable will be to follow baldly nationalistic policies, to assert prerogatives specific to one country or to one region of a country in order to clear the system of its previously slavish, if not always truthful, adherence to "internationalist" demands. Such elements can be seen in the political discourse almost everywhere in Eastern Europe and played an important part in the political campaign and elections in Hungary and Czechoslovakia. It also put some new governments, for example, the Czechoslovak and Bulgarian, in the political bind of trying to respond to the demands of long suppressed nationalities while avoiding a political backlash that would rob them of national support and cohesion.

The ethnic issue within the East European states looms large on the horizon for several governments. It is also clear that it is not and will not remain a "domestic" issue as newly open relationships allow for cross national criticism and pressure. In the past, long-simmering disputes were passed over in silence in the name of "fraternal unity" in the Warsaw Pact. Faced with contrasting demands, it will be a secure government indeed that resists the allure of aggressive nationalist policies.

✦

THE SEARCH FOR ECONOMIC AND INTERNATIONAL ALTERNATIVES

The new governments also have in common the search for economic alternatives. All have recognized the need to move away from the state- and party-dominated system practiced till now, and some parties and leaders have made Milton Friedman sound like the minister of state planning. The problems facing each of the economies are similar in form if not degree: state-subsidized enterprises; a lack of competition and real prices; nominal full employment but, in practice, an underemployed work force; huge unsatisfied consumer demand, contributing to inestimable monetary "overhangs" in the economy; inefficiency and environmental damage in the extraction and use of resources; and insufficient integration into the world economy. All of these problems must be faced using an inadequate and technologically backward infrastructure. Communications systems, computer systems, road systems, and sewage systems all must be built or rebuilt.

To make the dilemma even more acute, progress must be accomplished in a way that causes the least social pain. Not because the new governments are altruistic but because they know, as governments before them did not, that they and their policies can and will be subject to public assessment and, quite possibly, rejection.

The states of the region are not facing these daunting tasks totally alone. Most have received pledges of economic assistance from the world's major industrial states, although Romania was recently excluded because of the miners' rampage against demonstrating students. Most have also made their petitions to the International Monetary Fund and the World Bank and sought commercial credits and Western joint ventures to help their economies. This is part of an overall redefinition of their international relationships, which each are undergoing. In the most extreme case, East Germany, this involves its disappearance as a separate independent country. Less dramatic but equally significant changes are being pursued by the other states. Hungary has announced its intention to withdraw from the Warsaw Pact. Czechoslovakia has undertaken the most active diplomatic efforts as it seeks to create a new central and West European reference group to replace its enforced presence in the "Eastern" neighborhood.

For all of the states of the region this redefinition has meant, above all, a shift in relations with the region's two major powers: the Soviet Union and a united Germany. In the latter case this has taken the form of supporting the national aspirations of the German people as a whole while ensuring that in the process their own peace of mind—and [that] of Europe—is not threatened. This has the most immediacy for Poland but its government and those of the other East European states seem eager to look beyond the new political map to the new economic force with which they must reckon and from which they hope to benefit. For the time being, absorbing East Germany is likely to preoccupy a good deal of Germany's economic effort; but with that accomplished and on the basis of an already strong presence in the region, Germany can be expected to play a major role in East European economic recovery.

On the Eastern dance floor it is not simply a question of changing the music but of which partner will lead. Seeking out this new relationship need not, as Polish leaders have made clear, mean reverting to a hostile relationship or even in this case the immediate withdrawal of Soviet troops. But it is clear that it will mean for Poland and for the rest of the East European states the opportunity to practice policies which accord with their national needs as defined in Prague or Budapest rather than Moscow. Such policies had always been pursued more or less discreetly before Gorbachev, but they will now be asserted publicly, especially if new governments want to retain public support, and within policy frameworks that are no longer so narrowly defined. Thus, we will certainly see more assertion of national interests evident in the shift to world economic prices in Soviet–East European trade, the continued erosion of the Warsaw Pact, and very likely the complete dissolution of the moribund Council for Mutual Economic Assistance.

It is unlikely, however, that this shift will mean an upsurge in provocative challenges to Moscow. For one thing, what could be more challenging than the removal of the communist party? Or the complete absorption of a fraternal ally by an old enemy? The revolutions of 1989 have already produced consequences that Moscow has shown it can—or must—live with. It is not hard to imagine issues which could bring to the fore a dangerous test of wills between the USSR and a former ally, such as territorial questions with Poland or Romania. Yet it seems evident that neither the new government in Warsaw nor the not so new one in Bucharest wants to press such issues.

But such actions too may be tempting for the new governments, as they search for ways to appeal to an uncertain and newly demanding population. They will be eager to avoid the displeasure that the prescribed economic medicines seem to entail. They will be eager to do things that are both effective and popular, and the two will not always coincide. And they will be faced with their choices in a less controlled, increasingly noisy, and more complex environment, both at home and all around them. Those in power now are those who asked their people to give power to them. They may well discover the truth of Oscar Wilde's adage: the two worst things in the world are not getting what you want . . . and getting it.

The Elections Compared and Assessed

✦

Vladimir V. Kusin

A veteran observer of Eastern Europe at Radio Free Europe searches out the similarities and differences revealed in the several elections held in the area between June 1989 (Poland) and June 1990 (Czechoslovakia).

In the space of the year between June 1989 and June 1990, multiparty elections were held in all six countries that once comprised the Soviet bloc. After the Polish general elections in June 1989, which were open only partly to genuine contest, all the other elections were free of the restrictions that had been placed on them. Irregularities and intimidation did occur in some countries, mainly Romania and Bulgaria, and allegations were made but not proved that more votes had been counted than cast in some constituencies in Romania. But election results were apparently not rigged anywhere.

All the elections marked progress toward a democratic political future, although to differing extents. Yet even the elections could not ensure that this course would be pursued with equal dedication and at the same determined pace in each country. Communist rule in its neo-Stalinist (Brezhnevist) incarnation seems to have come to an end, but reform-communist and cryptocommunist elements remained strong in some countries and dominant in others. The elections themselves were, of course, of momentous importance; but creating and consolidating democratic regimes will be the real test. For, after over four decades of communist rule, the Central and East European societies must deal with problems elections alone cannot solve.

✦

ELECTORAL SYSTEMS

The Polish election in June 1989 (with its prearranged restrictions) was based on multimember constituencies and majority voting. Bulgaria combined proportional representation with majority voting along the lines of the West German system. Half of the 400 seats were allocated by party lists while the other half were contested in

Vladimir V. Kusin, "The Elections Compared and Assessed," from *Report on Eastern Europe*, July 13, 1990, pp. 38–46. Reprinted with the permission of Radio Free Europe/Radio Liberty.

single-member constituencies according to the majority system. A second round was necessary in places where no majority had been achieved. Hungary's very complicated system, sometimes referred to as the most complex in Europe, combined voting in single-member constituencies with voting for regional and national party tickets. There, too, a second round was required. Czechoslovakia, Romania, and East Germany converted votes into seats according to variations on the proportional representation formula only; in Romania, representatives of small minorities were given seats irrespective of the results.

Hungary made parliamentary representation conditional on a party's receiving at least 4% of the votes. In Czechoslovakia the hurdle was 5% for the Federal Assembly and the Czech National Council (the parliament of the Czech Republic). It was 3% for the Slovak National Council (the parliament of the Slovak Republic) in order to make representation more accessible to the smaller national minorities residing in that part of the country.

The Czech and Slovak National Councils have been vested with limited legislative powers since the country was federalized in 1968, but the supremacy of federal laws and institutions has been retained. It is one of the major declared intentions of the newly elected federal and national parliaments to reapportion legislative and executive powers so as to make the two constituent republics sovereign. It has been said that federal Czechoslovakia will only be strong when both republics are strong. The new arrangements will be reflected in three constitutions: the Czech, the Slovak, and the federal. Voters in Czechoslovakia elected the federal and the national parliaments at the same time.

The Polish, Romanian, and Czechoslovak parliaments all have a second chamber. The Polish Senate provides the voivodships with regional representation, while the Czechoslovak House of Nations protects the Slovaks against centralistic Czech tendencies. The division of labor between the Romanian Assembly of Deputies and the Senate is not quite clear and may be constitutionally regulated by the newly elected legislature.

Despite their differences, the various electoral laws were mostly adaptations of Western procedures. It can be expected that at least some of the newly elected parliaments will want to amend these laws before the next general elections. The Poles will obviously eliminate the pre-election arrangement that reserved seats for the Communists. A simpler system may be brought into operation in Hungary, and the Czechoslovaks may give up their exclusive focus on party tickets.

✦

THE CAMPAIGN

The special Polish case aside, campaigning in East Germany, Hungary, and Czechoslovakia was free of major disturbances. Results were tallied in these countries with no apparent incidences of fraud. The one interfering factor—the old communist secret services—derived from the very regimes the elections in these three countries sought to overcome. A number of candidates and party figures in East Germany and

Czechoslovakia withdrew after allegations that they had been connected with the secret police, and there was a scandal in Hungary when it was reported that some opposition figures were still under surveillance. In Romania and Bulgaria, complaints were lodged against former communist parties who apparently pressured and even intimidated voters, and some Western governments and organizations felt it necessary to criticize these practices publicly. International teams observed the elections in every country except Poland. In all countries the communist and excommunist contestants could take advantage of their established mechanisms (secretariats, the media) as well as of the fear of change that lingered in the less-educated segments of the electorate.

◆

THE TURNOUT

Voter turnout was high everywhere except in Poland and Hungary. In East Germany it stood at 93%, in Czechoslovakia at 96%, in Bulgaria at 90% in the first and 75% in the second round, and in Romania at 86%. In Poland 62% voted in the first round and just over 25% in the second round of the partly free elections of June 1989; 42% turned out for the local elections in May 1990. In Hungary 65% cast ballots in the first round and 45% in the second round. Lower turnouts were recorded in the two countries with the longest histories of political change. In the other four countries, which had undergone sudden and rapid revolutions, the public evidently understood that the elections were a critical test that was to bring the old regimes to a definitive end. Spain and Portugal also had larger than usual turnouts in their first elections following the collapse of the authoritarian systems there in the 1970s.

◆

COMMUNIST PARTIES IN THE CONTEST

The Polish election in June 1989, the Hungarian election in March 1990, and the Czechoslovak election in June 1990 were contested by communist parties or, in the Hungarian case, by a residual communist group, under their traditional names: the Polish United Workers' Party (PUWP), the Hungarian Socialist Workers' Party (HSWP), and the Czechoslovak Communist Party (CPCS). The CPCS is the only communist party in the former bloc that has refused to change its name so far. It may still do so at a congress later this year, but the fairly good showing it made under its old designation may strengthen the position of those opposing the change.

After the Polish contest, the PUWP broke up into two self-styled social democratic parties (Social Democracy of the Republic of Poland, and the Social Democratic Union), both of which fared abysmally in the May 1990 local elections.

The other parties renamed themselves and some split up before the contest, no doubt in order to increase their appeal to the majority of the electorate, which had been showing unmistakable anti-communist leanings during the campaigns. The East German Socialist Unity Party (SED) became the Party of Democratic Socialism (PDS). The Hungarian Socialist Workers' Party split: one group retained the old

The Composition of Eastern Europe's New Parliaments

BULGARIA

Date of Election: June 10 and 17, 1990

Type of Legislature: 400-member single chamber

Electoral Mode: Half the seats were elected from party lists on the basis of proportional representation. The other 200 were elected by single-member constituencies on the basis of majority vote, with run-off elections on June 17 in constituencies where no candidate secured 50% of the poll.

Name of Party (or Alliance)	Number of Seats
Bulgarian Socialist Party (excommunist)	211
Union of Democratic Forces	144
Movement for Rights and Freedoms (Muslim)	23
Bulgarian Agrarian National Union	16
Fatherland Union	2
Fatherland Party of Labor	1
Social Democratic Party (non-Marxist)	1
Independents	2
Total	400

Source: Tables on pp. 590–595 compiled by Vladimir V. Kusin with assistance from Barbara Donovan, Vera Gavrilov, Judith Pataki, Louisa Vinton, Roman Stefanowski, Dan Ionescu, Vlad Socor, and Peter Martin.

CZECHOSLOVAKIA

Date of Election: June 8–9, 1990

Type of Legislature: The Federal Assembly contains 300 seats divided into two chambers: the House of People (with 150 members, 101 from the Czech Lands and 49 from Slovakia) and the House of Nations (with 150 members, 75 from each republic). Also elected were the republican parliaments, that is, the Czech National Council (200 members) and the Slovak National Council (150 members).

Electoral Mode: All seats were elected from party lists on the basis of proportional representation. A minimum 5% of the poll was required to win representation in the Federal Assembly and Czech National Council; and a 3% minimum was required for the Slovak National Council.

Czech and Slovak National Councils

Name of Party	Number of Seats	
	Czech Lands	Slovakia
Civic Forum	123	—
Public Against Violence	—	48
Communist Party of Czechoslovakia	32	22
Society for Moravia and Silesia	22	—
Christian Democratic Union	19	—
Christian Democratic Movement	—	31
Slovak National Party	—	22
Coexistence	—	14
Democratic Party	—	7
Green Party	—	6
Liberal Democratic Party	4	—
Total	200	150

Federal Assembly
Both Chambers Combined

Name of Party (Alliance)	Number of Seats
Civic Forum/Public Against Violence*	168
Communist Party of Czechoslovakia	47
Christian Democratic Union/Christian Democratic Movement	40
Movement for Self-Governing Democracy/Society for Moravia and Silesia	16
Slovak National Party	15
Coexistence/Hungarian Christian Democratic Movement	12
Liberal Democratic Party	2
Total	300

*Of the 170 mandates obtained by the Civic Forum/Public Against Violence in the election, two are now held by the Liberal Democratic Party, which ran under Civic Forum's umbrella but has since set itself up as an independent group.

House of the People

Name of Party (Alliance)	Number of Seats
Civic Forum/Public Against Violence	85
Communist Party of Czechoslovakia	23
Christian Democratic Union/Christian Democratic Movement	20
Movement for Self-Governing Democracy/Society for Moravia and Silesia	9
Slovak National Party	6
Coexistence/Hungarian Christian Democratic Movement	5
Liberal Democratic Party	2
Total	150

House of the Nations

Name of Party	Number of Seats Czech Lands	Slovakia
Civic Forum	50	—
Public Against Violence	—	33
Communist Party of Czechoslovakia	12	12
Christian Democratic Union	6	—
Christian Democratic Movement	—	14
Society for Moravia and Silesia	7	—
Slovak National Party	—	9
Coexistence	—	7
Total	75	75

POLAND

Date of Election: June 4 and 18, 1989

Type of Legislature: The 560-member National Assembly comprises two chambers: the Sejm (with 460 members, representing electoral districts) and the Senate (with 100 members, representing *voivodships*).

Electoral Mode: 65% of the seats in the Sejm were reserved for Communists and their allies, while the seats in the Senate were all freely contested. Voting took place in multimember districts (where a 50% majority was required). An additional national list of 35 unopposed luminaries was posted; when many on this list failed to secure a stipulated 50% support in the poll, however, they were replaced for the second round of voting. This mode was an *ad hoc* agreement and is not likely to be used again.

| | Seats in | | | |
| | Sejm | | Senate | |
Name of Party	1989*	1990*	1989	1990
Citizens' Parliamentary Caucus (Solidarity) including:	161	157	99	99
Confederation for Independent Poland	1	1	1	1
Polish Socialist Party	2	2	1	1
Christian Democratic Labor Party	1	1	1	1
Christian Democrats	—	44	—	6
Polish Peasant Party (Solidarity)	—	22	—	—
Christian National Union	—	5	—	1
Liberal Democratic Congress	—	3	—	2
Communists in 1989/Ex-Communists in 1990:				
Polish United Workers' Party	173	—	—	—
Democratic Left Parliamentary Club	—	113	—	—
Social Democratic Union (Fiszbach)	—	42	—	—
Independent Deputies' Club	—	9	—	—
United Peasant Party (now the Polish Peasant Party)	76	79	—	1
Democratic Party	27	23	—	—
Former Proregime Christian Groups:				
PAX	10	10	—	—
Christian Social Union	8	8	—	—
Polish Catholic Social Union	5	5	—	—
Independent and Unaffiliated	—	14	1	—

*Changes between June 1989 and July 1990 reflect realignments in the Sejm and Senate and the internal diversification of the Citizens' Parliamentary Congress. Some affiliations are not clearly stated; some figures may not be entirely accurate.

EAST GERMANY

Date of Election: March 18, 1990
Type of Legislature: 400-member single chamber
Electoral Mode: All seats were filled from party lists by proportional representation.

Name of Party (Alliance)	Number of Seats
Christian Democratic Union	163
Social Democrats	88
Party of Democratic Socialism (excommunist)	66
German Social Union	25
Free Democrats	23
Alliance '90	12
Democratic Farmers' Party	10
Green Party	8
Democratic Awakening	4
United Left	1
Total	400

HUNGARY

Date of Election: March 25 and April 8, 1990
Type of Legislature: 386-member single chamber (including 8 deputies coopted after voting to represent national minorities).
Electoral Mode: A complicated system of district, regional, and national party lists as well as majority voting in single-member constituencies.

Name of Party (Alliance)	Number of Seats
Hungarian Democratic Forum	164
Alliance of Free Democrats	92
Independent Smallholders' Party	44
Hungarian Socialist Party (excommunist)	33
Alliance of Young Democrats	21
Christian Democratic Party	21
Agrarian Alliance	1
Independents	6
Single candidates representing two parties	4
Total	386

ROMANIA

Date of Election: May 20, 1990

Type of Legislature: The 515-member parliament comprises two chambers: the Deputies' Assembly (396 members) and the Senate (119 members). So far no clear division of labor between the two has emerged.

Electoral Mode: Voting was on the basis of party lists as well as individual candidates. Seats were allocated according to proportional representation within electoral districts, except for nine seats allocated to specified national minorities failing to win representation (namely, Armenians, Bulgarians, Serbs, Lippovan, Czechs and Slovaks, Greeks, Poles, Ukrainians, Turks, and Tatars).

Name of Party (Alliance)	Deputies' Assembly	Senate
National Salvation Front (including crypto-Communists)	263	92
Hungarian Democratic Union	29	12
National Liberal Party	29	9
National Peasants' Party	12	1
Romanian Ecological Movement	12	1
Alliance for Unity of Romanians	9	2
Democratic Agrarian Party	9	—
Romanian Ecological Party	8	1
Independents	—	1
Romanian Social Democratic Party	5	—
Social Democratic Party of Romania	2	—
Centrist Democratic Group	2	—
Labor Democratic Party	1	—
Free Exchange Party	1	—
National Reconstruction Party	1	—
Free Democratic Youth Party	1	—
"Brătianu" Liberal Union	1	—
The Germans' Democratic Forum	1	—
The Romanies' Democratic Forum	1	—
Plus the nine national minorities named above, with one seat each	9	—
Total	396	119

name, the other became the Hungarian Socialist Party (HSP). The Romanian Communist Party (RCP), which collapsed during the revolt against Nicolae Ceauşescu last December, retained some members and a great many officials under the name the National Salvation Front (NSF). (Most observers regard the NSF as the RCP's heir.) The Bulgarian Communist Party (BCP) became the Bulgarian Socialist Party (BSP).

The election platforms on which the Communists, however now named, ran shared what could be called an advanced reformist orientation that included multiparty parliamentarism, a free-market economy—but here each retained some measure of the state sector's size and influence—cultural and ideological liberalization, and an acceptance of the need for rapprochement with Western democratic institutions. Similarly, they all vowed to part ways with a dogmatic past they admitted had been noxious and, above all, unsuccessful.

In the somewhat singular case of Poland (June 1989), the PUWP failed to get a single seat in the Senate; but before the elections, it had already negotiated 65% of seats in the lower house for itself and its satellites. After the split at the last PUWP congress in January 1990, some former PUWP deputies did not join either of the two new "social-democratic" groups, which now have small and rather apathetic factions in parliament. In the May 1990 local government elections, one group received less than 0.3% and the other an even lower percentage of the vote. It is believed that some former communist candidates running for local councils failed to declare their party affiliation, as it was not mandatory to do so. Thus, the number of former Communists now serving as councilors may, in fact, be greater than the low percentage suggests. For all practical purposes, however, organized communism has died in Poland.

In Hungary the HSP won 8.5% of the vote, the HSWP won 3.7%. The reconstructed Czechoslovak communist party received 13.6%, and the East German PDS 16.3%. The East German PDS faces an uncertain future, as it is the only one of Central and Eastern Europe's former communist parties that will have to contest another election soon: the all-German election that will probably be held in December 1990. It is not likely that it will be able to retain its electoral support as unification progresses.

In Romania and Bulgaria the former Communists were the real winners. The NSF won a landslide victory, garnering 66.3% of the votes for the lower house and 67.0% for the Senate. The Bulgarian Socialist Party won 47.5% in that part of the election that was based on proportional representation, and it secured a sufficient number of seats in majority voting in single-member constituencies to register an absolute majority of 211 of the 400 available seats.

The conclusion must be that the cryptocommunist and former communist parties performed unevenly but, on the whole, not too badly. While the PSWP only retains seats in the Polish Sejm due to its extra-electoral agreement—now viewed as thoroughly obsolete—reconstituted communist parties remain in power in Romania and Bulgaria. The CPCS is the second largest party in Czechoslovakia, holding 47 of the 300 Federal Assembly seats. In both Hungary and East Germany the Communists have little legislative influence despite their parliamentary bases, holding only 33 of Hungary's 376 parliamentary seats and 66 of the GDR's 400.

It is not clear at this stage whether the Bulgarian former Communists will be able to form a coalition government with the defeated opposition, as they said they would like to do. The Bulgarian opposition parties have repeatedly rejected the notion. The new Romanian government does not include members of the opposition, but it does have a number of professionals who can be considered "technocratic" rather than purely political appointees. The NSF remains, however, fully in command. A government composed of both Communists and non-Communists exists in Poland by previous agreement and, obviously, pending the next general election. The Hungarian and East German governments contain no Communists, while the Czechoslovak election winners, the Civic Forum and the Public Against Violence, have included in the new cabinet on an individual basis several former Communists who quit the party only recently. The CPCS is not represented in the government as a party, but it has pledged to play the role of a "constructive opposition." It has said it will not automatically vote against the government only because of its position as an opposition party.

◆

NONCOMMUNIST ALLIANCES

The Hungarian Democratic Forum, a kind of alliance itself at first, soon developed into a political party and contested the election as such. The same can be said of the Hungarian Alliance of Free Democrats.

The several alliances that contested the East German elections all fared badly. The largest of them, Alliance '90, which many people thought best embodied the original philosophy of the East German revolution, won just over 600,000 votes and only 21 of 400 seats. The dominant feature of the East German election process was not the appearance of novel blocs but rather its parallels with the West German system.

In Romania, the NSF's main rivals did not establish an umbrella organization but chose to contest the elections as individual political parties. The victorious cryptocommunist NSF claims to be an alliance, but in fact leading officials of the Ceauşescu regime direct it. The NSF made no visible or significant attempts to negotiate with any possible partners.

The Bulgarian Union of Democratic Forces (UDF) unites ten founding organizations and six collective members that joined subsequently. There was not enough time for the member groups to crystallize into parties with clearly definable profiles, but the UDF collectively can be said to have advocated liberal democratic views tinged with social democratic influences. The UDF was able to mobilize large masses of people for its election rallies and protest demonstrations, and it obtained a respectable 144 seats in the 400-seat legislature. For the run-off elections in single-member districts, the UDF won promises of support from opposition parties no longer in the contest. It is conceivable that at least a measure of cooperation between the UDF and the other opposition parties in the new parliament will continue; the former Communists have a majority of only 11 seats. Protests against undemocratic practices during the election campaign continue in Bulgaria to date.

Unlike Solidarity in Poland and the Civic Forum in Czechoslovakia, the UDF seems to have acted more like an electoral coalition than a group of organizations united in the belief that alliance-building ought to replace party politics. The UDF's constituent groups knew they had to unite in order to stand any chance of defeating the former Communists. Moreover, after the BSP's rather narrow victory, the opposition groups may well conclude that they must remain united (at least during the new parliament's 18-month tenure) if they are to advocate noncommunist viewpoints with any degree of success.

Two alliances (or "broad churches") turned out to be decisive winners: the Polish Solidarity and, jointly as well as separately, the Czech Civic Forum and the Slovak Public Against Violence.

The idea of converting Solidarity into one or several political parties has not yet been acted upon for a variety of reasons. These include the genuine efforts being made to overcome what many see as the disadvantage deriving from the rather amorphous concept that holds the movement together. Furthermore, there is a dispute between those seeking to stabilize political support for Tadeusz Mazowiecki's government and those who believe that this stability is, in fact, stagnation that has slowed the pace of political change. A natural struggle for political influence among member groups and individuals also appears to be involved.

The Civic Forum and the Public Against Violence also appear to be headed toward political diversification. One component group, the Democratic Initiative, has already set itself up independently as the Liberal Democratic Party—a somewhat surprising move, as its political creed seemed to lie closer than any other group's to the Civic Forum's philosophy. Both the Civic Forum and the Public Against Violence are beginning to realize that it is difficult to practice politics without at least a rudimentary party structure. An attempt is being made to organize party-political life from below, and the Civic Forum's local groups have now been told to set up clubs as embryonic party cells. If this move meets with approval from the Civic Forum's followers, the clubs could then create networks within their districts and, eventually, central agencies and offices. It has been stressed that the structure arising from this base will not only be able to operate with a minimum amount of bureaucratic support but will also not overshadow the Civic Forum's image as a loose association of democratic thinkers and innovators. The Civic Forum would then function at two linked levels: through party-political activists in the clubs, and through the intellectually empathetic followers who adhere to the movement's general aims but dislike organizational ties. Jointly, the Civic Forum and its sister organization the Public Against Violence hold 168 of the 300 Federal Assembly seats. The Civic Forum has a majority (123 out of 200) in the Czech National Council, the Public Against Violence a plurality (48 out of 150) in the Slovak National Council.

If the former communist parties did not perform equally well or equally badly in each country, neither did the new alliances. Some failed altogether (GDR). Some gave up the notion of aligning disparate elements (Hungary). Some performed impressively (Bulgaria), and some scored convincing victories (Poland and Czechoslovakia).

◆

THE ETHNIC FACTOR

In Romania, the Hungarian Democratic Federation of Romania, which represents the country's largest ethnic minority, will form the main opposition in both houses of the newly elected Romanian parliament. It polled over 1,000,000 votes and has 29 seats in the 396-member Assembly of Deputies and 12 in the 119-member Senate. The Movement for Rights and Freedoms will be the third-largest party in Bulgaria, with 23 seats in the 400-strong Grand National Assembly. Although ostensibly not an ethnic organization, its primary support came from the Turkish minority. The Slovak National Party (usually seen as separatist) will have 15 deputies in the 300-member Federal Assembly and 22 in the 150-member Slovak National Council. The Society for Moravia and Silesia has seven seats in the Federal Assembly and twenty-two in the 200-strong Czech National Council. The Hungarian minority party in Czechoslovakia ("Coexistence") sends 12 representatives to the Federal Assembly and 14 to the Slovak National Council. Another ethnic Hungarian group, Democratic Initiative, ran under the aegis of the Civic Forum and the Public Against Violence. While no ethnic party gained access to the Hungarian parliament, 26 of the 376 representatives are said to be of non-Hungarian descent. Each of the eight minorities living in Hungary will also be allocated a parliamentary seat.

These are very respectable results, reflecting the national aspirations for which Central and Eastern Europe have long been known. Rightly or wrongly, they also reflect these minorities' sense of the injustices they have suffered. The results also mean that the new regimes will not be allowed to drop the ethnic question from their political agendas, no matter how urgent other issues may seem.

It should be noted that the large Gypsy (Romany) populations in Central and Eastern Europe have not been able to secure parliamentary representation through independent parties, although one of the five Gypsy groups in Romania was allocated a seat, as were other small minority parties. A Gypsy Party that competed in Slovakia failed to win the 3% of the vote necessary to be seated in the National Council. It polled fewer than 25,000 votes, or 0.7%, although there may be as many as 500,000 Gypsies in Slovakia. There will, however, be a handful of individual Romany deputies in all three Czechoslovak parliaments who ran on other party tickets. The Civic Forum's constituent member groups include a Romany Initiative.

◆

THE "HISTORICAL PARTIES"

Parties that had existed before the communist takeovers did not generally do well in their efforts to stage an electoral comeback. The 40-year hiatus between their earlier lives and their present resurrections turned out to be a handicap they were unable to overcome. Although some of them assumed that their histories would automatically provide them with political legitimacy, the voters—the majority of whom were voting in free multiparty elections for the first time—seemed unimpressed.

What these parties had done before the communist takeovers and, in some cases, during the years of communist rule evidently also held little appeal for postcommunist voters.

Among the newly resurrected "historical parties" that had been banned during the communist era, the Social Democrats in East Germany performed best with 88 seats, or over 2,500,000 votes. Their comrades did not, however, get elected to the parliaments in either Czechoslovakia or Hungary, for in both countries they garnered no more than just over 3% of the votes. There is one independent Social Democratic deputy in the Bulgarian parliament who adds the attribute "non-Marxist" to his party's name. A Social Democratic group that ran under the auspices of the Bulgarian UDF will hold 23 seats and plans to act as an opposition force. Two Social Democratic groups won representation in Romania, one with five and the other with two deputies. The Hungarian Independent Smallholders' Party has 44 of the 386 seats and is the Democratic Forum's government partner. In Romania, the National Liberal Party won 29 seats and the National Peasants' Party 12, compared with the NSF's 263 seats.

The "historical parties" that the Communists had allowed to exist as their satellites fared even worse. Only one of four such parties in Czechoslovakia cleared the 5% hurdle for the Federal Assembly, and that only after changing its name from Party of Renewal to Slovak Democratic Party and co-opting a new leadership, including some previously exiled politicians. The Bulgarian Agrarian National Union in Bulgaria has only 16 seats in the 400-member parliament.

The pre-election agreement governing the distribution of seats in Poland and the virtual reproduction of the West German party-political structure in East Germany make the amount of parliamentary representation the "historical parties" earned in these countries somewhat misleading. Even so, the East German Christian Democratic Union, a rather docile fellow-traveler during the SED years, came out a clear winner, the only such case throughout Central and Eastern Europe. It polled 4,700,000 votes, gaining 163 of the 400 seats.

◆

THE GREENS

According to both observers and opinion polls, the environmentalist groups stood a good chance in the elections. But the electorate failed the "green" parties. Not even the dire state of the environment could bridge the gap between ecological concerns and practical "universal" politics. The Greens' inability to enlarge their focus is generally thought to hamper their progress, despite a small and faithful following, in Western Europe as well. There are no separate Green parties in the Polish, Czechoslovak federal, Hungarian, and Bulgarian parliaments. In East Germany the Greens won eight seats out of 400. The Romanian Ecological Party, which was critical of the NSF, secured eight out of 396 seats in the Romanian assembly and one in the 119-strong Senate. The Romanian Ecological Movement, which is associated with the NSF, holds 12 mandates in the lower house and one in the Senate. In the Slovak National Council the Greens have six of the 150 seats. Ecological groups ran several candidates under the umbrella of the Czech Civic Forum and the Bulgarian Union of Democratic Forces, thus acquiring some parliamentary representation within larger groups. Ecoglasnost will have 15 deputies in the 400-member Bulgarian assembly. On the whole, however, the environmental lobbies will be able to exert significant pressure on the new political establishments only from outside the legislatures.

◆

"VOTES LOST"

In Hungary and Czechoslovakia, where a party had to receive a set percentage of votes in order to gain parliamentary representation, there is some concern that a fairly large section of the voting public remains unrepresented. Votes for parties that did not receive the mandatory percentage were transferred, according to a complex formula, to those who cleared the hurdle. In Czechoslovakia, out of twenty-two competing parties, six gained seats in the Federal Assembly, four in the Czech National Council, and seven in the Slovak National Council. Some 17% of those who went to the polls voted for parties that did not gain seats in any representative assembly. There is some campaigning to mobilize these "lost" voters for a kind of "extraparliamentary opposition," but the idea is vague and can hardly have a practical impact. More probably, the small parties will either work hard to improve their standing in the voters' eyes before the next elections, transform themselves into interest and pressure groups, or dissolve and let their members fuse with the larger groups.

◆

THE NEW REGIMES

Observers have noted that in the GDR and Hungary, right-wing or right-of-center parties scored victories; and some Western commentators saw postcommunist Central and Eastern Europe's move toward political conservatism as a logical corollary of the democratization process. Furthermore, the winners of the Polish, East German, and Hungarian elections all had strong religious bases for their political programs: Catholic in the case of Solidarity and Protestant in the case of the East German CDU and DSU as well as the Hungarian Democratic Forum and one of its coalition partners (also a Christian Democratic Party). This led some people to conclude that the part of anticommunist resistance that had rested on religious or Church-related principles would project itself into voting results everywhere.

The other three contests did not quite corroborate the "religious" and "right-wing" hypotheses. In Bulgaria and Romania, such dissent as had existed was not religiously or ecclesiastically inspired and failed to produce a political party capable of mounting a successful electoral challenge. In Czechoslovakia, the secular and liberal components of political beliefs—a traditional outlook, a history of dissent, and methods of analyzing current problems and proposing solutions—motivated voters more decisively than the largely Catholic orientation of the Christian Democratic Union coalition, which polled 13.3% in the federal elections, obtaining 40 seats out of the 300 in the Federal Assembly. Even in Slovakia, with its Catholic tradition, the CDU's showing was lower than expected at 19.2%, or 31 seats out of 150.

Moreover, none of these three countries moved to the right in the accepted sense of the word. "Liberal democratic" is perhaps the best description of the Civic Forum's political outlook. The former Communists' electoral victories in Bulgaria and Romania placed these two countries among the left-governed states of Europe. Their leftism is, of course, already reformist rather than dogmatic and may become even more so. In the meantime, some observers see the turmoil within Solidarity's ranks as the embryonic division of what many regarded as a solidly Catholic and right-ist organization into left and right factions.

It would perhaps be best not to measure the results of the first free elections in Central and Eastern Europe against the traditional left-to-right continuum. The elections all moved their respective societies away from the fossilized leftism of communist politics and from Soviet domination. In this sense, they can all be seen as a movement to the right, but they were at the same time part of a process through which the nascent democracies sought a place in the all-European order rather than in the West's conventional political spectrum. In the end, it matters less at the close of the 20th century than it did in its first half whether a democratic country has a leftist or a right-ist government. Democracy has become the decisive factor holding the large and still growing territory of the political center together. This democratic mainstream extends in both directions and absorbs more and more of the ground that used to be the domain of the traditional democratic left and right. The extremes at both ends of the spectrum are becoming increasingly confined to political adventurists, notorious malcontents, and professional agitators. Joining the mainstream is Central and Eastern Europe's main preoccupation, not joining a right or left, even if developments in Romania may yet disprove this conclusion.

Democracy, Debt, Double Standards

◆

Sophie Gherardi

Using Latin America for comparison, a *Le Monde* (Paris) correspondent examines the economic plight of Eastern Europe rooted in the heavy burden of external debt carried by these countries.

In response to popular pressure, nation after nation—half of a continent—throws off dictatorship for pluralism and free elections. Eastern Europe at the end of the 1980s? No, Latin America at the beginning of the 1980s. A contagious freedom struck the Western Hemisphere, resulting in the overthrow of military juntas: Ecuador in 1979, Peru in 1980, Bolivia in 1982, Argentina in 1983, Uruguay in 1984, and Brazil in 1985. Since then, these countries and several in Central America, as well as Chile and Paraguay, have experienced democratic successions.

The fall of Latin America's military regimes was applauded by the Western democracies but without any torrent of enthusiasm—except, perhaps, for the election of Raúl Alfonsín in Argentina, which has always somehow seemed more "European." This is in striking contrast to the lyrical response to the progressive collapse of Eastern Europe's communist regimes in 1989.

The seven countries that make up Eastern Europe saw their net debt balloon by more than $15 billion in 1989 to $114.5 billion, according to provisional estimates of the Organization for Economic Cooperation and Development (OECD). The OECD maintains that these countries, with the exception of Bulgaria, are experiencing less difficulty paying their debts now than they were in the early 1980s (if one takes, as criteria, net interest payments in relation to export earnings). If one can speak of a deteriorating financial situation, however, the reason is that indebtedness is growing while the economies are not: Poland and Hungary are experiencing recessions, while the Soviet Union, Czechoslovakia, and East Germany have each suffered a 1-percent decline in growth.

It became obvious to the West that Poland, Hungary, and East Germany, then Czechoslovakia, Bulgaria, and finally Romania would require assistance to avoid stumbling over their economic problems. Food supplies, grants, loans, improved terms of trade, technical assistance—all forms of aid—were announced and are beginning to be delivered in what has turned into a bidding contest of sorts. With the entry of the International Monetary Fund (IMF) and World Bank, the diligence of the European Community, and the creation of a European Bank for Reconstruction and Development, it is clear that the East European countries will not be abandoned as they journey—painfully—toward free-market economies.

At the same time, the Western countries have made no mystery of the political conditions that they are attaching to their aid. The so-called Group of 24 that is coordinating the delivery of aid to the East is demanding "firm commitments" concerning "law-based rule, respect of human rights, the establishment of a multi-party system, and the holding of free and fair elections in the course of 1990." As of early March, total financial commitments of Western nations and multilateral organizations to the East European countries have risen to some $16 billion. To this one must add the exceptionally favorable terms for the rescheduling of more than $9 billion of Poland's debt (out of a total of nearly $40 billion) by its creditor countries, the Paris Club. No one seems to mind that the rich countries are risking important resources on countries that are heavily indebted and whose economic prospects are not good. They are aiding democracy. But why, then, do they not do the same for Latin America?

Consider how much money the six largest Latin American countries that restored democracy between 1979 and 1985 have received. In 1979, Argentina, Bolivia, Brazil, Ecuador, Peru, and Uruguay together received $9 billion in aid; in 1985, the amount totaled only $3.3 billion. By that time the debt burden of these countries had risen to $192 billion, and annual service on the debt was more than $11 billion. An OECD document entitled, "Financing the External Debt of Developing Countries," finds that debt assistance in Latin America declined dramatically between 1981 and 1988: from $64.1 billion at the beginning of this period to $22.7 billion by the end.

The debt crisis, brought on by Mexico's inability to meet its scheduled payment in the summer of 1982, marked a turning point for the region. Commercial bank loans dried up, as did direct investments. Only public development assistance increased: Public charity had replaced business. Brazil, Argentina, Bolivia, Peru, and Ecuador, among others, have benefited from successive reschedulings of their debt. But nothing has been done to compensate for the disengagement of the banks and private investors from the region.

Unlike their counterparts in Eastern Europe, the countries of Latin America were not subject to any real political conditions—not in the 1970s, when the banks saw in Latin America the "markets of tomorrow" and disbursed credits while turning a blind eye toward authoritarian regimes and capital flight, estimated at $20 billion a year. (Chile, whose military dictatorship earned a certain notoriety, received more than $1 billion in 1980 and $2.2 billion in 1982. As in the rest of Latin America, its payments abroad precipitously began to exceed the income it received.) Then these same banks slowly turned off the spigot, leaving the newly established democracies in the 1980s to wrestle with over-indebted, non-egalitarian, and impoverished economies. The international community responded largely by imposing harsh economic policies in exchange for new multilateral credits—an approach that was meant to restore confidence to private lenders, which it by no means did. At no time was there any public or private collective effort to help Latin America pull through because it had become democratic again.

The countries of Latin America cannot disclaim all responsibility for the deterioration of their economies. Loans were not always put to good use, bloated public sectors helped produce enormous deficits, and policies governing foreign investment often resembled attempts to attract flies with vinegar. "Don't forget that, in the final analysis, these governments are masters of their decisions, even if they often shift responsibility onto the international organizations," says a World Bank official.

It is here where the comparison with Eastern Europe is rich in lessons. For the most part, aid for Eastern Europe is in the form of loans. But these countries—with the exception of Romania, which paid back its debt at the price of fearsome pauperization—have attained, even surpassed, levels of debt that are considered excessive in the Latin American context. The ratio of total debt to gross domestic product is 65 percent in the case of Hungary and 63 percent for Poland, as opposed to 60 percent for Argentina and 30 percent for Brazil. Unless the West forgives a portion of Eastern Europe's already existing debt, it risks entangling these countries further in a spiral of debt, which is what happened in Latin America.

Moreover, the austerity policies recommended by the IMF—which are already being applied in Poland and, to a lesser degree, in Hungary—have a depressive effect on economic activity and on living standards (as they have had in Latin America). Why should the East European countries, which know nothing of the market economy, be expected to do better than the powerful economies of Argentina and Brazil? Barring a rapid economic turnaround, the new regimes in the East will bear responsibility, in the eyes of their publics, for an economic slump.

Years of Grime and Grunge
Will Take Decades to Clean

✦

Girard C. Steichen

Even the environmentally aware leaders of the East European countries are inclined to postpone dealing with pollution on grounds that more basic economic problems must be addressed first. This dispatch to the *Christian Science Monitor* suggests the enormity of the environmental damage that has accumulated in Eastern Europe under communist rule.

Along the pocked banks of the Mulde River, Klaus Petrovsky navigates around small churning pools of luminescent goo, carefully sidestepping gurgling, spumy runoff from an ancient chemical complex nearby.

Across the turbid river, a cloud of orange-yellow vapor rises from a tangle of patched and rusty pipes.

"There's a different leak and a different smell every day," says Mr. Petrovsky, an inspection engineer at the air-quality control office in Bitterfeld, a town southwest of Berlin in former East Germany.

A few hundred miles to the southeast in northern Bohemia, the heart of Czechoslovakia's coal mining and industrial region, acid rain and strip-mining have transformed once verdant fields and forests into a moonscape.

In Romania's notorious "black town" of Copsa Mica, 150 miles north of Bucharest, houses, trees, and grass are so coated with soot from a nearby chemical plant that the town looks as if it had been soaked in ink.

Along the most congested, exhaust-fume-filled streets in Budapest, the amount of lead found in the blood of toddlers is barely considered safe for brawny factory workers. And throughout Eastern Europe infant mortality rates are reported higher than the European average. Miscarriages are common, and life expectancy is 10 years below the European average, according to recent studies.

From the Baltic to the Black Sea, the new democratic governments of Eastern

Girard C. Steichen, "Years of Grime and Grunge Will Take Decades to Clean," from *Christian Science Monitor,* April 25, 1991. Reprinted by permission of the author.

Europe are facing an ecological disaster, a nightmare legacy of four decades of communist mismanagement.

Environmental studies now indicate that the damage done to Eastern Europe, long suppressed under communist rule, is even more devastating than previously suspected.

Experts say it will take decades to clean up the East-bloc mess and that the costs will be withering—an almost impossible burden for cash-strapped countries struggling to implement painful economic reforms.

In eastern Germany alone, new studies indicate that more than $125 billion will be needed to bring the region up to standards long in place in western Germany. The IFO Institute for Economic Research in Munich said in a report released April 15 that water, air, and ground contamination in many parts of former East Germany "have reached catastrophic proportions."

The Bonn government has already earmarked millions of marks for ambitious cleanup projects, and officials contend acceptable standards can be achieved by the end of the century.

"The environmental gulf between eastern and western Germany will be eliminated by the year 2000," says Germany's optimistic federal environment minister, Klaus Töpfer.

Residents in eastern Germany can at least count on deep coffers in Bonn to improve their lot. A similar pace will be much harder to attain for Germany's impoverished eastern neighbors.

But help has been promised. The European Community and the United States have pledged substantial assistance, and many cleanup projects are now under way.

The EC's Phare program is currently funding several programs, including the construction of sludge disposal units at Prague's sewage-treatment plant, silt dredging at Hungary's popular Lake Balaton resort, and water-quality monitoring stations along the disastrously polluted Elbe River in eastern Germany. Throughout the region, untreated sewage is routinely pumped directly into rivers and coastal waters. Industrial wastes and runoff from the excessive use of fertilizers on vast farm cooperatives compound the problem.

A Regional Environmental Center was set up in Budapest last year with the help of a $5 million grant from the United States and matching assistance from the EC and the Hungarian government.

The center is meant to be a clearinghouse for information about the environment throughout Eastern Europe. "We are building a system to quickly identify environmental problems and trends," says Peter Hardi, the center's executive director. He says the center is already involved in more than 250 projects. "We're finally starting to make some progress."

Many of the worst polluters, like the sprawling and leaky former Chemical Combine in Bitterfeld, are being gradually shut down.

More will certainly follow as obsolete and uncompetitive state-run enterprises in Eastern Europe continue to collapse as market economies take over.

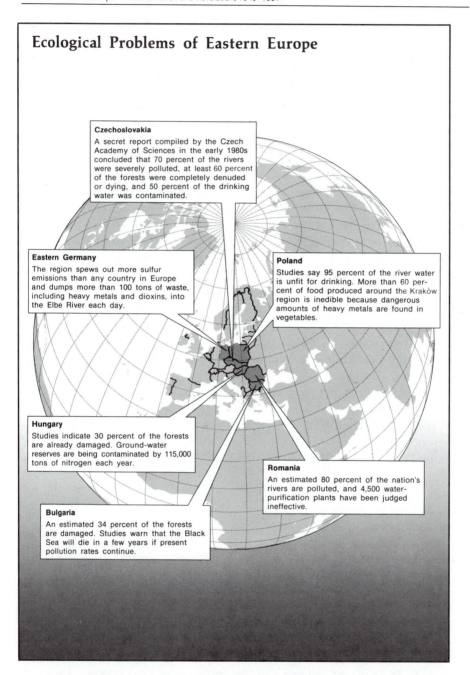

Ecological Problems of Eastern Europe

Czechoslovakia

A secret report compiled by the Czech Academy of Sciences in the early 1980s concluded that 70 percent of the rivers were severely polluted, at least 60 percent of the forests were completely denuded or dying, and 50 percent of the drinking water was contaminated.

Eastern Germany

The region spews out more sulfur emissions than any country in Europe and dumps more than 100 tons of waste, including heavy metals and dioxins, into the Elbe River each day.

Poland

Studies say 95 percent of the river water is unfit for drinking. More than 60 percent of food produced around the Kraków region is inedible because dangerous amounts of heavy metals are found in vegetables.

Hungary

Studies indicate 30 percent of the forests are already damaged. Ground-water reserves are being contaminated by 115,000 tons of nitrogen each year.

Romania

An estimated 80 percent of the nation's rivers are polluted, and 4,500 water-purification plants have been judged ineffective.

Bulgaria

An estimated 34 percent of the forests are damaged. Studies warn that the Black Sea will die in a few years if present pollution rates continue.

In addition, programs to replace the widespread use of lignite coal are being put into place. Decades of reliance on the cheap, plentiful, but dirty coal to fire furnaces and power plants has taken a staggering toll on cities and towns. Residents trudge through thick, acrid hazes that sting the eyes and choke the throat. Buildings and monuments are black and pitted.

Emission standards for automobiles are also being phased in, and new laws are being drafted to force companies to comply with more stringent environmental controls.

In Bulgaria, the government has promised to invest $15 million to upgrade safety at the nation's lone nuclear-power plant, considered to be one of the most dangerous in the region. Throughout the former East bloc, dozens of unsafe and obsolete nuclear reactors are still on line.

Officials in Western and Eastern Europe caution that some of the damage may be irreparable.

"We knew the situation over there was bad, but not this very, very bad," Erica Terpstra, a politician from the Netherlands, told a recent environmental conference in Florence, Italy.

Part V

Reflection and Outlook

♦ *It would be foolhardy at this stage in a process that clearly has a long course ahead of it to attempt prediction. Instead, this section offers a variety of viewpoints on the meaning of the events of 1989–1990 and on the tendencies that can be discerned. The commentators are either thoughtful East European or astute Western observers. They include critics of prior realities in the Soviet bloc and sympathizers with socialist principle; often these two roles are combined in one person, for those who know most about the Marxian socialist tradition have frequently been the severest critics of what passed for socialism in Eastern Europe. The occasional note of optimism is free of any inclination to gloat, and what may sound pessimistic is more aptly regarded as healthy skepticism about quick or easy solutions.*

The editor thought it advisable to avoid the more facile observations encountered all too often in Western discussion, especially the view of the "new revolution" as a simple vindication of Western policies, a tribute to hard lines of one sort or other, or an emblem of the superior qualities of capitalism. Ideological dogmatism got Eastern Europe into a lot of trouble, and more of the same will not improve our understanding of what is afoot in the region. The former client states have rediscovered the meaning of sovereignty, but after so many years it is hardly to be expected that they immediately know exactly what to do with it.

Marxism and Morality:
Reflections on the Revolutions of 1989

◆

Steven Lukes

One of the misleading habits of public discourse in the United States is the uncritical equation of Marxism with communism. Here the author of *Marxism and Morality,* a professor at the European University Institute in Florence, Italy, is at pains to dissociate Marxism from the long experience of communist rule in Eastern Europe and to show how its informing principles have a continuing relevance to the transformation under way in that region—even though the backlash there against official Marxism-Leninism might seem to deny this relevance.

In January 1990, as I write this piece, it is probably still too early to have an adequate understanding of the significance of last year's momentous events in China, the Soviet Union, and Eastern Europe. It is, however, already clear that the basic tenets of kremlinology stand in need of revision. Almost daily, transformations occur that academic orthodoxy had previously declared systemically impossible. The theory of revolutionary change needs drastic attention in the face of the democratic revolutions of Eastern Europe: revolutions that occurred without war between states or within them (apart from Rumania), without fanaticism or vanguards, undertaken in a self-limiting manner for goals that were limited and procedural rather than global and visionary. In general, the social scientists studying communist regimes should perhaps reflect on their collective failure to foresee even the possibility of most of what occurred. Perhaps that failure has something to do with their virtually total neglect of the moral dimension of political life. For it is a striking fact that morally motivated actions and reactions played a central role in all these events, from the Polish Round Table, at which the authorities and the Solidarity Opposition negotiated a partially

Steven Lukes, "Marxism and Morality: Reflections on the Revolutions of 1989," from *Ethics and International Affairs,* no. 4, 1990, pp. 19–31. Reprinted by permission of the Carnegie Council on Ethics and International Affairs.

free election between February and April of 1989, through the demonstrations and massacre in Tiananmen Square to the fall of Ceauşescu. All these events took the form both of a rejection of a prevailing type of political morality and of a common popular impulse to establish an alternative.

One way of interpreting the significance of these events, now prevalent among journalistic and political commentators, is to see them simply as the collapse of one political ideology and the triumph of its rival. Thus, for *Newsweek* (January 1, 1990), "1989 was the year the communist god finally failed." Others would extend the failure to the socialist project as a whole, and still others to the very identity of the left itself. Conversely, according to the *International Herald Tribune* (January 15, 1990), "the revolutions of 1989 [were] dominated by the ideals of pluralistic democracy and civil rights, a region-wide triumph for Western liberalism." Others, who take such liberalism to be inseparable from a more or less unbridled capitalism, see the revolutions as marking the definitive failure of a century-long experiment in social, economic, and political progress and a return to the market-based system it was intended to transform and supersede.

There is, doubtless, much to be said for these interpretations. Certainly, there is no shortage of voices in Eastern Europe, nor indeed in the Soviet Union, speaking enthusiastically in favor of such interpretations, particularly for their more stringent and strident versions. Nevertheless, I propose to take a different, less ideological tack, by asking two connected questions about political morality. First, what were the distinctive features of the prevailing political morality of communist regimes that was so massively rejected? And second, in the name of what was the system rejected? What distinguished the alternative political morality to which the revolutionary movements of 1989 in turn appealed?

By "political morality" I mean a set of principles that can be characterized at a fairly high level of abstraction, that underlie different, particular political positions that may be taken up by those who share them at any given time, or across time. They are, as Ronald Dworkin says, "constitutive": "political positions that are valued for their own sake," such that "every failure fully to secure that position, or any decline in the degree to which it is secured, is *pro tanto* a loss in the value of the overall political arrangement." Derivative positions, by contrast, are "valued as strategies or means of achieving the constitutive positions." Thus, different derivative views on policies—about taxation, say, or education or, more generally, about the nature and scope of state intervention in the economy—may appeal to or be justified by the same set of constitutive principles; and likewise, clusters of such derivative views will replace one another over time, as, for example, New Deal liberalism replaced Old Deal liberalism (the example is Dworkin's). Of course, constitutive political positions may conflict with one another, for political moralities will almost inevitably embody conflicting values. But by a "political morality" I mean the underlying structure within which and by virtue of which political value judgments are made and justified by those who share it, and which sets limits to the *kinds* of judgments that can be made.

✦

I

What, by 1989, was the political morality of "Official Communism"? This may seem like an odd question to those who are impressed by the corruption and cynicism of the elites ruling these regimes. (Certainly 1989 was not lacking in lurid evidence of the former, notably from China, East Germany, Rumania, and Bulgaria.) Nor, by asking this question do I wish to imply that these regimes enjoyed a moral legitimacy among their populations. This is a complex question, and there have clearly been variations across the communist world in this respect: compare the German Democratic Republic with Poland or Czechoslovakia, or indeed Czechoslovakia before and after 1968. It is, furthermore, true, as Leszek Kołakowski has said, that in Poland at least by the mid-1980s, "Marxism both as an ideology and as a philosophy" had "become completely irrelevant. . . . Even the rulers [had] largely abandoned this notion and even its phrases." What is, however, indisputable, is that Marxism, of however deformed or debased a sort, has dominated, indeed monopolized, the public sphere of these societies for decades (seven in the case of the Soviet Union) and has provided the sole framework and discourse within which the governing elites could seek to justify their policies to their subjects, to themselves, and to the outside world. It is, therefore, worth trying to identify the constitutive features of that framework and discourse.

Marxism has always been a peculiarly bibliocentric creed. There were times of faith when the massive ideological apparatuses achieved success in inspiring hearts and shaping minds within the party and far beyond. In the subsequent times of demoralization, the propaganda machine remained intact, its wheels went on turning, and the flow of words in workplaces and offices, schools and universities, newspapers, radio, and television continued unabated, only now as "noise" blocking out alternative forms of thought and expression. Nevertheless, the words always related, directly or indirectly, to texts, and ultimately to the founding texts of the Marxist canon. And this was not just a question of the time-honored practice of quoting the founding fathers, but went deeper and wider. The old books and pamphlets set their mark on vocabulary and syntax, on conceptual apparatus, polemical style and forms of argumentation, indeed even furnished the criteria of what was to count as a valid argument.

This helps to explain the remarkable coherence and continuity of Marxism as a political morality across the entire continuum that ranges from its historically significant incarnations as a political ideology, propagated by political elites, to the most refined and intellectually sophisticated theories favored by intellectuals, orthodox or "critical." For different reasons the same corpus of texts served as meat and drink to both. My claim is that, viewed as a text-based structure of thought, the political morality of Marxism is more or less firmly imprinted on all the significant varieties of Marxism, official and deviant, vulgar and refined, deformed and revised.

What distinguishes Marxism as a political morality is that it is a morality of emancipation. It promises communism as universal freedom from the peculiar modern slavery of capitalism, through revolutionary struggle. The promise is (usually) long-term: the prospect of a world of abundance, cooperation, and social rationality—

the free association of producers whose communal relations have overcome egoism, in full collective control of both the natural and social worlds which have become transparent to them. The world from which they are to be emancipated is one of scarcity, private property, the dull compulsion, anarchy, and irrationality of market relations, exploitation, class domination, human degradation, reification, and alienation. The access to the promised realm of freedom is through struggle: hence the consistent appeal throughout the Marxist tradition of the metaphors of war, of strategy and alliances, of forward marches and glorious victories, and its ingrained suspicion of compromise. In short, as a political morality, Marxism is future-oriented: it is, indeed, a perfectionist form of long-range consequentialism. The practical question, "What is to be done?"—How to act? What policy to pursue?—is always to be answered only by calculating what course is likely to bring nearer the long-term goal, the leap into the realm of freedom. The anxiety generated by that question is, however, traditionally diminished by two further assumptions: that capitalism is doomed and has nowhere to go but to its death; and that history is on the side of the working-class struggle, that long-term objective processes are at work that favor, and perhaps eventually guarantee, the leap into freedom.

There is, of course, as the history of Marxism superabundantly shows, enormous scope for dispute about all the elements in this picture: about how exactly to characterize socialism and/or communism, and in particular how economic planning and political decision making are to proceed and relate to one another (on which the canon is notably unforthcoming); about what the essential evils of capitalism are, which ones have explanatory priority, and through what kind of crisis they will issue in death; and about the famous problem of the "transition"—how warlike will it be, and through what kind of war? How parliamentary? How reformist? All these sources of indeterminacy become all the more confusing, of course, as the two anxiety-diminishing assumptions referred to above lose their power to persuade.

But, even in the present confusion, it is clear that Marxism has always held, as a constitutive triad of positions: (1) that capitalism belongs to the realm of necessity; (2) that communism signifies the promised realm of a higher kind of social freedom; and (3) that emancipation into the latter from the former is a discontinuous change, a qualitative transformation of economy, polity, and culture. In this respect, Ernst Fischer was right to say that for Marxism:

> Only the future is interesting, the fullness of what is possible, not the straitjacket of what has already been, with its attempt to impose on us the illusion that, because things were thus and not otherwise, they belong to the realm of necessity.

From the perspective of Marxism, in short, certain necessary facts are, rather, historically contingent: falsely to suppose them to be necessary facts is to cling to an ideological fiction blocking human progress. Four such "facts" strike me as of central importance. I shall call them the facts of scarcity, particularity, pluralism, and limited rationality.

By "scarcity" I mean limits to desired goods. It may take at least the following four forms: (1) insufficiency of production inputs (e.g., raw materials) relative to production requirements; (2) insufficiency of produced goods relative to consumption requirements; (3) limits upon the joint achievability of different goals, resulting from external conditions (e.g., limitations of space or time); and (4) limits upon the joint achievability of different goals, resulting from the intrinsic nature of those goals (e.g., "positional goods"—we cannot all enjoy high status or the solitude of a neighborhood park). Marxism, in promising abundance, considers only (1) and (2), which it promises to overcome through the mastery of nature and through a superior form of economic and social organization, combined with appropriate changes in preferences brought about by higher communal relations. It has nothing to say about (3) and (4), nor does it address contemporary ecological concerns about the feasibility or costs of seeking to eliminate the obstacles that lead to insufficent production.

By "particularity" I mean that we are not all Kantians, or utilitarians: that human beings have their separate lives to live and are properly motivated by a whole range of distinct interests, from the purely personal through a whole gamut of more or less local or particular concerns, to the most abstract and universal. In deciding how to act, we rightly give weight, at different times, to demands or claims that have different sources, but include our commitments and loyalties to relationships and activities that are special and exclusive to us. Marxism as a political morality belongs with those monistic moralities that require individuals to adopt a single privileged standpoint that abstracts from this motivational complexity and range, in its particular case requiring individuals to act solely in the postulated universal interests of future generations—or to adopt the social identity and thus the perspective of the imminently victorious class, which, together with its particular perspective, will wither away into the universal perspective indicated. Without that extravagant assumption, Marxism has always had the greatest difficulty in linking its monistic motivational requirement with the likely motivations of actual people.

By "pluralism" I mean the coexistence of different views about what is of central importance and value in human life, of what John Rawls has called divergent "conceptions of the good," where the differences or divergences are not simply alternative ways of spelling out a set of common principles that the adherents of each could recognize as shared in common among them. Alternative moralities, religions, world views, value standpoints, etc., are in this way "pluralistic," implying alternative conceptual structures, priorities of value, and forms of life—all of which are unassimilable to one another without destroying what is constitutive of each. Marxism does not address the possibility of pluralism, thus understood, in a general form, nor, therefore, the question of how to respond to it. It simply assumes, in the manner of the Enlightenment, that humanity is progressing, along however dialectical a path, toward moral convergence. That is why it has always typically treated actual instances of pluralist divergencies—particular forms of religion or nationalism or indeed secular moralities such as utilitarianism—as deviations, if occasionally useful shortcuts (as Lenin saw nationalism), along that path.

Finally, by "limited rationality" I mean limits upon the capacity of human beings in real time to solve certain problems, theoretical and practical, or to do so without creating other problems that undermine their solution. These limits may be of various kinds—of access or ability to process information, of theoretical knowledge or the means to apply it—and they may result from human incapacities, or from the nature of the problem itself, from social complexity, for example, or from unavoidable risk or uncertainty. To such contemporary concerns, Marxism answers once more with the voice of the Enlightenment, this time with a Hegelian, teleological accent: mankind only sets itself such problems as it can solve. The future is not only radiant but transparent; the social and natural worlds are alike in being in principle amenable to full prediction and control.

Marxism denies that these four facts are necessary, but in doing so, what does it deny? Not merely that they are present in all actual societies that have reached a certain level of economic development and social complexity. Not merely that, on the best estimates, they will be so present in all empirically feasible societies. (Marxism, after all, proposes a discontinuous leap into the realm of freedom, which our best estimates could not therefore predict since they are based on present knowledge, and therefore draw the bounds of feasibility in the wrong place). To say that these facts are necessary is to say that we cannot conceive of developed and complex societies that do not exhibit them—or that we could only do so at an unacceptable cost, by abandoning too much of all the rest of what we know and believe. They are facts at the very center, rather than the periphery, of our cognitive universe. To imagine them otherwise, as Ernst Fischer says, is, for us, literally to imagine utopia.

I have argued that Marxism as a political morality takes scarcity, particularity, pluralism, and limited rationality to be false necessities, as historically surmountable (and, in its confidently optimistic phase, imminently so). What, then, follows from taking them to be real necessities? The most general answer to this question is, I suggest, the recognition of the need for principles of justice for the regulation of social life. For, taken together, these "necessary facts" can be seen as constituting what Rawls calls the "circumstance of justice." They are conditions that *must*, in the appropriate sense, face the citizens of every conceivable society of a certain complexity and level of development. Within any such society (I here leave aside the question of intersocietal relations), they imply the inevitability of various kinds of conflicts of interest that, given these facts, are structurally determined. One such conflict of interest takes the form of a distributive struggle, involving conflicting claims upon limited resources of various kinds. Second, there are the conflicts facing both individuals and decision-making bodies at all levels of society, standing in the overlap of multiple intersecting circles of interest—individual, familial, local, regional, national, international, ethnic, religious, occupational, recreational, commercial, political, and so on—and having to draw different lines between what is public and what is private, and allocate priorities. Third, there are cultural conflicts between different ways of life, expressing divergent value standpoints that cannot be flattened into "shared understandings" or "common meanings." Finally, there are policy conflicts over problems for which the "correct" solution is neither on offer, nor in the offing. To acknowledge all this is to accept that such a society can only have a chance of being both stable and democratically legitimate if its citizens are able, *as citizens,* to step back from all these conflicting interests and acknowledge, as binding upon them, a set of principles for the distribution of benefits and burdens, and for the assigning of rights to protect interests and corresponding obligations.

My argument has been that Marxism, official and unofficial, is constitutively inhospitable to this conclusion, essentially because it views all these conflicts as the pathologies of pre-history, and in particular as stemming from the anarchic production relations and class conflicts of capitalism. And it believes this in part just because it takes the facts of scarcity, particularity, pluralism, and limited rationality to be contingent, not necessary.

As supporting evidence, I would cite the consistent polemics that have characterized the Marxist canon, from Marx's *On the Jewish Question* onwards, against all talk of morality and, in particular, against the vocabulary of "justice" and "rights"—or, to be more precise, against the idea of believing in such notions, rather than adopting and propagating them, where appropriate, in the course of the struggle. So, in the *Critique of the Gotha Programme,* Marx writes of the notions of "equal right" and "fair distribution" as "ideological nonsense . . . ideas which in a certain period had some meaning but have now become obsolete verbal rubbish." In 1864, he apologized to Engels in the following terms: "I was obliged," he wrote, "to insert two phrases about 'duty' and 'right' into the Preamble to the Rules [of the International Working Men's Association], ditto 'truth, morality and justice' but these are placed in such a way that they can do no harm." "Justice," Engels once observed, is "but the ideologized, glorified expression of the existing economic relations, now from their conservative, and at other times from their revolutionary angle." But it was Lenin who put the whole matter most clearly. Speaking to a Komsomol Congress in 1920 he said:

> We say that our morality is entirely subordinated to the interests of the proletariat's class struggle. . . . Morality is what serves to destroy the old exploiting society and to unite all the working people around the proletariat, which is building up a new, a communist society. . . . To a communist all morality lies in this united discipline and conscious mass struggle against the exploiters. We do not believe in an eternal morality, and we expose the falseness of all the fables about morality.

But, surely, it will be said, Marxism has a powerful moral message. In particular, socialism portrays itself as being concerned primarily with issues of justice; Marxists have indeed had an honorable place in countless struggles against injustice and the violations of rights. Czechoslovakian President Havel himself recently, and eloquently, observed:

> There was a time when . . . for whole generations of the downtrodden and oppressed, the word socialism was a mesmerizing synonym for a just world, a time when for the ideal expressed in that word, people were capable of sacrificing years and years of their lives, and their very lives even.

But this objection misses the point. Of course Marxism has offered victims of injustice and oppression and those who sympathize with them an inspiring vision of a future free of both. This objection misses the inspirational core of that vision. What inspires those who grasp what Marxism promises is not the prospect of a complex, conflictual, pluralistic world regulated by principles of justice and the protections of rights, but rather the overcoming of the very conditions that require such principles and protections—the prospect of a world in which justice and rights, together with class conflict and the oppression of the state, will have withered away. Communists have promised an end to injustice and oppression. What they promise, however, is not justice and rights, but, rather, emancipation from the enslaving conditions that make them necessary.

✦

II

I turn, finally, to the second question I asked at the outset: to what, and because of what political morality, did the revolutionary movements of 1989—those that succeeded and those that did not, or have not yet—appeal? A proper academic answer to this question would doubtless distinguish among the different kinds of evidence required to answer it properly—the writings of intellectuals, the speeches of leaders, the slogans and graffiti, the responses of the crowds, the oral evidence of different kinds of participants, the impressions of journalists, etc.—each of which would be given its proper weight among the different, though increasingly interdependent movements, and even among the different stages of these ever faster moving events. Nevertheless, even without the benefit of these indispensable distinctions, which future scholarship will not fail to furnish, it already seems clear at this short distance from them that the revolutionary movements of 1989 were similar, at least with regard to the following decisive points.

First, they were citizens' movements and actively invoked the idea of citizenship. In virtually every case, they were appeals by and to citizens that implied a retraction from more particular and immediate commitments, loyalties, and interests. Hence the rhetoric of "round tables" and "forums," one of which was, indeed, civic and the other new in, among other things, just this respect. The students of Tiananmen Square were seeking to transcend their generational and occupational identity and speak in the name of the "people"; and indeed from mid–May, the demonstration expanded to over a million people, and included workers, party bureaucrats, professionals, and even units of the military. One of the slogans shouted in demonstrations in East Germany was "We are the people!" The point is perhaps most dramatically made by the insignificance of ethnic and religious factors in the Timişoara uprising. It originated with the protests of Hungarian Protestants, but these, emphatically, were not what it was *about*. Only in the Caucasus and in Yugoslavia, especially Serbia, does this commitment to a pluralism-encompassing citizenship seem to be seriously in jeopardy.

Second, these were movements that appealed to a sense of distributive justice and fairness. For they were protests against the arbitrary allocation of advantage and opportunity, against the failed command economy that was itself a major source of scarcity as well as injustice, and in general against a system governed by no rationally defensible distributive principle, in which, from the ordinary citizen's point of view:

> . . . "they" can do everything they want [to the citizen]—take away his passport, have him fired from his job, order him to move, send him to collect signatures against the Pershings, bar him from higher education, take away his driver's licence, build a factory producing mostly acid fumes right under his windows, pollute his milk with chemicals to a degree beyond belief, arrest him simply because he attended a rock concert, raise prices arbitrarily, any-time and for any reason, turn down all his humble petitions without cause, prescribe what he must read before all else, what he must demonstrate for, what he must sign, how many square feet his apartment may have, whom he may meet and whom he must avoid.

There was, of course, no unified agreement about what distributive principles *would* be just, only that they should prevail; though all, including the gracefully depart-ing elites, were further united in the view that they could only prevail if markets—including capital and labor markets—play a key role in both the transition to and functioning of the future economy. The burning question for the future is, of course, just what kind and what degree of public intervention in markets justice will require. One real possibility is that, in full recoil from real socialism, the post-revolutionary elites will embrace the full package of the counter-ideology of free-market liberalism, which, like Marxism but on different grounds, also rejects the very notion of "social justice." Such an outcome, occurring under conditions of economic decline and crisis and at the periphery of the world capitalist system, would indeed be a novel, late-twentieth-century version of the revolution betrayed.

Third, the uprisings were defensive movements, aimed at revolution in the name of procedural justice, the rule of law, the protection of individuals' basic consti-tutional rights and liberties—the Principles of 1789, as distinct from the positive social and economic rights added to them in the Universal Declaration of 1948. In part, they were directed at abuses and corruption by individuals (Ceauşescu, Honecker, Zhivkov) and by a whole political class, as in China. These were certainly important in mobilizing people over grievances that took visible and outrageous forms. But at root the issue was the rejection of an entire institutional system that worked through com-mand, restrained only through bargaining, and whose official rationale lay entirely in the future it promised rather than in its responsiveness to present, actual individuals' interests.

Moreover, there was one particular individual right that was of special signifi-cance in 1989: the right to free travel across frontiers. It was the mass effective exercise of this right and its subsequent recognition by the East German state that unleashed the East German events and all that followed from them. The right to leave one's country is, as Locke intimated, a right of particular significance, for only where it is effective can the according of consent to a regime or a system be a genuine choice. Clearly,

Egon Krenz, in granting it, hoped thereby to establish the legitimacy of the German Democratic Republic; at the time of this writing, that hope looks indeed forlorn.

Fourth, the revolutions of 1989 were pluralist movements that demanded an end to the monopoly of power by the communist, an end to the *nomenklatura,* to the euphemistically described "leading role" of the party, to "ghost parties" in false "alliances" playing proportional roles based on frozen statistics from the past, to the suppression of local, regional, and national issues, and to suppression of the real history (as in the Baltics) of how nations were incorporated into the Soviet Empire, and an end to the denial of expression to and institutional embodiment of cultural, notably ethnic and religious, identities. In part, the revolutions embodied the expression of this pluralism or diversity, but, more significantly, they also expressed, often very clearly, a vivid sense, unavailable to the ruling structures, of the value of it.

Finally, they were skeptical movements—utterly skeptical not only of the content of what socialism had promised, both materially and morally, but of the very cognitive pretensions of the ruling parties who had in any case lost their way and abandoned any serious claim to knowledge-based, let alone science-based, authority (though Ceauşescu went on claiming it to the end). This is, in part, obviously a result of the massive economic failure of the prevailing system, as well as justified doubts about all the various attempts to reform it from within, from the Hungarian economic reforms onwards. But it also exhibits a deeper and more universal trend: a new sense, arising out of "green" concerns, of the complexity and uncertainty of the interaction between Man and Nature, and, in consequence, an awareness of the ecological consequences of the old Promethean Marxist vision of ending human exploitation through the exploitation of nature.

These were, in short, revolutions, some attempted, some successful, against hubris—the hubris of individual leaders, political elites, and indeed of an entire political class. They were also revolutions against the hubris of an arbitrary and oppressive system—economic, social, and political—whose claims to legitimacy were no longer, for the most part, even proclaimed by its rulers. But, above all, they were revolutions against the hubris of a political morality that for decades sustained that system and its leaders. In this sense, they were revolutions of fallen expectations, revolutions in the name of freedom—but of freedom, in a sense Hegel never intended, as the recognition of necessity.

Democracy Before Socialism

✦

George Konrád

A famous Hungarian writer and critic of the communist regime
here restates the thesis, rooted in disillusionment with the
shape and style of Soviet socialism, that democracy is a prior
requirement for socialism or indeed any authentic social reform.

Every culture has a grammar; ours does, and so do those of the other Europeans. How do we distill ourselves into a text, how does the text arise from our texture? There are occasional, local, conditional, and relative grammatical rules of communication. There are intercultural agreements, too, permanent and universal. Our moral history lies in our progress toward these rules, through a succession of errors. In the world of the philosophers, these agreements stand out. Geniuses don't all sing in the same chorus, but they understand one another better than the blinkered majority who are prey to misunderstanding, to taking offense, and to squabbling. These rules together make up a methodology of social communication.

Our experience is that the undisturbed communication of metaphysically equal subjects is best assured by a carefully cultivated mutual respect. Liberal philosophy expresses with the greatest formal coherence our European culture's most considered agreements on how we should harmonize our interests. Such philosophy finds its social and political form in democracy. Liberalism is much more than the propaganda of those political parties that call upon its name. Liberalism is a political mentality mindful of the mutually acceptable rules of the game and how to develop them. It means intellectual rigor and an insistence on fair play. That is where the significance of liberalism is to be found, as well as the case for it.

Children who can't read yet can argue about what's all right in a game and what isn't all right, what's fair and what's not fair. Consciously or not, every sports fan shares a philosophy of fair play. Liberal democracy has no need to repress people's expression of their spontaneous sense of justice, or their debates about whether a given measure is a fair rule of the game, because such debates and corrections only make the system stronger. Dictatorship, on the other hand, is incorrigible in this respect. If it doesn't

George Konrád, "Democracy Before Socialism," from *Antipolitics*, Harcourt Brace Jovanovich, 1984, pp. 186–190.

repress the free discussion of legislation, it will be overthrown by law. Liberal philosophy creates stability; antiliberal philosophies produce instability.

Democracy has its own style, which follows from a strategy of learning. A learner believes it is more important to learn than to teach. Sensing how little is known of all the things that could be known, he is ironic; he sees that the unknown is the greater part. The heroes of the European intelligentsia have been learners and not teachers, experimenters rather than defenders of existing knowledge. A society that learns is the root idea of all utopias—a community of people living together according to wise ordinances, constantly reviewing and refining them, with thoroughness and care.

It is nonsense to suppose that any utopia would approve of censorship. A utopian society is one that has become a subject for itself, through free communication among personalities open to learning. By definition, society is self-shaping and experimental, since it is made up of individual human beings with wills of their own, and there is no commandment sent from some higher sphere that is superior to their will. All existing rules are human, devised by human beings, demanded and observed by them. Our rules cannot be directly derived from any hypothesis about God or history. They are our work, and if we don't like them we can make others instead. If a small group of people clings by force to rules that the majority accepts only under compulsion, sooner or later revolutions will breach those rules and alter them radically.

Real reform is possible only in liberal democracies, where the majority, after hearing out the views of the minority, can act to change the laws. In dictatorships, reform is pseudoreform—a softening of the dictatorship, a lifting of this or that onerous restriction forced on the majority, while at the same time the overall system of restraints and prohibitions imposed by the minority remains in force.

Human beings are in principle free with respect to one another, since they can either kill or come to terms with one another. Dictatorship doesn't really exist, even if it goes on for a long time, because it is so chancy. Anyone can kill the dictator. No one knows in advance who may become a tyrannicide. The wisest and most powerful tyrant cannot see into the mind of his most wretched and dull-witted servant. Hitlerism would have collapsed if the attempt on Hitler's life had succeeded. The constitutional democracy of the United States, on the other hand, remains undisturbed by the assassination of Presidents.

A society is more advanced the more it becomes a subject for itself, the more conscious it becomes of its own interests. Limited autonomy means a cruder culture, a society of people who are not much given to thinking. Where individuals are not free, society is not free either. If the individuals in socialist society are not free, socialism is not a society of freedom. It represents something cruder: a dictatorship in the face of which revolution is justified.

In a liberal democracy, socialist reforms can be adopted by parliamentary majority, according to the constitutional rules of the game. Democracy is more important and more basic than the reform of income and property relations. Democracy can include socialism, but one-party state socialism cannot include democracy. If it gives ground, citizens newly awakened to their dignity will destroy the rigidly centralized political structure.

A socialism that benefits the majority—whether by the just redistribution of income or by the just redistribution of power—is possible only in a society where the majority decides and the minority is free to voice its opinion without restriction. If the so-called achievements of socialism cannot be debated there is no democracy. It is a cardinal principle that the values of democracy precede those of socialism (while in no way denying them).

The political, artistic, and scientific avant-garde is the creation of learners, people who recognize neglected human possibilities. Tradition is a product of learning, but so too is the radical demand that action be justified not merely by images of the past but also by images that speak of an imagined future. The past has not been so wonderful as to make utopia superfluous.

It is a false learning model that ranks what each of us has learned higher or lower on some scale or other, instead of recognizing the mystic uniqueness of each human being. Ways of learning can be evaluated, nevertheless. Liberal democracy is a way to minimize violence in our relations. It is a philosophical affirmation that interests can be reconciled. This is demonstrated by the experience of an infinite number of exchanges.

Liberal democracy is a philosophical refutation of the belief that the interests of flesh-and-blood people can really be antagonistic, that antagonistic conflicts can be resolved only by struggle of the who-beats-whom or the I-kill-you-or-you-kill-me sort. In place of escalation of the struggle, liberal democracy recommends peaceful negotiation. Your killing me is not the only alternative to my killing you. The alternative to war is liberal transaction.

The philosophy of dictatorship applies the laws of the war of people against people to the coexistence of individuals. The philosophy of democracy tries to apply the rules of transaction among individuals to the coexistence of peoples. If I insist that power should derive from transaction, I am a democrat. I have a right to endorse the philosophy of democracy, and no one can prevent me from doing so.

Whose Revolution in Eastern Europe?

✦

Michael Howard

Pondering the implications of radical change in Eastern Europe, this author cautions against unrealistic expectations based on our own experience and against presuppositions that have nothing to do with either the problems or the desires peculiar to Eastern Europe. And he warns, appropriately, that the outcomes may not meet with our approval.

Casual tourists from the West, traveling in air-conditioned buses and staying in modern government-sponsored hotels, may be pleasantly surprised by their first sight of Central Europe. In what used to be East Germany the countryside looks as prosperous and cultivated as anywhere in the West. City centers have been tidied up and carefully rebuilt, while the apartment blocks on the outskirts are no worse than one would find in the United Kingdom—in some places rather better. In Poland agriculture is picturesquely archaic, and in the bustling small towns the people look as well clothed and fed as they would at home. In Czechoslovakia Prague sparkles like a jewel, its streets thronged with happy holidaymakers. As for Hungary, it is hard to realize one is no longer in the West: the huge plains being efficiently (to all appearances) harvested by echelons of combines; the signs of prosperous well-being in industrial centers like Miskolc; the weekenders crowding the shores of Lake Balaton; above all, Budapest, a city in its elegance still more comparable to Paris than Vienna—is there anything seriously wrong here? The region is certainly "backward" compared with Western Europe and the United States, but it always was. The cars and roads are smaller, the trains shabbier, the shops fewer and selling a more limited range of goods. But so it was with Spain or southern Italy a few decades ago, a "backwardness" almost attractive to the overfed, overurbanized Westerner and, anyhow, surely remediable by a judicious infusion of capital, technology, and expertise.

Appearances are not totally deceptive. The image of Eastern Europe as a miserable gulag oppressed by Soviet power was always overdrawn. Even in gulags prisoners find ways to get by. The system worked, up to a point. The hard work of the Germans, the vitality of the Poles, the ingenuity of the Hungarians, the canniness of the Czechs,

Michael Howard, "Whose Revolution in Eastern Europe?" from *London Review of Books,* October 25, 1990. Reprinted by permission of David Higham Associates Limited.

all made it work or found ways round it if it did not. Life was admittedly hell for the intellectuals and the entrepreneurial classes, all the people that we in the West knew and liked; all the people on whom the ultimate progress and prosperity of their country depended. But the industrial workers in the cities and the poorer workers on the land enjoyed a degree of security, if not indeed prosperity, undreamed of by their parents. No one was *very* badly off. Things were very slowly beginning to get better, much as they had been getting better in France in the last years of the *ancien régime*. With continued suppression of the malcontents, continued isolation from the West, so reasoned the apparatchiks, they might go on getting better—if they were not already as good as anyone could reasonably expect.

It is important to bear this in mind, for once the present excitement is over, and unless the new rulers manage the transition to a market economy with unusual skill, nostalgia for the good old days when the currency was stable and jobs were secure may become a serious problem. There is something a little disquieting about the way in which the new political elites blame their difficulties on the people they have to govern: on the sluggish reluctance of bureaucrats to take responsibility, on the unwillingness of peasants to take back the land so freely offered to them, on the reluctance to participate in elections, on the habits of black-market dealing and petty corruption that grew up under a command economy. The cynic may well recall Bertolt Brecht's advice to the East German regime after the Berlin uprising of 1953: Rather than elect a new government, they had better elect a new people. For "the masses," to use that inadequate term, had as little to do with the revolutions of 1989 as they had with those of 1848. The old order fell not as the result of a great popular upheaval but because it had lost self-confidence, was not prepared to defend itself, and crumbled at the first sign of urban insurrection. The exceptions, of course, were the Poles. There the Catholic Church had preserved across class barriers a stubborn and universal sense of national resistance that had gradually and peacefully found political expression in Solidarity: a body so clearly expressive of the national will that the regime prudently decided to admit it to a share of power. But the Czechs had been too effectively cowed, and the Hungarians were too well fed, to make trouble on a major scale. The Jakeš and Kádár regimes enjoyed the legitimacy of inertia, and that is not a force to be underrated. The passivity with which they allowed themselves to be swept away once it was clear that the Russians would not help them showed how little confidence they had in their own achievements. They did not even try, as Iliescu did in Romania, to recruit strong-arm squads from the factories or the collective farms to deal with the urban, largely bourgeois insurgents who overthrew them. "The masses" stood by and watched that overthrow with indifference, if not contempt.

Their successors in government are very conscious that they do not yet enjoy the support of those masses. They have been at pains to establish their democratic credentials by instituting pluralistic politics, free elections, and elaborate provision for "human rights," but they are deeply worried, as we have seen, by the apparent indifference of "the people" in whose name they have taken power. To blame this indifference on bad habits produced by forty years of communist rule is, however, wishful thinking. More likely it results from the caution of the good soldier Schweik, who has seen governments come and seen them go and will judge the new leaders not by their good intentions but by their results. Democracy has always been a fragile plant in Central Europe, let alone farther east. The survival of the new regimes, and perhaps of the ideals they incarnate, depends less on the democratic title deeds that appear so impressive in the West than on their capacity to make the economic system work more effectively than their predecessors did. The bottom line is not the ballot box but *la poule au pot*.

To survive, the new regimes have to solve two gigantic problems. The first is to modernize their economic infrastructure after forty years of stagnation and neglect. The second is to move from a command to a market economy—a task universally recognized to be urgent and necessary but that is bound to be, both politically and socially, deeply traumatic. The establishment of formal democratic structures will be relevant only insofar as it enables them to do so, whether through mobilizing public opinion or by attracting essential support from the West.

Those likely to do well in the new market economies of Central Europe are not the civilized, Western-oriented intellectuals who come to conferences and seminars and spend a term in American universities, but other elements not nearly so nice. They will be the former black-market operators and the former apparatchiks—insofar as the two categories are distinct. These are the people who have the contacts, the local influence, who know how to run things. These are, unfortunately, the kind of people without whom capitalism cannot get going in the first place or continue to function for very long—Balzacian creatures, such as those who laid the foundations for the prosperity of Western Europe and the United States. They will be distinctly unpopular with those who lack their dubious talents, and their activities may lead people to wonder whether there was not something to be said for socialism after all.

It would, therefore, not be surprising if quite bitter social conflict were to develop in Central Europe. In fact, the fundamental problems of the region are not political or economic. They are social. They have less to do with the mechanism of the state than with the habits of the community—with the nature, or the absence, of what Ralf Dahrendorf and others have called "civil society." There is nothing necessarily wrong with social conflict. The problem is how to create political systems that can contain that conflict and make it fruitful. Some Western models may be helpful and some techniques may be transferable, but only at a very superficial level. Fundamentally, what Central Europe needs today is not so much formal democracy on the Western model as strong governments commanding broad consensus, responsive to popular needs, and operating within the rule of law.

If multiparty democracy can produce such governments, well and good, but the going will be very tough. Even with Western support on an unimaginably lavish scale, the economic situation is likely to get worse before it can get better. And here the analogy with 1848—1848 in France, that is—does seem depressingly relevant. If the new political parties cannot produce political stability and economic prosperity, they will inherit the popular contempt that attached to the old order, and their destruction will be greeted with the same indifference.

There has been an unspoken assumption in the West that the only obstacle to the peoples of Central and Eastern Europe adopting Western values and structures has been the imposition by the Soviet Union of foreign ideology and foreign domination. It was assumed that once these political shackles were removed, the peoples could, like released prisoners, resume a "normal" political life.

However, the history of Central Europe has produced a political culture distinct from that of the West. There has not been the growth of self-governing institutions from the bottom, such as occurred in Anglo-Saxon societies, or the drastic destruction of the feudal order and the institution of a legal, administrative, and political framework based on a concept of the Rights of Man, which took place in Western Europe after 1789. In Central and Eastern Europe centuries of agrarian feudalism and authoritarian rule were bound to produce a political culture of acquiescence if not submission, tempered by skepticism and evasion. Vigorous individual enterprise was unlikely to flourish, and those most likely to promote it emigrated in large numbers to the United States. In particular, intellectuals unwilling to be assimilated into the mechanism of the state were forced into interior or actual emigration—a situation that won them sympathy from their colleagues abroad but tended to alienate them from their own peoples, of whom they too easily conceived an ideal image very different from the mundane reality. How can we, from such roots, expect model liberal democracies to emerge overnight?

It is important, therefore, not to expect too much too soon. Dramatic appeals have been made to the effect that "democracy" is under threat in Central Europe and that it is the duty of the West to pour in money in order to shore it up. There are certainly good reasons why we should provide the new regimes with all the help we can in order to modernize their economies—good, practical economic and ecological reasons—but such contributions will not necessarily safeguard "democracy." A "democratic" regime that depends on foreign support for its credibility is something of a contradiction in terms. Democracy is a matter of political habits, not of formal institutions, and the development of these habits takes time.

Above all, we must beware the Manichaean tendency, so prevalent in the United States, to divide the regimes into totalitarian or democratic, slave or free, and ignore the gradations that lie between. In Central Europe Marxism-Leninism, with all its cumbrous apparatuses of political and intellectual oppression, has been effectively and permanently destroyed. It did not work. But pluralistic democracy may not work either, at least not yet. If it does, it is likely to be along lines rather different from our own. We must accept that in the new "European house" envisioned by Mikhail Gorbachev there are likely to be many apartments, and that in some of them we may find ourselves not entirely comfortable.

The Triumph of Capitalism?

✦

Bogdan Denitch

Professor Denitch of City University of New York, known for his
publications on contemporary Yugoslavia, looks critically at the
wishful tendency to suppose that the collapse of communism is
identical to the victory of capitalism. He insists, quite properly,
that the situation is much more complex than that, and that
what eventuates in Eastern Europe will have had to come to
grips with local conditions, the most fundamental of which
make political resolutions prerequisites for viable economic
arrangements.

The familiar debate about the prospects for capitalism and socialism has taken a
sharp turn as a result of three new trends transforming the politics of the world. In
brief, these are the collapse of the communist dictatorships in Eastern Europe, the end
of the cold war, and the growing pace of European unification. Each by itself would
represent a major development; the three together mark a profound historical change.

One likely consequence will be a relative decline in the economic and military
position of the United States, with a consequent loss of moral and political authority.
This also means that the capitalism that will continue to dominate the world is likely
to have new and peculiar characteristics, rather different from those propounded by
Anglo-Saxon apologists. It will be a world capitalism without the familiar cold war;
without the United States as dominant power; without a threat, real or supposed, of
Soviet expansionism.

It will take some time for the magnitude of these changes to sink in. But, clearly,
the capitalism likely to prevail in Europe will be different from the American and
British models, perhaps in some instances sharply different. For capitalism is not an
abstract entity, beyond the impact of time and historical change. Nor is it simply an
economic system (whatever that might mean). It is a historically inflected and changing system, in which political, economic, and social arrangements interact.

Capitalism has its institutions and legal systems, its armed bodies of men, its
dominant ideology, and certain kinds of political relations on a world scale. It is also a

Bogdan Denitch, "The Triumph of Capitalism?" from *Dissent,* Spring 1990, pp. 177–180.

system in which the *political* rule of parties committed to its maintenance—as it exists in actuality, and not as a theoretical "model"—is necessary. This is true whether the dominant party is officially procapitalist or prolabor, conservative or social democratic. Seen from this perspective, capitalism is in considerable trouble in at least three places: Eastern Europe, Western Europe, and the Third World. Let me take these in order, keeping in mind that capitalism in trouble does not necessarily signify good news for democrats and socialists.

◆

EASTERN INFATUATION

Large sections of the East European intelligentsia, it is true, are now fascinated by the idea of "the market." That "market," however, has rather little to do with the market that functions in the real capitalist world. The talk about markets in former communist states often serves as a synonym or code word for seeing to it that the state and especially the party are deprived of control over the economy and society. In East European countries lacking a usable tradition of political democracy, the market that is now being introduced could well bring about what I'd call a process of "Mexicanization." Both Mexico and a "Mexicanized" Eastern Europe have to cope with giant superpowers pressing down upon them; both are or will be mixed economies with a powerful state sector, a corrupt yet vital private sector, an elite that includes technocrats, decent trade unionists, corrupt trade unionists, as well as the rich and the gangsters. We will have all of that in Eastern Europe, and whatever else, it will not be capitalism as described in textbooks or the kinds of prose poems about the "free market" that have been appearing in the American press. Rather, it will be a highly politicized system, with political dominance manifesting itself through the economy, although at least in part it will include a functioning market. But, *nota bene,* this market economy will be subject to considerable corruption as former bureaucrats of the nomenklatura join foreign investors in a scramble to grab the more lucrative chunks of the economy at knock-down prices. Happily, many of these people will lose their shirts—the fates are sometimes just.

My prediction is that after the kissing stops, some very grim economic and social issues will come up. The prognosis for a decent democratic outcome is best for those countries with powerful, old-fashioned trade unions struggling to make sure that the burden of social transformation is not borne entirely by industrial workers and other employees. Whatever else, the upheavals in Eastern Europe did not take place in order to abolish the crude but almost universal welfare systems. To the contrary, *improvements* in services, health, education, and pensions, not to speak of living standards, are expected to result from toppling the party dictatorships—and sooner rather than later.

The idea of introducing the raw market of Thatcherite capitalism is therefore—short of authoritarian repression—politically unviable, even if it were morally and economically desirable. Since the communist parties are now disabled, an authoritarian repression could come only from the right, or from a curious union of communist technocrats and nationalist populists. In consequence, the optimistic prognosis for

Eastern Europe would be for parliamentary democracies with strong unions, mixed economies, and a substantial socially owned or nationalized sector. In other words, a social-democratic type of neocorporatism, somewhat like the West European welfare states. The pessimistic prognosis is for a xenophobic nationalist-populist authoritarian neocorporatism with limited democracy. Neither represents quite the victory of capitalism now being celebrated in the Western press. And neither represents a victory of socialism.

✦

MITIGATING FACTORS IN THE WEST

In Western Europe capitalism is also facing peculiar circumstances. There are at least three forces that militate against capitalism as popularly understood in the United States and Great Britain: that is, the free market geared to profit maximization. That system is, of course, a myth, although a very powerful myth. There are a number of obstacles to such a mytho-poetic system dominating a unified European Community. First, powerful trade unions are allied to the social democratic parties, which have a plurality in the European parliament. Their prospects for increased political power are increasing. Second, the Catholic Church and the social-Christian parties allied with it do not take to possessive individualism with any more enthusiasm than do the social democrats—as a matter of fact, their formulation is that private property is acceptable provided society holds a mortgage on it. Presumably, this mortgage can be called in when the private property in question no longer serves socially acceptable ends. Third, others not exactly committed to free marketeering are the Eurocrats, an increasingly influential bureaucracy in the European Community in Brussels (against which Thatcher leads a valiant and, happily, losing struggle). The Eurocrats are economic and social interventionists or statists, anything but free marketeers. So the capitalism of Western Europe will be a sort of neocorporatist arrangement, with powerful trade unions, an advanced welfare state, and a great deal of controls—conscious, politically imposed controls over what can and cannot be done with the movement of capital and where investments should go and what social policies should be. That is, a capitalism modified and defanged by social democracy.

This will, of course, not be socialism as we democratic socialists understand it. It will, however, be a capitalism almost unrecognizable to American businessmen and their intellectual cheerleaders. It will be a capitalism somewhat like that in Sweden today. But that tells us that the political, social, and economic terrain that contemporary capitalism represents in real life is an enormously wide one, with the political and social outcomes not at all predictable. Once you have said a society is capitalist, you have not said much, or enough, about it. You are only *beginning* to describe that society.

The transition from feudalism to capitalism took centuries. A new postcapitalist order called socialism may also take centuries to develop. But it will make an enormous difference whether that development occurs in a society where labor and socialist parties are strong, where a measure of social justice is legislated, and where a democratic welfare state exists that is more egalitarian than the communism of the past forty years. (The difference in wages between a Swedish factory worker and a manager in the auto industry is one to three. That means the actual socioeconomic differences are smaller in Sweden than in the Soviet Union or Eastern Europe. So, when we say that Sweden is a capitalist society, that needs to be qualified over and over again.)

◆

BLOCKING DEMOCRACY IN THE THIRD WORLD

The third place in which capitalism is not in very good shape is the Third World. Despite the brief celebration of the economic results of the Chicago school in Chile, Brazil, Ghana, the Ivory Coast, and Argentina, it turns out that the notion that markets and capitalism necessarily bring about democracy is not true. Quite the contrary. Insisting on marketizing those economies, on having them abide by the rules of the International Monetary Fund (IMF) and the World Bank is an almost sure guarantee that democracy will be endangered. It is very hard to be democratic and carry out the World Bank's economic cure, which includes cutbacks in already miserly social spending, freezing wages, and letting prices find their natural level. The economic burden such a policy imposes on the working population is not one that any popular regime or democratic polity can bear.

Capitalism has triumphed in the Third World, but in a peculiar sense. As the communist bloc collapses, so does its model for the Third World collapse. The Soviet Union is no longer a convincing rival in the Third World. It is difficult to treat somebody as a convincing rival if he comes requesting loans and technological aid. What follows is that a main ideological prop in the Third World—the cold war—is now gone. This means, to use an old-fashioned term, that the contradictions of the capitalist system itself become the terrain of political struggle. No longer can one say (not that it was ever morally valid), "Yes, yes, we, or our paid thugs, murder nuns and priests, but there is a more dangerous communist menace." And one cannot keep saying "Free trade unions are a nice thing but of course we will postpone that until we defeat communist insurgency." Now that communism has defeated itself, the issues of social justice, trade union rights, public squalor and private wealth will become central. An open socialist party campaigning on these issues came within an inch of winning the first democratic election in Brazil since the end of decades of military regime rule.

Apologists for capitalism are not very good at fighting over these issues. Admiration for capitalism in real life is limited to a small section of the population. For example, most East Europeans I speak to love the market abstractly. The market they love means a guaranteed job for them and their children and relatives and of course their friends, cheap housing, public health, free education, and a pension. Provided they all have all these things they would love to have a market in which they could get jeans that fit. But that's not what the market is all about. Most of the free-market supporters in Eastern Europe would be utterly shocked at the poverty and social injustice imbedded in American society. Poor as most of the East European cities are, you will not find people sleeping in the streets. Nor in most of Western Europe.

The visible exception is Great Britain. Social brutality seems now to be an Anglo-American specialty. But once you can no longer wield the threat of dictatorial communism in political debate, a whole host of domestic social issues becomes truly urgent. Nor is it only the left that believes that America has desperately overdue social agendas if this is to be a minimally decent society. The smarter pundits of the American right, like Kevin Phillips, predict that in the nineties the pendulum will swing away from conservative dominance.

If, then, capitalism faces serious troubles, what has triumphed? What has triumphed is the notion that socialism is not something that can be wished into being overnight. What has triumphed is the notion that there may be an extremely long period of transition during which most countries will be a part of a single world market that is essentially capitalist. But what has not triumphed is the worldview of the Chicago school, Margaret Thatcher, Reaganauts, and the others; that peculiarly puritanical version of capitalism that is really a part of Anglo-Saxon exceptionalism.

◆

NECESSITY OF A DEMOCRATIC STATE

In Eastern Europe the goal of democratic movements has to be the creation of a legal order where the judiciary system is independent of the state, a richly varied civil society autonomous from the state and the dominant political parties, genuine mass democratic trade unions, and a multiparty parliamentary democracy. These are necessary but not sufficient prerequisites for a genuine democracy, which should also move toward workers' control in the workplace, popular grass-roots participatory authority in the various institutions, and the abolition of gender oppression. Such democratic socialist goals are not to be counterposed to the institutionalization of a democratic polity. Fighting for these goals requires stable democratic institutions and development of a democratic political culture. A parliamentary democracy with powerful unions, parties, and social movements is the optimal terrain on which to work for democratic change. This requires tolerance, a virtue rare enough anywhere and positively priceless in Eastern Europe, where common sense argues against pushing political and national differences to the limit, at least until democratic institutions develop firmness and stability.

Tolerance of differences is essential in order to build stable democratic regimes. It is the precondition for a democratic civic culture. That means no vengeance, no matter how justified, against former communist hard-liners, no attempts to illegalize communist parties, and above all no hunt for scapegoats in what will be grim times.

Eastern Europe is populated today with ghosts of chauvinist, populist, and right-wing corporatist parties. It is important to try to keep these ghosts quiet. Nationalism is the red meat of the organic "genuine" Heideggerian national community, all too easy to mobilize against a mere "cool" legal and rational democratic universalism. It is therefore a continual threat to those who would build a multiparty democratic order. Nor does it help the prospects for democracy that many of the reformist intellectuals in

Eastern Europe have fallen in love with the idea of the market. From love of that idea almost as much suffering may be visited on Eastern Europe as has been for the equally abstract idea of centralized planning. There seems to be no limit to how much suffering can be imposed on living bodies in the name of abstract ideas. That seems to be the original sin of intellectuals.

In Hungary national populists have already begun attacking "cosmopolitan," read Jewish, big-city liberals. Similar national populist attacks on economic reforms and pluralistic democracy, with or without anti-Semitic subtexts, can be expected in Poland, Romania, and Serbia. The road to democratization runs through perilous straits in Eastern Europe. That is why it is essential to help democratic institutions, trade unions, and civic groups with massive moral, political, and material support from the West.

Genuine democracy requires at least minimal commitment to social justice. Effective political equality is not consistent with great differences in wealth. Wealth all too easily translates into political power. The social solidarity required to make the sacrifices necessary for modernizing the East European economies cannot be generated with an untrammeled "pure" market economy. There is no such thing as a "pure" economic policy that can be isolated from social and political consequences. Professors Friedman and Sachs should be kept at a distance from policy making in Eastern Europe. Their policies are dangerous to democracy itself.

The Revolution of 1989:
The Unbearable Burden of History

✦

Jerzy Jedlicki

This cautionary note, from a professor at the Institute of History, Polish Academy of Sciences (Warsaw), reminded his listeners at a lecture in Washington, D.C., in June 1990 that the East European states must, in their attempts at reconstruction, reckon with problematical historical freight that is bound to condition the outcomes of their struggle to change.

One of the primary concerns of the revolution in Poland, but also in the rest of Eastern Europe, is the past. Unmarked graves of the victims of the *ancien régime* are searched out; the remains are uncovered, scrutinized, honored, and then reburied in consecrated ground. Monuments are demolished; they will soon be replaced by new ones or by those that were removed half a century earlier. Former street names and, occasionally, names of towns, are being restored. Hated emblems are cut out of the national flag and portraits are knocked off the walls and trampled upon. The Polish White Eagle is regaining its lost crown. Leaders whose names are connected with a memorable national defeat or with a former national upheaval are welcomed back, dead or alive, as a covenant between the old and the new times. Other leaders hurry to rebuild their political parties, which were crushed and outlawed long ago. New statesmen are compared to the old ones: Václav Havel to Tomáš Masaryk, Tadeusz Mazowiecki to Ignacy Paderewski, Lech Wałęsa to Józef Piłsudski. An ousted king sends a message to his former and perhaps also his future subjects in Romania. The Polish president-in-exile in London awaits a solemn declaration of independence, after which he will return to the country he left half a century ago, only to vest the legal instruments of power in the hands of his democratically elected "successor."

The new republic in Poland will undoubtedly be regarded as a direct continuation of the prewar republic; what existed in between will be enclosed in historical parentheses as if the Poles had lived all that time in a coma or in a state of intransigent resistance to the Soviet-imposed regime. Contemporary history is to be rewritten,

Jerzy Jedlicki "The Revolution of 1989: The Unbearable Burden of History," *Problems of Communism,* July–August 1990, pp. 39–45.

truth unearthed, children reeducated, responsibility established, and justice done. Newly emerging parties will no less fiercely argue about who is entitled to be the heir to the political legacy of Polish Peasant Party leader Wincenty Witos or National Democratic movement leader Roman Dmowski than about what is to be done here and now.

Unemployment is not going to threaten the historians in Eastern Europe, even if some of us will have to move to a research field closer to the interests of a larger public. These are indeed golden times for historians. But more seriously, what is the reason for this preoccupation with the past? Why are people becoming so excited when trying on this or that antiquated garb, or disposing of the debris of the past?

One answer is that all revolutions arouse historical consciousness. A revolution implies a reevaluation of a nation's history. Moreover, however paradoxical it might at first appear, the bigger the leap forward, the more anxiously we look backward. We assimilate the unknown to the known and persuade ourselves that the unprecedented enterprise we have just embarked upon is but a repetition of an old and familiar pattern.

However, other factors also underlie this interest in history in East European societies. Under the communist regimes, a broad range of recent history had been so distorted or doomed to oblivion that the moment of revolution became a moment of revelation, a moment of truth. Nations are coming back into possession of their history, regaining their memory, discovering their soldiers' graves scattered all over the world, reconstructing their traditions, singing their sacred, long forbidden songs and, unavoidably, creating new myths and legends in the process. So our present revolution is no less conservative than it is radical, and its Janus-like face looks both ways—into the future and into the past.

◆

THE LABORS OF SISYPHUS

But what if there is indeed a recurrence of historical patterns? After all, how many times in the last two centuries were the Poles (or the Hungarians or the Bulgarians for that matter) fighting, weapons or pens in hand, for their national independence? And how many democratic manifestos have been written by Central-Eastern Europeans (couldn't I just call them "Ceastropeans"?) at home or in exile? And how many times has censorship of the press been abolished? And how many times did each of the countries in this region take off on a new path of economic growth and modernization? Indeed, if all those peoples who live in the narrow space between the old Russian, German, Austrian, and Turkish empires share any basic experience and any common wisdom, it boils down to this: that no victory is ever final, no peace settlement is ever final, no frontiers are secure, and each generation must begin its work anew. There is no linear development in East European history, but rather a Sisyphus-like labor of ups and downs, of building and wrecking, where little depends on one's own ingenuity and perseverance. This sort of mild resignation—social psychologists call it "learned helplessness"—has been conditioned by a very real historical experience and has nothing in common with any fatalistic "Oriental metaphysics."

To be sure, this mood is by no means a general one. Resourceful, energetic people are certainly not lacking in either political or economic life. However, this passive attitude—resulting from the conviction that it is always "they" who decide our fate—is common enough to create a problem in the present period of revolutionary change.

Moreover, Poles have little confidence in the future. Some are not yet convinced that their nation is no longer a pawn in the hands of the big powers or an object of their patronage but has become an autonomous entity in both domestic and international politics. And yet, of the three main goals of each national revolution in Central Europe—independence, democracy, economic change—the first one, long regarded as the most distant and utopian, has been reached almost imperceptibly and with surprising ease, thanks to Big Brother's weakness and his newly acquired human face. Now that the Warsaw Pact's military control over the armies of its member-states is about to be formally renounced, one can safely say that the former "satellite countries" (unlike the seceding Soviet republics) are at last free of the Soviet grip, even if some of these countries grudgingly consent to tolerate the presence of Soviet troops on their territories for a limited period of time.

Still, the joy of regaining sovereignty is overshadowed by the feeling of insecurity. Some Poles fear the Russians: for does not history teach us that they never abandon what they have once conquered? Forced to withdraw today, they will return and retaliate at the first propitious moment. Poles also fear the Germans: for does not history teach us that their nature as ruthless imperialists will not change? And the specter of a new Rapallo agreement between the Soviets and the Germans appears to be the most threatening of all.

Some American commentators on East European events regard these fears as the irrational remnants of old prejudices created by circumstances that have long since passed into history; not so of course with their own worries and fears. For do they not warn that virulent nationalism in Eastern Europe is on the rise again, as it was in the 1920's? Is not Balkanization of the Balkans imminent? Will not 20 or so nationalities and ethnic groups, having broken the chains of enforced communist uniformity, rush at one another with their centuries-old grievances? Are not the Poles born and unrepentant anti-Semites? And does not history teach us that Eastern Europe, for all its admirable striving toward freedom, is always a red-hot caldron that one should stay clear of?

Of course, history teaches us all this and much more. History also teaches us that the Spanish are extremists inclined to slaughter themselves in bloody civil wars, that German patriots love their Kaisers and Führers and have no idea of democracy, and that the British cannot do without oppressing Ireland and the colonies. On top of this, however, history teaches us that historical conditions change, and national characters change with them.

◆

A RETURN TO EUROPE?

Yet, I cannot argue that Eastern Europe is now safe for democracy. As Bronisław Geremek has rightly said about Poland, "the prospects for freedom are secured, but those for democracy remain uncertain." This is so, however, not because this part of Europe lacks a tradition of democracy. Even if this were true (and it is not), an argument drawn from history would provide a poor basis for prediction. Nations can learn democracy. They can also sometimes forget what they had once learned.

The drive to democracy seems strong in most of Central Europe, but there are still many people for whom this word means little, if anything. In the May 27, 1990, local government elections in Poland, for example, 58 percent of those qualified to vote did not go to the polls. This low turnout is disturbing: such a large mass of people alienated from politics could one day become prey to populist demagogues.

These demagogues are already on the spot. In Poland, freedom of association and of the press has brought a whole array of phantoms from the past to the surface of political life. Dozens of right-wing parties are trying to attract followers with the use of nationalist, populist, or slightly veiled anti-Semitic slogans. Their reappearance has alarmed enlightened public opinion: on May 7 of this year—on the initiative of Jerzy Turowicz, the widely respected editor of the Catholic weekly newspaper *Tygodnik Powszechny*—42 intellectuals prominent in Polish politics, journalism, and the arts and sciences met in Cracow, where they signed a statement against chauvinism, anti-Semitism, and the manipulation of Christian values for narrow political purposes; the statement has found broad support among the Polish intelligentsia.

Understandably, Western experts and observers are sensitive to the undeniable threat that a resurgence of nationalism could pose to political stability and incipient democracy in Central Europe. One only wishes that they would pay equal attention to the resolute resistance offered to every public declaration of nationalist bigotry. After all, in Poland's recent local government elections, the right-wing parties won little public support. The Poles overwhelmingly voted for independent candidates or for those supported by the mainstream Solidarity citizens' committees.

"Of course," writes Adam Michnik, "the rejection of totalitarian communism must entail, to some extent, a return to the roots of national identity. This is precisely why one must ask what sort of roots they are and what sort of identity it is." Consequently, he distinguishes two intellectual or spiritual cultures that oppose each other in the 20th-century history of Hungary, Czechoslovakia, and Poland. One is the tradition of xenophobia and intolerance based on social fears and resentments. This legacy can only lead to national isolation and stagnation. The other tradition is the one of liberalism and open-mindedness, the idea of a "return to Europe."

A return to Europe! Every day the Polish press contains new articles about the conditions for our return to Europe. We return to Europe because we have just had our first free elections. We return to Europe because we expect Poland to become a member of the Council of Europe. However, we cannot return to Europe as long as our towns are dirty, our telephones do not work, our political parties are reactionary and parochial, and our mentality "Sovietized." Europe, then, is a measure, a goal, a dream.

A very old dream, one should add. It was dreamt as early as the second half of the 18th century when the Polish intellectual elite perceived that Poland had been left far behind the West European countries in every area, from agriculture and trade to the structure of government. It was precisely in that period that the geographical notion of the West acquired a special meaning as the center of a fast-changing world, of which such countries as Poland, Russia, Greece, and Spain became more or less remote and neglected peripheries. Similarly, at that time the notion of Europe began to shrink to the size of the few most advanced states, while for all others it remained more of an ideal than a reality.

The Ceastropeans responded in two ways to the challenge of modern civilization. Some acknowledged its superiority and eagerly learned from it; they borrowed its knowledge, ideas, institutions, technology, fashions, and customs, and they tried to imitate its achievements. At times, however, this response encouraged a contempt for their own national cultures as somewhat lower and less creative, or at least less mature, than those in Western Europe.

The other, defensive, response looked upon Western civilization as "false," cold, and morally corrupt, because it was seen to be materialistic, godless, mercantile, and rationalistic. By contrast, our Slavic civilization, or our own native culture, even if less sophisticated, was seen as being organic, spiritual, humane, based not upon greed but upon true Christian values.

This dichotomous model is best known from the history of Russia, but to some degree it was omnipresent throughout East-Central Europe. Over the course of the second half of the 19th century, however, the Romantic apologists for native cultures gave way to those intellectuals with a strong sense of belonging to an all-European cultural community (which also embraced countries overseas that were settled by Europeans).

The intellectual elites of every East European country undoubtedly belong to the all-European family, even if they were frequently treated as poor cousins and often felt that they were. But what about their native countries, where did these belong? The Westernizers in the East European nations had to acknowledge their peoples' economic backwardness, civilizational primitivism, poverty, and illiteracy—the accumulated results of the slow peripheral economic development that began in the 16th or 17th century. In the early modern period the reinforcement of serfdom in most of Eastern Europe resulted in the petrification of feudal structures in these societies. The landlords who monopolized both international trade and political power did not allow the growth of the entrepreneurial and commercial classes, and hence they hampered the development of towns and industry. Consequently, the eastern part of the continent practically ceased to take part in the creative work of European civilization, by which I mean pioneering efforts in science, technology, medicine, social organization, the evolution of the theory and practice of law, political thought, etc. Polish scholars, for instance, lost touch with Western philosophy and science during the time of John Locke and Isaac Newton. And later it was very hard to make up for lost time. When closer relations were reestablished in the second half of the 18th century, there could only be one direction of influence: from the west to the east (or to the south) of Europe.

There is no need here to recapitulate the efforts undertaken by the intelligentsias, entrepreneurs, and national governments to overcome underdevelopment of this part of Europe. Although this work was not in vain, the result was what is today called "semi-modernity": a peculiar blend of archaic and modern cultural traits that generates strong social conflicts and authoritarian temptations.

Whatever the results of repeated campaigns to spur economic modernization and improvements in education in Eastern Europe, these efforts could not overcome the negative impact first of the centuries-long national and political dependence on outside imperial powers, then of the destruction caused by two world wars. Thus, there seemed to be no way of narrowing the gap between the two parts of Europe and healing the acute inferiority complex of the less advanced half.

Although imposed by force, a new order called "people's democracy" was introduced at the end of World War II as an apparently quick and efficient means of modernization. In Poland, the communists (then carefully avoiding this name) implemented a long overdue agrarian reform and nationalized industry, steps which at that time were generally regarded as preconditions for economic growth. They guaranteed everybody's right to work; organized free reading and writing courses for illiterate adults; founded new schools, universities, and theaters; built modern steelworks; and initiated the reconstruction of Warsaw, which had been destroyed by the Nazis. In sum, they made great efforts to be seen as a genuine party of progress, capable of mobilizing the nation's energy and making up for centuries of backwardness and social injustice.

No wonder that many of those who shared progressive and democratic ideals were attracted by this program, even if they had good reasons to fear and distrust the Polish, and more so the Soviet, communists. Once again there appeared the hope that Eastern Europe would be able to catch up with and even outrun the West as far as the material bases for civilization were concerned, and yet to create a new society, free of the exploitation of man by man.

The hopes soon proved illusory, and the price paid for this mirage was exceptionally high. The communist measures, instead of erasing the civilizational division of Europe, fixed it in all its dimensions. This is the crucial paradox of an extreme radicalism that began by bidding defiance to the world and ended up as an ossified system of thought and institutions that was impervious to change and reform.

So the communist countries in East-Central Europe came full circle. Measured by virtually every indicator of the quality of life, these countries were still at or near the bottom of the European scale. In the 1980's, they were even lagging behind those fast developing South European countries, such as Spain and Greece, to which they had previously been compared.

Statistics aside, every traveler coming to Poland from the West instantly perceives the difference between the two; unfortunately, the difference is no less clear today than it was in the 18th century. Backwardness is not merely a result of poverty; nor can communists be blamed for everything, dirt, neglect, drunkenness, and bribery included. Rather, this backwardness is, in part at least, the legacy of the ages that neither capitalism, nor communism, neither "organic work," nor a revolution, neither economic incentives, nor evangelistic exhortations have as yet been able to overcome.

So now once again we Europeans on the eastern periphery are trying "to return to Europe," to the Europe of our dreams. These dreams are diverse. Many Ceastropeans dream about European (or for that matter American) wages, cars, and various other accoutrements of Western life; the "populace"—as the latest Central Intelligence Agency report on Eastern Europe informs—"is increasingly hungry for Western-style commodities." Politicians and economists dream about our joining a united Europe, although Zbigniew Brzezinski is warning the impatient Poles about the dangers of creating a new myth: inequalities among nations, he argues, will not disappear in the common European home.

For his part, the Polish poet and Nobel Laureate Czesław Miłosz, who has spent the last 40 years in France and America, is disenchanted. He simply cannot believe that the peoples of Central and Eastern Europe, who experienced nearly 50 years of totalitarianism, should now simply accept the supremacy of certain Western values: "Will the years of suffering under totalitarian rule be obliterated, erased and the people start from scratch? Should the thinkers, poets, and artists join their Western colleagues in the somewhat marginal role assigned to them in societies busy with selling and buying?"

Other intellectuals—formerly in opposition and now in the government—have been dreaming, like Jiří Dienstbier and Václav Havel in Czechoslovakia, of a "better Europe," conceived of as "a friendly community of independent nations" and the embodiment of certain values that we in the East have in short supply. Along a similar line, one Polish author wrote "that not so much our material or civilizational conditions, as the weakening or even loss of those values, which are a foundation of the European culture and tradition, have pushed us away from Europe."

But from which Europe? "Europe"—reminds Adam Michnik—"is not only [François] Mitterrand, but also [Jean Marie] Le Pen; not only [Richard von] Weizsäcker, but also the German [neo-fascist] Republican Party. The idea of a return to Europe may carry with it a radical anti-Russian rhetoric . . . but it can also stand for faith in the Europeanization of the entire part of our continent, including Russia itself."

So this guidepost, which points in the direction of Europe or the West, is rather ambiguous. All Ceastropeans want to leave behind, as soon as possible, the drab barracks of a "real no-longer-existing socialism." But the way to go is by no means clear. They know only one thing for sure: they must start from scratch.

Tadeusz Mazowiecki's government was the first to make the decision: back (or forward) to capitalism, free market, Europe, and the World Bank, as fast as possible, or even a little bit faster than possible. Many foreign advisers commend Poland for its valiant leap forward. First, say experts from Harvard, Chicago, and Oxford, it is generally agreed that denationalization of industry is the precondition for economic growth. Second, they say to the Poles, you have neither the time nor the resources to experiment, so you better choose a system that has worked elsewhere, and this system is free market capitalism. There is no viable alternative; go ahead and one day you will reach—so Jeffrey Sachs assures—an economy "very much in the style of the United States and even more closely in the style of Western Europe, [your] neighbors."

By God, do not listen to the sirens' songs that lure you to the cliffs!—warns another group of advisers. You want capitalism? But what kind of capitalism? A free market? There is no such thing as a free market. In the 19th century, there used to be something close to it, but certainly "for Eastern Europeans," cautions John Kenneth Galbraith, "pure and rigorous capitalism would be no more welcome than it would be for us." Hence, this free market rhetoric betrays "a mental vacuity of clinical proportions." Nor should one listen to those "who see the promise of prompt economic betterment arising out of short-term shock and hardship." "This is a moment," Professor Galbraith continues, "of great and welcome liberty in Eastern Europe. It would be tragic indeed were liberty to be identified there with unacceptable economic deprivation."

Others offer even more caustic appraisals. "Most of the free-market supporters in Eastern Europe would be utterly shocked at the poverty and social injustice imbedded in American society," writes Bogdan Denitch. In fact, the existence of a large underclass of outcasts living outside any civilization does not seem to enter into the calculus of those advocates of an unrestrained free market who like to see the world in black and white. "Nor does it help the prospects for democracy," to quote Denitch again, "that many of the reformist intellectuals in Eastern Europe have fallen in love with the idea of free market. From love of that idea almost as much suffering may be visited on Eastern Europe as has been for the abstract idea of centralized planning."

Moreover, warn other critics, Ceastropeans have no chance to compete with any of the advanced modern economies. They cannot possibly catch up with the West. Poland, for all practical purposes, has fallen into the Third World and even lags behind many developing countries. And "as for the Third World," says Lawrence Weschler, "go ask Brazil or the Philippines or Mexico about the Triumph of Capitalism." Indeed, the question of whether the economic reconstruction now under way in Poland would not bring its "Mexicanization" has started to arouse anxiety among the Poles themselves. In one recent discussion, two prominent Polish politicians even went so far as to wonder if the German-Polish border would become a European Rio Grande.

This could easily happen. And if it does happen, we will again see the invincible Polish smuggler cross the "Oder Rio" under cover of night to barter butter for VCR's in the street dust of the Potsdamer Platz; or smart people of all ages and professions crossing that same river in order to seek some seasonal work so menial that it is despised by Turks or Moroccans. Crossing with them, however, will also be talented Ceastropean mathematicians, biochemists, and sociologists whom we export by the hundreds, free of charge, to European and American universities and laboratories.

Should the division of Europe not be overcome, there is no hope for stabilization and all the ghosts of the past will haunt the European home. There is no better breeding ground for parochial nationalism than economic stagnation, the feeling of helplessness, and the fear of tomorrow.

◆

THE CHALLENGE

What future, then, can a skeptical Ceastropean intellectual predict for his country if he is to play the role of a prophet or a fortune teller (which he is so often expected to do)? Above all, he remembers what Edmund Burke and Alexis de Tocqueville knew so well: that there are many things—work habits, patterns of culture, beliefs, and prejudices—that revolutions cannot revolutionize. We carry the burden of the past on our shoulders, as both a gift and a curse. The historical legacy contains precious national values. But it also contains pernicious, non-functional traits that hamper progress. It is impossible to get rid of these traits at one blow, and one had better not try.

Yet, Ceastropeans should not yield to a historical fatalism that excuses all problems. If efforts aimed at modernization have failed so many times before, the only legitimate conclusion is that one must start again, especially now, when external conditions appear to be more favorable than ever before.

The task is by no means confined to economic recovery and transformation, important as they are. In order to keep pace with the more advanced part of Europe, Poland and its neighbors will have to develop their systems of communication, financial services, environmental protection, city management, health and welfare systems, education, scientific research, etc. All these areas badly need massive new injections not only of capital, but also of human energy, ideas, and skills. Both the enthusiasts of free trade and their opponents should have these civilizational needs in mind when they discuss the role of the state in the national economies of Eastern Europe.

Sole reliance on state initiative to solve pressing social problems has its own high costs, as the postwar era has shown. It is obvious that the communists' centralization of decision-making over the allocation of all resources prevented people from taking any initiative into their own hands, even with regard to their own neighborhoods. In Poland, only now are we witnessing the slow revival of voluntary associations to tackle public problems on the national and local levels. But it is still too early to say whether the new democratic government, particularly the city and commune councils elected in May, will be efficient and effective in sustaining this grass-roots initiative and public spirit.

But one must also beware of falling into the opposite extreme of the libertarian-conservative doctrine that wants to limit the state's initiative, means, and prerogatives to a minimum. In the conditions of poverty and underdevelopment in Eastern Europe, such an approach could easily result in blatant social inequalities and a breakdown of the economic and cultural infrastructure.

If Ceastropeans really want to "return to Europe," they will have to first find and then maintain a balance between disruptive party politics and a strong, stable, constitutional government; between liberated market forces and corrective redistribution of wealth; and between national sentiments and an all-European identity. Even in optimal circumstances and with massive foreign aid, the entrapments on the way are many and success is highly uncertain. This challenge is great indeed, especially for the younger generation, which now rebels against the historical legacy it has inherited. Whether the best and brightest among them will choose to make something of this opportunity, and not try to escape its burden, remains to be seen. In any case, it may well be that raising our standards of civilization—both technological and moral—will take more wits, enthusiasm, and endurance than it took to cut barbed wire fences, pull down walls, and drive out dictators.

Bright Prospects for Eastern Europe

✦

William Echikson

Writing from Paris in January 1991, this correspondent found
many reasons for a more optimistic assessment of the outlook
for successful economic and political reform, especially in Poland and Czechoslovakia.

Völker Ebermann is understandably anxious. Like thousands of other former
East Germans, he recently was laid off from his job, a victim of the economic reconstruction sweeping Germany following its reunification. After being trained to take
orders, will he be able to learn how to take initiative? Will he and his wife Karin be
able to cope with skyrocketing prices now that the old East German mark has
vanished?

But beneath this anxiety lies a deep sense of exhilaration. Extraordinary things
are now possible. A shiny new VCR sits in his apartment. He has just returned from
his first trip abroad—to England. The excitement shows on his face. "For the first
time in my life, I'm free," he says. "I can do what I want with my life."

When I think of Eastern Europe today, a year after the dramatic revolutions
brought down communism, I think of Völker. He has every reason to be anxious
about the future. But he has even more reason to rejoice and be confident.

The amazing has been accomplished. Multiparty elections have been held in
Poland, Czechoslovakia, Hungary, and Germany. Independent newspapers prolif-
erate. Public debate flourishes. People can travel without restrictions.

Remember that only a little more than a year ago, Václav Havel was in prison.
Today, he is Czechoslovakia's president. In Poland, Solidarity leader and Nobel peace
prize winner Lech Wałęsa has become president. Hungary is ruled by a coalition of
former opposition leaders. Even the Balkan backwaters of Romania and Bulgaria are
inching toward liberalization.

Despite the tragic events in Lithuania, few worry that the Soviet Union will
invade and crush the newfound freedom. Mikhail Gorbachev is too preoccupied with
problems at home to meddle abroad.

Germany is likely to remain the dominant country in the region. It represents a

William Echikson, "Bright Prospects for Eastern Europe," from *Christian Science Monitor,* January 31, 1991.

positive, prosperous, democratic example, one particularly valuable to the East Europeans because it too was built from the ashes of a failed dictatorship.

If the political climate looks relatively rosy, what about the economy? A conventional snapshot shows industrial production plunging, unemployment soaring, and incomes falling.

But the apparent signs of impending disaster actually suggest that a serious switch is under way to a market economy. The true disaster would be if factories continued to pour out unwanted products and sold them at a loss.

Restructuring is painful. It also is necessary. Pessimists forget the crucial message that today's factory closures open up the bright prospect of higher living standards in the long run. Newly unemployed Völker Ebermann knows this.

Official statistics mislead. In the past, most store shelves selling subsidized goods were empty. Now the subsidies are being ended—and so is the need to spend hours standing in queues. Estimates of falling production are based on comparisons with old communist figures, which bore little relation to reality.

Reform meanwhile has produced important successes. Foreign investment is beginning to pour into the region. A recent survey by the New York–based accounting firm DRT International showed that nearly all large West European companies plan to invest in the region over the next five years. About half of large US and Japanese firms have similar plans. "The survey leads us to believe that investment commitments of anywhere from $20 billion to $50 billion may well be on the drawing board for the next five years," says Thomas Presby, a DRT managing partner.

Private enterprise also is booming, especially in Poland. An astounding 300,000 new private firms sprang up there last year, and existing ones are expanding fast, according to economist Jeffrey Sachs, who helped author Warsaw's reform plan.

True, these advances mean harder work, higher prices, jobless queues, and social tensions. Many Poles find themselves spending most of their paychecks on food and rent. In one year, the price of a one-bedroom apartment in Warsaw has risen by 400 percent.

The new class of private entrepreneurs can pay. Beleaguered workers cannot. Most Polish wages have gone up less than 15 percent.

Three external shocks will aggravate these problems. First, East Germany's demise deprives the East Europeans of a major trade partner. In reunited Germany, struggling factories have rushed to cancel contracts with their former East European partners.

Second, starting Jan. 1, trade with the Soviet Union switched to hard currency. Instead of bartering their oil for shabby East-bloc goods, the Soviets now sell their oil at world market prices. And third, the East Europeans face an additional oil shock from the Gulf crisis.

Stable, strong government is needed to cushion these shocks and implement deep and difficult economic reforms. In Poland, Lech Wałęsa is committed to reform and vows to take no shortcuts. If anything, his prime minister, Jan Krzysztof Bielecki, promises a healthy dose of faster reform, with quicker privatization and greater opportunities for foreign investors.

Other East Europeans are also putting forth bold market programs. After hesitating for a year, Czechoslovakia embarked on the rapid reform road on Jan. 1. Hungary should not be far behind. These countries know where they want to go—to join the European Economic Community.

Freed from the unnatural graft of communism and given Western financial and political support, the countries of Eastern Europe have a good chance of developing into prosperous democracies.

Central and Eastern Europe over the Last Year: New Trends, Old Structures

◆

George Schöpflin

The author, a specialist in East European politics at the University of London, attempts to draw a balance between the promising features of the East European landscape in early 1991 and the obstacles that impede constructive reform. He suggests that the working class may hold the key to success insofar as it can learn to engage in the give-and-take of a modern democratic polity instead of holding to the adversarial style of nineteenth-century working-class postures. In addition, people in general will have to learn to regard the state as something other than the enemy.

The conventional picture of what has happened in Central and Eastern Europe in the last year is surprisingly straightforward. Communism ended, democracy was introduced, and the countries of the region were left to construct their own systems. All this took place in a benign international context and on the assumption that the West would be sympathetic and supportive, especially in the matter of providing credit, technology, and expertise.

Then, about half way through the year, this idyllic picture unfortunately came

George Schöpflin, "Central and Eastern Europe over the Last year: New Trends, Old Structures," from *Report on Eastern Europe,* February 15, 1991, pp. 26–28. Reprinted with the permission of Radio Free Europe/Radio Liberty.

face to face with the hard realities of postcommunism. Although new democratic institutions were set up, making them function in a democratic way has proved much more difficult than it seemed a year ago. Understandably at that time, few people wanted to point to the enormous problems that establishing democracies would entail. And then came a series of international crises that all but marginalized Central and Eastern Europe. The Gulf crisis entirely distracted the attention of the West; German reunification tied West Germany into a long-term program of reconstructing East Germany; and the collapse of the Soviet Union as an economic partner, together with the accelerating slide into repression by the end of the year, left the Central and East European states very exposed. The future looked bleak, indeed.

There is such a thing as being too pessimistic. It would be unjust to underestimate the genuine strides made toward creating more effective and more open political systems. The most important change in this connection is the complete disappearance of communism as a legitimating ideology.

Furthermore, for large sections of society, democracy must be more than a slogan, as it was in the communist period; it must comprise a genuinely open system, in which individuals and groups can participate freely in a political contest of interests. The rule of law, constitutional government, representation, and the separation of powers have all been received as part of the normal, natural order in Europe. Elections have been held throughout the area, and political parties capable of attracting the support of the bulk of the electorate have come into being. Parallel with this has been the equally widespread acceptance of the market. In the midst of the gloom, it is worth restating and emphasizing that the turning point of 1989–1990 constituted the best chance that the Central and East European region has ever had for building democratic systems.

The negative aspects of the process, however, are many and were clearly underestimated by both rulers and ruled. Perhaps this was as well, for if anyone had taken a "realistic" view of the future a year or more ago, the attempt to replace communism might not have been made. Yet a realistic approach to the task of establishing democracy is essential at this time, otherwise the democratic project will certainly fail. And realism today does involve the sort of hard look at the state of affairs in the region that some people will undoubtedly regard as being excessively pessimistic.

A crucial task, which has barely begun, is to understand that the societies left behind by communism have certain characteristics that make the establishment of democracy extremely difficult. The situation under postcommunism is very different indeed from that in Spain, Portugal, or Greece, where right-wing dictatorships never carried out the same kind of devastation that the Communists imposed. Above all, civil society survived and to some extent even flourished, with the result that the establishment of democracy was much easier than it is proving to be in Central and Eastern Europe.

Civil society is one of those elusive concepts more widely used than defined, but it evidently involves an autonomous society and a self-limiting state: in other words, a state that recognizes that the rule of law applies as much to itself as it does to citizens. This cannot be a purely legal definition, however. It involves issues of political power.

The actual exercise of power by the state must, therefore, take place within a legal and constitutional framework, certainly; but society must equally be prepared to accept this framework and act accordingly. In this sense, self-limitation applies throughout the political system.

Unfortunately, self-limitation does not have strong roots in Central and Eastern Europe. The communist system was explicitly based on the claim to total power, and the precommunist systems likewise claimed the right to act through the discretionary power of the state: the state was free to act unless expressly prevented from so doing. The constraints on the state must be legal, of course, but also political, economic, social, and so on, in such way that a dynamic but equilibrative order is the outcome.

The question in the postcommunist world is who has the interest to work toward the construction of such a system. Obviously, the intellectuals who played such a crucial role in delegitimating communism and legitimating democracy are to be counted in this category. But there are difficulties with leaving the assessment there. The intellectual delegitimation of the communist order was carried out by a kind of coalition, in which there was agreement only on the ending of the communist system and the introduction of democracy but not on the kind of democracy, the nature of the constitutional framework, the role of social autonomy, the range of individual choice, the function of the market, and so on. A year on, there is every sign that the original consensus is falling apart and that intellectuals throughout the area are split on questions such as the speed and extent of privatization, the relative roles of the market and the state in the economy, and the definition of national identity.

This may well have far-reaching consequences for the democratic project in another respect. The existence of an autonomous entrepreneurial stratum, a bourgeoisie, is a precondition for a functioning democracy. Without a bourgeoisie there is little hope that social mobility, which in any case is very seriously blocked in the post-communist world as a result of the narrowing of opportunities in politics and culture caused by communism, will become a realistic prospect for the bulk of the population. In other words, the argument here is that only economic mobility can offer sufficient opportunity to integrate the lower-status sections of society into the values of democracy. Democracy, it need hardly be added, is favored by the bourgeoisie because it offers provision for economic competition and the protection of private property, in its classical Western definition.

It is hard to see alternative forms of integration having much success. Political integration of a sort was tried under communism and failed. The political rewards that a system can provide are simply not enough to satisfy the population, so that from the 1960s onward, the Communists were forced to offer economic rewards as well; it was their failure to provide these economic benefits that led to their downfall. It is inconceivable that political integration could be attempted as an all-out strategy under postcommunism, though one can visualize partial and short-term political rewards (which might include symbolic mobilization around "the nation" or "the leader") being offered as a palliative for economic privation; but if they do not satisfy the material aspirations of society, these experiments will fail.

The question is, then, whether the intellectuals now enjoying their dominance over politics will have the foresight to advance the growth of a bourgeoisie in post-communist Central and Eastern Europe. The prospects are not good. Intellectuals are unlikely to be ready to yield their dominant position without a fight; and traditionally, the principal objective of intellectual activity has been criticism of the bourgeoisie. At first sight, this suggests that intellectuals are unlikely to make good midwives for a bourgeoisie.

In concrete terms, the evidence of the last year supports this proposition, though it must be added that everything is still so fluid in Central and Eastern Europe that it is dangerous to offer any firm predictions. The conflict in Poland between Tadeusz Mazowiecki's government of intellectuals and the populism adopted by Lech Wałęsa quite clearly turned on this issue, and the intellectuals lost. In Hungary and Czechoslovakia, the governments have been extremely slow in introducing measures that would foster the growth of an entrepreneurial class; and the distaste, if not actual disdain, felt by some intellectuals for money-making was certainly part of this, even if the distaste was hidden deep and was not immediately evident. Privatization still has a long way to go before the new bourgeoisie starts to emerge.

This, indeed, brings me to the heart of my argument about the state of Central and Eastern Europe as it appears at the end of 1990. As communism receded, it revealed a somewhat unexpected social landscape. Parts of this landscape were vaguely familiar from periods of weakened communist party rule, such as the Solidarity era, but only now is anything like a true picture emerging. The key issue in this context is the nature of the working class in the postcommunist countries.

Whereas in Western societies, the working class has by and large been successfully integrated into society, the polity, and the economy and there is a broad acceptance of a shared culture, this was not paralleled under communism. On the contrary, communism managed to create a working class very much in its own image. Just as Marx started from the time-bound assumptions of the 19th century in his depiction of the working class, so his successors in Central and Eastern Europe after 1948 set up a 19th-century industry, which automatically resulted in the emergence of a 19th-century working class with it.

What this means is that the working class tends to be concentrated in large or super-large enterprises, to rely on old-fashioned technologies, and to regard manual labor as superior to knowledge-based work. The blocking of social mobility has allowed this working class to mature, to acquire an internal cohesiveness, and to be defensive about its status. Not surprisingly, the values of this working class are narrow and it is impatient and reluctant to come to terms with complexity. It is not hostile to materialism as such; indeed, it aspires to Western levels of consumption, but it expects to acquire them overnight.

The difficulty with this state of affairs is that a working class of this particular kind is not likely to be well disposed toward the compromises, dealing, and horse-trading that democratic politics requires, in which there are no outright winners and no outright losers either. Instead, the possibility cannot be excluded that the postcommunist working class will become vulnerable to demagogic manipulation, especially as it sees its standard of living eroded by the growing economic crisis.

To an extent, manipulation through the use of populist slogans has already been evident in Poland: by Wałęsa and, for that matter, the surrealistic Stanisław Tyminski, whose success in gaining 25% of the vote in the presidential elections is a good indication of the vulnerability of the Polish working class. Something similar can be said of Romania, where President Ion Iliescu's use of the miners to put down his opponents' protests in June falls clearly into this pattern. The taxi-blockade in Hungary could also have shifted in this direction. The fact that it did not was partly the result of the moderation of Hungarian society, which has the least homogenized working class in the region, and partly because of the government's eventual recognition that a retreat on its part would bring its own reward.

The receding of communism has also brought to the fore the unresolved issues of national identity and nationalism in Central and Eastern Europe. The dangers of this have been exaggerated in the West, though they do exist. The real danger lies in any attempt to use nationalism as an instrument of political mobilization in areas where it is not directly relevant.

Nationalism is very potent, because it appeals to the emotional dimension in politics, but it only answers questions of identity; it has nothing to say on the redistribution of power, though it has regularly been used in this way. Serbs are not poor because they are Serbs (the message hammered home by Serbian President Slobodan Milosević with considerable success) but because their economy is in a bad state, since the reforms of the economic structure needed to modernize it have been blocked by Milosević. The temptation to use, or rather abuse, nationalism is very strong in an unfavorable situation; and the trouble is that once mobilization has taken place along these lines, it is difficult in the extreme to achieve quiescence.

On the other hand, if democratic structures are in place and democratic procedures are accepted, deep-rooted national questions can be solved. I suspect that this, in fact, is what will happen with the Hungarian minority in Slovakia and with Hungary, Slovakia, and the Czech Republic, as the commitment to make democracy work is strong enough on the part of all the actors. The failure of the Slovak National Party to make much of an impression in the local elections in November tends to support this optimistic assessment.

There is one further legacy of the communist period that is increasingly becoming a serious obstacle to democracy: this is the rather homogeneous picture that Central and East European societies have of themselves. On the whole, societies tend to see themselves ranged against the state, which is regarded as an alien or hostile body, over which the individual has little chance of making much of an impact—only society as a whole can do this. It is probably this sense of helplessness that contributed to the relatively low turnout in the various elections throughout the area.

This attitude made sense while society was engaged in a life-or-death struggle with the totalitarian communist system, but in an open system it is harmful. A democracy is not about a conflict between the state and society; it is a series of interactions and power-flows at every level, involving different social groups and different agencies of the state. Sometimes the state will dominate, but often enough it will not. And the state also has a role in intervening in the affairs of society to prevent an overmighty social organization from arrogating excessive power to itself. Too homogeneous a perception of the state-society relationship leads to a zero-sum view of politics, in which the gain of one party is automatically the loss of the other. Here, the strict dichotomy between state and society can only be prejudicial to the effective operation of democracy.

There is no easy conclusion. On balance, the year has seen enormous gains for democracy, but this does not mean that the coming years will be easy. No one has promised that.

By Way of Conclusion

◆ *Economists draw a distinction between risk and uncertainty. Risk is a normal condition in the sense of being subject to calculation; and if actuaries can assign odds or assess probability, it becomes possible to insure against failure. Uncertainty, on the other hand, is a condition that does not yield to such calculation; there is no basis for insurability. The condition called risk presupposes the continuation of a system in its fundamental character and, therefore, the reasonableness of projecting its trends and tendencies into the future. The condition of uncertainty occurs in abnormal circumstances when, for example, a given system is in disarray and the future is essentially unpredictable.*

Although we can argue, as I noted in the introduction, about what exactly counts as a revolution, it is not possible at this stage to say of Eastern Europe that it is undergoing revolution in the most basic Marxist sense of a transformation of the very foundations of social existence. Yet it is plain that important changes of diverse sorts are under way in the countries of the region. What we might want to say—and this is the sense in which I use the term "revolution" in this book—is that these societies have entered upon conditions of uncertainty and that revolution, social transformation, is an implicit possibility in those circumstances. Putting it more tersely: revolution is by its nature uncertain, not just risky; and, turning the formulation around, uncertainty contains the possibility of revolution. This is to say that, in Eastern Europe at the end of 1990, actuaries are helpless and all bets are off.

But like most generalizations about Eastern Europe, even that one admits of partial exceptions. For example, the absorption of the German Democratic Republic into the Federal Republic, while it occasions countless problems, has a measure of predictability about it; there is no doubt that the resulting social, economic, and polit-ical order will bear a strong resemblance to the known features of the dominant party, however discomfiting that may be to some individuals on both sides. At the moment of writing, it appears that Czechoslovakia has a firmer grip on the changes it is experiencing than do some of its neighbors. If that impression is borne out over a longer span of time, we might surmise that it is because Czechoslovakia can depend, in impalpable ways, on its own historical experience of a relatively modern and lib-eral social order.

Where such antecedents are lacking, as they are in most of Eastern Europe, there can be no reliable direction of change modeled on historical experience—just as it has never made much sense for people on the left to fear a "return to capitalism" in places that had experienced very little capitalist development in the first place. This is not to say that the past defines what is possible in the future, but only that a usable past provides guidance and, if not too remote, also skills that are helpful in reducing abnormal uncertainty to normal risk in the fashioning of a satisfactory future. It does not preordain that Czechoslovakia will be more successful than, say, Hungary or Poland in managing change constructively, only that it may help to explain why, at the moment, Czechoslovakia is displaying a stronger sense of direction and a clearer vision of the future it desires.

But there is something else that our proposition about the past does not say: there is no guarantee, in Czechoslovakia or elsewhere, that constructive elements of the past will be selected for present guidance, so we cannot assume that the construc-tive antecedents will be the ones that operate at a given time. Abraham Brumberg has cautioned us about "the deceits bred by faulty memory" that may tarnish efforts to realize the promise of the present moment. More concretely:

> *In some countries, we now watch the discredited order and equally discredited myths . . . giving way to virulent nationalism, ethnic hatreds and enthusiasm for unrestrained laissez faire. I fear that the demise of communism is to be accompanied not by the dispelling of the long shadow of history; it is to be accompanied by the erosion of tolerance and of historical memory. (Granta 30, Winter 1990.)*

(Only a few pages away, Andrei Sinyavsky records his concern about the potential in the Soviet Union for retrograde change, a resurgent nationalism buttressed by anti-Semitism.)

It is obvious, I believe, that the principle of self-determination of peoples is compatible with either the constructive or the destructive dimension of historical mem-ory. The experience of independence or, failing that, the experience of striving for independence, is virtually universal in Eastern Europe and bears conspicuously on the long-standing efforts of those countries to achieve first greater autonomy, then full independence from Soviet tutelage. These efforts can be seen both as a reenactment of the achievement of independence from the dynasties of an earlier time and as a companion piece to, if slightly more advanced than, the impulse to autonomy exhibited currently in several Soviet republics. We may want to suspend judgment regarding the prospect of dissolution of the Soviet federation, but it would be hard to think of the achievement of full sovereignty by the East European states as anything but positive and constructive.

Perhaps we should regard the regaining of lost independence and the recapture of previously attenuated sovereignty as a "normal"—that is, risky but not altogether uncertain—process, one that is at least somewhat predictable. But self-determination shades rapidly into particularism, an inclination that is lacking a usable past and therefore is quite unpredictable. Do we wish to assign the same status to the Albanian and Slovenian rumblings in Yugoslavia today that we accord the 1948 break with the Soviet Union. Are we as comfortable with Slovak discontent today as we were with Dubček's reform movement of 1968? What about the Turks in Bulgaria, the Hungarians in Romania, the Byelorussians in Poland? The particularisms are not new, only the fulsome expression of them; they are fruits of oppositional success.

One of the imponderables of opposition to a single, preferably external enemy or to the external enemy's local agents is that it masks all manner of secondary discontents. For a long time, many Western observers of the Soviet scene lumped together all of the Soviet dissenters, preferring to regard them as united foes of evil incarnate in the Soviet regime. Only gradually did we begin to notice the enormous differences among them, differences as to motivation as well as desired outcome. Although this was a defect in the observer, it did match up with one fact about the dissenters: they could also seem to themselves to be united in their opposition to the authorities; their differences were either obscured or deliberately set aside while they focused on the common target.

And so it has been in Eastern Europe. Each of the major upheavals of the era of Soviet domination took on the character of a national protest, if not always in its inception then certainly in popular memory. The appearance of unity masked a plethora of differences so long as the enemy and the enemy's agents stood their ground. Only when they withdrew (or were excised) did the former opposition discover and have to confront the diversity of viewpoints and objectives animating the various elements of the opposition. That is the difference, to take the most conspicuous example, between Solidarity as a social movement in 1980–1981 and Solidarity as an electoral contestant in 1989–1990. And that is, in turn, the difference between revolt and the attempt to govern.

To many observers, especially in the West, it has seemed that at least one feature of oppositional unity has survived. It is sometimes expressed as the defeat of socialism, sometimes as the victory of a market economy. To the credit of these observers, they usually preface their announcements of victory with strictures against gloating. What eludes them, however, is the extent to which the undeniable East European clamor against planned economy and the social system surrounding it is itself a response to excess rather than an endorsement of a rival system. In effect, the observers who were wrong in the past, mostly by reason of their undifferentiated hostility to all things Soviet, are validating their past mistakes by equally faulty estimates of the current situation.

There is one rule of virtually universal applicability to be extracted from the postwar history of Eastern Europe: when an already ossified socioeconomic system is imposed from without and reinforced by all manner of penalties and privileged rhetoric, the revulsion against it will be total, extending also to the vocabulary in which it is couched. After an extended stay in Warsaw in 1982, I received a letter from a Polish friend, a sociologist, saying that, while I probably would not understand, he was reading St. John of the Cross. But I did understand. When a vocabulary has been completely debased, as official rhetoric has debased public discourse in Eastern Europe, even authentic literature expressed in that vocabulary will seem repugnant.

It is of course not just a matter of language. The system that came to be known as "already existing socialism" has been rejected fully, along with just about everything remindful of it. This has as little to do with socialism or capitalism as the rejected system had to do with either. For people who have traditionally favored radical social change, this points to the terrible responsibility borne by those who turned a theory of society into a social dogma, fearing all correctives—upon which the survival of any system depends—as deviations from received truth. Radical social change then became a necessity, precisely in opposition to the imposed order.

Absent the effective unanimity that characterized that opposition, the forces of reconstruction in the societies of Eastern Europe are in the grips of uncertainty. They have no more reliable recipes for the reordering of economically disastrous circumstances than did the party that came to power in Russia in 1917. Their resentments are profound (and justified) and their expression of them is sometimes equally extreme—likewise at times their endorsement of extreme solutions. What they all know, however, is that they operate in the realm of uncertainty, that their problems are peculiarly their own, and that ready-made solutions will not be discovered somewhere else. Sensible observers will, for the time being, leave it at that.

Suggestions for Further Reading

❖ *In the period since World War II, Eastern Europe has generated a voluminous literature, both scholarly and popular. Not at all surprisingly, much of it bears the marks of the Cold War, which, it now takes some effort to recall, once represented genuine dangers and the authentic fears they engendered. Some of the earlier literature retains its value precisely because it adequately represents the Cold War state of mind. But by the same token, a good deal of the more recent literature has quickly lost its usefulness by artificially prolonging a Cold War mindset, a reminder that scholars too develop an investment in certain modes of interpretation that they dislike surrendering. Some scholars share with some journalists and public officials the blame for stubbornly defending outmoded versions of reality, but others of these groups of interpreters deserve credit for prompt adjustment to an ever-changing reality.*

Although it is necessary to be aware of such problematic aspects of a body of literature, their importance can be minimized in a modest set of suggestions like this one by focusing somewhat narrowly on identifying works that will be most helpful to students new to the field of inquiry. As students advance toward fuller understanding of the subject, they will inevitably encounter more elaborate bibliographical tools that aspire to do justice both to the richness and to the problematics of the literature. That is not the present purpose.

A development that does deserve mention here is the increasing availability of East European writings in English translation. Linguistic diversity has always been a problem, even for specialists, in this field of study. In some measure it accounts for undue reliance on sweeping but often shallow surveys of the entire region. One of the best ways of overcoming superficiality without yielding to an impossibly narrow or fragmented approach to the field is to make available a large and so far as possible representative assortment of texts from the area itself. This is happening more rapidly for Poland and Czechoslovakia than for Albania and Bulgaria, as one might expect, but it is an altogether welcome trend and one that is reflected in the suggestions that follow.

The emphasis here falls on books, both because they are the likeliest starting points for beginning students and because they typically afford fuller background information than do journal articles. But because books, by their nature, do not stay abreast of the most current developments, it is important to mention some of the better sources of current information. Among the major newspapers, the Christian

Science Monitor *has long provided outstanding coverage of Eastern Europe;* World Press Review *is noteworthy for the breadth of sources employed in its sections on Eastern Europe; and* Problems of Communism *provides both analysis and relative currency.* East Europe *and* Across Frontiers, *both deceased, remain valuable sources for the periods in which they were published, not least because both (especially the latter) included rich material in translation from East European sources.*

Several journals have, in response to the drama of 1989–1990, offered valuable special issues on the area: Current History *(December 1990);* Daedalus *(Winter 1990);* Dissent *(Spring 1990);* Granta *(Winter 1990); and* Social Research *(Summer 1990), the last especially valuable because its contributors are all East Europeans.*

Finally, there is nothing to compare, for a combination of timeliness and trenchant analysis, with Report on Eastern Europe, *issued by Radio Free Europe.*

Suggested readings are grouped by country, with two preceding sections on Soviet–East European relations and on the region as a whole. There is no separate historical section, since so many of the books cited include pertinent historical background.

Soviet–East European Relations

The initial assertion of Soviet hegemony in Eastern Europe is examined and set in the context of the history of Soviet expansion in Thomas T. Hammond, ed.: The Anatomy of Communist Takeovers *(New Haven, 1975). Valuable documentation of the manner in which that control evolved is supplied by Robert H. McNeal, ed.:* International Relations Among Communists *(Englewood Cliffs, N.J., 1967) and Robert V. Daniels, ed.:* A Documentary History of Communism, *2 vols. (New York, 1962).*

Robert L. Hutchings: Soviet–East European Relations *(Madison, Wis., 1983) and Christopher Jones:* Soviet Influence in Eastern Europe *(New York, 1980) both examine the relationship in general; Karen Dawisha:* Eastern Europe, Gorbachev, and Reform *(New York, 1990) brings the account down to the onset of the transformation still in progress. George Schöpflin:* The Soviet Union and Eastern Europe *(London, 1986) is another instructive account.*

Two of the instruments of Soviet influence are examined in an older study, Michael Kaser: Comecon *(London, 1967) and the more up-to-date David Holloway and Jane M. O. Sharp, eds.:* The Warsaw Pact *(Ithaca, 1984).*

A recent and useful anthology of salient texts, extending all the way to 1990, is Gale Stokes, ed.: From Stalinism to Pluralism *(New York, 1991); also Aurel Braun, ed.:* The Soviet–East European Relationship in the Gorbachev Era *(Boulder, 1990).*

Eastern Europe

A general political history of the region since 1945 is found in Joseph Roths-child: Return to Diversity *(New York, 1988). J. F. Brown:* Eastern Europe and Communist Rule *(Durham, N.C., 1988) concentrates on the period since 1956.*

Some older accounts remain useful, especially since more recent ones tend to slight the early years: R. V. Burks: The Dynamics of Communism in Eastern Europe *(Princeton, 1961); Ghita Ionescu:* The Politics of the European Communist States *(New York, 1967); Zbigniew K. Brzezinski:* The Soviet Bloc *(Cambridge, Mass., 1967); and William E. Griffith, ed.:* Communism in Europe, *2 vols. (Cambridge, Mass., 1964, 1966). A book that has lost none of its eloquence since its first appearance in 1953 is Czesław Miłosz:* The Captive Mind *(New York, 1981). Still important for the events of 1956 is the documentary collection, Paul Zinner, ed.:* National Communism and Popular Revolt in Eastern Europe *(New York, 1956).*

Useful studies of particular topics include Peter Bender: East Europe in Search of Security *(Baltimore, 1972); Jane Leftwich Curry, ed.:* Dissent in Eastern Europe *(New York, 1983); Radoslav Selucký:* Economic Reforms in Eastern Europe *(New York, 1972); Pedro Ramet:* Cross and Commissar *(Bloomington, Ind., 1987); Nigel Grant:* Society, Schools and Progress in Eastern Europe *(Oxford, 1969); and Vladmir Tismaneanu, ed.:* In Search of Civil Society: Independent Peace Movements in the Soviet Bloc *(New York, 1990).*

Among the many accounts of recent developments in the region are Elie Abel: The Shattered Bloc *(Boston, 1990), Charles Gaţi:* The Bloc That Failed *(Bloomington, Ind., 1990), and William Echikson:* Lighting the Night *(New York, 1990). Timothy Garton Ash, recognized as one of the foremost interpreters of contemporary Eastern Europe, has supplied two books,* The Magic Lantern *(New York, 1990) and* The Uses of Adversity *(New York, 1990). Provocative reflec-tions are also found in Ralf Dahrendorf:* Viewpoints on the Revolution in Europe *(New York, 1990).*

Among the essential critiques from within the region are the works of Milován Djilas, particularly The New Class *(New York, 1957). George Konrád and Ivan Szelényi extended that critical approach in* The Intellectuals on the Road to Class Power *(New York, 1979). Konrád's* Antipolitics *(New York, 1984) is also important, as is Svetozar Stojanović:* In Search of Democracy in Socialism *(Buffalo, N.Y., 1981). Although his own position has since changed somewhat, Leszek Kołakowski:* Toward a Marxist Humanism *(New York, 1968) remains a powerful commentary.*

Albania

As might be expected, Albania has not generated quantities of commentary, because of either prevailing unfamiliarity or perceived unimportance. The few works we do have therefore assume greater significance. Nicholas Pano: The People's Republic of Albania *(Baltimore, 1968) was an almost singular contribution for some time.* Harry Hamm: Albania: China's Beachhead in Europe *(London, 1962) was the other full-scale study. Now* Elez Biberaj: Albania: A Socialist Maverick *(Boulder, 1990) brings the account close enough to the present that Albania's participation in radical processes of change can be seen in parallel with developments in the rest of Eastern Europe.*

Bulgaria

The situation is only marginally better for Bulgaria. The most useful single volume is J. F. Brown: Bulgaria Under Communist Rule *(New York, 1970), though it is seriously dated. Of about the same vintage is* Peter John Georgeoff: The Social Education of Bulgarian Youth *(Minneapolis, 1968). A more recent work,* Robert J. McIntyre: Bulgaria: Politics, Economics and Society *(London, 1988), offers serious social analysis but stops short of the dramatic developments of the last two or three years.*

The Bulgarian economy has attracted more up-to-date attention: George R. Feiwel: Growth and Reforms in Centrally Planned Economies: The Lessons of the Bulgarian Experience *(New York, 1977) and* John R. Lampe: The Bulgarian Economy in the Twentieth Century *(London, 1986).*

In a class by itself of course is Todor Zhivkov: Modern Bulgaria *(New York, 1974), written by the former first secretary of the Bulgarian Communist Party and president of that country's State Council.*

Czechoslovakia

It is a kind of commentary on the bleakness of the Czechoslovak scene before the Prague Spring of 1968 and again after it until 1989 that so much of the literature on that country focuses on 1968. Even works of a more general nature, such as Tad Szulc: Czechoslovakia Since World War II *(New York, 1971) and* Zdenek Suda: Zealots and Rebels *(Stanford, 1980) devote considerable attention to the country's most interesting episode. Other works take on special significance in light of 1968, for example,* Jiří Pelikan, ed.: The Czechoslovak Political Trials, 1950–1954 *(Stanford, 1970), which resulted from a 1968 Commission of Inquiry.* Jan Milič Lochman: Church in a Marxist Society *(New York, 1970) leads up to and includes the 1968 experience.* Ivan Sviták: Man and His World *(New York, 1970) affords a glimpse of the kind of intellectual expression that informed the Prague Spring, as does Anthony Liehm:* The Politics of Culture *(New York, 1973). An edition of the contemporaneous work of Karel Kosík, the other major intellectual figure of that time, is now in preparation.*

These and other related tendencies form the subject of Vladimir V. Kusin: The Intellectual Origins of the Prague Spring *(Cambridge, Mass., 1971). More extensive coverage is provided in two titles by Galia Golan:* The Czechoslovak Reform Movement *(Cambridge, Mass., 1971) and* Reform Rule in Czechoslovakia *(Cambridge, Mass., 1973) stretching from 1962 to 1969. A brief account of the Soviet intervention itself is found in Colin Chapman:* August 21st: The Rape of Czechoslovakia *(Philadelphia, 1968). And, by way of contrast, H. Gordon Skilling offers a truly monumental study,* Czechoslovakia's Interrupted Revolution *(Princeton, 1976).*

Robin Alison Remington, ed.: Winter in Prague *(Cambridge, Mass., 1969) supplies extensive documentation for 1967–1969. The content of the reform movement is summed up incisively by Radoslav Selucký in* Czechoslovakia: The Plan That Failed *(London, 1970) and, somewhat differently, by another eyewitness, George Shaw Wheeler:* The Human Face of Socialism *(New York, 1973). Robert Littell:* The Czech Black Book *(New York, 1969) is the refutation by the Institute of History, Czechoslovak Academy of Sciences, of the Soviet version of the intervention.*

The story is carried forward by Vladimir V. Kusin in From Dubček to Charter 77 *(New York, 1978) and elaborated in various ways by the several contributors to Václav Havel et al.:* The Power of the Powerless *(Armonk, N.Y., 1985). Havel, the playwright elected president of Czechoslovakia in December 1989, is a principal source of interpretation of the most recent period in two books:* Living in Truth *(London, 1987) and* Disturbing the Peace *(New York, 1990).*

East Germany

It took the occupation powers several years to decide to integrate the zones of Germany into their respective alliance systems. It took the academic world a good bit longer to accept East Germany, the German Democratic Republic, as a part of Eastern Europe. Now that the GDR is being absorbed as part of the Federal Republic, it has again lost its East European status. The fact remains, however, that it was, for forty years, an integral part of the Soviet bloc. The books that deal with the GDR must of course be viewed in that light.

The first major treatment of East Germany, J. P. Nettl: The Eastern Zone and Soviet Policy in Germany, 1945–50 *(London, 1951), was followed by two studies that regarded the GDR as a fitting subject in its own right:* Welles Hangen: The Muted Revolution *(New York, 1966) and Jean Edward Smith:* Germany Beyond the Wall *(Boston, 1969). Scholarly acceptance was signaled by Arthur M. Hanhardt, Jr.:* The German Democratic Republic *(Baltimore, 1968), Peter C. Ludz:* The Changing Party Elite in East Germany *(Cambridge, Mass., 1972), and Lyman H. Legters, ed.:* The German Democratic Republic *(Boulder, 1978). Meanwhile, the early development of the economy had been treated in Wolfgang F. Stolper:* The Structure of the East German Economy *(Cambridge, Mass., 1960) and the brief revolt of 1953 in Arnulf Baring:* Uprising in East Germany, June 17, 1953 *(Ithaca, 1972).*

More recent studies include David Childs: The GDR: Moscow's German Ally *(London, 1983), Martin McCauley:* The German Democratic Republic Since 1945 *(London, 1984), A. James McAdams:* East Germany and Détente *(Cambridge, Mass., 1985), and Henry Krisch:* The German Democratic Republic *(Boulder, 1985). Special topics are examined in Thomas A. Baylis:* The Technical Intelligentsia and the East German Elite *(Berkeley, 1974), a subject of great importance for understanding the country's inner workings, and Raymond Bentley:* Technological Change in the German Democratic Republic *(Boulder, 1984).*

There is also a valuable series entitled Studies in GDR Culture and Society, *edited by Margy Gerber and published by University Press of America, which contains essays on various topics, many of them quite timely.*

Hungary

As with other countries of the region, Hungary illustrates the potency of dramatic events in stimulating scholars and other writers to produce books. The rather barren periods before and after 1956 are less than adequately covered in the literature, except in relation to the memory of 1956 or the anticipation of future change.

A sound general treatment of the early period is Bennett Kovrig: The Hungarian People's Republic *(Baltimore, 1970). The events of 1956 were examined first by Paul Zinner:* Revolution in Hungary *(New York, 1962), then in more popular treatment by Noel Barber:* Seven Days of Freedom *(New York, 1975). Melvin J. Lasky, ed.:* The Hungarian Revolution *(New York, 1957) provides a wealth of contemporaneous documentation; and Tamas Aczel, ed.:* Ten Years After *(New York, 1966) includes various retrospective reflections. A very personal account by Budapest's police chief at the time is Sandor Kopacsi:* In the Name of the Working Class *(New York, 1987).*

Two substantial studies of the Kádár period are William P. Robinson: The Pattern of Reform in Hungary *(New York, 1973) and William Shawcross:* Crime and Compromise *(New York, 1974). Miklós Haraszti has authored two books that convey some of the bleakness of life in this period:* A Worker in a Workers' State *(New York, 1977) and* The Velvet Prison: Artists Under State Socialism *(New York, 1987).*

The past decade has brought several useful contributions: Hans-Georg Hein-
rich: Hungary: Politics, Economics, and Society *(London, 1986), Charles*
Gaṭi: Hungary and the Soviet Bloc *(Durham, N.C., 1986), and the provoca-*
tive study by a leading Hungarian economist, János Kornai: The Road to a Free
Economy *(New York, 1990). And special mention must be made of the eloquent*
reflections of János Kis: Politics in Hungary: For a Democratic Alternative
(Boulder, 1989).

Poland

Even Stalin recognized that Poland was a special case among the neighbors
being subdued by the Soviet Union. The number, frequency, and intensity of Polish
deviations and revolts in the postwar period seems to validate Stalin's observation,
which in turn helps to explain the relative abundance of publications about Poland.
If we also reflect that Solidarity was, in 1980–1981, far and away the most
advanced of all postwar upheavals to that date, it becomes clear why the selection
process must be more rigorous in this section.

Two works may suffice for the early postwar period: James F. Morrison: The
Polish People's Republic *(Baltimore, 1968) and Nicholas Bethell:* Gomułka
(Harmondsworth, Eng., 1972), for Gomułka's career was nearly coterminous with
Poland's experience in the early years. Peter Raina: Political Opposition in Po-
land, 1954–1977 *(London, 1978) extends the story, as does Jakub Karpinski:*
Countdown *(New York, 1982) in a survey of the upheavals from 1956 onward.*
A more theoretical examination of Polish society is Władysław Majkowski: Peo-
ple's Poland: Patterns of Social Inequality and Conflict *(Westport, Conn.,*
1985).

Because the Roman Catholic Church has played such a prominent role in Po-
land, it is important to mention the prison notes of Stefan Cardinal Wyszyński: A
Freedom Within *(New York, 1983) and, for a later period, a theologian's charac-*
terization of Solidarity, Józef Tischner: The Spirit of Solidarity *(New York,*
1984).

Several works lead up to and set the stage for the events of 1980. An unusual
one is Jane Leftwich Curry, ed.: The Black Book of Polish Censorship *(New*
York, 1984). Abraham Brumberg, ed.: Poland: Genesis of a Revolution *(New*
York, 1983) contains some instructive essays. Among the most striking books to
come out of Poland at any time is Poland Today: The State of the Republic
(Armonk, N.Y., 1981), an account of the work of a discussion group, Experience
and the Future, that became an agenda for change and reconstruction. Another sort of
commentary is found in two books by Kazimierz Brandys: A Question of Reality
(London, 1981) and A Warsaw Diary, 1978–1981 *(New York, 1985).*

Among the many accounts of the Solidarity period, three of the most accessible are Daniel Singer: The Road to Gdansk *(New York, 1982), Neal Ascherson:* The Polish August *(New York, 1981), and Timothy Garton Ash:* The Polish Revolution: Solidarity *(New York, 1984). Lawrence Weschler has put his excellent* New Yorker *reports in book form,* The Passion of Poland *(New York, 1984). More theoretical is Alain Touraine:* Solidarity: Poland, 1980–81 *(New York, 1983).* The Book of Lech Wałęsa *(New York, 1982) contains numerous tributes to the Solidarity leader. And Adam Michnik, another important figure then and since, offers stimulating reflections in* Letters from Prison *(Berkeley, 1985). A wealth of documentation can be found in Stan Persky and Henry Flam, eds.:* The Solidarity Sourcebook *(Vancouver, B.C., 1982).*

Looking beyond 1980–1981, Leopold Labedz has edited a rich and varied set of writings in Poland Under Jaruzelski *(New York, 1984), and John Rensenbrink:* Poland Challenges a Divided World *(Baton Rouge, 1988) extends his analysis into the 1980s. Another useful collection of essays on the post-Solidarity period is Bronisław Misztal, ed.:* Poland After Solidarity *(New Brunswick, N.J., 1985).*

Romania

The early postwar period in Romania received, relatively speaking, a fair amount of attention. Ghita Ionescu examined Communism in Rumania, 1944–1962 *(London, 1964); David Floyd examined the relationship with the Soviet Union in* Rumania: *Russia's Dissident Ally (New York, 1965); and Stephen Fischer-Galați added* The Socialist Republic of Rumania *(Baltimore, 1969). The socioeconomic dimension was handled in Kenneth Jowitt:* Revolutionary Breakthroughs and National Development: The Case of Romania, 1944–1965 *(Berkeley, 1971) and in Trond Gilberg:* Modernization in Romania Since World War II *(New York, 1975).*

The story is brought closer to the present in Robert R. King: History of the Romanian Communist Party *(Stanford, 1980) and in Daniel N. Nelson, ed.:* Romania in the 1980s *(Boulder, 1981). Michael Shafir:* Romania: Politics, Economics, and Society *(London, 1985) sets the stage for the developments to come at the end of the decade. And a cluster of books addresses the last stage of Ceaușescu's reign: Daniel N. Nelson:* Romanian Politics in the Ceaușescu Era *(New York, 1988), Mary Ellen Fischer:* Nicolae Ceaușescu: A Study in Political Leadership *(Boulder, 1989), and Trond Gilberg:* Nationalism and Communism in Romania *(Boulder, 1990).*

Yugoslavia

The break between Tito and Stalin is the dominant event of the early postwar period in Yugoslavia; it was examined in detail in Adam Ulam: Titoism and the

Cominform *(Cambridge, Mass., 1952) and is the centerpiece of at least two other books: Vladimir Dedijer:* The Battle Stalin Lost *(New York, 1971) and A. Ross Johnson:* The Transformation of Communist Ideology: The Yugoslav Case, 1948–1953 *(Cambridge, 1972). The whole period is synthesized in M. George Zaninovich:* The Development of Socialist Yugoslavia *(Baltimore, 1968) and in Dennison Rusinow:* The Yugoslav Experiment, 1948–1974 *(London, 1977). Theoretical matters are more heavily stressed in Bogdan Denitch:* The Legitimation of a Revolution *(New Haven, 1976) and Harold Lydall:* Yugoslav Socialism: Theory and Practice *(Oxford, 1984).*

The special case of Milován Djilas is treated meticulously by Stephen Clissold: Djilas: The Progress of a Revolutionary *(New York, 1983). Djilas's own works are very numerous; the most pertinent here are* The New Class *(New York, 1957),* The Unperfect Society *(New York, 1969), and* Tito *(New York, 1980). Another variant of dissent centers on the so-called Praxis group of scholars. Gerson Sher has examined the case in* Praxis: Marxist Criticism and Dissent in Socialist Yugoslavia *(Bloomington, Ind., 1977). The group speaks for itself in Mihailo Marković and Robert S. Cohen:* Yugoslavia: The Rise and Fall of Socialist Humanism *(Nottingham, Eng., 1975).*

Tito's central position in Yugoslavia lasted in some ways beyond his death. George Hoffman and Fred Warner Neal accord him that central place in their Yugoslavia and the New Communism *(New York, 1962), as do two later works: Duncan Wilson:* Tito's Yugoslavia *(Cambridge, Mass., 1979) and Slobodan Stanković:* The End of the Tito Era *(Stanford, 1981).*

The special Yugoslav type of socialist economy is described by the country's leading economist, Branko Horvat: An Essay on Yugoslav Society *(White Plains, N.Y., 1969), as well as by Deborah Milenkovitch:* Plan and Market in Yugoslav Economic Thought *(New Haven, 1971). The particular features of self-management are emphasized in Jan Vanek:* The Economics of Workers' Management *(London, 1972) and Ljubo Sirc:* The Yugoslav Economy Under Self-Management *(New York, 1979).*

The present crisis of nationality conflict has deep roots, as was shown in an early study, Paul Shoup: Communism and the Yugoslav National Question *(New York, 1968). More up-to-date is Ivo Banac:* The National Question in Yugoslavia *(Ithaca, 1984).*

The most recent period is treated in Pedro Ramet, ed.: Yugoslavia in the 1980s *(Boulder, 1985), April Carter:* Democratic Reform in Yugoslavia *(Princeton, 1982), and Bogdan Denitch:* Limits and Possibilities *(Minneapolis, 1990).*

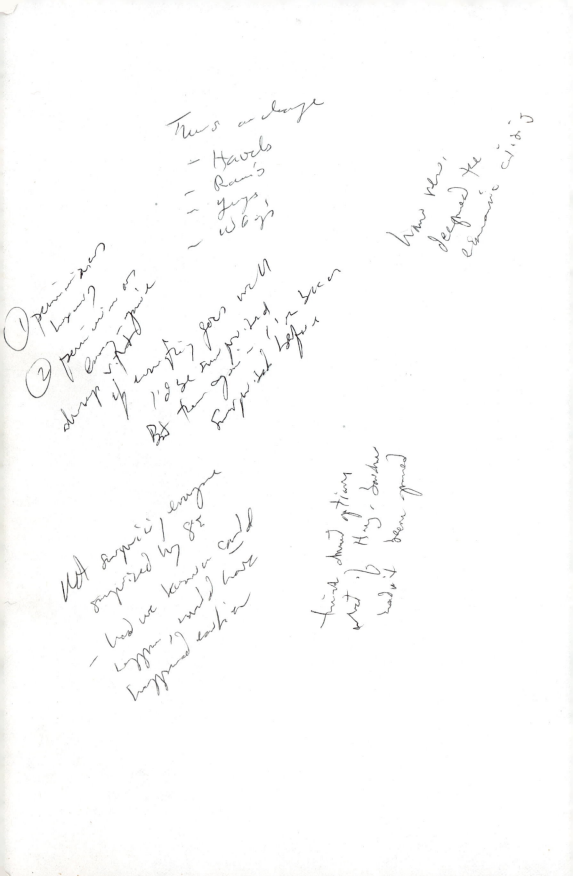